International Film Guide
2010

the definitive annual review of world cinema

edited by Ian Haydn Smith

46th edition

WALLFLOWER PRESS
LONDON & NEW YORK

Are you looking
for the next
blockbuster?

The Film & TV Zone, at The London Book Fair, brings together film & TV producers with over 300 literary agencies and publishers offering content with screen adaptation potential.

The seminar programme offers opportunities to gain and share knowledge while the networking events make The London Book Fair truly unmissable for the film & TV community.

Be a part of The London Book Fair 2010
www.londonbookfair.co.uk/ifg2010

Credits

Wallflower Press
97 Sclater Street
London
E1 6HR
tel: +44 (0)20 7729 9533
info@wallflowerpress.co.uk
www.wallflowerpress.co.uk

ISBN 978-1-906660-38-3

A catalogue record for this book is
available from the British Library

Copyright
© 2010 Wallflower Publishing Ltd

Printed and bound in the UK
by Scotprint, Haddington, Scotland

For information on sales and distribution in all territories worldwide,
please contact Wallflower Press on
info@wallflowerpress.co.uk

Editor
Ian Haydn Smith

Publisher
Yoram Allon, Wallflower Press

Founding Editor
Peter Cowie

Consultant Editor
Daniel Rosenthal

Editorial Assistant
Anne Hudson

Selected Contributors
Peter Calder, Nina Caplan,
Andrea Dittgen, Daniel Graham,
Philip Kemp, Ingrid Kopp,
Michelle Le Blanc, Benjamin Morgan,
Colin Odel, Ben Walters, Jason Wood,
Norman Yussof

Design
Elsa Mathern

Production
Tom Cabot

Photo Consultants
The Kobal Collection
www.picturedesk.com

International Advertising Manager
Sara Tyler
Europe, Film Festivals
tel: +44 (0)1349 854931
saraifg@aol.com

International Sales Consultants
Sherif Awad
Egypt, Iran, Turkey
mobile: +20 12 0827398
sherif_awad@link.net

Voula Georgakakou
Cyprus, Greece
mobile: +30 694 439 0510
voulageorg@yahoo.gr

Sheri Jennings
Italy
mobile: +39 335 831 5721
sheri.ifg@gmail.com

Anita Lewton
Belgium, France, Republic of Ireland,
United Kingdom
tel: +44 (0)7866 294766
anita.lewton@googlemail.com

Lisa Ray
Middle East, South East Asia,
South Africa
tel: +44 (0)7798 662955
l.ray@hotmail.co.uk

Front Cover
Pedro Almodóvar's **Broken Embraces** (Los abrazos rotos), *which appeared in competition at the 2009 Cannes
Film Festival.*

Contents

Michael Dwyer

As this publication was going to press, we were saddened to hear that Michael Dwyer had passed away. The Irish contributor to the IFG for twenty years, Michael was not so much a film critic in Ireland as one of its institutions. The founder of the Tralee Film Society, the Dublin Film Festival and its successor, the Jameson International Film Festival, he was also on the board of the Irish Museum of Modern Art. A champion of his country's cinema, he wrote with wit, intelligence and passion. To many he was the voice of Ireland on film. His generosity of spirit and his warmth as a human being was evident to anyone who worked with him or encountered him at the many festivals and events he attended over the decades. As Daniel Day-Lewis said in his tribute to him, 'I shall miss him. We all shall. He was a gentle man, a gentleman.'

Notes from the Editor

Welcome to the 2010 edition of the International Film Guide. One of the main aims of this guide is to present a review of the world's film-producing countries. Although each may be different in infrastructure, levels of output and the influence they have, both domestically and abroad, there are often issues in which national borders are inconsequential. Nowhere is this more apparent than in the impact of the economic downturn that hit financial markets in late 2008.

Many areas of the global film industry have suffered as a result of this crisis. It is not surprising, therefore, that the World Survey is smaller than last year (down from 123 to 112). Some countries have seen their filmmaking output reduced to zero due to a drop in investment from state and private sources. And many of the contributors highlight the problems producers and studios have faced in attempting to raise money for their projects.

There has also been the crippling impact of Swine flu (Argentina), an industrial dispute that saw cinemas closed for weeks (India) and the spectre of terrorism (Pakistan, Afghanistan and India again, following the Mumbai terrorist attack at the end of 2008).

However, against these events, 2009 will still go down as one of the most successful years in terms of audience figures. The economic downturn may have hit film production, but as in previous years when a recession has loomed, people look for escapism and once again their chosen entertainment has been cinema.

For the first time in history, an Austrian film was seen by over a million people domestically, while in Germany Michael Herbig's *Vicky the Viking* outpaced mainstream Hollywood releases. But it was the international figures

Ian Haydn Smith

for US productions that topped most box-office charts once again. Many US studios are recording their best years ever in terms of revenue, although this doesn't mean that the quality of the films released has improved. By late summer one could be forgiven for thinking that the majority of Hollywood's creative talent had chosen to work in animation or the younger market. *Coraline, Up, The Fantastic Mr Fox, Cloudy with a Chance of Meatballs* and *Where the Wild Things Are* all displayed a craft, wit and – more crucially – an intelligence in their scripts and execution that surpassed most 'mature' films. But at least there was one note of reassurance; no matter how brainless his previous films have been, we can always rely on Michael Bay to outdo himself.

For more information on the international box-office figures for 2009, go to the IFG website (www.internationalfilmguide.com) which also features regular news and festival circuit updates. The introduction of the website has enabled the International Film Guide to help increase the exposure of specific festivals and their activities through a variety of promotional platforms. The IFG now partners various international festivals, offering day-to-day coverage of events and screenings via the IFG Festival Spotlight as well as providing copies of the print edition for circulation to festival guests, jury members, plus directors/producers who have films in competition, etc. We were delighted to partner Black Nights, Cottbus, Kaunas, Transilvania and Zlin last year and in 2010 we look forward to also partnering BUFF, Baltic Film Festival Berlin, Cape Winelands, Era New Horizons, Fantasporto, Far East Film Festival, London Turkish Film Festival, Tampere, Vilnius and Visions du Réel. The coming months will also see a series of individual Spotlights, focusing on the work of cutting-edge production companies and speciality outfits, such as the Swedish digital effects house, Filmgate, whose profile is set to rise significantly throughout 2010.

One of the year's most important film festivals, the Berlinale, is subject of this guide's Festival Focus. German contributor Andrea Dittgen looks at how the festival has developed in the lead up to its 60th anniversary, including a timeline of significant moments in its history and profiles of the figures who have made the festival what it is today.

The Industry Focus shines a light on the grow-ing number of social network sites and their impact on the way films are made. Ingrid Kopp examines how organisations such as Shooting People, Massify and Wreckamovie are changing the face of independent filmmaking, and also how the traditional channels of distribution and exhibition are being replaced by the Internet.

Technology is also behind one of the year's biggest success stories. Long seen as little more than a gimmick, 3D is now an impressive revenue-generating platform. Ben Walters looks back on the earlier incarnations of this technol-ogy and suggests that, with recent innovations, the format is here to stay, a fact reinforced by the success of James Cameron's *Avatar*.

Some in the industry see 3D as a way to combat piracy and, once again, many of the country contributors discuss this problem and how it is crippling producers and studios. Pakistan in particular has suffered, with the government remaining too lax in their attempts to stem the illegal trade.

Although the more productive countries have been increasingly successful in clamping down on piracy, the economic downturn has also impacted mainstream DVD sales. However, niche companies have proven resilient, thanks to a core audience who hanker after quality releases. The format of this year's Home Entertainment section has changed in order to highlight the best of these labels, from Criterion, BFI and Masters of Cinema, to smaller labels such as Second Run and Microcinema, and other boutique companies that specialise in early cinema (Flicker Alley) or documentary (Artefact).

A Home Entertainment section will soon appear on the IFG website, offering regular reviews of the best releases and updates on how technology is changing the way we watch films at home. There will also be regular profiles of the best DVD labels, offering an insight into the films they choose to release and the lengths they go to in order to ensure each film can be seen in the way its director originally intended.

A final note about our Estonian contributor. Jaan Ruus is one of Europe's longest-standing film critics and a singular voice on cinema in his home country. He was honoured at this year's Tallinn Black Nights Film Festival with a Lifetime Achievement Award. Recognition of his work underpins the philosophy behind the Interna-tional Film Guide: to bring you the best writers on film and offer an overview of how cinema around the world is changing year-by-year.

Films of the Year – Editor's Choice
Hipsters (Valeriy Todorovskiy, Russia)
Up in the Air (Jason Reitman, USA)
The White Ribbon (Michael Haneke, Austria/ Germany/France/Italy)
A Prophet (Jacques Audiard, France)
Moon (Duncan Jones, UK)

Directors of the Year

Jacques Audiard by Nina Caplan

Here is a question that the CV of Jacques Audiard begs – one he may spend his entire career trying to answer: if you are the child of privilege, the son of a successful screenwriter who grew up outside Paris with *le tout* French film industry wandering through your lovely home, why do you end up obsessed with gangsters?

There is a threefold issue of inheritance here: personal, political and cinematic. Audiard's father, Michel, made his name writing screenplays with names like *Cop or Hood* and *Crooks In Clover*; he was particularly valued for the snap of his slang, a skill his son has inherited, although one that subtitles muffle. In politics, Audiard has made clear that he finds French attitudes despicable: *A Self-Made Hero* (*Un héros très discret*) deals with the pervasive fiction that France in the Second World War was a country full of Resistance heroes (as Mathieu Kassovitz, who plays the self-fictionalising hero of the title, has pointed out, if everyone in France had been a Resistance fighter, there would never have been a war). Audiard's most recent film, the superb prison drama *A Prophet* (*Un prophète*), looks at the injustices (including

racial divisions so draconian they don't require bars) within the prison system. The director is not a propagandist; these are the subjects that interest him, and he invariably uses them to service a shapely and romantic story. But it is less surprising, when you consider his problems with the French rule of law, that his characters should try to work around or outside it.

Cinematically, of course, France has as robust a lineage of gangster movies as America. Here again, subtitles let the Anglophone audience down: when Vincent Cassel's hood in *Read My Lips* (*Sur mes lèvres*) talks about 'les biftons' (the dosh), he is showing himself a good cinematic son of Jean Gabin and his 'grisbi' (dough) – just as his creator is demonstrating his own linguistic lineage (Gabin, the quintessential French gangster, was one of the friends of his father's wandering through that childhood home, and Audiard *père* wrote dialogue for him).

Jacques Audiard was born in 1952 in Paris, into a family of artists (his uncle and brother both also work in the film industry, and the sculptor Michel Audiard is another relative). He tried to turn his back on the family tradition,

A Prophet

claiming he would only go into film 'when I fail at everything else' and studying literature and philosophy with a possible view to becoming a teacher. However, things didn't turn out that way and he slipped into editing, then writing and eventually directing. 'As a writer you lack liberty,' he has said, 'so it is natural to try to gain more autonomy. I did it in three bounds by becoming a producer and then a director.' His wife, Marion Vernoux, is also a writer-director; the two collaborated on the script of *Venus Beauty Institute* but other than that appear to have stayed out of each other's professional lives. Audiard has, however, created a cinematic family for himself, perhaps in part homage to *la famille* Audiard, or maybe just because he tends to deal with anxiety-provoking topics; either way, his composer, Alexandre Desplat, and editor, Juliette Welfling, have worked on all five of the films he has directed. Other crew, and several actors, also pop up more than once in what is still, after all, a sparse oeuvre: Audiard was 42 when he directed his first film, *See How They Fall* (*Regarde les hommes tomber*), about a naïve young man (Mathieu Kassovitz) who becomes an assassin out of hero-worship for a played-out old gambler (Jean-Louis Trintignant). Fifteen years on (and despite having named John Huston as his favourite director, partly on the grounds that Huston slipped so easily between genres), Audiard is still making gangster films.

Or is he? A gangster belongs to a gang; Audiard's characters are invariably isolated – in fact it is their wish to join in, to belong, that leads them into criminal behaviour in the first place. Once there, these stymied individuals at last find an outlet for their hitherto untapped potential: in *A Self-Made Hero*, Albert (Mathieu Kassovitz), having failed to write a novel, gets to rewrite his own life; deaf, underrated Carla (Emmanuelle Devos) in *Read My Lips* can at last put her impressive talent for negotiation as well as her lipreading skills to good use – and win a man's appreciation for both; Malik (Tahar Rahim) in *A Prophet* discovers his formidable business abilities in the course of his struggle to survive the prison system. Even Tom

(Romaine Duris), the thwarted pianist in *The Beat That My Heart Skipped* (*De battre mon coeur s'est arrêté*), is very good at being a thug – at least until his love of classical music reasserts itself and his struggle for survival takes on a different emphasis.

Certainly, though, Audiard's characters tend to work outside the law. This seems less a tip of the trilby to daddy (fathers tend to get short shrift in the films themselves: either they're inadequate or they're invisible) than a wish to zoom in on the transactions that make up a life – gangsters, after all, play openly with power. They know that self-reinvention is expensive, in every sense, and they chalk the cost up more clearly than the rest of us.

They also use their brains fully, if unconventionally. The Audiard character is a chancer, a bright guy (or, in the case of Devos's Carla in *Read My Lips*, girl) afire with warped promise and incendiary disappointment. He is a romantic bright enough to know the dangers of that trait (rose-coloured spectacles obscure the view, and he needs clear sight in order to know when to duck). Only Kassovitz's character in *See How They Fall* lacks this intelligence (he has learning difficulties). But Kassovitz's Lieutenant-Colonel in *A Self-Made Hero*, dreaming himself up a past as a Resistance hero; Vincent Cassel's ex-con hoodlum and Emmanuelle Devos's deaf secretary in *Read My Lips* – an unlikely but enchanting couple of opportunists if ever there was one – and Romaine Duris's thuggish,

The Beat That My Heart Skipped

stymied piano player in *The Beat That My Heart Skipped* all pounce on opportunities and wrestle them into submission. Malik, the prophet of Audiard's most recent film (if *A Prophet* can be said to have an actual prophet), is no deviation. An unmoored youth who has wound up in prison for some unspecified crime, he grabs every chance offered to improve his lot and, despite being an Arab, winds up an integral part of the Corsican-run internal machinery of the prison. He may or may not be a prophet, but Malik is certainly a profiteer.

A Prophet

Read My Lips

So Audiard, in both the personal and the historical sense, has inherited his preoccupation with gangsters, and he is busily making the most of it. He is not a realist in the larger sense (his characters always get a happy ending, of sorts, which, given their multifarious disadvantages and misdemeanours, is about as fantastical as it gets), but on a more intimate level, he is. As a writer and director, he seems to be fuelled by an awareness of his own luck – a sense of 'there but for the grace of God go I' that's as potent as Benzedrine, and his characters are almost all graceless versions of their creator. They have powerful minds but have been taught only to use their fists (his films all bring up the biggest opposition in so-called civilisation, the one framed so beautifully in John Ford's *The Man Who Shot Liberty Valance*: the gun versus the law); they long to communicate but have no idea how. So Kassovitz's self-made hero writes himself – his invented persona is essentially a love

letter to the world, which makes it doubly bitter when he falls in love and realises that proper communication is impossible without truth. Audiard, the arch communicator, writes the rage of frustrated interaction really well: he knows that every love story is about the attempt, in a sense, to read someone else's lips.

It is this rage – born from the fear of remaining unheard, and therefore unloved – that causes Audiard's characters to lash out. Some of them use guns, some their hands; it's an opposition rendered clear in the case of Tom, in *The Beat That My Heart Skipped*, because his hands are used both as weapons and as instruments. Violence, after all, is a form of communication too – one that can be as powerful as speech. Or screenwriting.

Just as a punch is a way of telling somebody something, all art is an attempt to make contact, and *The Beat That My Heart Skipped* may be Audiard's saddest film because, while Duris escapes the seedy world of underhand property dealing, he becomes not a pianist but an amanuensis. Someone has heard him – Miao Lin (Linh Dam Pham), who was his piano teacher. But the world never will. The world doesn't quite hear Audiard as they might, either, because most of his dialogue is not listened to but read, on the screen, in translation. The title of the Duris film is a perfect example of this: in French, it is both poetic (*De battre mon coeur s'est arrêté*) and practical: *arrêter*, to stop, is the verb used when Duris's Tom talks of having quit piano playing. The whole film is about what has stopped that shouldn't have – his piano playing, his relationship with his father, his mother's life and therefore her playing – and what needs to begin. The awkward English title keeps the lovely dual meaning of *battre* – Tom beats time and beats people up – but it loses a great deal, not least the fluidity of the French. In the end, whatever your personal facility or the budget allocated to your self-expression, communication is never as easy as it sounds.

The darkness at the heart of all Audiard's films may spring partly from the knowledge of this dour truth. Tom will never be a pianist; Malik has become a link in a chain of violence that may one day end when another young upstart supercedes him as he has done with the Corsican capo, César (Niels Arestrup). In *Read My Lips*, Devos and Cassel may walk off into the sunset, hand in hand with a garbage bag of ill-gotten cash slung over each shoulder, but will he manage to stay straight? Is he really a candidate for the calm coupledom she seems to crave? Won't these two strong personalities end up clashing – always assuming that some greedy associate of the thugs they've ripped off doesn't come looking for payback and snuff those personalities out? As for Albert Dehousse, the self-made hero, he pays his debt to society but Audiard, in his most self-conscious film to date, throws up more questions about his character's future than he answers. Various talking heads disagree on what happened to Dehousse after prison; Jean-Louis Trintignant, supposedly the old Dehousse,

stares at the camera and asks us if he looks natural (has he made all of this up, too? Well, in a sense, yes). And most unsettling of all, the two lovely women Albert has romanced, lied to and abandoned forgive him and each other so enthusiastically that the whole scene becomes a joke. Sandrine Kiberlain and Anouk Grinberg gaze adoringly through the bars at their Albert (who has been put away, in the end, not for large-scale fraud but for bigamy), before slinking off together – to have dinner? To have sex? Either seems possible.

With another director, this could be written off as irritating male fantasy (in France especially, it seems, the myth of the unknowable but sexually available woman is still going strong). But Audiard is good at women. Devos's character in *Read My Lips* is superbly drawn (and deservedly won her a clutch of awards), but as importantly, she is the equal of the men he writes: Audiard's mistrust of hypocrisy (the anti-Semites who then claimed to have been Resistance fighters, the anti-Arab sentiment that spills over into the prison system) extends to sexism as well. It may be his finely tuned contempt for two-facedness that makes him such a sensitive portrayer of people caught between two worlds. Carla is a woman in an office full of men, a singleton, possibly even a virgin, in an atmosphere where even her boorish coworkers are married and cheating on their wives; and a deaf person surrounded by those who can hear, but who don't listen. These are powerful disadvantages… or are they simply powerful? After all, they barely see her, while she even sees what they say. And as anyone who has ever seen a gangster film knows, knowledge is power – especially knowledge that others don't realise you have. Her uncomfortable position between worlds – the perch of the eternal outsider – is the most useful asset she has.

All Audiard's people are like this: bold yet vulnerable, cunning yet needy, on the outside staring hungrily in like a succession of little match girls. The actors he chooses both portray and reflect this: he has said that he

Read My Lips

A Self-Made Hero

likes to cast virile men who nonetheless have something feminine about them, and Devos is a woman with a streak of masculinity about her. These people may move between worlds – negotiating public and private spaces, trying to adapt themselves but also manipulate others in their ceaseless quest for a better, more whole, more satisfying life – but they have also internalised that duality. They are masculine and feminine, open and closed, taken for granted yet never really accepted, lawbreakers who despise the criminal game and most of the other players (they are liars, but never hypocrites). Albert in *A Self-Made Hero* is a coward and a fantasist; he's almost pathologically detached, which enables him to play on everyone else's weaknesses, yet he concentrates all his abilities on the project to belong. Paul and Carla in *Read My Lips* are quintessential outsiders, at war with both the office – bourgeois respectability, if with a little baksheesh here and there – and the nightclub, where money comes in black plastic and the wrong move will get you not fired but killed. In *The Beat That My Heart Skipped*, Tom's division is clearest of all: he wants to express himself in music, to live for art, and to jettison the hardscrabble world of petty crime that is his father's legacy (his blowsy dad is almost a caricature of human failure – chain smoking, uncommunicative, a terrible businessman and forever getting his son further mixed up in the kind of persuasion that leaves scars). And Malik, who comes from nowhere, is the distilled essence of not-belonging: the Corsicans call him Arab, the Arabs deride him for working for the Corsicans and nobody else

cares if he lives, dies – or rots in jail, which is somewhere between the two. Is it their dual nationality, so to speak, that makes these people so preoccupied with communicating – learning languages (Malik) or dialects (Albert) or codes (Carla) or scores (Tom)? Their creator grew up in a dual world – a bourgeois home made comfortable by gangster slang – and his anxieties about communicating are as fascinating as they are profound: they impel him to remind us, incessantly, that he is trying to communicate – and that what he wants to say and what we choose to hear may not be the same. It's a common anxiety, of course, but rarely so elegantly played out: as director, Audiard will obscure part of the frame, or have a character speak directly to the audience, or fiddle with the sound as Devos does with her hearing aid. His soundtracks soothe us with strings even as he messes with our minds: in *The Beat That My Heart Skipped*, the jerky electro Romaine Duris listens to, brow furrowed as if having to concentrate on liking it, speaks eloquently of the kind of thug Tom isn't; the musicians we see onscreen in *A Self-Made Hero* remind us that Albert isn't the only person making up stories – or that, as Jean-Luc Godard put it, 'the only reality in a film is the reality of its own making'. Audiard's films are exceptionally stylish but the style often feels as if it's there to make that core anxiety palatable, like an insecure man who dresses beautifully – or a hoodlum whose mouthiness and swagger send signals about his toughness, his impregnability. Inside, of course, he's as soft and scared as the rest of

The Beat That My Heart Skipped

us. It is Audiard's great achievement to offer us both at once: gangster cool and the hot flush of self-doubt. This is what great cinema can do that people, even great people, can't: express itself fully and show only its best side, at the same time. This is what art has that violence doesn't – the capacity to eat cake and have it, or to fire guns yet kill no one.

If you're an artist, your elaborate lies may win you not a jail term but a clutch of Césars, international renown and the honour of having your fifth film represent your country in the 2010 Academy Award nominations. As Albert Dehousse puts it, 'la plus belle vie est celle qu'on invente', and Audiard – pen in hand, camera to eye and gun at his back, invents lives of peerless beauty. 'When death comes,' he has the old Dehousse say, 'we'll lie to it.' Death keeps coming. Audiard, we hope, has many more lies up his sleeve.

NINA CAPLAN is Arts Editor of *Time Out* magazine. In addition to film, she writes about photography, books, theatre, travel and food and drink.

Jacques Audiard filmography

[feature film directing credits only]

1994
REGARDE LES HOMMES TOMBER (See How They Fall)
Script: Jacques Audiard, Alain Le Henry. Photography: Gérard Sterin. Production Design: Jacques Rouxel. Editing: Juliette Welfling. Music: Alexandre Desplat. Players: Jean-Louis Trintignant (Marx), *Jean Yanne* (Simon), *Mathieu Kassovitz* (Johnny), *Bulle Ogier* (Louise), *Christine Pascal* (Sandrine), *Yvon Back* (Mickey), *Yves Verhoeven* (Homosexual), *Marc Citti* (Informer), *Roger Mollien* (Marlon), *Pierre Guillemin* (Mr. Vernoux), *Philippe du Janerand* (Merlin), *Rywka Wajsbrot* (Mme Rajenski), *Blats* (Donata). *Produced by Didier Haudepin. 90 mins*

1996
UN HÉROS TRÈS DISCRET
(A Self-Made Hero)
Script: Jacques Audiard, Alain Le Henry. Photography: Jean-Marc Fabre. Production Design: Michel Vandestien. Editing: Juliette Welfling. Music: Alexandre Desplat. Players: Mathieu Kassovitz (Albert Dehousse), *Anouk Grinberg* (Servane), *Sandrine Kiberlain* (Yvette), *Jean-Louis Trintignant* (Albert Dehousse), *Albert Dupontel* (Dionnet), *Nadia Barentin* (The General's Wife), *Bernard Bloch* (Ernst), *François Chattot* (Louvier), *Philippe Duclos* (Caron), *Danièle Lebrun* (Madame Dehousse), *Armand de Baudry d'Asson* (Englishman). *Produced by Patrick Godeau. 107 mins*

2001
SUR MES LÈVRES (Read My Lips)
Script: Jacques Audiard, Tonino Benacquista. Photography: Mathieu Vadepied. Production Design: Michel Barthélémy. Editing: Juliette Welfling. Music: Alexandre Desplat. Players: Vincent Cassel (Paul), *Emmanuelle Devos* (Carla), *Olivier Gourmet* (Marchand), *Olivier Perrier* (Masson), *Olivier Bonamy* (Annie), *Bernard Alane* (Morel), *Céline Samie* (Josie), *Pierre Diot* (Keller), *François Loriquet* (Jean-François), *Serge Boutleroff* (Mammouth), *David Saracino* (Richard Carambo), *Cristophe Vandevelde* (Louis Carambo). *Produced by Philippe Carcassonne, Jean-Louis Livi. 118 mins*

2005
DE BATTRE MON COEUR S'EST ARRÊTÉ
(The Beat That My Heart Skipped)
Script: Jacques Audiard, Tonino Benacquista. Photography: Stéphane Fontaine. Production Design: François Emmanuelli. Editing: Juliette Welflin. Music: Alexandre Desplat. Players: Romain Duris (Thomas Seyr), *Niels Arestrup* (Robert Seyr), *Jonathan Zaccaï* (Fabrice), *Gilles Cohen* (Sami), *Linh Dan Pham* (Miao Lin), *Aure Atika* (Aline), *Emmanuelle Devos* (Chris), *Anton Yakovlev* (Minskov), *Mélanie Laurent* (Minskov's Girlfriend). *Produced by Pascal Caucheteux. 108 mins*

2009
UN PROPHÈTE (A Prophet)
Script: Jacques Audiard, Thomas Bidegain. Photography: Stéphane Fontaine. Production Design: Michel Barthélémy. Editing: Juliette Welfling. Music: Alexandre Desplat. Players: Tahar Rahim (Malik El Djebena), *Niels Arestrup* (César Luciani), *Adel Bencherif* (Ryad), *Hichem Yacoubi* (Reyeb), *Reda Kateb* (Jordi), *Jean-Philippe Ricci* (Vettori), *Gilles Cohen* (Prof), *Antoine Basler* (Pilicci), *Leïla Bekhti* (Djamila), *Pierre Leccia* (Sampierro), *Foued Nassah* (Antaro), *Jean-Emmanuel Pagni* (Santi), *Frédéric Graziani* (Chef de détention), *Slimane Dazi* (Lattrache). *Produced by Lauranne Bourrachot, Martine Cassinelli. 155 mins*

Kathryn Bigelow by Philip Kemp

Action directors, it seems, are allowed to screw up now and again. Ridley and Tony Scott, Roland Emmerich, even the revered Clint Eastwood have all perpetrated the occasional box-office disaster, apparently without doing irrevocable major damage to their careers. It's only if – as so rarely happens – the action director in question is female that the rules seem to be different.

In the 1980s and 1990s Kathryn Bigelow looked like one of the most intriguing filmmakers working in American popular cinema, intent on subverting its conventions from within. Her background was unconventional for a film director. Born in 1951 in San Carlos, California, into a prosperous middle-class family, she studied painting at the San Francisco Art Institute until, at the age of 19, she won a scholarship to the Whitney Museum in New York, where her tutors included Susan Sontag and Richard Serra. Becoming active in the New York avant-garde art scene, she affiliated to Art and Language, the British-based group of conceptual artists

whose aim was the 'exploration of theoretical, literary and political topics through writing and painting', and worked as assistant to the performance artist Vito Acconci.

Increasingly, though, she found herself drawn to cinema. 'I felt painting was isolating and a little bit elitist,' she later explained, 'whereas film has the potential to become an incredible social tool with which you can reach a mass audience. Some painting requires a certain amount of knowledge or education on the part of the viewer to be appreciated. Film is not like that. It *must* be accessible to work within a cinematic context.' Accordingly she enrolled in Columbia University's Graduate School of Film, where she worked, among others, with Milos Forman and film theorist Peter Wollen.

Bigelow's 1978 graduate film, the 17-minute *The Set-Up*, mapped out in miniature her chosen territory as a filmmaker: a fascination with the testosterone world of masculinity and violence, tempered by a certain ironic critical distance. Two men (one of them played by Gary Busey) fight violently in an alley, while on the soundtrack the semioticians Sylvère Lotringer and Marshall Blonsky comment on and deconstruct the action. Her first feature followed four years later, co-written and co-directed with fellow Columbia film student Monty Montgomery. (It was Montgomery's sole foray into directing; he went on to become a producer, most notably on David Lynch's *Wild at Heart* and Jane Campion's *The Portrait of a Lady*.)

The Loveless gave fair notice of Bigelow's offbeat approach to genre cinema. Starting out from the classic set-up established by *The Wild One* and later productively mined by Roger Corman – a gang of black-leather-clad bikers, moody and sexy, sweep into an

The Loveless

all-American small town and disrupt its values – *The Loveless* slows down the action, putting a dreamy Sirkian spin on events and, taking a leaf out of Kenneth Anger's book *Scorpio Rising*, fetishising the gang's machines, clothing and accoutrements to the point of delirium. For all their apparent menace, the bikers (led by Willem Dafoe in his first major screen role) are essentially passive and self-absorbed; the film displaces the impulse to violence on to the respectable townsfolk.

The Loveless heralds elements that would recur throughout Bigelow's work. For her, as for Arthur Penn two decades earlier, 'a society has its mirror in its outcasts'. The bikers are the first of her self-contained groups of outsiders: seemingly defined by their opposition to conventional mores, they represent an alternative dark-side structure, respectable society's hidden needs and appetites made manifest. ('They're animals,' mutters one of the town's old-timers. 'Heck, I'd love to be them for a day or two.') And local teenager Telena (Marin Kanter) who latches eagerly on to the gang – and later shoots her sexually abusive father before killing herself – represents, with

her boyish figure and short hair, the first of Bigelow's gallery of androgynous heroines in a man's world.

The Loveless was cautiously received. Many reviewers found it slow and lacking in action. It wasn't a charge Bigelow would incur again. Around this time she experienced a cinematic epiphany. Her studies at Columbia had left her in thrall to European directors such as Fassbinder and Pasolini. Then one night she watched a double bill of *Mean Streets* and *The Wild Bunch*. 'It took all my semiotic Lacanian deconstructivist saturation and torqued it,' she recalled. 'I realised there's a more muscular approach to filmmaking that I found very inspiring.'

Following her own mantra – 'Rules are meant to be broken, boundaries are meant to be invaded, envelopes meant to be pushed, preconceptions challenged' – Bigelow rejigged the contours of the action genre, rejecting standard rollercoaster excursions in favour of cross-fertilising experiments in genre-bending. Her next film, *Near Dark*, an insidious vampire western tinged with noirish melancholy, also tosses in elements of star-crossed lovers romance and the counterculture road movie.

Near Dark

Set in the scoured flatlands of the American southwest and shot almost entirely at the magic hour, *Near Dark* pivots around a series of archetypal opposites – light and dark, love and death, nurturing and destroying – that intertwine and merge. Caleb (Adrian Pasdar), an Oklahoma farm-boy, finds himself torn between two families: in the light, his widowed father and self-assured little sister; lurking in the dark, the itinerant vampire clan into which he's inducted by the sensual Mae (Jenny Wright). The film's action highpoint comes when the clan trash a redneck bar and its patrons, watched with horrified fascination by Caleb. The scene's played with measured, almost courtly pacing, and leaves room for black humour. 'I hate it when they ain't bin shaved,' growls Severen (Bill Paxton) as he sinks his fangs into a biker's neck.

Bigelow followed it up with *Blue Steel*, a cop drama laced with horror-movie tropes; as if to underline the generic links, Bigelow cast as her lead the iconic queen of stalk'n'slash, Jamie Lee Curtis. In this film the fetishistic impulse turns yet more intense: in the credit sequence light caresses the contours of a handgun (a key factor in the plot) in extreme close-up, transforming it into an abstract study of curves and shadows. Curtis plays a rookie New York cop (unusually for Bigelow, a female protagonist) who, after a shoot-out in a late-night convenience store, acquires a lethal stalker: a market trader (Ron Silver) who, having stolen a gun from the shoot-out scene, becomes obsessed with her and with random killing, scratching her name on his bullets like twisted valentines.

By now, Bigelow was attracting attention as a woman not only working in the hitherto men-only field of action movies, but proving herself exceptionally adept at them. Her appearance – 6 ft tall, slim, strikingly attractive with long dark hair – added to the media's fascination. (*Vogue* described her as looking like 'the world's highest-paid dominatrix'.) She fielded persistent questions about her supposedly anomalous status with weary courtesy tinged

Blue Steel

with exasperation. 'I tend not to dignify it as a gender occupation. I see myself as a filmmaker, period. If other people find me a novelty that's their problem.' Her own style she summed up as 'visceral, high-impact, kinetic, cathartic'.

Her next film certainly ticked the first three boxes, though some reviewers found it more risible than cathartic. *Point Break* again melded genres, crossing a heist thriller with a surfing movie and tossing in a sky-diving episode for good measure. As before, Bigelow focuses on a group of social outsiders, this time a quartet of California surfing dudes who finance their pursuit by robbing banks as 'the Ex-Presidents', wearing rubber masks of Reagan, Carter, Nixon and LBJ. Their leader, Bodhi (Patrick Swayze), is much given to windy philosophical musings: 'This was never about money – it was about us against the system…. To those dead souls inching along the freeways in their metal coffins, we show them that the human spirit is still alive.'

Going up against the gang is an ambitious young FBI agent, Johnny Utah (Keanu Reeves),

Point Break

who takes up surfing in order to infiltrate their society. Though Johnny falls for a female surfer, Tyler (Lori Petty), another of Bigelow's short-haired androgynes, the film's strongest relationship is between him and Bodhi. This homoerotic bond, and the surfers' self-absorbed intensity ('Riding waves is a state of mind – it's that place where you lose yourself and you find yourself,' proclaims Bodhi), create a superheated mood in which the frequent absurdities of the plot dissolve into irrelevance. Bigelow's skill at staging action sequences hits virtuoso levels: in an on-foot chase sequence, her unbroken Steadicam hurtle through the alleys, gardens and houses of Santa Monica outdoes Scorsese's famous shot in *Goodfellas*.

Bigelow's first four features built her a strong niche following, pitching her midway between maverick and mainstream. *Strange Days* looked like her bid for major-pantheon status. An intricate, hugely ambitious vision of the millennium, it packs its dystopian sci-fi framework with elements of love story, noirish murder mystery and political satire, borrowing and creatively reworking influences from a dazzlingly eclectic range of sources: Hawks, Hitchcock, Scorsese, *Blade Runner*, *Peeping Tom* and cyberpunk fiction, to name but a few. As always, Bigelow brought an artist's visual sensibility to the film with stunning imagery, sweeping imperious camerawork and sculpted lighting. Her scrupulous attention to formal style, sometimes mistaken for emotional detachment, is counteracted by the dark romanticism that suffuses all her work.

Bigelow described *Strange Days* (co-scripted by her ex-husband, James Cameron, who also co-produced) as 'the ultimate Rorschach' – an artefact lending itself to as many interpretations as it has viewers. The action plays out in the dying hours of the 20th century in Los Angeles, a city quivering with Millennium fever and incipient racial violence. Ex-cop Lenny Nero (Ralph Fiennes) peddles 'clips' – recordings of other people's subjective experiences that can be played back directly through the cerebral cortex for the ultimate out-of-body high: virtual reality that's indistinguishable from real. But someone is using the technology to commit ingeniously sadistic murders, and the victims are coming dangerously close to Lenny. The plot asks more questions than it answers, though; the film nags and probes at our own voyeuristic tendencies, pushing us to react not only to what we're seeing but to our motives in wanting to watch it. But in presenting audiences with such a convoluted, demanding collage, inviting simultaneous engagement on a multiplicity of levels, Bigelow outpaced her public and the film stalled badly at the box office.

Strange Days

The Weight of Water

There followed a further debacle. *Company of Angels*, her long-planned concept of a Joan of Arc movie, fell victim to a clash with the project's executive producer, Luc Besson. Bigelow had chosen Clare Danes to play the Maid; Besson wanted to cast his then partner, Milla Jovovich. When Bigelow refused to accede, Besson withdrew his finance, two weeks before shooting was scheduled to start, and proceeded to make his own movie, *The Messenger* (1999), with Jovovich. That it proved just as ineptly conceived and direly miscast as Bigelow had predicted scarcely compensated for the loss of her cherished project. Another pet project, *Ohio*, about the 1970 Kent State shootings, languished for want of funding.

The failure of *Strange Days* badly dented Bigelow's career. Not for five years was she able to direct another film; and even then *The Weight of Water*, though completed in 2000, had to wait nearly two years for its US release. (In the UK it went straight to video.) This was Bigelow's first (and so far only) film adapted from another source, a novel by Anita Shreve. It traces two parallel stories: a double-murder case (based on a real-life incident) on an island off the New Hampshire coast in 1873, and the tensions and jealousies among a modern-day quartet on a yacht visiting the murder site while one of them, a photographer (Catherine McCormack), tries to unearth the truth behind the killings.

For once, a Bigelow film features neither cars nor guns, and for much of its length it feels

uncharacteristically quiet and low-key – though the claustrophobic atmosphere on the island in the period story is vivid and increasingly ominous, gradually building to a violent climax that envelops both stories. Vigorous as ever at this juncture, Bigelow's direction whips up twin physical and emotional storms; but the two stories never fully mesh, the dialogue all too often judders, and Elizabeth Hurley's crude vamping tips several of the modern-day scenes into farce.

Bigelow's next film was out before *The Weight of Water* received its belated release. At a budget of US$100 million, *K-19: The Widowmaker* was her most expensive film to date, and said to be the most expensive film yet directed by a woman. It's based on the real-life story of the catastrophic maiden voyage of the USSR's first nuclear submarine in 1961 at the height of the Cold War, only a few months before the Cuban Missile stand-off. Rushed into panicky production to counter the perceived US threat, launched with an inadequately trained crew, the ill-made sub heads out under the ice of the Bering Sea. Disasters mount, culminating in the nuclear reactor springing a leak.

Tension on board is heightened by the cumbersome double-command structure. The Party, doubting the commitment of Captain Polyanin (Liam Neeson), a humane commander who enjoys the loyalty of the crew, shoehorn in a doctrinaire martinet,

K-19: The Widowmaker

Captain Vostrikov (Harrison Ford), over Polyanin's head. Bigelow depicts an edgy, all-male culture of suspicion and accusation, intensified by the claustrophobic confines of the sub – which she had built exactly to scale, to preserve authenticity. *K-19* exerts a grim fascination and carries an intriguing (and, aptly enough, submerged) political subtext. But the constricted environment cramps Bigelow's expansive shooting style, restricting her largely to fast tracks forwards and back, and the plot is let down by an unconvincing change-of-heart development towards the end. Despite its substantial investment, *K-19* was dumped out on a midsummer release in the US, up against popcorn fare like *Spiderman* and *Men in Black II*, and predictably flopped. Its UK release, given minimal support, lasted barely a week.

Once again, Bigelow's career had suffered a bad knock, and it was six years before she released another film. When she did, it was to some of the best reviews she had received since *Near Dark*. *The Hurt Locker*, set in Iraq one year after Saddam Hussein's regime has been toppled, focused on the work of a three-man US Army bomb squad. When the sergeant in charge (a brief cameo from Guy Pearce) is killed by an IED, a new disposal expert, Sgt

The Hurt Locker

William James (Jeremy Renner), comes in to replace him. His two colleagues soon realise that James, though instinctively brilliant at his job, is a reckless wild card, high on adrenaline and endangering them all. Their company is nearing the end of its tour of duty; an on-screen countdown of days heightens the suspense.

The Hurt Locker opens with a quote from *New York Times* war correspondent Chris Hedges: 'The rush of battle is a potent and often lethal addiction, for war is a drug.' The script, by freelance journalist Mark Boal (who also scripted *In the Valley of Elah*) draws on his experiences when embedded with just such a squad in Iraq. Unlike other Iraq movies, *The Hurt Locker* passes no comment on the rightness or otherwise of the US-led invasion. Bigelow, who insisted on shooting in Jordan rather than in Morocco, South Africa or other less logistically problematic locations, simply aims, with visceral immediacy, to get us inside the heads of soldiers operating with that degree of danger in gruelling, always potentially hostile terrain. 'War's dirty little secret is that some men love it,' she says. 'I'm trying to unpack why, to look at what it means to be a hero in the context of 21st-century combat.' As ever, her action sequences are textbook examples of clarity, pace, timing and gut-churning tension. The nearest hint to a political comment comes when James arrives at what he thinks is Camp Liberty, to be told it's been renamed Camp Victory because 'it sounds better'.

The Hurt Locker won a number of awards following its premiere at the Venice Film Festival. In the wake of it, Kathryn Bigelow's stock is again riding high. But despite its acclaim, the film received only a relatively restricted release and, on past evidence, it may take only one box-office disappointment to knock her back to square one. It does seem that, if a woman has the audacity to choose to operate in an overwhelmingly male genre, she's only ever allowed to be as good as her last picture. And though Bigelow famously dislikes being labelled a 'woman director',

The Hurt Locker

it's known that, as her friend Willem Dafoe notes, she's repeatedly come under pressure from 'the boys' network in LA'. She herself, while insisting that her gender never causes her any problems during the making of a film (a view endorsed by those who have worked with her), adds, 'That's not to say that there isn't an inequality in the business. There is, but the prejudices are perceptual. It is a very competitive field and that can create some limitations. It's not that women can't make films, but that some people think they can't.'

Currently, Bigelow is working again with Mark Boal on a project called *Triple Frontier*, an action-adventure film set in the remote jungle zone where the borders of Argentina, Paraguay and Brazil come together, an area much favoured by organised crime and drug barons. It sounds like ideal material for one of the most intelligent, individual and technically accomplished of today's action directors, one who sees as her strategy to 'include genre elements which make you comfortable, and then I add other dimensions'. Let's hope none of those 'perceptual prejudices' get in her way this time.

PHILIP KEMP is a freelance writer and film historian, a regular contributor to *Sight and Sound*, *Total Film* and *DVD Review*, and teaches Film Journalism at the University of Leicester.

Kathryn Bigelow filmography

[feature film directing credits only]

1982
THE LOVELESS
Co-director: Monty Montgomery. Script: Kathryn Bigelow, Monty Montgomery. Photography: Doyle Smith. Production Design: Lilly Kilvert. Editing: Nancy Kanter. Music: Robert Gordon. Players: Willem Dafoe (Vance), Robert Gordon (Davis), Marin Kanter (Telena), J Don Ferguson (Tarver), Tina L'Hotsky (Sportster Debbie), Lawrence Matarese (La Ville), Danny Rosen (Ricky), Phillip Kimbrough (Hurley), Ken Call (Buck), Elizabeth Gans (Augusta), Margaret Jo Lee (Evie), John King (John), Bob Hannah (Sid), Jane Berman (Lady in T-Bird), AB Calloway (Truck Driver in Diner). Produced by A Kitman Ho and Grafton Nunes. 85 mins

1987
NEAR DARK
Script: Kathryn Bigelow, Eric Red. Photography: Adam Greenberg. Production Design: Stephen Altman. Editing: Howard E Smith. Music: Tangerine Dream. Players: Adrian Pasdar (Caleb Colton), Jenny Wright (Mae),

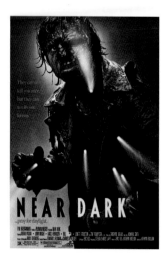

Lance Henriksen (Jesse Hooker), Bill Paxton (Severen), Jenette Goldstein (Diamondback), Tim Thomerson (Loy Colton), Joshua Miller (Homer), Marcie Leeds (Sarah Colton), Kenny Call (Deputy Sheriff), Ed Corbett (Ticket Seller), Troy Evans (Plainclothes Officer), Bill Cross (Sheriff Eakers), Roger Aaron Brown (Cajun Truck Driver), Thomas Wagner (Bartender), Robert Winley (Patron in Bar). Produced by Steven-Charles Jaffe. 94 mins

1989
BLUE STEEL
Script: Kathryn Bigelow, Eric Red. Photography: Amir Mokri. Production Design: Toby Corbett. Editing: Lee Percy. Music: Brad Fiedel. Players: Jamie Lee Curtis (Megan Turner), Ron Silver (Eugene Hunt), Clancy Brown (Nick Mann), Elizabeth Pena (Tracy Perez), Louise Fletcher (Shirley Turner), Philip Bosco (Frank Turner), Kevin Dunn

(Asst Chief Stanley Hoyt), *Richard Jenkins* (Attorney Mel Dawson), *Markus Flannagan (Husband)*, *Mary Mara* (Wife), *Skipp Lynch* (Instructor), *Mike Hodge* (Police Commissioner), *Mike Starr* (Superintendant), *Chris Walker* (Officer Jeff Travers), *Tom Sizemore* (Wool Cap). *Produced by Oliver Stone, Edward R Pressman. 102 mins*

1991
POINT BREAK
Script: Rick King, W Peter Iliff. Photography: Donald Peterman. Production Design: Peter Jamison. Editing: Howard Smith. Music: Mark Isham. Players: Patrick Swayze (Bodhi), *Keanu Reeves* (Johnny Utah), *Gary Busey* (Pappas), *Lori Petty* (Tyler), *John McGinley* (Ben Harp), *James Le Gros* (Roach), *John Philbin* (Nathanial), *Bojesse Christopher* (Grommet), *Julian Reyes* (Alvarez), *Daniel Beer* (Babbitt), *Chris Pedersen* (Bunker), *Vincent Klyn* (Warchild), *Anthony Kiedis* (Tone), *Dave Olson* (Archbold), *Lee Tergesen* (Rosie). *Produced by Peter Abrams, Robert L Levy. 120 mins*

1995
STRANGE DAYS
Script: James Cameron, Jay Cocks. Photography: Matthew F Leonetti. Production Design: Lilly Kilvert. Editing: Howard Smith. Music: Graeme Revell. Players: Ralph Fiennes (Lenny Nero), *Angela Bassett* (Lornette 'Mace' Mason), *Juliette Lewis* (Faith Justin), *Tom Sizemore* (Max Peltier), *Michael Wincott* (Philo Gant), *Vincent d'Onofrio* (Burton Steckler), *Glenn Plummer* (Jeriko One), *Brigitte Bako* (Iris), *Richard Edson* (Tick), *William Fichtner* (Dwayne Engelman), *Josef Sommer* (Palmer Strickland), *Joe Urla* (Keith), *Nicky Katt* (Joey Corto), *Michael Jace* (Wade Beemer), *Louise LeCavalier* (Cindy 'Vita' Minh). *Produced by James Cameron, Steven-Charles Jaffe. 145 mins*

2000
THE WEIGHT OF WATER
Script: Alice Arlen, Christopher Kyle. Photography: Adrian Biddle. Production Design: Karl Juliusson. Editing: Howard E Smith. Music: David Hirschfelder. Players: Catherine McCormack (Jean Janes), *Sean Penn* (Thomas Janes), *Sarah Polley* (Maren Hontvedt), *Ciaran Hinds* (Louis Wagner), *Josh Lucas* (Rich Janes), *Elizabeth Hurley* (Adaline Gunne), *Katrin Cartlidge* (Karen Christenson), *Vinessa Shaw* (Anethe Christenson), *Ulrich Thomsen* (John Hontvedt), *Anders W Berthelsen* (Evan Christenson), *Adam Curry* (Emil Ingerbretson), *Richard Donat* (Mr Plaisted), *Joseph Rutten* (Judge), *John Walf* (Defense Attorney), *John Maclaren* (Dr Parsons). *Produced by A Kitman Ho, Sigurjón Sighvatsson, Janet Yang. 113 mins*

2002
K-19: THE WIDOWMAKER
Script: Christopher Kyle, Louis Nowra. Photography: Jeff Cronenweth. Production Design: Karl Juliusson, Michael Novotny. Editing: Walter Murch. Music: Klaus Badelt. Players: Harrison Ford (Capt Alexei Vostrikov), *Liam Neeson* (Capt Mikhail Polyanin), *Peter Sarsgaard* (Lt Vadim Radtchinko), *Joss Ackland* (Marshal Zelentsov), *John Shrapnel* (Admiral Bratyeev), *Ravil Isyanov*

(Suslov), *James Ginty* (Anatoly), *Donald Sumpter* (Dr Gennadi Savran), *Ingvar Sigurdsson* (Chief Engineer Gorelov), *Michael Gladis* (Yevgeny Borzenkov), *Gerrit Vooren* (Voslensky), *Steve Cumyn* (Arseni), *Peter Oldring* (Vanya), *Peter Stebbings* (Kuryshev), *Christian Camargo* (Pavel). *Produced by Kathryn Bigelow, Edward S Feldman, Sigurjón Sighvatsson, Christine Whitaker. 138 mins*

2008
THE HURT LOCKER
Script: Mark Boal. Photography: Barry Ackroyd. Production Design: Karl Juliusson. Editing: Chris Innis, Bob Murawski. Music: Marco Beltrami, Buck Sanders. Players: Jeremy Renner (Sgt William James), *Anthony Mackie* (Sgt JT Sanborn), *Brian Geraghty* (Spc Owen Eldridge), *Guy Pearce* (Sgt Matt Thompson), *Ralph Fiennes* (Contractor Team Leader), *David Morse* (Colonel Reed), *Evangeline Lilly* (Connie James), *Christian Camargo* (Col John Cambridge), *Suhail Al-Dabbach* (Black Suit Man), *Christopher Sayegh* (Beckham), *Nabil Koni* (Professor Nabil), *Sam Spruell* (Contractor Charlie), *Sam Redford* (Contractor Jimmy), *Feisal Sadoun* (Contractor Feisal), *Barrie Rice* (Contractor Chris). *Produced by Kathryn Bigelow, Mark Boal, Nicolas Chartier, Greg Shapiro. 131 mins*

Park Chan-wook by Colin Odell and Michelle Le Blanc

One of the key figures in South Korean cinema, writer and director Park Chan-wook has created a body of work that is uncompromising in its depiction of violence, yet engrossing in its art-house sensibilities and tight scripting. Although commentators have often focused on the transgressive and visceral nature of his films, this belies the wider themes of alienation, fracture (social, mental, temporal and political) and morality that pervade his work. Time, perception and memory all play key roles in his often tragic tales of misunderstanding and retribution where characters tread a fine line between redemption and damnation. Park tempers his grim premises with dark humour, even as he shows that anyone, no matter how good, can be capable of terrible, horrific deeds and that humanity is something fragile and ultimately ephemeral.

Park was born in 1963. He grew up in Seoul, studying philosophy and aesthetics at Sogang University, where he was an active member of the photography club. A cinephile, he spent a large part of his student life watching films and was particularly influenced by Alfred Hitchcock. Indeed it was viewing *Vertigo* that convinced Park that he wanted to become a filmmaker. After graduation Park found himself a job on the production crew of Yu Young-jin's *Ggam-dong* and also began working as a film critic. He made his feature debut writing and directing *The Moon is What the Sun Dreams Of* (1992), a melodramatic gangster film. It was not a success, so Park reverted to film criticism, publishing a book of reviews, *Videodrome: The Discret Charm of Watching Films*, which reflected his passion for all things cinematic. After a five-year hiatus he returned to filmmaking, directing his second feature *Threesome* (*Samminjo*), a road film about a dysfunctional trio who travel around the country robbing houses. It carried many of the themes that would typify Park's later work, combining social issues with black humour. Again, the critical response was generally negative.

1999 was a pivotal year for the Korean film industry, a time when investment resulted in a series of impressive films that rivalled the increasingly popular US blockbusters. While filmgoers were flocking to see the political action thriller *Shiri*, the manga-noir of *Nowhere to Hide* or the controversial comedy *Attack the Gas Station*, Park produced a claustrophobic short film, *Judgement* (*Simpan*), which used mixed media to question the nature of identity and memory. Set in a mortuary, it follows the autopsy and identification of an unknown victim who has been recovered from the rubble of a collapsed department store. Shocked parents are convinced the deceased girl is theirs. Bizarrely, though, the overworked, beer-swilling mortuary attendant (who keeps his drinks nice and chilled in the body drawers) is convinced that the victim is actually his estranged daughter. The whole sorry situation is filmed by a TV crew to show the human side of the disaster. Park takes this premise and increases its macabre elements to the point of pitch-black comedy. The characters' motivations become more apparent and less pleasant when it becomes clear that the girl's identification could lead to financial remuneration. In many ways this is Park's most cynical and nihilistic film – one that doesn't offer redemption for any of its characters. It implicates not only the perpetrators but also the filmmakers and viewing audience – voyeurs sucked into other people's misery and moribund moralities. This questioning of morality provides the backbone not only to Park's films as a director but also as a screenwriter. Occasionally collaborating with Lee Mu-yeong, Park has written screenplays for various projects such as *Anarchists* (2000), the brutal kidnapping farce *The Humanist* (2001), the quirky Taekwondo sci-fi romance *A Bizarre Love Triangle* (2002), the drama *A Boy Who Went to Heaven* (2005) and the black comedy *Crush and Blush* (2008).

Park's first major feature-film release in Korea's new climate of cinematic strength was *Joint Security Area* (2000), a combination of thriller, mystery and political drama set around the DMZ, the demilitarised zone that divides North and South Korea in an uneasy truce. Two North Korean soldiers have been killed and one wounded in an incident at an outpost close to the zone. A South Korean soldier has confessed to the crime and the situation threatens to spiral into a major international incident. Sophie, working for the Neutral

Nations Supervisory Committee, seeks to find the truth – 'not who, but why'. Her investigations reveal a complicated situation because the men involved had secretly become friends, sharing evenings together following a series of chance encounters that led each to realise that there was genuine humanity on both sides of the border. The poignancy of these platonic relationships lies in the bonding between brothers, of a desire for Korea to be whole again. Ultimately, yearning is not enough and the tragedy in *Joint Security Area* lies in the inability of those in the present to forget the past. Park plays with time, through flashbacks and slow revelations, to paint a picture that, even as the pieces of the puzzle fall into place, creates a more complex situation rather than a simplistic one. With its assured performances and exemplary direction *Joint Security Area* became the highest-grossing film of 2000.

Sympathy for Mr Vengeance

Sympathy for Mr Vengeance marked the start of Park's 'Vengeance Trilogy', an almost Jacobean exploration of tragedy and revenge that offers a bleak insight into the human condition. Ryu, a deaf-mute with a loving temperament and pale-green hair, needs to find money to save his sister so that she can have a kidney transplant. Desperate, he turns to an underworld surgeon who agrees to remove one of Ryu's kidneys for a fee and give him one that's compatible to his sister. It's a con. He recovers consciousness with a kidney missing and his money gone. In order to raise the funds, Ryu hatches a plan with his politically active girlfriend, Young-mi, to engage

Joint Security Area

in the 'good kidnapping' of the daughter of Dong-jin, the man who sacked him from his day job. The plan goes horribly wrong despite their best intentions and the stage is set for acts of retribution from which no one can emerge unscathed.

Sympathy for Mr Vengeance paints a picture of society where the rich have no concept of the plight of the ordinary person, but it avoids painting its characters in broad Marxist strokes. Instead, the powerful backbone of *Sympathy for Mr Vengeance* is precisely that both Ryu and Dong-jin are good men, if misguided, hemmed in by their social status. Their need to exact vengeance on the people that have taken loved ones from them sets them on a path to damnation that taints not just them, but society as a whole. Park treats his viewers with intelligence; much of the action occurs between scenes so that key elements need to be pieced together to understand the whole. The barrage of inexorable tragedy, irredeemable characters, rape, torture and violence led to a mixed critical reaction in South Korea but raised Park's profile internationally.

In 2003, Park contributed to *If You Were Me*, a portmanteau of six short films commissioned by South Korea's National Human Rights Commission, tackling the theme of discrimination. Park's segment, *N.E.P.A.L. Never Ending Peace and Love*, tells the true story of a Nepalese immigrant, Chandra, who finds herself incarcerated in a Korean mental institution when she fails to pay for a bowl of noodles. Her lack of Korean language skills, coupled with well-meaning but ignorant police and medical staff, leads to over six years of imprisonment. Filmed mainly in black and white, the film implicates the viewer in Chandra's plight by alternating between documentary-style interviews with those involved, and claustrophobic point-of-view shots that leave the central character largely absent from the screen; a woman made invisible by others' incorrect perceptions. Many of the issues explored in this film resurfaced in Park's later films, particularly *Oldboy* and *I'm a Cyborg, but That's OK*.

Returning to retribution, the flamboyant and controversial *Oldboy* offered a different take on vengeance, eschewing prompt action for brooding and calculated planning, arguing that revenge is a dish not only best served cold but kept in the freezer well beyond its sell-by date. Oh Dae-su's plans to deliver a present to his daughter are put on hold when he is kidnapped and locked in a room for 15 years. His release is similarly abrupt. Emerging from a suitcase on top of a tower block at exactly the point he was kidnapped, Dae-su finds himself in a changed world. Sushi chef Mi-do provides some grounding in reality as Dae-su attempts to find the person responsible for taking his daughter and 15 years of his life. Adapted from the Japanese manga, the baroque nature of the premise helps temper some of the film's more extreme scenes (live octopus eating, tooth extraction by claw-hammer) with a plot about time and memory, of action and consequence. The mystery that is key to the film is spelled out by one of the characters when he states, 'It's not about why you were incarcerated for 15 years, it's about why you were released.' The final revelation is shocking, compounded by the fact that Dae-su's actions that led to his incarceration were so mundane that he had simply forgotten about them and was unaware of the dire consequences that had resulted. This twisted tale won the Grand Prix at Cannes and continues to have a broad following worldwide.

Oldboy

Cut

Park next turned his hand to *Cut*, a short film made as part of the *Three... Extremes* (2004) project that also featured entries from Fruit Chan and Miike Takashi. In *Cut*, a director making a vampire film finds himself bound by the waist with a ribbon that extends throughout a studio set. His pianist wife is strung like a human puppet, her fingers glued to the piano keys. Their captor gives the director an ultimatum – kill a helpless child or he'll chop the wife's fingers off, one by one. The fluid and ostentatious camerawork, coupled with the primary colour-design, emphasises the deliberate artifice of the film industry, but again Park sees this environment as a means of expressing mirrors and divides, of providing structure that is shattered by fate and action. The director's captor, a disgruntled extra, has placed his boss in this predicament because he sees the director not only as intelligent, rich and talented but also as a good person. This is Park's most postmodern and self-reflexive film. He would later tackle the vampire genre itself with *Thirst*.

The final part of the 'Vengeance Trilogy', *Sympathy for Lady Vengeance* (2005), shifted the emphasis to someone who knows exactly why she has been incarcerated and schemes her terrible revenge on that basis. Lee Guem-ja is a pious woman who uses her 13-year prison sentence to aid needy prisoners while serving time for the brutal murder of a child. Rehabilitation? Not quite. Guem-ja is innocent of the crime and her actions are anything but altruistic. The film also shows that the public

can become complicit in the crimes that are committed and that ordinary people are capable of becoming monsters, a theme that resonates in much of Park's work. In filming his star as a Catholic icon (backlit halo, head cocked sideways, a single tear trickling down her face), Park is not being ironic. Whatever the levels of cruelty and violence her retribution finally entails, she has made a sacrifice for her own daughter, putting duty above herself. The public desire for blood, money and power is seen as tainting society – Guem-ja's mockery of religious piety paradoxically makes her a more enlightened figure of self-sacrifice.

Sympathy for Lady Vengeance

I'm a Cyborg, but That's OK (2006) takes the themes of physical and mental disability shown in *Sympathy for Mr Vengeance* and *Never Ending Peace and Love* and weaves a complex blend of romance, comedy, science fiction and social commentary in its story of an ex-electronics factory worker, Cha Young-goon, who is admitted to a psychiatric hospital following an attempt to plug herself into the mains. Young-goon believes she is a cyborg and, as a result, refuses to eat, relying instead upon electrical batteries, her toes lighting up as her power levels increase. Her mission is to eradicate the hospital orderlies who were responsible for incarcerating her grandmother. When powered up she will unleash a stream of bullets from her fingers, the spent cartridge cases spilling from her mouth. Park's affinity with even the minor characters of the piece means that *I'm a Cyborg* never strays into mean-spirited mockery but instead uses

I'm a Cyborg, But That's OK

its cast to examine social conditions at a microcosmic level, exploring themes of fracture and dislocation. Memory and perception play multiple roles in the film through many of the characters, particularly a woman who has been given electro-shock therapy so often that she creates new stories for each of her fellow inmates due to amnesia – stories that do, however, have grains of truth. In what is set up as a bizarre romantic comedy (*Amelie* meets *One Flew Over the Cuckoo's Nest* meets *The Terminator*), *I'm a Cyborg* proves to be a rebuke of the social-care system and, despite its heroine's quest to dehumanise herself, a life-affirming story. It may be fantasy but Park's whimsical and imaginative candyfloss dream images emphasise the struggle to be human rather than trivialise it.

With the recent surge of interest in vampires, Park's latest feature, *Thirst*, offers an alternative perspective on the silver screen's most malleable monster. When priest Sang-hyan survives the deadly Emmanuel virus after receiving a blood transfusion, he becomes a vampire, drinking blood and lusting after sinful pleasures. He begins a passionate affair with Tae-ju, the downtrodden wife of an old friend, and together they indulge in a life of hedonism. But Sang-hyan cannot completely dispel his former life and his nagging conscience knows that this cannot continue forever. *Thirst* is a vampiric love story bursting with erotic sex and lashings of violence, an antidote to the chaste teen vampire films that are currently all the rage. Again, Park plays with the audience's expectations of how characters are supposed to behave. Sang-hyan, dressed in his priestly attire, comforts patients in hospital but later secretly drinks their blood. He is riddled with guilt but cannot help himself. When he falls for Tae-ju he doesn't realise how manipulative she is and eventually gives in to his dark desires – his innocence leading to his damnation. There is less social commentary in *Thirst* than in Park's other films. It is more an exploration of human desire and conscience. Park takes his time in telling this story and laces many of the scenes with his usual brand of wickedly black humour. He lays on plenty of gore as befits a horror film, and the sex scenes are languid and steamy – filled with lust and affection. The film picked up the Jury Prize at the Cannes Film Festival.

Park Chan-wook continues to provide thought-provoking genre cinema that questions the nature of morality and humanity. His unflinching depiction of violence is often tempered with dark comedy and strong visual stylisation.

COLIN ODELL and **MICHELLE LE BLANC** are authors, broadcasters and film journalists. They have written on David Lynch, Tim Burton, John Carpenter and horror and vampire films, among others. Their most recent book, *Studio Ghibli* (2009), explores the films of Miyazaki Hayao and Takahata Isao.

Thirst

Park Chan-wook
filmography

[feature film directing credits only]

1992
MOON IS THE SUN'S DREAM

*Script: Park Chan-wook. Players:
Bang Eun-hee, Lee Seung-chul, Nah
Hyun-hee, Song Seung-hwan.
103 mins*

1997
SAMINJO (Threesome)

*Script: Park Chan-wook.Production
Manager: Joh Neung-yeon. Players:
Jeong Seon-kyeong (Maria), Kim
Min-jong (Moon), Lee Kyun-young
(Ahn), Kim Bu-seon. 100 mins*

2000
GONGDONG GYEONGBI
GUYEOK JSA
(J.S.A.: Joint Security Area)

*Script: Park Chan-wook, Jeong
Seong-san, Kim Hyeon-seok, Lee
Mu-yeong. Photography: Kim
Sung-bok. Editing: Kim Sang-beom.
Music: Bang Jun-Seok, Jo Yeong-
wook. Players: Lee Yeong-ae (Maj.
Sophie E. Jean), Lee Byung-hun
(Sgt. Lee Soo-hyeok), Song Kang-ho
(Sgt. Oh Kyeong-pil), Kim Tae-woo
(Nam Sung-shik), Shin Ha-kyun
(Jeong Woo-jin). Produced by Eun
Soo Lee. 110 mins*

2002
BOKSUNEUN NAUI GEOT
(Sympathy for Mr. Vengeance)

*Script: Park Chan-wook, Lee Jae-
sun, Lee Jong-yong, Lee Mu-yeong.
Photography: Kim Byeong-Il.
Production Design: Choe Jung-hwa.
Editing: Kim Sang-beom. Players:
Song Kang-ho (Park Dong-jin), Shin
Ha-kyun (Ryu), Bae Du-na (Cha
Yeong-mi), Lim Ji-Eun (Cha Yeong-
mi), Lim Ji-Eun (Ryu's sister), Han
Bo-bae (Yun-sun), Kim Se-dong
(Chief of Staff), Lee Dae-yeon
(Choe). Produced by Lee Jae-sun,
Lim Jin-gyu. 121 mins*

2003
OLDBOY

*Script: Park Chan-wook, Lim chun-
hyeong, Hwang Jo-yun. Photography:
Chung Chung-hoon. Production
Design: Ryu Seong-hie. Editing: Kim
Sang-beom. Music: Shim Hyun-jung.
Players: Choi Min-sik (Oh Dae-su),
Yu Ji-tae (Lee Woo-jin), Kang
Hye-jeong (Mi-do), Ji Dae-han (No
Joo-hwan), Oh Dal-su (Park Cheol-
woong), Kim Byeong-ok (Mr Han),
Lee Seung-shin (Yoo Hyung-ja), Yun
Jin-seo (Lee Soo-ah). Produced by
Lim Seung-young. 120 mins*

2005
CHINJEOLHAN GEUMJASSI
(Sympathy for Lady Vengeance)

*Script: Park Chan-wook, Jeong Seo-
Gyeong. Photography: Chung Chung-
hoon. Production Design: Jo Hwa-
seong. Editing: Kim Jae-beom, Kim
Sang-beom. Music: Choi Seung-hyun.
Players: Lee Yeong-ae (Lee Geum-
ja), Choi Min-sik (Mr Baek), Tony
Barry (Stepfather, Australian), Anne
Cordiner (Stepmother, Australian),
Go Su-hee (Ma-nyeo), Kang Hye-
jeong (TV Announcer), Kim Bu-seon
(Woo So-young), Kim Byeong-ok
(Preacher), Kim Shi-hoo (Geun-
shik), Kwon Yea-young (Jenny),
Lee Dae-yeon (Prison Head), Lee
Seung-shin (Park yi-jeong). Produced
by Cho Young-wuk, Lee Chun-yeong,
Lee Tae-hun. 112 mins*

2006
SAIBOGUJIMAN KWENCHANA
(I'm a Cyborg, but That's OK)

*Script: Park Chan-wook, Jeong
Seo-Gyeong. Photography: Chung
Chung-hoon. Visual Effects: Lee
Jeon-hyeong. Editing: Kim Jae-beom,
Kim Sang-Beom. Music: Jo Yeong-
wook. Players: Lim Su-jeong (Cha
Young-goon), Rain (Park Il-sun),
Choi Hie-jin (Choi Seul-gi), Kim
Byeong-ok (Judge), Lee Yong-nyeo
(Young-goon's mother), Oh Dal-su
(Shin Duk-cheon), Yu Ho-jeong
(Il-sun's mother). Produced by Park
Chan-wook, Lee Chun-yeong.
105 mins*

2009
BAKJWI (Thirst)

*Script: Park Chan-wook, Jeong
Seo-Gyeong. Photography: Chung
Chung-hoon. Production Design:
Ryu Seong-hie. Editing: Kim Jae-
beom, Kim Sang-bum. Music: Cho
Young-ook. Players: Song Kang-ho
(Priest Sang-hyeon), Kim Ok-bin
(Tae-ju), Kim Hae-sook (Lady
Ra), Shin Ha-kyun (Kang-woo),
Park In-hwan (Priest Noh), Oh
Dal-su (Yeong-doo), Song Young-
chang (Seung-dae), Mercedes
Cabral (Evelyn), Eriq Ebouaney
(Immanuel). Produced by Park
Chan-wook, Ahn Soo-Hyun.
133 mins*

Claire Denis by Daniel Graham

Born in 1948 in Paris but raised in French colonial Africa where her Father worked as a Regional Administrator, Claire Denis' childhood was, by her own account, an itinerant one that may have later helped inform the remarkable sense of spatial and temporal displacement so prevalent in her work. Her father instilled in her an appreciation for geography that likely fostered an open mind towards peoples of other cultures and racial backgrounds, another of the director's ongoing thematic concerns. Her mother was a cinephile and would describe her favourite films to her, much the same way a novel might be recounted. An early love of adventure stories by writers such as Robert Louis Stevenson, Joseph Conrad and Jack London gave way to a later attraction to the works of Jim Thompson and William Faulkner, who left a long-lasting impression on Denis.

A brief spell studying economics and an internship at a television station was followed by entry into France's prestigious film school IDHEC (now known as FEMIS). Graduation in 1972 left Denis in a 'zombie-like' state, but

fortuitously she was given the chance to work for Jacques Rivette, the only director of the New Wave she held in high esteem. Despite her disinterest in pursuing a career and being possessed of a strongly individualistic temperament, Denis went on to spend several years working for directors as diverse as Jean-François Stévenin, Costa-Gavras and Wim Wenders. By 1988 Claire Denis was well and truly ready to embark on her own career as a feature film director.

1988 saw the release in France of Catherine Breillat's *36 Fillette*, Luc Besson's *The Big Blue* and Bruno Nuytten's *Camille Claudel*, as good a barometer of public taste at that time as any. It also marked the appearance of Claire Denis' first feature, *Chocolat*, which recounted her experiences growing up in French colonial Africa. It was a remarkable debut by any standard. Free of the usual uncertain sense of editing, it felt, looked and sounded like the work of a fully matured artist.

Chocolat is the story of a white French family living in Cameroon around the late1950s, only a few years before the country gained independence. Marc Dalens (François Cluzet) is a Regional Administrator whose travelling keeps him away from home and his wife, the beautiful but bored Aimée (Giulia Boschi). The story's narrator is their aptly named young daughter, France. When not barking orders at the various members of staff, Aimée fills her days with curious interludes between her and the striking Protée, the family servant, played with brimming intensity by Denis regular Isaach De Bankolé. These often threaten to become something more perilous than mere verbal exchange. Instead, Protée develops a more profound friendship with the young girl. Into this delicate mix of familial estrangement, sexual frustration, class structure, the shifting

Chocolat

state of race relations, a fading colonialism and geographical extremity comes an errant planeload of obtuse outsiders, both French and English, whose presence soon peels away the veneer that holds the Dalens family together. *Chocolat* is a highly assured, complex work, whose modesty nevertheless announced the arrival of a major new voice in cinema.

A Decade of Discovery

Denis followed the critical and commercial success of *Chocolat* with the 1989 documentary *Man No Run*, about the Cameroonian group, Les Têtes Brulées, who play a contemporary version of the ancient Bikutsi music; a uniquely hybrid form that made them stars in their own country and that brought them considerable success in France, where Denis first approached them about a film.

The 1990s proved an eclectic and progressive decade for Denis, as she worked in both cinema and television, including an episode

No Fear, No Die

of *Cinema, de notre temps*, entitled *Jacques Rivette – Le veilleur*. It was a conversational piece between Denis and co-director and interviewer Serge Daney and the French master, who discussed his life and career. Also in 1990, Denis released her second feature, *No Fear, No Die* (*S'en fout la mort*), which starred Jean-Claude Brialy, Solveig Dommartin and Isaach De Bankolé. The film took an unflinching look at the desperate measures a lack of money and, worse, a lack of hope, can bring about in people. It demonstrated Denis' growing confidence with actors of significantly varied backgrounds. The following year, she directed the short film *Keep It For Yourself* and took part in a portmanteau film, *Control l'oubli*, which was designed to act as an 'artists petition' to free a prominent figure of the Irian Jaya Separatist Movement, Thomas Wanggai.

I Can't Sleep

In 1994's *I Can't Sleep* (*J'ai pas sommeil*), a young Lithuanian woman, played by another Denis regular Yekaterina Golubeva, arrives in Paris to look for work and crashes with a distant relative. She encounters some dyed-in-the-wool bigotry, male chauvinism and police harassment before Denis segues into a parallel story of a young, gay, black man whose unspecified criminal associations eventually split asunder his already precarious existence. Rarely seen in the UK, *I Can't Sleep* seems, with hindsight, to be the best example of Denis' early career of the human landscape she would explore in years to come.

That same year, Claire Denis teamed up with actress Anne Wiazemsky, whom Robert Bresson had discovered many years earlier, to co-write *U.S. Go Home*, an episode from the television series *Tous les garçons et les filles de leur âge....* Commissioned by ARTE, *U.S. Go Home* was a compendium film in which ten filmmakers were asked to direct a film dealing with their youth. There were two stipulations, that a party scene be included and that reference be made to music that had a particularly strong impact upon them. Denis successfully took a fairly predictable set of ideas and turned them into something more personal and complex, yet with a real sense of the impermanence that marks one's teenage years. Future Denis regulars Grégoire Colin and Vincent Gallo were on hand to offer their compelling brand of physicality.

Nice, Very Nice followed in 1995, which was another episode from a television series in France, called *A propos de Nice, la suite.* Her fellow directors included Costa-Gavras, Abbas Kiarostami and Catherine Breillat. Made with Jean Vigo very much in mind, a reference made apparent in the series title, *Nice, Very Nice* took a semi-fictional look at modern life on the French Côte d'Azur. Again, Denis' episode fared well alongside her colleagues' instalments. Evident too was Denis' unfailing humanity and love of people, and her understanding of human nature, which overrides racial, cultural and gender backgrounds.

Nenette et Boni is set in the melting pot of Marseilles. nineteen-year-old hoodlum Boniface Pavone (Grégoire Colin) shows little concern for the lives of those around him nor indeed for his own future. Having inherited his late mother's flat, he passes his time with cruel and unusual pursuits, surely a warning sign to anyone bothered enough to care. When his younger sister Nenette (Alice Houri), herself no angel, enters the scene, things only become more complicated until 'Boni', as he is known, takes a more active interest in his sibling's future and by consequence his own. *Nenette et Boni* uses the familiar coming-of-age framework to deliver the more substantial and complex ideas of repressed emotion and the inability to come to terms with one's own desires, no matter how destructive they are. Distinguished by a keen eye for casting and an impartial camera that refuses to take sides, *Nenette et Boni* also marked the beginning of Denis' collaboration with The Tindersticks whose genre-defying music would go on to make such an important contribution to her films, reaching its apotheosis in *The Intruder.* Rarely has a filmmaker employed music in such an empathetic and inspired way and avoided cliché so assiduously. It seemed a match made in heaven.

Beau Travail

Beau Travail is one of the most convincing arguments for blurring the lines between cinema and other art forms. Inspired by Herman Melville's unfinished novella, *Billy Budd*, Denis' film could be described, at its most basic, as a power struggle within a small band of French Foreign Legion troops. Starring Denis Lavant and the charismatic Michel Subor (*Le Petit Soldat*), *Beau Travail* proves that 'beauty' just by itself can achieve profundity without textual justification. The cinematography of Denis regular Agnès Godard is ravishing and she must be counted as Denis' most significant ongoing collaborator, alongside editor Nelly Quettier.

Galoup (Denis Lavant) spends his days in idle retreat in a small flat in Marseilles reflecting on his past in the French Foreign Legion. As Sergeant of a small troop of soldiers stationed in the remote deserts of Djibouti, Galoup's primary task is to maintain discipline amongst his men. However, his feelings for a new recruit, the fine-featured young Sentain (Grégoire Colin), don't go unnoticed. Even their commanding officer, Bruno Forrestier (Michel Subor), harbours feelings for the young man, adding to the already palpable sense of tension set amidst the stunning geographical extremity of Djibouti.

For the casual viewer, *Beau Travail* may appear stunning but confusing. What Denis has achieved, however, is a film that cannot be approached or understood in a conventional way. In its perfect blend of image and sound, interpreting the narrative becomes redundant. It is a film whose sensuousness, above all else, is important. It is an impressive stylistic advance within Denis' work and contemporary European cinema in general.

2001's *Trouble Every Day* was another of Denis' many Parisian-based films that dealt non-tangentially with a set of strained relationships that intersect, only to suddenly part ways again. Here she tackles the idea of lives unconsciously affecting each other with a naturalness that has often escaped other filmmakers. A weakness throughout is Vincent Gallo, who fails to convince at any point, especially when he 'talks science' with a colleague. Denis' grasp of the real and the imagined falls short on this occasion whenever Gallo is on screen. An acquired taste, perhaps, but one that escaped this writer's palate.

Trouble Every Day sees a young American couple visit Paris on their honeymoon. Shane (Vincent Gallo) is a scientist whose pursuit of cannibalism carries him off the traditional honeymooners' path in search of old friend Léo (Alex Descas), another character with a taste for the macabre. Unable to grasp the true nature of his sickness, Shane seems doomed from the outset, not helped by the childlike demeanour of his new bride (Tricia Vessey). Meanwhile, Léo's wife Coré (Beatrice Dalle) notches up more than a few victims. A not entirely successful genre-bending experiment, *Trouble Every Day* still looks and feels utterly

Trouble Every Day

unique and daring when placed alongside the efforts of most other filmmakers who have attempted a similar approach. Why Denis chose the vampire film remains obscure, but the film succeeds at the very least on the level of sheer thematic boldness and originality, consistent with her body of work at large.

In 2004, Denis directed *Vendredi Soir*, which came about in an uncannily similar way to the film's plot. Denis and Emmanuèle Bernheim, author of the novel, were working on another film together when one day, over a glass of wine in a café, Denis proposed they drop the project and try something else. When Bernheim asked Denis what it was that she really wanted to work on, her synopsis breakdown was practically identical to the novel Bernheim had written.

Any adaptation of a novel is by definition subject to radical change and it was the absence of the novel's 'voiceover' and any other expository device that imbued the film with its mystery and near-magical ability to move the receptive viewer to a place both strange and beautiful. The sparsity of dialogue wasn't the film's only daring choice. Its lead was Valérie Lemercier, an actress better known for her comedic roles such as the 1993 mega-hit *Les Visiteurs*. Added to this, her unconventional beauty was considered 'intriguing' by the producers – a poorly veiled insult and one that had a profound effect on the actress. Yet the performance she produced is one of the most sensual and intoxicating in recent memory, along with the intensity and charisma of leading man Vincent Lindon. The reservoir of unspoken emotion that is ready to boil over by the final frame is a testament to the filmmaker's virtuosity with even the slightest of narrative threads.

Vendredi Soir takes place over the course of one night in Paris amidst the worst traffic jam in memory. Laure (Valérie Lemercier) is in a state of flux as she packs up all her belongings to move in with her lover. Stuck in an impossible gridlock that offers her a strange sense of security and privacy, she meets handsome stranger Jean (Vincent Lindon) with whom she enters into an ill-considered, fly-by-night love affair. Overtaken by emotion, Laure lets events overtake her, unaware of where they might lead her.

Vendredi Soir

One of the qualities of a great artist who endures is unpredictability. Not through a calculated approach to the ever-changing marketplace but through their own inability to know how they will feel in the future. In 2004, two years after her contribution to the compendium film *Ten Minutes Older: The Cello*, Denis embarked on her most ambitious film to date, *The Intruder* (*L'Intrus*). Its primary source of inspiration were the memoirs of Jean-Luc Nancy, which provide the film with its title and plot. In collaboration with Jean-Pol Fargeau, Denis' screenplay also borrowed freely from the diaries of painter Paul Gauguin and novelist Robert Louis Stevenson. *The*

The Intruder

Intruder (2004) tells the tale of the aging Louis Trebor (Michel Subor), a 'man's man', who takes off on a global search for a new heart and to track down his long lost son. Living a solitary existence amongst the forests of the Swiss/Franco border, Trebor embarks upon a part-imagined, part-experienced journey to the South Pacific, via Geneva, where he buys a new watch, and Pusan, in South Korea, where he buys a new heart. The epic voyage he takes acts as a physical and emotional rebirth for a man whose thoughts and feelings remain ambiguous throughout.

An initial viewing of *The Intruder* will most likely perplex, frustrate and even infuriate. Yet a second viewing makes complete sense of events, not in a textual, analytical way, but by trusting one's own intuition and relinquishing the need to 'understand'. Like *Beau Travail*, the experience is utterly unique. The stunning score by Stuart Staples of The Tindersticks plays no small part in this transformational effect. Somewhat reminiscent of the ECM 'sound', Staples' music is both ethereal and propulsive and evokes a mood of temporal awareness, intuitive thought without end. An exact musical correlative of the film, in fact.

2005's *Vers Mathilde* is an intimate documentary about French choreographer Mathilde Monnier, who is the director of the Centre Chorégraphique National de Montpellier Languedoc-Roussillon, in the South East of France. The empathy between Denis and Monnier is unmistakable, especially given Denis' own understanding of dance and choreography. Sadly its very limited theatrical distribution has prevented it from reaching a wider audience. The greater the understanding one has of Denis' work, the richer the reward to be found here when observing Monnier at work. It comes as something of a surprise that Denis hasn't made more documentaries about like-minded artists given her intuitive understanding of Monnier's work.

35 Shots of Rum

Denis effortlessly reverted to a more traditional form of storytelling in 2008 with *35 Shots of Rum* (*35 Rhum*). It centres on the relationship between Lionel, a Parisian train driver, and his young student daughter, Joséphine. Lionel makes just enough money to sustain a spartan yet comfortable existence while his bright young daughter studies social sciences, hoping one day to make a better life for herself. When a recently retired colleague of Lionel's takes his own life, he is forced to reassess the things that matter most to him and to finally come to terms with the death of his wife. He's also keen to see Joséphine seek her independence, as hard as this will be for him in her absence. Their charming neighbour Noé (Grégoire Colin) courts Joséphine but her attention lies elsewhere, while their other neighbour Gabrielle (Nicole Dogué) has eyes for the sullen but handsome Lionel.

35 Shots of Rum was proof positive of Denis' total mastery and confidence behind the camera. Tellingly, she has described herself as a fragile person in normal life, when not directing, but that directing a film makes her strong. One could hardly guess such a disparity exists given the profound humanity and assurance evident in this film. Again, Denis' artistry elevates an essentially mundane set of circumstances to the realm of transcendent realism; a realistic style that captures and distils feelings well beyond the 'everyday', using the simplest of means. However, *35 Shots of Rum* is far from pretentious. It is a direct film that bravely never succumbs to waving the 'race' flag despite its unmistakable milieu. Newcomer Mati Diop and Denis regular Alex Descas both turn in impressively naturalistic performances, full of unforced humanity and hope amidst the ceaseless grind of working-class life that is modern-day existence for the large majority of the world's population.

35 Shots of Rum

Claire Denis returned to the African continent in 2009, with *White Material*. Isabelle Huppert plays Maria, a coffee plantation owner struggling in the face of an impending coup, with increasingly resentful workers and an idle teenage son whose ominous silence speaks volumes about the privileged environment in which they live. The pairing of France's most audacious actress and its most innovative film director is enough to grab one's attention, but this is neither a tepid vehicle for a great actress or a poorly conceived mismatch of talent. Instead we have another fresh chapter in the Claire Denis story. If it feels like similar territory, then this may be a signal that Denis will once again defy expectation and move in a new or different direction. When compared to the work of most other contemporary directors, many of whom are more highly regarded, *White Material* stands out as a persuasive reminder of Denis' singular

White Material

strength of vision and profound understanding of human beings in all their weakness and strength, beauty of spirit and ugliness of heart.

In response to the question of the formation of her distinctive style already evident in her debut film some 22 years ago, Denis has this to say: 'I knew even before I was working on my first film... you can invent a style in your mind but what happens on set is what is in [the film]. For the style is not something I can choose on the set. It's the way the script is written. It's already a choice of lens I can say. It's already a choice of point of view in the script. So therefore if suddenly on the set I thought I was attracted to choose a style or whatever I would be afraid. I would be afraid to betray the script, to betray

what I believe in. As soon as I start editing with the editor it shows as a natural thing... like the pure nature of the film.'

Despite the undoubted artistry of Claire Denis' work, any suggestion to this effect is, in true modesty, rebuked by the filmmaker, who is only too aware of the fragile, inter-dependent nature of filmmaking: 'It's a sort of painful situation because cinema is not known for artists. I don't take myself for an artist. I try to make a film as honestly as I can... I don't try to translate my personal story but I try to say something about the world. Therefore I think if I manage to make a film with a little budget, a small budget, to not spend too much money and to have a producer who understands me, who believes me, an actor who can touch you, I think I am still very lucky.'

DANIEL GRAHAM is a freelance film critic who has written for various publications and interviewed many filmmakers and practitioners. He has also written and directed eight short films that have played at film festivals throughout the UK and France.

Claire Denis filmography

[feature film directing credits only]

1988
CHOCOLAT
Script: Claire Denis, Jean-Pol Fargeau. Photography: Robert Alazraki. Production Design: Thierry Flamand. Editing: Monica Coleman, Claudine Merlin and Sylvie Quester. Music: Abdullah Ibrahim. Players: Isaach De Bankolé (Protée), *Giulia Boschi* (Aimée Dalens), *François Cluzet* (Marc Dalens), *Jean-Claude Adelin* (Luc), *Laurent Arnal* (Machinard), *Jean Bediebe* (Prosper), *Jean-Quentin Châtelain* (Courbassol), *Emmanuelle Chaulet* (Mireille Machinard), *Kenneth*

Cranham (Boothby), *Jacques Denis* (Joseph Delpich), *Cécile Ducasse* (France enfant), *Clementine Essono* (Marie-Jeanne), *Didier Flamand* (Capt. Védrine), *Esssindi Mindja* (Blaise). *Produced by Alain Belmondo, Gérard Crosnier.*
105 mins

1990
S'EN FOUT LA MORT
(No Fear, No Die)
Script: Claire Denis, Jean-Pol Fargeau. Photography: Pascal Marti. Production Design: Jean-Jacques Caziot. Editing: Dominique Auvray. Music: Abdullah Ibrahim. Players: Isaach De Bankolé (Dah), *Alex Descas* (Jocelyn), *Solveig Dommartin* (Toni), *Christopher*

Buchholz (Michel), *Jean-Claude Brialy* (Pierre Ardennes), *Christa Lang* (Toni's Mother), *Gilbert Felmar* (TiEmile), *Daniel Bellus* (Henri), *François Oloa Biloa* (François), *Pipo Sarguera* (Pipo), *Alain Banicles* (Inspector), *Valérie Monnet* (The Girl). *Produced by Francis Boespflug, Philippe Carcassonne. 90 mins*

1994
J'AI PAS SOMMEIL (I Can't Sleep)
Script: Claire Denis. Photography: Agnès Godard. Production Design: Arnaud de Moleron and Thierry Flamand. Editing: Nelly Quettier. Music: Jean-Louis Murat, John Pattison. Players: Yekaterina Golubeva (Daiga), *Richard Courcet*

(Camille), *Vincent Dupont* (Raphael), *Laurent Grévill* (le docteur), *Alex Descas* (Theo), *Irina Grjebina* (Mina), *Tolsty* (Ossip), *Line Renaud* (Ninon), *Béatrice Dalle* (Mona), *Sophie Simon* (Alice), *Patrick Grandperret* (Abel). *Produced by Bruno Pésery. 110 mins*

1996
NÉNETTE ET BONI
Script: Claire Denis, Jean-Pol Fargeau. Photography: Pascal Marti. Production Design: Arnaud de Moleron. Editing: Yann Dedet. Music: Tindersticks. Players: Grégoire Colin (Boni), *Alice Houri* (Nénette), *Jacques Nolot* (Monsier Luminaire), *Valeria Bruni Tedeschi* (Baker's wife), *Vincent Gallo* (Vincenzo Brown), *Malek Brahimi* (Malek), *Gérard Meylan* (Uncle), *Sébastien Pons* (Boni's friend), *Mounir Aïssa* (Boni's friend), *Christophe Carmona* (Boni's friend), *Djellali El'Ouzeri* (Boni's friend), *Alex Descas* (Le gynécologue), *Jamila Farah* (Midwife), *Agnes Regolo* (Radiologist), *Pepette* (L'assistante sociale). *Produced by Georges Benayoun. 103 mins*

1999
BEAU TRAVAIL
Script: Claire Denis, Jean-Pol Fargeau. Photography: Agnès Godard. Production Design: Arnaud de Moleron. Editing: Nelly Quettier. Music: Charles Henri de Pierrefeu, Eran Zur. Players: Denis Lavant (Galoup), *Michel Subor* (Commander Bruno Forestier), *Grégoire Colin* (Gilles Sentain), *Richard Courcet* (Legionnaire), *Nicholas Duvauchelle* (Legionnaire), *Adiatou Massudi* (Legionnaire), *Mickael Ravovski* (Legionnaire), *Dan Herzberg* (Legionnaire), *Giuseppe Molino* (Legionnaire), *Marta Tafesse Kassa* (Young Woman), *Gianfranco Poddighe* (Legionnaire), *Marc Veh* (Legionnaire), *Thong Duy Nguyen*

(Legionnaire), *Jean-Yves Vivet* (Legionnaire), *Bernado Montet* (Legionnaire), *Dimitri Tsiapknis* (Legionnaire), *Djamel Zemali* (Legionnaire), *Abdelkader Bouti* (Legionnaire). *Produced by Patrick Grandperret. 93 mins*

2001
TROUBLE EVERY DAY
Script: Claire Denis, Jean-Pol Fargeau. Photography: Agnès Godard. Production Design: Arnaud de Moleron. Editing: Nelly Quettier. Music: Tindersticks. Players: Vincent Gallo (Shane), *Tricia Vessey* (June), *Béatrice Dalle* (Coré), *Alex Descas* (Léo), *Florence Loiret* (Christelle), *Nicholas Duvauchelle* (Erwan), *Raphaël Neal* (Ludo), *José Garcia* (Choart), *Hélène Lapiower* (Malécot), *Marilu Marini* (Friessen), *Aurore Clément* (Jeanne). *Produced by Georges Banayoun, Philippe Liégeois, Jean-Michel Rey. 101 mins*

2002
VENDREDI SOIR (Friday Night)
Script: Emmenuèle Bernheim. Photography: Agnès Godard. Production Design: Katia Wyszkop. Editing: Nelly Quettier. Music: Dickon Hinchliffe. Players: Valérie Lemercier (Laure), *Vincent Lindon* (Jean), *Hélène de Saint-Père* (Marie). *Produced by Bruno Pésery. 90 mins*

2004
L'INTRUS (The Intruder)
Script: Claire Denis, Jean-Pol Fargeau. Photography: Agnès Godard. Production Design: Arnaud de Moleron. Editing: Nelly Quettier. Music: S.A. Staples. Players: Michel Subor (Louis Trebor), *Grégoire Colin* (Sidney), *Yekaterina Golubeva* (Young Russian woman), *Bambou* (Pharmacist), *Florence Loiret* (Antoinette), *Lolita Chammah* (The Wild Woman), *Alex Descas* (The Priest), *Dong-ho Kim* (Ship owner), *Henri Tetainanuarii* (Henri), *Jean-Marc Teriipaia* (Tony), *Anna*

Tetuaveroa (The Mother), *Béatrice Dalle* (Queen of the Northern Hemisphere). *Produced by Humbert Balsan. 130 mins*

2008
35 RHUMS (35 Shots of Rum)
Script: Claire Denis, Jean-Pol Fargeau. Photography: Agnès Godard. Production Design: Arnaud de Moleron. Editing: Guy Lecorne. Music: Tindersticks. Players: Alex Descas (Lionel), *Mati Diop* (Joséphine), *Nicole Dogue* (Gabrielle), *Grégoire Colin* (Noé), *Jean-Christophe Folly* (Ruben), *Djédjé Apali* (Martial), *Eriq Ebouaney* (Blanchard), *Ingrid Caven* (La tante allemande), *Julieth Mars Toussaint* (René), *Mary Pie* (Lina). *Produced by Bruno Pésery. 100 mins*

2009
WHITE MATERIAL
Script: Claire Denis, Marie N'Diaye. Photography: Yves Cape. Production Design: Abiassi Sanit-Père. Editing: Guy Lecorne. Music: Stuart Staples. Players: Isabelle Huppert (Maria), *Isaach De Bankolé* (The Boxer), *Christophe Lambert* (André Vial), *Nicholas Duvauchelle* (Manuel Vial), *William Nadylam* (Chérif), *Adéle Ado* (Lucie), *Ali Barkai* (Jeep), *Daniel Tchangang* (José), *Michel Subor* (Henri Vial). *Produced by Pascal Cauchetaux. 100 mins*

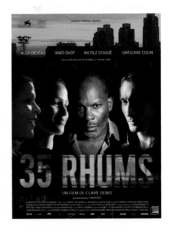

John Hillcoat by Jason Wood

A characteristically uncompromising film, John Hillcoat's adaptation of Cormac McCarthy's Pulitzer Prize-winning novel, *The Road*, depicts a planet in the throes of a seemingly irreversible demise. An unforgiving world, familiar from those previously evoked in *Ghosts... of the Civil Dead*, *To Have and To Hold* and *The Proposition*, the savage outlook is this time leavened by the faintly perceptible notes of optimism that Hillcoat found central to the book: 'The bleakness for me is just a backdrop, and the gestures towards hope that the film makes are that much more special because of the tremendous obstacles that the characters are up against.' Hillcoat's most high-profile assignment yet, *The Road* can also be seen as a summation of the director's fascination with desperate people in hostile situations, who are driven to extremes of behaviour in order to survive.

A graduate of Australia's Swinburne Film School, where he produced the celebrated shorts *The Blonde's Date With Death* and *Frankie and Johnny*, John Hillcoat went on to forge a successful career as a director and editor of music videos for The Birthday Party, INXS, Crowded House and Depeche Mode. *Ghosts... of the Civil Dead* was his first foray into features and marked the arrival of a distinctive and visceral filmmaking talent.

Nominated for nine Australian Film Institute Awards, *Ghosts... of the Civil Dead* was born of three years of exhaustive research into maximum-security prisons. Based on actual events that occurred in the project's gestation period, the film, an incisive and biting piece of polemical social commentary, also draws extensively on the writings and experiences of Jack Henry Abbott who, after a lifetime of incarceration, hanged himself in his cell. Abbott also gave the film its title, writing, 'As long as I am nothing but a ghost of the civil dead, I can do nothing.' Michel Foucault was another influence, particularly the writer's theory that the prison structure is an agent of the state to legitimise the use of violent and excessive force against its citizens.

Set within the despairing confines of Central Industrial Prison, a privatised, state-of-the-art correctional unit surrounded by a vast and inhospitable desert, the film opens during a lockdown situation, in which all prisoners are returned to their cells with privileges denied. Unfolding in flashback, following the formation of a committee founded to report on the lead up to the incident, the film focuses on the activities of inmate Wenzil (Dave Field), Officer David B. Yale (Mike Bishop), and a maniacal psychopath (Nick Cave, shorn of his trademark crow-black mane) in their stoking of tension, conflict, retribution and violence.

Co-written by Hillcoat and producer Evan English, the film was produced by the ironically named Correctional Services (in association with Outlaw Values), and was made on the understanding that all the 'artistic participants' retained creative and economic control. This would in part explain the stark documentary aesthetic and its refusal to sweeten the portrait of a corrupt and dehumanising prison scheme that adopts a strategy of violence and humiliation in the name of discipline and control. Establishing a working relationship with Chris Kennedy, the production pesigner who would become integral to Hillcoat's nihilistic vision, *Ghosts... of the Civil Dead* also cemented the enduring alliance with Nick Cave, who as well as appearing in front of the camera, co-composed the film's ethereal score with Blixa Bargeld and Mick Harvey. Cave and Hillcoat first met in Melbourne in the late 1970s and bonded over similar interests in music and literature.

Ghosts... of the Civil Dead

Not emerging until almost ten years later, *To Have and To Hold* was greeted with great expectation, but regarded as a disappointment. Travelling extensively on the festival circuit and given a limited release in a number of territories, the project signalled an ambitious undertaking fatally undone by an apparent lack of conviction on the part of its makers. Hillcoat is himself dismissive, claiming that 'it has the distinction of being flawed in every department'.

Jack (Tchéky Karyo), a projectionist working in a small village on the Sepik River, in Papua New Guinea, appears to enjoy a bucolic

existence. Passing the days screening violent action movies to the captivated locals at a makeshift cinema, Jack shares his relatively tranquil life with his alluring wife, Rose (Anni Finsterer), and a number of local associates. Two years later, after a tragic boating accident, a chance meeting in a Melbourne bookshop with a romantic novelist named Kate (Rachel Griffiths) re-ignites the flames of passion. Bearing an uncanny resemblance to Jack's deceased spouse, Kate finds herself the subject of a whirlwind courtship and travels back with Jack to his remote idyll. After an initial honeymoon period it soon becomes clear that Jack's feelings are the result of a process of emotional transference, and with the local youths' thirst for violent images becoming increasingly insatiable, events begin to spiral dangerously out of control.

Further establishing a motif of having location function as a character in its own right, this brooding tale of obsessive, ill-fated love again addresses issues relating to isolation and violence. Clearly favouring atmosphere and tone over a wholly credible narrative, the film's two protagonists, though well played, are also a little too thinly sketched. Hillcoat's frank appraisal of his own film is, however, perhaps a little harsh. Sumptuously shot by Andrew de Groot, the film exerts a strange fascination and builds to a memorable denouement. The Cave, Bargeld and Harvey score also worms its way under the skin and the film is notable for coaxing Scott Walker from a self-imposed artistic exile to perform on the soundtrack.

Jointly inspired by his combination of cruel realism and poetry, Hillcoat and Cave conspired in their ambition to adapt Michael Ondaatje's *The Collected Works of Billy the Kid*. A recreation of the life of the legendary outlaw that synthesises poetry and prose, the attempts to acquire the rights were scuppered by the sudden and unexpected success of Ondaatje's *The English Patient*. Retaining a similarly intoxicating blend of brutality and lyricism, Hillcoat's next film, *The Proposition*, would not arrive until five years later.

The Proposition

Steeped in admiration for a number of 1970s American westerns (the spirit of Peckinpah, whose *Pat Garrett and Billy the Kid* is visually referenced, looms large), Cave and Hillcoat's primary aim was to embrace the history of Australia and its own genre of bush-ranging films. 'I thought the ingredients of struggling with the climate, the clash of cultures, that kind of lyrical, mythical quality of the power of the landscape hadn't been fully explored,' commented Hillcoat. Originally enlisted to write the score, Cave's impatience with the length of time it was taking for a script to be completed precipitated his own undertaking of the task. The result, later claimed to have been written in a little over three weeks, is a remarkably sparse yet intelligent analysis of savagery, tenderness and beauty. Set around the end of the nineteenth century, it pits the British administration in a desolate corner of the Australian outback against a family of Irish bushrangers, with the native aboriginal population aligned with and against both.

A British lawman dispatched to bring order to the colonies at any cost manages to capture Mikey (Richard Wilson) and Charlie (Guy Pearce), two younger members of the notorious Burns Brothers gang. Dispensing his own brand of barbaric justice to men wanted for various acts of general atrocity, the lawman, Captain Stanley (Ray Winstone), explains to Charlie that it is the elder brother, Arthur (Danny Huston), that the authorities really want. The proposition is thus struck. If Charlie brings in Arthur by Christmas Day (seven days hence), Mikey's life will be spared. If not, he will be

hanged. An exchange that will involve the death of at least one brother, Charlie's thankless dilemma is further complicated by a circling coterie of mercenary bounty hunters, led by the reptilian Jellon Lamb (John Hurt). Meanwhile, Captain Stanley also grapples with his own tormentors: arrogant superiors and incompetent subordinates, a desperately subdued wife (Emily Watson), and the debilitating migraines that hint at his own sense of failure concerning the enormity of his task.

Marshalling fine performances from an impressive ensemble cast, with Pearce, for whom Cave wrote the role as well as lobbying for his participation, especially outstanding, *The Proposition* boasts numerous technical merits. It is beautifully shot, with French cinematographer Benoît Delhomme teasing out the contrasting properties of the outback (shooting largely took place in Winton, Queensland with the British performers suffering terribly in the heat), while Craig Walmsley's sound design exists in perfect harmony with the profoundly melancholic and dread-inducing Nick Cave/Warren Ellis score.

The Proposition

Violent, though never for a moment gratuitous (slow-motion is avoided and, in one instance, the camera pans outside a room where a beating is taking place, registering the horror on the face of a bystander forced to listen to the cries of the victim), the film is at pains to depict the moral hopelessness of the times in which the characters exist, linking them directly to their environment's unforgiving elements. Hillcoat recalled, 'We wanted to show all the kinds of aggression from that time, including the black-on-black violence. For us, the film was about the physical and psychological effects of violence and we didn't want to shy away from how brutal those times were. What we wanted to linger on was not the violence itself, but how people are affected by it.'

Certainly one of the finest films to emerge from Australia in recent years, *The Proposition* was met with almost unanimous critical acclaim. Writing in *Sight and Sound*, Nick Roddick equated it with the first years of the Australian cinema renaissance in the 1970s, 'where the tension between a hostile landscape and a country in search of a civilised identity, between freedom and compromise, forged a new mythic structure'.

Having read Cormac McCarthy's *The Road* in manuscript form (*Blood Meridian* is credited as another inspiration for *The Proposition*) Hillcoat was in a favourable position to avoid a repeat of the Michael Ondaatje experience. By the time the novel had chimed with the public and Joel and Ethan Coen had translated the author's *No Country For Old Men* to the screen, Hillcoat was already signed up to direct. Initially wary of the challenge of bringing the world McCarthy depicts to the screen, and of sustaining the intensity of the Father/ Son relationship at the heart of the novel for an entire film, Hillcoat adopted the 'overriding philosophy that it would be better to fall flat on my face rather than not try at all because it seemed too tough'.

A terrifying glimpse into a possible future, an unnamed man (Viggo Mortensen) and his son (Kodi Smit-McPhee) travel through a post-apocalyptic landscape, ten years after the world has been ravaged by an unspecified catastrophe that has eradicated all energy, power, vegetation, food and human decency. The road the pair travels is littered with corpses and its surrounding ash-grey landscapes are patrolled by marauding gangs who feast on the flesh of the living in order to survive. Following the once magnificent American highways west towards the ocean, the pair seeks refuge in

the woods and abandoned structures they find along the way. Food and comfort is minimal, but there are odd moments of relief and the innate goodness of the young boy acts as a spur for the man to carry on.

The Road

Diverting from the source material only in the occasional flashbacks to the man's life with his wife (Charlize Theron) and in its expansion of minor characters, *The Road* functions effectively as a chilling morality tale and as a road movie, horror film and compelling love story. What is perhaps most impressive about the endeavour is the relative avoidance of CGI and the attendant clichés of the apocalypse genre, in favour of an approach more firmly grounded in reality.

Founded on Hillcoat's desire to create a frighteningly familiar world – with the image of the millions of homeless as a guiding visual principle – the production team, headed by Chris Kennedy, decided to look at 'the small apocalypses that have happened already'. Shooting in a post-Katrina New Orleans, Oregon, Mount St. Helens and Pennsylvania, Hillcoat captures a natural and authentic sense of devastation and deprivation. 'For the crew, these locations lent an added poignancy, but for the actors also it was something else for them to naturally react to. When half of your crew have been through the experience of Katrina it offers an incredible series of parallels with the story you are trying to tell.' A number of images in the film are also genuine, including the 70mm Imax shot of abandoned boats on the freeway, taken two days after Katrina hit. The billowing smoke that appears in the background of a number of sequences is reproduced from news footage of the terrorist attacks on 11 September 2001.

The approach to graphic imagery is again minimalist and deliberately low key. The sequence featuring the discovery of a cellar housing humans captured and kept for human consumption is all the more terrifying for what is indicated rather than actually revealed. Perhaps the most disturbing moment is when one of the cannibalistic hunters (Garret Dillahunt) feasts his eyes upon the boy and hungrily sniffs his scent. Hillcoat, with economy and subtlety, suggests that the man's physical and mental state is more animal than human.

Having previously left lengthy gaps between projects, John Hillcoat's rising reputation and the high visibility of *The Road* seem likely to ensure that he will not be absent from our screens for long. He has been linked to a string of projects. He is definitely planning a fifth collaboration with Nick Cave (who composed the score for *The Road* with Warren Ellis), who will return to scriptwriting duties with *The Wettest Country in the World*. John Hilllcoat promises it will be a comedy.

JASON WOOD is a film programmer and contributor to *Sight and Sound* and the *Guardian*. He has also published several books on cinema.

John Hillcoat filmography

[feature film directing credits only]

1988
GHOSTS... OF THE CIVIL DEAD
Script: Nick Cave, Gene Conkie, Evan English, John Hillcoat and Hugo Race. Photography: Paul Goldman and Graham Wood. Production Design: Chris Kennedy. Editing: Stewart Young. Music: Blixa Bargeld, Nick Cave and Mick Harvey. Players: David Field (Wenzil), Mike Bishop (David Yale), Chris DeRose (Grezner), Kevin Mackey (Glover), Dave Mason (Lilly), Nick Cave (Maynard), Bogdan Koca (Waychek), Freddo Dierck (Robbins), Vincent Gil (Ruben), Ian Mortimer (Jack), Mick King (Edwin Neal), Angelo Papadopoulos (John Bird). Produced by Evan English. 93 mins

1996
TO HAVE AND TO HOLD
Script: Gene Conkie and John Hillcoat. Photography: Andrew de Groot. Production Design: Chris Kennedy. Editing: Stewart Young. Music: Blixa Bargeld, Nick Cave and

Mick Harvey. Players: Tchéky Karyo (Jack), Rachel Griffiths (Kate), Steve Jacobs (Sal), Anni Finisterer (Rose), David Field (Stevie), Larry Lavai (James), John Parinjo (Noah), Ura Eri (Gabby). Produced by Denise Patience. 99 mins

2005
THE PROPOSITION
Script: Nick Cave. Photography: Benoît Delhomme. Production Design: Chris Kennedy. Editing: Jon Gregory. Music: Nick Cave and Warren Ellis. Players: Guy Pearce (Charlie Burns), Ray Winstone (Captain Stanley), Danny Huston (Arthur Burns), Emily Watson (Martha Stanley), Richard Wilson (Mike Burns), John Hurt (Jellon Lamb), David Wenham (Eden Fletcher), Noah Taylor (Brian O'Leary), David Gulpilil (Jacko), Robert Morgan (Sergeant Lawrence). Produced by Chris Brown, Chiara Menage and Cat Villiers. 104 mins

2009
THE ROAD
Script: Joe Penhall. Photography: Javier Aguirresarobe. Production

Design: Chris Kennedy. Editing: Jon Gregory. Music: Nick Cave and Warren Ellis. Players: Viggo Mortensen (Man), Kodi Smit-McPhee (Boy), Charlize Theron (Woman), Robert Duvall (Old Man), Guy Pearce (Veteran), Molly Parker (Motherly Woman), Michael Kenneth Williams (The Thief), Garret Dillahunt (Gang Member), Bob Jennings (Bearded Man), Agnes Herrmann (Archer's Wife). Produced by Paula Mae Schwartz, Steve Schwartz and Nick Wechsler. 119 mins

In Memoriam

YASMIN AHMAD
7 January 1958 – 25 July 2009

The demise of Malaysia's acclaimed filmmaker
Yasmin Ahmad was described by many as a
great loss to contemporary Malaysian cinema.
Yasmin managed to direct six feature films
– *Rabun* (2003), *Sepet* (2004), *Gubra* (2006),
Mukhsin (2006), *Muallaf* (2008) and *Talentime*
(2009). Her works – both feature films and her
work in commercials – garnered international
accolades. At home, Yasmin's works never
failed to engender controversy, as they dared
to confront accepted norms and practices
within the volatile mix of cultures and religious
beliefs in Malaysia. A gifted storyteller with
sharp, astute observations on Malaysian
society, Yasmin has left an indelible legacy, as
manifest in all her works. – *Norman Yussof*

Yasmin Ahmad

KEN ANNAKIN
10 August 1914 – 22 April 2009

Ken Annakin's directorial career fizzled out
in television, but for four prolific decades
his oeuvre tended towards pyrotechnics. A
journeyman in every sense of the word, he
was born in Yorkshire, saw action in the RAF
during World War Two and directed stars as
diverse as Kenneth Williams (*The Seekers*,
1954) and Yul Brynner (*The Long Duel*, 1967).
Despite Annakin's military nous and with Henry
Fonda in a leading role, *The Battle of the Bulge*
(1965) swashbuckled more than it convinced,
suggesting that Disney adventures like *Third
Man on the Mountain* (1959) and *Swiss Family
Robinson* (1960) suited his palate more. He
did shoot the British exteriors for Darryl F.
Zanuck's *The Longest Day* (1962) with enough
panache to get his own shot at a big-budget
flyer, the Zanuck-financed *Those Magnificent
Men in Their Flying Machines* (1965), for which
he co-wrote the Academy Award-nominated
screenplay. – *Benjamin Morgan*

STEVEN BACH
29 April 1938 – 25 March 2009

Steven Bach was a graduate of the Sorbonne
who enjoyed a distinguished second career
as a lecturer in film at Columbia University.
Posterity, however, will doubtless cast him
in a less illustrious role: as the producer
responsible for one of the biggest box-office
flops of all time. When Michael Cimino
pitched *Heaven's Gate* (1980) to Bach, then
vice-president of United Artists, Cimino was
fresh from *The Deer Hunter* (1978) and had
the world at his feet. Bach gave the nod, as
he had to *Raging Bull* (1980) and *The French
Lieutenant's Woman* (1981). His excellent
book, *Final Cut: Art, Money and EGO in the
Making of 'Heaven's Gate' the Film That
Sank United Artists* remains one of the finest
accounts of the foibles of filmmaking in
Hollywood. – *Benjamin Morgan*

PÉTER BACSÓ
6 January 1928 – 11 March 2009

The Slovak-born Hungarian filmmaker Péter Bacsó never achieved the international profile of his contemporary Miklós Jancsó, perhaps because his black comedies lacked the art-house cachet of Jancsó's austere output. Nor did Bacsó, an ironist in a po-faced age, have an easy ride domestically: strict censorship and his friendship with the executed reformer Imre Nagy dogged his early career. All the more remarkable, then, that with *The Witness* (*A tanú*, 1969), *Oh, Bloody Life!* (*Te rongyos élet*, 1985) and his screenplay for Károly Makk's *Love* (*Szerelem*, 1971), Bacsó has left us a searing celluloid indictment of the Stalinist regime of 1949–56, arguably Hungary's darkest era. – *Benjamin Morgan*

BARRY BARCLAY
12 May 1944 – 19 February 2008

Writer, director, a bold and provocative thinker who could be a quite infuriating human being, Barclay was indisputably New Zealand's greatest documentarian. His landmark 1974 television series *Tangata Whenua* ('people of the land', which is how Maori refer to themselves) showed his skill for intimate filmmaking and his output – not prolific but always penetrating – over the rest of his career continued in that vein. Yet it is worth remembering that his 1987 feature *Ngati* (the first by a Maori director) captured better than any other local film what makes this

Barry Barclay

country tick. What was striking about his work was that, from the minutely observed experiences of small communities, he extracted overarching, even universal truths. In everything, Barclay always zoomed in close. His intention, so often and so elegantly achieved, was that the viewer emerged with a deeper and broader perspective. – *Peter Calder*

Claude Berri

CLAUDE BERRI
1 July 1934 – 12 January 2009

By the time Claude Berri adapted Marcel Pagnol's *Jean de Florette* and *Manon des Sources* (both 1986), catapulting Gérard Depardieu to international stardom and establishing Provence as the summer destination of choice for millions of rapt cinemagoers, he was already a pillar of the French film industry, with a body of work as director, producer and distributor extending far beyond the realms of the picturesque. He began as an actor, with a role in Chabrol's *The Girls* (*Les Bonnes Femmes*, 1960) before an Academy Award for his short *The Chicken* (*Le Poulet*, 1962) kick-started his career behind the lens. *The Two of Us* (*Le Vieil Homme et l'Enfant*, 1966) is characteristically autobiographical, based on his experiences as a Jewish child during World War Two. Berri's later work was aimed at the mainstream, eschewing the political preoccupations of the New Wave in favour of commercially oriented screenplays like *Male of the Century* (*Le Mâle du Siècle*, 1975) and yet another lavish literary adaptation (*Germinal*, 1993). – *Benjamin Morgan*

KATHLEEN BYRON
11 January 1921 – 18 January 2009

There are few moments in cinema that will ever match the intoxicating blend of fear, fascination and allure that was Kathleen Byron's appearance, as the psychotic Sister Ruth, in the climactic moments of Powell and Pressburger's *Black Narcissus* (1947). It was her third collaboration with the Archers, after her brief turn as a heavenly clerk in *A Matter of Life and Death* (1946) and *The Silver Fleet* (1943, which they produced). Arguably her finest performance for them was opposite her *Narcissus* co-star David Farrah, playing the girlfriend of an alcoholic bomb-disposal expert in *The Small Back Room* (1949). That film allowed her more scope to display her talent and she excelled in the role. A career in film and television followed, which was consistent if mostly unremarkable. Sadly, illness prevented her playing Lauren Bacall's sister in Lars von Trier's *Dogville*. But future screenings of her most famous work will remind audiences of what a luminous presence Kathleen Byron was on the screen.
– Ian Haydn Smith

JACK CARDIFF
19 September 1914 – 22 April 2009

One of the greatest cinematographers in the history of cinema and the recipient of an Academy Award for his work on *Black Narcissus*, Jack Cardiff grew up in a family of vaudevillians. In 1936, After a few years as a cameraman, he volunteered to attend a course on colour photography, which led to his filming the first colour film in the UK, *Wings of the Morning* (1937). Ironically, his first collaboration with Michael Powell, on *A Matter of Life and Death* (1946), involved shooting the black-and-white afterlife sequences. However, it was for his lush, colour imagery, on films such as *The Red Shoes* (1948), *The Black Rose* (1950), *The African Queen* (1951), *The Barefoot Contessa* (1954), *War and Peace* (1956) and *The Vikings* (1958), that he will be remembered. His directing career was less successful, with a

Jack Cardiff

solid adaptation of *Sons and Lovers* (1960), an aborted Erroll Flynn adventure and one of the iconic films of the late 1960s, *The Girl on a Motorcycle* (1968). The 1996 autobiography, *Magic Hour: A Life in Movies*, is a fascinating account of the development of cinema by one of its true innovators. – Benjamin Morgan

SIMON CHANNING WILLIAMS
10 June 1945 – 11 April 2009

The producer Simon Channing Williams made up one half of one of the most fertile producer-director partnerships in recent European cinema. But his collaborations with Mike Leigh tell only part of the story of a dogged and socially engaged career at the heart of the British film industry. Channing Williams served as first assistant director on Leigh's television drama *Grown Ups* (1980) and, when Leigh returned to feature filmmaking with *High Hopes* (1988), his former assistant was on hand to produce. The company the two founded, Thin Man, would finance the vast majority of Leigh's subsequent work, from *Naked* (1993) to *Happy-Go-Lucky* (2008). Channing Williams also forged a fruitful relationship with a younger generation of filmmakers, including Fernando Meirelles; it was during production of Meirelles' *The Constant Gardener* (2005) that his attention was drawn to the dreadful

conditions of the Nairobi slums, for whose benefit he established a charitable trust.
– *Benjamin Morgan*

JOHN HUGHES
February 18 1950 – 6 August 2009

For a generation of American adolescents, the films of John Hughes offered an antidote to the strictures of home and school life, pointing the way instead to a principled and liberating 'slacker' ethos. Indeed, it could be said that with films like *The Breakfast Club* (1985) and *Ferris Bueller's Day Off* (1986), Hughes spawned his own teen-movie subgenre, one that was to scale heights in the early work of Richard Linklater, only to mutate less fruitfully into the *American Pie* franchise. But before giving the Brat Pack to the world, Hughes had also rejuvenated the ailing *National Lampoon* series, casting Chevy Chase as a typically overbearing parent in *National Lampoon's Vacation* (1983). There was always more that was cute than cutting about even his most anxious rebels. In this light, his progression from teen drama to pre-teen slapstick as producer and writer on *Home Alone* (1990) was perhaps not altogether surprising.
– *Benjamin Morgan*

John Hughes

MAURICE JARRE
13 September 1924 – 29 March 2009

Maurice Jarre would be regarded as an important composer in his own right even if his collaborations with David Lean had not produced three truly memorable film scores. *Lawrence of Arabia* (1962), *Dr Zhivago* (1965) and *A Passage to India* (1984) won an Oscar apiece for their music, which lent epic force to Lean's sweeping canvases. Urged by his parents to become an engineer, Jarre held out for a music scholarship and his intransigence paid rich dividends: besides Lean, his collaborators included Jacques Demy (*Le Bel Indifférent*, 1957), Alfred Hitchcock (*Topaz*, 1969) and John Huston (*The Man Who Would Be King*, 1976). Jarre's success in film perhaps owed much to his versatility: in the 1980s his experiments with electronic music, particularly synthesisers, made him the composer of choice for a new, brasher generation of filmmakers and he wrote scores for, amongst others, George Miller (*Mad Max Beyond Thunderdome*, 1985) and Adrian Lyne (*Fatal Attraction*, 1987). – *Benjamin Morgan*

FEROZ KHAN
25 September 1939 – 27 April 2009

Pin-up and producer, Feroz Khan was instrumental in making Bollywood cinema a force to be reckoned with beyond the Indian sub-continent. After moving to Mumbai from his native Bangalore in the early 1960s, he eked out an acting apprenticeship in low-budget thrillers before a role as the charismatic prodigal son in the drama *Oonche Log* (1965) brought him to the attention of the wider Indian public. His profile rose and by 1972 he had the financial clout to produce, direct and star in his first big hit, *Aprah*, a slick action movie which, like much of Khan's best work, combines traditional Bollywood motifs with storylines pinched from Hollywood. A string of box-office successes followed, including the 'curry western' *Khotte Sikkey* (1974), *Dharmatma* (1975), a Bollywood take on *The Godfather*, and *Qurbani* (1980), a tortuous

besides novels, short stories and politically engaged screenplays such as *A Face in the Crowd* (1957), another collaboration with Kazan, he also wrote a sequence of insightful memoirs on his time in Hollywood.
– *Benjamin Morgan*

Patrick Swayze

PATRICK SWAYZE
18 August 1952 – 14 September 2009

In many ways a highly unlikely leading man, Patrick Swayze took Hollywood by storm in two phenomenally successful films before a series of crises in his personal life effected a career reversal from which he had not yet fully recovered at the time of his death. A former ballet professional, Swayze made a dazzling crossover to cinema in Emile Ardolino's *Dirty Dancing* (1987), a camp-drenched musical romance about a dance instructor from the wrong side of the tracks. *Dirty Dancing*, like Jerry Zucker's *Ghost* (1990), in which Swayze's murdered banker lovingly haunts his grieving widow, pulled off a very contemporary trick, managing to both be a runaway commercial hit upon release and acquire 'cult' status in the years that followed. The 1990s must have seemed agonisingly fallow after such beginnings, but a terrifying performance in another 'cult' smash, *Donnie Darko* (2001), and successful outings on Broadway and in the West End suggested a new upward trajectory which was sadly never permitted to peak. – *Benjamin Morgan*

HOWARD ZIEFF
21 October 1927 – 22 February 2009

Howard Zieff made an unstuttering transition from advertising to filmmaking in the mid-1970s, retaining the populist smarts he had developed in the short medium and leavening them with a comedian's sense of a durable conceit. His debut, *Slither* (1973), played fast and loose with the crime genre, while *Hearts of the West* (1975), with Jeff Bridges, and *The Main Event* (1979), with Barbra Streisand, paid worthy homage to the B-Western and the screwball comedy respectively. Then his biggest success arrived with the boot-camp rom-com *Private Benjamin* (1980), which garnered an Oscar nomination for its star, Goldie Hawn. The 1980s proved a lean decade and the Preston Sturges remake *Unfaithfully Yours* (1984) only one of several conspicuous flops, but Zieff bounced back into the limelight in schmaltzy fashion with *My Girl* (1991) and *My Girl 2* (1994), a franchise that, for all its defects, coaxed undeniably memorable performances from child actors Macaulay Culkin and Anna Chlumsky. – *Benjamin Morgan*

Amongst those who also passed away in 2009...

HERCULES BELVILLE (b. 8 June 1939)
BETSY BLAIR (b. 11 December 1923)
DAVID CARRADINE (b. 8 December 1936)
MARILYN CHAMBERS (b. 22 April 1952)
DOM DELUISE (b. 1 August 1933)
ROY EDWARD DISNEY (b. 10 January 1930)
DMMINICK DUNNE (b. 29 October 1925)
FARRAH FAWCETT (b. 2 February 1947)
VILKO FILAK (b. 14 February 1950)
LARRY GELBART (b. 25 February 1928)
HENRY GIBSON (b. 21 September 1935)
PAT HINGLE (b. 19 July 1924)
EDWARD JUDD (b. 4 October 1932)
TROY KENNEDY MARTIN (b. 15 February 1932)
KARL MALDEN (b. 22 March 1912)
RICARDO MONTALBAN (b. 25 November 1920)
RON SILVER (b. 2 July 1946)
RICHARD TODD (b. 11 June 1919)
KEITH WATERHOUSE (b. 6 February 1929)
JAMES WHITMORE (b. 1 October 1921)

Industry Focus: The Social Media Revolution

The Social Media Revolution – Film Networks, Technology and the Future
by Ingrid Kopp

The Internet has changed significantly in just a few years. We now take the participatory web for granted and it seems completely natural for people to upload a video and tag it, comment on other people's blog posts, or tweet about what they are doing at any given moment. This is the read/write web, where sites are dynamic and driven by the communities that use them, often uploading their content to them. Facebook, YouTube and their ilk make you feel like they have been around forever and that Web 2.0 is old news.

However, it is a little startling to remember that this brave new world only emerged after the first dot-com bubble imploded in 2001. Facebook was founded as recently as 2004 and YouTube in 2005. Even early social network trailblazers like Friendster and MySpace were only founded in 2002 and 2003 respectively. The influence of these networks is undeniable. More than 350 million people currently use Facebook, according to its founder Mark Zuckerberg, and YouTube is the second-largest search engine in the world after Google.

It has taken most filmmakers some time to adopt these new technologies. Clay Shirky, an expert on the collaborative possibilities of the web has noted that 'tools don't get socially interesting until they get technologically boring... when everybody is able take them for granted'. Shirky explains the innovative possibilities of these mass conversations and shows how, unlike previous technologies like the telephone and the television, the 'Internet has native support for groups *and* conversations at the same time'. This is the power of many to many, as conversations flow in all directions at once, as opposed to one to one (telephone) or one to many (television). Moreover, all the old mediums have migrated to the Internet and live side by side; as you're streaming online video you can engage in a Skype video chat. When a new consumer joins this media landscape, they simultaneously become a producer. Shirky sees this as truly revolutionary: 'It's as if when you bought a book they threw in the printing press for free.'

Social media is powerful. The Obama election campaign demonstrated this in the US, creating a new political environment with MyBO, an online community of supporters and organisers. Facebook and Twitter have been blocked in countries like China, although the powers that be are finding it increasingly hard to control something as decentralised as social media, where every citizen is also a potential journalist and commentator. Such sites have also rapidly developed as communication tools, much like email and text messaging, the key difference being that this communication is public and reaching many people at the same time.

So, with such a spread of activity and cross-media application, how has this filtered down into the more traditional landscape of film production, from the development of the original project, through to its distribution and exhibition? What specifically film-oriented websites have emerged to capitalise on the possibilities of these new technologies?

The Film Network

Shooting People (www.shootingpeople.org) was founded way back in 1998 – the same year that Google became incorporated – by Jess Search and Cath Le Couteur, who were making a short film and wanted to find a better way to tap into their network of filmmaking friends. They worked on the principle of six degrees of separation: that someone would know someone who knew someone who could get something done. Shooting People began as a simple email bulletin with website that was little more than a page where people could sign up to receive the emails. Over the years it has developed, along with the available technology, into a fully interactive website where members can create profiles, upload their films, contact each other and rate and comment on each other's work. The site also includes RSS feeds from blogs and Twitter to create a wider conversation around independent film.

The Shooting People website

The original intention of Shooting People – solely dealing with members wanting to find crew and equipment – still exists elsewhere, on sites that offer a one-stop shop for all production assistance. Simple listing and directory services such as **ProductionHub** (www.productionhub.com) and **Mandy** (www.mandy.com) have given filmmakers access to the resources they require for their projects.

However, like Shooting People, a number of sites have realised the potential to go beyond a directory function, creating communities with more sophisticated demands and the filmmaking tools to match them. **Massify** (www.massify.com) is one such site. It encourages filmmakers to connect, collaborate and create. Cast and crew jobs or calls for qualified assistance are advertised, but it is also possible to set up a personal profile and find collaborators for projects. Massify have also established partnerships with Killer Films and Lionsgate in order to gain more industry exposure.

Star Wreck: In the Pirkinning

At the DIY end of the spectrum, **Wreckamovie** (www.wreckamovie.com) is an online collaborative film community that emerged from the making of *Star Wreck: In the Pirkinning*, a feature-length, collaboratively created sci-fi parody. Here, people can upload information about their films in progress and then create tasks and solicit help.

However, social media and networks are only effective when a critical mass of people actually use them. Similar networks are springing up around the world, but it is this factor that can determine their success – being able to attract active communities of filmmakers, and often their audiences too, and keep them engaged. Sometimes this can mean honing in on a specific area and dominating by being *the* site for anyone working in that environment.

Some networks do this by devoting themselves exclusively to a particular genre,

The Documentary Filmmakers Group website

such as documentary. **D-Word** (www.d-word. com) is a forum-based community of over 2,000 documentary filmmakers worldwide. It began in 1996 as a series of online journal entries by filmmaker Doug Block, who was writing about his experiences making and selling his feature documentary, *Home Page*. It is notable that the best sites for filmmakers often evolve organically in this way. **The Documentary Filmmakers Group** (DFG, www.dfgdocs.com) is a UK-based group, who use their website to provide resources and training information, as well as a blog-based community component. **The European Documentary Network** (EDN, www.edn. dk) does a similar job with a Europe-wide focus. **4Docs** (www.4docs.org.uk) recently re-launched in the UK as a home for short documentaries. It is not a network as such, but it has a very useful wiki that anyone can contribute to. Based on their experience running the Good Pitch at film festivals, Britdoc

The 4Docs website

have recently released **Goodfilm** (www. goodfilm.org/) as an online platform to connect films and filmmakers with the Third Sector. This is a new trend in social-issue filmmaking and it makes sense as avenues of funding dry up and filmmakers discover the power of a solid outreach campaign.

Creating New Avenues for Publicity and Funding

More commercial ventures are also emerging. **Genius Rocket** (www.geniusrocket.com) is a crowdsourced creative marketing platform where brands can tap into the online community in order to get work produced cheaply. In a similar vein, **Poptent** (www. poptent.net) allows creatives to connect with companies and brands for commercial work. **Placevine** (www.placevine.com) is an online service connecting brands with content. Companies are seeing the value of user-generated marketing, which is ideally both cheap and genuine. However, this can sometimes backfire. When GM gave people the opportunity to create an ad for the Chevy Tahoe, environmentalists used it as an opportunity to point out the ridiculousness of selling rugged, gas-guzzling SUVs to customers living nowhere near a snowy mountain. Other sites are using crowdsourcing to allow filmmakers to pitch their projects and raise funds using a microfunding model. The most notable examples are **IndieGoGo** (www. indiegogo.com) and new kid on the block, **Kickstarter** (www.kickstarter.com). 'The opportunity to start small and then be found is bigger than ever,' says IndieGoGo's co-founder Slava Rubin. 'Crowdfunding is in its infancy. There is still a lot of runway for it to take off.'

Some filmmakers are using their own websites to raise funds for both production and distribution. British filmmaker Franny Armstrong did this with her most recent film, *The Age of Stupid*. Over €850,000 of the film's budget was contributed by more than 600 people. **Indie Screenings** (www. indiescreenings.net), a new DVD distribution

The Indie Screenings website

tool, evolved out of the film's innovative distribution campaign. It automates community screenings by allowing anyone in the world to order a DVD copy of *The Age of Stupid* to screen and then return it. Once all the screening details have been added on the site, the software automatically calculates the screening fee. At the moment, only *The Age of Stupid* is available through Indie Screenings, but more films will soon be added to the site. *Four Eyed Monsters* co-director Arin Crumley used Kickstarter to raise funds for a new user-generated film screening tool called **OpenIndie** (www.openindie.com), which is currently in development but will likely make some waves in 2010.

Franny Armstrong's **The Age of Stupid**

Creating New Distribution Channels

Filmmakers are increasingly using the power of the web for distribution. Robert Greenwald used the experience of screening *Wal-Mart:*

The High Cost of Low Price on 7,000 screens simultaneously to start **Brave New Theaters** (www.bravenewtheaters.com), which allows anyone to host their own screening of any of the films available through the site. Filmmakers decide how much to charge for their DVD and then whoever is hosting the screening simply clicks through to buy it. Film screenings are then added to the website and are searchable by zip code in the US. Another new avenue for filmmakers is the online premiere. Sally Potter's *Rage* premiered in episodic form for mobile phones on **Babelgum** (www.babelgum.com), an Internet and mobile TV platform, at the same time as the cinema and DVD release.

Sally Potter's **Rage**

People are increasingly experimenting with new distribution options as traditional windows collapse and many films are offered bad deals or not picked up for distribution at all. Some filmmakers have leveraged these possibilities in very inventive ways. Brett Gaylor created **Open Source Cinema** (www.opensourcecinema.org) to allow people to remix footage for the film that became *RIP: A Remix Manifesto*, which explores the complex world of copyright, from the work of the mash-up artist Girl Talk to new forms of music in Brazil and attempts to work against the monopolisation of the pharmaceutical industry.

Following the Radiohead model, whereby the group made available their album 'In Rainbows' to listeners for a fee that each listener felt they should pay, people are sometimes now given the option to can download a copy of a film

RIP: A remix Manifesto

for a price they decide. Nina Paley made her animated feature *Sita Sings the Blues* available to audiences across a variety of different platforms, at different price points, including the opportunity to download it for free. She makes her motives clear on her website: 'I hereby give *Sita Sings the Blues* to you. Like all culture, it belongs to you already, but I am making it explicit with a Creative Commons Attribution-Share Alike License. Please distribute, copy, share, archive, and show *Sita Sings the Blues*. From the shared culture it came, and back into the shared culture it goes.'

Nina Paley's **Sita Sings the Blues**

Employing Existing Sites

Filmmakers are also using non-film related networking sites, like Facebook, MySpace, YouTube, LinkedIn and Twitter, for everything from crewing-up to marketing their distribution campaigns. They are creating communities around blogs and websites, and utilising all the free tools that are now available to forge a rich media environment, as well as a feedback loop between themselves and their audiences. This relationship often begins right from the start of a project's life. The people behind *Lost Zombies* made clever use of the Ning social-network platform to create the world's first user-generated Zombie documentary. Some other tools available include live streaming, forums, and real-time chat. Web applications have emerged to service this new world, where filmmakers use many sites simultaneously. For example, tools like Tubemogul allow filmmakers to upload their video to many sites at once and keep track of all the metrics.

On the set of the music video 'Wake the Dead', part of **Lost Zombies**

Some Distance to Go

The music business is ahead of film in terms of available web tools to allow musicians to create, tour and sell merchandise. Musicians like Zoe Keating and Amanda Palmer have created an astounding fan base around their work with no record company to support them (or to get in their way). Napster online file sharing began in 1999, so the music business has had to adapt to all-things-digital ahead of film.

But although film lags behind the music industry, there are innovative new sites emerging. These are necessary because traditional distribution and marketing models for independent film are crumbling at a time when technology is becoming both ubiquitous and cheap, meaning an increasing number of people are making films and competing to get them seen. Filmmakers have a great deal to learn from other fields and disciplines.

The web is *disintermediated* and so there is a new focus on the audience and on filmmakers using the available technology to connect directly with their fans. Creatives can talk to and sell to their fans directly, thereby skipping the middlemen. These social networks are practical production tools, but they also allow for new ways of storytelling and of engaging audiences in the creative process. Filmmakers are networking with other filmmakers to get advice, crew and equipment, but they are also conversing with their audiences, or rather with the people formerly known as the audience. Convergence culture is upon us – user-generated content and social media is anywhere that people can go online. There are many more amateurs than professionals and they can all talk to each other. Filmmakers who tap into the creative possibilities of this are reaping the rewards.

There is still, however, a marketing gap for filmmakers without money for a decent P&A spend and a good publicist. This is something Netflix's Ted Sarandos calls the 'cold start on the Internet'. The web has become less about searchability and more about findability so filmmakers need to identify their audience early on in the production process and go where their audience lives online, fish where the fish are, as it were. Filmmakers who can do this, and are able to create conversations and calls to action with their audience, are ahead of the game. As Boing Boing blog co-editor and bona fide member of the digerati Cory Doctorow says, 'Conversation not content is king.' There is a value in any kind of relationship that can never be copied because, unlike content, these relationships are not reducible to bits.

Filmmakers need new tools and they need to look beyond film to find adequate solutions. Lance Weiler, ever ahead of the curve, set up the **Workbook Project** (workbookproject.com) to explore ways of bridging the gap between technology and entertainment. Weiler is helping filmmakers to explore new ways of extending the storytelling experience, often using social-media tools that already exist as part of the story itself. Weiler is also a big advocate of filmmakers connecting and engaging with their audiences through the creative use of technology.

We are discovering the power of ideas when they are shared. Mass conversations lead to true innovation on a massive scale. This can be seen in all the films that are funded through IndieGoGo or Kickstarter, crewed and cast through Shooting People or Massify and distributed through Babelgum or one of the myriad other online video sites. It remains to be seen how far filmmakers can use social networks and social media to emerge from the ashes of the current distribution quagmire. The web tools already out there are just the first steps but there are already enormous benefits to be gained by filmmakers of any genre and at any stage of their careers using them. It is always just a question of the right tools for the job. And if they don't exist, they need to be built.

INGRID KOPP lives in New York and is director of the US office of Shooting People. She writes about film and technology for various publications and teaches digital bootcamp workshops for filmmakers. She began her career in the documentaries department at Channel 4 in the UK and still works as a documentary programming consultant.

Special Focus: The New 3D Cinema

The New 3D Cinema

by Ben Walters

In 2005, a young company called RealD demonstrated to Walt Disney Pictures its new digital 3D projection system, which used a single projector, rather than two, and glasses with polarised grey lenses rather than the two-colour anaglyph technique. Disney were so impressed that they reconfigured their latest computer-animated feature, *Chicken Little*, which was already in production, as a stereoscopic film. Since then, a fully fledged boom has developed that, unlike earlier 3D crazes, shows no sign of being a flash in the pan. The sky will not fall on this trend any time soon – but a number of chicken-and-egg questions about the technology's commercial and artistic uses remain unresolved.

Although various kinds of stereoscopic filmmaking have been in existence for as long as motion pictures themselves – Eadweard Muybridge, William Friese-Greene and Abel Gance were among early experimenters – the technology only attained widespread traction in the 1950s. The 3D craze that began in November 1952 with the release of *Bwana Devil* yielded around 50 feature films and numerous supporting items, from cartoons to newsreels. But, hobbled by unreliable technology and over-reliance on novelty effects, it lasted barely a year and few mourned its passing. The early 1980s saw another spate of 3D pictures but similar problems applied: mediocre content relying on shock-value application of stereo space exhibited via technology that was prone to errors and could even cause discomfort for

viewers. Following this short-lived resurgence, the format lingered on largely in IMAX documentaries and bespoke programming for theme parks.

The new wave of digital 3D films has already proven more sustainable than the crazes of the 1950s and 1980s in longevity and profitability, and the number of titles looks likely to overtake those produced in the 1950s within a year or two. Since *Chicken Little*, more than two dozen films have been released in RealD's digital 3D format and at least 17 more are scheduled for release in 2010 from major Hollywood studios, which, like audiences, have been convinced by the reliability and user-friendliness of the digital system in comparison to its analogue predecessors. These titles include *Shrek Forever After* from DreamWorks Animation, which now produces all its films in 3D, and Tim Burton's *Alice in Wonderland* from Disney. European productions include the children's animations, *Animals United* and *The Little Medic* from Germany and, in the UK, a *Postman Pat* feature and *Streetdance 3D*, starring Charlotte Rampling and George

Chicken Little

Tim Burton's **Alice in Wonderland**

Sampson, the young dancer featured on
ITV's *Britain's Got Talent*. New entries in the
Hellraiser, *Tron* and *Spy Kids* franchises, as
well as the debut feature from the Blue Man
Group of performers, will also use the format.

The bottom line also seems sound. *Monsters
vs Aliens* more or less single handedly boosted
DreamWorks Animation to strong profits
in the third quarter of 2009; it was shown
in 3D on only 20% of screens but these
accounted for more than 40% of the film's
takings. Stereoscopic showings of *Ice Age 3*
and *Cloudy with a Chance of Meatballs* were
comparably more profitable than 'flat', or
two-dimensional, screenings, and Disney's *A
Christmas Carol* opened at the top of the US
chart in November 2009. Some analysts at
September's 3D Entertainment Summit in Los
Angeles last September even maintained that
3D films could take the credit for American box-
office returns being in profit for the summer
2009 period. Multiplex owners reported that a
screen showing a 3D film could be expected to
generate up to nine times the profit of a screen
showing a 'flat' programme. Some of the
delegates, whose number had doubled to 500

Ice Age 3

since 2008, had vested interests in the success
of the technology but many more were simply
interested in what was best for the industry.
Even so, reported *Variety*, 'No one at the
summit voices suspicions that the current 3D
wave is a passing fad.'

Cloudy with a Chance of Meatballs

In fact, the problem was not whether
audiences were willing to pay a premium to
watch films in stereo but whether cinemas
were able to meet the demand: limited screen
availability was leading to cannibalisation
of profits as a thriving picture was booted
out mid-run to make way for the next 3D
film that required its screen. Indeed, the
renovation of cinema screens to allow for
digital 3D projection remains one of the major
stumbling blocks to wider entrenchment of
the technology and the subject of a protracted
debate between distributors and exhibitors
over who should bear the costs. The economic
collapse of autumn 2008 put paid to a hard-
won billion-dollar deal between studios and
US cinema chains that would have greatly
expanded the number of screens; the resulting
lag between 3D films produced and 3D
screens available to show them partly accounts
for the bottleneck effect reported above.

But even if screen pick-up has been slower
than the industry had hoped, it has still
been considerable: between January and
November 2009, the number of 3D-viable
American screens rose from 900 to nearly
2,000, and was expected to reach 2,500 for
the December release by Twentieth Century
Fox of James Cameron's long-gestating 3D
epic *Avatar* – fewer than the 3,000 Fox and

Disney had hoped to see by year's end but of the same order of magnitude. Internationally, the number rose over the same period from around 1,000 to around 3,200, with the UK and China each boasting 400 screens and other European nations not far off. Russia and Mexico saw significant growth and Egypt's first 15 3D screens were being installed in time to show *Avatar*.

There are other encouraging signs. Prime Focus, an Indian post-production conglomerate with substantial Hollywood connections, recently announced the launch of View-D, a high-profile 2D-to-3D conversion service that could be used to reconfigure a host of features if the releases of retroactively 3D-rendered 'flat' pictures – such as the first two *Toy Story* films, released in 2009, and *Beauty and the Beast*, scheduled for release in 2011 – prove successful. And, in another sign of entrenchment, the University of Southern California announced an interdisciplinary programme at the School of Cinematic Arts to start in 2010, focusing on technological and aesthetic concerns in 3D filmmaking. 'We're getting so many requests from industry to provide them with this kind of background in stereoscopic imaging,' said USC professor Perry Hoberman.

Nor is such engagement restricted to content: the technology is also undergoing dynamic development. Presently, RealD dominates the digital 3D imaging market with their polarised-lens system. (Disney Digital 3D is a variation on the system.) Another company, Trioscopics, has developed a new green-and-magenta anaglyph system, which could be adapted for use with current digital-projection formats, perhaps at a lower price than polarised imaging. And, partly in response to the slower-than-expected conversion of digital screens, Technicolor has developed a new celluloid 3D system compatible with conventional projectors. Intended as a stopgap solution, it has angered major cheerleaders for digital 3D, including Disney and Fox, but has the support of Paramount, Universal, Warner Bros

and other large studios and unquestionably has potential application in parts of the world where large-scale digital take-up is not likely in the foreseeable future.

The Hollywood studios' new enthusiasm for 3D has been characterised by some as representing a bulwark against piracy and 3D films certainly constitute a relatively novel form of spectacle presently unavailable on home-entertainment platforms. But, as the studios know very well, this distinction might not persist much longer. The technology for domestic 3D broadcasting already exists (and has been on sale in Japan for some years) and is being actively developed. In November, Sony, a major player in both feature production and home entertainment, announced plans yoking the corporation's future success to 3D technology across a variety of platforms, including TV, PlayStation and Blu-ray content as well as films. While Sony expects a billion-dollar loss over the 2009–10 business year, it anticipates making $11 billion dollars in 2012–13 from 3D-related products alone. Disney has also been exploring home 3D, through its sports channel, ESPN. In September, a test broadcast of an American football match was hailed as a technological success within the industry and, although not widely seen by general audiences, garnered positive responses from test viewers.

It has also been suggested that the gaming sector would be a prominent force in driving domestic 3D but challenges to that assumption have already appeared. Tests of

James Cameron's **Avatar**

the 3D functions included in *James Cameron's Avatar: The Game*, released in November 2009, prompted complaints about image quality and processing speed. It remains to be seen whether these are teething problems or insurmountable obstacles.

Up!

More than a decade in development, *Avatar* has acquired the status of standard-bearer for the new 3D revolution, even the picture on whose fortunes the technology's future depends. In fact, there would now seem to be sufficient entrenchment of 3D in mainstream film exhibition that even its box-office failure would not scupper the format. It might, however, have repercussions for its artistic development. To date, 3D has acquired a solid toehold in certain genres – horror and music or dance films – and is on the way to dominating others, such as computer-animated features. Filmmakers working in these areas have not simply exploited the potential for coming-at-you! shocks but have also proven adept at utilising deep cinematic space for expressive purposes. Animated features like *Up!* and *A Christmas Carol* have used aerial

compositions with multiple shifting planes to good effect, while deep space can also enhance suspense for horror films. Cameron's *Avatar* demonstrated a confident grasp of stereoscopic space, eschewing novelty effects for impressive aerial vistas and compellingly shot alien dogfights.

What remains open to question is whether 3D will remain a niche area associated with certain genres or be embraced by big-name studio directors and art-house auteurs. As we saw above, Tim Burton has taken the plunge and Steven Soderbergh has announced plans for a stereoscopic rock-opera version of *Cleopatra*, though these seem to have been shelved. If *Avatar* – which at the time of writing had enjoyed a strong opening weekend at the global box office – proves a great success, it could encourage other established directors to take the technology seriously; even if it does not, Steven Spielberg's *Tintin: Secret of the Unicorn*, due for release in December 2011, will be another test case. In principle, there is no reason the technology shouldn't be put to creative, imaginative use by talented directors interested in the expressive use of space. Experimental filmmaker Ken Jacobs has already got stuck in, following in the footsteps of Norman McLaren, who produced 3D work in the 1950s, creating beguiling and discombobulating effects.

3D is not going anywhere for the foreseeable future. The questions that remain – whether it will remain in cinemas or migrate to the home, and whether its use will remain restricted to particular genres or be seriously explored as a means of artistic expression – will be determined by a number of factors, of which, as so often in filmmaking, the most important will be the bottom line.

A Christmas Carol

BEN WALTERS is the author of books about Orson Welles, *The Office* and (with JM Tyree) *The Big Lebowski*, and contributes regularly to *Film Quarterly*, the *Guardian*, *Sight & Sound* and *Time Out*.

Home Entertainment by Ian Haydn Smith

This section, an annual round-up of some of the best DVD releases from the last year, has changed its format. Rather than focus on titles geographically, sections are divided by label. This will offer a greater overview of the work of each label and will complement more in-depth profiles of them in the regular Home Entertainment Spotlights that will appear on the IFG website (www.internationalfilmguide.com, which will also feature an extended version of this article).

The Criterion Collection
(Region 1)

Started in 1984, the Criterion Collection has become the gold standard of DVD – and now Blu-ray – releases. They have consistently delivered on their mission statement of 'gathering the greatest films from around the world and publishing them in editions that offer the highest technical quality and award-winning, original supplements'. And as technology has moved on, so has Criterion's willingness to try out new formats (including an online cinematheque), while remaining true to its commitment to 'publishing the defining moments of cinema for a wider and wider audience'.

In addition to the exceptional quality of their releases – much of the work being done in-house, with skilled staff and state-of-the-art facilities – Criterion works, wherever they can, with a film's director and/or cinematographer, to ensure the image is exactly how it was meant to be presented. Such high quality is further enhanced by the plethora of extras included with each film and stunning designs and packaging, as well as booklets with essays by many of the world's top critics and writers. The result is a library that anyone with anything more than a passing interest in film could not fail but be stunned by.

Michael Ritchie's **Downhill Racer** (1969) has, for too long, been one of the more overlooked films of the new Hollywood that emerged out of the 1960s. Played with an icy narcissism by Robert Redford, David Chappellet's ruthless ascension through the ranks of the international skiing circuit underpins one of the bleakest films made about sport and the pursuit of victory. Thrillingly shot (*Variety's* Todd McCarthy informs us, in his insightful essay in the accompanying booklet, that the handheld POV camerawork had never been done before) and adopting the semi-documentary style that works so well in Ritchie's later *The Candidate*

Downhill Racer

(1972), the new restoration highlights the beauty of Bryan Probyn's crisp cinematography. **Extras:** A fine booklet, with images recalling the aspirational Time&Life photo-style; a promotional featurette; a recording of a 1977 AFI seminar given by Ritchie; the original theatrical trailer; new video interviews with Redford, the film's writer, editor and production manager, as well as downhill skier and technical adviser, Joe Jay Jalbert.

Whit Stillman's eighties-set **The Last Days of Disco** (1998) sees Kate Beckinsale and Chloë Sevigny play two employees of a publishing house who spend their nights carousing through the city's trendy bars and venues. Unlike other films exploring New York's nightclub past, the film stands out for its lack of sentimentality and Stillman's biting dialogue. Although less remembered than Quentin Tarantino's on-screen film discussions, Charlotte's (a career-best performance by Beckinsale) take on Disney's *Lady and the Tramp* (1955) is hilarious. With

The Last Days of Disco

its wit, sophistication and intelligence, *The Last Days of Disco*, whose restoration was approved by the director, makes Stillman's decade-long absence from the cinema all the more regrettable. **Extras:** A booklet with a short essay by novelist David Schickler; a commentary by Stillman, Sevigny and Chris Eigman; a number of deleted scenes; a featurette; the theatrical trailer; and an audio recording of Stillman reading from his book, *The Last Days of Disco, with Cocktails at Petrossian Afterwards*.

The Human Condition

Masaki Kobayashi's epic, nine-and-a-half-hour **The Human Condition** (1959–61) was adapted from Junpei Gomikawa's mammoth six-volume novel. Split into three parts, it is, as Philip Kemp points out in his insightful accompanying essay, 'one of the most monumental acts of personal expiation in all cinematic history'. It traces the arduous journey of Kaji, played by Tatsuya Nakadai, from the supervisor at a labour camp to an infantryman in the Imperial Army and finally Soviet POW, who attempts to rise above the inhumanity of the world around him, only to realise that the more he holds on to his personal sense of morality, the greater his hardship. The sheer scale of the undertaking is remarkable, but that Kobayashi never loses focus on Kaji and the disparity between his attempt to maintain his dignity and the callous inhumanity of those around him reinforces both the film's message and its relevance. **Extras:** An informative booklet; excerpts from a video interview with the director; a new video interview with Tatsuya Nakadai; a video appreciation of Kobayashi and his film; and the film's Japanese theatrical trailers.

Another epic undertaking by Criterion is the box set, **The Golden Age of Television** (1953–58). It features eight television plays that were originally broadcast live, presenting the world of theatre and literature to a mainstream audience. These productions are often startling in their rawness and feature an impressive roll-call of actors, including Andy Griffith, Julie Harris, Kim Hunter, Paul Newman, Jack Palance, George Peppard, Mickey Rooney and Mel Tormé. There are also a few surprises. Ernest Borgnine may have won an Academy Award for his performance in the titular role of Paddy Chayefsky's play, but Rod Steiger's Marty is no less impressive. Likewise, in John Frankenheimer's 1958 version of *Days of Wine and Roses*, Cliff Robertson and Piper Laurie present a more harrowing account of addiction than Jack Lemmon and Lee Remick attempted, just four years later, in Blake Edwards' film adaptation of J.P. Miller's play, which was originally commissioned for television. **Extras:** Even by Criterion's usual high standards, Ron Simon's notes in the accompanying booklet are a treasure trove of fascinating facts and insights; commentaries by a number of the directors; and interviews with many of the plays' cast members.

Roberto Rossellini has been served well by Criterion and Eclipse over the last year, along with the release of his war trilogy this year. Though lesser known than *Rome Open City* (1945), *Paisan* (1946) and *Germany Year Zero* (1948), **Il generale Della Rovere** (1961) is a bridge between those earlier neorealist works and his more challenging historical works of the 1960s and 1970s. Moreover, the film is arguably one of the director's most accessible. In a role that hints at Italy's duality during the Second World War, adapted from journalist Indo Montanelli's controversial historical novel about Nazi collaborator and spy Giovanni Bertoni, Vittorio De Sica plays con artist

Emanuele Bardone. He takes on the role of an army colonel in order to dupe people out of their money, before transforming once again into a stooge for the Nazis. De Sica is excellent in the central role, while the screenplay by Montanelli, Sergio Amidei and Diego Fabbri refuses to simplify the roles people are forced to play in a country occupied by a hostile force. **Extras:** The booklet features an essay by James Monaco and an excerpt of an interview with Indo Montanelli; interviews with Isabella, Renzo and Ingrid Rossellini; a visual essay by Rossellini biographer Tag Gallagher; and the original theatrical trailer.

The Taking of Power by Louis XIV

The Taking of Power by Louis XIV (1966) was Roberto Rossellini's move from cinema, which he announced was dead, to television, and remains the most famous work of this final period of his career. Although many of his practices rarely changed over the years – his later films were still mostly populated by non-professional actors – his approach here takes on a more essayistic feel, presenting a diarised account of historical events, though never lacking the humanism that permeated all his work. If *Il generale Della Rovere* explored the nature of myth and the malleability of truth, Rossellini's account of the Sun King was successful in taking the myth and making him human. His attention to detailing everyday life in the court of Louis XIV helped redefine the costume drama. **Extras:** A booklet essay by critic Colin McCabe; a video interview with the film's artistic adviser, script supervisor and second-unit director; and a multimedia essay by Rossellini biographer Tag Gallagher.

That Hamilton Woman

A more full-blooded account of history dominates Alexander Korda's **That Hamilton Woman** (1941). Made as propaganda for the British war effort, Laurence Olivier and Vivien Leigh revel in their roles as Horatio Nelson and his lover, Lady Hamilton. It was Winston Churchill's favourite film and featured enough romance and battle scenes to sate the appetites of both sexes on its release, and thanks to its charming star couple; and Korda's sense of the epic, it remains a fabulously extravagant adventure. ***Extras:*** A booklet essay by critic Molly Haskell; a new video recording with Alexander Korda's nephew Michael; an audio commentary by film historian Ian Christie; a promotional radio piece for the film; and the original theatrical trailer.

Eclipse
(Region 1)

The younger sibling of Criterion, Eclipse is an impressive series, releasing 'lost, forgotten, or overshadowed classics in simple, affordable editions'. From its first collection, featuring the early films of Ingmar Bergman, Eclipse has become a fascinating outlet for lesser-known

directors such as Larisa Shepitko and Raymond Bernard together with the films of William Klein, the early and later works of Yasujiro Ozu (the former featuring the sublime *I Was Born, But...*) and the musicals of Ernst Lubitsch. (A Home Entertainment Spotlight on all Eclipse releases, with a film-by-film guide through each collection will appear on the IFG website in spring.)

For those enticed by *The Taking of Power by Louis XIV*, **Rossellini's History Films** is a must. The collection features *The Age of Medici* (1972), *Cartesius* (1974) and *Blaise Pascal* (1972), all of which were produced for television and employ the same technique as *Louis XIV*, of bringing history to life whilst avoiding the trappings of heritage cinema. *Blaise Pascal* is arguably the most intriguing of the three, detailing the controversies and debates that dominated that philosopher scientist's life.

The Age of Medici

Like *That Hamilton Woman*, **Alexander Korda's Private Lives** is the polar opposite of Rossellini's austere worlds. Bawdy and fruity, though never descending to coarse vulgarity, *The Private Life of Henry VIII* (1933), *The Rise of Catherine the Great* (1934), *The Private Life of Don Juan* (1934) and *Rembrandt* (1936) are the finest productions by London Films, which made the most of their lavish budgets (as Michael Koresky points out in his liner notes, *Catherine the Great*'s €60,000 budget soon spiralled to €127,868). As befitting his love of grandeur and the grand, Korda found his perfect stars in Douglas Fairbanks and Charles Laughton, who each dominate two films. Laughton, in particular, is a delight, imbuing

The Private Life of Henry VIII

Henry VIII and Rembrandt with a lust for everything that life has to offer.

Continuing the Eclipse series' strand of Japanese directors, **Travels with Hiroshi Shimizu** and **Nakkatsu Noir** present two very different takes on Japanese society. Though little known nowadays, Shimizu's films were quiet, understated studies of contemporary life. Present in this collection are *Japanese Girls at the Harbour* (1933), *The Masseurs and a Woman* (1938), *Ornamental Hairpin* (1941) and arguably the best film in the collection, *Mr. Thank You* (1936), which details a young bus driver's fascination with a beautiful passenger.

Fans of Seijun Suzuki's *Tokyo Drifter* (1966) and *Branded to Kill* (1967) may want to check out the collection of Japanese noirs from the country's oldest film studio, Nikkatsu. Pared down to their existential basics, these tautly directed thrillers pit tough, embittered protagonists against criminals, cops and the system. Their titles say it all: *I am Waiting* (1957), *Rusty Knife* (1958), *Take Aim at the*

A Colt is My Passport

Police Van (1960), *Cruel Gun Story* (1964) and *A Colt is My Passport* (1967). The latter is a marvel of genre-bending ingenuity. What begins as a straightforward set-up, with a perfectly executed hit, transforms by its climax into a modern-day western, replete with a shootout on an empty, arid landscape.

Facets
(Region 1)

One of the oldest labels in the US, Facets was founded in 1975 as a non-profit organisation with a mission to 'preserve, to present and to distribute independent, world and classic film, and to educate adults and children in the art and legacy of film'. Through a combination of revenue generation, subscription fees and artistic grants, Facets has built up an eclectic library of films. It also offers its local Chicago audience a wide-ranging programme at their Cinémathèque. They also have a film school for those wishing to learn more about film and are closely involved in education events, such as the Chicago International Children's Film Festival.

Facets offers the chance to rent or purchase titles from an extensive catalogue, with a particularly strong focus on Eastern Europe.

Black Peter (1963) was the feature debut of Milos Forman. It was shot concurrently with *Talent Competition* (aka *If Only They Ain't Had Them Bands*), which was the second of two medium-length films released together (available in a fine edition from Second Run DVD). A coming-of-age narrative shot in a documentary style and, like so much of the director's early work, drawing humour out of generational conflict, it is a finely observed drama that hints at the work that was to come. Unfortunately, the transfer is a little rough, resulting in a film whose quality is, at best, patchy. **Extras:** An interview with Milos Forman and a simple booklet with biographical material.

Of significantly better quality (particularly when compared with previous versions of the film) is the **Grigori Kozinstev Collection**, featuring his most acclaimed Shakespearean adaptations, *Hamlet* (1964) and *King Lear* (1971). The latter is stunning and, along with Kurosawa's *Ran* (1985), is the best film version of Shakespeare's tragedy. ***Extras:*** Nicely produced booklets with biographies of the director, adaptor Boris Pasternak and composer Dimitri Shostakovich, as well as essays; the disc features an introduction by Peter Sellars.

The Nose

The Animation of Alexeïeff is an impressive collection of animated films by the Russian-born, Paris-based animator, Alexandre Alexeïeff, and his wife, Claire Parker. The collection includes many of the animator's advertising films (1935–64) and Norman McLaren's 1973 documentary about pinscreen animation. There is also an excellent booklet with essays by Susan Doll and Dominique Willoughby. All of which goes some way to appreciating the beauty of the collection's core feature, Alexeïeff's five pinscreen films: *En Passant* (1944), *The Nose* (1963), *Pictures at an Exhibition* (1972), *Three Moods* (1980) and the earliest work in the collection, the sublime *Night on Bald Mountain* (1933).

One of the most surprising releases of the year was **Goldstein** (1964), the directorial debut of Philip Kaufman. Described by Jean Renoir as 'the best American film I have seen in 20 years', it tells the story of a tramp (Lou Gilbert) who emerges from the waters of Lake Michigan and wanders the streets of Chicago. Like Hal Ashby's *Being There* (1979), Kaufman's

film works well as an engaging profile of an eccentric and an occasionally sharp assessment of contemporary society. An early example of American independent filmmaking, it wears the influence of the Nouvelle Vague, particularly in the street scenes, but also shares the same lightness of spirit that characterised the Czech New Wave. Above all, it offers the chance to see a Chicago that has long since disappeared. ***Extras:*** An interview with Philip Kaufman; a booklet featuring a profile of the director and the fascinating essay, 'Touring Chicago with Goldstein'.

Milestone Films
(Region 1)

Founded in 1990 by Dennis Doros & Amy Heller, who dedicated themselves to 'discovering and distributing films of enduring artistry from both yesterday and today'. It has an excellent track record of releasing important – both socially and cinematically – works. In 2008 they released Charles Burnett's *Killer of Sheep* (later released on Region 2 by the BFI) to much acclaim.

The Exiles

Milestone score once again with their release of Kent Mackenzie's groundbreaking **The Exiles** (1961). An attempt to re-address the way Native Americans were represented on film, it was inspired by an article that appeared in *Harper's* magazine, which detailed the government's attempts to reclaim reservation land. Mackenzie set about creating a narrative whose 'concern with physical reality', like his favourite filmmakers, 'was not for its own sake, but to create living and vital images, and symbols from recognisable elements of everyday life'.

The resulting film is a powerful portrait of life for a group of Native Americans living in the Bunker Hill district of Los Angeles, as they drink, party, dance and fight their way through one night. Beautifully restored, *The Exiles*, like *Killer of Sheep* before it, is a welcome addition to the canon of films that have been missing for so long from US film culture. **Extras:** Four short films by Mackenzie, including *Bunker Hill* (1956), the inspiration for *The Exiles*; excerpts from Thom Anderson's *Los Angeles Plays Itself*, which brought the film's existence to light; a commentary by novelist Sherman Alexie and critic Sean Axmaker; short films by Robert Kirste and Greg Kimble; and an episode of WNYC's *The Leonard Lopate Show* with Sherman Alexie and Charles Burnett.

Microcinema DVD
(Region 1)

Microcinema has created an impressive platform for 'the acquisition, exhibition, and distribution of independently produced moving images of an artistic and socially relevant nature'. Across a broad range of subjects, the label has released works that range from 'art film and video, music-driven visuals, ambient media, works about art and artists, and documentaries representative of current global issues and artistic trends'.

Having released numerous animated compilations in the past, Microcinema recently focused attention on the films of Bill Plympton with two collections, **Dog Days** (2004–8) and **Bill's Dirty Shorts** (1997–2002). For those familiar with his Academy Award nominated *Your Face* (1987) and *Guard Dog* (2004), or the popular *The Tune* (1992), *Dirty Shorts*, with titles such as *Sex & Violence* (1997), *More Sex & Violence* (1998) and *Krazy*

Guide Dog

Kock (2004), may come as something of a surprise. The more recent collection, including the hilarious *Dog* series, is better behaved, but both discs highlight the dexterity and imagination of this singular artist. **Extras:** Both collections feature commentaries and commercial work, while *Dog Days* includes music videos, TV interviews and a variety of other animated material.

Adding to the growing library of available Luis Buñuel films, **Death in the Garden** (1956) is the rare opportunity to watch one of the filmmaker's few colour, mid-period films. A thriller with signature surreal touches and featuring fine performances by Georges Marchal, Simone Signoret, Michel Piccoli and Charles Vanel, it shows how versatile the director's work was prior to his better-known late period. The quality of the image is mostly fine, as it should be (we are told it was

Death in the Garden

Tokyo Sonata

the current state of global economic unease, Teruyuki Kagawa plays an executive who is unable to face his redundancy, pretending to carry on his life as though nothing has changed, at least keeping up the pretence in front of his family. A similar theme was explored in Laurent Cantet's *Time Out* (2001) and John Lanchester's novel *Mr Philips*. Where Kurosawa's film excels is in the growing sense of unease faced by the central character. A master of mood and unsettling atmospheres, as witnessed in his earlier *Pulse* (2001), here Kurosawa turns the everyday into a horror story, as all hope for the businessman begins to fade. **Extras:** A 'making of' documentary; the film's Tokyo premiere; a Q&A; a DVD discussion; a booklet featuring the director's statement and an extended essay by writer B. Kite.

MoC's second Antonioni release, **Il Grido** (1957), is a fine example of why the label is held in such high regard. Like *La Notte* (1961) before it, the quality of the transfer is as high as one has come to expect. Made before the

Il Grido

director's more critically acclaimed work in the 1960s, the film is a fascinating insight into the development of his style. **Extras:** A superb booklet featuring an excerpt from William Arrowsmith's 'Antonioni: The Poet of Images', detailed notes and an interview with Antonioni; previously unseen footage; the original Italian theatrical trailer.

La Tête Contre Les Murs (1959) is MoC's second Georges Franju release (last year's *Judex* [1963] and *Nuits rouges* [1974] were released together). The director's feature debut, it is a tale of one man's fight for survival in the confines of a psychiatric ward, where he has been committed on the request of his father, worried about his son's wayward behaviour. What begins as a battle between generations becomes far more unsettling, as the young man fights for his sanity against Pierre Brasseur's authoritarian psychiatrist. **Extras:** A booklet featuring an article by Raymond Durgnat, an interview with Franju and a piece by Jean-Luc Godard; the original French theatrical trailer; recently filmed interviews with Jean-Pierre Mocky and Charles Aznavour.

Nous ne vieillirons pas ensemble

MoC is also presenting three very different features from Maurice Pialat: **Passe ton bac d'abord** (1979), **Nous ne vieillirons pas ensemble** (1972) and **La Gueule Ouverte** (1974). The most recent of these, which rounded off a remarkable series of unsentimental and bleak works from the 1970s, details the travails of a group of students who are reaching the end of the schooldays and are mostly unsure about the future. Their lives are punctuated by arguments, violence, sex and the futile activity of adolescents adrift and unsure of their place in the world. Not that the couple at the centre of *Nous ne vieillirons pas ensemble* feels any more comfortable. Based on Pialat's semi-autobiographical novel, his depiction of the disintegration of a couple's relationship would seem harsh if not for his humanism. And, finally, there is *La Gueule Ouverte*, whose account of a terminally ill woman (a remarkable performance by Monique Mélinand) is, at times, as painful for the audience to watch as it is for the woman's family to deal with. Adrian Martin correctly asserts in his essay accompanying the DVD that Pialat's bleakest film not only casts asunder most other films described as 'devastating', but also critics' very use of the word. And though it makes for uncomfortable viewing, it is an essential piece of cinema. ***Extras:*** Each release features a booklet with essays and interviews. The DVDs feature copious interview footage, shorts, documentaries and conversations.

Another excellent release, Jean-Luc Godard's **Une Femme Mariée, fragments d'un film tourné en 1964 en noir et blanc**, is accompanied by a booklet so encyclopaedic, it takes less time to watch the film than it does to read it. It is an excellent accompaniment to a film that has been out of circulation for too long. Macha Méril replaced Anna Karina as the female

Une Femme Mariée

lead, whose life is dissected into vignettes, detailing moments from it and the men who pass through it. Like so many of Godard's earlier films, it still surprises to see how fresh the film looks after 45 years. ***Extras:*** Aside from the booklet, the DVD features a trailer for the film that was created and edited by Godard.

BFI
(Region 2)

The last few years have seen many changes in the British Film Institute's DVD output. There has been reduction in the number of contemporary world titles that came out following a limited theatrical release and a greater focus on British archives, as well as the championing of work by both acclaimed and lesser-known filmmakers.

Winstanley

Two fine examples of this are Kevin Brownlow and Andrew Mollo's **Winstanley** (1975) and Bill Douglas's **Comrades** (1987), both of which document pivotal moments in British history. Douglas's film details the struggle of the Tolpuddle Martyrs, a group of Dorset labourers whose trade-union activities saw them transported to Australia. Adopting a similar approach to that of his earlier work, Douglas creates a drama that examines the basic rights that every human should reasonably expect, only to see them undermined by the forces of commerce and the state. His unforced style never preaches, instead allowing time for us to familiarise ourselves with the characters, which only accentuates the sense of injustice

Comrades

meted out to workers who only wish to receive a fair day's pay and to be treated as human beings. ***Extras:*** The booklet features essays and an interview; a documentary on the filmmaker; a recent interview with cast members; an on-location news report; the original theatrical trailer; a short film co-scripted by Douglas; and a series of interviews with him from 1978.

Brownlow and Mollo's film is set two centuries before *Comrades*, in 1649, when a small group known as the Diggers created a settlement in Surrey county, in the south east of England. Led by the visionary Gerrard Winstanley, their utopian way of life was crushed under the yolk of local suspicions and the concerns of landowners in fear of any threat to the status quo. Like Douglas's film, *Winstanley* excels in its depiction of a people who believe they have the right to live a life in quiet dignity and away from forces of coercion and exploitation. ***Extras:*** A booklet featuring articles and reviews; new interview with the directors; a 'making of' featurette; and Kevin Brownlow's short film about the last weekend of Glasgow's tram system.

Two collections of films by Frank Borzage draw attention to the visual poetry of the early Hollywood director. **Frank Borzage: Volume One** includes *7th Heaven* (1927) and *Street Angel* (1928), which both star Janet Gaynor and Charles Farrell. The former, based on a successful stage play, is one of Borzage's better-known films. It tells of the love affair between a Parisian street waif

and a Montmartre sewage worker, and gave the director the best platform to explore the mysticism of romantic love. *Street Angel* never quite achieves the same rhapsodic heights (although its street cred increased when American Music Club wrote a score for it), but in the way that Frank Capra's least convincing material still kept his audience's attention rapt, Borzage casts a powerful spell with his story of a painter who falls in love with a woman on the run from the law, who joins a travelling circus. ***Extras:*** There are no extras except for a booklet featuring essays by Joe McElhaney and Janey Bergstrom.

Frank Borzage: Volume Two includes *Lucky Star* (1929) and *Liliom* (1920), which once again feature favourite leading man Charles Farrell, along with Janet Gaynor and Rose Hobart. It is perhaps in the first, lesser-known film (only recently re-discovered and restored) that one can appreciate what an asset Farrell was and how Borzage realised the treasure he had in this underrated leading man. His physical dexterity – it would take me a little longer to scale a telegraph pole – not to mention the charisma he displays, mark him out as an actor in need of re-evaluation. *Lucky Star*'s narrative is yet another variation on the earlier volume's love-struck couples. Once again, it is the intensity of Borzage's gaze and the spell he casts over us that matters. Even with the absence of Gaynor, *Liliom* still has its pleasures. Based on the Ferenc Molnar play

Lucky Star

and later remade as *Carousel*, it might lack the earlier films' warmth, but its value as a curio amongst Borzage's silent work makes it worth seeing. ***Extras:*** A commentary to *Lucky Star* by Tom Gunning; a booklet with Gunning's extended essay on the director's career, along with essays on the two films; and *The River* (1929), Borzage's 55-minute masterpiece of unbridled eroticism.

BFI Flipside
(Region 2)

The films released so far under the BFI Flipside label justify its inclusion separately of the main body of releases. As the BFI's Sam Dunn points out, 'We have recently begun to focus on a number of areas of British filmmaking in order – we hope – to tell a kind of forgotten history of British cinema and provide a platform for long-neglected and often challenging films.' These films may not be to everyone's taste, but together they present a fascinating look at British life from the point of view of a singular group of filmmakers. (A more detailed overview of BFI Flipside will appear on the IFG website's Home Entertainment Spotlight in spring.)

Anyone looking for the UK equivalent of Franco Prosperi and Gualtiero Jacopetti could do worse than seek out Arnold L. Miller's **London in the Raw** (1964) and **Primitive London** (1965), which guide us through some of the seedier sites of the capital during the height of the Swinging Sixties. The combination of documentary footage and staged action works more effectively in the later film, with an amusing host highlighting the difference between the mods, rockers and beatniks that roam the city's streets and fill its drinking holes. But we're never too far away from a quick cut back to some stripper or young woman in various states of undress. The film also features British comedian Barry Cryer in a bizarre sketch about broadcast advertising that punctuates perhaps too much of the film. ***Extras:*** Both films are worth acquiring for their extras alone.

Primitive London

London in the Raw includes an alternative cut of the film, the original trailer and three 'London Sketches': *Strip* (1966), a behind-the-scenes look at working life in a strip club on Old Compton Street in London's West End; *Chelsea Bridge Boys* (1965) comprises of a series of interviews with bikers, inter-cut with footage out on the road with them; and *Pub* (1962) documents life in a typical East End boozer, whose impressionistic style makes it a fascinating companion piece to Terence Davies' *Distant Voices, Still Lives*. An accompanying booklet includes essays, reviews and biographies. *Primitive London* features a dramatised documentary about a group of striptease artistes, *Carousella* (1965); interviews with a stripper, nightclub owner and stripclub manager; and a booklet featuring an excellent essay by novelist, London expert and psychogeographer, Iain Sinclair.

Any attempt to describe the narrative of Richard Lester's adaptation of Spike Milligan and John Antrobus's play **The Bed Sitting Room** (1969) is bound to fail. Suffice to say it is the work of at least one mad genius and a host of willing participants. The cast, who 'star in order of height', play survivors from a global catastrophe, left to roam a devastated land. The result falls somewhere between Ionescu, Beckett, *Hellzapoppin*, and a dose of Milligan's own television series, *Q*. ***Extras:*** Interviews with Lester, Milligan and Peter Cook and a booklet featuring an essay by Michael Brooke.

Herostratus

One of the genuine surprises so far from the Flipside collection is Don Levy's **Herostratus** (1967). Not only do its themes resonate even as powerfully today, it is astonishing to see how much it influenced later films such as *Performance* (1970) and *A Clockwork Orange* (1971). Michael Gothard plays a young poet who employs a bloated advertising guru to sell his suicide as a mass-media event. Along the way, Levy employs a variety of effects, both narrative and visual, to discomfort, disorientate and provoke. The result is a riveting, troubling and often ravishing piece of experimental cinema. ***Extras:*** Three shorts by Don Levy, including his student film, *Ten Thousand Talents*, with a voiceover by Peter Cook; an audio interview with the director; and a booklet whose essays explore Levy's life and the genesis of his remarkable film.

Second Run
(Region 2)

One of the outstanding UK-based boutique labels, Second Run has consistently surprised with its output. The label champions 'niche-market films' that 'anyone who seriously cares about cinema would want in their collection'. The care and attention lavished on these films – wherever possible with the co-operation of the film's director – has given the label a unique status in a short amount of time. The extras tend to be perfunctory, but they are made up for by the films themselves, allowing audiences to watch such remarkable titles as Frantisek Vlácil's *Marketa Lazarová* and Artur Aristakisyan's *Palms*, as well as more familiar titles by Apichatpong Weerasethakul and Miklós Jancsó.

Celia (1988) might at first seem an odd choice for Second Run. But their first Australian title, directed by Ann Turner, is an overlooked gem that ranks alongside the best accounts of childhood, stripping away the rose-tinted view that adults prescribe it and emphasising the powerful imagination and the cruelty that children can be capable of. Though often compared with Truffaut's debut, for me Turner's film ranks alongside Victor Erice's *The Spirit of the Beehive* (1973) in detailing how easily children move between reality and their own dream world. ***Extras:*** An interview with Ann Turner and a booklet featuring essays and *The Hobyahs* – the traditional folk tale featured in the film.

Daisies

Věra Chytilová's **Daisies** (1966) is yet another excellent addition to Second Run's impressive catalogue of Czech New Wave films. It is certainly one of the most anarchic. With its series of happenings, staged by two sisters rebelling against bourgeois life, it was described by its director as a 'philosophical documentary in the form of a farce'. The result is fascinating, intriguing and a reminder of how inventive Czech cinema was in the 1960s. And, of course, it looks fabulous. ***Extras:*** Jasmina Blaževič's documentary about Chytilová and a booklet featuring an essay by critic Peter Hames.

Artificial Eye
(Region 2)

Arguably the UK's most prominent first-run release label for European and art-house releases, Artificial Eye has built up an impressive back catalogue of titles from some of the world's greatest directors. Although most releases feature limited extras, the label's choice of titles is impeccable.

Artificial Eye's centrepiece last year was the mammoth **The Essential Michael Haneke**. It features every release by the Austrian auteur, from *The Seventh Continent* (1989) to the US remake of *Funny Games* (2007) and also includes the rarely seen adaptation of Franz Kafka's *The Castle* (1997). Though best not to watch too many of his films back-to-back without a therapist present, the collection highlights how the themes that have preoccupied Haneke (our relationship to the media, an unwillingness to face up to past actions and how we rarely take responsibility for present ones) have developed over the years, along with his sophistication as a filmmaker. ***Extras:*** Interviews; theatrical trailers; the documentary *24 Realities per Second*; and 'making of' documentaries for *Code Unknown* (2000), *Time of the Wolf* (2003) and *Hidden* (2005).

Hidden

The release of **Paris Vu Par** (1965) is evidence that good portmanteau films are possible. But then what else would you expect when the segments were shot in different Paris locations by Claude Chabrol (*La Muette*), Eric Rohmer (*Place d'Etoile*), Jean-Daniel Pollet (*Rue Saint Denis*), Jean Rouche (*Gare du Nord*), Jean Douchet (*Saint Germain des Prés*) and Jean-Luc Godard (*Monparnasse and Levellons*). The latter's expansion on a narrative element of *Une femme est une femme* (1961), which was shot

by Albert Maysles, finds the director in playful form and features a sensual jazz score. Taken as a whole, the anthology, which was produced by Barbet Schroeder, beautifully captures life on the streets of Paris in the mid-1960s.

Orlando

Released in the wake of last year's disappointing *Rage*, **Orlando** (1992) is a reminder of what an exciting filmmaker Sally Potter can be. In a role she seemed born to play, Tilda Swinton excels as Virginia Woolf's eponymous hero(ine), who witnesses the passing of time and how societal structures have constantly sought to maintain the gender imbalance. ***Extras:*** documentary featurettes; a selected scene commentary by Potter; an interview with Potter; the Venice Film Festival press conference; and the original theatrical trailer.

Optimum Releasing
(Region 2)

Like Artificial Eye, Optimum Releasing handles first-run releases (including last year's best horror film, *Orphan*), while simultaneously building up an impressive back catalogue of mostly mainstream international releases and classics of world cinema, under the categories of Optimum Home Entertainment, Optimum Asia and Optimum Classic.

The label's best release of the year was **The London Collection**, comprising *Pool of London* (1951), *The Small World of Sammy Lee* (1963), *The Yellow Balloon* (1953), *Sparrows Can't Sing* (1963), *Les Bicyclettes de Belsize*

(1969) and *The London Nobody Knows* (1967). Though not quite as adventurous as BFI Flipside in their evocation of metropolitan life, there is much to treasure in this collection, whether it's the gripping cat-and-mouse pursuit at the end of J. Lee Thompson's 1953 B-thriller, a view of London from the point of view of a young man in love with a model in the 1969 short by Douglas Hickox, or Ealing director Basil Dearden's evocative take on dock life in *Pool of London*, which was also the first UK film to feature an interracial relationship. The real treasure, however, is James Mason's entertaining guide to the nooks and crannies of *The London Nobody Knows*. Sadly, the box set features no extras.

Le Cercle rouge

Though they have been released as separate titles elsewhere (the BFI's editions feature an impressive array of extras), those uninitiated in the world of France's premiere crime director could find no better place to start than with **The Jean-Pierre Melville Boxset**. *Bob Le Flambeur* (1956), *Léon Morin, prêtre* (1961), *Le Doulos* (1962), *Army of Shadows* (1969), *Le Cercle rouge* (1970) and *Un flic* (1972) cover the filmmaker's investigation into the criminal mind and the set also includes his stunning 1969 drama about the role played by the Resistance during the Second World War.

Leon (1994) was clearly modelled on another Melville film, *Le samouraï* (1967), but whether it can be considered a masterpiece depends on how highly one regards Luc Besson's operatic style. Optimum has released five of the director's films. The good news is that *The*

Subway

Messenger: The Story of Joan of Arc is not one of them. Starting with the impressive, low-budget sci-fi thriller, **The Last Battle** (1983), the releases cover the earlier, better part of the director's career. Unsurprisingly, **Subway** (1985) remains the standout film. Along with Jean-Jacques Beineix and Leos Carax, Besson spearheaded the *Cinema du Look* movement in the 1980s and *Subway* was his calling card. Style over substance it may be, but what style, as we follow Christophe Lambert and Isabelle Adjani through the Parisian underground system. Things went a little awry with **The Big Blue** (1988) which, though stunning to look at and thrilling in its underwater sequences, is just a very silly story about a man who gives up Rosanna Arquette to hang out with some dolphins. More impressive is Besson's narrative-free paean to the beauty of the deep, **Atlantis** (1991); a rhapsody of underwater images, set to Eric Serra's syrupy score, which fails to avoid sentimentality but makes one think Besson would be more fun in a submergible than James Cameron.

Gran Casino (1947) was the first of Luis Buñuel's Mexican films and the closest he came to genre filmmaking. As such, the pleasure lies in watching him bend the rules. Nowhere is this more apparent than in the opening number, when the film's romantic lead, Jorge Negrete, sings from a dirty prison cell with a chorus comprising a motley collection of unkempt cellmates. ***Extras:*** A featurette on Buñuel's work.

Arrow
(Region 2)

Arrow films, who recently released the 2009 Foreign Language Academy Award winner, *Departures*, run the gamut, from classics of world cinema to the best of cult, erotica and the downright strange.

With their new offshoot, Arrow Video, the label has released one bona fide video nasty, a late work by a master of giallo and the debut feature of a second-generation horror filmmaker. Though never held in the same high regard as many of his peers, Lucio Fulci's **The House by the Cemetery** (1981) features a number of impressive set-pieces. What plot there is revolves around a family that move to a house whose basement is occupied by the animated, flesh-eating corpse of a once revered scientist. Unwilling to pay attention to even the most obvious signs that they should look to rent elsewhere, the family move only to meet an over-the-top end. Though clearly adept at scaring the bejesus out of his audience, Fulci lacks the basic rudiments of film grammar to hold one's attention between his scenes of bloodletting. Nevertheless, this is one of his more coherent films. ***Extras:*** Trailers; a TV spot; a deleted scene; and a fine documentary on the director.

The House by the Cemetery

Dario Argento's **Sleepless** (2001) opens with one of his best set-ups – a grisly murder on a train. Starring Max von Sydow, who must by now surely have starred in more dodgy films than Udo Kier, this late entry in the director's career, about a crazed serial killer returning after two decade's silence, is hardly his best. But it is more coherent than many of his recent films that have received international distribution and occasionally unnerves. ***Extras:*** A 'making of' featurette; a trailer; and an excellent documentary on the giallo tradition, with contributions by an astute Joe Dante and Troma's Lloyd Kaufman.

Sleepless

Macabre (1980), Lamberto Bava's feature debut, lacks the spark and visual flare of even his father's most average films. Set in New Orleans and channelling an awful Tennessee Williams production, the film opens with the death of the central character's lover, then catches up with her a year later, still unable to get over her loss. What follows is less a tale of intrigue than an extended wait for the final act when things simmer to a climax when they should boil. That said, the final shot and fake 'true story' explanation offer the one hilarious moment in the film. ***Extras:*** An introduction by Lamberto Bava, a trailer and an average documentary on the halcyon days of Italian horror.

Two lesser-known titles by Jules Dassin are a welcome addition to a growing number of releases by a director whose work has often been maligned. **Brute Force** (1947) and **The**

Naked City (1948) were made shortly before Dassin was forced to leave the US following an investigation by the House of Un-American Activities Commission. Both are hardboiled crime dramas, shot in crisp black and white, and featuring solid central performances by, respectively, Burt Lancaster and Barry Fitzgerald. As the tough con in a brutal penitentiary, Lancaster is a classic Dassin anti-hero, hell-bent on breaking the system that is trying to buckle him. With its introduction that harks back to the cautionary G-Men narratives that Warners distributed in the 1930s, *The Naked City* blends a straightforward police procedural with excellent footage taken on the streets of Manhattan.

Second Sight
(Region 2)

Second Sight have often surprised with their releases, offering Region 2 viewers the opportunity to enjoy many classics and overlooked titles. Nowhere is this better in evidence than last year's exquisite *Picnic at Hanging Rock* (1975) box set, which offered two versions of the film and a host of fascinating extras.

Michelangelo Antonioni's **Beyond the Clouds** (1994) is a series of short stories, shot with the help of Wim Wenders, which explores notions of infatuation, jealousy and the mysteries of human relationships. John Malkovich is our guide through each of the four stories, only one of which, featuring Vincent Perez as a man who falls for Irène Jacob's nun-to-be, sustains interest. Antonioni's camera is fluid and graceful, but his narratives smack of superficiality. ***Extras:*** An audio essay by critic Seymour Chatman and a 'making of' documentary by Enrica Antonioni.

For those willing to work a little more for their pleasure, both Raul Ruiz's **Time Regained** (1999) and Alain Robbe-Grillet's **La Belle Captive** (1983) have much to offer. The latter plays out like a disturbing dream, opening with a chance encounter, a night of passion and the mysterious disappearance of a woman who may not have existed in the first place. Like David Lynch's last few films, particularly *Lost Highway* (1997), *La Belle Captive* leaves the viewer unsettled. ***Extras:*** Audio commentary.

La Belle Captive

Time Regained is arguably the best attempt to date to adapt Proust's novel – or, at least, the last volume of it – for the screen. And, for the most part, it works. Ruiz moves seamlessly through time, introducing us to the myriad characters who float in and out of the author's memories, whilst avoiding the trappings of heritage cinema.

Along with *Fat City* (1972), **Wise Blood** (1979) is John Huston's other great film of the 1970s and one that feels perfectly at home with the new wave of directors that changed the face of Hollywood. Brad Dourif has never been better as the Vietnam vet who returns home and opens 'The Church Without Christ'. Tearing apart the hypocrisy of the sanctimonious, Huston's bile-filled drama speaks as much about America under the Bush administration as it did about the US when it was first released. ***Extras:*** Interviews with cast and crew.

Arguably Second Sight's most pleasurable release and screening in a stunningly restored edition is Max Ophul's final film, **Lola Montès** (1955). Martine Carol plays the lead in a film that was dismissed by many critics upon first release, but is now regarded as a masterpiece. In the way he employed the carousel to spin the narrative thread of *La ronde* (1950),

Lola Montès

Ophuls uses the circus to explore the life of 'the most scandalous woman in the world'. The result, like the best of Jean Cocteau and Michael Powell, is simply magical. **Extras:** A commentary by Ophuls expert Susan White and a feature documentary on the making of the film.

Documentaries

Founded in 2008, Artefact Films (Region 2) is the only UK-based DVD label to specialise solely in non-fiction and documentary films, championing both new releases and classic titles. Though most feature few, if any, extras, the choice available is impressive. Of the numerous releases from last year, three stand out. Barbara Kopple's 1976 Academy Award winner, **Harlan County U.S.A.**, details a miners strike in Kentucky that saw a corporation attempt to use any means to break an intractable workface that had been forced into a state of abject poverty by low wages. A timeless account of corporate greed, it ranks

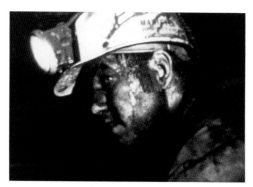

Harlan County U.S.A.

alongside the best of Pennebaker, Maysles and Wiseman within the canon of American documentary film.

War Photographer (2001) is Swiss filmmaker Christian Frei's profile of James Nachtwey, who records humanity's most depraved and desperate acts in times of war. Yet what Frei witnesses is not the cliché of the browbeaten cynic, but a humanist who believes that his recording these events might make a difference, no matter how small.

War Photographer

Injustice of a different kind can be found in the case of Brenton Butler, a 15-year-old who, in 2000, was arrested for the murder of a white woman. It was a crime he clearly did not commit and one he was arrested for because of the colour of his skin. Jean-Xavier de Lestrade's **Murder on a Sunday Morning** (2001) is a documentary-as-thriller – an excellent account of rough justice presented with the gusto of a taut crime drama. A deserving winner of the 2002 Academy Award for Best Documentary Feature, it is also a depressing exposé of thinly veiled racism in the American justice system.

From Strike Force Entertainment (Region 2) come two novel collections. **Public Information Films of the British Home Front** presents an anthology of films designed to keep Britain safe in the lead up to and during the Second World War. With titles like 'Careless Talk Costs Lives', 'Food Flashes', 'Is Your Journey Necessary?' and the entertaining 'Dig for Victory', these films are a fascinating addition to the many collections documenting domestic life in Britain during the war. **The Wrecker** (1928) is a 14-minute film, with a score by acclaimed silent film composer Neil Brand, of the destruction of a train on the then soon-to-be-abandoned Basingstoke to Alton branch. Shot with 22 cameras, it is still regarded as the most spectacular British rail crash ever filmed. It is accompanied by supporting documentaries and interviews.

Encounters at the End of the World

Encounters in the Natural World, released by Revolver (Region 2), is a collection of Werner Herzog documentaries that span his career: *The Flying Doctors of East Africa* (1969), *La Soufrière* (1977), *Grizzly Man* (2005), *The White Diamond* (2004) and *Encounters at the End of the World* (2007). Although the first three films have been previously available, gathered together these titles are, in many ways, less about their individual subjects than the man who made them and his spirit of adventure. Even his earliest films show Herzog's desire to throw himself into precarious situations or highlight his fascination with characters whose actions defy logic. The most recent film comes complete with hours of extras.

Coinciding with the 40th anniversary of the first lunar landing, a number of documentaries have been made available. MoC released the sublime **For All Mankind** (1989), Al Reinert's lyrical account of the NASA lunar missions, which uses footage and the unidentified (unless you wish to choose that option) voices of astronauts from all missions to present

For All Mankind

one single, universal voyage. The result is breathtaking and is accompanied by Brian Eno and Daniel Lanois' ethereal score. As would be expected of the label, there are a multitude of extras. The recent **In the Shadow of the Moon** (Film4, Region 2) is the perfect companion to Reinert's film. It features new interviews with every astronaut who landed on the moon, except for Neil Armstrong, as well as previously unseen footage (along with another hour's worth of footage and interviews in the extras). Less successful is Theo Kamecke's **Moonwalk One**, (The Attic Room, Region 2). Long believed to have perished, a print was only recently discovered. Although it features some interesting footage, the film is very much of its time and suffers as a result. Arguably the oddest, but compelling, addition to the NASA-themed documentaries is **The Sky at Night: Apollo 11, A Night to Remember** (BBC, Region 2). Across two hours, Sir Patrick Moore narrates

In the Shadow of the Moon

the experience of reporting live on the Apollo moon landing, cutting back to the original footage. Unlike *Moonwalk One*, there is no attempt to capture a zeigeist moment. It is just a group of passionate astronomers and scientists who can't believe their luck in playing a part in one of the greatest human achievements.

The BFI continues its sterling run of documentary releases. **Portrait of a Miner** is one of its most remarkable collections. One only need watch the 1953 information film, *The Shovel*, to see how much attention and research has gone into the production of this two-disc set. As with previous BFI documentary releases, the collection features a detailed booklet, with essays and annotated notes on each film. No less impressive are volumes two and three of the GPO Film Unit Collection: **We Live in Two Worlds** and **If War Should Come**. It takes the collection from 1936–1941 and feature such treasures as *Nightmail* (1936), Norman McLaren's *Love on the Wing* (1938), *Penny Journey* (1938), *London Can Take It!* (1940) and *Christmas Under Fire* (1941), the transitional film that saw the GPO Film Unit come under the aegis of the MOI and eventually become the Crown Film Unit. (An overview of the BFI's documentary archival output will shortly appear as a Spotlight on the IFG website.)

Few recent documentary portraits are as heartfelt as Isaac Juliien's wonderful **Derek** (2008), a tribute to, and remembrance of, one of the UK's most daring independent filmmakers and artists, Derek Jarman. Julien's documentary is written and narrated by Tilda Swinton and features Jarman in conversation with Colin McCabe, as well as excerpts from his films and archive footage. With a plethora of extras, it is a wonderful homage to a gifted and important voice who played such an important role in the cultural life of Britain across three decades.

For anyone who believes television was always dumbed down, the BBC's re-issue of the

Face-to-Face series, which ran from 1959–62, should change their minds. What surprises most is not the fact that a television interview format once existed that was capable of asking difficult and challenging questions, but that it was one that was broadcast to, and watched by, millions of people. From Bertrand Russell, Sterling Moss and Evelyn Waugh, to Carl Jung, Martin Luther King and Tony Hancock, the series understood that no matter whether the guest was a celebrity, politician, artist or sports personality, dig deep enough, whilst refraining from condescension or mockery, and a fascinating story will surface. That it did so across most of the 34 interviews is a testament to the skill of the producer-presenter team of Hugh Burnett and John Freeman.

DVD Releases of the Year
Downhill Racer (Criterion)
The Human Condition (Criterion)
Goldstein (Facets)
The Exiles (Milestone)
Miss Mend (Flicker Alley)
La Gueule Ouverte (Masters of Cinema)
Une Femme Mariée (Masters of Cinema)
Winstanley (BFI)
Herostratus (BFI Flipside)
The Essential Michael Haneke (Artificial Eye)
Lola Montès (Second Sight)
Derek (BFI)

Derek

Key DVD labels

Ian Haydn Smith profiles the essential distributors of world cinema in the English language

Arrow Films

A strong range of films across the spectrum of world cinema, some with a fine array of extras.
www.arrowfilms.co.uk

Artefact Films

A new UK documentary label, featuring an impressive roster of international titles.
www.artefactmedia.com

Artificial Eye

A major UK label, whose extensive catalogue reflects the best in contemporary and art-house releases.
www.artificial-eye.com

Axiom Films

High-quality presentation of new and classic releases, running the gamut of world cinema and the arts.
www.axiomfilms.co.uk

BFI (& BFI Flipside)

Now an essential DVD label, covering world cinema, animation, documentary and archive material, as well as experimental film.
http://filmstore.bfi.org.uk

Criterion (& Eclipse)

The benchmark of excellence amongst DVD labels, now spearheading the future with the impressive Online Cinematheque.
www.criterion.com

Facets

An eclectic and wide-ranging selection of films from around the world.
www.facets.org

Flicker Alley

Specialising in pre-sound and early film, this label has quickly established itself as one of the best.
www.flickeralley.com

Masters of Cinema

MoC match Criterion, both in transfer quality and the extensive extras and accompanying booklets.
www.eurekavideo.co.uk/moc

Milestone

A US label, whose recent releases are a mark of high quality.
www.milestonefilms.com

Mr Bongo

The handful of releases from this relatively new label display a refreshing daring in choice and design.
www.buymrbongo.com

Optimum World

One of the most expansive UK labels, covering all genres and tastes.
www.optimumreleasing.com

Microcinema

One of the best collections of underground and experimental films from North America.
www.microcinemadvd.com

Second Run DVD

An excellent collection of must-have titles by many directors who have dropped off the cinematic radar.
www.secondrundvd.com

Second Sight

An eclectic collection of films and TV programmes, ranging from classical Hollywood to contemporary world cinema.
www.secondsightfilms.co.uk

Soda Pictures

A diverse catalogue populated with some of the best contemporary world cinema releases.
www.sodapictures.com

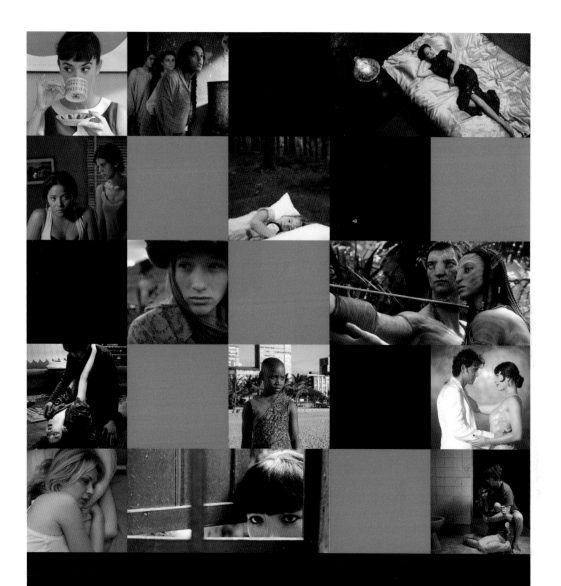

World Survey

6 continents | 112 countries | 1,000s of films...

Sand in your shoes, a smile on your face…

That would be the best way to describe Production Manager Henrik Griesner as he drove his way up the dunes, with a few bouncing members of his crew in the back seat. *Christmas in the Desert* is a German made-for-TV film that shot for three weeks in the UAE. Others might have said 'a big kid in a big sand box'.

The United Arab Emirates does have sand, lots of sand; but we also have crystal clear waters, white beaches, glorious palms, famous architecture, heritage sites and striking mountains. If the story fits, it's a great place to film; and Abu Dhabi Film Commission (ADFC) has much to offer the international filmmaking community. Our Locations and Production Support department is dedicated to providing a growing database of high-quality location photos, all with GPS locations.

These guys live to get out of the office, and most times armed with a camera and a 4-wheel drive. They have over ten years of experience in the UAE as location scouts, DPs, and location managers; and have worked on films like *Syriana* (2005) and *The Kingdom* (2007) and the recently released *City of Life* (2009). They have the local connections to production support, and the knowledge to

help see a project through. ADFC recently accredited and processed shooting permits for over 27 international broadcast teams shooting in Abu Dhabi for the final F1 race in 2009.

For new filmmakers, Abu Dhabi Film Commission offers the Aflam Qaseera (short film) production fund, New Voices documentary and drama production internship schemes, giving real production opportunities to emerging talent and production companies in the UAE. The Low Budget Feature Film Fund will see five low-budget feature films produced as part of a New Producers Development Programme linking production finance with production, international market events, and eventual distribution.

The Emirates Media Skills Training Council is the start of an ongoing forum to maintain a dialogue and connection between media educators and media companies to help ensure programme outcomes and student skills match industry needs. Green Kids on Screen will see a visual storytelling film culture begin early in elementary and secondary schools. Four students from Abu Dhabi were recently sent by ADFC to Mira Nair's Maisha Film Lab, in Kampala, Uganda. Film production master classes will become

لجـــنــــــة أبـوظـــبي للأفــلام
ABU DHABI FILM COMMISSION

لجـــنـــــــة أبــوظــبـــي للأفـــلام
ABU DHABI FILM COMMISSION

You have a story?
Film It.

film.gov.ae

Permits for filming in public locations
Script clearances and advice on approvals
Initial scouting for potential locations
Support for location filming

أبـوظـبـي للـثـقـافـة و الـتـراث
ABU DHABI CULTURE & HERITAGE

available throughout the Emirates. The award-winning WETA workshop recently gave public demonstrations on prosthetic makeup for film as part of the Emirates Film Competition during Middle East International Film Festival.

ADFC also assists in the development of the film and TV industry in Abu Dhabi, nurturing new talent and contributing to the promotion of Arab culture through film and television. And realising this ambition is becoming easier, with some help from our friends. The film, TV and media industries in Abu Dhabi are currently entering an exciting growth phase. New production opportunities are emerging, new broadcasters are about to go live and major international media organisations are actively setting up bases in the city.

Twofour54 is one company that provides a multifaceted approach to supporting the local and regional industries with extensive training, content creation, and production programmes. The strength of MEIFF, the Emirates Film

Competition and Shasha Grant all contribute to a vibrant time. This year, over 40 leading media professionals joined ADFC's Circle Conference discussing the issues most relevant to our industry and our region. We believe that each one of our guests helped contribute to building a strong and sustainable industry for the future.

The Shasha Grant is the Abu Dhabi Film Commission's US$100,000 international screenwriting competition, designed to identify, develop and launch the careers of outstanding Arab writers and filmmakers. The programme exposes emerging filmmakers to high-level industry decision makers and facilitates financing for talented writers and directors from around the world. The 2008 Shasha winner has a script currently in production with Fox Pictures.

The Abu Dhabi Authority for Culture and Heritage and the government of Abu Dhabi continue to have a clear vision and strong commitment to the success of Abu Dhabi Film Commission, the Film and Television industry, and to the arts. The Sadyaat Island Project is under construction and will house a state-of-the-art performing arts centre, the Guggenheim Museum, and the Louvre.

Studios are being built; stories are being written; films are on the way. It is indeed an exciting time to be a filmmaker in Abu Dhabi and the UAE. You might get some sand in your shoes, but you're sure to leave with a smile on your face.

Afghanistan Sandra Schäfer

There is still no public film funding in Afghanistan and few filmmakers succeed in finding international co-producers. On both a domestic and international level, there is a lack of an all-encompassing policy for film funds and education. Hence, in 2009, only short films were produced, either self-financed or through the support of local production companies or international aid agencies. Not surprisingly, the poor production conditions had an obvious effect on the quality of films.

Nassir Alqas, now living in Germany, self-funded his short, **Voice** (*Seda*), the first film he has made in Kabul since 1990. Shot on digital, it opens with the painful cry of a woman, convincingly performed by actress Sabera Mehraban, whose face we never actually see. In the neighbourhood, which is kept awake by the cries, it is finally a young boy who has the courage to call a doctor. Angered and outraged by the medics' appearance, the husband waves an axe at them, even though they have come to help the woman. Her death underpins the director's concerns about the patriarchal structure that still exists in the country.

Mirwais Rekab's experimental short **1+1=1** is also dedicated to the women who live in this patriarchal societal structure. Rekab's impressive film uses no dialogue and relies on a story whose chronology has been reversed. Hence, we see a woman selling a whip to a merchant, which in the next scene is used by her husband to beat her. A teacher in a classroom writes the formula 1+1=1 on the blackboard. The students, men and women, giggle. To decipher the film's plot, one has to understand the provocative meaning of the formula, with which the teacher determines the equality of men and women.

In Rada Akbar's poetic short, **Shattered Hopes**, her role as a media officer for GTZ foregrounds the fight for survival experienced by refugees in a camp in Kabul. In addition to interviews, Rada Akbar employs a lyrical voiceover to highlight the plight and living conditions of these refugees.

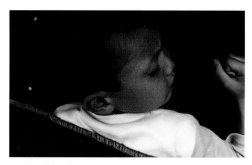

Sayed Jalil Hussaini's **The Angels of Earth**

Director Sayed Jalil Hussaini made two shorts in 2009: **Devious** (*Birahe*) and **The Angels of Earth** (*Freshta Ahee Roy Zameen*). In *Devious*, a man strolls along the streets of Kabul. A hand-held camera follows him, while piano music accompanies the scenes, which are inter-cut with sequences from the past: a motorbike accident at night and the man's unsuccessful attempt to profit from a failed robbery he witnessed. In *Angels of Earth*, Kabul is depicted as a place where everyone's sole thought is of survival. A boy who dreams of flying to visit his deceased mother in heaven, walks with arms spread like a bird through the park. But the angels in this film can also be found on Earth. In the midst of poverty, an economic condition that can degrade the individual, there is a character who maintains respect for others. His actions prove to have a profound impact on those around him.

Noor Hussainian's **Wall** (*Diwar*) is an amateurishly filmed short about a hopeless situation. An illiterate boy earning his money as a car washer finds his way to school blocked by an insurmountable brick wall.

Internationally produced documentaries dominated festivals around the world. Ian Olds' impressive, award-winning **Fixer** sketches a complex picture of the work of journalist Ajmal Naqshbandi, who was murdered following his kidnapping, unlike his Italian colleague, who was released. Olds opens with the murder so that he can detail the difficult negotiations that took place between foreign journalists, radical Taliban groups and the local authorities in the months leading up to Naqshbandi's death. The court case, staged for western journalists and based on a democratic model, mirrors the complicated relationship between western reconstruction aid and the stubbornness of local systems. Through uncovering the reasons for Naqshbandis murder, the film reveals how he became a victim of the power struggle that existed between the Taliban and the Karzai government.

Ian Olds' **Fixer**

British director Havana Marking's **Afghan Star** focuses on a popular and seemingly harmless topic. She portrays the selection of singers who are chosen for the popular televised amateur singing competition, 'Afghan Star'. Amidst thousands of contestants are three women. This portrait makes clear the different personal approaches to music, ethnic conflict and the extreme moral pressures that weigh on the female contestants.

Havana Marking's **Afghan Star**

Helga Reidemeister's documentary **War and Love in Kabul** (*Mein Herz sieht die Welt schwarz, eine Liebe in Kabul*) is about a relationship in Kabul that continued, despite forced marriage, the injuries of war and years of separation. In long, quiet shots, filmed on 16mm, cameraman Lars Barthel captures the fraught familial relations, as well as the brief encounters between the two lovers. The participants criticise the patriarchal, egotistical behaviour of the head of the family to the camera, but soon change their tone when he is present.

Dina Saqeb's documentary about the participation of the only Afghan sportswoman at the Beijing Olympics is currently in the final stages of production, as is a feature about the famous Persian poet Maulana, by Latif Ahmadi. The award winning director of *Osama*, Siddiq Barmak, is also in pre-production on his new film.

The year's best films
1+1=1 (Mirwais Rekab)
The Angels of Earth (Sayed Jalil Hussaini)
Voice (Nassir Alqas)
Fixer (Ian Olds)
Afghan Star (Havana Marking)

Quotes of the year

'If we keep quiet today, our whole society will be affected tomorrow.' DIANA SAQEB.

'They are like extras for our films, but extras that can come out of their houses to make demonstrations for the benefit of some political parties or some political figures.' SIDDIQ BARMAK, *talking about the counter-demonstrators during the protests against the Shiite Personal Status Law in Kabul in spring 2009.*

Directory

All Tel/Fax numbers begin (+93)

Afghan-Film, Grand Masood Ave 2, Kabul. Tel: 20 210279.

Azim-Film, Kabul. Tel: 70 282097.

Barmak-Film, Kabul. sbf@barmakfilm.com. www.barmakfilm.com.

BASA-Afghan Cinema Club.Tel: 75 2028910. basa@inbox.com. www.basafilm.com.

Basa-Film, District 6, Street 1, House No: 38, Karte Se Kabul. Tel: 799 345962, 700 083908. cacakabul@gmail.com. www.afghanistancinemaclub.com.

Cinema Magazine, Afghan Film, Grand Masood Ave 2, Kabul. Tel: 79 314303. cinema_mag@yahoo.com.

Filmmakers Union, Kabul. Tel: 79 375530. cinemaf@hotmail.com.

Kabul Film festival, www.kabulfilmfestival.org.

Second Take Gender and Society in Cinema, www.mazefilm.de. www.basafilm.com.

Roya Cinematic House Production, Herat. Tel: 40 441437.

Saba Film, Kabul. Tel: 70 246827.

Star Group, Kabul. Tel: 799 533292.

SANDRA SCHÄFER is a filmmaker, curator and writer. She has worked on projects in cooperation with filmmakers and activists in Kabul and Berlin since 2002, including the film festivals Second Take, Splice In and Kabul/Teheran 1979ff. Her book *Stagings: Kabul, Film & Production of Representation* was published in 2009.

Algeria Maryam Touzani

Making films in Algeria is not a simple task and finding distribution, both domestically and abroad, can be just as difficult. The lack of financial aid for filmmakers and the absence of training for professionals in the film industry has obstructed cinema production. Yet, against all odds and via different routes, Algerian films are crossing borders and finding their way into the world's finest festivals. It is a fact, nonetheless, that most successful Algerian films are co-produced with France.

Rachid Bouchareb's **London River** was nominated for the Golden Bear at the Berlinale, with Malian actor Sotigui Kouyaté winning the Silver Bear for Best Actor. Bouchareb, born in Paris to Algerian parents, took part in the Berlinale with the feature film *Little Senegal* in 2001 and again in 2004 with the short *Le Vilain Petit Poussin*. The director of the acclaimed *Days of Glory* recounts the story of Ousmane and Mrs Sommers, played by award-winning British actress Brenda Blethyn, two ordinary people whose paths cross when they travel to London in search of their missing children, following the July 2005 terrorist attacks.

Rachid Bouchareb's **London River**

Bouchareb explores race and prejudice as Ousmane, a Muslim, and Mrs Sommers, a Christian, put aside their religious differences, giving each other the strength to continue their search. Bouchareb's film is not directly about the attacks, but their impact on the lives of ordinary people.

Merzak Allouache's **Harragas**

Merzak Allouache's **Harragas** screened at Venice Days at the Venice Film Festival. The veteran director recounts a group of young Algerians' odyssey across the Mediterranean to Spain, in search of a better life. After two recent comedies, *Chouchou* and *Bab el Web*, Allaouche delves into a profound issue, exploring the growing tragedy of illegal immigration through this perilous journey.

Ben Boulaid reiterates the fact that history is undoubtedly an ingrained issue in Algerian cinema. Directed by Ahmed Rachedi, the film retraces the life of national hero Ben Boulaid, popularly known as 'the lion of Algeria', and his role in the Algerian revolution. Backed by a relatively high budget of 230 million Dinars, the film attempts to shed light on a turbulent period from the country's past.

Ahmed Rachedi's **Ben Boulaid**

Abdelkrim Bahloul's **Voyage to Algiers** (*Le Voyage à Alger*), inspired by a true story, depicts the struggle of an Algerian martyr's widow, whose house (left to her by a French man just a few months after independence) has been expropriated by a local chief. Having lost faith in the local authorities, she decides to make the journey to the capital with her six children, in order to seek the help of the president.

Malek Bensmaïl is the director of more than a dozen documentaries. In his latest film, **China is Still Far** (*La Chine est Encore Loin*), he chronicles life in a remote village in the Aurès Mountains that, over half a century ago, became the 'cradle of the Algerian Revolution'. As he films the everyday existence of its inhabitants, particularly the schoolchildren, he explores the spread of knowledge and education in a shattered country. In the Muslim culture, it is said that one should seek knowledge, even if it means going to China, hence the title's suggestion that education remains a major problem.

Djamila Sahraoui returned to the cinema with **Ouardia Once had Sons** (*Ouardia avait Deux Enfants*). It is the story of a mother who slowly learns to overcome her grief and continue living following the death of her son, Tarik, a soldier who was probably killed by his own brother, Ali, the leader of an Islamist group.

Among the best short films of the year was Sabrina Draoui's **Tell Me if You Know** (*Dis Moi si Tu Sais*), in which two friends, for whom speaking about love and sex is a complicated matter, have an important conversation before going to class. In Khaled Benaïssa's short, **They Stopped Speaking** (*Ils se Sont Tus*), a radio conductor returns home at dawn following a long night's work, hoping to sleep. Unfortunately for him, the city is only just waking up. During the 23 minutes of Samia Chala's short documentary, **The Hair Salon** (*Le Salon de Coiffure*), women talk about life and love, while their male hairdressers express the difficulty of performing their job in Algerian society.

In 2009, The Pan-African Cultural Festival returned to Algeria after 40 years, highlighting the newly vested interest in culture. Even if cinema in Algeria currently seems to be an unprofitable sector, it constitutes an important part of the country's cultural identity. Though disapproved of by many, if co-productions offer a country deprived of its own images the opportunity to revive its cinematic landscape, their place seems altogether legitimate.

The year's best films
London River (Rachid Bouchareb)
Harragas (Merzak Allouache)

Quote of the year
'*London River* is first and foremost a human drama, about how people react to events such as these, how they come together in the same place and forge a connection.' RACHID BOUCHAREB, *director of* **London River.**

Directory
All Tel/Fax numbers begin (+213)
Cinémathèque Algérienne, 49 rue Larbi Ben M'Hidi, Algiers. Tel: (2) 737 548. Fax: (2) 738 246. www.cinematheque.art.dz.

MARYAM TOUZANI is a freelance journalist based in Morocco and working internationally, specialising in art and culture.

Argentina Alfredo Friedlander

Cinema attendance and the number of films released (almost 300 features) stayed at the same level as last year. July saw a dramatic reduction in admission figures – approximately 2.5 million – due to swine flu. A surge in attendance over the last quarter of 2009 redressed this imbalance.

On average, half the films released were from the United States, including a number of co-productions with the UK. Second came Argentina and third France, with the rest mainly European productions, particularly from Italy and, to a lesser extent, the UK and Spain. Few films came from Asian countries.

As in previous years, the task of listing the exact number of Argentine releases remains almost impossible, as some films are shown once or twice a week in a single cinema. Their number should be around 75, a similar quantity to 2008.

The Cannes Film Festival featured no Argentine films, a sharp contrast to last year's five entries. There were few domestic releases at other festivals, but San Sebastián Film Festival did screen Juan José Campanella's **Secret of her Eyes** (*El secreto de sus ojos*)

Juan José Campanella's **Secret of her Eyes**

in its official competition. It is the story of a judicial employee, Benjamin Esposito (Ricardo Darin), who writes a novel about a murder that took place in Buenos Aires in 1974, in which he was an indirect protagonist. Writing the book leads him to investigate his own past during a period when Argentina's history was marked by violence and death. He also ruminates on his unexpressed love for a female supervisor (Soledad Villamil).

The 11th Buenos Aires International Film Festival (BAFICI) screened almost 400 films, some of which featured in the national and international competition strands. Miguel Gomes' overlong Portuguese feature, **Our Beloved Month of August** (*Aquele querido mês de agosto*), won the International Competition. The prize for the best local film went to Alejo Moguillansky's **Castro**, about a man who flees Buenos Aires with his girlfriend, leaving behind a group of friends.

The 23rd International Film Festival of Mar del Plata returned to its original November slot with veteran filmmaker José Martínez Suárez as its new director. Hirokazu Kore-Eda's **Still Walking** won the International Competition while Amat Escalante's Mexican production, **Los Bastardos**, took the prize for the best film from Latin America. A third competition reserved to Argentine films saw Kris Nikilson's **Diletante** and Jorge Leandro Colás' **Parador Retiro** sharing the award.

The most important local production during 2009 was *Secret of her Eyes*. It was number one at the box office for over ten weeks in late summer and has gone on to become the biggest commercial success of the year, with attendance figures exceeding two million. It was even able to displace *Ice Age 3*, which was released at the height of concerns over swine flu in the country.

Fernando E. Solanas, director of *The Hour of the Furnaces*, continued with his series of documentaries about Argentina. The fifth chapter, **Uprisen Land – Part I: Impure Gold** (*Tierra sublevada – Parte I: Oro impuro*), attacks the exploitation of Argentina's mineral resources, which the director states does not bring prosperity to the inhabitants of several provinces rich in precious metals. All it brings for locals is environmental contamination. Unfortunately, the film failed to perform well at the box office, unlike his previous film, *The Next Station*.

Mundo Alas: An Alternative Tour, *directed by Sebastián Schindel, Fernando Molnar and Leon Gieco*

Another striking documentary was **Mundo Alas: An Alternative Tour** (*Mundo Alas*) directed by Sebastián Schindel, Fernando Molnar and musician Leon Gieco. It is a touching film, documenting a tour organised by Gieco with a group of handicapped musicians and singers around several Argentine provinces.

There were some disappointing new films by acclaimed directors. Carlos Sorin's **The Window** (*La ventana*) was about an old man close to his death, while *XXY* director Lucia Puenzo's **The Fish Child** (*El niño pez*) told the story of a teenager from an exclusive suburban neighbourhood in Argentina who is in love with a Paraguayan maid. The film lacked strength, despite the presence of Inés Efrón, who was better cast in the comedy **Lovely Loneliness** (*Amorosa soledad*), co-directed by Martin

Carranza and Victoria Galardi, in which she plays a teenager abandoned by her boyfriend, who makes a resolution to stay single for the next three years in order to avoid heartbreak.

The comedy genre was also well represented by newcomer Hernán Goldfrid's **Hold On... Please!** (*Musica en espera*), about a composer (Diego Peretti) desperately seeking a song for a film. He finds the perfect tune when he calls his bank and is placed on hold. Unable to find the song that played whilst he was waiting, the bank manager (Natalia Oreiro) promises to help him on the condition that he will pretend to be her fiancé when her mother, played by the impressive Norma Aleandro, arrives from Spain.

Aleandro also appeared in Rodrigo Grande's **A Question of Principles** (*Cuestión de principios*), a dramatic story about a civil servant (Federico Luppi) who refuses to sell an old volume containing a photo of his father to Pablo Echarri's young supervisor, who needs this edition to complete his collection. Echarri was one of the main characters in another succesful drama, directed by Marcelo Piñeyro. **The Widows of Thursdays** (*Las viudas de los jueves*), based on a local bestseller, is a mystery that takes place in a private country club where three yuppies are found dead in a swimming pool.

Marilú Marini in Diego Sabanés' **Made Up Memories**

Diego Sabanés' **Made Up Memories** (*Mentiras piadosas*) is loosely based on some short stories by the late Julio Cortazar, one of Argentina's greatest writers. An excellent atmosphere and fine performance by Marilú Marini and Claudio Tolcachir did not help the film at the box office.

Pablo Fendrik's first two films, **The Mugger** and **Blood Appears**, which had screened at Cannes Critics' Week in the past, were finally and almost simultaneously released in Argentina. Arturo Goetz starred in both films, with *The Mugger* impressing the most.

Mention should be made of Fernando Diaz's second feature, **The Stranger** (*La extranjera*), about an introverted woman, played by María Laura Cali, who lives in Barcelona and is obliged to return home in order to decide what to do with the ranch she inherited from her late grandfather. An excellent atmosphere and fine acting makes for a compelling film.

Teresa Constantini's **Felicitas**

Teresa Constantini's **Felicitas**, an historical drama based on a true story that took place during the 19th century, was something of a disappointment. A costly production by Argentine standards, it tells of the tragic end of Felicitas Guerrero, who was forced by her father to marry a wealthy older man. It performed quite well at the local box office but prospects for international distribution are slim.

The year's best films
Secret of her Eyes (Juan José Campanella)
Hold On... Please! (Hernán Goldfrid)
Made Up Memories (Diego Sabanés)
Mundo Alas: An Alternative Tour
(L. Gieco, S. Schindel & F. Molnar)
The Mugger (Pablo Fendrik)

Quote of the year
'I am very happy. Every time I enter a race my aim is to win. But it is true that there are races

in which one can feel proud from the very moment you have the possibility to compete. The possibility of being nominated for the Oscar is a very important issue.' JUAN JOSÉ CAMPANELLA *on Argentina choosing* **Secret of her Eyes** *as its representative at the 2010 Academy Awards.*

Directory
All Tel/Fax numbers begin (+54)
Critics Association of Argentina, Maipu 621 Planta Baja, 1006 Buenos Aires. Tel/Fax: 4322 6625. cinecronistas@yahoo.com.
Directors Association of Argentina (DAC), Lavalle 1444, 7° Y, 1048 Buenos Aires. Tel/Fax: 4372 9822. dac1@infovia.com.ar. www.dacdirectoresdecine. com.ar.
Directors of Photography Association, San Lorenzo 3845, Olivos, 1636 Buenos Aires. Tel/Fax: 4790 2633. adf@ba.net. www.adfcine.com.ar.
Exhibitors Federation of Argentina, Ayacucho 457, 1° 13, Buenos Aires. Tel/Fax: 4953 1234. empcinemato@infovia.com.ar.
Film University, Pasaje Guifra 330, 1064 Buenos Aires. Tel: 4300 1413. Fax: 4300 1581. fuc@ucine. edu.ar. www.ucine.edu.ar.
General Producers Association, Lavalle 1860, 1051 Buenos Aires. Tel/Fax: 4371 3430. argentinasonofilm@impsat1.com.ar.
National Cinema Organisation (INCAA), Lima 319, 1073 Buenos Aires. Tel: 6779 0900. Fax: 4383 0029. info@incaa.gov.ar.
Pablo Hicken Museum and Library, Defensa 1220, 1143 Buenos Aires. Tel: 4300 5967. www. museudelcinedb@yahoo.com.ar.
Producers Guild of Argentina (FAPCA), Godoy Cruz 1540, 1414 Buenos Aires. Tel: 4777 7200. Fax: 4778 0046. recepcion@patagonik.com.ar.
Sindicato de la Industria Cinematográfia de Argentina (SICA), Juncal 2029, 1116 Buenos Aires. Tel: 4806 0208. Fax: 4806 7544. sica@sicacine. com.ar. www.sicacine.com.ar.

ALFREDO FRIEDLANDER is a member of the Asociación de Cronistas Cinematográficos de Argentina. He writes regularly for www. leedor.com and presents movies at the 56-year-old Cine Club Núcleo.

Armenia Susanna Harutyunyan

Armenia applied for entry to EURIMAGES, which should offer new opportunities for European co-productions. Armenian producers have waited some time for this step, which should make a difference considering the limited state subsidies for film production. In 2010, subsidies for the national film industry will remain the same in the previous two years, at USD$1.6 million. The amount set aside for film production is USD$771,000, with USD$295,000 for animated films and USD$130,000 for documentaries.

At the same time, the state subsidies for the participation of Armenian films in festivals and the presentation of national product at leading film markets has increased as a result of the participation of Armenian films at the Cannes film market over the last two years, supported by the Armenian National Cinema Centre. Documentaries, feature films, short films and projects in post-production were all represented. The Armenian stand attracted festival programmers, distributors and a range of other industry professionals. We hope this is one more step towards the integration of Armenian cinema within the global cinematic landscape.

The catalyst for this process has been the circulation of Armenian films at international film festivals. Harutyun Khachatryan's **Border**, an Armenian and Netherlands co-production with Hubert Bals Fund participation, has become the most visible Armenian festival participant throughout 2009. This docu-drama, which surveys the landscape following the country's war with Azerbaijan in the late 1990s from the perspective of a 'she-buffalo', was presented at major film festivals, picking up

Harutyun Khachatryan's **Border**

numerous prizes, including the Platinum Remy at the Houston International Film Festival and the first prize at Antalya's Golden Orange film festival and Spain's Gijón film festival.

Among the new Armenian films that were premiered at the end of 2009, Suren Babayan's **Don't Look In The Mirror** (*Mi Najir Hajelun*) tells the story of an artist-turned-model who has hit hard times and is faced with no choice but to sell his possessions. When he looks into a mirror, he does not see himself but the faces of strangers, who turn out to be the various facets of his own ego. The experience forces him to seek forgiveness at his parents' graveside, begging for mercy, help and, ultimately, the restoration of faith.

The main character of Vigen Chaldranyan's **Maestro** is a famous musician, living in his fragile world of music and art. Any intrusion from reality into this world, or the political crises reflected in the open struggle between the ruling party and opposition, breaks his internal harmony, threatening profound tragedy or even self-destruction. The film explores the troubles that vex artists who have to balance their life and the life around them with the demands of art and intellect.

Aram Shahbazyan's **Chnchik**

Several local features are in production and will be completed in early 2010. One of them is Mikayel Vatinyan's **Joan and Voices** (*Jannan ev Dzajner*), the study of a woman who travels throughout Armenia, interviewing people about their lifes in an attempt to find meaning in her own existence. Aram Shahbazyan's **Chnchik** promises to be a unique drama. It looks at a small village's everyday life as seen through the drama of a family and a village girl who is distanced from this world.

The main venue of the 2009 Golden Apricot Film Festival

The year's best films
Border (Harutyun Khachatryan)
Don't Look In The Mirror (Suren Babayan)
Maestro (Vigen Chaldranyan)
Quote of the year
'I have just finished watching *Border*. It was an overwhelming experience for me. So much depth and search! So many amazing visual ideas, one after another, carrying me into places I didn't know cinema could reach!' *American director* **ROB NILSSON**, *commenting on Harutyun Khachatryan's* **Border**.

Directory
All Tel/Fax numbers begin (+374)
Armenian Association of Film Critics & Cinema Journalists, #3, Moskovyan Str., 0001 Yerevan. Tel/Fax: 10 52 10 47. aafccj@arminco.com. www.arm-cinema.am.
Armenian National Cinema Centre, 38, Pushkin Str., Yerevan. Tel/Fax: 10 51 82 30 (31). abovyans@yahoo.com.
Golden Apricot Fund for Cinema Development, 3 Moskovyan Str., 0001, Yerevan. Tel/Fax: 10 52 10 42 (62). info@gaiff.am. www.gaiff.am.

SUSANNA HARUTYUNYAN graduated in film criticism from Moscow State Cinema Institute in 1987. She has been film expert of the daily *Respublika Armenia* since 1991 and is president of Armenia's Association of Film Critics and Cinema Journalists (the Armenian National Section of FIPRESCI) and Artistic Director of the Golden Apricot Yerevan International Film Festival.

ABU DHABI FILM COMMISSION

Australia Peter Thompson

Australian cinema bounced back to life in 2009. So far, the global financial meltdown has had little visible effect. Audiences were in no doubt: they lifted box-office revenue to over AUS$900 million, up 16% on 2008, which was itself a record year. More significantly, Australian-made feature films found significant support.

Leading the way was **Mao's Last Dancer**, produced by Jane Scott, directed by Bruce Beresford and featuring Chi Cao, Joan Chen, Amanda Schull, Bruce Greenwood, Kyle McLachlan, Jack Thompson and a large supporting cast. Adapted from Li Cunxin's bestselling memoir, it tells of his rise from abject poverty to favouritism as Madame

Mao's leading dancer and his ultimate defection to the West. An audience favourite in Toronto, the film had earned around AUS$14 million domestically by December 2009.

Scott Hicks' **The Boys Are Back**

Released late in the year, Scott Hicks' **The Boys Are Back** was also performing strongly at the time of writing. Featuring Clive Owen as the recently widowed father of two lively sons, played by George MacKay and Nicholas McAnulty, it's an accessible and moving story about the peaks and pitfalls of single parenthood. Emma Booth also adds lustre to the cast.

One aspect of the 2009 releases was the presence of internationally known Australian filmmakers, often more conspicuous for their absence from home turf. As well as Beresford and Hicks, Jane Campion also had a major new film. Others not so instantly recognised, but well into their creative maturity, include Ana Kokkinos, Robert Connolly, David Caesar, Sarah Watt and Sue Brooks.

The digital revolution has been hailed for burying technical and economic barriers to film production and unleashing a tidal wave of young talent. This wave is certainly under way, but the new filmmakers still have some

Bruce Beresford's **Mao's Last Dancer**

way to go to find their audience. Instead, people have responded more to experienced hands controlling the directorial reins. With **Blessed**, Ana Kokkinos returned to *Head On* territory. As with that 1998 film, the action is compressed into 24 hours as six young people face harrowing existential crises. The first half tells the stories through the principle characters' eyes, while the latter half adopts the perspective of their parents. It drew great performances from Deborra-Lee Furness, Miranda Otto and particularly Frances O'Connor, back in Australia after a long sojourn abroad.

Anthony LaPaglia in Robert Connolly's **Balibo**

Balibo, co-written by pre-eminent dramatist David Williamson and director Robert Connolly, explores the deaths of six Australian journalists in East Timor during the Indonesian invasion of 1975. The complicated flashback structure undermines the impact of the story, and the hard questions dealing with American and Australian complicity in the invasion are brushed over. However, the film received positive critical attention, inspired by its obvious passion and fine performances by Anthony LaPaglia, Oscar Isaac, Damon Gameau and others.

David Caesar has satisfied a long-held ambition with **Prime Mover**. Featuring Michael Dorman, Emily Barclay, Ben Mendelsohn and a clutch of veteran Australians, it's an intimate, surprisingly gentle portrait of lives lived under the economic hammer. Dorman plays Thomas, a country boy smitten, as most young men are, by the mystical power of the internal combustion engine. Thomas goes heavily into debt to buy his first big rig but the real

David Caesar's **Prime Mover**

hardships of the long-haul trucker's life never completely erase his romantic illusions.

The diversity of the 45 features released in 2009 is greatly enriched by three striking contributions from indigenous filmmakers. Warwick Thornton was awarded the Camera d'Or at Cannes, a brace of domestic prizes and universal acclaim for **Samson and Delilah**. The subject matter is hopelessly grim on the surface: two teenagers trapped in the vicious circle of neglect and abuse in a remote Outback settlement. Samson (Rowan MacNamara) is addicted to petrol-sniffing which still kills too many young people, while Delilah (Marissa Gibson) is ritually blamed for the death of her artist grandmother. But there is a deep bond between the two that

Warwick Thornton's **Samson and Delilah**

endures even the hardships of homelessness in the desert city of Alice Springs. No other dramatic film has portrayed this social reality so uncompromisingly, but Thornton also has an extraordinarily poetic sensibility that lifts his narrative to another level. It was the Australian film of the year and the only one so far to make back its entire budget (AUS$1.6 million) at the box office and went on to collect seven prizes at the Australian Film Institute Awards.

Rachel Perkins' **Bran Nue Dae**

One cannot help but be encouraged by the emergence of indigenous filmmaking, not only because the voices of the first Australians were ignored for so long, but also because their work is, like Thornton's, so distinctive. In **Bran Nue Dae**, Rachel Perkins has brought the eponymous stage musical to the screen, featuring a mostly indigenous cast alongside the likes of Geoffrey Rush. It's a wonderful, shaggy dog of a movie, full of foot-tapping, catchy tunes, moderating some of the harsh realities of Aboriginal life that intrude. Something of a companion piece, Richard Frankland's road movie, **Stone Bros.** is being cleverly billed as the first indigenous comedy in 200 years. In sharp contrast to *Samson and Delilah*, but similar to *Bran Nue Dae*, it suggests that humour can be a real and effective survival tool.

It seems more than coincidence that at least five of 2009's more notable films were directed by actors, or former actors. Again, one suspects that actual hands-on experience, even if it is in front of the camera, can serve the director's craft well. Notable in this

regard is Eric Bana, who has transformed his obsession with his Ford GT Falcon coupe – the same car Mad Max drives – into a meditation on a number of interlocking themes: growing up, friendship, 'hooning' around in fast cars, the temptations of money and the responsibilities of fatherhood. Like his acting, his documentary **Love the Beast** exhibits thoughtful intelligence, enlisting Jay Leno, Jeremy Clarkson and Dr Phil among others on his tour of the male psyche.

It has been a long journey for Rachel Ward, who dipped a toe briefly in the Hollywood pond but opted instead for family life in Australia with her actor/producer partner, Bryan Brown, playing in local films and campaigning for the rights of disadvantaged youths. But judging by the solid achievement of her feature-length directorial debut, **Beautiful Kate**, she has found her true calling. Patriarchy, alienation, lost love and even incest make a dangerous, if not entirely original, brew. The casting and the performances, notably from young Sophie Lowe in the title role, are particularly strong, but Ward shows other skills as well, handling the emotional tangles with conspicuous maturity.

Rachel Ward's **Beautiful Kate**

Notable character actor David Field made his directing debut with the violent, raggedly emotional **The Combination**. Drawing occasionally overwrought performances from his mostly inexperienced cast, the film is really the personal vision of the writer George Basha, who plays the central Lebanese-

Austria Gunnar Landsgesell

What turned out to be quite a successful year for Austrian filmmakers had, at the same time, a genuinely schizophrenic feel to it. While audiences for domestic films passed the million mark for the first time at the national box office and films by Austrian filmmakers attracted acclaim at film festivals, politicians appeared to have lost interest.

The Austrian film industry is small, with filmmakers working under precarious and fragile conditions, while their producers are almost entirely dependent on public funding. 2009 saw another appeal to the authorities for tax incentives in order to boost the annual production, although these cries appeared to fall on deaf ears. The budget for film production is always scarce, so when the subsidy of the Austrian Broadcasting Corporation (ORF) was cut dramatically, the treasury promised to step in by establishing a film fund similar to the German Federal Film Fund (DFFF). As yet, that fund has yet to materialise. But there are hopes it will emerge in 2010.

The serious condition of the Austrian film in- dustry notwithstanding, the filmmaking scene seems not only to have preserved its identity, it has experienced a watershed in creative activity. After bringing home the Oscar for the first time (for *The Counterfeiters*) in 2008, Austria was once again nominated for the Best Foreign Language Film Academy Award. Götz Spielmann's *Revanche* was not only a great success, it also confirmed the artistry of the so-called *Nouvelle Vague Viennoise*.

With his ninth Cannes Festival entry, Austrian director Michael Haneke finally won the Palme d'Or for the German-Austrian co-production,

Michael Haneke's Palme d'Or winner, **The White Ribbon**

The White Ribbon (*Das weiße Band*). Christian Berger, one of the most outstanding Austrian cinematographers, brought a stark beauty to Haneke's extensive portrait of rural life, with clear, crisp imagery, often in long shot, accentuating the characters' relationship with the world around them.

Jessica Hausner, clearly influenced by Haneke's work, advanced her own personal style of storytelling with **Lourdes**, which was in competition at the Venice Film Festival. It is about a woman who is miraculously healed at the famous French destination for Christian pilgrims. The film rejects spectacle,

Shirin Neshat's **Women Without Men**

any superficial visual style and defies simple explanation. Hausner instead focuses on the structural aspects of the place and the inner dynamics of the community of peripatetic miracle-seekers. The production collective Coop99, which Hausner is a member of, has collaborated on two other extraordinary projects: the impressive video artist Shirin Neshat's **Women Without Men** is a poetic fragment about subversion in Iran in 1953; while **Pepperminta**, by Swiss visual artist Pipilotti Rist, translates emotions into child-like colours. The latter is an anarchic piece, containing only traces of a narrative.

Tizza Covi and Rainer Frimmel's **La Pivellina**

Austrian films are often identified by a harsh realism, coolly portraying the daily life of the lower classes. Tizza Covi and Rainer Frimmel's **La Pivellina** features elements of this approach, but also goes against the grain. A variation on the docu-drama, it explores the life of a family belonging to a travelling circus, located somewhere on the outskirts of a city in Northern Italy. An abandoned child found on a playground is at the centre of this portrait of lives full of uncertainty, love and longing. It was awarded the Best European Film in Cannes' Quinzaine des Realisateurs and is an emotionally powerful companion to their earlier circus-based film, *Babooska*.

Israeli director Yoav Shamir's **Defamation** raises the provocative question of what form anti-Semitism takes in the 21st century. Joining the New York-based Anti-Defamation League (ADF) on their journey to Eastern Europe, Israel and other locations, Shamir

Yoav Shamir's **Defamation**

attempts to decipher the subtle differences that divide criticism of Israel and anti-Jewish, racist stereotypes. Like its subject, *Defamation* is a film on the edge. A similar investigative approach can be seen in Werner Boote's **Plastic Planet**, which looks at the wasteful use of packaging and its cluttering up of the world. Less an explorative documentary than one in which the director's opinion is, from the outset, firmly set in stone, Boote's style is not dissimilar to Michael Moore's combative, research-lite approach.

Michael Glawogger, who is known for such spectacular works as *Workingman's Death* and *Megacities*, oscillated once again between documentary and fiction with **Kill Daddy Goodnight** (*Das Vaterspiel*), an adaptation of the novel by Austrian author Josef Haslinger. Weaving three different narratives and timeframes together, it tells the story of three families and the guilt and anger that exists between fathers and sons. The spectre of fascism is the backdrop to this ambitious film,

Michael Glawogger's **Kill Daddy Goodnight**

Kurt Ockermueller's **Echte Wiener**

which goes some way to showing that even the most un-filmable of novels can be brought to the screen.

For 2010, we can expect more of the recently 'discovered' national comedies that accounted for the year's impressive box-office results. **Echte Wiener** and **Kottan ermittelt** are spin-offs from television series that were extremely popular in the 1970s. However, it is unlikely the humour of *Echte Wiener* would travel well outside Austria's borders. It portrays the typical Viennese habitant: grumpy, offensive, naïve and as such, a funny character. The sale of 370,000 tickets made it one of the most successful Austrian movies in history.

Other projects include **Der Kameramörder** by Robert Adrian Pejo, which focuses on the impact on two couples of the appearance of a snuff film. And with **Im Keller**, notorious filmmaker Ulrich Seidl enters the cellars of private households, searching for the skeletons in the Austrian closet.

The year's best films
La Pivellina (Tizza Covi, Rainer Frimmel)
The White Ribbon (Michael Haneke)
Little Alien (Nina Kusturica)
Lourdes (Jessica Hausner)
Women Without Men (Shirin Neshat)

Quote of the year
'Austrian cinema lacks stars. Look at Cannes-winner Christoph Waltz (Inglourious Basterds). Quentin Tarantino has shown with this Austrian actor, how to create stars.' *Unknown producer in Vienna.*

Directory
All Tel/Fax numbers begin (+43)
Austrian Film Museum, Augustinerstr 1, A-1010 Vienna, Tel: (1) 533 7054-0. Fax: (1) 533 7054-25. office@filmmuseum.at. www.filmmuseum.at.
Filmarchiv Austria, Obere Augartenstr 1, A-1020 Vienna. Tel: (1) 216 1300. Fax: (1) 216 1300-100. augarten@filmarchiv.at. www.filmarchiv.at.
Association of Austrian Film Directors, c/o checkpointmedia Multimediaproduktionen AG, Seilerstätte 30, A-1010 Vienna. Tel/Fax: (1) 513 0000-0. Fax: (1) 513 0000-11. www.austrian-directors.com.
Association of Austrian Film Producers, Speisingerstrasse 121, A-1230 Vienna. Tel/Fax: (1) 888 9622. aafp@austrian-film.com. www.austrian-film.com.
Association of the Audiovisual & Film Industry, Wiedner Hauptstrasse 53, PO Box 327, A-1045 Vienna. Tel: (1) 5010 53010. Fax: (1) 5010 5276. film@fafo.at. www.fafo.at.
Austrian Film Commission, Stiftgasse 6, A-1070 Vienna. Tel: (1) 526 33 23-0. Fax: (1) 526 6801. office@afc.at. www.afc.at.
Austrian Film Institute (OFI), Spittelberggasse 3, A-1070 Vienna. Tel: (1) 526 9730-400. Fax: (1) 526 9730-440. office@filminstitut.at. www.filminstitut.at.
Location Austria, Opernring 3, A-1010 Vienna. Tel: (1) 588 5836. Fax: (1) 586 8659. office@location-austria.at. www.location-austria.at.
Vienna Film Fund, Stiftgasse 6, A-1070 Vienna. Tel: 526 5088. Fax: 526 5020. office@filmfonds-wien.at. www.filmfonds-wien.at.

GUNNAR LANDSGESELL is a freelance writer for *Blickpunkt: Film, FORMAT, kolik, ray film magazin* and is chief editor of the human rights magazine *MOMENT.*

Jessica Hausner's **Lourdes**

Belgium Erik Martens

A sense of crisis pervades Belgium. It's not just the country's economy, which is in a comparable state to everywhere else in the world, but a problem at the core of national institutions. For a few years, the political system has experienced great difficulty in bringing together politicians from the two (actually, even three) national language communities. Every day newspapers publish new stories to demonstrate that governing Belgium is more difficult than finding the Holy Grail.

Fortunately we do have a small local cinema that is performing rather well. At the beginning of 2009, Eric Van Looy's noir thriller **Loft** set a new all-time box-office record, with approximately 1,200,000 Belgians going to see it. Apart from Van Looy's personal triumph, a significant number of films were selected for international festivals. Most striking were this year's four Cannes selections: **The Misfortunates** (*De helaasheid der dingen*) by Felix van Groeningen; **Lost Persons Area** by Caroline Strubbe; **Altiplano** by Peter Brosens and Jessica Woodworth; and the animated film, **A Town called Panic** (*Panique au village*), by Stéphane Aubier and Vincent Patar.

The most successful in terms of profile was *The Misfortunates*. In one of the film's most memorable scenes, the five brothers Strobbe go on their annual bicycle race in their local town, Reetveerdegem. To increase public interest, they perform it naked. At Cannes, where the film played in the Directors' Fortnight, Felix van Groeningen and the main cast repeated the scene, parading naked along the Croisette, which certainly helped to attract national and international attention. In contrast to the debuting or sophomore directors who are the majority of filmmakers behind the year's

Felix van Groeningen's **The Misfortunates**

releases, van Groeningen is a third-time director. And, once again, he manages to create a unique world. *The Misfortunates* presents a grotesque social underclass dominated by filth, alcoholism, financial problems and occasional violence. The film is based on Dimitri Verhulst's bestselling novel in which 13-year-old Gunther experiences great difficulty in escaping his bleak background in order to become a writer. Although van Groeningen goes some way towards visualising the novel's depravity, the film was surprisingly popular at Flemish cinemas.

Pieter Van Hees' first feature, **Dirty Mind**, occupies a similar niche. It features popular TV comic Wim Helsen as the shy Diego, who crashes his car and wakes up transformed into the bold and uninhibited stuntman, Tony T. The curious case of Diego/Tony T. and his so-called 'frontal syndrome' interests neurologist Jaana, who wants to cure him. Obviously Diego prefers to stay as Tony. The comic implications are evident, but its serious undertone is less convincing. *Dirty Mind* was selected for the *Variety* Critics' Choice at the Karlovy Vary Festival, although back at home it failed to attract the same audience interest as *The Misfortunates*.

On the whole, style was a predominant issue in the Dutch-speaking part of Belgium; obviously so for Van Hees and van Groeningen, but also for Caroline Strubbe, Dorothee van den Berghe and Fien Troch. And if we consider Patrice Toye and her late-2008 release, *Nowhere Man*, as part of this year's 'Female Wave', then it did temporarily provide a little counterweight to the traditional male director's dominance. It would be unjust, however, to think of these films merely as one cohesive movement: the differences between them are significant.

A personal favourite is Fien Troch's **Nowhere Man**, in which the director re-examines themes she introduced in her 2005 debut feature, *Someone Else's Happiness*, of parents mourning the loss of a child and experiencing difficulty in communicating with each another. The title is English, but the protagonists speak French, unusual for a Flemish film. Lukas (Bruno Todeschini) and Grace (Emmanuelle Devos) perform their roles with great delicacy. Shot mainly in close-up, the film creates an intimate mood. Although it may lack substance, the film's artistic achievement is, nevertheless, considerable.

Dorothee van den Berghe's **My Queen Karo**

As far as image is concerned, Dorothee van den Berghe's second feature, **My Queen Karo**, is utterly enchanting. The film retraces young Karo's confusing experiences in the 1970s, when the family lived in a commune in Amsterdam. The father is a free-love idealist. But Karo, like her mother, feels ill at ease with the mores of the period. The film's photography and the creation of young Karo's world are very poetic. But, once again, characters lack a certain depth.

Although a lack of coherence and sense of being lost are central to *Lost Persons Area*, the fact that the film itself suffers from these elements somewhat undermines it. Bettina, Marcus and their daughter Bettina live in some unidentified industrial wasteland, amidst pylons and power-line cables. In the beginning they seem quite connected with the environment, but then an accident changes everything. Caroline Strubbe conveys this feeling using a shaky camera style, which feels a little tired. On the other hand, the film did attract acclaim at the Cannes Festival. It was also awarded a Best Film prize at the Tout Ecran Festival in Geneva and has been selected for numerous international festivals.

Peter Brosens and Jessica Woodworth are by no means newcomers. Both of them have a number of documentary films to their names, but as far as feature work is concerned *Altiplano* is only their second outing. In their 'globalist' approach to their subject, they are quite unique in Belgium. 2006's *Khadak* took place in Mongolia, within the context of large industrial companies exploiting the land and its people. *Altiplano* takes the viewer to a mining site in Peru where industry has a devastating impact upon local communities. Expectations were high after *Khadak*, but *Altiplano*'s ambitious artistic agenda is somewhat overcharged. Photographer Grace is married to Max, a cataract surgeon. Grace has experienced traumatic events in Iraq, only to lose her husband in Peru. Added to this is the story of Saturnina and the village of Turubamba, which suffers severe ecological problems due to a

Peter Brosens and Jessica Woodworth's **Altiplano**

mercury spill from a local mine. Brosens and Woodworth are stretched beyond their limit in a film where less could have been more.

Stijn Coninx's filmmaking involves a more populist approach to storytelling. **Sister Smile** (*Soeur Sourire*) is based on a fragment of Belgian collective memory: the story of sister Jeanine Deckers, who became world famous as the Singing Nun with her hit song, 'Dominique'. The French-language film plays out in warm nostalgic tones, with Jeanine Deckers engagingly played by Cécile de France. Apart from being a crazy singing nun, Jeanine was a complex case, whose life involved darker elements, which Coninx chooses not to deal with too explicitly. As a result, what remains is a somewhat superficial account of the singer's life.

Joachim Lafosse's **Free Student**

Joachim Lafosse's cinema couldn't be more opposite. It never embellishes or aims for 'great images', but it digs into where it hurts and becomes uncomfortable for the viewer. Dramatically speaking, it is intensely stimulating cinema. It operates both on the emotional and the intellectual level. Like most of his previous films, **Free Student** (*Elève libre*) deals with the often problematic relationship between parents and their children. Sixteen-year-old Jonas has lost all interest in school. Then one day he meets Pierre, who is willing to give him free private lessons so that he will be able to pass his exams. The film explores the line where transmission and tuition ends, and manipulation and exploitation begins. Yves Hanchar's **No Hard Feelings!** (*Sans*

rancune) deals with more or less the same issue. Laurent Matagne is sent to a boarding school where a French teacher has a great influence on the boy's intellectual evolution. He is also responsible for Laurent's decision to become a writer. And, believe it or not, Laurent will also learn that his teacher is his father!

Nabil Ben Yadir's **The Barons**

On the whole, French-speaking cinema in Belgium is a more verbal enterprise than its Flemish counterpart. Take, for instance, **The Barons** (*Les barons*) by first-time director Nabil Ben Yadir. The film consists of people talking to one another. Even the main character, Hassan (Nader Boussandel), talks to himself. He dreams of becoming a stand-up comedian, but in order to do this, as well as win over his great love, Malika, he has to deal with his father and friends. *The Barons* is this year's great surprise in Belgian cinema; an inventive social comedy, it features the smartest and funniest dialogue in years.

Simon Konianski (*Les folles aventures de Simon Konianski*) is no less talkative. A likeable comedy about a character called Simon (Jonathan Zaccaï) who struggles with his old father and the woman who left him, the film also deals, on a more philosophical level, with Judaism. Micha Wald's comedy is occasionally a wildly extravagant film, featuring a playful musical score and a fine performance by Nassim Ben Abdeloumen as Simon's son, Hadrien.

Manuel Poutte's **Distant Tremors** (*Les tremblements lointains*) is visually daring in its attempt to show audiences the difference between western and African approaches to life. A young woman is in love with a young Senegalese man, which brings her into conflict with her father, a doctor who runs a local hospital. Poutte's atmospheric approach is quite effective throughout.

Finally, outside all categories, there is Aubier and Patar's wildly anarchistic animated feature, *A Town Called Panic*. It is difficult to summarise the plot, so let's keep it simple: 'Cowboy' and 'Indian' plan to buy 'Horse' a number of bricks so that he can construct a barbecue for his birthday. But something goes terribly wrong with the order and, from then on, fast pacing and absurdist humour dominate. The characters are Playmobil toys, so technological innovation is minimal. But that is precisely what the film is all about – a joyful slice of Dada-style animation.

Mark Mertens and Wim Bien's **Luke and Lucy & The Texas Rangers**

At the other side of the linguistic border, a totally different team of animated filmmakers, supervised by Mark Mertens and Wim Bien, created **Luke and Lucy & The Texas Rangers** (*Suske en Wiske & de Texaskrakkers*). The computer-generated film is based on the popular cartoon series by Willy Vandersteen. The story is pretty conventional compared to *A Town called Panic*: Luke and Lucy become Texas Rangers in order to combat evil Jim Parasite. It is nicely designed, but lacks the spark of inspiration. If *Panic* is this year's fastest-paced Belgian film, *Luke and Lucy* is most definitely the slowest.

To summarise 2009, there were no huge box-office hits like *Loft*, but numerous small artful features, many of which were not without merit. And to the future? No doubt Dutch-speaking Belgians are curious to see how crime thriller *Dossier K.*, the long-anticipated successor to Eric Van Looy's 2007 hit, *The Alzheimer Case*, will perform. On the French-

speaking side, **Mr. Nobody** by veteran Jaco Van Dormael is eagerly awaited. The film was screened at the Venice Film Festival, where it received a technical prize. It is hoped that Belgians will like it for more that that.

The year's best films
The Barons (Nabil Ben Yadir)
Free Student (Joachim Lafosse)
Distant Tremors (Manuel Poutte)
Unspoken (Fien Troch)
My Queen Karo (Dorothee van den Berghe)

Quote of the year
'It's my life, these are my friends. I opened my front door and I filmed my street. The people I know. The neighbourhood I grew up in.'
Director NABIL BEN YADIR *on* The Barons.

Directory
All Tel/Fax numbers begin (+32)
Royal Belgian Film Archive, 3 rue Ravenstein, 1000 Brussels. Tel: (2) 551 19 00. Fax: (2) 551 19. info@cinematek.be. www.cinematek.be.
Communauté Française de Belgique. Le Centre du Cinéma et de l'Audiovisuel, Boulevard Léopold II 44, 1080 Bruxelles. Tel: (2) 413 35 01. Fax: (2) 413 20 68. www.cfwb.be/av.
Wallonie Bruxelles Images (WBI), Place Flagey 18, 1050 Bruxelles. Tel: (2) 223 23 04. Fax: (2) 218 34 24. info@wbimages.be. www.wbimages.be.
Wallimage, Rue du Onze Novembre 6, 7000 Mons. Tel: (6) 540 40 33. Fax: (6) 540 40 39. info@wallimage.be. www.wallimage.be.
Ministry of the Flemish Community. Media & Film, Arenbergstraat 9, 1000 Brussels. Tel: (2) 553 45 50. Fax: (2) 553 45 79. film@vlaanderen.be. www.flanders.be.
Flemish Audiovisual Fund (VAF), Bischoffsheimlaan 38, 1000 Brussels. Tel: (2) 226 06 30. Fax: (2) 219 19 36. info@vaf.be. www.vaf.be.
Flanders Image, Bischoffsheimlaan 38, 1000 Brussels. Tel: (2) 226 06 30. Fax: (2) 219 19 36. flandersimage@vaf.be. www.flandersimage.com.

ERIK MARTENS is editor of the DVD releases at the Royal Belgian Film Archive and film critic for different media.

Bolivia José Sánchez-H.

Production in Bolivia is undergoing some significant changes, with co-productions generating jobs and offering the opportunity to learn and share new technologies. The accessibility of digital formats has helped bring production costs down, allowing first-time directors to make films. Some productions are also making use of higher-end digital formats, such as the Red camera. But in a world divided over which format to use, support for celluloid remains strong.

One of the most accomplished films of 2009 was Thomas Kröntaler's Spanish-language drama **Write Me Postcards to Copacabana** (*Escríbeme postales a Copacabana*), about the lives and dreams of a girl, her mother and grandmother. Based on German writer Stefanie Kremser's book, which she adapted, this Bolivian/German film was co-produced by Italian-born Bolivian director Paolo Agazzi. It features Julia Hernández as Alfonsina, a 13-year-old girl who asks tourists to send her postcards as a way for her to see the world. Carla Ortíz is Rosa, Alfonsina's mother, a flight attendant trying to fix her life, and Agar Delós plays the role of Alfonsina's grandmother, who spends her days remembering her deceased German husband. It was filmed on 35mm.

On its opening weekend, Juan Carlos Valdivia's **Southern District** (*Zona Sur*) was the most viewed film of the year, attracting an audience of 5,877. *Hannah Montana: The Movie* occupied second place with 2,999 viewers. For Valdivia, who had previously directed *American Visa* and *Jonah and the Pink Whale*, *Southern District* was a personal film that presented an intimate portrait of a wealthy family as they faced the unavoidable social changes taking place across the country, albeit from

Filming Juan Carlos Valdivia's **Southern District**

the confines of their home in one of the most exclusive neighbourhoods of La Paz. Shot on digital using the Red camera, Valdivia's film gradually reveals his characters' inability to cope with their new reality.

Red, Yellow and Green (*Rojo, amarillo y verde*) by Sergio Bastani, Rodrigo Bellot and Martín Boulocq was adapted from three short stories. A 30-year-old mother with cancer faces death; a boy becomes lost after leaving his house and finds himself part of a new adventure; and an orphaned young man wants a mother. The filmmakers' intention was to present a portrait of their society, highlighting the conflicts people face on a daily basis, and to tell stories with a universal theme. Again, the production was shot using Red technology.

Of the other fine recent releases, Germán Monje's drama, **Worker's Hospital** (*Hospital obrero*), told the story of six patients whose experiences create a bond of friendship between them. Most of the characters were played by elderly non-professional actors. Alejandro Pereira Doria Medina's first feature, **To See One Self** (*Verse*), explored the issue of immigration and the emotional impact it has on families. A mother who is left by herself

Germán Monje's **Worker's Hospital**

after the departure of her only son must face the question that haunts her: what is there left in life to live for and for whom to live it. Meanwhile, Tomás Bascopé's more commercial feature debut, **The Elevator** (*El ascensor*), had three robbers trapped in an elevator for three days, their captivity forcing them to find a way to survive without killing each other.

Tomás Bascopé's **The Elevator**

Another recent co-production, between Bolivia and Japan, was Toshifumi Matsushita's **The Gift From Mother Earth** (*El regalo de la pachamama*), a coming-of-age story of a 13-year-old Quechua boy named Kunturi and his relationship with his family. The film employs the surreal landscape of Bolivia, such as the Uyuni Salt Lake, which was beautifully photographed in Super-16 to great effect.

A documentary worth mentioning, valuable as a document of a little-known culture, is **Tentayape** by Roberto Alem Rojo. It focused on members of the Guarani, who live in the state of Chuquisaca, in the isolated community that gives the film its title.

Rodrigo Ayala Bluske's comedy, **Stories of Wine, Cognac and the Bedroom** (*Historias de vino, singani y alcoba*), set amongst the Tarija culture, located in the southern part of Bolivia, plays up the humour that characterises the area. It revolves around seven characters who become embroiled in various madcap situations and features performances by Andrea Camponovo and Toto Vaca.

Hugo Torrico's **Ecoman the Movie** (*Ecoman la película*) employs action, comedy and romance in its story of a superhero whose mission is to protect the natural world. Like many superheroes, Ecoman has a vulnerability that weakens him. In this case it is the destruction of the environment. The film is targeted at children in order to raise awareness about green issues.

Diego Torres' **Loves of Fire** (*Amores de lumbre*) is a vivid take on a contemporary love triangle between two women who work as masseuses and their relationship with a writer they meet, played by veteran actor Jorge Ortíz.

Given the lack of state support due to the worldwide economic conditions, co-productions seem likely to continue in the future. Some of these include co-directing, as in the case of two young filmmakers, Bolivian Yashira Jordan and Argentinian Nadia Lozano, who are planning to direct **The Heiresses** (*Las herederas*) together. The script tells the story of a landowner who leaves his money to the women in his life. Gathered in an office, they all discover things about themselves and their past with the man they all thought they knew.

Toshifumi Matsushita's **The Gift From Mother Earth**

Thomas Kröntaler's **Write Me Postcards to Copacabana**

The year's best films
Write Me Postcards to Copacabana
(Thomas Kröntaler)
Southern District (Juan Carlos Valdivia)
Red, Yellow and Green (Sergio Bastani,
Rodrigo Bellot, Martín Boulocq)
The Gift From Mother Earth
(Toshifumi Matsushita)
Tentayape (Roberto Alem Rojo)

Quote of the year
'I wanted to break loose from the dialect of
film language that tells a story by juxtaposing
images, or by shooting coverage. Nor did I
want to follow the characters and thus impose
a sequential plot to the story. The camera
here is part of the film's leitmotif, a part of its
essence.' JUAN CARLOS VALDIVIA, *writer and
director of* **Southern District**.

Directory
All Tel/Fax numbers begin (+591)
Cinemateca Boliviana, Calle Oscar Soria,
Prolongación Federico Zuazo s/n, Casilla 9933,
La Paz. Tel: (2) 211 8759.
informaciones@cinematecaboliviana.org.
www.cinematecaboliviana.org.
Consejo Nacional de Cine (CONACINE), Calle
Montevideo, Edificio Requimia, Piso 8, La Paz. Tel:
(2) 244 4759. contacto@conacine.net.
www.conacine.net.

JOSÉ SÁNCHEZ-H. is a filmmaker and author
of *The Art and Politics of Bolivian Cinema*. He
teaches in the department of Film and Electronic Art at California State University, Long Beach.

Bosnia & Herzegovina Rada Sesić

It is estimated that in Bosnia and Herzegovina, a country with four million inhabitants, only some five or six cinemas, together accommodating approximately 20 screens, have survived the war and are in the painful process of transition. Some big cities and regional centres like Mostar, Tuzla, Jajce or Travnik don't even have a single cinema. Sarajevo, with its 400,000 residents, until recently only had three cinemas. A new multiplex now caters to the capital's audience.

Jasmila Zbanic's **On The Path**

The Sarajevo Film Festival, which uses only one regular cinema venue and a huge open-air screen, still manages to attract over 100,000 spectators to its events. This summer's feature competition did not feature a Bosnian film, although three new feature films were due to be finished. With the working title **On The Path** (*Na putu*), the new film by Jasmila Zbanic (Berlinale winner with her debut, *Grbavica*) is eagerly awaited. This daring and talented female director will once again address a politically contentious and socially relevant issue, telling the story of a happy young couple whose relationship is put under immense strain when the man, after losing his job, starts working at a religious camp set up by

Wahhabis, the movement of ultra-conservative Muslims. As in her previous film, the director has cast actors from Slovenia, Croatia and Serbia, as well as Bosnia and Herzegovina.

Nedzad Begovic's **Jasmina** opens in war-torn Sarajevo, where an old woman escapes with baby Jasmina to a small provincial location on the Croatian coast. Living in a friend's apartment, she struggles to make ends meet. Her next-door neighbour is the local drunkard and a brutal man who transforms into a sober and caring babysitter, looking after the child when the grandmother becomes terminally ill, a drama that dominates the later stages of the film.

Adis Bakrac's debut, **Bare Skin** (*Gola koža*), is set in an orphanage in Sarajevo, where children have to confront gang fights and bullying, while the guardians struggle to find the best educational approach. At the same time, local criminals are intimidating the orphans into committing petty crimes. Central to the drama is the sensitive Alen, who believes that his parents are famous journalists who have only temporarily placed him in the care of the orphanage. His world crumbles when he finds out his mother conceived him after being raped.

Some fine shorts were made by newcomers, such as Elmir Jukic's **Mother** (*Majka*), whose central character is closely linked to the tragic events that unfolded in Srebrenica. As performed by Jasna Zalica, the character remains silent throughout the film. Amra Mehic's diploma film, **The Ruin** (*Zgariste*), features a man forced out of his home during the war, only to return to set the place on fire. He discovers a new occupant, of a different ethnic background, living in it, which causes huge tension.

Documentary production was quite meagre, with just two stand-out films: Timur Makarevic's **Anybody** (*Iko*) and **Believers** (*Vjernici*), by Namik Kabil. The first evokes the metaphysical spirit of nature in a poetic, non-narrative and meditative journey through idyllic landscapes, set against an impressive electronic score. *Believers* also challenges cinematic form through the use of photographs accompanied by personal stories. Focusing on a multi-ethnic choir in Sarajevo that performs religious works, it features an impressive dynamic.

Elmir Jukic's **Mother**

Timur Makarevic's **Anybody**

There was great news that the animator Midhat Ajanovic, who left Sarajevo for Sweden, has been returning to the city more often, making films here once again. His **Point of Mouth** reminisces about growing up in his hometown.

The poetic animated film by Faruk Sabanovic, **Birds Like Us**, is still in progress. His producers have found another backer from Turkey and the extra financial boost will help this ambitious, feature length animated debut from Bosnia and Herzegovina to finally reach cinemas.

Sarajevo's Arts Academy Direction Department celebrated its 20th anniversary. Amongst all the graduates, from the first inductees to those recently entering the film industry, some 250 prestigious film awards have been won, including an Academy Award for *No Man's Land* and the Golden Bear for *Grbavica*.

The year's best films
Anybody (Timur Makarevic)
Jasmina (Nedzad Begovic)
Mother (Elmir Jukic)

Directory
All Tel/Fax numbers begin (+387)
Academy for Performing Arts, Obala, Sarajevo. Tel/Fax: 665 304.
Association of Filmmakers, Strosmajerova 1, Sarajevo. Tel: 667 452.
Cinematheque of Bosnia & Herzegovina, Alipasina 19, Sarajevo. Tel/Fax: 668 678. kinoteka@bih.net.ba.

RADA SESIĆ is a film critic, curator and a festival programmer based in the Netherlands. She is programme advisor of IFFR and one of the selectors of IDFA, also heading the documentary competition at SFF and lecturing at the Dutch Institute for film education (NIF).

Brazil Nelson Hoineff

From a commercial point of view, 2009 was one of the best years in recent memory for Brazilian cinema. Market share by the end of the year will be between 17% and 18% – a huge increase compared to the traditional 10%.

This increase in Brazilian cinema's fortunes was due to a number of commercially successful films, led by **If I Were You: Part 2** (*Se eu fosse você 2*). Produced by Total Entertainment and directed by Daniel Filho, the sequel to the light comedy in which a wife and husband change roles after an inexplicable accident attracted six million viewers. Filho, who already saw success with the original *If I Were You*, is currently in post-production on his new film, **Chico Xavier**, an extremely popular Brazilian paranormal tale.

Daniel Filho's **If I Were You: Part 2**

There is also much riding on the success of **Lula, the Son of Brazil** (*Lula, o filho do Brasil*), a biography of president Luiz Inacio Lula da Silva, produced by Luiz Carlos Barreto and directed by his son, Fabio Barreto. *Lula* is so far one of the most expensive films ever shot in Brazil (nearly USD$9 million) and will open on 1 January 2010 across approximately 500

Fabio Barreto's **Lula, the Son of Brazil**

screens – almost 25% of all available screens in the country. Even before its premiere, the film has been the subject of heavy criticism in the Brazilian press, not necessarily for the quality of its content but for its means of production. The influential news magazine, *Veja*, ran a cover story filled with accusations about how the film is being used for propagandist purposes. The country will face a presidential election in October 2010 and the magazine claimed that companies investing in the film, although they did not use public money, have strong links with the federal government. Similar accusations featured in the leading daily papers *O Globo, Folha de S.Paulo* and *O Estado de S.Paulo.*

Many other films contributed to the increase of market share for Brazilian films. Among them is another sequel, **The Normals: Part 2** (*Os Normais parte 2*), based on a popular television series and directed by José Alvarenga Jr., who also directed **The Coach** (*Divã*). Each film drew more than two million viewers, while Cláudio Torres' **The Invisible Woman** (*A mulher invisível*), also a comedy based on TV characters, attracted an audience of 2.5 million. These figures represent a

Cláudio Torres' **The Invisible Woman**

success for the alliance between independent producers, the media firm Globo Filmes and favourable tax laws, particularly Article 3, which allows foreign distributors more leeway to invest in Brazilian films.

Many other production incentives became effective in 2009, led by the FSA (Setorial Fund for Audiovisual), a fund administered by Ancine (the official agency for cinema) and Finep (a government agency for the funding of commercial studies and projects). The authorities in São Paulo have also played an important role in film production. And last September, the governments of the state and city of Rio de Janeiro announced several investments for the area, including funds of nearly USD$9 million provided by BNDES (a government-controlled development bank), as well as state stock funds, for film and television production.

Among the foreign films, *Twilight: New Moon* was a phenomenon, selling 1.4 million tickets in its first weekend, the second-biggest opening of the decade in Brazil, an unexpected surprise for the industry.

Total viewers for films will have reached 100 million in 2009 (against 89.1 million in 2008), with the average ticket price slightly above USD$4.61, according to *Filme B* magazine. In December, Convecom, a national conference called by the government to discuss new regulation of the media and telecommunications in the country, took place. Among the many proposals was the rebirth

of Embrafilme, the old government agency closed in 1992, which for many years was responsible for funding local film production.

Directory

All Tel/Fax numbers begin (+55)

ANCINE (National Agency for Cinema), Praça Pio X, 54, 10th Floor, 22091-040 Rio de Janeiro. Tel: (21) 3849 1339. www.ancine.gov.br.

Brazilian Cinema Congress (CBC), (Federation of Cinema Unions/Associations), Rua Cerro Cora 550, Sala 19, 05061-100 São Paulo. Tel/Fax: (11) 3021 8505. congressocinema@hotmail.com. www.congressocinema.com.br.

Cinemateca Brasileira, Largo Senador Raul Cardoso, Vila Clementino 207, 04021-070 São Paulo. Tel: (11) 5084 2318. Fax: (11) 5575 9264. info@cinemateca.com.br. www.cinemateca.com.br.

Grupo Novo de Cinema, (Distributor), Rua Capitao Salomao 42, 22271-040 Rio de Janeiro. Tel: (21) 2539 1538. braziliancinema@braziliancinema.com. www.gnctv.com.br.

Ministry of Culture, Films & Festivals Dept, Esplanada dos Ministerios, Bloco B, 3rd Floor, 70068-900 Brasilia. www.cultura.gov.br.

NELSON HOINEFF is a film critic, vice president of the Association of Film Critics of Rio de Janeiro and president of the Institute of Television Studies.

Bulgaria Pavlina Jeleva

Bulgarian cinema started 2009 with great expectations for its future. The long-awaited increase of the national support to €9.5 million was finally announced. The Bulgarian National Film Archive marked its 50th anniversary with a year-long programme, beginning with the 1911 film, *Opening of the Great National Assembly in Veliko Tarnovo.*

Nadejda Koseva's **Omelette**, part of the first Bulgarian omnibus, **15**, portraying a young mother unsuccessfully trying to feed her child in 1996, received an Honorable Mention among the seven international shorts screened at the Sundance Film Festival. Meanwhile, Petar Popzlatev's 1989 film, *The Countess*, which tells the true story of 18-year-old Sybilla and her rebellion against totalitarianism through drug use, was chosen for the Berlinale programme to commemorate the 20th anniversary of the fall of the Berlin Wall.

Kamen Kalev's **Eastern Plays**

Georgy Djulgerov's **The Goat**

Known for his original blend of popular beliefs and rituals, Georgy Djulgerov opened the Sofia Film Festival with his much-anticipated **The Goat** (*Kozelat*), narrating the story of an animal that descends from the heavens on a mystical mission. Kamen Kalev's debut, **Eastern Plays** (*Iztochni piessi*), a sad and sensitive look at Sofia's underground youth, was selected for

the Directors' Fortnight at Cannes and received a nomination for the European LUX Prize, as well as picking up the Sakura Grand Prix at the Tokyo Film Festival, along with the Best Director and Best Actor awards.

The world premiere of Ivan Cherkelov's dramatic and deeply personal **Crayfish** (*Razi*), about two friends who become killing instruments in the hands of competing criminals, took place at the Moscow Film Festival.

Janos Edelenyi's popular Hungarian/Bulgarian/ UK/Dutch hit, **Prima Primavera**, which details the cross-border journey of a mentally disabled 55-year-old man (Andor Lukáts) and a kindhearted gypsy girl (Vessela Kazakova), picked up the Best Actress prize and a special award at the Varna Film Festival. Stephan Komandarev's **The World is Big and Salvation Lurks Around the Corner** (*Svetat e goliam i spassenie debne ot vsiakade*), which tells the story of a character's return to life with the help of the ancient game of backgammon, continued its impressive festival marathon and was announced as the Bulgarian entry for the 2010 Academy Awards.

Inspired by a strange novel from 1933 on the future death of the Romanian town of Sulina, the beautifully shot and intelligent **Europolis: The Town of the Delta** (*Evropolis: gradat na deltata*) brought to director Kostadin Bonev a fully deserved Golden Rhyton for best documentary at the Bulgarian festival of animation and non-fiction film.

On an international level, six-time Academy Award nominee Peter Weir shot the Siberian section of his World War II drama, **The Way Back**, on the impressive Vitosha Mountain, using international stars (Colin Farrell, Ed Harris) as well as local talent (Zahari Baharov). The imaginary journey of the Neanderthal nomad, Ao, across Europe and his eventual meeting with the Homo sapiens girl, Aki, was the story behind the epic **Ao: The Last Neanderthal**, which brought French director Jacques Malaterre to the Bulgarian capital.

Unfortunately, after a strong initial engagement with positive changes in film legislation by the new administration at the Ministry of Culture, it became clear that a serious cut in financial support was planned for 2010. The Bulgarian film community tried to defend its legitimate rights in all possible ways and received valuable European advocacy. In a letter from 23 November, the FERA president, István Szabó, expressed his unconditional support to Bulgarian filmmakers, stating: 'It has now been brought to our attention that the Bulgarian government plans to cut the Film Fund by 57%. The Federation of European Film Directors wishes to make clear its extreme concern at these massive proposed cuts – the like of which would suffocate the film industry in any European country.'

PAVLINA JELEVA is a film critic and journalist, regularly contributing to many Bulgarian newspapers and magazines. Having been national representative on the boards of Eurimages and FIPRESCI, she is now artistic and foreign-relations director of her own film company.

Ivan Cherkelov's **Crayfish**

The year's best films
Crayfish (Ivan Cherkelov)
Eastern Plays (Kamen Kalev)
The Goat (Georgy Djulgerov)
Europolis: The Town of the Delta (Konstantin Bonev, docu)
Omelette (Nadejda Koseva, short)

Quote of the year
'There is a real danger for a dozen of new Bulgarian feature films, supported in 2009 not to be made.' *The new NFC director* **ALEXANDER DONEV** *summarises the current situation for Bulgarian filmmakers.*

Directory
All Tel/Fax numbers begin (+359)
Ministry of Culture, 17 Stamboliiski St, 1000 Sofia. Tel: (2) 980 6191. Fax: (2) 981 8559. www.culture.government.bg.
National Film Centre, 2A Dondukov Blvd, 1000 Sofia. Tel: (2) 987 4096. Fax: (2) 987 3626. www.nfc.bg.
Bulgarian National Television, 29 San Stefano St, 1000 Sofia. Tel: (2) 985 591. Fax: (2) 987 1871. www.bnt.bg.
National Academy of Theatre & Film Arts, 108A Rakovski Street, 1000 Sofia. Tel: (2) 9231 231/233.
Bulgarian National Film Library, 36 Gurko St, 1000 Sofia. Tel: (2) 987 0296. Fax: (2) 987 6004 bnf. bg/en/film_library/ or www.ceebd.co.uk/ceeed/un/bg/bg023.htm.
Bulgarian Film Producers Association, Tel: (2) 8860 5350. Fax: (2) 963 0661. geopoly@gmail.com.
Union of Bulgarian Film Makers, 67 Dondukov Blvd, 1504 Sofia. Tel: (2) 946 1068. Fax: (2) 946 1069. www.filmmakersbg.org.

Canada Tom McSorley

Canadian cinema continued its internationalist trend – onscreen and off – on all levels, from production and financing to narrative content. Indeed, Canada's screens hosted a considerable number of notable international figures in 2009: Morgan Freeman, Iggy Pop, Alice Cooper, Malcolm MacDowell, Liam Neeson, Julianne Moore, Amanda Seyfried, Patricia Clarkson, and Woody Harrelson appear in various Canadian films. Freeman was in Paul Saltzman's documentary **Prom Night In Mississippi**, which recorded the actor's attempts to end racism in his home town; Pop, Cooper, and MacDowell starred in Rob Stefaniuk's kinetic and clever vampire film, **Suck**; Neeson, Moore and Seyfried were in Atom Egoyan's international co-production, **Chloe**, a re-make of Anne Fontaine's **Nathalie**; Clarkson appeared in Ruba Nadda's **Cairo Time**, a quiet, intimate portrait of a middle-aged woman who strikes up an intense friendship with an Egyptian man; and Harrelson was in Peter Stebbing's poignant study of male delusion and imaginary heroism, **Defendor**.

Crossing borders in the other direction, Quebec director Jean-Marc Vallee worked in the UK, directing **The Young Victoria**,

Dilip Mehta's **Cooking With Stella**

a costume drama about a youthful Queen Victoria (the historical ironies of a Quebecois directing a film about an English monarch are multiple and delicious) starring Emily Blunt and Rupert Friend. Dilip Mehta (brother of acclaimed director Deepa Mehta) sets his engaging cross-cultural tale, **Cooking With Stella**, in New Delhi. It is the story of an Indian woman, Stella (Seema Biswas), who works in the home of Canadian diplomats, Michael and Maya (Don McKellar and Lisa Ray). Although she is befriended by the diplomats, Stella steals from them and even fakes her own abduction in order to extort the ransom money offered by the Canadian embassy.

Despite the impact of the global economic crisis and the threat of public funding cuts to the arts in Canada, the last year yielded much hope for the future of the country's cinema in the form of several impressive feature-film debuts from both French and English-speaking regions. Arguably the most dramatic debut came from Montreal's Xavier Dolan, a mere 20 years old when **I Killed My Mother** was invited to Cannes and walked away with three prizes from the Directors' Fortnight. Dolan wrote, directed, and starred in this autobiographical story of a young gay

Jean-Marc Vallee's **The Young Victoria**

Xavier Dolan's **I Killed My Mother**

man's struggles with his sexual identity and his exasperating relationship with his mother. Also from Montreal, Simon Galiero's **Clouds Over The City** was a poetic existential drama about an aging, disillusioned writer, which cleverly cast veteran independent Quebec directors Jean Pierre Lefebvre and Robert Morin in prominent roles. Alexandre Franchi's **The Wild Hunt** is a stylish and perceptive drama about a man searching for his ex-girlfriend in the murky world between reality and fiction that is the medieval role-playing sub-culture in contemporary Quebec. Franchi's is a surprisingly original contribution to an already vast body of work dealing with Canadian confusion over identity.

Set in Toronto in 1988, writer-director David Bezmozgis' debut, **Victoria Day**, is a finely observed, psychologically nuanced portrait of a teenager coming to terms with the disappearance of his ice hockey team-mate. Examining the murky territory between how one imagines one's life to be and how it really is also propels the assured first feature, **Crackie**, from Newfoundland director Sherry White. The tale of a young woman trying to cope with feckless, absent parents, a domineering grandmother, and her own emerging sexuality and need for love, *Crackie* is a coming-of-age tale with an intelligent, idiosyncratic accent. Sook Yin Lee's appealing, Patricia Rozema-esque **Year of the Carnivore** examines the quirky figure of Sammy Smalls (Cristin Milioti), another young woman searching for love and meaning, while working as an undercover security guard at a grocery store.

In English-speaking Canada, several veteran filmmakers produced new works in the last year. Vancouver-based Bruce Sweeney's **Excited** is a taut, deadpan comedy about golf club owner Kevin's (Cam Cronin) search for love and a solution to his not entirely unrelated problems of meddling parents and premature ejaculation. Carl Bessai's **Cole** is a sensitive though not completely successful tale of Cole Chambers (Richard de Klerk), a young man from a troubled small-town family who falls in love with a black woman, Serafina (Kandyse McClure), while taking writing classes in faraway Vancouver. Talented director Reg Harkema's latest, **Leslie, My Name Is Evil**, is an awkward, tonally inconsistent drama of one young woman's destructive attraction to the cult of Charles Manson.

Sherry White's **Crackie**

In Quebec, veteran auteur Marc Andre Forcier's disappointingly conventional **I Remember** chronicles a famous strike in Quebec during the politically repressive period of the 1940s. Bernard Emond's **The Gift**, on the other hand, is a masterful conclusion to his 'faith, hope and charity' trilogy (following *The Novena* and *Summit Circle*) that follows a disillusioned urban doctor into a remote mining town as she attempts to revive her belief in medicine as a vocation. Denis Cote's

Denis Cote's **Carcasses**

Carcasses is a hybrid documentary-drama about a rural junkyard owner who collects the corpses of cars, who, one day, is visited by four young adults with Down's syndrome. While the observational documentary and dramatic narrative do not mesh comfortably, this film confirms Cote's fearless approach to cinematic style. Ricardo Trogi's **1981**, meanwhile, offers an offbeat, ironic memoir of growing up within an Italian family in Montreal.

Certainly the most intense film from Quebec is Denis Villeneuve's historical drama, **Polytechnique**. On December 6, 1989, a 24-year-old man walked into a classroom at Montreal's Ecole Polytechnique, separated the female engineering students from the rest of the class and gunned them down. His rampage, fuelled by a deep-seated hatred of 'feminists' (revealed in his suicide note), took the lives of 14 young women before he turned the gun on himself. The film is a harrowing reconstruction of that fateful day, based on the testimony of those who survived. The film follows the atrocious event from the perspectives of the killer (Maxim Gaudette), a student who survived, Valerie (Karine Vanasse),

Denis Villeneuve's **Polytechnique**

and Jean-Sebastien (Sebastien Huberdeau), her classmate who feels tremendous guilt for not having attempted to stop the assassin. Alternating perspectives and flashing forward and backward in time, the tautly constructed 77-minute film is mature, non-sensational, and sensitive. Villeneuve's film does not avert its eyes from the terror of this traumatic event, but it also depicts the struggle of the survivors as they try to remember and forget at the same time. **Polytechnique** is as honest as it is unsettling, and resists the temptation to explain the atrocity. Instead, it attempts to be a cinematic version of public art, an act of collective memory.

Canadian documentary filmmaking had another strong year: Kevin McMahon's **Waterlife** is a disquieting assessment of the fate of the Great Lakes water system; Richard Brouillette's **Encirclement** delivers an absorbing, if visually pedestrian, excursion into the pathological discourses of neo-liberalist economics; Sarah Goodman's **When We Were Boys** is an incisive, observant film about boys in a Toronto private school being groomed to be future elites; Peter Mettler's arresting portrait of the massive Alberta Tar Sands oil extraction wastelands, **Petropolis**, is constructed entirely out of astonishing aerial views of the refinery and surrounding landscape; and Neil Diamond's **Reel Injun** intelligently assembles and critiques the shifting representations of aboriginal peoples across decades of cinema history.

Canada's other renowned cinematic tradition, the experimental film (launched by Norman MacLaren and continued by Michael Snow *et al*), flexed its avant-garde muscles in 2009, with three feature films. Philip Hoffman's **All Fall Down**, a striking palimpsest of personal memory and regional Canadian history, premiered at the Berlinale. Mike Hoolboom's **Mark** is an elegiac portrait of his recently deceased friend and film editor. John Greyson's formally freewheeling **Fig Trees** also premiered at the Berlinale. Described by Greyson as an 'operatic documentary', it is a

John Greyson's **Fig Trees**

multifaceted portrait of two renowned AIDS activists who work tirelessly to provide anti-retroviral drugs to countries around the world. They appear in various guises: as themselves in actual archival footage and news reports; as quasi-fictional characters; as figures in an opera by Gertrude Stein, who takes them to Niagara Falls. Saint Teresa of Avila also makes an appearance. Now that's internationalism.

The year's best films
Polytechnique (Denis Villeneuve)
Crackie (Sherry White)
Petropolis (Peter Mettler)
La Donation (Bernard Emond)
Waterlife (Kevin McMahon)

Quote of the year
'It was heroic.' ATOM EGOYAN, *describing the return of Liam Neeson (after the sudden death of his wife, Natasha Richardson, in a skiing accident) to Toronto to finish shooting his remaining scenes in* **Chloe***.*

Directory
All Tel/Fax numbers begin with (+1)
Academy of Canadian Cinema & Television, 172 King St E, Toronto, Ontario, M5A 1J3. Tel: (416) 366 2227. Fax: (416) 366 8454. www.academy.ca.
Canadian Motion Picture Distributors Association (CMPDA), 22 St Clair Ave E, Suite 1603, Toronto, Ontario, M4T 2S4. Tel: (416) 961 1888. Fax: (416) 968 1016.
Canadian Film & Television Production Association, 151 Slater Street, Suite 605, Ottawa, Ontario, K1P 5H3. Tel: (613) 233 1444. Fax: (613) 233 0073. ottawa@cftpa.ca.

La Cinémathèque Québécoise, 335 Blvd de Maisonneuve E, Montreal, Quebec, H2X 1K1.Tel: (514) 842 9763. Fax: (514) 842 1816. info@cinematheque.qc.ca. www.cinematheque.qc.ca.
Directors Guild of Canada, 1 Eglinton Ave E, Suite 604, Toronto, Ontario, M4P 3A1. Tel: (416) 482 6640. Fax: (416) 486 6639. www.dgc.ca.
Motion Picture Theatre Associations of Canada, 146 Bloor Street W, 2nd Floor, Toronto, Ontario, M5S 1P3. Tel: (416) 969 7057. Fax: (416) 969 9852. www.mptac.ca.
National Archives of Canada, Visual & Sound Archives, 344 Wellington St, Ottawa, Ontario, K1A 0N3. Tel: (613) 995 5138. Fax: (613) 995 6274. www.archive.ca.
National Film Board of Canada, PO Box 6100, Station Centre-Ville, Montreal, Quebec, H3C 3H5. Tel: (514) 283 9246. Fax: (514) 283 8971. www.nfb.ca.
Telefilm Canada, 360 St Jacques Street W, Suite 700, Montreal, Quebec, H2Y 4A9. Tel: (514) 283 6363. Fax: (514) 283 8212. www.telefilm.gc.ca.

TOM McSORLEY is Executive Director of the Canadian Film Institute in Ottawa, a Sessional Lecturer in Film Studies at Carleton University, film critic for CBC Radio One, and a Contributing Editor to *POV* Magazine.

Bernard Emond's **La Donation**

Chile Hugo Díaz Gutiérrez

2008's record of 22 features is unlikely to be repeated in 2009, considering that only nine new films had been released at the time of writing. The obvious factor is the global financial crisis. That said, timely financial policies made by Michelle Bachellet's administration offered protection to the country and to cinema promotion funds in particular. But although the government helps in encouraging creativity across a variety of areas, it still can't solve marketing and distribution problems. There is little shortage of new talent, but at the same time there is no guarantee of a sustained career for people in the industry.

Victor Uribe's gangster-themed short, **A Sacred Day** (*Un Día Sagrado*), which was selected for the Mar del Plata film festival, is a good example of the new blood in the industry. As is Rodrigo Jara Lizana's medium-length documentary, **Andergraun**, about the punk music movement in the southern Chilean city of Valdivia. Both independent works have received an amazing response from industry inner circles, but have lacked public recognition.

At the end of 2008, Cristián Galaz and Andrea Ugalde's **The Gift** (*El Regalo*) was a surprise hit. Known for *The Sentimental Teaser*, Galaz proved again how to make a film that

Sebastián Lelio's **Christmas**

generated word-of-mouth recommendations. The light comedy, about a group of sexagenarians who go on vacation, find themselves in trouble and fall in love, was the top-grossing film at the box office.

The Sky, the Earth and the Rain, *directed by Jose Luis Torres Leiva*

Jose Luis Torres Leiva's **The Sky, the Earth and the Rain** (*El Cielo, La Tierra y la Lluvia*) was less successful with audiences. Shot in Valdivia, this box-office failure was nevertheless one of the most acclaimed films of the year. A contemplative vision of three characters and their relationship to the environment around them, it is poetic, intimate and meditative in pace, with a story so low key an audience could be forgiven for thinking there was none.

Sebastián Lelio (formerly known as Sebastián Campos), who debuted with the award-winning *The Sacred Family*, returned with **Christmas** (*Navidad*). The film tells the story of three dysfunctional teenagers who share their afflictions and passions in an abandoned house on Christmas Eve. An interesting melodrama, it was presented at the Quinzaine des Réalisateurs in Cannes, receiving mixed reviews on its release in Chile.

Another significant feature was Sebastián Silva's **The Maid** (*La Nana*), which generated

 لجنة أبوظبي للأفلام
ABU DHABI FILM COMMISSION

Sebastian Silva's **The Maid**

critical consensus as a more mature work compared to his earlier *Life Kills Me*. The comedy-drama centres on an embittered woman who has been serving a wealthy family for 23 years and mistakenly believes she has been accepted as part of it, only to have her illusion shattered when a new maid is hired to help her with her chores. Catalina Saavedra received a World Cinema award at the Sundance Film Festival for her excellent performance as the maid.

The Chilean submission to the 2010 Academy Awards for Best Foreign Film is Miguel Littín's **Dawson, Island 10** (*Dawson, Isla 10*). It is based on Sergio Bitar's memoir (one of Bachellet's ministers) of his experiences as in an inmate at Dawson Island prison during the early days of Pinochet's regime. Featuring impressive performances and excellent camerawork, it is let down by a weak script, which favours vignettes over a linear narrative. The film's nomination appears to have more to do with politics than artistic merit.

Miguel Littín's **Dawson, Island 10**

The consequences of Pinochet's regime are better shown in Ignacio Agüero and Fernando Villagran's script of **Agustín's Newspaper** (*El Diario de Agustín*). Agüero's documentary features six journalism students who investigate the connection between *El Mercurio* (the oldest and most powerful newspaper in Chile, operated by Agustín Edwards) and cases of human rights violations during Pinochet's rule. It was received indifferently by Chile's right-wing press, which contrasted with the praise it received from critics and artists, who awarded the film with an Altazor award (created by Chilean artists for artists).

The year's best films
Agustín's Newspaper (Ignacio Agüero)
The Maid (Sebastián Silva)
Christmas (Sebastián Lelio)
The Gift (Cristián Galaz and Andrea Ugalde)
Dawson, Island 10 (Miguel Littín)

Quote of the year
'Unlike my previous films which nobody cares about, with this issue I was walking on eggs.'
IGNACIO AGÜERO, *explaining to the press how daring he was to make* **Agustín's Newspaper**.

Directory
All Tel/Fax numbers begin (+56)
Consejo Nacional de la Cultura y las Artes, Fondo de Fomento Audiovisual, Plaza Sotomayor 233, Valparaíso. Tel: (32) 232 66 12. claudia.gutierrez@consejodelacultura.cl. www.consejodelacultura.cl .
Corporación de Fomento de la Producción (CORFO), Moneda 921, Santiago. Tel: (2) 631 85 97. Fax: (2) 671 77 35. lordonez@corfo.cl. www.corfo.cl.
Ministerio de Relaciones Exteriores, Dirección de Asuntos Culturales, Teatinos 180, Santiago. Tel: (2) 679 44 07. Fax: (2) 699 07 83. acillero@minrel.gov.cl. www.minrel.cl.

Hugo Díaz Gutiérrez is a journalist, screenwriter, film critic, and former editor of the Catalogue of the Valdivia International film Festival.

China Luna Lin

'Booming' is one word to describe the Chinese film industry in 2009. As the country's overall economy struggles to maintain the 8% growth rate against the global credit crunch, the film market has achieved an estimated 38% growth. The theory that the box office can benefit during times of recession seems to have been proven right in mainland China. Cinemas in major cities were packed in early 2009, during the worst period of the economic crisis. And the impressive box-office figures continued through the year.

Romantic comedies are favourite among Chinese audiences this year. Though rarely successful in the past, the genre has become a major trend over the last 12 months. A continuing trend is the historical film, often featuring strong patriotic themes. The biggest of these, coinciding with celebrations around the 60th anniversary of the Chinese communist state, was **The Founding of A Republic** (*Jian Guo Da Ye*). Directed by Han Sanping and Huang Jianxin, the film tells the story of the Chinese civil war in 1947 and details the establishment of Mao Zedong's

Han Sanping and Huang Jianxin's **The Founding of A Republic**

People's Republic of China in 1949. Some 200 Chinese stars performed in the state-funded film, including Jet Li, Jackie Chan, Zhang Ziyi, Zhao Wei, and Andy Lau. The film was released across a record number of screens and launched at a time when there was little competition from Hollywood. As expected, it became the biggest Chinese-language film ever, grossing US$59.7 million.

China's box-office revenue has been growing steadily over the past five years, with an increase of roughly 20% each year. However, growth in 2009 was surprisingly high, reaching 38%, as estimated by the Chinese State Administration of Radio, Film and Television (SARFT). Its statistics show that, up to mid-November, box-office revenue had reached US$644.22 million and estimated that the total gross would reach US$878.48 million. The cinema business continued to grow, with 4,500 screens in operation by the end of October 2009, increasing 606 screens from the previous year.

The fast increase in the country's cinemas, particularly multiplexes developed within large shopping malls, is the main driving force behind box-office growth. Beijing's cinema managers' analyses that more and more young or middle-class people in the country go to multiplexes and shopping malls shows a significant change in lifestyle habits. And as China's major cities were less affected by the economic crisis, city dwellers generally see cinema going as an affordable form of entertainment.

If the country's middle class is more willing to go to the cinema, the romantic comedy genre is likely to increase in popularity. Feng Xiaogang's **If You Are the One** (*Fei Cheng*

Wu Rao) is one good example. Starring Shu Qi and Ge You, the film is about a rich middle-aged man's journey to find his 'Miss Right' through ads in the personals, but falling for a stewardess who is in love with a married man. Ge You's excellent performance, as a sincere man seeking true love, not only wins the heart of the leading lady, it also captured the hearts of audience members. In a film market dominated by action, *If You Are the One* is a new trendsetter. It was the first romantic comedy to score a breakout success at the box office, attracting USD$51.24 million and taking top place for the whole of the eight months leading up to the release of *The Founding of A Republic*.

Feng Xiaogang's **If You Are the One**

Young filmmaker Jin Yimeng's **Sophie's Revenge** (*Fei Chang Wan Mei*) was another successful romantic comedy. Zhang Ziyi plays a cartoonist who tries to win back her fiancé (Korean star So Ji-sub), who ditched her for a movie actress (Fan Bingbing). Zhang's girl-next-door look is a welcome break from her action-woman image. Despite the all-too-familiar plot, no different to the average Hollywood 'chick flick', the film features good production values and decent performances, which helped it drum up USD$14.05 million. The success of these two films has given film distributors and producers a degree of confidence about the future box-office prospects of romantic comedies in the country.

Two films looked back to the Nanking massacre, which took place prior to the outbreak of the Second World War. Lu Chuan's

Lu Chuan's **City of Life and Death**

City of Life and Death (*Nanjing Nanjing*) used powerful black-and-white images to revisit the massacre. In the place of a sensational plot accusing the Japanese of brutality, Lu's visually impressive film cleverly tells the story from a Japanese soldier's point of view, focusing on the cruelty of war and the humanity that remains between aggressor and survivor. The China-German co-production, **John Rabe**, directed by Florian Gallenberger, is a faithful biopic about the German merchant Rabe's heroic deeds in rescuing tens of thousands of Chinese civilians from the massacre.

Florian Gallenberger's **John Rabe**

Compared with 2008, there seems to be less government control on production. Fewer films had their shooting permit rejected or were banned from being screened. The production environment is significantly smoother. The total production figures rose from 406 films in 2008 to 450. The subject matter of films was also more diverse.

Wang Jing's **Invisible Killer**

Wang Jing's **Invisible Killer** (*Wu Xing Sha*) is a social thriller adapted from a true incident: a police detective investigates a headless woman's murder only to unravel a notorious extramarital affair that has been carried out online. The victim and her lover were both 'Internet fugitives', hunted by the so-called Human Flesh Search. The suspenseful film gripped with its controlled atmosphere and dealt impressively with the issue of Internet abuse.

Cow (*Dou Niu*), directed by Guan Hu, is a witty black comedy about a stubborn peasant's somewhat strange relationship with a cow. Together they survive the inferno of the Second World War, are pursued by bandits and experience other hardships. Huang Bo's vivid portrayal of a countryman of resource and Guan Hu's magical-realist storytelling made *Cow* an enjoyable film that attracted both art-house and general audiences.

Guan Hu's **Cow**

Berlin Golden Bear-winning director Wang Quanan once again worked with the actress Yu Nan on the melancholy **Weaving Girl** (*Fang Zhi Gu Niang*). She portrays a strong-willed woman working in a textile factory in Xi'an, who bravely defies the inhuman working conditions, but discovers she has leukaemia, an illness whose cure she cannot afford. Through his portrait of this stoic woman, Wang offers a biting social critique. It won the Jury Grand Prix and FIPRESCI award at the Montreal World Film Festival. But again, like his previous *Tuya's Marriage*, the film still struggles for a domestic release.

Chen Kuo-fu and Gao Qunshu's **The Message**

At the end of the year, private production power house Huayi Brothers presented **The Message** (*Feng Sheng*), an espionage thriller co-directed by Chen Kuo-fu and Gao Qunshu. The star-laden film, with Zhou Xun, Fan Bingbing and Huang Xiaoming, is set during the Second World War. Five suspects imprisoned in an isolated castle try to discover the mole in the Japan-controlled government and the key behind the assassination of Japanese officials. The impressive script, meticulous production design and superb performances appealed to audiences. It attracted US$33.89 million at the box office and drew positive responses from critics, who regarded it as the first Chinese-language film to be made in the style of a mainstream Hollywood product.

In terms of future productions, recruiting international talent and producing Hollywood-style local-language genre films is likely to increase. However, the target audience of such films will be more focused on mainland

China. Cross-region co-productions have proven to be a successful model, particularly films such as *Warlords* and *Red Cliff*. These gain more of their revenue from the mainland than other co-production regions, such as Hong Kong, Japan and Korea. 'Now that the mainland has become the biggest market for Chinese-language films, it is time for a mainland company to be the major investor of co-produced Chinese-language films,' said Yu Dong of Bona International Film Group. 'And the films we make will be more China-centric,' said Hong Kong director Peter Chan, who established, with Yu Dong, a Beijing-based production company, Cinema Popular, to produce Chinese-language films.

As China's film market expands and the box-office revenue continues to grow, the international industry has raised the perennial question: when will China loosen its restrictions on foreign films? Currently, all foreign releases in China are imported by state-owned China Film Group Corporation and only allowed distribution through China Film Group or Huaxia Film Distribution, another state-owned company. However, last August, responding to the US Trade Representative's 2007 complaint, a WTO ruling ordered China to stop forcing US content owners to use government-controlled distribution companies. Although the ruling did not address the country's 20-film per year import quota, the ruling will likely put pressure on China to open its market for competition.

Following China's appeal in September, the case is now with the WTO's appeals tribunal and will likely reach a result by the end of 2009. Beijing-based cinema manager Gao Jun estimates that expanding the import quota and opening up the market will happen soon. As for the exact date, the whole world is watching.

LUNA LIN is a Beijing-based journalist who contributes to Beijing-based *City Weekend* magazine and Shanghai-based *Modern Weekly* magazine.

Wang Quanan's **Weaving Girl**

The year's best films
The Message (Chen Kuo-fu, Gao Qunshu)
Cow (Guan Hu)
City of Life and Death (Lu Chuan)
Weaving Girl (Wang Quanan)
Invisible Killer (Wang Jing)

Quote of the year
'I'm probably one of the few filmmakers in China with good credits for investment. I almost never let my investors lose money. Before, we get the money from the government. Now, we get it from the bankers. No matter where it comes from, it is money. The most fundamental thing as a filmmaker is to use other people's money reasonably. You can't burn it!' ZHANG YIMOU *interviewed in 'China Entrepreneur' magazine.*

Directory
All Tel/Fax numbers begin (+86)
Beijing Film Academy, 4 Xitucheng Rd, Haidian District, Beijing 100088. Tel: (10) 8204 8899. http:www.bfa.edu.cn.
Beijing Film Studio, 77 Beisanhuan Central Rd, Haidan District, Beijing 100088. Tel: (10) 6200 3191. Fax: (10) 6201 2059.
China Film Archive, 3 Wenhuiyuan Rd, Xiao Xiao Xitian, Haidian District, Beijing 100088. Tel: (10) 6225 4422. chinafilm@cbn.com.cn.
China National Film Museum, 9, Nanying Rd, Beijing 100015. Tel: (10) 64319548. cnfm2007@yahoo.com.cn.

Colombia Jaime E. Manrique & Pedro Adrián Zuluaga

Jorge Navas' **The Blood and the Rain**

2009 was declared the year of the internationalisation of Colombian cinema by the national film authorities. And although it is true that the participation of national films at international festivals has increased, there is still no real strategy to access the international market.

Colombia was guest country at Mexico's Guadalajara Film Festival in March. Actor Andrés Parra was awarded the Best Actor prize for his portrayal of a priest tormented by doubts and caught up in the middle of the Colombian conflict in Luis Alberto Restrepo's **The Passion of Gabriel** (*La pasión de Gabriel*). Regardless of its clear social content, the film was marked by the televisual style that has influenced a whole generation of filmmakers.

Luis Alberto Restrepo's **The Passion of Gabriel**

The main event of the year was the participation of Ciro Guerra's **The Wind Journeys** (*Los viajes del viento*) in Un certain regard at the Cannes Film Festival. Guerra is a member of a new breed of Colombian filmmakers under 35 who have been trained in film, social communication, or advertising, and are interested in transgressing the limits of conventional narrative.

Two other films form part of this renovation of the national cinema. Oscar Ruiz Navia's contemplative **Crab Trap** (*El vuelco del cangrejo*) screened in the Toronto Film Festival, while Jorge Navas' **The Blood and the Rain** (*La sangre y la lluvia*), which explored urban violence, was selected for Venice Days, part of the Venice Film Festival.

The three features mentioned are only linked by the age of the filmmakers and the risk they take in trying to do something outside the norm. *The Wind Journeys* follows a member of the Colombian folk music tradition, *Vallenato*, as he travels through the Caribbean landscape, thus updating an old legend of a man who confronts the devil and beats him in a music duel. The more politically complex *Crab Trap* is set within a community of African Colombians in the Colombian Pacific region. The staging is as idyllic as that of *The Wind Journeys*, but the film fleshes out the clash between white colonisers and native traditions. Lastly, *The Blood and the Rain* takes place during six hours of a sordid night in Bogotá, as two characters try to share their fears and loneliness.

These three films move from a decomposed and chaotic city to a rural world where traditional and modern values clash. The political and social conflict – a recurrent theme in Colombian cinema – is not ignored in these works, but it is approached in an indirect and less dogmatic way. All three were internationally co-produced.

It is also worth mentioning two documentaries that have attracted success at international festivals. **Bagatela**, by Jorge Caballero, reflects the way in which petty crimes are dealt with in Colombia, while Camilo Botero's **16memorias** (*16 memories*) recovers and reinvents a family's film archive from the 50s and 60s.

Camilo Botero's **16memorias**

The paradox of the alleged internationalisation of Colombian cinema is that it arrives when the local box office for local films has diminished. What we can see in the near future is a shift where the audience, the industry and the people who actually make films may not have the same interests.

The year's best films
Crab Trap (Oscar Ruiz Navia)
The Wind Journeys (Ciro Guerra)
The Blood and the Rain (Jorge Navas)
Bagatela (Jorge Caballero)
Rojo Red (Juan Manuel Betancourt)

Quote of the year
'There is a discussion, still at a precarious level, about how to narrate or construct a Colombian film language. A lot of people want to speak about the reality, but there is no aesthetic idea of how to express or transmit such reality.' CIRO GUERRA, *director of the film* The Wind Journeys.

Directory
All Tel/Fax numbers begin (+57)
Colombian Association of Documentary Film Directors, Calle 34, No 6-59, Bogotá.
Tel: (1) 2459961. alados@aladoscolombia.com. www.aladoscolombia.com.
Colombian Film Archives, Carrera 13, No 13-24, Piso 9, Bogotá. Tel: (1) 2815241. Fax: (1) 3421485. info@patrimoniofilmico.org.co. www.patrimoniofilmico.org.co.
Colombian Film Commission, Calle 35, No 4-89, Bogotá. Tel: (1) 2870103. Fax: (1) 2884828. info@filmingcolombia.com. www.filmingcolombia.com.
Film Promotion Fund, Calle 35, No 4-89, Bogotá. Tel: (1) 2870103. Fax: (1) 2884828. claudiatriana@proimagenescolombia. www.proimagenescolombia.com.
Ministry of Culture, Film Division, Calle 35, No 4-89, Bogotá. Tel: (1) 2882995. Fax: (1) 2855690. cine@mincultura.gov.co. www.mincultura.gov.co.
Kinetoscopio Magazine, Carrera 45, No 53-24, Medellín. Tel: (4) 5134444. Fax: (4) 5132666. kinetoscopio@kinetoscopio.com. www.kinetoscopio.com.
Cinemateca Distrital, Carrera 7, No 22-79, Bogotá. Tel: (1) 2837798. Fax: (1) 3343451. direccioncinemateca@fgaa.gov.co. www.cinematecadistrital.gov.co.

JAIME E. MANRIQUE is a journalist and director of the showcases In Vitro Visual and Imaginaton. **PEDRO ADRIÁN ZULUAGA** is a journalist and film critic who has contributed to Colombian and international magazines and newspapers.

Ciro Guerra's **The Wind Journeys**

Croatia — Tomislav Kurelec

Instead of the usual six to seven movies per year, Croatia produced ten in 2009. It doesn't mean that the global economic crisis has avoided the country, as it will likely affect production next year. Of the releases, there were three exceptional films. Each dealt, more or less, with the war for independence during the 1990s. A good number of films have been made on this topic over the last 15 years, but only a few are very good.

Branko Schmidt's **Metastases**

The winner of the national festival in Pula, Branko Schmidt's **Metastases** (*Metastaze*) is a contemporary story, but the protagonists and their actions are determined by their involvement in the war. Now they are living on the edge, with no hope for their future in a society they helped to create. One of four friends returns after a year-long attempt to cure his drug addiction, another is still a junkie and the most sensible third has become an alcoholic who is only able to display affection towards homeless cats. Then there is the wife beater, who also bullies supporters of visiting football clubs, people of other nationalities, or anybody he dislikes, for whatever reason. Combining intense naturalism and black comedy, Schmidt has succeeded in a very powerful and grotesque portrait of one side of Croatian society.

The same level of quality was reached by Antonio Nuić's **Donkey** (*Kenjac*), the winner of the critics' prize. Set in 1995, the war is far away, an as yet undefined threat and certainly less dangerous than Boro's family problems. After seven years, Boro, his son Luka, and his wife, with whom he constantly quarrels, return to his home village. Boro is not on speaking terms with his father, whom he blames for the death of his mother. Most of these problems could be resolved if the family members were not as stubborn as the donkey that stands in the courtyard, waiting to be sold to some Italian restaurant as a 'gastronomic speciality'. The boy senses the tension between the adults and becomes attached to the donkey. The grandfather, who has also become estranged from the family, is the only one who understands the boy's feelings. This changes the dynamic inside the family and helps to heal the years of conflict. The film tells us that the characters can only achieve fulfilment in harmony with the nature of their homeland, as symbolised by the donkey. Nuić's direction offers much space for the actors to invest in their roles while shaping a very precise and engaging family drama.

Antonio Nuić's **Donkey**

After a number of high-quality documentaries, Zvonimir Jurić and Goran Dević have joined

Ivo Gregurević in Zvonimir Jurić and Goran Devič's **The Blacks**

forces to make **The Blacks** (*Crnci*), which won the Best Director award at Pula and Cottbus. It is one of the best films about the last war in Croatia. In a town under siege, the black-clad platoon of commandos are charged with sabotage and killing the civilians of the opposing side. Engaged in rescuing their fellow soldiers behind enemy lines, they discover that they have been killed. Although the ceasefire has just been announced and the order to demobilise has been given, their leader decides to take them on a revenge mission. The theme is provocative, particularly due to the story's similarity to the most notorious case of Croatian war crimes. Interestingly, the filmmakers began by choosing the actors they most admired and only after that did they look for a story, one that would suit their cast. There are no enemies or civilians present in the film, only the soldiers in black who themselves rarely speak. The energy and the strong physical presence of the actors make the long, actionless scenes exceptionally tense. Combined with the precise attention to detail, the result is an impressive picture of the horror of war.

As a country in transition and experiencing extensive social change, Croatia could be an inspiration for many intriguing film stories, but it seems that the majority of domestic filmmakers are not convinced that it could interest the public quite enough. Even renowned directors have injected some elements of fantasy into their contemporary stories. In **The Man Under the Table** (*Čovjek ispod stola*), Neven Hitrec shows a gallery of picturesque characters drifting around a suburban market. Struggling to survive, only

the most naive or mentally handicapped fail to lose human values and it takes the help of an angel for good to prevail. Dejan Šorak's **In the Land of Wonders** (*U zemlji čudesa*) is the story of poor girl Alica, who has contracted cancer from collecting and selling cartridge cases containing depleted uranium on the black market. Searching for medical care, she arrives in Zagreb, which appears like a land of wonders to her. Both films have a number of interesting sequences, but the blending of fantasy and reality is not always convincing.

Although 2009 saw a 20% growth in ticket sales, Croatian films (except the very successful *Metastases*) failed to attract audiences. With the economic crisis and probable cuts in state help, the near future of the Croatian cinema looks less than promising.

The year's best films
Metastases (Branko Schmidt)
Donkey (Antonio Nuić)
The Blacks (Zvonimir Jurić and Goran Dević)
In the Land of Wonders (Dejan Šorak)
The Man Under the Table (Neven Hitrec)

Quote of the year
'Simply we have to react. We need changes. We can't be only the observers reconciled to the disturbing situations.' BRANKO SCHMIDT *on the social content of* **Metastases**.

Directory
All Tel/Fax numbers begin with (+385)
Hrvatski filmski savez (Croatian Film Clubs' Association), Tuškanac 1, 10000 Zagreb. Tel/Fax: (1) 484 8764. vera@hfs.hr.
HAVC – Hrvatski audiovizualni centar (Croatian Audiovisual Centre), Zvonimirova 20, 10000 Zagreb. Tel: (1) 465 5439. Fax: (1) 465 5442. info@havc.hr.

TOMISLAV KURELEC has been a film critic since 1965, mostly on radio and television. He has directed five short films and many television items. Since 2007, he has been the artistic director of the festival Days of the Croatian Cinema in Zagreb.

Cuba Jorge Yglesias

Two very different films enjoyed great success in 2009: **The Horn of Plenty** (*El cuerno de la abundancia*), a comedy by Juan Carlos Tabío, and **The Broken Gods** (*Los dioses rotos*), by Ernesto Daranas. *The Horn of Plenty* deals with the shock of a family living in the imaginary town of Yaragüey upon receiving the news that they are about to inherit a significant sum of money and the hilarious consequences this has for their small community. *The Broken Gods*, Cuba´s choice to compete for Best Foreign Film at the 2010 Academy Awards, is the first feature to look at prostitution on the island. Bathetic and predictable, it tells the story of a university professor who explores the history of Yarini, a famous Cuban pimp who lived at the beginning of the 20th century. The film's fast-paced narrative combines the narcissism of a music video with a picture-postcard image of Afro-Cuban religions.

Juan Carlos Tabío's **The Horn of Plenty**

Some well-known works of Cuban literature were recently adapted. **The Thin Prize** (*El premio flaco*), defined by its director Juan Carlos Cremata as a 'sad comedy', is a classic of Cuban theatre and mostly comprises close-ups. **City in Red** (*Ciudad en rojo*), by Rebeca Chávez, is based on *Bertillón 166*, a José Soler

Ernesto Daranas's **The Broken Gods**

Puig novel about the city of Santiago de Cuba in the final years of the 1950s.

The strangest note was sounded by a low-budget feature, made in the spirit of exploitation cinema. **Molina´s Ferozz** is the story of Red Riding Hood retold by the most independent of Cuban film-makers, Jorge Molina. Veering dangerously towards unintentional parody, the film is the reverse of traditional TV soap operas – a raunchy joke where sex and violence always come together.

We stay (*Nos quedamos*), a documentary by Armando Capó, reinstates the importance of mise-en-scène in presenting reality. Employing

Rebeca Chávez's **City in Red**

the carnivalesque and collage as strategies of representation, the film focuses on a family waiting for a dangerous hurricane in a decrepit, bee-ridden house, itself a metaphor for Cuba´s state of disarray. After this remarkable work, Capó made **Tide** (*La Marea*), a portrait of a 'man without history' – an alcoholic living an isolated life on a small island off Santiago de Cuba bay. An apparently uninteresting character gives life to a contemplative piece that is an example of pure cinema.

Armando Capó's **Tide**

Armando Capó's **We Stay**

An increasing number of documentaries reveal the dark side of Cuba´s reality. In **Close Up**, Damián Saínz and Roger Gutiérrez interview young people who gather together at night in a park within the well-attended G Avenue in Havana. There they form groups inspired by emo, vampirism, lycanthropy and so on. Jessica Rodríguez´s **Near High Heels** (*Tacones cercanos*) is a portrait of Mariposa (Butterfly), a transvestite who finds sexual and personal gratification in selling his/her body for sex. **Rara Avis**, by Rolando Rosabal, restores the image of Jorge Mañach (1898–1961), a leading intellectual figure of the pre-Revolutionary Cuba who left the island in 1960 following a disagreement with the socialist character of the new regime and whose work was banned for many years. In **Thebes** (*Tebas*), Maysel Bello and Luis Alejandro P. Méndez juxtapose the testimony of the writer Antón Arrufat, another victim of state censorship, with that of a government official. Together, these documentaries prove how times in Cuba are changing.

The year's best films
Molina's Ferozz (Jorge Molina)
We Stay (Armando Capó)
Tide (Armando Capó)
Close Up (Damián Saínz and Roger Gutiérrez)
Rara Avis (Rolando Rosabal)

Quote of the year
'I feel so happy when a man pays to have sex with me. I enjoy what I do, I love to prostitute myself: I'm a natural born prostitute' BUTTERFLY *the transvestite in* **Near High Heels.**

Directory
All Tel/Fax numbers begin (+53)
Cuban Institute of Art and Cinema Industry (ICAIC), Calle 23, No 1155, Entre 8 & 10, Vedado, Havana. Tel: (7) 8383650. Fax: 8333281. internacional@icaic.cu. www.cubacine.cu.
Escuela Internacional de Cine y TV, Carretera Vereda Nueva, Km 4½, San Antonio de Los Baños. Tel: (47) 383152. Fax: 382366. eictv@eictv.org.cu. www.eictv.org.
Festival Internacional del Nuevo Cine Latinoamericano, Calle 2, No 411, Entre 17 & 19, Vedado, Havana, Cuba CP 10400. festival@festival.icaic.cu. habanafest@festival.icaic.cu (World Registration). www.habanafilmfestival.com.

JORGE YGLESIAS is a poet and movie critic, and Professor of Film History and Chair of Humanities at the International School of Film and Television of San Antonio de los Baños, Cuba.

Cyprus Ninos-Feneck Mikelidis

Although the crisis regarding the exhibition of films continues, with only American productions attracting audiences, the Film Funding Committee, part of the Ministry of Education and Culture, continues its policy of funding short and feature films. With this year's budget of €1.5 million (an increase over last year), the Committee has funded seven shorts, three documentaries, four feature films for development and two for script development, with three short films and seven documentaries already produced. Eleven feature films are reaching the final stage of development, and are expected to start production soon.

Already completed this year is **Guilt** by Vassilis Mazomenos (co-produced with Greece), with Michael Chapesis' **Dinner with My Sisters** in post-production. Mazomenos' film covers 50 years of Cyprus history, opening in the late 1950s and ending in the last years of the century, from British occupation and the fight for freedom to Independence and the Turkish occupation. This is seen through the memories – or nightmares – of an ex-arms dealer who is undergoing a crucial operation. Mazomenos, known for a number of avant-garde films, has made a stylised film with a slow, harrowing rhythm and incorporating, with some panache, ideas from Kafka and Welles.

A family conflict is at the centre of Michael Chapesis' film, co-produced with the UK. The protagonist is Dr. Michael, who returns from England to investigate his father's death and becomes involved with his three sisters and the caretaker of the parental home. This leads to a conflict and the discovery of a terrible secret.

Non-American films which, due to the current distribution, are not available to the public are at least screened during various cultural events and small festivals, which are supported by the state, such as Cyprus Film Days 2009, Short Film Festivals for Greek films, as well as Greek-Cypriot and Turkish-Cypriot films (with prizes given to the Cypriot films). Costas Yiallouridis' humorous film, **Application Instructions** (*Odigies hriseos*), was awarded the prize for Best Short Film. There are also the various programmes by the Nicosia Film Society, which this year included strands on French, Romanian and Indian cinema as well as a series of documentary screenings. Next year, a number of film festivals and events will celebrate the 50th anniversary of the Republic of Cyprus.

As for the semi-independent Cultural Institution, which was promised by the new Minister of Education and Culture, it is still being looked into. It will hopefully offer a solution to many of the current problems regarding film financing, production and distribution.

The year's best films
Guilt (Vassilis Mazomenos)
Application Instructions (Costas Yiallouridis)

Quote of the year
'Are we bastards? What are we? The affliction of Hellenism starts from our weakness to answer this question?' VASSILIS MAZOMENOS, *the director of* Guilt.

NINOS-FENECK MIKELIDIS is an historian of Greek Cinema and film critic for *Eleftherotypia* daily newspaper. He is also the founder and director of the Panorama of European Cinema film festival in Athens.

FILMING in CYPRUS

Locations, Incentives, Resources

There's always a new world to discover.

Cyprus lies at the crossroads of three continents, where East
meets West, where deep blue seas, sandy beaches,
captivating forests, breathtaking mountains, unique
archaeological sites, monasteries, churches and enchanting
locations await for you to discover them.

Probably your next filming destination.

The "all in one" Filming Destination

One Island. One natural Studio with almost 360 days of Sunshine...

Ministry of Education and Culture of Cyprus
Cultural Department (Cinema Advisory Committee)
Kimonos and Thoukididou, 1434 Nicosia, Cyprus
Tel.: 0035722800982 Fax.: 0035722809506
Email: echristo@cytanet.com.cy   http:www.moec.gov.cy

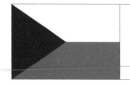

Czech Republic Eva Zaoralovà

The Czech film industry saw some important developments during the course of 2009. In particular, there were the negotiations on the amendment of the law governing the audiovisual sphere, which would guarantee greater support for the growth of the Czech film industry from the State Fund for Cinematography. There were also discussions on the procedures governing cinema digitalisation. Cinema audience figures continue to rise and, apart from *Bathory* (see IFG 2009), four Czech films made it into the 2008 Top 10.

The economic crisis hasn't affected production for the time being and the number of films produced in 2009 will be more then 25

features and 15 feature-length documentaries. Comedies and fairytales repeatedly come out on top as the most popular genres, generally appreciated more by audiences than critics. The comedy by Marie Poledňáková, **You Kiss Like a God** (*Líbáš jako bůh*), about stormy passion, infidelity and divorce, is likely to have attracted over a million viewers by the end of its run. Other notable comedies include **Thawing Out** (*Sněženky a machři po 25 letech*), where director Viktor Tauš followed on from the famous 1982 film by Karel Smyczek, about a high-school class who go off on a skiing course. Jan Hřebejk's comedy **Shameless** (*Nestyda*) was also a hit with audiences, with the popular Jiří Macháček playing a habitual

adulterer, as was **Grapes** (*Bobule*), by debuting director Tomáš Bařina, about a petty crook who gets his comeuppance.

2009 was also a good year for Czech filmmakers who were looking to gain recognition abroad. Zuzana Kirschnerova-Špidlova, a student at Prague's FAMU, won the Cinéfondation section at Cannes her film **Baba** (*Bába, 21*), a bleak study of the contradictory states of mind of a girl obliged to look after her infirm grandmother 24 hours a day. Young director Julius Ševčík was awarded Best Director in Shanghai for his drama **Angels Gone** (*Normal*), based on a serial-killer case that unfolded in Germany in 1931. Director Maria Procházková received an invitation to the Berlin Film Festival, where her film **Who's Afraid of the Wolf?** (*Kdopak by se vlka bál?*) was screened in the Generation competition. The director combined the story of a little girl whose parents are divorced with animated sequences expressing the girl's fears and hopes. International Critics' Week in Venice welcomed the first film by another young female director, Mira Fornayová's **Foxes** (*Lištičky*), the tale of two sisters working as au pairs in Ireland in an attempt to forget their past. While neither film won an award, both revived interest in new Czech film: *Foxes* was invited to the 53rd London Film Festival, where other Czech films were also screened. They include *Who's Afraid of the Wolf?* and the experimental film by Czech New Wave member Jan Němec, **The Ferrari Dino Girl** (*Holka Ferrari Dino*), a highly unusual and authentic testimony of the occupation of Czechoslovakia in August 1968. London festival audiences also had the opportunity

Marek Najbrt's **Protector**

to see Marko Skop's winning documentary from the Karlovy Vary Film Festival, **Osadne** (*Osadné*), a humorous and touching account of how 'one East Slovak village forges its way into Europe'. The chief representative of Czech film production at the festival was Marek Najbrt's second film, **Protector** (*Protektor*), which concerns a man who tries to protect his Jewish wife by collaborating with the enemy during the Nazi occupation. The Czech Film Academy have nominated the film as their entry for the 2010 Academy Awards.

Filip Renč's **Guard No. 47**

Czech productions continue to tour the festival circuit. Tiburon Film Festival in the US awarded several prizes to Filip Renč's psychological drama about jealousy, **Guard No. 47** (*Hlídač č. 47*), which also screened in competition at the Troia Festival in Portugal. The 20-minute spine-chiller, **Seance** (*Seance*), a spiritist piece by student Robin Kašpařík, was a hit in Chicago and at other American film events.

Following on from Juraj Jakubisko's successful *Bathory*, another film inspired by a legendary historical figure arrived in cinemas. This time it was the Slovak outlaw Jánošík, who lived in the late nineteenth and early twentieth centuries and whose life and death has been

Marko Skop's **Osadne**

the focus of Czechoslovak literature, as well as a film from the 1930s. The new Czech co-production was filmed in Slovakia and Poland by Agniezska Holland and her daughter Kasia Adamik. Due to financial difficulties, **The True Story of Janosik and Uhorcik** (*Jánošík*) suffered a long production schedule, which had a detrimental effect on the final film.

Dan Svátek's The Hour You Don't Know

Tomáš Mašín's Three Seasons in Hell

Like Marek Najbrt, two other debuting directors have also sought inspiration in events from the recent past, although they are too young to have any personal recollections of the periods in question. Lenka Kny, in **You Cannot Escape Your Shadows** (*Stínu neutečeš*), conveys the harsh experiences of a young lawyer confronted with the breakdown of her grandparents' marriage. Tomáš Mašín, who has a series of successful commercials behind him, fared better commercially with **Three Seasons in Hell** (*3 sezóny v pekle*). His critically acclaimed film is set in post-war Czechoslovakia, where developments following the Communist putsch of 1948 affect the lives of a young couple. The bittersweet comedy **An Earthly Paradise for the Eyes** (*Zemský ráj to na pohled*) is the work of experienced director Irena Pavlásková and screenwriter Tereza Boučková, daughter of the celebrated and controversial novelist, Pavel Kohout. The film traces the years following the end of the Prague Spring, which was brutally repressed by the arrival of Soviet tanks and culminated in the persecution of everyone involved in Charter 77.

Czech cinema has also seen an increase in contemporary themes. Zdenek Tyc's **El Paso**

(*El Paso*), about a Romany woman who refuses to place her seven children in institutional care following the death of her husband, examines prejudice towards ethnic minorities. The real-life case of a series of mysterious deaths in a rural hospital caused by a hospital attendant who secretly injects patients with lethal doses of heparin is the subject of Dan Svátek's 'noirish' thriller, **The Hour You Don't Know** (*Hodinu nevíš*). Documentary filmmaker Robert Sedláček came up with a homely rural comedy that ridicules the current political scene in his sophomore feature, **Men in the Rut** (*Muži v říji*), while Vít Pancíř's **Sister** (*Sestra*), a sombre love story based on Jáchym Topol's experimental novel, is distinguished by its intriguing style.

The way filmmakers view the current state of society is increasingly reflected in documentaries, many of which have attracted acclaim from critics and sizeable audiences. After the success last year of *René*, which won the Prix ARTE, the Award for Best European Documentary in 2008, Helena Třeštíková is now completing **Katka** (*Katka*), which captures various stages in the life of a young female drug addict from footage shot over a lengthy period. Slovakian director Peter Kerekeš' **Cooking History** (*Jak se vaří dějiny*) collected a series of awards from important international film festivals, as did Jana Ševčíková's **Gyumri** (*Gyumri*), which detailed the consequences of the devastating earthquake in Armenia during the 1990s. Other documentary films attracted considerable attention

BRINGING CZECH FILMS TO THE WORLD

at both Czech and foreign festivals. The International Documentary Film Festival in Jihlava profiled a collection of 12 promising new documentaries, among them **The Obscurantist and His Lineage** (*Tmář a jeho rod*), the latest work from the guru of young Czech documentary filmmakers, Karel Vachek.

Two animated films deserve a special mention. Young artist and animator Jan Tománek chose for his debut **Goat Story – The Old Prague Legends** (*Kozí příběh – Pověsti staré Prahy*), a comic story shot in the style of the popular *Shrek*. The engaging, poetic and playful film about toys in an old attic, **In the Attic – Who Has a Birthday Today?** (*Na půdě aneb Kdo má dneska narozeniny*), whose charm will appeal to children and adults alike, is the work of Jiří Barta, creator of the internationally recognised 1985 animated work, *The Pied Piper*.

Jiří Barta's **In the Attic – Who Has a Birthday Today?**

Alice Nellis is currently involved in preparations for two noteworthy projects: **Mamas & Papas** tells the story of a couple who are unsuccessfully trying for a baby, while **Lidice** returns to the past to re-visit the village that was razed to the ground by the Nazi occupiers in 1942, following the assassination of Reinhard Heydrich.

The year's best films

Three Seasons in Hell (Tomáš Mašín)
Protector (Marek Najbrt)
The Ferrari Dino Girl (Jan Němec)
In the Attic – Who Has a Birthday Today?
(Jiří Barta)
Who is Afraid of the Wolf?
(Mária Procházková)

Quote of the year

'Doubts accompany me constantly and everywhere. Given that self-reflection helps, I consider that a useful part of filmmaking.'
MAREK NAJBRT, *writer and director of* **Protector**.

Directory

All Tel/Fax numbers begin (+420)
Association of Czech Filmmakers (FITES), Pod Nuselskymi Schody 3, 120 00 Prague 2. Tel: (2) 691 0310. Fax: (2) 691 1375.
Association of Producers, Národní 28, 110 00 Prague 1. Tel: (2) 2110 5321. Fax: (2) 2110 5303. www.apa.iol.cz.
Czech Film & Television Academy, Na Îertvách 40, 180 00 Prague 8. Tel: (2) 8482 1356. Fax: (2) 8482 1341.
Czech Film Center, Národní 28, 110 00 Prague 1. Tel: (2) 2110 5302. Fax: (2) 2110 5303. www.filmcenter.cz.
FAMU, Film & Television Faculty, Academy of Performing Arts, Smetanovo 2, 116 65 Prague 1. Tel: (2) 2422 9176. Fax: (2) 2423 0285. kamera@f.amu.cz. Dean: Karel Kochman.
Ministry of Culture, Audiovisual Dept, Milady Horákové 139, 160 00 Prague 6. Tel: (2) 5708 5310. Fax: (2) 2431 8155.
National Film Archive, Malesická 12, 130 00 Prague 3. Tel: (2) 7177 0509. Fax: (2) 7177 0501. nfa@nfa.cz. www.nfa.cz.

EVA ZAORALOVÀ is Artistic Director of the Karlovy Vary International Film Festival, editor of *Film a doba* magazine and author of books on Czech, French and Italian cinema.

Maria Procházková's **Who's Afraid of the Wolf?**

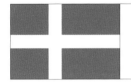
ABU DHABI FILM COMMISSION

Denmark Christian Monggaard

While 2008 was a record year for Danish cinema, selling the largest number of tickets for home-grown films in more than 30 years (4.3 million), 2009 turned out to be the worst in recent history. The 20 films released by early November had sold a paltry two million tickets and with only five more Danish films slated for release for the rest of the year – of which none had the promise or the time to make an impression at the box office – things were not looking great financially.

Of the films released, only a handful succeeded in bringing something new and exciting to the table, while other films either underperformed or disappointed in terms of style and content. The gap between art house and mainstream is widening, making it difficult to finance the smaller, artistically flavoured films, and many production companies are struggling to make a profit, some actually fighting for their existence.

If it hadn't been for Lars von Trier's latest film, **Antichrist**, which created waves all over the world, beginning with its international premiere at the Cannes Film Festival, and first-time director Martin Zandvliet's **Applause** (*Applaus*),

Paprika Steen in Martin Zandvliet's **Applause**

which made an international star out of actress Paprika Steen, 2009 would have also been a depressing year creatively. Although they didn't make much money at the Danish box office, the two films, different as they are, gave local audiences something to talk about, and the film industry and Danish Film Institute something to be proud of.

Charlotte Gainsbourg and Willem Dafoe in Lars von Trier's **Antichrist**

The much-hyped *Antichrist* is a harrowing, visually stunning and thematically rich variation on the horror film, about a married couple, played by Charlotte Gainsbourg and Willem Dafoe, who lose their young son while making love. They retreat to an isolated cabin in the woods where strange and violent events occur. The film has divided audiences – critics in Cannes were either visibly shaken or downright angry – but in Denmark it was hailed as yet another strong piece of art from one of the world's most uncompromising, genre-bending and interesting auteurs.

Antichrist sold 83,000 tickets locally, which is impressive for a film this challenging and well above the distributor's estimate of 50,000 tickets. It was the best for Lars von Trier since *Dogville* (2003), which sold 110,000 tickets.

Von Trier's biggest hit in Denmark remains *Breaking the Waves* (1996), with almost 300,000 admissions.

Martin Zandvliet's Cassavetes-inspired *Applause* was only seen by 30,000 people, but this intense and superbly acted chamber piece about an actress (Paprika Steen) who tries to reconnect with her children and life in general after sobering up made headlines when Steen won the Best Actress Award at the Karlovy Vary International Film Festival. The film was then shown at the Toronto International Film Festival and Steen again became the toast of the town. Of the 20 films released by early November 2009, nine were feature debuts, an unusually high number, and all but one suffered at the box office. This is bad news for the Danish Film Institute, which is responsible for supporting Danish cinema and administering schemes that favour cheaply made debuts.

The Buddhist comedy, **Sorte kugler**, did make a splash at the box office. The film was written and directed by the very popular stand-up comedian and actor Anders 'Anden' Matthesen and became the most successful film of the year, with more than 400,000 admissions. *Sorte kugler*, a modestly budgeted film made without the customary financial support from the Danish Film Institute (which means that those films supported by the institute only sold around 1.5 million tickets, which just isn't good enough) is a funny, albeit somewhat didactic, film about a man with a bleak outlook on life, played by Matthesen, who through a metaphysical game show learns to appreciate himself and the people around him.

Heidi Maria Faisst's **The Blessing**

Of the debuts, Heidi Maria Faisst's powerful and touching **The Blessing** (*Velsignelsen*), about a young woman who suffers from post-natal depression, was the most accomplished. Unfortunately, it was the least-seen Danish feature film, with just 1,489 admissions.

Rumle Hammerich's **Headhunter**

The latest, exquisitely made film from veteran director Nils Malmros sold 175,000 tickets. **Aching Hearts** (*Kærestesorger*) sees Malmros revisit his youth with a universal story about burgeoning adulthood. Rumle Hammerich made a comeback with the slick, effective corporate thriller **Headhunter** (*Headhunter*), which sold a solid 218,000 tickets and brought together two of Denmark's best actors, Lars Mikkelsen and the aging Henning Moritzen, who played the paedophile patriarch in Thomas Vinterberg's *Festen*.

Ole Bornedal's **Deliver Us from Evil**

In contrast, Ole Bornedal preached loud and manically about good and evil in rural Denmark, in the visually captivating but ultimately tiring **Deliver Us from Evil** (*Fri os fra det onde*). The film only sold 28,000 tickets. Across the board, any 'message' films had difficulty connecting with Danish audiences.

Of the half a dozen films made for children and families in 2009, only Charlotte Sachs Bostrup's **Karla and Katrine** (*Karla og Katrine*) did any significant business, with 175,000 admissions. The film was based on popular book by former supermodel Renée Toft Simonsen and was a decent follow-up to Bostrup's own *Karla's World*, about a pre-teenage girl and her often confusing, painful life.

The Apple & the Worm (*Æblet & Ormen*), Anders Morgenthaler's third feature film, after *Ecco* and the award-winning *Princess*, was an irreverent and amusing 2D-animated parable for 5 to 9-year-olds about a very unsympathetic apple, but it was only seen by 5,400 people in the first weekend, perhaps because it missed its target audience with its grown-up dialogue and a storyline that was too sophisticated.

Anders Morgenthaler's **The Apple & the Worm**

The actress Hella Joof, who had been honing her skills as a director with a couple of comedy-dramas, returned with her best film to date, **Hush Little Baby** (*Se min kjole*). It was a riveting, youth-oriented story about three girls who travel across Denmark in search of a new life. Although the film received positive reviews, less than 50,000 people saw it.

A few Danish documentaries made it into the cinemas. Of those, talented director Michael Noer's entertaining **The Wild Hearts** (*De vilde hjerter*), about a gang of hedonistic moped riders, attracted the best reviews, while Anders Riis-Hansen's **Blekingegadebanden**

Charlotte Sachs Bostrup's **Karla and Katrine**

was seen by the largest audience (73,000). Still, the numbers were disappointing, considering that the film was based on a bestselling account of real events: the dramatic story of a group of Danish left-wing radicals who performed a string of brutal bank robberies throughout the 1970s and 1980s and had ties to the Palestinian terrorist organisation, PFLP.

The poor ticket sales for Danish films are bound to prompt some soul searching at the Danish Film Institute, especially as overall ticket sales in Danish cinemas haven't dipped.

The Institute and the various associations representing the different branches of the film industry are gearing up for negotiations with the politicians about a new, four-year film agreement that would cover the period 2011–14. And the better the ticket sales, the stronger the industry's hand in negotiating with the Danish parliament, which more often than not has to be convinced of the benefit of government subsidies for Danish film.

Hella Joof's **Hush Little Baby**

The current, much-criticised film settlement moved subsidies from artistic films to more commercial fare and also transferred power from the Danish Film Institute to the two public service TV stations, DR and TV2, who are obliged by law to invest money in Danish cinema. Thus the more commercially minded stations are increasingly a deciding factor when it comes to financing new films, more so than the Danish Film Institute. Not surprisingly, this is an issue when it comes to the subject of diversity.

Early in 2009, the CEO at the Danish Film Institute, Henrik Bo Nielsen, discussed revising the support system, inviting 300 people from the Danish film industry to participate in an 'Ask & Listen' process. Its aim was to identify the major problems the industry faces and to find a common ground, making it easier for the industry to negotiate as a whole with politicians.

On a more positive note, in terms of quality and pure commercial power, 2010 appears more positive than 2009. Some of the most popular Danish directors are finishing new films, which will be released over the next year: Per Fly, Susanne Bier, Nicolas Winding Refn, Christoffer Boe, Erik Clausen, Thomas Vinterberg and Nikolaj Arcel. It could turn out to be quite a cinematic feast.

The year's best films
Antichrist (Lars von Trier)
Applause (Martin Zandvliet)
Hush Little Baby (Hella Joof)
The Blessing (Heidi Maria Faisst)
Aching Hearts (Nils Malmros)

Nils Malmros' **Aching Hearts**

Quote of the year
'Debate is always a good thing in life and in society. I like that kind of response. I don't take it personally. A lot of journalists have talked more about me than about the film. "Do you hate women?" they ask, and then I have to tell them, that there is something called fiction. I don't hate women. I try really hard, but it is not possible.' **LARS VON TRIER**, *talking about the harsh reactions to* **Antichrist** *and accusations of him being a misogynist.*

Directory
All Tel/Fax numbers begin (+45)
Danish Film Institute/Archive & Cinematheque (DFI), Gothersgade 55, DK-1123 Copenhagen K. Tel: 3374 3400. Fax: 3374 3401. dfi@dfi.dk. www.dfi.dk. Also publishes the film magazine, *Film*.
Danish Actors' Association (DSF), Sankt Knuds Vej 26, DK-1903 Frederiksberg C. Tel: 3324 2200. Fax: 3324 8159. dsf@skuespillerforbundet.dk. www.skuespillerforbundet.dk.
Danish Film Directors (DF), Vermundsgade 19, 2nd Floor, DK-2100 Copenhagen Ø. Tel: 3583 8005. Fax: 3583 8006. mail@filmdir.dk. www.filmdir.dk.
Danish Film Distributors' Association (FAFID), Sundkrogsgade 9, DK-2100 Copenhagen Ø. Tel: 3363 9684. Fax: 3363 9660. www.fafid.dk.
Danish Film Studios, Blomstervaenget 52, DK-2800 Lyngby. Tel: 4587 2700. Fax: 4587 2705. ddf@filmstudie.dk. www.filmstudie.dk.
Danish Producers' Association, Bernhard Bangs Allé 25, DK-2000 Frederiksberg. Tel: 3386 2880. Fax: 3386 2888. info@pro-f.dk. www.producent-foreningen.dk.
National Film School of Denmark, Theodor Christensen's Plads 1, DK-1437 Copenhagen K. Tel: 3268 6400. Fax: 3268 6410. info@filmskolen.dk. www.filmskolen.dk.

CHRISTIAN MONGGAARD is a film critic and the film editor at the daily Danish newspaper *Information*. He freelances for various monthly magazines in Denmark and Norway, serves on FIPRESCI juries and writes books on films. In 2007 he authored a book on Nordic cinema for the San Sebastián Film Festival.

ل جـنـة أبـوظـبـي للأفـلام
ABU DHABI FILM COMMISSION

Ecuador Gabriela Alemán

Once again, documentary filmmaking dominated local film production in 2009. Although most films concentrated on human rights and the social problems of the country, some took other approaches. Joe Berlinger's international co-production **Crudo**, filmed with a large Ecuadorian crew, attracted the most attention. It focused on the problems between indigenous groups from the Ecuadorian Amazon and Chevron-Texaco. Pocho Alvarez's **Open Mines, Broken Rights** (*A Cielo Abierto, Derechos Minados*) concentrated on communities where gold and copper deposits had been discovered and detailed the locals' fight to protect their water resources and traditional way of life. Alvarez also made a beautiful film about the culture of Manabí and their popular poetry (*amor fino*), **Ale y Dumas, One is Two and Two are One** (*Ale y Dumas, uno es dos y dos son uno*). Jorge Luis Narváez's **Alpachaca,**

Dirt Bridge (*Alpachaca, Puente de Tierra*) was the first documentary to focus on the history and peoples of the Chota Valley (the geographical locus of slavery in Ecuador), while Alex Schlenker's **Chigualeros** was about a salsa group from Esmeraldas, another of the strong Afro regions of Ecuador. Karina Vivanco's **Galapagos, Patrimony or Humanity?** (*Galápagos, ¿Patrimonio o Humanidad?*) aimed for a non-judgemental account of the environmental situation on the famous islands in light of their growing population.

Juan Pablo Rovayo's **Eyes That Don't See, Esmeraldas 2008**

Two recent films were directed by Juan Pablo Rovayo: **Eyes That Don't See, Esmeraldas 2008** (*Ojos que no ven, Esmeraldas 2008*) and **Making Sense** (*Consentido*). Rovayo and his crew visited different communities and prisons around Ecuador, teaching the basics of film production. They later edited the footage shot by these people, releasing it as these well-received films. **The Memory of Quito** (*Memory of Quito*), by Mauricio Velasco, explores the social mores of Quito through a series of old photographs. Tito Molina, a native of Ecuador who now lives in Spain, shot one of the most cinematic productions of the year, the beautiful **Why do the Chestnuts Die?**

Joe Berlinger's **Crudo**

Youssry Nasrallah's **Tell Us, Scheherazade**

towards the end of the year in the action hit, **Cousins** (*Awlad El-Am*). She played a housewife who discovers that her husband is a Mossad spy, with an Egyptian agent, played by Karim Abdelaziz, coming to her rescue.

The Traveller was the feature debut by writer-director Ahmed Maher. It received its premiere in competition at the Venice Film Festival before going on to open the Middle East International Film Festival. Influenced by the Italian filmmakers Fellini and Visconti, Maher, who studied filmmaking and visual arts in Italy, favoured stunning compositions and fluid camera movement over a dramatic narrative or conventional character development in telling the story of three separate days in one man's life. Egyptian screen legend Omar Sharif appears in the final third of the film, as the older Hassan, who tries to locate his grandson in order to find meaning to the journey that was his life. It was the first feature in 30 years to be produced by the Egyptian Ministry of Culture. The last was Chady Abdel Salam's

Ahmed Maher's **The Traveller**

The Mummy from 1969, which was restored in 2009 with support from Martin Scorsese's World Cinema Fund.

In 2010, a number of Egyptian actors will be co-starring in major foreign productions, including Khaled Nabawy in Doug Liman's **Fair Game**, Khalid Abdalla in Paul Greengrass's **Green Zone** and Sayed Badreya in Yan Vizinberg's **Cargo**.

The year's best films
Mechano (Mahmoud Kamel)
Tell Us, Scheherazade (Yousry Nasrallah)
The Traveller (Ahmed Maher)
Cousins (Sherif Arafa)
One-Zero (Kamla Abou-Zekri)

Quote of the year
'I wanted to prove our society wrong; Egyptian women are not weak or fragile because they play a strong role in daily life. Thousands of families rely on women like Fawzia to survive. She broke all the traditions to deal with men throughout her feelings.' *Screenwriter* HANAA ATTIA *discussing her film* **Fawzeya's Special Blend**

Directory
All Tel/Fax numbers begin (+20)
Chamber of Film Industry, 1195 Kornish El Nil, Industries Union Bldg, Cairo. Tel: 578 5111. Fax: 575 1583.
Egyptian Radio & TV Union, Kornish El Nil, Maspero St, Cairo. Tel: 576 0014. Fax: 579 9316.
National Egyptian Film Archive, c/o Egyptian Film Centre, City of Arts, Al Ahram Rd, Guiza. Tel: 585 4801. Fax: 585 4701. President: Dr Mohamed Kamel El Kalyobi.
National Film Centre, Al-Ahram Ave, Giza. Tel: 585 4801. Fax: 585 4701.

SHERIF AWAD is an Egyptian based film/art critic who also curates cinema and art focuses across Europe. Besides his contribution to Arab and European publications, he produces TV shows in the pan-Arab area.

EGYPTIAN MEDIA PRODUCTION CITY CO.

MEDIA FREE ZONE

65 TV. & CINEMA STUDIOS
16 OUTDOOR SHOOTING AREAS
POST & PRE-PRODUCTION
STATE OF THE ART TECH. SERVICES
HOTEL & CONVENTION CENTER

SHOT IN 2008:
THE JUNIOR OLSEN GANG
AND THE BLACK GOLD (NORWAY)

PRE-PRODUCTION:
RAMSES 2 THE GREAT VOYAGE (FRANCE)
THE LAST PHARAOH (UK)
DYNASTY ZERO (GERMANY)
YOUNG CLEOPATRA (UK)
THE EXODUS SCROLLS (USA)

ALL IN 1 PLACE

Highly competitive Prices
All kinds of Shooting Permits
Pre-scouting
Excellent Weather Conditions

EMPC

P.O.BOX: 31   Post Code: 12568
6th Of OCTOBER CITY, EGYPT
Email: ycrizkallah@empc.com.eg

Tel.: +(202) 38555310 - 38555311
Fax: +(202) 38555314
Mob.: +(202)0165504546

w w w . e m p c . c o m . e g

EGYPTIAN MEDIA CITY IN 2010

Established in the year 1997, **The Egyptian Media Production City** (EMPC) is set 30 km away from Downtown Cairo and 10 km away from the Giza Pyramids, thus representing a central location for not only indoor shooting, but outdoor shooting as well where the sky is clear all year long. Logistically, EMPC is provided with the latest state-of-the-art equipment, as well as experienced technicians and crews who work in local and international TV, Cinema and ads productions. EMPC comprises 65 video and cinema studios and 16 outdoor shooting locations with a variety of architectural and historical designs including Pharaonic, Islamic, Bedouin, rural, jungle, and military areas, just to name a few.

There is also the Magic Land entertainment park suitable for shooting children programs, a five-star hotel to accommodate visiting crews, pre and post-production facilities and the Nile Sat uplinks with transcontinental footprints.

EMPC also operates under the umbrella of the Media Free Zone, which gives its clients tax-free unconstrained imports on their shooting equipment. Cinema City is also a major EMPC division that comprises soundstages, printing facilities, sound unit and camera.

With a major success and established reputation throughout the whole world, EMPC is continuing its leadership in film and TV production with major international companies coming to use its facilities. The 2010 projects scheduled to shoot in EMPC include, *Ramses II, The Great Voyage*, a docu-drama that spans over the ages starting from ancient Egypt till the 21st century. Directed by Guillaume Hecht and Valerie Girie, the ninety minute is a co-production between the French company **Les films du Scribe** and **EMPC** that will entirely be shot on location at EMPC facilities, in January 2010. Also, in the first quarter of 2010, *Dynasty Zero*, a four-part documentary on ancient Egypt produced by **Gruppe 5**, a Cologne based film production company for **ZDF**, is scheduled to be shot at EMPC. Acclaimed British filmmaker Christopher Miles will be also helming *The Last Pharaoh*, an EMPC co-production of a WWII epic drama revolving around the last Egyptian king, Farouk the First.

Estonia Jaan Ruus

From the remarkable high of 2007, when ten long features were produced in Estonia, the last year saw that figure reduced by half. Producers make their money through television advertising and turn to 'making art' only when subsidised by state funds.

Of the films produced in 2009, the one worth mentioning is Veiko Õunpuu's symbolic morality tale, **The Temptation of St. Tony** (*Püha Tõnu kiusamine*), which depicts a manager's *via dolorosa* in a tough, bleak world that has lost its meaning and appears to have run its course. The film includes the influence of David Lynch and Federico Fellini, amongst many others.

An air of superficiality dominated two coming-of-age stories about youngsters from broken families. Hanno Salonen's **Vasha**, which focused on the bond between an Estonian schoolboy and a Chechen man in multinational Estonia, employed a revenge narrative as the film's moral driving force. It attempted to be a thriller, but remained too one-track to interest. Andrus Tuisk's road movie, **Bank Robbery** (*Pangarööv*), saw a masculine and crude ex-convict become the role model for a young man in search of a father figure. The boy's character is slowly revealed as the pair travel

Hannes Kaljujärv in Andrus Tuisk's **Bank Robbery**

through Estonia, but, once again, the lack of drama ultimately became too monotonous.

Liina Paakspuu's debut, **A Wish Tree** (*Soovide puu*), was another film that relied on grotesque characters in its presentation of a young, naive country girl arriving in the city. Another debut, Rasmus Merivoo's children's film **Buratino, Son of Pinocchio** (*Buratino*), which used live actors to bring to life Carlo Collodi's/Aleksei Tolstoi's well-known fairytale, was bold but lacked skill in its execution.

Several documentaries boasted a higher level of artistic merit. Jaak Kilmi's mockumentary **Disco and Atomic War** (*Disko ja tuumasõda*) created a mystic aura around the Finnish television programmes that reached Estonia,

Liina Paakspuu's **A Wish Tree**

from across the Gulf of Finland, during the Soviet era. The film ridiculed the KGB's efforts to stop the transmissions reaching Estonian homes. Meelis Muhu's **Wedding in Kihnu** (*Kihnu pulm*) enthusiastically captured the revitalisation of national customs in Estonia.

A new generation inspired by the long tradition of wildlife filmmakers emerged. Joosep Matjus's **Old Man and the Moose** (*Vanamees ja põder*) is a poetic account of a man who speaks the 'language of the moose', while Vasili Sarana's **Return of the Musk Ox** (*Muskusveise tagasitulek*) attracted acclaim at wildlife film festivals for its detailing the existence of the creatures that live within the wilds of the arctic.

Jaak Kilmi and Kuir Aarma's **Disco and Atomic War**

Another documentary, Erle Veber's **State Traitor** (*Riigireetur*), received a great deal of attention because of its subject matter: for a long time, the high-ranking Estonian Defence Ministry official, Herman Simm, sold NATO military secrets to the Russian Foreign Intelligence Service, prior to being caught in 2008.

Animation, though increasingly marginalised for wider audiences, is creating sharp, potent and surreal visions, as seen in Priit and Olga Pärn's **Divers in the Rain** (*Tuukrid vihmas*) and Jelena Girlin ja Mari-Liis Bassovskaja's stop-motion film **Oranus**.

Priit and Olga Pärn's **Divers in the Rain**

Class, Ilmar Raag's feature about school violence, which originally screened in 2007, has found success touring festivals, receiving over 20 awards, including those given by audiences and young viewers.

The maximum state subsidy for a single feature is €0.46 million: €0.4 million from the Estonian Film Foundation and €0.06 million from the Estonian Cultural Endowment. In 2010, the Estonian government will cut the total film subsidies to €3.16 million, which is roughly 25% compared to 2008's figures. It essentially means the loss of funding for two features per year.

Cinema attendance has remained largely stable in the past few years, albeit considerably low (1.22 per capita). The average price of a cinema ticket has also remained at the 2005 level (approximately €4.50). However, the new Baltic Cinamon multiplex cinema chain, which opened its doors in Tallinn in 2009 and boasts seven viewing halls and 1,600 seats, quickly forced Coca Cola Plaza – the capital's first multiplex cinema, which had enjoyed a monopoly in the city – to cut its evening ticket prices by as much as 50%, to €4.20.

The number of releases has also increased. In 2007, 145 new foreign films opened in Estonia.

The figure increased to 166 in 2008. Box-office figures have remained the same and the annual top ten films have always included at least one domestic release.

A new two-hall art-house cinema, which opened in October 2009, now regularly screens Estonian classics. The celebration of Estonian film's 100th anniversary takes place in 2012.

Estonia now hosts five international film festivals. The most prominent of them, Tallinn Black Nights Film Festival, even has three specialised programmes in addition to the main programme. Producers are also interested in the Baltic Events film market, which is held under the auspices of Black Nights. It was at this market in 2009 that inventors Kaspar and Kaur Kallas, from Digital Sputnik media studio, unveiled new digital cameras, produced with international co-operation. Oscar-winner *Slumdog Millionaire* was filmed using one of these 'Silicon Imaging 2K' cameras, the hardware of which was produced by Digital Sputnik. It was also used by Arko Okk to shoot **Where the Poetry Ends** (*Seal, kus lõpeb luule*), a documentary overview of Estonian life. Another version of the camera allows the fast representation of 3-D footage, cutting post-production costs significantly.

Digital public television station ETV 2 is regularly showing film classics. Public Estonian National Broadcasting has spent €0.4 million to launch the digitisation of its audiovisual archives and will make them available for home viewing. Estonian film life is indeed full of energy.

The year's best films
The Temptation of St. Tony (Veiko Õunpuu)
Disco and Atomic War
(Jaak Kilmi and Kiur Aarma)
Old Man and the Moose (Joosep Matjus)
Divers in the Rain (Priit Pärn and Olga Pärn)

Quote of the year
'If you like bad films, then you are probably a simple-minded and kind-hearted person.' *Film critic* **MARGIT ADORF**, *discussing the selection of Estonia's 'Worst Film of the Year'.*

Veiko Õunpuu's The Temptation of St. Tony

Directory
All Tel/Fax numbers begin (+372)
Estonian Film Foundation, Uus 3, 10111 Tallinn. Tel: (6) 276 060. Fax: (6) 276 061. film@efsa.ee. www.efsa.ee.
Estonian Association of Film Journalists, Narva mnt 11 E, 10151 Tallinn. Tel: (6) 5533 894. Fax: (6) 698 154. jaan@ekspress.ee.
Estonian Filmmakers Union, Uus 3, 10111 Tallinn. Tel: (6) 464 164. Fax: (6) 464 068. kinoliit@kinoliit.ee. www.kinoliit.ee.
Association of Estonian Film Producers, Lootuse pst 62, 11616 Tallinn. Tel: (6) 5646 7769 produtsendid@produtsendid.ee.
Union of Estonian Cameramen, Faehlmanni 12, 15029 Tallinn. Tel: 5662 3069. Fax: (6) 568 401. bogavideo@hot.ee.
Association of Professional Actors of Estonia, Uus 5, 10111 Tallinn. Tel: (6) 464 512. Fax: (6) 464 516 enliit@enliit.ee. www.enliit.ee.
Estonian National Archive's Film Archive, Ristiku 84, 10318 Tallinn. Tel: (6) 938 613. Fax: (6) 938 611. filmiarhiiv@ra.ee. www.filmi.arhiiv.ee.
Media Desk Estonia c/o Estonian Film Foundation, Uus 3, 10111 Tallinn. Tel: (6) 276 065. Fax: (6) 276 061. mediadesk@efsa.ee. www.mediadesk.efsa.ee.
Tallinn University's Baltic Film and Media School, Sütiste tee 21, 13419 Tallinn. Tel: (6) 268 124. Fax: (6) 268 108. info.bf@tlu.ee.

JAAN RUUS works as a film critic for the leading Estonian weekly, *Eesti Ekspress*. He is the founder of Estonian FIPRESCI and the Artistic Director of Tallinn Black Nights Film Festival's competition programme.

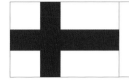

Finland Antti Selkokari

The last year was a breakthrough for Finnish debuts. Out of a total of 16 premieres, six were made by first-time directors. These included two debuts played to the Finnish strong suit – feature-length documentaries. Of those, Annika Grof's **Within Limits** (*Liikkumavara*) followed a parliamentary committee preparing the law that set the fees for health care. By recording the endless discussions of the committee, Grof distills some illuminating and frustrating facts. The mighty clerks in the ministry of finance had already decided the guidelines regarding national health centre user fees, leaving one feeling sorry for the politicians, who are left to act merely as a rubber stamp for decisions that are made on their behalf.

Annika Grof's **Within Limits**

The other documentary is Oskari Pastila's **Basket Case** (*Täynnä tarmoa*), which follows the B-league basketball club, Porvoon Tarmo, and how it treats its foreign support players. In recording the machinations of the club, from the incomprehensible behaviour of the management, who seem to have no clue as to who to hire, even down to some players' inability to handle a ball, let alone play properly, through to the relationship between team members from different cultures, Pastila

creates a no-holds-barred documentary whose humour is derived from unintentionally hilarious situations.

Jukka-Pekka Valkeapää's **The Visitor**

In recent years, the Finnish filmmaking climate has favoured crowd-pleasing genre films. However, the appearance of Jukka-Pekka Valkeapää's **The Visitor** (*Muukalainen*) indicated some kind of change. Valkeapää's diploma film from the University of industrial arts in Helsinki was one of the most talked-about feature debuts, winning trophies at several film festivals. The slow-paced drama, set in a pastoral landscape, clearly showed the influence of Andrei Tarkovsky as it followed a young boy whose only company is his mother and a horse. The appearance of a male visitor brings about a change in this underwhelming film, which is little more than a series of tableaux.

As much as *The Visitor* may have initially seemed a blip on the radar, there were other signs of filmmakers' willingness to do more than churn out 'cannon fodder' for the multiplexes. In Klaus Härö's **Letter to Father Jacob** (*Postia pappi Jaakobille*), a hardened ex-con is assigned to work as a secretary for an

Kaarina Hazard in Klaus Härö's **Letter to Father Jacob**

old priest, whose infirmity permits him the one joy of answering letters from those asking for his help. The film was aided immensely by the performances of its main actors: veteran Heikki Nousiainen was perfect in the role of the priest without a parish, while outspoken intellectual and feminist, Kaarina Hazard, convinced as the ex-con. The film features echoes of Ingmar Bergman, particularly *Winter Light*, but remains a distinctive and original piece of filmmaking.

Zaida Bergroth, whose previous short films showed great promise, chose a well-known Finnish play, Antti Raivio's **Last Cowboy Standing** (*Skavabölen pojat*), for her feature debut. The story covers several decades in the lives of two competing brothers in a tempestuous family. The film successfully explores both the fragility and frustrations of fraternal relationships.

Zaida Bergroth's **Last Cowboy Standing**

The year's most popular Finnish film was Aleksi Mäkelä's **Hellsinki** (*Rööperi*). It attracted 255,954 admissions. Mäkelä employed his

schtick of male camaraderie and violence, combined with petty crime, structuring the narrative around a collection of interviews concerning the history of Helsinki's most notorious neighbourhood between 1955 and 2005. However, Mäkelä failed in his attempt to make the great Finnish gangster film. The story of a group of childhood friends who move from bootlegging to drug dealing never fulfils its potential. The director displayed skill in capturing the period atmosphere and frenzy of youth, however, as well as drawing fine performances from the cast. This was enough to catapult the film to the top of the box office.

Aleksi Mäkelä's **Hellsinki**

Two veteran filmmakers returned to the screen. Mika Kaurismäki followed up last year's *Three Wise Men* with an adaptation of Petri Karra's first novel, **The House of Branching Love** (*Haarautuvan rakkauden talo*), which explores the lives of a middle-aged, middle-class couple. A farce in the broadest sense, it presents the soured marriage of a family therapist and business trainer. Discussion of a civilised, well-behaved divorce soon disappears amidst arguments and recriminations. The actors shine with the material, but Kaurismäki should have been bolder with his adaptation. However, audiences flocked to the film, securing a modest success with 74,000 admissions.

Jörn Donner last made a feature in 1978, with *Men Can't Be Raped*. Since that time, he has been busy directing films for television and writing books. His new film, **Kuulustelu**, tells a true story, about the interrogation of a Soviet spy sent to Finland during the Second World War. Donner handles the film with a refreshing sparseness, mainly using close-up shots of the two leads. The story plays out as a battle of wills between the Soviet, Finnish-born woman (Minna Haapkylä) and a civilised officer from the Finnish army (Hannu-Pekka Björkman). Donner uses history as a canvas upon which he paints the portrait of an idealistic communist breaking under the pressure of the situation.

Dome Karukoski followed his 2008 success, *Home of the Dark Butterflies*, with another story of youth under pressure. In **Forbidden Fruit** (*Kielletty hedelmä*) the protagonists are two girls, childhood friends from the same village. The more independent of the girls, fed up with the restrictions of a conservative religious sect governing life at home, escapes to Helsinki. The patriarchs of the village press the other girl to find her friend and bring her home. The film surprises with the turns it takes, capturing the moodiness and conflicted emotions of youth, while successfully avoiding any easy resolution.

Dome Karukoski's **Forbidden Fruit**

The Finnish box office seems to have survived the harsh economy with barely a scratch. By September 2009, admissions showed a 4% rise over the previous year. There were two year-end releases: **Backwood Philosopher** (*Havukka-ahon ajattelija*) and **Under the North Star** (*Täällä pohjantähden alla*). Both will likely reap commercial rewards well into 2010. Each play to Finnish appetites – popular novels and bucolic setting. With *Under the North Star*,

Timo Koivusalo has adapted the first part of a trilogy by the seminal Finnish writer, Väinö Linna, who chronicled the lives of a peasant family that join the Finnish Civil War in 1918, taking the side of the labour movement and becoming socialist guards. Linna's trilogy has had a huge impact on Finnish self-identity. Unfortunately, Koivusalo produced a turgid, three-hour film, which will be followed by a second part in October 2010.

Kari Väänänen adapted the work of another popular novelist, the recently deceased Veikko Huovinen. *Backwood Philosopher* is a story of a ruminative, self-taught thinker and lumberjack, Konsta Pylkkänen, played by Kai Lehtinen, who enjoys poking fun at authority figures. He is assigned to guide two biologists from Helsinki University into the woods of Eastern Finland. Sadly, Väänänen tries too hard to breathe life into his film, losing the subtle ironies of Huovinen's source.

The year's best films
Letter to Father Jacob (Klaus Härö)
Last Cowboy Standing (Zaida Bergroth)
Within Limits (Annika Grof)
Kuulustelu (Jörn Donner)
Forbidden Fruit (Dome Karukoski)

Quote of the year
'My Finnish colleagues should pay more attention to their choice of shooting locations than to concentrate solely on the substance and actors of their films.' *Director* KLAUS HÄRÖ *encourages his fellow directors to choose their locations more carefully.*

Directory
All Tel/Fax numbers begin (+358)
Finnish Film Foundation, Kanavakatu 12, FIN-00160. Tel: (9) 622 0300. Fax: (9) 622 0305. ses@ses.fi. www.ses.fi.

ANTTI SELKOKARI is a freelance film critic and journalist, who lives in Helsinki.

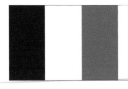

لـجـنـــة أبـــوظـبـــي لـلأفـــلام
ABU DHABI FILM COMMISSION

France Michel Ciment

The economic crisis does not seem to have affected the French cinemagoing public. During periods of depression, the need for entertainment has been proven to be greater than usual. Whatever the reasons, 2008 ended with a record attendance of 189.71 million spectators, up 6.7% on the previous year and the second-best performance in 25 years. And French films fared particularly well, with an audience of 86.14 million – or a market share of 45.4% – their highest level since 1984. With 44%, the American cinema had to concede first place – an unusual result – but it nevertheless attracted 83.43 million viewers. Due to an increase in the price of the cinema ticket, box-office figures increased by 7.7%. Compared to the decline in Italy (4.1%) and Spain (7.6%), as well as the small increase in the UK (1.1%) and Germany (3.2%), the state of cinema in France looked rather promising, even if the geographical diversity of the films on offer has become a matter of concern. European films attracted 16.59 million people (down 25.1%), while non-European, non-American product represented a miserable 1.9% of the market, with 3.55 million viewers.

A total of 555 films were released during the year (as against 573 in 2007) and, as usual, comedy was the most popular genre, with 116 films screened (21% of the films released, but 34.6% at the box office), the most successful of which were French. Animated films also struck a chord with audiences, with 9.8% of the market share for 22 films, which was slightly less than usual. Documentaries, though numerous (58 were released throughout the year), once again proved to be less than popular (1% of the market). Art-house films represented 20% of the releases and box-

office, almost half of them of French origin. They fared better in Paris and its outskirts, although the increase in cinema attendance was stronger in the provinces. All in all, an annual average of 3.24 seats per person was achieved, some kind of a record, but – a bad omen for the future – people aged more than 35 represented 54% of the audience, with senior citizens representing 31.5%. The decline in attendance among the young (less than 25) who favour Internet or DVDs might create a real problem in the years to come.

French cinema fared rather well on the foreign markets with 84.2 million spectators abroad, 15 films having been seen by more than one million cinemagoers. Western Europe and North America were the best outlets with Germany, Japan and Russia the countries most fond of Gallic features. Production proved once more very prolific (too much so?) with 240 films (an increase of 12) and a progression in investment of 25.5%, for a total of €1 billion. Belgium, Italy and Germany were privileged partners, while not one single film was shot with a British participation. Again, television was a crucial partner: 92 films were produced with the main

Alain Resnais's **Wild Grass**

channels (up 15.5%), while private stations Canal + and TPS contributed, respectively, to the financing of 142 and 46 films.

A total of 46 films received money in advance from the CNC, among which 18 were debuts and seven second features, proof once more of the constant transfusion of new blood into the industry. Distribution was on a par with the production. An average of 12 films opened each week, making it an impossible challenge for small productions with scant resources to publicise their films. To meet this considerable flux of releases, 11 multiplexes opened in 2008 (making a total of 164), while 5,418 screens (up 86) in 2,076 theatres (136 of them equipped for digital presentation) were active across the country.

The French scene, characterised by the co-existence of several generations of filmmakers, was particularly buoyed by the vitality and inspiration of the elder statesmen; a phenomenon practically unique compared to other countries, where the odd Manoel de Oliveira or Andrzej Wajda fim are the exception. Alain Resnais (born 1922) was given a grand reception with **Wild Grass** (*les Herbes folles*), both at the Cannes Film Festival where it won a special prize and at the opening night of the New York Film Festival. For the first time in his life, Resnais adapted a novel (Christian Gailly's *l'Incident*) as faithfully as possible, while still making it very much his own. His long flirt with surrealism was particularly conspicuous in a story full of fantasy and surprises, where a married man becomes infatuated with a woman whose bag he has found in a parking lot and whom he will eventually meet very late in the film. As usual, sombre thoughts circulate, but the tone remains decidedly light and whimsical. As to be expected, the direction is superb, as is the design, lighting and performances, particularly those of Sabine Azéma and André Dussollier.

Though he is Resnais' contemporary, Claude Chabrol (born 1930) is also his exact opposite. While the former renews himself constantly,

Chabrol has remained the chronicler of bourgeois life. **Bellamy** is one of his best recent efforts, an investigation *à la* Simenon with Gérard Depardieu as a detective who investigates an insurance swindle. The beguilingly leisurely style of the actor matches his director's easygoing *mise en scène*, which reveals an artist completely in command.

Claude Chabrol's **Bellamy**

Alain Cavalier (born 1931) spent much of the last two decades away from commercial cinema, instead shooting more private subjects with a video camera. With **Irène**, he has finally created his signature work. Its subject is the death of his wife in the early 1970s. The relationship between his voiceover and the fragments of reality that he films (photographs, still-lifes, landscapes, letters, etc), are all reminders of his loved one, creating a powerful emotional experience; a kind of *Vertigo* in the autobiographical realm.

Alain Cavalier's **Irène**

Jacques Rivette (born 1928), a decidedly uneven director, was not at his best in **Around a Small Mountain** (*36 Vues du pic Saint-Loup*), a rather plodding comedy about life in a circus, which lacked the charm, verbal invention and lightness of touch that the story required.

At the other end of the spectrum, as if in riposte to the old guard, some newcomers have shown signs of talent even if, for the most part, they are not of the same calibre. **The French Kissers** (*Les Beaux Gosses*) by Riad Sattouf, a comic-strip artist, is a funny and inventive portrayal of some high-school boys and their relationship with girls. **Spy(ies)** (*Espion(s)*), by Nicolas Saada, is a classical spy story with a keen sense of the genre, while Nassim Amaouch's **Goodbye Gary** (*Adieu Gary*) is an evocative account of family life in a former industrial district that has become a ghost town. Best of all is 27-year-old Léa Fehner's **Silent Voice** (*Qu'un seul tienne et les autres suivront*), where the destinies of three characters become intertwined in the waiting room of a prison: a young girl is in love with a man facing incarceration, an Algerian mother tries to understand the murder of her son in France; and a man in his thirties wants to find meaning to his life. This powerful drama turned out to be the most revelatory film of the year.

Riad Sattouf's **The French Kissers**

Some of the best films came from the middle generation. Winning the Grand Prix at Cannes and the Best Film in the London Film Festival, **A Prophet** (*Un prophète*) confirmed Jacques Audiard as one of the country's top directors. His fifth feature is among the best prison films ever made; a complex and intriguing portrait of a young man of North African origin who discovers his own identity and potential as he survives a clan war (between, at varying

times, Corsicans, Arabs and Italians) inside and outside prison. Brilliantly performed by newcomer Tahar Rahim and with Niels Arestrup as the Corsican boss, the film displays Audiard's trademark taut style, his use of violence and an expansive, emotionally engaging narrative that constantly surprises.

Jacques Audiard's **A Prophet**

Cedric Kahn's **Regrets** (*Les Regrets*), featuring Valéria Bruni-Tedeschi and Yvan Attal, and Stéphane Brizé's **Mademoiselle Chambon**, with Sandrine Kiberlain and Vincent Lindon, were two subtle and moving love stories that did not end well. In the former, a man meets a woman he has ended a relationship with ten years earlier. She has married, given birth to a child, divorced, and lives with different partner. He is also married but tries to re-establish the broken bond. As usual, Kahn adopts a swift, dynamic style, bolstering a thin storyline with a compelling and dramatic tension. In Brizé's film, another married man is attracted to his child's schoolmistress. This shy manual worker is suddenly confronted by an emotional

Stéphane Brizé's **Mademoiselle Chambon**

dilemma that changes his life. The moral and psychological tale is a French *forte* that can become tedious. But here, in both cases, the challenge is met with a real sensibility.

Bertrand Tavernier has never been satisfied working in one specific genre. His filmography testifies to the diversity he so much admired in the great Hollywood directors. **In the Electric Mist** is, strictly speaking, an American film (production, location, cast and language), yet its director gives it a distinctive touch. It may surprise as it is not plot-oriented, instead prioritising atmosphere and colourful characterisation, particularly that of the protagonist (Tommy Lee Jones), a detective investigating a murder case in the bayous of Louisiana. Adapted from a novel by the great writer James Lee Burke, the film has the flavour of real Americana.

Bertrand Tavernier's **In the Electric Mist**

With two films in competition, **Ricky** in Berlin and **The Refuge** (*Le refuge*) in San Sebastián, François Ozon proved once again that he is one of the most eclectic, daring and prolific filmmakers at work in France. *Ricky* is the fantastic tale of a baby with wings who flies higher and higher, and is protected by the love of his mother. A metaphor on the state of being different, it both provokes and teases. *The Refuge* is another kind of exercise. It is spare and unadorned, harking back to some of Ozon's best films (such as *Under the Sand*). The exceptional Isabelle Carré, one of the best actresses at work today, discovers she is pregnant (as she was in real life) after her

François Ozon's **Ricky**

lover has died of an overdose. She decides to go to the countryside, cutting herself from society. However, she is visited by her dead companion's half-brother, a homosexual, who changes her relationship to the world.

Supreme visual artist Bruno Dumont's **Hadewijch** has divided audiences and critics. Less composed than his earlier films, it is also more enigmatic, making it difficult for the viewer to perceive the director's point of view. A novice in a convent devoted to the love of Christ encounters a group of Muslim fundamentalists and participates in their terrorist activities. Julie Sokolowski is a model of Bressonian inscrutability, while Dumont is more ascetic than ever in his portrayal of a Paris that inspires him less than the austere beauty of the northern landscapes.

Patrice Chéreau, another highly idiosyncratic director, has recently focused on the confrontation between two characters (*Intimacy*, *Son frère*, *Gabrielle*). In **Persecution** (*Persécution*), he extends his chamber style to three participants: a couple on the verge of splitting up and a homosexual intruder. Chéreau brings his actors (Charlotte Gainsbourg, Romain Duris and Jean Hughes Anglade) to fever pitch, in the process creating a Dostoyevskian atmosphere full of sound and fury.

A trend of dealing with subjects inspired by real events has become increasingly popular. It has provoked various responses from the media, not always linked to the cinematic aspects of the films. However, some directors

Claude and Nathan Miller's **I'm Glad That My Mother is Alive**

have found genuine inspiration in the world at large. In **I'm Glad That My Mother is Alive** (*Je suis heureux que ma mère soit vivante*), Claude Miller and his son Nathan made a powerful film about a young man who was adopted, decides to find out who his real mother is and finally resolves to kill her. The unknown actor – but future star – Vincent Rottiers and some unfamiliar faces lend credibility to this unusual real-life story.

Pierre Trividic and Patrick Mario Bernard adapted Annie Ernaux's autobiographical text 'L'Occupation' for **The Other One** (*l'Autre*), about the ravages of jealousy, where a woman who has decided to leave her companion discovers that he has a new mistress. We never see the other woman but witness the obsession that ultimately becomes destructive. It features a haunting and compelling performance by Venice Film Festival award winner, Dominique Blanc.

In **Rapt**, Lucas Belvaux recreated the kidnapping of a famous banker who was kept prisoner by a group of hoodlums awaiting his ransom. While captive, his private life is disclosed in the press and his business associates abandon him. Yvan Attal offers another stunning performance, with the remarkable Anne Consigny playing the wife, hurt by revelations in the press about her husband's infidelities. André Téchiné was less successful in **The Girl on the Train** (*la Fille du RER*), where too many characters and incidents dilute what was a potentially strong central theme: a mythomaniac convinces the

media and the people in her life that she was assaulted on the subway by a gang of anti-Semites. Meanwhile, Xavier Giannoli's **In the Beginning** (*À l'origine*) featured an excellent François Cluzet as a swindler who manages to sell a highway project to a provincial northern town. Finally, illegal immigration is dealt with head-on in Philippe Lioret's powerful **Welcome**. A swimming teacher, convincingly played by Vincent Lindon, helps a young Turk to swim across the English Channel in order to meet his beloved in London. Lioret, a rising star among French filmmakers, blended a strong, realistic style with a subtle handling of repressed emotions.

Philippe Lioret's **Welcome**

Documentaries are, of course, a more straightforward way to deal with present or past realities. Among the releases, one should single out **La danse, le ballet de l'Opéra de Paris**. Frederic Wiseman offers both a dazzling look at an institution and one of the great cinematic tributes to classical dance. Denis Gheerbrant's **La République Marseille** is an investigation across seven parts into the southern city, its social and economic conditions and its motley population. In **My**

Serge Bromberg's **Henri-Georges Clouzot's Inferno**

Oceans *directed by Jacques Perrin and Jacques Cluzaud*

Greatest Escape (*Ne me libérez pas, je m'en charge*), Fabienne Godet interviews an ex-convict famous for his daring escape from prison. Serge Bromberg's **Henri-Georges Clouzot's Inferno** (*L'enfer d'Henri-Georges Clouzot*) investigates the Clouzot film that was never finished and where Romy Schneider, at 24, was at the peak of her beauty. Finally, **Oceans** by Jacques Perrin and Jacques Cluzaud is a masterpiece about life under water where reality reveals itself in more fantastic ways than Hollywood films like *Jurassic Park*. These are extraordinary images that one has rarely seen the likes of before.

Jean-Pierre Jeunet's **Micmacs**

Among the dozens of comedies, most of which are hard to export, one should mention Jean-Pierre Jeunet's **Micmacs** (*Micmacs à tire-larigot*), a film in the spirit of Jacques Tati, with its collection of odd-balls, circus performers and tramps who fight against weapon manufacturers and merchants in a picturesque Paris, and Bruno Podalydès **Park Benches** (*Bancs publics (Versailles Rive Droite)*), an

uneven but highly original film, *à la* Altman, about the denizens of Versailles.

The year's best films
Wild Grass (Alain Resnais)
Irène (Alain Cavalier)
I'm Glad That My Mother is Alive
(Claude Miller and Nathan Miller)
A Prophet (Jacques Audiard)
Welcome (Philippe Lioret)

Directory
All Tel/Fax numbers begin (+33)
Archives du Film, 7 bis rue Alexandre Turpault, 78395 Bois d'Arcy. Tel: (1) 3014 8000. Fax: (1) 3460 5225.
Cahiers du Cinema, 9 passage de la Boule Blanche, 75012 Paris. Tel: (1) 5344 7575. Fax: (1) 4343 9504. cducinema@lemonde.fr.
Centre National de la Cinématographie, 12 rue de Lubeck, 75016 Paris. Tel: (1) 4434 3440. Fax: (1) 4755 0491. webmaster@cnc.fr. www.cnc.fr.
Cinémathèque de Toulouse, BP 824, 31080 Toulouse Cedex 6. Tel: (5) 6230 3010. Fax: (5) 6230 3012. contact@lacinemathequedetoulouse.com. www.lacinemathequedetoulouse.com.
Cinémathèque Française, 4 rue de Longchamp, 75116 Paris. Tel: (1) 5365 7474. Fax: (1) 5365 7465. contact@cinemathequefrancaise.com. www.cinematequefrancaise.com.
Ile de France Film Commision, 11 rue du Colisée, 75008 Paris. Tel: (1) 5688 1280. Fax: (1) 5688 1219. idf-film@idf-film.com. www.iledefrance-film.com.
Institut Lumière, 25 rue du Premier-Film, BP 8051, 69352 Lyon Cedex 8. Tel: (4) 7878 1895. Fax: (4) 7878 3656. contact@institut-lumiere.org. www.institut-lumiere.org.
Positif, 3 rue Lhomond, 75005 Paris. Tel: (1) 4432 0590. Fax: (1) 4432 0591. www.johnmichelleplace.com.
Unifrance, 4 Villa Bosquet, 75007 Paris. Tel: (1) 4753 9580. Fax: (1) 4705 9655. info@unifrance.org. www.unifrance.org.

MICHEL CIMENT is president of FIPRESCI, a member of the editorial board of *Positif*, a radio producer and author of more than a dozen books on cinema.

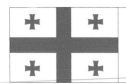

Georgia Nino Ekvtimishvili

Five of the ten films playing at cinemas in Tbilisi at the end of 2009 were Georgian productions. The most remarkable was a Georgian-Kazakh co-production, Giorgi Ovashvili's feature debut, **The Other Bank** (*Gagma Napiri*), about a 12-year-old refugee from Abkhazia, who travels alone from Tbilisi to his homeland in search of his father, who has remained in Abkhazia during the war, following a heart attack. First shown at the Berlinale, the film had already taken part in 11 international film festivals, picking up numerous prizes. It is Georgia's official entry for the 2010 Academy Awards and is shortlisted for the European Film Academy European Discovery Award.

Tredo Bekauri in Giorgi Ovashvili's **The Other Bank**

Irakli Faniashvili's short, **Sergo the Rogue** (*Sergo Gotorani*), also dealt with the plight of Abkhazian refugees. Adopting a documentary style, the film features real refugees from Abkhazia in its tale of a little boy whose family lives in a poor suburb of Tbilisi and struggles to survive on a daily basis.

Vano Burduli's **Conflict Zone** (*Konfliktis Zona*) portrays the post-Soviet Caucasus as a large expanse troubled by ethnic conflicts. A Tbilisi drug addict, gambler and Sukhumi sniper travel together to Karabakh in order to buy

missiles from Azeries for the Georgian military in Abkhazia. Acclaimed by critics, Burduli's film won the Perspectives Competition at the Moscow International Film Festival.

Vano Burduli's **Conflict Zone**

War continued to dominate Georgian cinema throughout the year. Miguel Angel Jimenez Colmenar, in his Spanish-Georgian feature debut **Ori**, tells two stories which take place following the recent five-day Russia-Georgia conflict. The fighting may have stopped, but for those suffering from grief and sadness in the post-war silence, it still rages. Often, the faces of those who are silent express more than words ever could. Salome Jashi's short, expressionistic documentary, **Speechless** (*Dadumebulebi*), was made immediately after the Russia-

Miguel Angel Jimenez Colmenar's **Ori**

Irakli Faniashvili's **Sergo The Rogue**

Georgia ceasefire. The camera looks into the eyes of people who experienced the conflict first-hand. A stranger is on the verge of crying, a young man drifts into a restless sleep, a girl covers her eyes with her hand. They are all speechless.

Nutsa Alexi-Meskhishvili's short comedy-drama, **The Happiness** (*Bedniereba*), tells the story of one Georgian family, where the wife, who works illegally in Italy, is not able to attend her husband's funeral in Georgia. She decides to participate in the ceremony via her mobile phone. Neighbours and relatives attending the burial listen to her voice through large loudspeakers. The film was awarded a special diploma at the Venice Film Festival.

2010 sees the first Georgian co-production with a Hollywood studio. Renny Harlin's untitled drama is based on actual events that took place during the recent Russia-Georgia war. Meanwhile, Serb director Emir Kusturica turned down an offer from a Russian studio to shoot a film about the same conflict.

In order to attract foreign filmmakers and expand the local industry, the Georgian Film Centre has succeeded in tabling the possibility of introducing lucrative tax breaks. If these are approved, foreign investors could see a return of 25% on investments over USD$500,000.

NINO EKVTIMISHVILI is a freelance journalist who specialises in cinema and art in Georgia.

The year's best films
The Other Bank (Giorgi Ovashvili)
Ori (Miguel Angel Jimenez Colmenar)
Sergo The Rogue (Irakli Faniashvili)
Speechless (Salome Jashi)

Quote of the year
'We want to bring the film to Abkhazian and Ossetian spectators. This war is a sorrow of all of us. Abkhazians as Georgians are victims in this conflict.' GIORGI OVASHVILI *talking about* The Other Bank.

Directory
All Tel/Fax numbers begin (+995)
Film Studio – Remka, 36 Kostava St., 0179 Tbilisi. Tel: (32) 990 542. Fax: (32) 933 871. remka@remkafilm.ge. www.remkafilm.ge.
Georgian National Film Center, 164, Davit Agmashenebeli Av., 0112 Tbilisi. Tel: (32) 34 29 75, (32) 34 28 97. office@filmcenter.ge.
Independent Filmmakers' Association – South Caucasus (IFA-SC), Head Office – Georgia, Niko Nikoladze Street 1, Apt. 12, 0108 Tbilisi. Tel: (32) 93 12 50. Fax: (32) 50 60 68. ifasc@ifasc.org.ge.
Ministry of Culture, Sport and Monument Protection, 4 Marjvena Sanapiro St., 0105 Tbilisi. Tel: (32) 98 74 30. info@mc.gov.ge.
Sakdoc Film – 2007, 121 Zemo Vedzisi St., 0160 Tbilisi. Tel: (93) 24 32 72/(93) 32 39 29. info@sakdoc.ge. www.sakdoc.ge.
Sanguko Films, 7 Tamarashvili St., 0162 Tbilisi. Tel: (32) 22 40 61. info@sanguko.ge. www.sanguko.ge.
Shota Rustaveli Theater and Cinema State University of Georgia, 19, Rustaveli Av., 0108 Tbilisi. Tel: (32) 99 94 11. Fax: (32) 99 05 75. info@tafu.edu.ge. www.tafu.edu.ge.
Studio 99, 10 Sharashidze St., 0162 Tbilisi. Tel: (32) 220 79064. Fax: (32) 230 412. Berlin office: Greifenhagener Str. 26, D-10437 Berlin, Germany. Tel: (+49 30) 44031861. Fax: (+49 30) 44031860.
Taia Group Ltd., 74, Chavchavadze Ave., 0162 Tbilisi. Tel: (32) 912 945. Fax: (32) 253 072.
Tbilisi International Film Festival (Georgia), 164, David Agmashenebeli Av., 0112 Tbilisi. Tel: (32) 35 67 60. office@tbilisifilmfestival.ge. www.tbilisifilmfestival.ge.

Germany Andrea Dittgen

A little red-haired boy wearing a strange-looking helmet with horns dominated the domestic box office. **Vicky the Viking** (*Wickie und die starken Männer*), a humorous adventure film for children by popular comedian, actor and director Michael Herbig, was the year's surprise hit, with 4.8 million admissions. It was outpaced only by two international blockbusters: *Ice Age 3* and *Harry Potter and the Half-Blood Prince*. Despite the global economic crisis, German films in 2009 equalled 2004's business, a notable year when 36.7 million cinemagoers went to see local releases.

Jonas Hämmerle in Michael Herbig's **Vicky the Viking**

Vicky wasn't alone. 2009 was the year of children's film in German cinema. Vivian Naefe's **Wild Chicks and Life** (*Die wilden Hühner und das Leben*), the last entry in the successful series about a girls' gang tricking boys and teachers, and in turn being struck by first love, offered new settings with a well-constructed plot. It turned out to be the best of the three films based on the children's books. Only 500,000 people saw the male equivalent, **Gangs**, by Rainer Matsutani, a variation on the franchise *The Wild Soccer Bunch 1-5*, with Jimi Blue Ochsenknecht

once again playing the lead. **Lilly the Witch: The Dragon and the Magic Book** (*Hexe Lilli – Der Drache und das magische Buch*) was also an adaptation, with caves, girls and secrets thrown into the mix. Austrian director Stefan Ruzowitzky seamlessly mixed real life and fantasy scenes in a film that contrasted starkly with his previous, Academy Award-winning effort, *The Counterfeiters*. Half a million children saw Tony Loeser and Jesper Møller's animated film, **Friends Forever** (*Mullewapp*). Combining stories from the book series of the same name, about the friendship between animals in a barn, the old-fashioned, but lovingly drawn, adventure featured vivid colours and singing, hitting exactly the right note for younger viewers. Even Piet De Rycker and Thilo Rothkirch's more conventionally animated adaptation of the serial about a courageous little girl, **Laura's Star and the Mysterious Dragon Nian** (*Lauras Stern und der geheimnisvolle Drache Nian*), was seen by 500,000 viewers.

Eleven German productions or co-productions passed the benchmark of one million admissions, even before the Christmas-blockbuster season. Most of them were comedies, with two featuring lowbrow jokes

Simon Verhoeven's **Männerherzen**

and stereotypes geared towards German men who don't want to grow up. **Männerherzen** (literally, *Men's Hearts*) by Simon Verhoeven and **Männersache** (*Men's Stuff*) by Gernot Roll each attracted two million viewers. The former starred the permanent womaniser Til Schweiger, now in his 40s, with the latter featuring the nerdy comedian Mario Barth.

Shot in local dialect to ridicule regionally challenged German politicians just prior to the German elections, **Horst Schlämmer – I Run for Chancellor** (*Horst Schlämmer – Isch kandidiere*) marks the first appearance of TV satirist Hape Kerkeling as everyman Horst Schlämmer. Admittedly, it was only funny for a short time, but helped to push up domestic ticket sales.

Hape Kerkeling in **Horst Schlämmer – I Run for Chancellor**

German audiences loved **Pope Joan** (*Die Päpstin*) by Sönke Wortmann, the adaptation of a ninth century story about a woman who disguised herself as a man and rose through the Vatican's ranks, eventually becoming pope. Many people doubted that comedy specialist Wortmann was the right director for an English-language, big-budget period film, a mixture of art-house and action movie, even after his successful football documentary, *Germany: a Summer's Fairytale*. Another literary adaptation that passed the one-million-admission mark, **Desert Flower** (*Wüstenblume*) by Sherry Hormann, was based on the bestselling book by Waris Dirie, about her life as a girl from Somalia, sold into marriage and eventually becoming a supermodel and UN spokeswoman against female circumcision. Hormann

Johanna Wokalek in Sönke Wortmann's **Pope Joan**

succeeded in making a Hollywood-style film with a slight European touch. Former short film Academy Award winner Florian Gallenberger tried to do the same with more money and fewer clichés. But the long-awaited **John Rabe**, a true story about the German businessman who saved more than 200,000 Chinese during the Nanjing massacre in 1937–38, featuring domestic stars Ulrich Tukur and Daniel Brühl, only attracted 168,000 viewers.

When it comes to the biopic, it seems that Germans prefer women's stories, perhaps because their life can be more rebellious or fascinating. **Hilde**, about the famous singer and actress Hildegard Knef, who was the first naked woman on screen in German post-war cinema, was directed by Kai Wessel. **Effi Briest**, the remake – after R.W. Fassbinder – of Theodor Fontaine's novel by Hermine Huntgeburt, starred Julia Jentsch in the title role. Sadly, Margarethe von Trotta's **Vision – The Life of Hildegard von Bingen** (*Vision – Aus dem Leben der Hildegard von Bingen*), about a nun, mystic, poet and scientist of the 12th century who founded a cloister for women, was arid and tedious. Each of these films was watched by an audience of 400,000.

All these films, as well as approximately 80 other productions, received money from the German Federal Film Fund (DFFF), which offered for the third consecutive year a total of €60 million in aid. But for the first time, German-American co-productions not only benefited from DFFF, they also proved to be a domestic success. Stephen Daldry's **The**

Reader (*Der Vorleser*), adapted from Bernard Schlink's international bestseller, attracted 2.2 million admissions, while Quentin Tarantino's brilliant Nazi satire, **Inglourious Basterds**, followed with 2.1 million admissions. Even Bryan Singer's **Valkyrie** (*Operation Walküre*) was seen by 1.3 million people.

History is a beloved subject in German cinema, which might explain the genesis of **Germany 09**, an omnibus-film by 13 leading directors (led by Tom Tykwer) about the state of Germany. It attempted to capture the mood around the twentieth anniversary of the fall of the Berlin Wall, whilst alluding to the classic 1978 political portmanteau, *Germany in Autumn*. The new interpretation surprised with its wide range of themes and genres, from the politics of the past (a fantasised discussion between philosopher Susan Sontag, terrorist Ulrike Meinhof and a young female director in 1969) to globalisation (Tom Tykwer's story of a globetrotting businessman ending up in similar hotels across the world). Widely discussed at the Berlinale, the film failed at the box office because of its length (153 minutes) and high-mindedness.

Angela Schanelec's **First Day**, *part of* Germany 09

Tykwer's thriller **The International**, about an agent fighting the world of finance, was technically impressive but maybe too elaborate ,and ultimately failed to ignite the box office (700,000 admissons). However, its set-piece shoot-out in New York's Guggenheim museum has earned it a place in film history.

The more demanding **The White Ribbon** (*Das weiße Band*) by Austrian director Michael

Michael Haneke's **The White Ribbon**

Haneke turned out to be an art-house hit, with 300,000 viewers, after winning the Palme d'Or in Cannes. Prior to the outbreak of the First World War, strange occurrences take place in a Protestant village in northern Germany. People are hurt or die in mysterious circumstances. Shot in black and white, Haneke focuses on the village children, perfectly creating an old-fashioned horror film, which nevertheless offers no clues as to what is going on. No other German production of 2009 made such a strong and long-lasting impression on viewers.

Back to genre films, Fatih Akin's first comedy, **Soul Kitchen**, plays out like a Heimat film. However, it is not located in the country but in Hamburg, where people of various nationalities act like villagers in the 'Soul Kitchen' restaurant. Akin focuses on love, economics and family ties between Germans and immigrants, who are quick to adapt to their new surroundings. Excellent timing and the use of soul music link the fates and fortunes of the characters, who struggle to survive the financial crisis.

Film production in Germany continued at an impressive level. More than 100 features were shot and most were of a remarkably high quality. However, the majority of the production and distribution companies were forced to downsize as a result of the economic crisis.

The most important topic in the industry was how to finance the digitalisation of cinemas, an inevitable move with the new rafter of 3D films soon to be released. Which is where the biggest problem lies in Germany these days.

There is government money available for digitalisation, but there is an ongoing disagreement between theatre owners – who have to pay a levy – and the state funding bodies. The levy was disputed by some theatre chains, throwing a wrench into the digital expansion project.

No one but veteran Wim Wenders was shooting in digital 3D. His new documentary, **Pina**, about the legendary German dancer and choreographer Pina Bausch, will be released in 2011.

In the meantime, forthcoming films include **Goethe!** by Philipp Stölzl, about the great love of the young, passionate German poet. There are the sequels, **Lilly the Witch: Trip to Mandolan** (Hexe Lilli – Reise nach Mandolan) and **Zweiohrküken**, Til Schweiger's follow-up to the 2008 romantic comedy and box-office hit, Rabbit without Ears. And finally, **Jew Süß – Film without Conscience** (Jud Süß – Film ohne Gewissen) by Oskar Roehler.

The year's best films
The White Ribbon (Michael Haneke)
Germany 09 (Fatih Akin, Wolfgang Becker, Sylke Enders, Dominik Graf, Martin Gressmann, Christoph Hochhäusler, Romuald Karmakar, Nicolette Krebitz, Dani Levy, Angela Schanelec, Hans Steinbichler, Isabelle Stever, Tom Tykwer, Hans Weingarten)
Pope Joan (Sönke Wortmann)
Soul Kitchen (Fatih Akin)
John Rabe (Florian Gallenberger)

Quotes of the year
'The power of cinema is going to bring down the Third Reich. And I get a big kick out of that.' QUENTIN TARANTINO, *explaining* **Inglourious Basterds.**

ANDREA DITTGEN is a film critic and editor of the daily newspaper *Die Rheinpfalz* and also a contributor to the magazine *Filmdienst*. She is a member of the board of the German Film Critics Association and web editor for the International Federation of Film Critics (www. fipresci.org).

'It's like sitting in a privileged row in the theatre.' WIM WENDERS, *on shooting his documentary* **Pina** *in digital 3D.*

Directory
All Tel/Fax numbers begin (+49)
Deutsches Filminstitut-DIF, Schaumainkai 41, 60596 Frankfurt am Main. Tel: (69) 961 2200. Fax: (69) 620 060. info@deutsches-filminstitut.de. www. deutsches-filminstitut.de.
Deutsches Filmmuseum Frankfurt am Main, Schaumainkai 41, 60596 Frankfurt am Main. Tel: (69) 2123 8830. Fax: (69) 2123 7881. info@ deutsches-filmmuseum.de. www.deutsches-filmmuseum.de.
Federal Film Board (FFA), Grosse Praesidentenstr 9, 10178 Berlin. Tel: (30) 275 770. Fax: (30) 2757 7111. www.ffa.de.
Filmmuseum Berlin-Deutsche Kinemathek, Potsdamer Str 2, 10785 Berlin. Tel: (30) 300 9030. Fax: (30) 3009 0313. info@filmmuseum-berlin.de. www. filmmuseum-berlin.de.
German Films Service & Marketing GmbH, Herzog-Wilhelm-Strasse 16, 80331 Munich. Tel: (89) 599 787-0. Fax: (89) 599 78730. info@german-films. de. www.german-films.de.
Münchner Stadtmuseum/Filmmuseum, St Jakobsplatz 1, 80331 Munich. Tel: (89) 2332 2348. Fax: (89) 2332 3931. filmmuseum@muenchen.de. www. stadtmuseum-online.de/filmmu.htm.
New German Film Producers Association, Agnesstr 14, 80798 Munich. Tel: (89) 271 7430. Fax: (89) 271 9728. ag-spielfilm@t-online.de.
Umbrella Organisation of the Film Industry, Kreuzberger Ring 56, 65205 Wiesbaden. Tel: (611) 778 9114. Fax: (611) 778 9169. statistik@spio-fsk.de.

Fatih Akin's **Soul Kitchen**

Greece Ninos-Feneck Mikelidis

Notwithstanding the comparatively small amount of money spent on film production (the Greek Film Centre received only €3.5 million in 2009), the number of completed feature films rose above 40 in the last year. This rise was due in part to the use of digital technology. However, most of these films have yet to be distributed.

Farcical, knockabout comedies, mainly made for home-consumption and employing stars from television, as well as parodies of foreign films and remakes of classic Greek comedies were the most successful films at the box office. These enabled production companies to invest in other projects.

The most important film of the year was the second part of Theo Angelopoulos' trilogy (following on from *The Weeping Meadow*), **The Dust of Time** (*I Skoni tou chronou*). It deals with the hopes and disappointments of the Left, as witnessed by a film director who is trying to record the odyssey of his parents over 50 years; from the civil war in Greece, continuing through the story of the self-exiled Greek communists in Tashkent, and ending with the fall of the Berlin Wall. Angelopoulos takes us on a journey through time and

Theo Angelopoulos' **The Dust of Time**

memory, featuring a series of stunning images, which highlight the betrayal of an ideology.

Personal relationships and a lack of human contact are at the centre of Alexandros Avranas' first feature, **Without**. It tells the story of a young couple and their child, who live out their daily lives without love, existing in a Kafkaesque hell from which they cannot escape. Avranas details their existence through a series of small, well-structured, expressionistic scenes.

Panos Koutras' **A Woman's Way**

Panos Koutras' **A Woman's Way** (*Strella*), shown in the Panorama Section of the Berlin Film Festival, deals with the love story between a recently released convict and Strella, a young transsexual prostitute who, somewhere in the middle of the plot, is revealed to be the man's lost son. Successfully incorporating elements of ancient Greek tragedy into his plot, Koutras' portrait of Strella is almost documentary in style and is accompanied by provocative dialogue, explicit sex and a fair amount of subversive humour, before the film reaches its unexpected ending.

Dogtooth (*Kynodontas*), the second film by Yorgos Lanthimos and winner of Un Certain

Regard prize at the Cannes Film Festival, is about a middle-class couple who keep their three teenage children imprisoned in their well-protected house, deceiving them about what is happening in the world. Lanthimos' allegory of the socio-political state of middle-class society features some interesting ideas in its detached approach and use of humour. However, the naïve dialogue and deliberately slow tempo, not to mention the clumsy handling of different styles, diminish the film's impact.

Pantelis Voulgaris' **Deep Soul** (*Psyhi Vathia*) is set in 1949, the last year of the Greek civil war. It is viewed through the eyes of two brothers fighting on different sides – the communist guerrillas and the army of the right-wing government, which is supported by the US. the director's approach is straightforward, frequently tinged with melodrama and features some impressive battle scenes in his account of political reconciliation. However, superficial characterisation and an oversimplification of the process that took place lead to significant historical errors.

Yiorgos Angelkos in Pantelis Voulgaris' **Deep Soul**

In Philippos Tsitos' comedy, **Plato's Academy** (*Akademia Platonos*), the protagonist, the racist Greek owner of a haberdashery who, together with his bigoted friends, sits outside his store and makes fun of Albanians, discovers that his roots are Albanian. Although the plot is thin and direction lacks real muscle, the film's humour and sharp dialogue shine through, and Antonis Kafetzopoulos gives an

Antonis Kafetzopoulos (centre) on set in Philippos Tsitos' **Plato's Academy**

excellent central performance, which won him the Best Actor award at the Locarno Film Festival.

Dimitris Kollatos returned to the cinema after a long break to make one of his best films, **The Testament of Father Jean Melies**. The story of a present-day country priest, influenced by an atheist priest from seventeenth-century France, it gave the director an opportunity to present the priest's life through austere black-and-white imagery, strongly reminiscent of Bresson.

Cantine (*Kantina*), the first feature by Stavros Kaplanidis, was written by filmmaker Stavros Tsiolis. A day in the life of a fast-food truck owner, it features clever dialogue, original gags and solid direction, resulting in a pleasing, low-profile, Jacques Tati-style comedy.

In Pericles Hoursoglu's **The Caretaker**, a married man with two children takes over as caretaker of a building where his mother lives. What begins as an amusing comedy, mid-way through transforms into a drama, losing its impact and tempo along the way.

The decline of an aristocratic family in Corfu and the ascent of the new middle class at the beginning of the twentieth-century, as seen through the tragic love affair between a young aristocratic girl and a poor, romantic intellectual, is the subject of Toni Lycouresis' **Slaves in Their Own Chains** (*Sklavi sta desma tous*). Winner of the state prize for best film, it is a flat, overlong drama that resembles a costume series made by the BBC.

Four documentaries managed to find their way into cinemas. Stelios Haralambopoulos' **The Night That Fernando Pessoa Met Constantine Cavafy** (*Ti nyhta pou o Fernando Pessoa synantise ton Konstantino Cavafy*) is an ingenious combination of documentary and fiction that presents a fictional meeting between the titular characters. Alida Dimitriou's **Life Among the Rocks** (*I zoi stous vrahous*) is a gripping account, based on the testimonies of 33 women who fought in the Democratic Army during the civil war, of their tribulations during captivity followed by their years in exile. Fotos Lambrinos' **Captain Kemal, the Comrade** (*Kapetan Kemal, o syntrofos*) sees the 92-year-old Turk, Mihri Beli, recount his adventures in the 40s, during the Greek civil war, when he fought in the mountains as a guerrilla with the left-wing Democratic Army. Finally, Elias Yiannakakis and Evi Karabatsou's **Makronissos** documents the nightmarish lives of exiled communists on the island of Makronissos.

Fotos Lambrinos' documentary **Captain Kemal, the Comrade**

There are a number of new films that have yet to find distribution and others currently in post-production. Among these are Yiannis Economides' **Knifer**, Nicos Panayiotopoulos' **Fruit Trees of Athens**, Margarita Mandas' **Gold Dust**, Vassilis Mazomenos' **Guilt**, Sotiris Goritsas' **Ap' ta kokkala Vgalmeni**, Vardis Marinakis' **Black Meadow** and Dimitris Atanitis' **Madonna Calls Fassbinder**, amongst numerous others.

The last year was marked by the decision of the majority of Greek directors and producers (the so-called 'Film-Makers in the Mist') to abstain from submitting their films for state prizes and from participating in the Thessaloniki Film Festival. The decision followed the previous right-wing government's refusal to proceed with passing a new bill to aid the industry, as well as changing the statutes regarding state prizes. As a result, of the 43 domestic films produced during last year, only eight screened at the festival and no prizes were handed out.

In addition to their demands for a new cinema law, the 64 filmmakers and producers who agreed to boycott the festival also demanded:

a) Immediate implementation of the 1.5% revenue promised (which would come from the films screening on television channels).
b) The immediate reinstatement of the special tax on cinema tickets, which would be recouped by producers (a clause that existed in the law but was never implemented).
c) Developmental measures for investment in films.

Their stand continued after last October's elections, when the new Socialist government took over, with filmmakers waiting for the new Minister of Culture to proceed with the introduction of a new law.

After the Thessaloniki Film Festival, the 'Filmmakers in the Mist' initiated the creation of a Hellenic Academy of Cinema, which will in future give prizes to Greek films. More than 100 figures from all areas of the industry have joined, including Theo Angelopoulos, Michael Cacoyiannis, Pantelis Voulgaris and Nicos Koundouros.

NINOS-FENECK MIKELIDIS is an historian of Greek Cinema and film critic for *Eleftherotypia* daily newspaper. He is also the founder and director of the Panorama of European Cinema film festival in Athens.

ABU DHABI FILM COMMISSION

Theo Angelopoulos' The Dust of Time

The year's best films

The Dust of Time (Theo Angelopoulos)
Life Among the Rocks (Alida Dimitriou)
Captain Kemal, the Comrade
(Fotos Lambrinos)
Cantine (Stavros Kaplanidis)
A Woman's Way (Panos Koutras)
Without (Alexandros Avranas)

Quote of the year

'A nation without memory is a nation without a future.' ALIDA DIMITRIOU, *director of* Life Among the Rocks.

Directory

All Tel/Fax numbers begin (+30)
Association of Independent Producers of Audiovisual Works (SAPOE), 30 Aegialias, 151 25 Maroussi. Tel: (210) 683 3212. Fax: (210) 683 3606. sapoe-gr@otenet.gr.
Greek Film Centre, President: George Papalios, 7, Dionysiou Aeropagitou, 117 42 Athens. Tel: (210) 367 8500. Fax: (210) 364 8269. info@gfc.gr. www.gfc.gr.
Greek Film, Theatre & Television Directors Guild, 11 Tossitsa, 106 83 Athens. Tel: (210) 822 8936. Fax: (210) 821 1390. ees@ath.forthnet.gr.
Hellenic Ministry of Culture, 20 Bouboulinas, 106 82 Athens. Tel: (210) 820 1100. w3admin@culture. gr. http://culture.gr.
Hellenic Film Academy, 12 Athinas Street, 182 33, Athens. press@fogfilms.org.
Union of Greek Film Directors and Producers, 33 Methonis, 106 83 Athens. Tel: (210) 825 3065. Fax: (210) 825 3065.
Union of Greek Film, TV & Audiovisual Sector Technicians (ETEKT-OT), 25 Valtetsiou, 106 80 Athens. Tel: (210) 360 2379/361 5675. Fax: (210) 361 6442. etekt-ot@ath.forthnet.gr.

Hong Kong Tim Youngs

Few Hong Kong films performed spectacularly at the domestic box office in 2009, but mid-year successes and steady investment across the border in China have given some cause for optimism. Faced with a sustained lack of interest at home, local filmmakers have busied themselves for years trying to hit the right mark with mainland audiences – their efforts moving into a higher gear since the 2003 trade agreement that opened up co-production arrangements as a way to access China's cinemas. And, halfway through 2009, things seemed to be paying off with a diverse collection of releases performing well across the border. Spearheading a summer surge were Alan Mak and Felix Chong's sleek surveillance thriller **Overheard** (*Sit ting fung wan*), Brian Tse's animated piglet picture **McDull** (*Mcdull heung dong dong*) and Wong Jing's scrappy imperial-palace farce, **On His Majesty's Secret Service** (*Dai loi mak tam 009*), all attracting strong mainland grosses. The business appeal of drawing in China's cinemagoers is hard to ignore: *Overheard* nabbed USD$13.2 million in China and only USD$2 million domestically; for Wong's picture, the difference was USD$14.6 million to USD$1.1 million.

Gains in China ranked alongside improved figures in Hong Kong. 2008 had seen a slight increase, to 53, in Mandarin- and Cantonese-language films, after only 50 came out the year before. There was also a small rise in grosses. In 2009, the number passed 60, with summer alone witnessing a doubling in that season's offerings. Film buffs loyal to the local film scene could find several treats in the year's line-up. The new *McDull*, (aka *McDull Kung Fu Kindergarten*), is the third entry in the intelligent, charming, animated franchise, which

captures the riches of Hong Kong's culture and local concerns, even though this time the porcine protagonist is packed off to a martial-arts school deep in the heart of China. Meanwhile, *Overheard*, a strong performer locally, integrated the staples of a police procedural thriller with lashings of corporate fraud and financial troubles to chime with the times.

Other films drew a buzz both in Hong Kong and at festivals in the West. Johnnie To saw his **Vengeance** (*Fuk sau*) appear in the main competition at Cannes. A rare Hong Kong-France joint venture, To's film followed a Gallic assassin descending on Macau to slay the gang that killed his daughter's family. The director also continues to nurture promising filmmakers at his Milkyway Image production house. The year's big-screen treat from there was Soi Cheang's **Accident** (*Yi ngoi*). A hit-squad film with not a gun in sight, it delivered scenes featuring complex urban traps, a novel twist for a staple Hong Kong genre product.

Johnny Hallyday in Johnnie To's **Vengeance**

Also acquitting themselves well in the thriller department were Herman Yau, the prolific director of four 2009 releases (and cinematographer on two more), and Dante

Nick Cheung and Nicholas Tse in Dante Lam's **The Beast Stalker**

Lam. Yau's **Turning Point** (*Laughing Gor ji bin jit*) was a spin-off from a television series featuring a popular undercover-police character, but the director's mastery of the genre meant those unfamiliar with the character could still be swept up in the action. Yau then released **Rebellion** (*Tong mun*), a tongue-in-cheek gangland saga focusing on an underworld flunky's boozy night from hell. Lam began 2009 with acclaim for **The Beast Stalker** (*Ching yan*), a taut crime thriller about a young cop becoming a vigilante in order to save a barrister's kidnapped daughter. Tense, gritty and with some wonderful performances (Nick Cheung won the Hong Kong Film Awards' Best Actor award for his villainous role), Lam's success prompted production on two further thrillers, to be released in 2010: **Fire of Conscience** (*Fo lung*) and **Stool Pigeon** (*Sin yan*). Wong Jing, best known for his broad approach to comedy and drama, also turned his hand to crime, with the 1970s-set **I Corrupt All Cops** (*Gum chin dai kwok*). He was also co-director, with Billy Chung, on **To Live and Die in Mongkok** (*Wong gok gaam yuk*).

Other highlights could be found in dramas, comedies and historical epics. John Woo completed **Red Cliff II** (*Chi bi*), the final instalment of Asia's most expensive film. Having detailed the extensive backstory in *Red Cliff*, the explosive second part recreated the immense battle with considerable aplomb. Wilson Yip's wartime drama **Ip Man** (*Yip Man*)

was a biopic about a southern Chinese kung-fu master who once taught Bruce Lee. The film continued Hong Kong's quality-driven, staunchly patriotic, martial-arts filmmaking tradition.

Donnie Yen in Wilson Yip's **Ip Man**

Art-house director Yonfan relocated to Taiwan for the lavishly shot **Prince of Tears** (*Lei wangzi*), setting a family story against the anti-communist witchhunts that took place on the island during the 1950s. Ann Hui followed the low-budget *The Way We Are* with the searing domestic-violence saga, **Night and Fog** (*Tin Shui Wai dik yeh yu mo*). Based on true events in a small town, the film examined a suspicious death in a family, detailing the parents' relationship while also paying attention to cross-border migration and the role of social services. Wai Ka-fai's **Written By** (*Joi sang ho*) delivered an offbeat mix of family tragedy and all-out fantasy, which featured crafty narrative tricks in its story of a group of car-accident victims.

Zhang Jingchu and Simon Yam in Ann Hui's **Night and Fog**

Cheung King-Wai's documentary **KJ: Music and Life**

The independent scene also thrived in 2009, with more releases in commercial cinemas, showcases and local film festivals. The year's most unexpected success was the documentary **KJ: Music and Life** (*Yam ngok yan sang*), directed by *Night and Fog* writer Cheung King-wai. Chronicling the growing pains of a child prodigy with an independent streak, and spanning a six-year timeline, the film benefited from its limited-release schedule. Sell-out shows, no more than two a day, began in July and continued into late-November, after it had picked up the Best Documentary and Best Editing prizes at Taiwan's Golden Horse Awards. Another popular independent release was Philip Yung's **Glamorous Youth** (*Ming mei si kwong*), deftly capturing Hong Kong–China relations at a personal level within a well-measured – even sexy – drama.

2009's Chinese New Year saw the big guns come out for Andrew Lau's **Look for a Star** (*Yau lung hei fung*), featuring Andy Lau in a glitzy, Macau-set romantic comedy. Yet the season's box-office winner was a cheap-looking comedy, Vincent Kok's **All's Well Ends Well 2009** (*Ga yau hei si 2009*). A romantic comedy, it tapped into the tradition of cheery, family-friendly buffoonery for an impressively lucrative holiday run. Better laughs arrived late in the year with the little-seen, low-budget quickie, **Split Second Murders** (*Sei sun sor liu*), a teen-idol-driven comedy of errors built around a comic artist's series of encounters – with passersby, triads and his girlfriend – that soon descends into chaos. Herman Yau's assured direction allowed the mostly

inexperienced cast to come across naturally, playing up themes of fate and greed, alongside sly, local pop-culture references.

Local cinemagoers should be thankful that Hong Kong topics are still presented front and centre in the works of Yau and other key mid-budget filmmakers, who manage to make films without co-production arrangements (or strive to sustain some semblance of local character on the screen). But for larger-budgeted films, the growth of the China market and its funding channels can mean that catering to Hong Kong audiences is secondary to serving mainland interests. Because of this, not all films reach China, the most recent high-profile case being Derek Yee's **Shinjuku Incident** (*Sun suk si gin*). The ambitious Jackie Chan thriller about Japanese triads and the Chinese diaspora proved too much for mainland censors, so the Hong Kong producers cut their losses and chose not to release it there.

Derek Yee's **Shinjuku Incident**

Creativity also continues to suffer in these co-production ventures. Even when different cuts of a film are made for the two markets, plot developments pandering to China's censorship (such as having all of a film's wrongdoers punished or killed) can be glaring or disruptive, and some genres, such as horror, are just not allowed in China. There are also concerns about retaining the local identity that so marked out the city's filmmaking scene, with fears that it could be watered down or lost completely in co-productions. When the local take on *Transformers*-style robot wars, Jeff Lau's **Kung Fu Cyborg: Metallic Attraction** (*Gei hei hap*), appeared in late summer, it was based around a Chinese small-town romance featuring a police officer, with barely a few Hong Kong elements remaining, beyond the members of cast and crew. Nevertheless, investment from China means Hongkongers can expect such compromised titles to be a constant from now on.

The year closed with **The Storm Warriors** (*Fung Wan II*), the Pang Brothers' effects-laden sequel to the 1998 comic-based fantasy, *The Storm Riders*. It was released alongside Teddy Chen's star-laden early twentieth century action saga, **Bodyguards and Assassins** (*Sup yuet wai sing*).

Filmmakers have pencilled in a breakneck release schedule for the start of 2010. By early November, ten co-productions were lined up for a three-week window around the Chinese New Year holiday, including Eric Tsang and Patrick Kong's festive-season ensemble comedy **72 Tenants of Prosperity** (*72 kar jouh ha*) and Herman Yau's **All's Well Ends Well 2010** (*Ga yau hei si 2010*). With the pace of releases gradually increasing, fans of Hong Kong cinema, whether at home, in China or beyond, will be hoping that filmmakers can maintain such stamina for the rest of the year.

The year's best films
KJ (Cheung King-wai)
McDull (Brian Tse)
The Beast Stalker (Dante Lam)
Accident (Soi Cheang)
Night and Fog (Ann Hui)

Quote of the year
'We are making films that have Chinese audiences more in mind. It's very difficult not to be completely China-centric.' *Producer* PETER CHAN *on high-budget co-productions with mainland Chinese partners.*

TIM YOUNGS is a Hong Kong-based writer and a consultant on Hong Kong cinema for the Udine Far East Film Festival and the Venice Film Festival.

Directory
All Tel/Fax numbers begin (+852)
Hong Kong Film Archive, 50 Lei King Rd, Sai Wan Ho. Tel: 2739 2139. Fax: 2311 5229. www.filmarchive.gov.hk.
Film Services Office, 40/F, Revenue Tower, 5 Gloucester Road, Wan Chai. Tel: 2594 5745. Fax: 2824 0595. www.fso-tela.gov.hk.
Federation of Hong Kong Filmmakers, 2/F, 35 Ho Man Tin St, Ho Man Tin, Kowloon. Tel: 2194 6955. Fax: 2194 6255. www.hkfilmmakers.com.
Hong Kong Film Directors' Guild, 2/F, 35 Ho Man Tin St, Ho Man Tin, Kowloon. Tel: 2760 0331. Fax: 2713 2373. www.hkfdg.com.
Hong Kong International Film Festival Society, 21/F, Millennium City 3, 370 Kwun Tong Rd, Kwun Tong. Tel: 2970 3300. Fax 2970 3011. www.hkiff.org.hk.
Hong Kong, Kowloon and New Territories Motion Picture Industry Association (MPIA), Unit 1201, New Kowloon Plaza, 38 Tai Kok Tsui Rd, Kowloon. Tel: 2311 2692. Fax: 2311 1178. www.mpia.org.hk.
Hong Kong Film Awards Association, Room 1601–1602, Austin Tower, 22–26 Austin Ave, Tsim Sha Tsui, Kowloon. Tel: 2367 7892. Fax: 2723 9597. www.hkfaa.com.

Richie Jen, left, and Louis Koo in Soi Cheang's **Accident**

Hungary John Cunningham

As well as being the anniversary of the collapse of the Berlin Wall, an event partly precipitated by the opening of Hungary's western border with Austria, 2009 was also the 40th anniversary of the Hungarian Film Week. Although it started in the southern city of Pécs (European City of Culture in 2010) it soon moved to the capital, where it has been ensconced ever since. There was therefore a buzz of anticipation as delegates and guests gathered for this annual film festival in the new surroundings of a somewhat uninviting cinema complex (no improvement on the Mamut shopping mall and cinema, where the event had been held for the last few years). It was, however, a mixed bag of films on offer and it proved difficult to single out any one film as outstanding. Nevertheless, there was a promising display of new young talent and, if none of them quite left a major impression, at the very least there was a demonstration of things to come. Of the 18 feature films in competition, seven were debuts.

Although newcomers were prominent, veterans also had films on show, most notably Péter Bacsó's **Virtually a Virgin** (*Majdnem szüz*), which followed the story of a young

Péter Bacsó's **Virtually a Virgin**

woman released from an institution only to fall into prostitution. Bacsó was given a thoroughly deserved lifetime achievement award, but this was followed by the sad news, only a few months later, that the 81-year-old had died.

Simon Szabó's **Paper Planes**

Debut director Oszkár Viktor Nagy's slow-moving and intensely atmospheric **Father's Acre** (*Apaföld*) told a moving and powerful tale of generational tension as a father (János Derzsi) returns from prison to begin a new life with his son (Tamás Ravász), working on a vineyard he has purchased. No doubt an impressive debut with some fine cinematography (from Tamás Dobos), but possibly too derivative of Kornél Mundruczó and Béla Tarr. Simon Szabó's **Paper Planes** (*Papírrepülők*), an urban kaleidoscope of sex, drugs and rap music, won praise for its no-holds-barred portrayal of the lifestyle of Budapest's teenagers. The Golden Reel Award went to **Lost Times** (*Utolsó idök*) by first-time director, Áron Mátyássy. It was another intense film, this time set in the east of Hungary where Iván (Jószef Kadás), a car mechanic, lives with his mentally handicapped sister, Eszter (Teréz Vass), who is raped. Iván takes the law into his own hands to seek revenge.

Áron Mátyássy's **Lost Times**

This rather heavy diet of serious 'art' films was broken by Gábor Herendi's follow-up to his 2001 success, *A Kind of America*. With the same popular actors (including Csaba Pindroch) and, more or less, the same basic plot, **A Kind of America 2** (*Valami Amerika 2*) recycled the formulaic crime caper/comedy and ludicrous money-making schemes of the earlier film. Although it has subsequently proved to be very popular with domestic audiences, it reaped no prizes at the Film Week, where juries tend not to favour comedies. Another comedy was Tamás Keményffy's **Fluke** (*Mázli*), where Hungarian villagers, having accidentally broken an oil pipeline, cash in on their good luck. The intervention of an Austrian oil executive provides ample scope for a 'yokels vs. city slicker' farce and some muted social comment, reminiscent of the British Ealing comedy, *Passport to Pimlico*. **Prank** (*Tréfa*), directed by Péter Gárdos, won the Best Director award. It is set in 1912, at a provincial school run by a group of easy-going

Péter Gárdos' **Prank**

priests whose cosy, relaxed world is disrupted by the arrival of a new teacher, the stern Father Weigel (Tamás Lengyel), who is appalled by the laxity he encounters. Based on a novella by popular Hungarian writer Dezső Kostalyáni, this is a warm and tender film with some fine performances, not least by Ferenc Takács, the well-known Budapest academic and man-about-town turned character actor. Although not in competition, Gergely Fonyó's **Made in Hungary** had the audience rocking in the aisles with a tale of youthful rebellion, romance and rock 'n' roll, set in 1950s Hungary.

Gergely Fonyó's **Made in Hungaria**

Márta Mészáros, who was chair of the Film Week Jury, was also busy with her latest release, **The Last Report from Anna** (*Az utolsó jelentes*), which appeared just in time to make it into this edition of the guide. Following the pattern of her previous film, it looks at yet another historical and political figure, the Social Democrat activist, Anna Kéthly (Enikő Eszenyi), who opposed the right-wing drift of Hungarian society in the 20s and 30s, only to fall foul of the Stalinist dictatorship of Mátyás Rákosi in the 1950s.

Audiences and devotees of two of Hungary's most revered filmmakers will have to wait until 2010 to see their latest offerings. The 88-year-old veteran Miklós Jancsó returns to the screen with **So Much for Justice!** (*Oda az igazság!*). Almost finished at the time of going to press and probably scheduled to open the 2010 Budapest Film Week, this promises to be a departure from Jancsó's previous zany, burlesque, 'Budapest' films and a return to a historical topic – the fate of the young Hungarian king Matthias Corvinus. Béla Tarr's much-anticipated **The Turin Horse**, helped by a grant of €240,000 from the Council of Europe Film Fund, Eurimages, is currently in production and scheduled to premiere at Cannes in 2010. The film is loosely based around an incident attributed to Nietzsche while he was staying in Turin. Whether or not this will be Tarr's last film (as he has stated) remains to be seen.

In the domestic market, *Valami Amerika 2* was the best-performing Hungarian film (448,321 viewers) making it the third most popular film overall, behind the latest *Harry Potter* and *Ice Age* franchise entries. The second most popular Hungarian film was *Made in Hungaria* (223,892). So far, the Hungarian film industry seems to be weathering the international recession relatively well and foreign production companies are still being attracted to Hungary, with its range of impressive facilities, expertise and generous tax incentives. The Korda Studios at Etlek, on the outskirts of Budapest, are currently hosting a major US production, **The Season of the Witch**, starring Nicolas Cage. Most commentators are of the opinion that, in terms of attracting foreign production, Hungary is now outstripping its former rival, the Czech Republic.

The year's best films
Made in Hungaria (Gergely Fonyó)
Prank (Péter Gárdos)
Father's Acre (Oszkár Viktor Nagy)
Lost Times (Áron Mátyássy)
Fluke (Tamás Keményffy)

Oszkár Viktor Nagy's **Father's Acre**

Quote of the year
'Directors in Hungary make films with long breaks between them and struggle to sustain themselves. On the other hand, when I finished the film school I quickly discovered the disease of the Hungarian cinema: the script. Most of the directors write their own, and not all of them are good writers.' LÁSZLÓ KÁNTOR, *Head of Új Budapest Filmstudió.*

Directory
All Tel/Fax numbers begin (+36)
Association of Hungarian Filmmakers, Városligeti fasor 38. Budapest, Hungary-1068. filmszov@t-online.hu.
Association of Hungarian Producers, Eszter utca 7/B. Budapest, Hungary-1022. mail@mpsz.org.hu, www.mpsz.org.hu.
Hungarian Directors Guild, Ráday utca 31/K., Budapest, Hungary-1092. mrc@filmjus.hu. www.mmrc.hu.
Hungarian Film Alliance (Magyar Filmunió), 38 Városligeti fasor, Budapest, Hungary - 1068. Tel: (1) 351 7760, 351-7761. Fax: (1) 352 6734. filmunio@filunion.hu.
Hungarian Independent Producers Associations, Róna utca 174. Budapest, Hungary-1145. eurofilm@t-online.hu.
Hungarian National Film Archive, Budakeszi út 51/E. Budapest, Hungary-1021. www.filmintezet. hu.
Hungarian Society of Cinematographers (H.S.C.), Róna utca 174. Budapest, Hungary-1145. hsc@hscmot.hu. www.hscmot.hu.
MEDIA Desk Hungary, Városligeti fasor 38. Budapest, Hungary-1068, info@mediadesk.hu. www.mediadesk.hu.
Motion Picture Public Foundation of Hungary Városligeti fasor 38. Budapest, Hungary-1068. mmka@mmka.hu. www.mmka.hu.
National Film Office, Wesselényi utca 16. Budapest, Hungary-1075. info@filmoffice.hu. www.nationalfilmoffice.hu.

JOHN CUNNINGHAM is Senior Lecturer in Stage and Screen at Sheffield Hallam University, UK. He is also Principal Editor of *Studies in Eastern European Cinema*, a new journal which will appear in early 2010.

Iceland Eddie Cockrell

When national crises strike, artists can rally a country. During 2009, as the abrupt failure of Iceland's top three banks threw one of the world's most admired societies into unprecedented social tumult and personal strife, this is precisely what transpired.

In fact, the year's story arc couldn't have been scripted to greater dramatic effect. January began on a note of enlightened optimism with the release of **The Sunshine Boy**, acclaimed veteran Fridrik Thor Fridriksson's first documentary in nearly three decades. Taking its name from the term of affection producer Margret Dagmar Ericsdottir has for her autistic son Keli, this is a focused, inspiring global inquiry into alternative treatments. Following the film's North American premiere at the Toronto festival, trade paper *Variety* correctly anointed it 'a mystery replete with miracles'.

In April, the government bumped the all-important offshore producer tax credit from 14% to 20%, keeping Iceland on pace with Hungary, the Czech Republic and France, in the forefront of such schemes. Sadly, at the time of writing that same government was proposing a 34% cut in domestic film funding – a margin greater than all other proposed arts cuts combined.

The year's fourth month also saw the release of **Dreamland**, a probing documentary by Thorfinnur Gudnason and Andri Snaer Magnason charting the country's difficult passage in building a massive aluminium smelter in the east fjords. Perhaps reflecting the activist anger of the populace, *Dreamland* played for a remarkable 11 weeks in local cinemas and subsequently premiered in competition at the International Documentary Festival Amsterdam.

Following a summer given over to dependably attractive Hollywood product – *The Hangover* became the year's top-grossing import, following *Mamma Mia!* in 2008 – October opened with the debut of perhaps the year's strongest and most cautionary film.

A mere eight months after the violence that greeted the government's stonewalling of the economic crisis, filmmaker Helgi Felixson had assembled visceral footage of the unrest and valuable background material into the meticulously probing documentary **God Bless Iceland**. The personalities may be of little

interest to those outside the country, but the emotion on display as citizens gathered to express their anger and anguish is universal.

Julius Kemp's **Reykjavik Whale Watching Massacre**

Early September also saw the release of the bluntly titled **Reykjavik Whale Watching Massacre**, which did just what it said on the tin as a group of tourists succumb to a demented fishing family. Despite genuinely gory genre thrills and the appearance of native Icelander Gunnar Hansen – Leatherface in the original *Texas Chainsaw Massacre* – RWWM had the great misfortune to open opposite both *Up* and *Inglourious Basterds*.

The holidays approached, and in the manner of audiences the world over, Icelanders seemed far more interested in comfortable escapist fare than horror films or documentaries.

Thus came director Bragi Thor Hinriksson's **The Big Rescue**, which built on the man-child personality of small-screen comedian Sveppi (Sverrir Thor Sverrisson) to tell a family-skewed adventure story massaged with agreeably cheesy special effects. Following close on Sveppi's heels was first-time director Thorsteinn Bjarnason's low-key comedy **Johannes**, which proved such an effective showcase for popular comedian Thorhallur Sigurdsson, as a put-upon art teacher and good Samaritan, that it immediately took top place in the box-office chart.

At the time of writing, critics were praising the newest local release, veteran filmmaker Hilmar Oddsson's **December**. Set during the holidays,

the film follows selfish musician Jonni (Tomas Lemarquis from *Noi Albinoi*) as he returns home from a mysteriously abrupt three-year hiatus in Argentina. He has no choice but to put aside his own ambitions in order to help his family and friends as they cope with emotional and economic uncertainty. In both subject matter and approach, *December* is perfectly timed to entertain at home and illuminate abroad.

Speaking of *Noi Albinoi*, missing from the year's release roster, but already acquired for American distribution, is Dagur Kari's English-language drama, **The Good Heart**. *There Will Be Blood's* Paul Dano stars as a fragile, homeless New Yorker taken in by Brian Cox's abrasive and unhealthy publican. Though dismissed at Toronto as 'arthouse hokum' by *Variety*, the film's affectionate grunge lingers, in much the way the ensemble passages of *Million Dollar Hotel* and the whole of *Barfly* give a scruffy dignity to the downtrodden.

Dagur Kari's **The Good Heart**

Of special note amongst the year's dozen long documentaries is the immensely atmospheric 45-minute essay film, **The Mysteries of Snae-fellsjokul**. French filmmaker Jean Michel Roux's satisfying follow-up to his 2002 full-length investigation into the *Invisible World* is another nature-documentary-as-otherworldly-thriller about the mysteries of the eponymous volcano in western Iceland, selected by Jules Verne as the gateway in *Journey to the Centre of the Earth*.

On the business front, the five home-grown dramatic features unveiled during 2009 are down from eight the previous year. The domestic box office for all releases totalled approximately USD$10.2 million from the period January–October 2009, a USD$2.8 million dip from the same period in 2008.

The annual Edda awards, which bestow honours on worthy Icelandic films, was delayed from late 2009 to the first quarter of 2010. There were assurances that the reasons for this were only partly financial.

No less than a dozen promising feature-length dramas and documentaries are in the pipeline. Highlights include *Children and Parents* director Ragnar Bragason's **Bjarnfredarson**; Valdis Oskarsdottir's *Country Wedding* follow-up, **Kings Road**; and Fridriksson's **Mamma Gogo**, which addresses his mother's debilitating Alzheimer's condition.

Conspicuous by his low profile in 2009 was *Jar City* director Baltasar Kormakur. While finishing the English-language **Inhale** (previously known as *Run for Her Life*) with Dermot Mulroney, Diane Kruger, Rosanna Arquette and Sam Shepard, he has also been tipped as director of an American remake of *Reykjavik-Rotterdam*. Mark Wahlberg will produce and star.

Thirty years after the creation of the contemporary Icelandic film movement, the industry faces some of its toughest challenges. Yet with the talent of its artists, determination of its proponents and proven support of its domestic fan base, there is confidence that Icelandic cinema will survive, and thrive.

The year's best films
God Bless Iceland (Helgi Felixson)
The Sunshine Boy (Fridrik Thor Fridriksson)
December (Hilmar Oddsson)
The Mysteries of Snaefellsjokul (Jean Michel Roux)
Reykjavik Whale Watching Massacre (Julius Kemp)

Quotes of the year
'If the currency devalues, then the grants and investments we receive from abroad will be more valuable to us. And sales abroad are worth more too. It's like the fishing industry, which is very happy as they effectively get double for their catches.' **Reykjavik Whale Watching Massacre** *producer/director* JULIUS KEMP *on the silver lining of currency devaluation.*

Directory
All Tel/Fax numbers begin (+354)
Association of Film-Rights Holder in Iceland, Laugavegur 182, 105 Reykjavík. Fax: 588 3800. smais@smais.is. www.smais.is.
Association of Icelandic Film Directors, Túngata 14, 101 Reykjavík. Fax: 562 7171. f.thor@icecorp.is.
Association of Icelandic Film Producers, Túngata 14, PO Box 5367, 125 Reykjavík. Tel: 863 3057. Fax: 555 3065. sik@producers.is. www.producers.is.
Film in Iceland Agency, Borgartún 35, 105 Reykjavík. Tel: 561 5200. Fax: 511 4040. ininfo@filminiceland.com. www.filminiceland.com.
Icelandic Film Centre, Túngata 14, 101 Reykjavík. Tel: 562 3580. Fax: 562 7171. info@icelandicfilm-centre.is. www.icelandicfilmcentre.is.
Icelandic Film Makers Association, Túngata 14, PO Box 1652, 121 Reykjavík. filmmakers@filmmakers.is. www.filmmakers.is.
Icelandic Film & Television Academy/EDDA Awards, Túngata 14, 101 Reykjavík. Tel: 562 3580. Fax: 562 7171. bjorn@reykjavikfilms.com.
National Film Archive of Iceland, Hvaleyrarbraut 13, 220 Hafnarfjordur. Tel: 565 5993. Fax: 565 5994. kvikmyndasafn@kvikmyndasafn.is.
Statistics Iceland, Borgartún 21a, 150 Reykjavík. Tel: 528 1000. Fax: 528 1099. information@statice.is. www.statice.is/Statistics/Culture/Cinemas.

EDDIE COCKRELL is a film critic and consulting programmer whose reviews have appeared in *Variety*, *The Washington Post*, *The Sydney Morning Herald* and *The Australian*.

Jean Michel Roux's **The Mysteries of Snaefellsjokul**

India Uma Da Cunha

Increasingly – and disconcertingly – the over-used term 'Bollywood' is taken to represent all Indian cinema. It does not. It began – and should still be seen – as a description of the Hindi film scene and, within that, of the song-and-dance, star-studded blockbuster emanating from India's film capital, Bombay (now Mumbai). A look at the statistics of films made in 20 of the country's regional dialects would set the record straight.

India is still the world leader in film production. In 2008, it made 1,325 features. But, of these, only 286 were in Hindi, the national language. Over half were in the four main South Indian languages (Telugu – 286, Tamil – 175, Kannada – 162 and Malayalam – 88). But there is little doubt that India's film business is dominated by the power, wealth and manic popularity of the Bollywood film. Today, it also enjoys a lucrative and expanding international market. At home, it has sidelined art-house and regional cinema.

However, at the end of 2009 it seemed like Bollywood's time of reckoning had arrived. Internationally, India's film business is at an all-time high, but the vast domestic market was still trying to recover from a year of unprecedented setbacks. The first blow followed hard on the heels of the terrorist attacks in Mumbai, which prompted a grieving, conscience-stricken nation to stay away from cinemas, which lay abandoned for weeks. The release at Christmas of Aamir Khan's aggressively promoted **Ghajini**, a pyschological thriller about a man's short-term memory igniting his killer instincts, jolted people back into the cinemas. Then came the adrenalin rush of Danny Boyle's *Slumdog Millionaire*, with its bagful of Oscars.

The bombings led to a delay in the planned December 2008 shoot of ITV's *A Passage to India*. However, boosted by *Slumdog Millionaire*'s popularity, international crews began heading for Indian shores in early 2009. By September, the country saw Julia Roberts tackling village life in North India for **Eat, Pray, Love**, directed by Ryan Murphy. And in December, Sir Ben Kingsley arrived in Goa to raise funds for his proposed epic film on the creation of the Taj Mahal.

March 2009 saw a confrontation between distributors and producers, and the six national multiplex chains, over a revision of how box-office receipts were to be divided. With neither side giving in, distributors suspended all new releases from being screened at multiplexes, daring the latter to survive with no revenue. Producers also suffered by this action, paying tax on their huge loans and freezing (exorbitantly priced) productions. The impasse led to a ruinous 61-day nationwide shutdown by multiplexes, consternation over mounting losses among producers, cancelled shoots and a logjam

Aamir Khan's **Ghajini**

of pending films. Finally a compromise was reached which benefited the distributors and producers. The strike was lifted and new releases once again appeared in cinemas, but not without some concern for the future.

Vivek Sharma's **Who Can See the Future?**

The fears were well founded. The public were used to famine and refused to feast. The first release, Vivek Sharma's **Who Can See the Future?** (*Kal Kissne Dekha*), about an idealistic young man's ability to see into the future, failed to predict its own doom. It was followed by a unique series of big-budget disasters. Diwali festival prize-winning releases in October performed miserably. Even sure-fire male stars, like Akshay Kumar in **Blue** ('the most expensive film and first deep-sea thriller to be made in India'), performed miserably. Ashutosh Gowariker's **What's Your Sun Sign?** (*What's Your Raashee?*), with Priyanka Chopra playing 12 different roles, each representing a different Zodiac sign, also failed. Zoya Akhtar's

Akshay Kumar in **Blue**

Zoya Akhtar's **Luck By Chance**

exhilarating debut feature **Luck By Chance**, an incisive, star-studded spectacle dealing with the callous chicanery that underlines Bollywood success, failed to attract a large audience, but played well to an urban niche.

Post-Diwali releases also collapsed: '*London Dreams* a loser: *Aladdin* a disaster', hollered *Screen*, India's bellwether trade weekly. The first, directed by Vipul Shah, tells of two childhood friends who realise their dreams of becoming famous rock stars. The second is a special-effects film, directed by Sujoy Ghosh, about an orphan who, as a young man, is pursued by Amitabh Bachchan's solicitous and quirky genie.

Kabir Khan's **New York**

Not all films were doomed. Two mid-year releases transformed into unexpected successes and enthused dejected producers. They were Kabir Khan's **New York**, starring John Abraham and Katrina Kaif, about an immigrant Indian's suspected terrorist links,

Imtiaz Ali's **Love Nowadays**

which connect him to his former campus romance and loyalties; and Imtiaz Ali's **Love Nowadays** (*Love Aaj Kal*), starring Saif Ali Khan, Deepika Padukone, Rishi Kapoor and Neetu Singh as two couples, one living in the present and the other in the past, and their differing ideas about romance.

Prabhu Deva's **Wanted**

The year-end registered just two hits. Prabhu Deva's **Wanted**, released mid-September, led by a large margin, proving that Salman Khan was still a dependable draw. It is about an assassin who mercilessly wipes out his boss's enemies but himself becomes a target. The other was Rajkumar Santoshi's **The Amazing Story of A Weird Love** (*Ajab Prem Ki Ghazab Kahani*) starring new heartthrobs, Ranbir Kapoor and Katrina Kaif in a romantic caper about an irresponsible youth who kidnaps the woman he loves, who then makes him mend his ways.

With film appearing to be a less secure source of profit, both banks and traditional financiers

backed away, seeing as even average-scale films need a US$10 million investment, with 60% going to stars and top technicians. The Reserve Bank of India's move to encourage legitimate funding for India's film production, an attempt to reduce the amount of illicit money invested in it, made little headway. The film industry's complex structure defeated even the smartest banks and corporate houses. Looking ahead, Bollywood has a US$100 million stake in big releases over just three months, from December 2009 to February 2010. Normally, these films are held back from this period as it leads up to the final examinations at the nation's universities. But the multiplex closure forced a change of strategy. The launches include Shahrukh Khan in Karan Johar's **My Name is Khan**, Salman Khan in Anil Sharma's **The Brave** (*Veer*), Aamir Khan in Rajkumar Hirani's **Three Idiots** and Amitabh Bachchan in a back-to-back trio: R. Balki's **Father** (*Paa*), Leena Yadav's **A Poker Game** (*Teen Patti*) and Ram Gopal Varma's **The News(s) Battle** (*Rann*). There are also several low-budget films slated for an early 2010 release.

India's presence on the international scene continues to prosper and impress. At the 2008 Cannes Film Festival, Amit Khanna, Chairman of Reliance Big Entertainment, stunned the media by announcing a billion-dollar investment by the end of 2009 in production, distribution and the exhibition of Indian films around the world. The next day he announced further development funding in conjunction with companies owned by Tom

Rajkumar Santoshi's **The Amazing Story of A Weird Love**

R. Balki's **Father**

Hanks, Brad Pitt, Nicolas Cage and George Clooney, among others. A year later, the same company struck a US$825 million production deal with DreamWorks Studio partners, Steven Spielberg and Stacey Snider.

Also making history in India was Dev Benegal's **Road Movie**, which was pre-sold to Fortissimo before filming even began. Premiering at the Toronto Film Festival, the film follows a young man who drives an antique Chevy full of old film projectors and who discovers life on the Indian highway. Fortissimo also picked up its first Hindi-language documentary, Rajesh S. Jala's **The Children of the Pyre**, about seven children who make a living at the country's busiest cremation ground.

Hollywood's animation industry, led by major studios such as Warner Bros., Disney, Pixar, Sony and MGM, have, for some time, outsourced work to Mumbai's animation and CGI talent, including such features as *Spider Man 3*, *Blood Diamond*, *The Chronicles of Narnia*, *Click*, *Shrek 3* and *A Night at the Museum*. The international ties are multiplying and strengthening.

Mumbai's Crest Animation Production recently entered into a three-film co-production deal with Los Angeles-based Lionsgate. Currently in production is **Alpha and Omega**, budgeted at US$25 million, which marks the first Hollywood film to be funded entirely by an Indian company. Within India, the US$324 million animation industry is catering to an ever-growing audience. So many films now employ animation and digital techniques, and animation features themselves are becoming more numerous.

India-centric films also brought honour to the country. The American documentary, **Smile Pinki**, directed by Megan Mylan, about an Indian doctor's selfless mission to provide cleft-lip surgery free of charge to under-privileged children, won the 2009 Academy Award for Best Short Documentary. Oscars also came India's way via *Slumdog Millionaire*: Best Original Song (A. R. Rahman and Gulzar); Best Original Music (A. R. Rahman); and Best Sound Mixing (Resul Pookutty).

Faiza Ahmad Khan's hilarious documentary, **Supermen of Malegaon**, was popular at international festivals. It is an account of one man, his small camera and a tiny crew attempting their own, home-spun version of *Superman*, with a little imagination standing in for special effects.

The struggling art-house features and films featuring lesser-known, regional dialects are

Rajesh S. Jala's **The Children of the Pyre**

Laxmikant Shetgaonkar's **The Man Beyond The Bridge**

managing to survive thanks to financial support from government-related institutions. The most visible is the Mumbai-based National Film Development Corporation of India (NFDC), which brings in quality films from leading world film festivals. At the Toronto Film Festival, a small NFDC film, Laxmikant Shetgaonkar's **The Man Beyond The Bridge** (*Paltadacho Munis*), walked away with the FIPRESCI Prize. Made in Konkani, a minor regional dialect, it is set in a forest and follows the struggles of an unlikely pair, the forest caretaker and a deranged woman he befriends. Films made in the Marathi language also continued to display an impressive degree of marketability, led by Satish Manwar's **The Damned Rain**, a devastating presentation of the country's rising spate of farmer suicides.

Satish Manwar's **The Damned Rain**

There are around 20 dialects in which films are gaining ground. They include: Marathi with 116 films; Bhojpuri, a Hindi dialect, with 68 films; Bengali with 66; Gujarati with 49; Oriya with

20; Punjabi with 11; and ten English-language films. There is also Assamese, Rajasthani, Tulu, Maithili and many others. With each passing year, the language of a remote region asserts its identity and makes a mark on the register of India's cinema. And on this chart, Bollywood does not figure.

The larger, film-related corporations are nurturing India's rich source of known and new talent. Over 2008–9, Reliance Big Pictures has funded close to ten films by some of India's most renowned directors: Shyam Benegal, Saeed Mirza, MS Sathyu, Rituparno Ghosh and Buddhadeb Dasgupta, with their work reaching the world's top film festivals.

Ayan Mukerji's **Wake Up Sid**

Leading production house UTV has for a time been generating strong new talent. In 2009, it backed one of India's most original filmmakers, Vishal Bhardwaj, known for his films *Maqbool* and *Omkara*, Indian adaptations of Shakespeare's *Macbeth* and *Othello*. His mid-August release, **Scoundrel** (*Kaminey*), was about identical twins raised in Mumbai's biggest slum. Newcomer Ayan Mukerji's **Wake Up Sid**, a UTV October release about a spoilt, rich college brat in Mumbai, played well to young urbanites. The company also signed a three-year, nine-film deal with hot-shot director Anurag Kashyap, who recently served on the Venice Film Festival's International Jury.

The production house run by superstar Aamir Khan has an unfailing record for delivering creatively challenging fare that plays well at the box office. It produced the forthcoming **Peepli Live**, by debuting writer-director Anusha Rizvi, which has the honour of being the first Indian feature selected for competition at the Sundance Film Festival. The film details the media frenzy that follows an impoverished farmer's announcement that he intends to commit suicide in order for his family to be granted government compensation.

India continues to attract the world's filmmakers. From Italy, Italo Spinelli is in Kolkata shooting his first feature **What's Behind a Blouse** (*Choli ke Peeche*), based on a Mahashweta Devi story and starring Irrfan Khan as a wildlife photographer. From Britain comes Leslie Udwin who is completing **West is West**, a companion piece to the highly successful *East is East*. From Australia, Claire McCarthy shot her feature film **The Waiting City** in Kolkata. Dilip Mehta (Deepa Mehta's brother, who is also an acclaimed photographer) presented his Canadian offering, **Cooking with Stella**, which was shot in Delhi and premiered at Toronto. Deepa Mehta and Salman Rushdie have completed their script of **Midnight's Children**, and Mira Nair's next film is said to be based on Mohsin Hamid's novel, **The Reluctant Fundamentalist**.

The year's best films

The Damned Rain (Satish Manwar)
Luck By Chance (Zoya Akhtar)
Supermen of Malegaon
(Faiza Ahmad Khan) (documentary)
The Children of the Pyre
(Rajesh S. Jala) (documentary)
The Man Beyond The Bridge
(Laxmikant Shetgaonkar)

UMA DA CUNHA is based in Mumbai. She edits the quarterly *Film India Worldwide* and works as a researcher and freelance journalist on film and also as a programmer for international film festivals, specialising in new Indian cinema. She organises specialised film industry events.

Quotes of the year

'More often than not, Indian films cannot travel because either their narrative techniques are not comprehensible to Western audiences, the acting is not naturalistic enough, or the subject matter is not universal.' LIZ SHACKLETON, *Screen International, 20 November, 2009.*

'I have nothing against my face. Never had. It's loved by women just like my voice. ' *Actor* OM PURI.

Directory

All Tel/Fax numbers begin (+91)
Film & Television Institute of India, Law College Rd, Pune 411 004. Tel: (20) 543 1817/3016/0017. www.ftiindia.com.
Film Federation of India, B/3 Everest Bldg, Tardeo, Bombay 400 034. Tel/Fax: (22) 2351 5531. Fax: 2352 2062. supransen22@hotmail.com.
Film Producers Guild of India, G-1, Morya House, Veera Industrial Estate, OShiwara Link Road, Andheri (W), Mumbai 400 053. Tel: (22) 5691 0662/2673 3065. Fax: (22) 5691 0661. tfpgoli1@vsnl.net. www.filmguildindia.com.
National Film Archive of India, Law College Rd, Pune 411 004. Tel: (20) 565 8049. Fax: (20) 567 0027. nfai@vsnl.net.
National Film Development Corporation Ltd, Discovery of India Bldg, Nehru Centre, Dr Annie Besant Rd, Worli, Bombay 400 018. Tel: (22) 2492 6410. www.nfdcindia.com.
Central Board of Film Certification, Bharat Bhavan, 91 E Walkeshwar Road, Mumbai 400 006. Tel: (22) 2362 5770. Fax: (22) 2369 0083. rocbfcmum@rediffmail.com.

Zoya Akhtar's **Luck By Chance**

Indonesia Lisabona Rahman

Indonesia's new film bill was passed by its parliament in early September, much to the local film scene's surprise. The new bill, which is set to complicate bureaucratic procedures with regard to production and distribution, was met with strong opposition from the industry and independent filmmakers alike.

The number of local productions this year steadily increased and the market share for local films continued to rise, but the Indonesian government seems to have its own ideas about how to treat the re-emerging film industry. Many members of the local industry were worried that the new bill would hold back growth.

Though still dominated by sex comedies and horror, the local scene actually witnessed a much richer variety of films compared to the previous year, starting with Joko Anwar's thriller **Forbidden Door** (*Pintu Terlarang*), which told the story of a man haunted by a dark family secret. It received the Best Film award at South Korea's Puchon International Fantastic Film Festival.

Joko Anwar's **Forbidden Door**

In August, action-film fans applauded the genre's return to the local film scene. The martial-arts blockbuster **Merantau Warrior** (*Merantau*) was directed by Gareth Evans and

Teddy Soeriaatmadja's **Ruma Maida**

featured the *silat* athlete Iko Uwais, whose character embarks on a search for self-identity as he enters adulthood. Historical drama also made a comeback with director Yadi Sugandi's **The Red and the White** (*Merah Putih*), which was released in time for Independence Day. It features a group of guerrilla soldiers attempting to overcome their personal conflicts due to their different cultural backgrounds during the war for independence. Another historical drama set during the same period, **Ruma Maida**, was directed by Teddy Soeriaatmadja. It focused less on the war and more on its tragic love story, witnessed through flashbacks from the present.

The first local animated film in six years, Philip Mitchell's **Sing to the Dawn** (*Meraih Mimpi*), was a co-production between Indonesia and Singapore. It was released in English and Indonesian versions and is based on a Singaporean novel about a village girl and her dream of experiencing a world beyond her home.

With more films to choose from, the audience numbers per title decreased from last year. However, the estimated total audience for local films this year is expected to exceed 60 million, roughly the same as 2008.

The industry has welcomed more newcomers. Besides Yadi Sugandi, there are at least three other first-time directors worth noting. Ifa Isfansyah's **Garuda in My Heart** (*Garuda di Dadaku*) tells the story of a boy who wants to pursue his dream of becoming a football player, against the wishes of his family. Ari Sihasale's **King**, on the other hand, is about a boy fulfilling his father's dream to become a badminton champion. An independent production blending documentary and fiction styles, Sammaria Simanjuntak's **Love** (*cin(T) a*) boldly addresses the relationship between people from different religious backgrounds, something still forbidden by Indonesian marriage law. The story takes place in contemporary Indonesia, where both terrorism and the law threaten any form of religious pluralism. These films received fairly positive responses from critics and audiences.

Chaerul Umam's **Love and Prayer Beads**

There were many sequels to last year's more popular releases, but most experienced only modest success. Two attempted to lure audiences around the Idul Fitri holiday period and represented the decade's two most commercially successful strands: romantic comedy and religious drama. In Hanung Bramantyo's **Get Married 2**, Mae – a boyish, urban-village Cinderella – is trying to bear a child for her prince. Their relationship goes sour at some point, so Mae's best friends (they're all boys) try to mend things. Chaerul Umam's **Love and Prayer Beads** (*Ketika Cinta Bertasbih*), the story of a prestigious Muslim university graduate from Cairo and his love

life, has attempted to increase its box-office takings by organising screenings to Indonesian immigrants overseas. As this article was being written, both sequels are still touring the country's cinemas and have so far attracted over 1.5 million people.

The end of the year will see the release of Riri Riza's much-anticipated **The Dreamer** (*Sang Pemimpi*), the sequel to last year's box-office hit, *The Rainbow Troops*, about a group of boys growing up on the tin-mining island of Belitong.

The year's best films
Jermal (Ravi L. Bharwani, Rayya Makarim, Utawa Tresno)
Love (Sammaria Simanjuntak)
Forbidden Door (Joko Anwar)

Quote of the year
'There is no point in setting a 60 per cent quota for Indonesian movies. When people are flooded with low-quality movies, they will simply walk away from Indonesian movies and it will make things even more difficult for us.' MIRA LESMANA *(producer) on the new screen-quota policy in the new Film Law.*

Directory
All Tel/Fax numbers begin (+62)
Ministry of Information for Film & Video, Departement Penerangan RI, Jalan Merdeka Barat 9, Gedung Belakang, Jakarta Pusat. Tel: 384 1260. Fax: 386 0830.
Ministry of Tourism, Art and Culture, Jalan Medan Merdeka Barat 17, Jakarta 10110. Tel: 383 8000/381 0123. Fax: 386 0210. http://gateway. deparsenibud.go.id.

LISABONA RAHMAN is a Jakarta-based freelance writer on film. She is Programming Manager of community cinema *Kineforum – The Jakarta Arts Council.*

Iran Kamyar Mohsenin

In its new phase of development, Iranian cinema has moved away from the characteristics (beguilingly simple narratives blending fiction and documentary approaches) that led to international recognition over the last three decades. This has also changed the emphasis on locations, with more narratives set in urban areas as opposed to rural settings. Deaking with sophisticated and problematic issues, these stories have a greater appeal amongst the larger metropolitan audiences.

Unfortunately, no matter how successful individual domestic releases are, the shortage of cinemas and the increasing expense of production have proven to be major obstacles in the development and growth of the industry. With over 200 feature films produced in 2009 and less than 300 cinemas across the whole country, overproduction or the lack of exhibition facilities are decisive challenges for the future of Iranian cinema.

The domestic market is dominated by clichéd comedies, many of which are little more than vehicles for stars of film and television. However, the incredible success of Masoud Dehnamaki's **The Expelled 2** (*Ekhrji-ha 2*) showed that inventive films were still capable of attracting an audience. After his sensational debut hit with the *The Expelled*, Dehnamaki moved from the war front to prisoner-of-war camps for the sequel, again employing familiar comedy routines within the narrative. The film was premiered out of competition at the Fajr International Film Festival, before going on to earn over US$7 million at the domestic box office. The biggest financial success in Iranian film history, *The Expelled 2* was not without controversy, attracting as much ire from some critics as it did acclaim from others.

Asghar Farhadi's **About Elly**

Away from the mainstream, some films attracted attention at various international festivals. The prominent Iranian release of the year was undoubtedly Asghar Farhadi's **About Elly** (*Darbare-ye Elly*), the Iranian submission to the 2010 Academy Awards and a winner at Fajr, Berlin and Tribeca. After *Dancing in the Dust*, *Beautiful City* and *Fireworks Wednesday*, Farhadi once again explored the human condition, this time chronicling the disappearance of a young woman, who joins a group of people on a trip to the seaside, but is abandoned and lost to the sea. A keenly observed drama about hasty judgements and how people respond under pressure, the strength of the film lies in its suspenseful narrative, recalling Michelangelo Antonioni's most acclaimed work. Enhanced by excellent performances and impressive handheld camerawork, it is a milestone in Iranian cinema.

A number of other filmmakers attracted international attention. Abdolreza Kahani's Karlovy Vary winner, **Twenty** (*Bist*), dealt with the impoverished employees in a mourning- and wedding-reception hall, who receive notice from its owner that they have just 20 days to find a new job before it is closed. With

PROMOTING
IRANIAN CINEMA

FARABI
CINEMA FOUNDATION

PRODUCTION, CO- PRODUCTION
ACQUISITIONS, SALES
DISTRIBUTION

INTERNATIONAL AFFAIRS
13, Delbar Alley, Toos St., Valiye Asr Ave.,Tehran 19617, Iran.
Tel: +98 (21) 22741252-4, 22734939
Fax: +98 (21) 22734953
E-mail: fcf1@dpi.net.ir/intl@fcf.ir

strong performances, *Twenty* interweaves stories of unhappiness, solitude, failure and death. Beginning in a social-realist style, complemented by cinematographer Masood Salami's naturalistic imagery, Kahani's film suddenly transforms into something stranger when the strict employer turns into a forgiving angel. Echoing the fears and worries that accompany a great depression, *Twenty* offered audiences hope for radical change.

Bahman Ghobadi's **Nobody Knows about the Persian Cats**

Abdolreza Kahani's **Twenty**

Hamid Nematollah found a different way of approaching power and poverty in **The Penniless** (*Bi-pouli*). He traced the decline of one person, who is a fashion designer when the film begins, only to descend to being an unemployed liar. Nematollah effectively employs comedy, approaching tragic moments from a different perspective. With its subtle characterisation, inventive humour and sharp dialogue, *The Penniless* marks an attempt to break away from familiar territory in more artistically oriented Iranian films, where even the simplest of situations are viewed through a dark and gloomy eye. Maziar Miri's **The Book of the Law** (*Ketab-e Ghanoun*), which detailed the marriage of an Iranian man to a Lebanese woman, was another thought-provoking and crowd-pleasing comedy of manners.

Mohsen Amiryousefi's **The Fire Keeper** (*Atashkar*) took a comical look at the life of a foundry worker and his preoccupation with vasectomy. A bitter black comedy, everything revolves around this melancholic man. Sadly, the film lacked the wit and intelligence of the

director's 2004 comedy, *Bitter Dream*, about an undertaker's obsession with death. However, *The Fire Keeper* received the innovation award at the Montreal World Film Festival, where Mohammad Reza Vatandoust's first film, **When the Lemons Turned Yellow...** (*Vaghti Limou-ha Zard Shodand...*), also screened. The story of everlasting love blossoming in the middle of a war, it was awarded the Silver Zenith. With its stunning impressionistic imagery, Vatandoust's debut just manages to carry off its melodramatic plot.

A worthy winner at Taormina Film Festival was Ensieh Shah-Hosseini's **Penalty**, which depicts a decisive football match that impacts on the lives of a group of poor children and their families in the southern part of the country. An emotionally engaging and all-too-humane film, its realist aesthetic was spiced with humorous moments. Tahimineh Milani, one of the country's leading female filmmakers, took a different course with her latest film, **Superstar** (*Superstar*). With shades of Hermann Hesse, it followed a young man in moral decline, who looks at himself and the life he is leading after encountering a mysterious girl. Interestingly, the man is a film star and so Milani's narrative looked inwards at the state of the Iranian film industry and caused considerable controversy.

Also, Parviz Shahbazi returned with the cryptic film, **Karat 14** (*Ayyar Chahardah*), about a convict's actions following his release from prison. Crosscutting between past and present, including the heist that saw the man incarcerated, Shahbazi played with perceptions of reality and how vulnerable our interpretation of it can actually be. An eccentric mixture of the director's vision, combined with elements of Kiarostami and tropes of the western genre, *Karat 14* was a favourite amongst local critics.

The last year also saw the return of a few great directors to Iranian cinema. Masoud Kimiaie revived the mood of his 1969 classic, *Qaisar*, in **The Trial in the Streets** (*Mohakemeh dar Khiaban*), a story of betrayal, doubt and revenge. Meanwhile, Bahram Beizai criticised Iranian film-production processes in **When We Are All Sleeping** (*Vaghti hameh khabim*). And, in **Doubt** (*Tardid*), Varouzh Karim-Massihi presented an Iranian variation on *Hamlet*, which won the Fajr Film Festival's Best Film Award.

Finally, Bahman Ghobadi's **Nobody Knows about the Persian Cats** (*Kasi az gorbeh-ha-ye irani khabar nadareh*), a fast-paced tale about Iranian underground musicians, was well received at Cannes.

Abdolreza Kahani's **Twenty**

The year's best films
About Elly (Asghar Farhadi)
The Penniless (Hamid Nematollah)
Karat 14 (Parviz Shahbazi)
The Book of the Law (Maziar Miri)
Twenty (Abdolreza Kahani)

Quote of the year
'It is not possible to omit the film permits from the process of filmmaking. But we have just two issues in mind: preventing insults to religious beliefs and stopping the moral decline to save the family lives. If these two issues were not ignored, we would have not been witnessing the reduction in the annual rates of the admissions from 57 million to 13 million in the recent years.' *Deputy Minister* JAVAD SHAMAGHDARI.

Directory
All Tel/Fax numbers begin (+98)
Farabi Cinema Foundation – International Affairs, Tel: (21) 22741254. Fax: (21) 22734953. fcf1@dpi.net.ir.
IRIB Media Trade, Tel: (21) 22548032. Fax: (21) 22551914. info@iribmediatrade.com.
Documentary and Experimental Film Center, Tel: (21) 88511241. Fax: (21) 88511242. naderi@defc.ir.
Iranian Young Cinema Society, Tel: (21) 88773114. Fax: (21) 88779073. varshochi@iycs.ir.

KAMYAR MOHSENIN has worked as a film critic and TV host in film programmes for the last 15 years. He is also in charge of Research in International Affairs for the Farabi Cinema Foundation.

Asghar Farhadi's **About Elly**

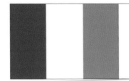

Ireland Donald Clarke

Few countries have been quite so scarred by the current economic downturn as Ireland. So it was hardly surprising that much of the conversation at the nation's film festivals turned to belt-tightening strategies. Although some very interesting domestic films premiered this year – notably Ken Wardrop's **His & Hers**, Conor Horgan's **One Hundred Mornings** and Tomm Moore's **The Secret of Kells** – the main topic of debate remained the state of the Irish Film Board. On 16 July, the Special Group on Public Service Numbers and Expenditure Programmes, an advisory body established to recommend cuts in public spending, published a report that, among many other things, called for the abolition of the board and the amalgamation of its funding duties with those of Enterprise Ireland. Such a decision would significantly alter – many irate filmmakers would say 'damage' – the lines of communication between the film sector and state funders.

Ken Wardrop's **His & Hers**

Did the uncertainty lead to a degree of caution among distributors? Well, it was notable that, whereas 2008 saw a swathe of (all too often sub-standard) Irish films making it into cinemas, this year there were far fewer domestic pictures at the multiplex. Nonetheless, two very decent Irish films did receive a release early on in the year. Joel Conroy's visually overpowering **Waveriders**, a

Joel Conroy's **Waveriders**

study of Irish surfing and the nation's influence on the sport worldwide, included stunning photography and some surprising insights on the Ulsterman who reinvigorated surf culture in early-twentieth-century Hawaii. *The Secret of Kells*, an animated feature dealing with the creation of 'The Book of Kells' – the nation's famous medieval illuminated gospel – proved to be a strange, sumptuous film featuring fine voice work from the likes of Brendan Gleeson and Mick Lally. Released by Disney, the picture won the Dublin Film Critics Circle prize for best Irish feature at the Jameson Dublin International Film Festival and the audience prize at the Edinburgh Film Festival.

As Christmas loomed, two Irish comedies – Stephen Burke's **Happy Ever Afters** and Lisa Mulcahy's **Situations Vacant** – arrived in commercial cinemas. But domestic pictures were, for most of the year, hard to locate in the high street.

That noted, visitors to the main festivals would have detected little evidence of any crisis in Irish filmmaking. Also premiering at the Dublin International Film Festival was the delightfully eccentric **Eamon**. Later reviewed warmly at the Toronto Film Festival, Margaret Corkery's

Margaret Corkery's **Eamon**

comedy follows a squabbling couple as they holiday with their troublesome child in a bleak seaside resort. Combining quirky surrealism with darker moods, the film finds Corkery maintaining the quality of her early shorts, while stretching confidently into the longer form.

Other highlights of the Dublin Festival included a public interview with Liam Neeson and a characteristically noisy performance by the Canadian heavy metal band Anvil following a screening of the self-explanatory *Anvil: The Story of Anvil*.

The main launching platform for new Irish features remains the Galway Film Fleadh in July and the 2009 jamboree saw an exciting array of premieres. Long lauded for his excellent shorts – indeed, he has already received a retrospective at the Cork Film Festival – Ken Wardrop stunned audiences with his quasi-documentary *His & Hers*. Beginning with a shot of a baby and ending with a perky nonagenarian lady, the picture invites a sizeable collection of females from the Irish midlands, appearing in order of their age, to comment upon the men in their lives. Impressively sure of his own voice, the director somehow persuades the viewer to believe that each woman is talking about the same man. Greeted with warm applause, the picture deservedly went on to win the audience prize at the Fleadh.

Also worthy of mention was the canny, evocative, post-apocalyptic drama by Conor Horgan, *One Hundred Mornings*. Beautifully

shot in washed-out watercolours by Suzie Lavelle, the film sends four young people to a remote cabin following a vaguely defined collapse in western society. Featuring contained, committed performances by Suzie Lavelle, Kelly Campbell, Alex Reid and Rory Keenan, the film tells its unhappy story through a neat arc, but it never feels forced or overworked. Distributors may be nervous about reviewers drawing unhelpful parallels with John Hillcoat's *The Road*, but the film deserves a commercial release.

Fans of John Carney's *Once*, the breakout hit of 2007, may have been slightly taken aback by the raucous **Zonad**. Co-written and co-directed with Kieran Carney, John's brother, this achingly funny film follows a drunken layabout who, mistaken for an alien, persuades the gullible inhabitants of a small Irish town to provide him with sex, sausages and booze. Set in an odd amalgam of 1950s America and contemporary Ireland, the film does strain at the constrictions of its tiny budget, but it's so stupidly amusing that it would seem churlish to complain.

Neil Jordan's **Ondine**

Still absorbing news about their employer's potential abolition, representatives of the Irish Film Board put on a brave face and proudly presented five features funded or co-funded by the body at September's Toronto Film Festival. Neil Jordan's **Ondine** (Colin Farrell finds a mermaid), Jordan Scott's **Cracks** (Ridley's daughter directs a school drama), Carter Gunn and Ross McDonnell's **Colony** (a documentary about missing bees) and Ian Fitzgibbon's **Perrier's Bounty** (comic villainy

Jordan Scott's **Cracks**

from distinguished writer Mark O'Rowe) joined Corkery's *Eamon* at the festival.

The board's rising mood was boosted further in October when the Renewed Programme for Government, a new agreement hammered out between the ruling Fianna Fáil and Green parties, appeared to offer assurances that the coalition was minded to ignore pleas for abolition of the board. One of the five commitments to the arts stated that: 'We will ensure that the supports provided by the Film Board are maintained in order to realise the potential of Irish filmmaking.'

At time of writing, the country is still waiting a final decision in the December budget, but it seems that the organisation – founded in 1980, abolished in 1987, reconstituted in 1993 – may be safe for another year. Cuts are, however, inevitable. Hard times will be with us for some while to come.

The year's best films

One Hundred Mornings (Conor Horgan)
His & Hers (Ken Wardrop)
The Secret of Kells (Tomm Moore)
Waveriders (Joel Conroy)
Eamon (Margaret Corkery)

Quotes of the year

'Oh, every time I see Anthony Hopkins I think I'm just getting away with it. I have always felt that I have, to some extent, been getting away with it.' LIAM NEESON *chats at the Jameson Dublin International Film Festival.*

'What happened during the 1960s and 1970s here was disgraceful: people were denied the right to see 700 films. When they did eventually appear, as was the case with *Casablanca* and *The Graduate*, significant sections of plot were often excised.' JOHN KELLEHER, *proud liberal, retires as a reforming Director of the Irish Film Classification Office.*

Directory

All Tel/Fax numbers begin (+353)
Film Censor's Office, 16 Harcourt Terrace, Dublin 2. Tel: (1) 799 6100. Fax: (1) 676 1898. info@ifco.gov.ie.
Film Institute of Ireland, 6 Eustace St, Dublin 2. Tel: (1) 679 5744. Fax: (1) 679 9657. www.fii.ie.
Irish Film Board, Rockfort House, St Augustine St, Galway, Co Galway. Tel: (91) 561 398. Fax: (91) 561 405. www.filmboard.ie.
Screen Directors Guild of Ireland, 18 Eustace St, Temple Bar, Dublin 2. Tel: (1) 633 7433. Fax: (1) 478 4807. info@sdgi.ie.
Screen Producers Ireland, The Studio Bldg, Meeting House Sq, Temple Bar, Dublin 2. Tel: (1) 671 3525. Fax: (1) 671 4292. www.screenproducers-ireland.com.

DONALD CLARKE is a film critic and feature writer for *The Irish Times*. A graduate of Trinity College Dublin, he makes frequent appearances on RTÉ radio and is a regular panellist on the television arts show, *The View*. He has also written two successful short films – *My Dinner With Oswald* and *Pitch 'n' Putt with Beckett 'n' Joyce* – the latter of which he also directed.

Tomm Moore's **The Secret of Kells**

Israel Dan Fainaru

The age of introspection is over. For a while, everybody talked about Israeli cinema coming of age, finally discussing real, intimate issues instead of addressing topics way over its head, such as the Middle East conflict. But after *Beaufort*, *Waltz with Bashir*, and now **Lebanon**, the wind seems to be changing. Politics has re-entered films, though not quite in the same way it once used to figure.

Shmuel Maoz's **Lebanon**

Lebanon, this year's Golden Lion recipient in Venice, is based on the personal experience of writer/director Shmuel Maoz and has the ferocious intensity of a nightmare that time has failed to efface. The visualization of Maoz's memories, which have been haunting him for over twenty years, is a tour de force. It was shot entirely within the confines of a tank (albeit a set which looked like a tank), depicting the hallucinatory first day of the war through the eyes of an 18 year-old gunner. Evidently still tormented by his personal demons, Maoz took 3 years to bring his vision to the screen.

Although it is arguably this year's Israeli flag bearer on the international stage, its reception at home was more subdued. The intransigence of Maoz's approach, the intentional absence of any psychological depth and, most of all, the grimness of the subject and its treatment, has kept some viewers away. Cynics, meanwhile, have once again brought up the old accusation against a type of film they call 'shoot and cry', about Israelis who pretend to justify their war records by shedding tears of sorrow over themselves and their victims. In this case, however, even the cynics had to concede the tears were sincere.

The Israeli critical and commercial success of the year was **Ajami**, by first-time directors Scandar Copti and Yaron Shani; one an Arab, the other a Jew. They wrote the script with the help of an amateur cast that rehearsed for ten months before shooting in pseudo-documentary style on the streets of one of the less privileged Jaffa slums, which gives the film its title. Its protagonists are Christians, Muslims and Jews. It opens with the murder of a Muslim boy on the street, proceeding later with the murder of a Jew by a bunch of Arab boys on another street and ends in a free-for-all shootout in an underground parking lot, triggered by a variety of reasons including drugs, race and sheer rage. A stunning portrait of the uneasy relations between all these communities in a small, crime-infested territory, it serves as an allegory for the entire country. Though shot chronologically,

Scandar Copti and Yaron Shani's **Ajami**

the film is divided into chapters, each one covering the same time period and inviting the audience to reach conclusions that are disproved in the next chapter, leading to a tragic ending, in which everyone shares the guilt and no solution is found. Unveiled in Cannes's Directors' Fortnight, it dominated the Israeli Academy Awards and will represent the country at the 2010 Oscars.

Keren Yedaya's **Jaffa**

Sharon Maymon and Erez Tadmor's **A Matter of Size**

The undisputed box-office champion of the year is likely to be **A Matter of Size** (*Sipur Gadol*) by another two debutants, Sharon Maymon and Erez Tadmor, an innocent crowd pleaser about four overweight gentlemen who, once they realise that all their efforts to lose weight are in vain, decide it's wiser and far more rewarding to form a Sumo team where they can display their massive physiques. Since its debut at Tribeca, it has gathered momentum at international festivals, marking one of the very rare instances of an Israeli film whose success lies in its value as entertainment and not because of some political or social statement.

In a record year that featured no less than 25 new films, almost double the average Israeli output, there are many that could be discussed. The best included **Eyes Wide Open** (*Eynaim Pekuchoth*), Hayim Tabakman's homosexual love story that drew attention in Cannes, mostly because it takes place in Jerusalem's Ultra-Orthodox community. Keren Yedaya's **Jaffa** (*Kalat Hayam*) was a somewhat limp follow-up to her award-winning *Or*,

which tried but failed in its attempt to employ a Romeo & Juliet-style Mediterranean melodrama to deal with Jewish-Arab relations. Using the same locations as *Ajami*, it never really integrated them in a plot that ultimately failed to catch fire. Renen Schorr returned after a self-imposed silence of over 20 years with **The Loners** (*Habodedim*). Two young Russian-born soldiers rebel against the Israeli military establishment in a film that doesn't quite make up its mind which of the main issues it raises it actually wants to tackle. As for **There Were Nights** (*Hayu Leylot*), Roni Ninio seems too intimately related to the subject he has chosen to dare to explore the heart of the matter. It is the true story of his father, a well-known theatre director, who was sent to jail for tax evasion.

Renen Schorr's **The Loners**

There was a long list of documentary releases. Among them was Dana Goren's **Diplomat**, about a former luxury hotel that was turned into a home for hundreds of Russian emigrants caught between the world they left behind and the one they have not yet entered. Anat Tzuria's

Black Bus (*Soreret*) was the final part of a trilogy dedicated to the state of women in the Ultra-Orthodox Jewish community, this time focusing on the fate of young women who choose to leave the community for the secular world. Both films look set for international distribution.

Anat Tzuria's **Black Bus**

Considering the number of foreign investors currently interested in Israeli films, it might look like business is better than ever. Probably true, but neither the local distributors nor the TV channels, which should be part of the game, seem particularly eager to recognise it. Finding screens for domestic films when United King, the main investor in Israeli cinema and a powerful exhibitor in its own right, is not involved remains a serious problem. The Israeli Film Fund is now offering additional help to producers who wish to administer their own distribution, as happened with *Ajami*. As for broadcasters, only two of the six operating in the country are respecting the letter of the law and investing in films. Some claim that business is bad and they can't afford it. Unless they are compelled to respect their obligations, there is no other obvious partner to share the burden of production. And all the relative generosity of the Treasury, which pledged to keep supporting cinema at the same level it has been doing, may not be enough to keep production going.

DAN FAINARU is co-editor of Israel's only film magazine, *Cinematheque*, and a former director of the Israeli Film Institute. He reviews regularly for *Screen International*.

The year's best films

Ajami (Skander Kopti, Yaron Shani)
Lebanon (Shmuel Maoz)
The Loners (Renen Schorr)
A Matter of Size
(Sharon Maymon, Erez Tadmor)
Black Bus (Anat Tzuria)

Quote of the year

'ARTE, a French broadcaster, is putting more money into Israeli films than all our own broadcasters put together.' MAREK ROZENBAUM, *President of the Producers Association, at the Israeli Film Academy annual ceremony.*

Directory

All Tel/Fax numbers begin (+972)
Israel Film Archive, Jerusalem Film Centre, Derech Hebron, PO Box 8561, Jerusalem 91083. Tel: (2) 565 4333. Fax: (2) 565 4335. jer-cin@jer-cin. org.il. www.jer-cin.org.il.
Israel Film Fund, 12 Yehudith Blvd, Tel Aviv 67016. Tel: (2) 562 8180. Fax: (2) 562 5992. info@filmfund. org.il. www.filmfund.org.il.
Israeli Film Council, 14 Hamasger St, PO Box 57577, Tel Aviv 61575. Tel: (3) 636 7288. Fax: (3) 639 0098. etic@most.gov.il.
Tel Aviv Cinema Project, 29, Idelson St, Tel Aviv 65241. Tel. (2) 525 5020. info@cinemaproject.co.il. www.cinemaproject.org.il.
The New Fund for Cinema and Television, 112, Hayarkon St, Tel Aviv. Tel. (3) 522 0909. info@nfct. org.il. www.nfct.org.il.

Shmuel Maoz's **Lebanon**

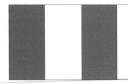

Italy Lorenzo Codelli

Despite the economic crisis, Italians are spending more money on entertainment and attending the cinema remains their most popular pastime. During the first six months of 2009, 55.5 million tickets were sold (an increase of 1.8% over the previous year). Of course, most audiences are enthralled by Hollywood blockbusters and locally produced 'fast-food' vehicles. Escapist portmanteau farces such as Giovanni Veronesi's **Italians** or Fausto Brizzi's **Ex**, the first exploiting clichés about Italians abroad while the latter offers up truisms about ex-lovers, proved very popular. Their veteran producers, Aurelio De Laurentiis and Fulvio Lucisano, know perfectly well how to homogenise old and new stars, and how to launch them through massive promotional campaigns.

Giovanni Veronesi's **Italians**

Industry mammoth, Medusa, has gone overboard in its efforts to launch their €35 million extravaganza, **Baaria**, with Silvio Berlusconi himself – owner of Medusa and of almost everything else in Italy – loudly heralding his product prior to its Venice Film Festival premiere. With *Baarìa*, Giuseppe Tornatore wished to create his own kind of *1900*, an epic focusing on his father, a Communist trade unionist, who struggled for

Giuseppe Tornatore's **Baarìa**

private happiness and social justice, from the Fascist era until the late 1960s, in Bagheria ('Baaria' in local jargon), Sicily. Instead of Bernardo Bertolucci's operatic, utopian vision, Tornatore has opted for a cartoonish approach, pasting together repetitive scenes peopled by an army of caricatures. Sicilian comedians, running and shouting non-stop and deafened by Ennio Morricone's bombastic score, push hard to enliven this barely concealed remake of *Cinema Paradiso*, Tornatore's spectacularly successful 1988 Oscar winner. His very superficial approach to Italian history, and particularly to the bloody roots of the Sicilian mafia, curtails any autobiographical veracity. *Baarìa* was shot over two years at Tarak Ben Ammar's studios in Tunisia, using hundreds of local technicians and extras. Consequently, Tornatore (who had already shot *Malena* in Morocco) could be called Italy's major 'outsourcing filmmaker'.

Using a much smaller budget from Medusa, Michele Placido falls into a similar trap – or is it a *trend* induced by TV moguls? – with his autobiographical **The Big Dream** (*Il grande sogno*). It is a bland attempt to reconstruct his experiences as a proletarian cop 'truncheoning' revolutionary students circa 1968. Jasmine

Michele Placido's **The Big Dream**

Trinca, exquisitely embodying a bespectacled bourgeois Maoist who falls for her 'class enemy', deserved the Marcello Mastroianni Award as 'Best Discovery' at Venice. Her character reminds us constantly of her subtler and far more moving role in Marco Tullio Giordana's *The Best of Youth*, a classic study of the 1960s generation. By contrast, in **The First Line** (*La prima linea*), Renato De Maria tackles the rise and fall of a real couple of terrorist killers from the 1970s. His brave but convoluted and mostly uninspired film was the year's favourite target of reactionaries and censors.

Amusing himself once again with fragments of memories and myths from his Felliniesque teenager's misadventures, Pupi Avati's **Margherita Bar's Friends** (*Gli amici del Bar Margherita*) contemplates a grotesque microcosm of life, where chatting and plotting takes place daily in an old Bologna pub. It is a case of 1950s nostalgia galore, enhanced by Lucio Dalla's superb score and a cast of largely sympathetic, clownish characters.

Pupi Avati's **Margherita Bar's Friends**

Though failing to get even a mention from the Cannes Film Festival's Competition jury, **Vincere** represents yet another masterstroke from Marco Bellocchio. The mature phase of this once insurgent and aggressive director confirms more and more that his fists are still in his pocket – to paraphrase the title of his most celebrated film – and that he is still stoking the fires of political angst. Unveiling the secret story of young Benito Mussolini's first wife and son, Bellocchio analyses the psychological and political mechanisms of power within a fearful regime ruled by the church and dominated by aggressive levels of machismo; an era not too different from today. Filippo Timi's and Giovanna Mezzogiorno's devilish performances, as tormentor and butchered victim, are in tune with the extraordinary virtuosity of the film's montage sequences, overseen by Bellocchio's devoted partner Francesca Calvelli, which blend newsreels, silent films and melodramatic climaxes.

Filippo Timi and Giovanna Mezzogiorno in Marco Bellochio's **Vincere**

The infamous 1944 Marzabotto massacre of 800 civilians by the Nazis is presented through the innocent eyes of a peasant girl in Giorgio Diritti's **The Man Who Will Come** (*L'uomo che verrà*). A pupil of both Pupi Avati and Ermanno Olmi, Diritti has received several awards for his directorial debut, *The Wind Blows Round*, which received little distribution. With his second opus, he paints a multi-layered fresco of rural life under duress. It is influenced by *The Tree of the Wooden Clogs'* subdued austerity and features professional actors side by side with real country people, all talking in strict Emilian dialect, which is subtitled in Italian.

Giorgio Diritti's **The Man Who Will Come**

In **The White Space** (*Lo spazio bianco*), Cristina Comencini explores the unstable soul of a mother anxious to know if her prematurely born baby will survive or not. Luca Bigazzi's luminous camerawork and Margherita Buy's fluid acting boost Comencini's heart-warming weepie.

Among the most interesting debutants of the year was Giuseppe Capotondi, a commercials director who appears to want to adopt the style of Dario Argento's early giallos and their sinister mood. His thriller, **The Double Hour** (*La doppia ora*), traces the double life of a Slovenian waitress, played by Russian actress Ksenia Rappoport, who received the Best Actress award at Venice.

Giuseppe Capotondi's **The Double Hour**

Giuseppe Piccioni's nicely crafted romance, **Giulia Doesn't Date at Night** (*Giulia non esce la sera*), like Marco Risi's Neapolitan camorra drama **Fortapàsc**, Marco Amenta's vivid anti-mafia exposé **The Sicilian Rebel** (*La siciliana ribelle*), and Alessandro Angelini's father-and-

son match, **Rise Your Head** (*Alza la testa*), was praised by critics but failed to attract a large audience.

Comedies 'Italian style' are not a completely lost genre, even if contemporary farceurs look rather fangless when compared with Dino Risi or Marco Ferreri. Luca Lucini's **Married Today** (*Oggi sposi*) and Umberto Riccioni Carteni's **Different from Whom?** (*Diverso da chi?*) are typical of the Cattleya company's box-office-oriented satires, blending sex and social topics in an elegant, often inoffensive way. Also from Riccardo Tozzi's Cattleya production house, Francesca Archibugi's **A Matter of Heart** (*Questione di cuore*) is a colourful, hospital-set tragi-comedy starring popular actors Kim Rossi Stuart and Antonio Albanese. Will these films be as successful abroad as Risi's and Ferreri's in their time? One suspects that current filmmakers do not care, nor dare, enough to export their 'made in Italy' commodities.

The Berlusconi government is not only curtailing its already meagre support of the film industry, it is also encouraging its ministers to cannonade filmmakers at random as 'state profiteers'. Such scandalous attacks against artists have not been seen anywhere in Europe since Stalin, Mussolini and Hitler's regimes. Those same shameless ministers are also injecting public money into explicit right-wing propaganda. Take, for instance, Renzo Martinelli's **Red Beard** (*Barbarossa*), a racist Barbarian tract, or Michele Soavi's fascistic saga, **Blood of the Losers** (*Il sangue dei vinti*), both straining to preach revised history lessons. Predictably, they flopped, but they will unfortunately be resurrected all too soon on television, in much longer – and deadlier – versions.

Maestro Ermanno Olmi directed two assured, idiosyncratic documentaries in a row. **Mother Earth** (*Terra madre*) was applauded at the Berlinale, while **Wine Cliffs** (*Rupi del vino*) graced the Rome Film Festival. He is encouraging us to rediscover the lost pleasures of slow food and healthy drinking.

ABU DHABI FILM COMMISSION

Ermanno Olmi's **Mother Earth**

His Virgilian poem, devoted to Valtellina's vine-dressers who work in vineyards exactly like their Middle Age predecessors, made some people a little less pessimistic about the future.

Though Federico Fellini has never been forgotten in Italy, it was Paris that celebrated his genius, thanks to an inventive exhibition at Jeu de Pomme Museum, which was linked to handsome DVD editions and illustrated books. Sergio Leone's anniversary was magnificently celebrated at Lyon's Lumière Festival with brand-new restorations, while New York's Lincoln Centre honoured neorealism with brand new prints.

Next season should offer us a few gifts, such as Nanni Moretti's **We Got the Pope** (*Abbiamo il Papa*), Daniele Luchetti's **Our Life** (*La nostra vita*) and Mario Martone's **We Believed** (*Noi credevamo*).

LORENZO CODELLI is on the board of Cineteca del Friuli, a Cannes Film Festival adviser and a regular contributor to *Positif* and other cinema-related publications.

The year's best films
Vincere (Marco Bellocchio)
Margherita Bar's Friends (Pupi Avati)
The Man Who Will Come (Giorgio Diritti)
Wine Cliffs (Ermanno Olmi)
The White Space (Cristina Comencini)

Quote of the year
'Mussolini was indeed the first politician who used his image to impose himself.' **Vincere** *director* MARCO BELLOCCHIO.

Directory
All Tel/Fax numbers begin (+39)
Filmitalia-Cinecittà, Via Tuscolana 1055, 00173 Rome. Tel. (6) 722 861. Fax: (6) 7228 6324. www.filmitalia.org/mission.asp?lang=ing.
Cineteca del Comune, Via Riva di Reno, 40122 Bologna. Tel: (51) 204 820. www.cinetecadibologna.it.
Cineteca del Friuli, Via Bini 50, Palazzo Gurisatti, 33013 Gemona del Friuli, Udine. Tel: (4) 3298 0458. Fax: (4) 3297 0542. cdf@cinetecadelfriuli.org. http://cinetecadelfriuli.org.
Cineteca Nazionale, Via Tuscolana 1524, 00173 Rome. Tel: (6) 722 941. www.snc.it.
Fondazione Cineteca Italiana, Villa Reale, Via Palestro 16, 20121 Milan. Tel: (2) 799 224. Fax: (2) 798 289. info@cinetecamilano.it. www.cinetecamilano.it.
Fondazione Federico Fellini, Via Oberdan 1, 47900 Rimini. Tel (541) 50085. Fax: (541) 57378. fondazione@federicofellini.it. www.federicofellini.it/.
Museo Nazionale del Cinema, Via Montebello 15, 10124 Turin. Tel: (11) 812 2814. www.museonazionaledelcinema.org.

Margherita Buy in Cristina Comencini's **The White Space**

Japan Katsuta Tomomi

More than 400 domestic films, along with a similar number of foreign films, opened in Japan by the end of 2009, dozens of which generated over one billion yen in revenue, the marker of a commercial hit. The box-office gross is likely to equal the previous year, aided by strong local blockbusters produced by television networks and the major studios, Toho, Toei and Shochiku.

However, everyone in the industry has recognised that the situation is more stagnant than stable. While annual admissions have changed little over the last few years, blockbusters are taking a larger part of the box-office share than ever and the decline in foreign film consumption has showed no signs of stopping. Independent distributors have been struggling to survive, with the recent bankruptcy of Wise Policy and Movie Eye being seen by many in the industry as exemplifying everything that is currently wrong. And rumours suggest that other distributors may follow suit.

Toho, the largest studio and distributor, has long been the partner of choice for the networks, because of its size and strong marketing operation. So far this year, five of its films have surpassed three billion yen at the box office. At the top of the list is **Rookies** (*Rukiizu: Sotsugyo*), an adaptation of the popular television drama that was produced by TBS, about a high-school baseball team comprising delinquent students who dream of going to the Koshien High School baseball tournament. **Gokusen The Movie** (*Gokusen The movie*) earned 3.5 billion yen. The big-screen adaptation of NTV's comedy, it features a high-school teacher who is also the heir apparent of a crime syndicate. Despite featuring TV drama clichés,

with predictable storylines and excessive emotions, the films had strong appeal amongst the series' original fans, many of whom come from territories outside Japan.

However, the networks have also been looking for something new, even taking on more challenging material. TBS and Shochiku released Takaita Yojiro's *Departures* in September 2008, whose approach to death – the central character prepares dead bodies – dealt with a Japanese taboo head-on. The film won numerous local and international awards, including the Grand Prix in Montreal and the Academy Award for Best Foreign Language Film. It eventually raked in six billion yen.

Kimura Daisaku's The Summit: A Chronicle of Stones

Kimura Daisaku, the 70-year-old cinematographer, made his directorial debut with **The Summit: A Chronicle of Stones** (*Tsurugi-dake: ten no ki*). It recounts the true story of a group of surveyors who were the first to ascend the previously unconqued Mt. Tsurugi-dake in 1907. In his search for authenticity, Kimura led his cast and crew to the summit of the mountain in a shoot that took over two years to complete. Co-produced with Toei and Fuji TV stations, the director succeeded in bringing the breathtaking images of the mountain and the passion of those earlier explorers to the screen.

Fuji TV and Toho were responsible for releasing one of the year's most critically acclaimed films, Negishi Kichitaro's **Villon's Wife** (*Viyon no Tsuma: Outou to Tanpopo*). An adaptation of Dazai Osamu's popular novel, it is set in Tokyo following the Second World War and follows the wife of a decadent writer, whose sense of hope casts a light on the dark shadow of war and economic turmoil.

Negishi Kichitaro's **Villon's Wife**

Miike Takashi, the most prolific director in Japan and acclaimed internationally as a cult master, has found new admirers, in the form of mainstream producers, following the box-office success of 2007's *Crows-Episode 0*, a manga-inspired action film about high-school delinquents. He scored again with its sequel, **Crows II** (*Kuroozu Zero II*), and also **Yatterman** (*Yattaaman*), an action comedy based on a popular animated television series from the 1970s. Both films grossed more than three billion yen. Exploring various genres and

Miike Takashi's **Yatterman**

adept at playing to market demands, Miike unmistakably carved his signature with his visual style and twisted narratives. Independent films took a lower profile in

Koreeda Hirokazu's **Air Doll**

2009, but some titles still attracted critics and audiences. The young Nishikawa Miwa directed **Dear Doctor**, about a fraudulent medical practitioner in a remote village. Along with a familiar con plot, Nishikawa raises serious questions about the blurred boundaries between truth and lies, at the same time exploring the problems of a lack of medical expertise in the country's more remote regions. Koreeda Hirokazu explored the hollowness of the urbanites in **Air Doll** (*Kuuki Ningyo*), in which a life-size, blow-up doll develops a soul. Koreeda follows the doll through the lonely metropolitan environment in a film that ultimately conveys both the sweetness and bitter side of human relationships. The film benefited greatly from the brilliant performance of Korean actress Bea Doo-Na, bringing to life this surreal fantasy. Ogata Akira's comedy-drama **Noriben – The Recipe of Fortune** (*Nonchan Noriben*), about a single mother facing the harsh realities of life whilst developing her skills as a cook, highlighted the immaturity of adults in Japanese society. Meanwhile, cult director Sono Shion rebelled against traditional Japanese filmmaking with **Love Exposure** (*Ai No Mukidashi*), an epic love story with a chaotic blend of lust, perversion, violence and religion. Running close to four hours, this dazzling rollercoaster of a film features powerful images that never bore. Pia Film Festival, a competition for independent filmmakers, is a fertile source of new talent. In 2009, two filmmakers made splendid debuts: Ichii Masahide with **Naked of Defenses** (*Mubobi*), a psychological drama; and Naito Takatsugu with **The Dark Harbour** (*Futoko*), an off-beat, Kaurismaki-style romantic comedy.

Hosoda Mamoru's **Summer Wars**

There was a retrospective of Japanese anime, entitled *Manga Impact*, at the Locarno Film Festival, which was intended to offer European audiences some perspective on the genre. The latest anime release, Hosoda Mamoru's **Summer Wars**, screened in competition at the festival. Set in the near future, the film depicts a war between a large family and an avatar that has thrown the world into chaos. It is an outstanding film that blends state-of-the-art sci-fi with a more conventional, heart-warming family story. Anno Hideaki's **Evangelion: 2.0 You Can (Not) Advance** (*Evangerion Shin Gekijoban: Ha*) was another of the year's animated sensations. Originally a television series in the early 1990s, it is set in the future, where human beings are fighting a war against aliens, called 'shito' or 'apostles', using robots piloted by teenagers. It received an enthusiastic response from fans of the

Anno Hideaki's **Evangelion: 2.0 You Can (Not) Advance**

genre and required very little promotion to turn in a profit.

Documentaries are receiving wider theatrical releases, thanks to the attention of a small but committed audience. Veteran director Heneda Sumiko's **A Story of Manchurian Settler Communities** (*Aa, Manmo Kaitakudan*) follows the survivors of the Manchurian settler communities in northeast China during World War II. At the end of the war, millions of Japanese settlers died in Manchukuo, on their way home. Haneda collected the testimonies of the survivors and followed their footsteps in China in order to record the tragedy. Matsue Tetsuaki's **Annyong Yumika** (*Annyon Yumika*) is the story of the now-deceased queen of porn. Searching for her lost film that was shot in South Korea, Tetsuaki reveals what life was like on set, highlighting the affection those who worked with her felt for the actress. **Mental** (*Seishin*) is the second feature-documentary by Soda Kazuhiro. His film was shot in a mental clinic, detailing the daily lives of the patients and employees of a facility that is normally concealed from the public eye. Adopting Frederic Wiseman's patient approach, Soda blurs the simple diagnoses of sane and insane.

Soda Kazuhiro's **Mental**

In 2010, internationally acclaimed directors such as Kitano Takeshi and Yamada Yoji will release new films, alongside the many domestic blockbusters that will bolster the box office. However, with little sign of change for the fate of foreign films, the ominous clouds currently hanging over the industry are unlikely to be dispelled any time soon.

Nishikawa Miwa's **Dear Doctor**

The year's best films
Dear Doctor (Nishikawa Miwa)
Villon's Wife (Negishi Kichitaro)
Noriben – The Recipe of Fortune (Ogata Akira)
Summer Wars (Hosoda Mamoru)
Air Doll (Koreeda Hirokazu)

Quote of the year
'The one and only thing I did as a director
was to bring the actors up to the mountains.
Shooting was like a documentary. I asked
them not to act but to react and to express
with honesty their reactions to the severe
environment and nature. All I had to do was
not miss the right moment to record them.'
KIMURA DAISAKU, *talking about the shooting of*
The Summit: A Chronicle of Stones.

Directory
All Tel/Fax numbers begin (+81)
Kawakita Memorial Film Institute, Kawakita
Memorial Bldg, 18 Ichiban-cho, Chiyoda-ku, Tokyo
102-0082. Tel: 3265 3281. Fax: 3265 3276. info@
kawakita-film.or.jp. www.kawakita-film.or.jp.
Motion Picture Producers Association of Japan,
Tokyu Ginza Bldg 3F, 2-15-2 Ginza, Chuo-ku, Tokyo
104-0061. Tel: 3547 1800. Fax: 3547 0909. eiren@
mc.neweb.ne.jp.
National Film Center, 3-7-6 Kyobashi, Chuo-ku,
Tokyo 104-0031. Tel: 5777 8600. www.momat.go.jp.

KATSUTA TOMOMI is a journalist for the
Mainichi newspapers in charge of films. He
recently published a book about an actress,
Kagawa Kyoko, who performed in the films of
Kurosawa, Mizoguchi, Naruse and Ozu.

Kazakhstan Gulnara Abikeyeva

2009 can be seen as the breakthrough year for cinema in Kazakhstan. The strategy of producing films changed completely. Previously, Kazakh productions were mainly art-house affairs, seeking success at international film festivals. The new trend leans towards the production of commercial films, with the desire to conquer a Kazakh audience and play a part in the Russian film market. Within the last year, there were 17 features produced, half of which were made at the national film studio, Kazakhfilm, with the rest produced privately.

Sabit Kurmanbekov's **Seker**

Ermek Tursynov's **Kelin**

The most talked-about film of the year was Ermek Tursynov's **Kelin**. It is set in the third and fourth centuries and its story of three men – a hunter, shepherd and artist – vying for the affections of one woman is told without dialogue. The film screened at film festivals in Taormina, Montreal and Pusan. It will represent Kazakhstan in the Best Foreign Film category at next year's Academy Awards.

Sabit Kurmanbekov's **Seker** was another artistic highlight of the year. It is a story of a girl whose father raised her as a boy until she was 13, when her school head insisted that she dress appropriately. This touching story of a young girl's coming-of-age, with its

beautiful images of life in the countryside, is a testament to the spirit of Kazakh culture.

Between 2005 and 2009, director Bahyt Gafu made a series of 31 visually stunning documentaries. Dealing with various aspects of Kazakh life, they explored the country's geography and its people, detailing how they have moved across the land throughout history. A direct contrast to any officially sanctioned chronicle, **9th Territory of the World** presents audiences with a deeply personal vision.

Bahyt Gafu's **9th Territory of the World**

Two of the most popular films of the year were both privately funded productions: Zhanna Issabayeva's **Oypirmai, or My Dear Children** and Akhan Satayev's mystical thriller, **Strayed**.

Akhan Satayev's **Strayed**

Issabayeva's film tells the story of a mother who visits her four grown children in order to ask for money for her youngest son's wedding ceremony. There is a great deal of humour and irony relating to Kazakh customs and traditions, but the film's central theme is a celebration of unity and the value of the Kazakh family. The film also features some wonderful dancing that is more inspired by Indian culture. *Strayed* is an atypical Kazakh story, featuring a family who become lost in the Steppe region. The father eventually falls asleep in his car, only to wake up and discover his wife and son gone. Elements of mysticism are built upon western archetypes, and the repentance of the main character can be perceived more as a product of Christian beliefs. Russian actor Andrey Merzlikin plays the lead, with the hope of attracting Russian distributors.

Although the appearance of Russian actors in Kazakh films is increasingly common, it is no guarantee that a film will automatically

Renat Davletiyarov's **The Irony of Love**

be distributed there. It explains why Kazakhfilm is hiring Russian film directors and producers such as Timur Bekmambetov, Renat Davletiyarov and Egor Konchalovsky. Bekmambetov is working on **The Code of the Golden Warrior**, based on an ancient Kazakh myth. Davletiyarov is producing **The Irony of Love**, a comedy about an affair between a Russian man and a Kazakh woman that originated as a bet. Konchalovsky is directing a grand military drama, **The Afghan**, about events during the Soviet occupation of Afghanistan. It is hoped that all these projects will bring commercial success to Kazakhfilm, from both Kazakhstan and Russia.

Zhanna Issabayeva's **Oypirmai, or My Dear Children**

The year's best films
Seker (Sabit Kurmanbekov)
Kelin (Ermek Tursynov)
Oypirmai, or My Dear Children
(Zhanna Issabayeva)
Strayed (Akhan Satayev)
9th Territory of the World (Bahyt Gafu)

Quote of the year
'I would really hope that the film *Code of the Golden Warrior* would be famous for the number of people that have watched it and not for the PR-campaign that would be held for it.'
Director TIMUR BEKMAMBETOV

GULNARA ABIKEYEVA is a Kazakh film researcher and film critic and an author of five books about the cinema of Central Asia. She is Art Director of the 'Eurasia' Film Festival that is held annually in Almaty, Kazakhstan.

Lithuania Ilona Jurkonytė

In recent years, cinema exhibition has been among the most profitable businesses in Lithuania. But this has had little effect on either national film production or distribution. The domestic film market's box-office share was just 1.95%. This can be directly linked to the fact that Lithuania still has no established institution to regulate the local industry. Discussions regarding the establishment of a national film centre date back to 2003. Ironically, while local audiences prefer American films, Lithuanian productions successfully screen at international film festivals.

Gytis Lukšas' **Vortex**

Gytis Lukšas returned to feature filmmaking for the first time since 1997 with **Vortex** (*Duburys*), Lithuania's entry for the 2010 Academy Awards. Scripted by novelist

Romualdas Granauskas, the film details daily life under the Soviet occupation. Representing the younger generation and offering no signs of the country's Soviet past was Ignas Miškinis' **Low Lights** (*Artimos šviesos*). His fascination with street life, both in terms of attitude and language, fed into his presentation of the modern condition in contemporary Lithuania. The film links three characters, lost in their daily routines and losing a sense of meaning in their lives, who travel the empty streets at night. In doing so they rediscover a new side to each other. The first Lithuanian feature to be supported by Eurimages, it received the Best Film prize at the national awards.

Like many young filmmakers, Giedrė Beinoriūtė has chosen to write and direct her own films. In contrast to Miškinis' film, **Balcony** (*Balkonas*) takes a closer look at Lithuania's Soviet past, revelling in colourful, nostalgic childhood memories of life in the 1980s, which most of her generation would be able to relate to. It details an 11-year-old's first 'real' date. Its warm, evocative atmosphere, which appealed to younger audiences as well as Beinoriūtė's generation, won plaudits at numerous international festivals. **Flowers**

Giedrė Beinoriūtė's **Balcony**

(*Gėlės*), by Giedrius Zubavičius, was presented in competition at the Tampere International Short Film Festival. Again, the film has great appeal for younger audiences, telling the story of children who sell flowers in cafes and on the streets of Vilnius. However, although the film is visually beautiful, its characters lack motivation.

Documentary currently dominates Lithuanian film production, with the majority of productions made for television. Romas Lileikis' **The Shadow of Heaven** (*Dangaus šešėlis*) was the year's best non-fiction feature, focusing on the life and work of the Lithuanian composer and painter, Mikalojus Konstantinas Čiurlonis. A legend who was regarded as one of the great geniuses of Lithuanian cultural life, the film's international appeal may nevertheless be limited. **The Bug Trainer** featured the efforts of Rasa Miškinytė, Donatas Ulvydas and Linas Augutis from Lithuania, as well as Marek Skrobecki from Poland. It profiles the life of Ladislas Starewitch, a pioneer of puppet animation,

The Bug Trainer

which was first created in Kaunas at the beginning of the 20th century. A fascinating documentary, ii continues to be a draw at festivals. Giedrė Žickytė's **Baras** profiled the colourful personality of filmmaker, actor and lead singer of the avant-garde band Ir visa tai, kas yra gražu, yra gražu, Artūras Barysas. It received a national award for best television documentary. A final biographical documentary, Agnė Marcinkevičiūtė's' **Dance in the Desert** (*Šokis dykumoje*), looked at the life of the recently deceased Lithuanian writer, Jurga Ivanauskaitė. It was an original attempt to re-enact some elements of this personality's

Giedrė Žickytė's **Baras**

life through a symbolic style of dance. The prognosis of the Lithuanian economic situation is not great. In January, the Cultural Ministry of the Republic of Lithuania budgeted €2.86 million for production and distribution. However, by May there were significant cuts across the public sector. The film budget shrank by 30% to €1.99 million, lower than the previous year's figure.

The last year has clearly not been easy for Lithuanian cinema. However, discussions regarding the establishment of a national film institution have been revived. According to representatives of the Cultural Ministry, there are plans afoot to reform the Film Law by the end of 2010. But there remains no set plan for the creation of an official film body. So the future of production and distribution remains in limbo, with self-regulation by the market clearly failing in offering a variety of Lithuanian releases to the local audience.

No matter how complicated (or simplified) official policies regarding the audiovisual sector are in Lithuania, a significant number of premieres lie on the horizon. In 2010, no fewer than 14 documentaries will be completed, as well as 10 feature premieres. These include co-productions such as Kristijonas Vildžiūnas' **Back to Your Arms** (*Kai apkabinsiu tave*), Saulius Drunga's **Anarchy in Žirmūnai** (*Anarchija Žirmūnuose*) and Šarūnas Bartas' **Neither Before, Nor After** (*Lisabona 02*).

Saulius Drunga's **Anarchy in Žirmūnai**

National history will play an important role in future productions, with two projects focusing on the Soviet exiling of Lithuanian citizens to Siberia: Audrius Juzėnas's **Excursionist** (*Ekskursantė*) and Inesa Kurklietytė's **Madonna of Siberia** (*Sibiro Madona*). Both films are competing for additional public funding, as another historical project is in pre-production. Raimundas Banionis' **Žalgiris: The Iron Day** (*Žalgiris – geležies diena*) which recounts the crucial battle of Tannenberg in 1410 and is set to premiere in time for its 600th anniversary, drew €3.5 million from a special fund.

There are hopes that, with changes in official policy, Lithuania will be able to brand itself not only as a location for foreign studio productions, but as a country of great creative potential.

The year's best films
Balcony (Giedrė Beinoriūtė)
Baras (Giedrė Žickytė)
Vortex (Gytis Lukšas)
The Bug Trainer (Rasa Miškinytė, Donatas Ulvydas, Linas Augutis and Marek Skrobecki)
The Shadow of Heaven (Romas Lileikis)

Quote of the year
'According to the governmental programme, in 2011 there are plans to establish a Cinema Department within the Cultural Ministry of the Republic of Lithuania. [Local] filmmakers have serious hopes that such a department will bring national cinema back to normal conditions by coordinating the creative initiatives and state's support (Lithuania is the only EU country which has no separate national cinema institution).' *Quoted from an official letter (7 November, 2009) sent to the President of Lithuania, Dalia Grybauskaitė, Prime Minister Andrius Kubilius and the Minister of the Cultural Ministry of the Republic of Lithuania, signed by the representative of the Lithuanian Filmmakers' Union,* LINAS VILDŽIŪNAS.

Directory
All Tel/Fax numbers begin (+370)
The Ministry of Culture of Republic of Lithuania, J. Basanavičiaus g. 5, LT-01118 Vilnius. Tel: (5) 219 3400. Fax: (5) 262 3120. culture@lrkm.lt. www.lrkm.lt.
Lithuanian Filmmakers Union, Vasario 16-osios g. 13 / Šermukšnių g. 1, LT-01002 Vilnius. Tel/Fax: (5) 212 0759. info@kinosajunga.lt. www.kinosajunga.lt.
Lithuanian Theatre, Music and Cinema Museum, Vilniaus g. 41, LT-01119 Vilnius.Tel/Fax: (5) 262 2406. ltmkm@takas.lt http://teatras.mch.mii.lt.
Lithuanian Central State Archives, O. Milašiaus g. 21, LT-10102 Vilnius. Tel: (5) 247 7811. Fax: (5) 276 5318. lcva@archyvai.lt www.archyvai.lt.
www.lfc.lt (Information about Lithuanian film online). info@lfc.lt.

ILONA JURKONYTĖ is a director of Kaunas International Film Festival, a journalist writing about film and art for cultural magazine *Miesto IQ*, and co-author of the Internet portal about Lithuanian film, www.lfc.lt.

Luxembourg Boyd van Hoeij

In recent years, the Luxembourg film industry has gained in both reputation and visibility. In 2009, two Luxembourg co-productions premiered at Cannes: Stéphane Aubier and Vincent Patar's stop-motion animated comedy, **A Town Called Panic** (*Panique au village*), and French director Marina de Van's thriller, **Don't Look Back** (*Ne te retourne pas*). The films couldn't be more different and perfectly illustrate the breadth and diversity of the projects (at least partially) made in Luxembourg.

International co-productions are still the lifeblood of the industry, with over a dozen European features co-produced last year. The shoots educate the small pool of Luxembourg filmmaking talent, who can then invest their know-how in local projects. The results of this long-term objective are beginning to be seen.

Evidence of the current surge in creativity by the local filmmaking community can be seen in Thierry Schiel, the director of the CGI-animated and narrative-driven features *Tristan and Isolde* and *The Adventures of Renny the Fox*. He has returned to the short form in order to refuel himself, both creatively and artistically. The resulting dialogue-free **Fog** (*Le vieil homme dans le brouillard*) is a visually arresting short that recounts the story of an old man who is depressed after the loss of his wife and child. Schiel's use of CGI animation here veers away from the traditional style of his features and is pushed into a promising new realm.

Fog is one of two shorts that attracted attention for their lack of dialogue. The other was **Morgenrot**, directed by Jeff Desom. One of the brightest young talents, his *Morgenrot* is a spellbinding visual experience in which a burning piano falls from a skyscraper in 1920s

Sean Biggerstaff in Jeff Desom's **X on a Map**

New York (in a combination of photo-collage and animation). In Desom's live-action **X on a Map**, a young cartographer falls in love with a colleague in an eerily monotonous office. He tries to win her heart by showing her a film (the film-within-a-film is its weakest element). Desom's whimsical and inventive work derives its power from toying with different genre elements.

Fred Neuen's **Vault**, though hampered by a practically non-existent CGI budget, shows a flair for atmosphere in its story of creepy things lurking in the vaults of a bank. Saesa Kiyokawa's **Routine**, about a bus driver's mysterious passenger, also wears its generic influences clearly, but it remains an effective entertainment.

Fred Neuen's **Vault**

Ben Andrews' **Dawning**

Relying on a single twist for effect is Ben Andrews' **Dawning**. Like the previously mentioned shorts, it was shot, somewhat incongruously, in English. Though technically impressive, the story of a man who wakes up unable to remember the boozy night before underlines the Achilles heel of current Luxembourg films: weak writing.

Nicolas Steil's **Draft Dodgers**

Three 2009 features also suffer from underdeveloped screenplays and strange language choices. Interestingly, with the local industry still in its adolescence, all three focus on protagonists in their teens. Producer-turned-director Nicolas Steil's **Draft Dodgers** (*Réfractaire*) centres on a Luxembourger (French actor Grégoire Leprince-Ringuet) who hides in the disused part of a mine in order to escape conscription following Luxembourg's annexation by Nazi Germany. Lacking scope and vigour, the old-school Second World War drama does showcase young French acting talent alongside Luxembourg character actors, who include Thierry van Werveke. Though inspired by local history, the film struggled to achieve the success of several recent wartime-themed documentaries, with the use of French rather than Luxembourgish a likely factor.

Jean-Claude Schlim's AIDS drama **House of Boys** also features a Luxembourg protagonist, but here he speaks English. The often overly sincere love story centres on a gay pupil (Brit Layke Anderson) who escapes to Amsterdam in the 1980s, where he finds employment in the eponymous nightclub of Madame (German veteran Udo Kier). Though not emotionally specific enough to overcome the fact it could have been made 20 years ago, *House* does showcase a talent to watch out for and the supporting cast, which includes Stephen Fry and an impressive Steven Webb as a pre-op transsexual, shines.

Jean-Claude Schlim's **House of Boys**

Young, London-schooled Max Jacoby made the most idiosyncratic and (overly) ambitious film of the year with **Dust**, a post-apocalyptic tale of dizygotic twins living in a nameless, Mitteleuropa-looking country. While suggestively atmospheric, the film's storytelling is so oblique the narrative runs hollow, as Jacoby combines beautiful shots with a mise-en-scene that betrays his lack of experience. And, like Schlim, Jacoby lacks a clear grasp of the nuances of the English language, with the inexperienced leads looking stranded.

Max Jacoby's **Dust**

ABU DHABI FILM COMMISSION

More lived-in and authentic is **Reste Bien, Mec** by Adolf El Assal, a 'guerrilla film' about local youngsters with musical aspirations. Shot and distributed outside the mainstream, the multi-lingual, music video-inspired film successfully found its audience. Assal has since lined up a project with Film Fund money.

Thierry Van Werveke in Andy Bausch's **InThierryView**

On the documentary front, Georges Fautsch's medium-length **Magno Tripudio**, about the historic dancing procession in the pilgrims' town of Echternach, and Andy Bausch's feature, **InThierryView**, about cult actor and Bausch discovery, Thierry Van Werveke, impressed. A modest box-office hit, the unsentimental *InThierryView* in part came about because of its star's deteriorating health (he died a month after the premiere). Both Fautsch and Bausch used a multi-faceted collage approach that ensured their films remained lively and interesting.

Jacques Molitor's **Bonobo**

2010 might be the year of young producer Bernard Michaux, whose promising slate not only includes the latest documentary from creative wunderkind Beryl Koltz (she is also working on a feature), but also the first

features of Jeff Desom and Jacques Molitor (whose short **Bonobo** was not as strong as his Locarno-selected 2008 title *En Compagnie de la poussière*). Molitor's film, as well as a children's film in development, will be mainly in Luxemburgish.

The year's best films
Morgenrot (Jeff Desom)
Routine (Saesa Kiyokawa)
House of Boys (Jean-Claude Schlim)
Draft Dodgers (Nicolas Steil)
InThierryView (Andy Bausch)

Jeff Desom's **Morgenrot**

Quote of the year
'It is important to produce films with a Luxembourg identity, also to create something that will ultimately be recognisable and sellable abroad, but it will be hard to find something that unites all the Luxembourg movies. It will definitely not be the language.'
Producer BERNARD MICHAUX.

Directory
All Tel/Fax numbers begin (+352)
Film Fund Luxembourg, Maison de Cassal, 5 rue Large, L-1917 Luxembourg. Tel: 2478 2065. Fax: 22 09 63. info@filmfund.etat.lu. http://en.filmfund.lu.

BOYD VAN HOEIJ is a freelance film writer, a contributing critic of US trade paper *Variety*, Benelux correspondent for cineuropa.org and film editor of *Winq* magazine.

Malaysia Norman Yusoff

2009 witnessed little improvement for Malaysian cinema in terms of both commercial and critical achievements. Around 26 films were released across mainstream and non-mainstream cinema circuits. Of these, only a few emerged as box-office hits. That said, the new generation of filmmakers continued to make films in an unconventional, disparate way, resulting in accolades on the international stage.

Yeoh Joon Han's **Sell Out!** is a well-crafted, inventive and refreshingly witty musical comedy that went on to win the Young Cinema Award at the Venice Film Festival. It pokes fun at the greed of the media, as well as Malaysian attitudes towards the arts and entertainment. Unsurprisingly, it failed commercially.

Yeoh Joon Han's **Sell Out!**

Chris Chong's **Karaoke** was screened during the Directors' Fortnight at the Cannes Film Festival, making it just the second Malaysian feature to screen there, after U-Wei Haji Saari's *The Arsonis*, in 1995. *Karaoke* was also awarded the Maverick prize at the Calgary International Film Festival. In its languid and meditative style, the film focuses on a young man who returns from the city to his village, dreaming of taking over the family karaoke business. In parts a social satire and a meditation on individual

Chris Chong's **Karaoke**

responsibility, it employs long takes to allow the story to unfold, heightening its raw power. A poetic and intelligent feature debut, the film offered hope for the younger generation of Malaysian filmmakers.

Talentime was the late Yasmin Ahmad's swan song. It was released a few months before her sudden demise in July, which shocked the whole nation. She sets her sights on the insidiousness of racism in a heartbreaking love story that follows the forbidden relationship between a Malay girl and an Indian boy. The film exposed the unacknowledged racial prejudice that permeates contemporary Malaysian society. It won the Best Director and Best Screenplay awards at the Malaysian Film Festival.

It was heartening that Yasmin's previous film, *The Convert*, was finally given a general release at the end of the year. The film earned recognition at the Tokyo International Film Festival, with a Special Mention in the Best Asian-Middle Eastern Film category.

Afdlin Shauki's **Papadom**, a family-oriented comedy-drama, about a protective, domineering father and his adolescent daughter, emerged as one of the year's box-office hits, also winning the Best Film award at the Malaysian Film Festival. Afdlin attracted local cinemagoers with a mix of outlandish humour and saccharine-tinged melancholy.

As usual, a significant number of films were churned out in order to make a fast profit. These included: **Jangan Pandang Belakang Congkak**, which spoofed previous horror hits and went on to gross over RM6 million; **Bohsia – Jangan Pilih Jalan Hitam**, a didactic teen-oriented social drama; and **Jangan Tegur**, a formulaic local horror from a producer associated with the genre.

Bohsia – Jangan Pilih Jalan Hitam

Lembing Awang Pulang ke Dayang, a period piece that chronicled a Johorean (one of the states in Malaysia) legend about a bloody love affair in the late 18th century, was the year's biggest debacle. A laughably bad, cheap-looking epic, it might have delivered on the promise of retelling a significant local tale, but failed miserably in just about every other aspect, from poor production values and atrocious acting to a chronically weak screenplay. The film, not surprisingly, did not ignite the box office.

The creative and commercial failure of *Lembing Awang Pulang ke Dayang* also raised more intrinsic issues about the state of the local industry and how it is financed. It was made with the support of the government through a loan scheme. The Malaysian press claimed

that the government's RM50 million feature-film scheme to boost the country's film industry, had come unstuck. The key players in the industry urged that the loan scheme be reviewed and managed properly in future, so that only 'real producers' benefit from it.

The year's best films
Sell Out! (Yeoh Joon Han)
Karaoke (Chris Chong)
Talentime (Yasmin Ahmad)

Quotes of the year
'Yasmin Ahmad left a vibrant legacy, and it is still strange to talk about her in the past tense.' **AMIR MUHAMMAD**, *film director and author of 'Yasmin Ahmad's Films'*.

'With *Karaoke*, Malaysia again proves that its film industry has the potential to create works by recognisable auteurs that can occasionally and surprisingly reshape the potential of film as a language. The world has already begun to take notice and I only hope Malaysian audiences take this opportunity to encounter the on-screen world of Chris Chong.' **BENJAMIN McKAY**, *columnist, film writer and academic, summing up his insightful article on* **Karaoke**, *which appeared in the local magazine 'Off the Edge'*.

Directory
All Tel/Fax numbers begin (+603)
National Film Development Corporation (FINAS), Studio Merdeka Complex, Hulu Kelang, 68000 Ampang, Selangor. Tel: 41041300. Fax: 41068509. finas@po.jaring.my. www.finas.gov.my.
Malaysia Institute of Integrative Media, Centre for Film and Broadcasting, No. 1, Jalan 9/27 A, Section 5 Wangsa Maju, Kuala Lumpur 53300. Tel: 4142 2422. Fax: 4142 8422.

NORMAN YUSOFF teaches film studies at the Faculty of Artistic & Creative Technology, Universiti Teknologi MARA, Malaysia. He is the co-founder and editor of *Jurnal Skrin Malaysia* (Malaysian Screen Journal), Malaysia's only academic journal for film and television.

Malta Daniel Rosenthal

Though government support for local filmmakers continued in 2008–09, with one narrative short and three documentaries tapping the Ministry of Finance, Economy and Investment's €230,000 development and production fund, the vast majority of film and TV production in Malta continued to come from visiting projects. They were lured by the islands' varied locations and the ministry's incentive scheme, which offers a cash rebate of up to 22% on EU-eligible expenditure in Malta by qualifying productions.

Luisa Bonello, Malta's Film Commissioner, said that apart from the first few months of 2009, when a number of Malta-bound projects lost their financing in the credit crunch, 2009 'had been a pretty good year. We picked up momentum in the spring and have kept going since then.' At press time, a €15 million European feature film was prepping for a two-month shoot early in 2010, with Malta doubling for Iraq, while the island also stood in for Istanbul for British television's *Poirot: Murder on the Orient Express*.

Other notable visitors in 2009 included two German television projects, mini-series *The Golgotha File*, a series, *Father Kastell*, and a

Bollywood romance, **Will You Cross the Sky?**, *shooting in Birgu*

Russian television series, *The Last Meeting*. Joining the long list of Bollywood productions to have filmed in Europe in recent years, **Will You Cross the Sky?** (*Vinnai Thankdi Varuvaya*), directed by Gautham Menon and featuring music and songs by Oscar-winner A.R. Rahman, used Maltese locations, including the streets of Birgu and the coast of Gozo, for its youth-oriented love story, starring Trisha Krishnan and Simbu, whose characters, Jessica and Neru, enjoy a romantic interlude on the islands.

Yevgeny Pashkevich's Latvian feature, **Gulfstream Under the Iceberg**, which tells three love stories linked by a mythological, time-travelling figure, Lilith, used several locations and the water tanks of Mediterranean Film Studios (MFS).

Other productions at MFS in 2009 included *Moby Dick* and a major Japanese TV series. The former is a $25.5m German–Canadian two-part television film of Melville's classic nautical adventure, directed by Mike Barker (*To Kill a King*), scripted by Nigel Williams and starring William Hurt as Captain Ahab, Ethan Hawke as first officer Starbuck and Gillian Anderson as Ahab's wife; the latter is the epic, 13-part *Cloud Above the Slope* (*Saka no ue no kumo*), co-directed by Takafumi Kimura and Taku Kato. The series dramatises the Russo-Japanese war of 1904–05. Four months of pre-production work went into the building of two 40-metre sections of warships and several interior sets at MFS, for about an hour's worth of scenes. Four years in the making, this production from NHK, Japan's largest broadcaster, also filmed in Japan, Russia and London.

Alejandro Amenábar's breakout Spanish success, **Agora**

Spaniard Alejandro Amenábar's epic *Agora*, which in 2008 built massive sets on Malta to replicate ancient Alexandria, and used Maltese landscapes to double for Egypt, became a major box-office success in the director's native country in autumn 2009 and was scheduled for release in other countries in 2010. Finally, the second series of the Norwegian/Swedish reality TV show *Champion*

of Champions (*Mesternes Mester*) took up residence on Malta in September 2009, filming at numerous locations as teams of former champion Norwegian and Swedish sportsmen sought to avoid elimination in a series of physical and mental challenges (running, a giant game of checkers), while also being filmed cooking and relaxing in their luxurious villas. The first, Spanish-shot series produced extremely high ratings, which explains why the Malta Tourism Authority, sensing a huge promotional opportunity across 12 hours of prime-time television in Norway and Sweden, had fought to bring this show to the islands against rival bids from Greece, Sicily and Spain.

Quote of the year

'Sometimes journalists asked why we filmed *Agora* in Malta. I say this was the only place this film could have been shot the way we did it.' **Agora** *director,* ALEJANDRO AMENABAR.

Directory

All Tel/Fax numbers begin (+356)
Malta Film Commission, Caraffa Stores, Cottonera Waterfront, Vittoriosa BRG 1721. Tel: 2180 9135. Fax: 2780 9136. info@mfc.com.mt www.mfc.com.mt.
Mediterranean Film Studios, St. Rocco Street, Kalkara KKR3000. Tel: 2166 8194 (production) / 2137 8852 (admin). Fax: 2138 3357. www.mfsstudios.com.

DANIEL ROSENTHAL was Editor of *IFG* from 2002 to 2006. He is the author of *100 Shakespeare Films* (BFI, 2007) and teaches 'Shakespeare on Film' and 'Arts Journalism' classes for the International Programmes department of Pembroke College, Cambridge. He is completing *The National Theatre Story*, a major new history of Britain's flagship theatre, for Oberon Books.

Mexico Carlos Bonfil

Although the global financial crisis prevailing in Western societies affects many developing countries in Latin America, it had a particularly strong effect on the Mexican economy, so closely linked to the United States via the North American Free Trade Agreement (NAFTA). A steadily growing rate of unemployment has reduced to a shambles what appeared to be the federal government's confidence in neo-liberal formulas for economic recovery. Among those sectors most heavily affected by this crisis are education, health and culture, which are continuously threatened with unrelenting budgetary cuts. Cinema is no exception in this matter, in spite of the official claim that the production of new films is being steadily supported.

It would be difficult to deny the fact that Mexican film production has maintained a surprising stability (70 films per year, as opposed to little more than one or two dozen in previous years) over the past two years. This has been the result of new policies that reduce taxes for those enterprises investing in cinema. The immediate outcome of this financial support has been an increase in the number of films produced, although there was no correlative rise in their artistic quality.

Many investors were somewhat discouraged by the poor box-office performance of some films they supported, with many young filmmakers, whose interests lie in more personal projects, producing a kind of cinema that has little appeal for large audiences. In this vicious circle, cinema can only be effectively supported if it complies with Hollywood's narrative formulas, the format that dominates, at nearly 90%, most Mexican screens.

It is no surprise then that when a proposed amendment to the Federal Law of Cinema sought to guarantee that local films stayed for a minimum of three weeks on the exhibition circuit, the main exhibitor chains showed a strong negative reaction. Along with this is a steady reluctance from distributors to promote independent Mexican cinema. Instead, they focus their attention on local productions from directors who have, in the past, proved their knack at grasping the advantages and solid rewards of light entertainment.

For long periods, particularly the fruitful decades of the seventies and the nineties, the government played a key role in financing and promoting Mexican cinema. The work of many filmmakers contributed to enhancing the idea of a booming film industry and of an official engagement favouring the arts. This idea of the State as a benefactor of national culture was highly publicised both domestically and abroad, and in many ways it still is. At the turn of the new century, however, a conservative government has displayed an increasing detachment from such efforts. Its record of defending the local film industry has repeatedly been highlighted

Gerardo Naranjo's **I'm Gonna Explode**

by many industry figures as inconsistent and erratic. This is particularly true when it comes to renegotiating the NAFTA in order to control the growing presence of American films, thus guaranteeing better conditions for the distribution and exhibition of local productions. As a result of this situation, the Mexican film industry lies stagnant, with local talent searching for better working conditions abroad. And yet some bureaucratic figures still celebrate the 'recovery' of film production. As some independent filmmakers put it, the true accomplishment is not to produce 70 films a year, but to create a legal framework to secure their survival at the box office.

A good number of Mexican films are of a quality to deserve and justify larger support. Not only do they succeed in attracting attention and acclaim at international film festivals, they have also proved to be efficient in developing new strategies of joint financing and alternative distribution. Nevertheless, these are isolated efforts that hardly contribute to a true strengthening of a national film industry. Tellingly, some titles in 2009 betrayed the prevailing mood of disenchantment among industry figures, concerning both their own difficulties in producing films and the collective moral strain resulting from the economic crisis. **I'm Gonna Explode** (*Voy a explotar*), the second feature by Gerardo Naranjo, whose previous film, *Drama/Mex*, was widely acclaimed, offers a Godardian take on a dark romantic story of two teenagers disconnecting themselves from the adult world through rebellion and violence. Rejecting traditional moral values, the director offered a glimpse of political corruption, family decay and the chilling nonchalance of the country's ruling class.

Julián Hernández's **Furious Sun, Furious Sky** (*Rabioso sol, rabioso cielo*) is a three-hour story of homosexual passion transformed into a mystical tale. The filmmaker chose an abstract narrative, alternating colour and black-and-white photography to illustrate, through symbolism and use of the landscape, the state of the characters' minds and the impossibility

Giovanna Zacarías in Julián Hernández's **Furious Sun, Furious Sky**

of absolute love in modern society. It is an ambitious and uneven work that runs against the grain of conventional narrative in Mexico.

Alberto Cortez's **Heart of Time** (*Corazón del tiempo*) unfolds in a Zapatista rural community – an autonomous territory in southern Mexico ruled by indigenous rebels. After writing the folk tale of unrequited love, the director shot his film whilst living with the community that features in it for three years. The film succeeds in vividly portraying the hitherto unexplored daily life of this world.

Alberto Cortez's **Heart of Time**

Documentary films have also provided interesting incursions into marginal urban communities. Luis Rincón's **The Forgotten Tree** (*El árbol olvidado*) revisits the locations where Luis Buñuel's Mexican masterpiece, *Los olvidados*, was filmed almost 60 years ago. It is troubling to see how little those miserable conditions of life have changed. Four young characters trapped in the routine of drug abuse and petty crime attempt to escape from poverty, only

Roberto Hernández and Geoffrey Smith's **Presumed Guilty**

to see their efforts fail. Moral disenchantment dominates Roberto Hernández and Geoffrey Smith's **Presumed Guilty** (*Presunto culpable*). Hernández, a lawyer, recorded the case of a man framed by the police for a crime he didn't commit and for which he was sentenced to 20 years. As they expose the practice of policemen randomly choosing scapegoats in order to claim that an effective battle is being waged against crime, the film exposes a nightmare of social injustice and political corruption.

In contrast with these grim views of Mexican society and individual revolt, 2009 has also been a year that witnessed the unexpected return

Rigoberto Perezcano's **Clueless**

of comedy. One of the biggest surprises was Rigoberto Perezcano's feature debut, **Clueless** (*Norteado*). It is the story of Antonio who, after several unsuccessful attempts to cross the US border, is trapped in the frontier town of Tijuana, where he is pursued by two women. After resisting this double amorous assault, he tries once again to cross into the US. Illegal migration, a subject often dealt with in dramatic terms, appears here in a different light that is creatively accomplished and entertaining.

Hansel Ramírez in Jaime Ruiz Ibañez's **Half of the World**

Jaime Ruiz Ibañez's debut feature, **Half of the World** (*La mitad del mundo*), is another tale of seduction. A mentally stunted and malicious young man suddenly becomes the sexual pet of a group of middle-aged women in a small town where prejudices and moral hypocrisy abound. Although the plot initially appears to lack subtlety, the director turns the celebration of life and sexual freedom into a parable of mass intolerance and revenge against non-orthodox behaviour. The comedy and melodramatic elements work well together, with irony and good humour ensuring the film remains satisfying throughout.

A similar blend of genres is to be found in Humberto Hinojosa's first feature, **Black Sheep** (*Oveja negra*), in which two friends herding sheep at a ranch concoct a plan for stealing the beasts and selling them in order to fund their migration to the United States. Things turn sour when one of them falls in love with the boss's daughter and has to confront her violent fiancé. The film is a tribute to old-fashioned Mexican comedies, and although violence and crime are present, a clever twist

Humberto Hinojosa Oscariz's **Black Sheep**

in the narrative finally drives the film to an unexpected and gratifying solution.

Lastly, another comedy, Gerardo Tort's **Round Trip** (*Viaje redondo*), tells the story of two young women who, during a journey they share, explore their own identity and sexuality. In a cinema where male identities and struggles are the dominant narrative force, this romantic tale of female friendship, which also deals with existential uncertainties and repressed desires, rings of novelty and freshness.

Gerardo Tort's **Round Trip**

The fact that none of the films mentioned was able to remain for longer than two weeks in the national box office charts, thus failing to recover their initial investment, while other routine works of dubious quality outnumber

them to become the most reliable product for distributors and exhibitors alike, makes clear the extent of the current crisis in the Mexican film industry.

The year's best films
Clueless (Rigoberto Perezcano)
Presumed Guilty
(Roberto Hernández and Geoffrey Smith)
Black Sheep (Humberto Hinojosa)
Round Trip (Gerardo Tort)
I'm Gonna Explode (Gerardo Naranjo)

Quote of the year
'What could we possibly expect from a country with no images and no stories of its own to tell?' *Head of IMCINE (Instituto Mexicano de Cinematografía)*, **MARINA STAVENHAGUEN.**

Directory
All Tel/Fax numbers begin (+52)
Cineteca Nacional, Avenida México-Coyoacán 389, Col Xoco, México DF. Tel: 1253 9314. www. cinetecanacional.net.
Association of Mexican Film Producers & Distributors, Avenida División del Norte 2462, Piso 8, Colonia Portales, México DF. Tel: 5688 0705. Fax: 5688 7251.
Cinema Production Workers Syndicate (STPC), Plateros 109 Col San José Insurgentes, México DF. Tel: 5680 6292. cctpc@terra.com.mx.
Dirección General de Radio, Televisión y Cine-matografía (RTC), Roma 41, Col Juárez, México DF. Tel: 5140 8010. ecardenas@segob.gob.mx.
Instituto Mexicano de Cinematografía (IMCINE), Insurgentes Sur 674 Col del Valle, CP 03100, México DF. Tel: 5448 5300. mercaint@ institutomexicanodecinematografía.gob.mx.

CARLOS BONFIL is a film critic, contributing a weekly article on cinema to *La Journada*, a leading Mexican newspaper. He is the author of *Through the Mirror: Mexican Cinema and its Audience* (1994).

Morocco Maryam Touzani

Moroccan films struggle for visibility in a market dominated by international productions. Hollywood takes almost half the total box-office revenue and also screens the largest number of films. Indian cinema, of which Morocco has been an avid consumer for decades, is close behind in terms of exhibition. Local and Egyptian productions follow, with significantly fewer films.

Although cinemagoers appear to be mainly attracted to Hollywood and Bollywood products, interest does appear to be shifting. Proof of this was Nabil Ayouch's *Whatever Lola Wants*, which remained popular throughout 2009, scoring a record for the number of weeks it screened in cinemas. Nourredine Lakhmari's *Casa-negra* also showed stamina and, although opinions were extremely divided on the film, it attracted a large audience.

In Abdelhamid Zoughi's first feature, **Nothing is Eternal** (*Kharboucha*), a beautiful singer and poet, living amongst a peaceful tribe, is taken hostage by the terrifying chief of a neighbouring region. After *The Boy from Tangier*, Moumen Smihi returned with **Les Cris de Jeunes Filles des Hirondelles**, which unfolds in Tangier in 1955 and tells the story of

15-year-old Larbi Salmi, the son of a theologian, who is obsessed with the opposite sex. His mother introduces him to Rabea, an attractive young girl fascinated by love stories. Mohamed Mernich's **Tamazight Oufella** tells the story of an isolated village in the mountains, whose inhabitants have requested the construction of a road. When Alili returns home from France, with money he has won from a lottery, he decides to finance the construction of the road, giving the villagers hope. Mohamed Chrif Tribak's debut, **Time of Comrades** (*Le Temps des Camarades*), recounts the story of Rahil, who at the beginning of the 1990s chose to pursue a university education against her family's will. In doing so, she discovers the growing influence of Islam. Mohammed Ahed Bensouda's **Tale of a Mchaouchi Wrestler** (*Histoire d'un Lutteur Mchaouchi*) revives the traditional martial art of Lamchaoucha, with the main protagonist, Slimane, challenging a tyrannical wrestling champion, who wants to marry the woman he loves, to a winner-takes-all wrestling match.

Documentary films over the last year fared better in terms of quality. *Tanger, le Rêve des Brûleurs* director Leila Kilani returned with **Our Forbidden Places** (*Nos Lieux Interdits*),

Mohammed Ahed Bensouda's **Tale of a Mchaouchi Wrestler**

which attracted much critical acclaim, winning her awards at a number of festivals. In 2004, the King of Morocco launched an Equity and Reconciliation Commission to investigate state violence during the 'years of lead'. Kilani's film delves into that particular period as it accompanies four families in their search for the truth. With **I Loved so Much…** (*J'ai Tant Aimé*), Dalila Ennard continues to focus on portraits of women and their daily lives, as it follows Fadma, a joyful 75-year-old woman who begs for a living at a very popular site. This singular woman, who at the age of 20 was engaged by the French army as a prostitute to accompany Moroccan soldiers during the Indo-China war, asks France to recognise her in the same way as the veterans, claiming that she also took part in the war effort.

After the success of *El Ejido, The Law of Profit*, Jawad Rhalib returned with **The Damned of the Sea** (*Les Damnés de la Mer*), looking at the thousands of Moroccan fishermen who travel to Dakhla, in the south of the Sahara, in order to make a living. The experience is often a gruelling challenge, with little reward.

The closure of cinemas remains an issue of concern in Morocco. For some, the solution has been to construct multiplexes, which have begun to appear throughout the country. However, due to the enormous cost of building them, ticket prices have become prohibitively expensive, thus not answering the problem of finding a way to make cinema available to everyone. Images for Everyone (Images pour Tous), created by filmmakers Nabil Ayouch and Mohamed Layadi, is a new initiative with an important social and cultural scope. Through the creation of 50 small cinemas – each with a capacity of around 100 – in rural areas and suburbs, which screen films on DVD, the project aims to allow a significant number of Moroccans access to film.

According to statistics produced in recent years, cinema is just not part of Moroccan leisure activities. Indeed, 60% of Moroccans go less than once a year to the cinema, or not at all. Though they claim to enjoy cinema, one of the problems seems to reside in films available. For cinema to survive and flourish, making it accessible to everyone is vital. After all, what is the point of making films if they cannot be watched?

The year's best films
The Damned of the Sea (Jawad Rhalib)
Our Forbidden Places (Leila Kilani)

Quote of the year
'A people can only exist through the wealth that its culture, its heritage, its traditions, and its customs provide. My goal was to make an entertainment film tied to our cultural richness.' MOHAMMED AHED BENSOUDA, *director of* **Tale of a Mchaouchi Wrestler**.

MARYAM TOUZANI is a freelance journalist based in Morocco and working internationally, specialising in art and culture.

Jawad Rhalib's **The Damned of the Sea**

Mozambique Martin P. Botha

A major focus on recent filmmaking in Mozambique formed part of the 2009 African Film Festival in Leuven, Belgium. The festival co-director, Dr Guido Convents, presented a fascinating historical overview of Mozambican cinema. Several recent features, documentaries and shorts were included in the retrospective. The organisers of the African Film Festival also signed a co-operation agreement with Dockanema, the Maputo-based international documentary film festival set up by leading filmmaker, Pedro Pimenta.

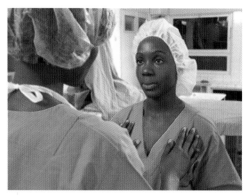

João Luis Sol de Carvalho's **Another Man's Garden**

João Luis Sol de Carvalho's **Another Man's Garden** (*O Jardin do Outro Homem*) is a tense and uplifting tale that illustrates the barriers women face in seeking an education in Mozambique. Sophia, an aspiring medical student, receives no moral or financial support from her family. When an error in judgement leaves her vulnerable to ruin at the corrupt school, her female colleagues help her fight patriarchal attitudes. De Carvalho has dedicated the film to the courage of young women who continue to strive against the odds, proving that educating a girl is not a waste of time in a land, where it is perceived

that 'sending a girl to school is like watering another man's garden'.

Licinio Azevedo's *The Great Bazaar* was also included in the retrospective. The film focuses on two boys with different experiences and goals, who meet up in a sprawling African market. One is looking for a job, to get back what was stolen from him and return home. The other will do anything to avoid having to go back with his family. They become friends and together they reinvent the world. Azevedo's latest documentary is **Night Lodgers** (*Hóspedes da Noite*). During the colonial era, the Grande Hotel in the city of Beira was the largest in Mozambique. It included 350 rooms, luxurious suites, as well as an Olympic-size swimming pool. The building, which is now in ruins and has no electricity or running water, is currently inhabited by 3,500 people. Some have been living there for 20 years. As well as the rooms, the foyers, corridors, service areas and the basement all serve as residences. With little natural light, it is permanently night-time there, yet there is no trace of sadness or self-pity in Azevedo's luminous documentary.

Licinio Azevedo's **Night Lodgers**

Teresa Prata's **Sleepwalking Land**

At the time of writing, the Mozambican production company Elbano Multimedia started work on Azevedo's new feature, **Virgin Margarida**. Also written by Azevedo, the film is being produced by Pimenta, a well-known filmmaker in the Southern African region. Set just after Mozambique's independence, it tells the story of a young girl caught between events that will change her destiny forever. In a time of radical social and political transformation, where people are judged by their ideological stance, she maintains the ingeniousness of her peasant background. She has to die for people around her to realise that life goes beyond the good intentions of any ideology. Azevedo said in an interview that the original story was written eight years ago and was inspired by research he did for one of his documentaries: 'The current script has been developed over the past three years, partly in collaboration with DV8 Films' script workshops. Financing the project started two years ago.' *Virgin Margarida* is described as a universal story set in an atmosphere of enormous social and political tension. Azevedo believes audiences will appreciate its proximity to actual events: 'Also, the drama takes place mostly amongst women. This is a story of women in a time when men decide their destiny.'

Teresa Prata's **Sleepwalking Land** (*Terra Sonâmbula*) also deals with war-torn Mozambique. Muidinga, a young boy, searches for his parents. He is accompanied by Tuihir, an elderly man, who takes him under his wing.

Tuihir teaches Muidinga a series of life lessons in how to survive during the civil war. The travellers come upon a burnt-out bus and decide to make this their home. Inside the bus, Muidinga finds a notebook used as a journal by one of the passengers. He reads it aloud at night to keep himself and Tuihir company.

As the film progresses, Tuihir becomes increasingly interested in learning about Mrs. Farida whom the author, Kindzu, writes about. Despite Tuihir's insistence that he not think about his parents, Muidinga refuses to believe they are dead and begins to wonder if Mrs. Farida is his mother. Muidinga leads the reluctant Tuihir on a journey to find Mrs. Farida, in a film that blends a coming-of-age drama with a variation on Homer's *The Odyssey*.

The year's best films
Sleepwalking Land (Teresa Prata)
Night Lodgers (Licinio Azevedo)

Quote of the year
'When I had doubts about the project, the film that helped me during those seven years before shooting was *Come and See* by Elem Klimov. Because it's a film about war, and because of the personal story of the director – it took him ten years to make it. When I had doubts that I could make my own movie, I watched parts of his movie and it helped me to go on.' *Director* **TERESA PRATA** *talks about* **Sleepwalking Land**, *a project that took seven years to complete.*

MARTIN P. BOTHA has published five books on South African cinema, including an anthology on post-apartheid cinema entitled *Marginal Lives and Painful Pasts: South African Cinema After Apartheid*. He is a professor of film studies in the Centre for Film and Media Studies at the University of Cape Town. He was awarded a Global Film Award at the Ischia Global Film and Music Film Festival for his lifetime contribution to the South African film industry.

Netherlands Leo Bankersen

Women rule! It didn't go unnoticed that the four features representing Dutch cinema at the Berlin festival were all made by women. Mijke de Jong's 2008 release, *Katia's Sister*, about a 13-year-old girl struggling because of neglect was selected for the Generation section. The Forum presented the improvised circus drama *Calimucho* (also from 2008) by Eugenie Jansen, together with the visually stunning myth, **Winter Silence** (*Winterstilte*), the first feature by Sonja Wyss.

Also in Forum, and arguably the most impressive of the four, was the psychological drama **Can Go Through Skin** (*Kan door huid heen*). Debuting writer-director Esther Rots received much praise for the way she entered the mind of an emotionally scarred young woman (Rifka Lodeizen) who is trying to rebuild her life.

Rifka Lodeizen in Esther Rots' **Can Go Through Skin**

While this manifestation of female talent could have been a coincidence, more evidence of the trend was displayed in January, when the Netherlands Film Fund handed out the annual prizes for artistic success (based on international festival selections). It turned out that seven of the eight films awarded were directed by women.

Stephen Rea and Lotte Verbeek in **Nothing Personal**

To top if off, **Nothing Personal**, by Polish-Dutch director Urszula Antoniak, was a winner at Locarno. Later on, this sensitive study of loneliness, with an almost wordless yet very expressive performance by previously unknown Dutch actress Lotte Verbeek, who plays opposite Stephen Rea, was awarded Golden Calves for best film, best direction, best photography and best sound at the Netherlands Film Festival in Utrecht.

Is this a Dutch new wave? Nobody seems to be sure. It's not really a movement, but there seems to be a shared sensitivity for films that rely more on character and mise-en-scène than just the story – films where a great deal is actually going on beneath the surface.

At the Netherlands Film Festival, the phrase *Dutch Angle* (originally a cinematic term for a canted image) was introduced as a label and marketing tool for this kind of Dutch auteur cinema, which is recognised by international festivals but currently not by the domestic audience.

Simone van Dusseldorp's **Frogs & Toads**

It should be mentioned that finding an audience abroad is usually as difficult as finding one for Dutch films locally. Being a festival darling is one thing, but actually selling your film is another. Alex van Warmerdam's black comedy, **The Last Days of Emma Blank** (*De laatste dagen van Emma Blank*) and 2008 domestic hit *Winter in Wartime* sold relatively well. But *Can Go Through Skin*, like so many other local films, is having a tough time being sold.

Dutch mainstream film continued to perform reasonably well at the box office, though the peak market share of 2008 (17.6%) is unlikely to be met this time. By the end of October it stood at 11% and will likely round off at 12% by the end of 2009.

As usual, a fair slice of the box-office pie was taken by films aimed at teens and pre-teens, such as Dave Schram's **Lover or Loser**

Dave Schram's **Lover or Loser**

(*Lover of loser*), in which 15 year-old Eva is in danger of falling victim to an unsuitable boyfriend and sexual abuse. The fourth in the successful series of adaptations of novels by popular author Carry Slee, it offered reliable production values and young characters the target audience could relate to. The film was never going to play well with critics, but their opinions carry little truck with this kind of film.

Simone van Dusseldorp's **Frogs & Toads**

A most charming film for young children was **Frogs & Toads** (*Kikkerdril*), in which a simple search for frogspawn turns into an exciting adventure for two six-year-olds. Perfectly tailored for the youngest audience by director Simone van Dusseldorp, it also proved to be a delight for grown-ups.

Ben Sombogaart's **The Storm**

After the success of *Bride Flight*, Ben Sombogaart directed another big hit, **The Storm** (*De storm*). The fictional story of a young unmarried mother (Sylvia Hoeks) in a desperate search for her lost child, it is set against the spectacular backdrop of the storm that broke the dikes of Zeeland in 1953. The unusual move – at least for Dutch cinema – of employing extensive digital effects helped immensely in recreating the flood.

Will Koopman's thriller **The Dark House** (*Terug naar de kust*) also attracted a large audience. And hopes are high for another late-autumn release, Producer Reinout Oerlemans' directorial debut, **A Woman Goes to the Doctor** (*Komt een vrouw bij de dokter*), which is also based on a bestselling novel. It tells the story of a man torn between his love for his dying wife (Carice van Houten) and his desire for other women.

The audience favourite at the Netherlands Film Festival was Danyael Sugawara's **Upstream** (*Alles stroomt*), a sensitive drama in which a mother and her son struggle to let go of each other. The youth jury at the festival favoured Mark de Cloe's **Life in One Day** (*Het leven uit een dag*), a slightly experimental fable in split-screen about love in both an ideal and a real world.

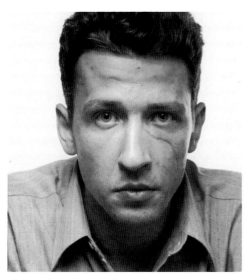

Aliona van der Horst's **Boris Ryzhy**

The Dutch documentary tradition continued with a number of fine films. One of the most thought provoking was Renzo Martens' **Episode III: Enjoy Poverty**. While travelling in the Congo he asks disturbing questions about the relationship between poverty and aid. Aliona van der Horst's **Boris Ryzhy**, about the Russian poet who hung himself at the age of 26, was the favourite of the critics' jury

at the Netherlands Film Festival. In her moving portrait, Van der Horst connects the tragedy of this young man with that of post-perestroika Russia.

Coco Schrijber's **Bloody Mondays & Stawberry Pies**

Coco Schrijber's **Bloody Mondays & Strawberry Pies**, an intriguing essay on boredom, was fascinating to watch, with striking images and a voiceover by John Malkovich. It performed well on the international festival circuit. Also wonderful for the big screen and almost classical in appearance was **Remembering Holland** (*Denkend aan Holland*) in which Jan Wouter van der Reijen allows us the viewpoint of artists who find their inspiration in the rivers that meander through the Dutch landscape.

Jan Wouter van der Reijen's **Remembering Holland**

This year's edition of the Netherlands Film Festival was the last under the much-praised leadership of Doreen Boonekamp, who from 3 October took over directing the Netherlands Film Fund. An important transfer, it is expected that Boonekamp will be able to steer the Fund out of the controversy that has surrounded it. Willemien van Aalst succeeded Boonekamp as festival director.

While the Netherlands Film Festival is an excellent showcase for Dutch cinema, the country's most important festival is the International Film Festival Rotterdam. While the 2009 attendance of 341,000 was a little below previous years, it is still quite miraculous considering the uncompromising nature of the programming and the lack of well-known stars. It would have been nice, of course, to see Danny Boyle introduce audience favourite *Slumdog Millionaire*, but Rotterdam was proud to welcome interesting filmmakers like Claire Denis and Alexei Balabanov.

The country focus was on young Turkish cinema. There was also an impressive overview of Asian horror. Guy Maddin, Nanouk Leopold and Carlos Reygadas were commissioned to make shorts for giant outdoor projections and *Sopranos* actor Michael Imperioli directed the opening film, *The Hungry Ghosts*, all of which gives some indication of the extraordinary range of this festival.

This 38th edition was also the first to be completely supervised by new director Rutger Wolfson, who decided to stay on after an interim appointment. Wolfson has not opted for major changes so far, although he has streamlined the programme. The adventurous auteur cinema, often by young makers (there were 14 of them in the Tiger Competition), along with a very strong market place for producers and distributors, remain the core features of IFFR.

Some confusion surrounded the Dutch Oscar entry this year. *Winter in Wartime* was chosen, but only after it was discovered that **The Silent Army** was not going to meet the Academy's requirements. An African-set thriller about child soldiers, *The Silent Army* is actually the heavily re-edited version of the film that premiered in December 2008 under the title

Jean van de Velde's **The Silent Army**

White Light. After removing the music and the flashback structure, Jean van de Velde saw his film selected for Un Certain Regard at Cannes, but such changes did not accord with the Academy's policy.

2010 will begin with a reshuffling of the Dutch film landscape, when the Filmmuseum, the promotional agency Holland Film, the Dutch Institute for Film Education and the organisation for experimental film, Filmbank, merge into a single agency for Dutch film.

Some 2010 releases to look out for are **Brownian Movement**, an international co-production by Nanouk Leopold (*Wolfsbergen*) about a couple in crisis, and **Tirza**, Rudolf van den Berg's adaptation of the bestseller by Arnon Grunberg.

Productive director Ben Sombogaart is working on a number of projects, among them **Isabelle**, based on a novel by Tessa de Loo, whose *Twin Sisters* he adapted successfully in 2002. And be prepared for a most unexpected approach to a historical event from the Second World War, as Ineke Smits imagines it in her poetic and even surreal **The Aviatrix of Kazbek** (*De vliegenierster van Kazbek*).

LEO BANKERSEN is a freelance film critic, contributing regularly to *de Filmkrant*, the largest independent film magazine in the Netherlands.

Renzo Martens' **Episode III: Enjoy Poverty**

The year's best films
Nothing Personal (Urszula Antoniak)
Boris Ryzhy (Aliona van der Horst)
Can Go Through Skin (Esther Rots)
Episode III: Enjoy Poverty (Renzo Martens)
Frogs & Toads (Simone van Dusseldorp)

Quotes of the year
'Aspirations. I'd rather see a filmmaker fail miserably while taking a big risk, than having him follow the well-trodden road that was tried and tested by others.' URSZULA ANTONIAK, *when asked what Dutch cinema would need.*

'Why, for heaven's sake, would you put money and energy in a film without having the aim to improve the world?' *Enfant terrible* CYRUS FRISCH, *explaining his ambitions, while still impressed by the emotional audience response to* **Dazzle**, *his idiosyncratic plea against indifference shown at the BAFICI festival in Buenos Aires.*

Directory
All Tel/Fax numbers begin (+31)
Association of Dutch Film Critics (KNF), PO Box 10650, 1001 ER Amsterdam. Tel: (6) 2153 4555. info@filmjournalisten.nl. www.filmjournalisten.nl.
Cobo Fund, PO Box 26444, Postvak M54, 1202 JJ Hilversum. Tel: (35) 677 5348. Fax: (35) 677 1955. cobo@cobofonds.nl. www.cobofonds.nl. Contact: Jeanine Hage.
Dutch Federation for Cinematography (NFC), PO Box 143, 1180 AC Amstelveen. Tel: (20) 426 6100. Fax: (20) 426 6110. info@nvbbureau.nl. www. nfcstatistiek.nl/index2.html. Contact: Wilco Wolfers.
Filmmuseum, Sandra den Hamer, Vondelpark 3, PO Box 74782, 1070 BT Amsterdam. Tel: (20) 589

1400. Fax: (20) 683 3401. info@filmmuseum.nl. www.filmmuseum.nl.
Holland Film, Claudia Landsberger, Jan Luykenstraat 2, 1071 CM Amsterdam. Tel: (20) 570 7575. Fax: (20) 570 7570. hf@hollandfilm.nl. www. hollandfilm.nl.
International Film Festival Rotterdam, PO Box 21696, 3001 AR Rotterdam. Tel: (10) 890 9090. Fax: (10) 890 9091. tiger@filmfestivalrotterdam.com. www.filmfestivalrotterdam.com.
Ministry of Education, Culture and Science, Arts Dept, PO Box 16375, 2500 BJ Den Haag. Tel: (70) 412 3456. Fax: (70) 412 3450. www.minocw.nl.
Netherlands Film and Television Academy (NFTA), Markenplein 1, 1011 MV Amsterdam. Tel: (20) 527 7333. Fax: (20) 527 7344. info@filmacademie.nl. www.filmacademie.nl. Contact: Willem Capteyn.
Netherlands Film Festival, Willemien van Aalst, PO Box 1581, 3500 BN Utrecht. Tel: (30) 230 3800. Fax: (30) 230 3801. info@filmfestival.nl. www.filmfestival.nl.
Netherlands Film Fund, Jan Luykenstraat 2, 1071 CM Amsterdam. Tel: (20) 570 7676. Fax: (20) 570 7689. info@filmfonds.nl. www.filmfund.nl. Contact: Doreen Boonekamp.
Netherlands Institute for Animation Film (NIAf), PO Box 9358, 5000 HJ Tilburg. Tel: (13) 532 4070. Fax: (13) 580 0057. niaf@niaf.nl. www.niaf.nl. Contact: Ton Crone.
Netherlands Institute for Sound and Vision, PO Box 1060, 1200 BB Hilversum. Tel: (35) 677 8035. klantenservice@beeldengeluid.nl. instituut. beeldengeluid.nl.
Rotterdam Media Fund, Lloydstraat 9F, 3025 EA Rotterdam. Tel: (10) 436 0747. Fax: (10) 436 0553. info@rff.rotterdam.nl. www.rff.rotterdam.nl. Contact: Jacques van Heijningen.

Urszula Antoniak's **Nothing Personal**

ABU DHABI FILM COMMISSION

New Zealand Peter Calder

Niki Caro's **The Vintner's Luck**

t's a safe bet that no other country produced a film in the last year about fiftysomething lesbian twin country-and-western singers who like nothing so much as a good yodel. But in New Zealand, it was a no-brainer. The producers professed delighted astonishment, but **Topp Twins: Untouchable Girls** was always going to be a winner. So it proved. The film, directed by Leanne Pooley, took a healthy US$1.5m – outperforming *Fahrenheit 9/11* to set a local box-office record for a documentary, at least until the Michael Jackson film **This Is It** opened in October.

Topp Twins, *Linda and Jools*

The intimate portrait and affectionate history of two women who are household names at home, in the spheres of both entertainment and political activism, also performed well on the international festival circuit, winning audience awards at Toronto and Melbourne.

Topp Twins was the notable crowd-pleaser of an uneven year in which the most keenly anticipated release turned out to be a major disappointment. Niki Caro, whose breakthrough was the surprise 2002 hit *Whale Rider*, adapted an international bestseller by

local novelist Elizabeth Knox. **The Vintner's Luck** was an obscure and often incoherent magical-realist allegory which, despite high production values, remained mired in the mud of its vineyard setting. The hostile trade-press reviews following its Toronto premiere were echoed at home.

Much more gratifying was **The Strength of Water**, the feature debut of Armagan Ballantyne, whose films have long been fixtures on the festival circuit. The film, shot in an isolated Maori community in the north of the country, with non-professionals in the main child roles, is a simple and uplifting drama about twins forced apart by an unexpected tragedy. Both Ballantyne and Maori writer

Armagan Ballantyne's debut **The Strength of Water**

Briar Grace-Smith, a noted local playwright, had the benefit of workshopping the project at the Sundance lab, and the long development process – too often lacking in local films – paid off handsomely.

Also deeply satisfying was **Dean Spanley**, the second feature by Toa Fraser, an Edwardian-set yarn about an old man healing his stilted relationship with his son. Judged best film at the local awards – it also garnered a supporting-actor gong for Peter O'Toole – the film turned a shaggy-dog tale into a beautiful story of loss and redemption. The NZ-UK co-production attracted some criticism at home for its British theme, but New Zealanders occupied all the key creative posts.

Jonathan King's **Under the Mountain**

At the time of going to press, **Under the Mountain**, the new film by Jonathan King, who made the splatter spoof *Black Sheep* in 2006, was unseen here but it had received a critical mauling at Toronto. The kidult thriller based on a fantasy classic by a prolific local author was made as a television series a few decades ago, but the advance word on the new version is not good.

The only other significant release was **Separation City**, directed by Australian-based ex-pat Paul Middleditch, but notable mainly because of its writer. The multi-talented Tom Scott, who virtually invented satirical political journalism in New Zealand and is one of the country's best newspaper cartoonists, has also penned critically acclaimed work for the stage and small screen. *Separation City*, which has been in development since the 1980s under the title *The Truth About Men*, was a wistful rumination on mid-life malaise and infidelity. Although there is a sure feel for certain emotional realities, it felt dated and its attempts at poignancy were undermined by Scott's penchant for smart one-liners.

The local industry mourned the passing of pioneer Maori filmmaker Barry Barclay, unquestionably our greatest and most influential documentary filmmaker, whose feature debut *Ngati* in 1987 was the first directed by a member of an indigenous people. A portrait-of-the-artist documentary, **The Camera on the Shore**, by Barclay's long-time buddy Graeme Tuckett, which premiered at the country's main film festival, was a fitting tribute.

The small but vigorous short-film community continued to nurture new talent. Notable were **Poppy**, a CGI animation of a touching true episode in the First World War, and **The Six Dollar Fifty Man**, about a young dreamer's triumph over his tormentors.

Big changes are afoot at the New Zealand Film Commission, the state- and lottery-funded film bank, which is the primary financier for project development – though less so for feature productions, which now routinely have to seek most of their finance from pre-sales or co-production agreements. The commission's chief executive Ruth Harley left to take up the equivalent position with Film Australia, with her sales and marketing director, Kathleen Drumm, the face of the commission at festival sales desks, following her soon afterwards. Harley's replacement is an Australian: Graeme Mason, who was at Polygram Filmed Entertainment in its glory days. He has impressed as a thoughtful executive who listens well to industry concerns and has been welcomed as a change from his micro-managing and widely unpopular predecessor.

Meanwhile, the new National (conservative) Government ordered a wholesale review of the commission, which was to be conducted, in partnership with an Australian academic, by Peter Jackson. The name must have chilled a few bloodstreams in the commission's offices, since Jackson has been a vocal critic of the organisation for years (in March he said the films it had made over the past ten years were 'the most disappointing in [the history of] our 30-year-old modern film industry'). At press time, it was understood that the review's report – or at least a draft of it – was on the desk of the minister responsible, but Jackson's absence, to publicise the December release of his new film, **The Lovely Bones**, seemed likely to delay its public release until well into 2010.

The credit crunch and recession hit the cash-poor local business harder than in 2008 and, as a result, the production slate is pretty lean for the year ahead. The industry was alarmed at changes to the taxation law, which removed incentives for investors, including presales to distributors. But a well-established scheme offering a 15 per cent rebate on local spending by foreign productions – and a recent new one providing an even more generous 40 per cent refund to local companies – seems to be having the desired effect. Film New Zealand, which markets the country's locations, infrastructure and creative personnel, reports that income from overseas-funded films shot and produced here jumped almost 80 per cent in the past year, as productions such as *The Adventures of Tintin: The Secret of the Unicorn*, *District 9* and *The Lovely Bones*, all produced by Jackson, *The Day the Earth Stood Still*, and James Cameron's *Avatar* set up shop here.

The year's best films
Topp Twins: Untouchable Girls
(Leanne Pooley)
The Strength of Water (Armagan Ballantyne)
Dean Spanley (Toa Fraser)
Lost in Wonderland (documentary)
(Zoe McIntosh)
Poppy (short film) (James Cunningham)

Quotes of the year
'Only communist countries still have a government agency in the sales role.' JOHN BARNETT, *New Zealand's most prolific screen producer, and one of the Film Commission's most strident critics.*

'The slightly scary thing is that the politicians like the sound of what he says so much. Peter has done some amazing things but... he has not worked at the level [of] the rest of the industry for a very long time.' DAVE GIBSON *of production company Gibson Group on the selection of Peter Jackson to review the Commission.*

Directory
All Tel/Fax numbers begin (+64)
Film New Zealand, PO Box 24142, Wellington. Tel: (4) 385 0766. Fax: (4) 384 5840. info@filmnz.org.nz. www.filmnz.com.
New Zealand Film Archive, PO Box 11449, Wellington. Tel: (4) 384 7647. Fax: (4) 382 9595. nzfa@actrix.gen.nz. www.filmarchive.org.nz.
New Zealand Film Commission, PO Box 11546, Wellington. Tel: (4) 382 7680. Fax: (4) 384 9719. marketing@nzfilm.co.nz.
Ministry of Economic Development, 33 Bowen St, PO Box 1473, Wellington. Tel: (4) 472 0030. Fax: (4) 473 4638. www.med.govt.nz.
Office of Film & Literature Classification, PO Box 1999, Wellington. Tel: (64) 471 6770. Fax: (4) 471 6781. information@censorship.govt.nz.
Screen Production & Development Association (SPADA), PO Box 9567, Wellington. Tel: (4) 939 6934. Fax: (4) 939 6935. info@spada.co.nz.

PETER CALDER is the chief film critic for the *New Zealand Herald*, the country's major newspaper.

James Cunningham's **Poppy**

Nigeria Steve Ayorinde

Nigerian cinema, otherwise known as Nollywood, began 2009 as the world's second-largest producer of feature films. In 2006, the Global Cinema Survey for film releases, conducted by the UNESCO Institute for Statistics, ranked Nollywood, with 872 movies shot on digital video, ahead of Hollywood, whose output was 485. Only India was ahead, with 1,091 films. Though the figures have altered, the ranking remain the same.

That said, the industry experienced a major lull in production in 2009, with releases sliding to less than 400, according to Emeka Mba, the Director General of the National Film and Video Censors Board. In a year of global recession and a financial crisis that shook many banks in Nigeria, Nollywood suffered badly. And with audiences now insisting on better quality product, directors such as Zeb Ejiro and Kingsley Omoife have been forced to return to television, to produce soap operas.

Two films stood out. Actress Stephanie Okereke's directorial debut, **Through the Glass**, was a romantic thriller set in an immigrant district in Los Angeles where Stephanie, following a serious car accident, has gone to recover. The film was not necessarily the perfect combination of Nollywood and Hollywood styles, although it did feature as many white actors as black in the cast. Nevertheless, it offered what an industry suffering a dry spell at the cinemas needed – a star-studded premiere and a bona fide hit.

What Okereke's film lacked in terms of compelling content and technical skill was what Kunle Afolayan's **The Figurine**, a moving blend of horror, adventure, love and tragedy set across two periods, offered in abundance. By far the most ambitious and outstanding Nigerian film

of the year, *The Figurine* is a technical and artistic success for the banker-turned-filmmaker/actor. A five-city road-show premiere, including Ghana and London, ensured enough publicity to guarantee a box-office hit, with the total revenue earned yet to be calculated, since the release was only at the beginning of October. Critics admired the film more than Afolayan's previous effort, *Irapada*, which nevertheless won an award at the African Movie Academy Awards and was selected for the London International Film Festival.

On the set of Kunle Afolayan's **The Figurine**

Low-budget popular releases in the indigenous Yoruba language also appeared on the radar, making a powerful impact at video clubs. Foluke Daramola's **The Appointed Time** (*Wakati Eda*), a didactic story of trials and adversity, and Dotun Taylor's **A Thousand Miles** (*Egberun Maili*), a fast-paced action thriller based on a real-life story, were audience favourites.

Similarly, though they may be late entries in the declining market, the romantic thriller **Guilty Pleasures**, jointly directed by actor Desmond Elliot and Daniel Ademinokan, as

On the set of Moses Inwang's **Nollywood Hustlers**

well as a stylishly wry thriller, **Nollywood Hustlers**, directed by Moses Inwang, served as the core Nollywood offerings of the year.

The year's best documentary choices came from Femi Odugbemi with **Bariga Boy**, a docu-drama telling the story of a boy and the deprived area of the city he lives in, and **Ibadan, Cradle of Nigerian Literati**. The film celebrated key historical and literary achievements of Nigeria and extolled the rich past of the ancient city of Ibadan, in which the nation's premier university is located. It was founded in 1948 and was the alma mater of Nigeria's first generation of literary giants and cultural icons.

It is still being voiced, albeit in hushed tones, that some in Nollywood are still in denial about the fact that cinemas and major international festivals, as opposed to the traditional platform of video clubs, are the future.

Mahmood Ali-Balogun's big-budget urban drama, **Tango With Me**, has started shooting in Lagos with an American crew. Like Jeta Amata's 2006 epic drama, *Amazing Grace*, Ali-Balogun is filming with 35mm – a rare thing in Nollywood.

The year could be described as Dickson Iroegbu's simply on account of the buzz around his next project, **Child Soldier**, a tragic adventure with which he hopes to bring the plight of child soldiers in Africa to the world's attention. He has succeeded in discussing the project at every film forum and requires US$2million,

an almost unrealistic big budget by Nollywood standards, with which to shoot the film.

Actress Shan George is also trying her hand at directing and has picked a Spanish script, hoping for a Nigerian-Spanish collaboration with **Super Zebra Man**, a cross-continental thriller about love and betrayal. At the same time, actor/producer Saheed Balogun is looking for an international break with **You or Me**, a multi-layered story of identity crisis that is set both in the United States and Nigeria.

The lull in the home market has forced Nollywood to seek new frontiers in 2010. Another endorsement from Oprah Winfrey would be welcome, similar to the one she gave the industry in September, when she described actress Genevieve Nnaji as the 'Julia Roberts of Nollywood', during the 'Meet the Most Famous People in the World' episode of her talk show.

The year's best films
The Figurine (Kunle Afolayan)
Bariga Boy (Femi Odugbemi)
Guilty Pleasures
(Desmond Elliot and Daniel Ademinokan)
Through the Glass (Stephanie Okereke)
The Appointed Time (Foluke Daramola)

Quote of the year
'What we are producing now are home videos, and it's not right to judge them by the quality of what we see in the cinemas. If we want to begin to produce what will be good enough for the cinemas, in terms of content and technical quality, then we must be ready to put in everything that is required.' PETER IGHO, *producer/manager, Nigerian Television Authority, saying Nollywood might have revived film production in Nigeria but has not yet graduated into proper filmmaking.*

STEVE AYORINDE is a film critic and Editor of *The PUNCH*, Nigeria's highest-selling quality daily. He is a member of FIPRESCI and is on the jury of the African Movie Academy Awards (AMAA). He is the author of *Masterpieces: A Critic's Timeless Reports*.

Norway Trond Olav Svendsen

An account of the past year might best begin with a note on the box-office results, as 2009 began with the biggest success in Norwegian film history. Joachim Rønning and Espen Sandberg's *Max Manus*, released in December 2008, tells the story of a Norwegian resistance fighter during the Second World War. It turned out to be the perfect home-grown blockbuster, with close to 1.2 million tickets sold – in a country with just 4.6 million inhabitants. The film is closely connected to a specific Norwegian historical/ myth from the war. It deals with the forming of a famous resistance group in Oslo after the German attack in the spring of 1940, and follows the group's exploits during five years of occupation. It has a comic-strip quality – in a positive sense – with strong visuals and a fast pace. The treatment of the various dilemmas of the occupation is brief and not always in accordance with fact, but at the same time it has an appealing sincerity. The film ends in 1945 with one of its best scenes, when the hero (Aksel Hennie) is drunk, as the Germans surrender, wondering what to do next. The answer is to get married to his female contact in neutral Sweden, played by newcomer Agnes Kittelsen, who gives the film's best performance.

Tommy Wirkola's **Dead Snow**

With a couple of other films, such as Nils Gaup's *The Kautokeino Rebellion*, *Max Manus* helped to make 2008 the best commercial year ever for Norwegian cinema. Home product accounted for 22.4% of all cinema tickets sold. It was, of course, an impossible act to follow. By autumn, it became clear that the earnings of the next 20 films together barely matched *Max Manus'* impressive takings. There was a box-office hit in January, however, with **Dead Snow** (*Død snø*), a splatter film about rotting Nazi zombies creating terror amid the wintery landscape of northern Norway. Director Tommy Wirkola, of *Kill Buljo* fame, knows what modern genre filmmaking is about and effectively juggles elements of fright and fun.

After this, audiences divided themselves equally among a number of films, many of

Joachim Rønning and Espen Sandberg's **Max Manus**

Pål Jackman's **Shooting the Sun**

which had something to commend them. In **Shooting the Sun** (*Jernanger*), Pål Jackman tells the story of a middle-aged bartender who reflects on his missed opportunities. The film is not fleshed out enough dramatically, but features a great performance by veteran actor Bjørn Sundquist in what must be close to his 80th role. The award-winning **North** (*Nord*), directed by Rune Denstad Langlo and scripted by Erlend Loe, is an eccentric road movie, set in northern Norway. Anders Baasmo Christiansen is excellent as the skier who has a mental breakdown and begins a journey northwards on his snowmobile. The various individuals he encounters along the way are portrayed with an unassuming humour. **Vegas**, directed by Gunnar Vikene, offers a fresh look at troubled teenage life, with fine performances all round, particularly by young Karoline Stemre as the unruly Marianne.

Rune Denstad's **North**

Two good films arrived in early autumn. **The Angel** (*Engelen*), directed by the noted documentary filmmaker Margreth Olin, is the story of Lea (Maria Bonnevie) who becomes

a heroin addict and prostitute who decides to surrender her child to foster parents. The story is hardly original, the title is forgettable and the *mise-en-scene* is often static. However, a voiceover by the director is put to good use as the story flashes back and forth in time and the film ultimately makes a strong impression, mostly for its compassion. Olin's involvement in Lea's plight is genuine and moving. Some of the simple scenes, such as Lea's surrender of her child, work splendidly. And as the desparate woman, Maria Bonnevie is excellent. With her background in Swedish and Norwegian theatre, her performance is as convincing technically as it is emotionally.

Marie Bonnevie in Margreth Olin's **The Angel**

Upperdog is the sophomore feature by Sara Johnsen. The focal point of the story is the reunion of Axel (Herman Sabado) and Yanne (Bang Chau), a brother and sister born in Asia and adopted by two different Norwegian families, one belonging to the upper class and the other working class. At the centre of the drama is a young Polish woman, Maria

Sara Johnsen's **Upperdog**

(Agnieszka Grochowska), who works as a cleaner in the wealthy home of the brother. She embarks on an affair with the handsome young man, even though he is cold and not particularly likeable, and is ultimately responsible for bringing the siblings together. Johnsen has a knack for a kind of distanced intimacy; an observational approach that maintains an emotional space between the characters, which gradually engages the audience. Politics plays a role (the film features a soldier who served in Afghanistan), but it is handled subtly, without resorting to grand statements. There is also a lightness to the film; it is both playful and serious, like some of the works by Mozart that litter the soundtrack.

In September, the Labour/Socialist/Centre coalition was re-elected. Perhaps their cinema policy helped? Relying on the oil-fuelled economy, the coalition's policy has been one of unprecedented generosity, resulting in a large output of features. But in the place of what could have been a deluge of meaningless quota films, many directors and scriptwriters with something to say are making a living from producing insightful and popular films in this small nation. We can look forward to good things in the years to come.

The year's best films
Upperdog (Sara Johnsen)
The Angel (Margreth Olin)
Shooting the Sun (Pål Jackman)
Vegas (Gunnar Vikene)
North (Rune Denstad Langlo)

Karoline Stemre in Gunnar Vikene's **Vegas**

Quote of the year
'When people had seen *Max Manus* their Norwegian quota was full. Some cinemagoers think that way.' IVAR KØHN, *film consultant, explaining the box-office results.*

Directory
All Tel/Fax numbers begin (+47)
Henie-Onstad Art Centre, Sonja Henie vei 31, 1311 Høvikodden. Tel: 6780 4880. post@hok.no
Norwegian Film Institute, PO Box 482 Sentrum, 0105 Oslo. Tel: 2247 4500. Fax: 2247 4599. post@ nfi.no. www.nfi.no. Contact: Lise Gustavson.
Norwegian Film Development, Dronningens gt 16, 0152 Oslo. Tel: 2282 2400. Fax: 2282 2422. mail@nfu.no. Contact: Kirsten Bryhni.
Norwegian Film and TV Producers Association, Dronningens gt. 16, 0152 Oslo. Tel: 2311 9311. Fax: 2311 9316. leif@produsentforeningen.no, Contact: Leif Holst Jensen.
Norwegian Film Workers Association, Dronningens gt. 16, 0152 Oslo. Tel: 2247 4640. Fax: 2247 4689. post@filmforbundet.no, Contact: Sverre Pedersen.
Norwegian Media Authority, Nygata 4, 1607 Fredrikstad, Tel: 6930 1200. Fax: 6930 1201, post@ medietilsynet.no, Contact: Tom Thoresen.

Margreth Olin's **The Angel**

TROND OLAV SVENDSEN is a historian from the University of Oslo. He has worked as a newspaper film critic and an editor in the Oslo publishing house of Kunnskapsforlaget. Among his publications is a theatre and film encyclopedia.

Pakistan Aijaz Gul

The last year has once again seen a downward slide in the quality and quantity of films being produced in Pakistan. There were only 25 feature films, compared with 50 releases in 2004. Competition from Indian films, which are of significantly higher quality, also placed a burden on Urdu films. And in terms of content, the violence shown so openly in recent years now sits uncomfortably with the actual violence that erupts regularly on the country's streets.

After peace returned to the Swat valley in September 2009, Pushto action films were popular with audiences. This followed the paucity of cinema activity under the Taliban's reign, where they closed down cinemas, music venues and shops selling CDs or videos. Pushto films also played well because they are not being shown on cable television.

Imports from Hollywood and Bollywood are now being released religiously every Friday, occupying the most prominent cinemas. This continues to be good news for importers and exhibitors, but the resentment and outrage of producers and large sections of the local film industry still festers, as it denies them the best venues for domestic releases. At the same time, the number of cinemas has reduced from 700 to less than 200 in recent years. However, with the flood of popular imports, a number of single-screen cinemas are being renovated and some urban areas are seeing the introduction of multiplexes.

Major Hollywood titles like *Star Trek*, *Hotel for Dogs*, *Transformers 2*, *Ice Age 3* and *G.I. Joe* showed only modest returns due to rampant piracy. Pirated DVDs are being sold everywhere, including Sunday markets, often for

A cinema in Rawalpindi showing the Punjabi film **Rascal**

as little as US$0.50. Copyright violation is a major issue and the industry has called for the government to control it. PEMRA (Pakistan Electronic Media Regulatory Authority), with all the cable operators under its strict domain, has done little to stop this menace. In addition to DVD piracy, there are illegal cable operators who pay no royalties to the producers or distributors when screening their films. Added to this problem is the threat of violence outside people's doors, leaving them concerned about their own safety and thus staying inside with the illegal cable stations and pirated DVDs.

The state does not promote film studies in schools, colleges or universities, and seeking funding for films from the government is a convoluted process, which has been known to encourage nepotism and corruption. Such things need to change and the authorities need to play more of a role in promotional and development activities within the industry.

AIJAZ GUL is a film critic. He has published four books, the latest on singer-actress Noorjehan. He is a member of FIPRESCI and NETPAC (Network for the Promotion of Asian Cinema).

Peru Isaac Léon Frías

The highlight of Peruvian cinema in 2009 was the success of Claudia Llosa's Spanish-Peruvian co-production, **The Milk of Sorrow** (*La teta asustada*), which received both the Golden Bear and FIPRESCI Award for best film at the Berlin Film Festival. It was the first time that a Peruvian film participated in the International Competition at the Berlinale and the announcement came as a welcome surprise.

Héctor Gálvez's **Paradise**

Claudia Llosa's **The Milk of Sorrow**

The film is about the daughter of a woman who was raped during a violent period of the country's recent past (1980–1992) and the trauma that is transferred, by breast milk, from the mother to daughter – the 'milk of sorrow'. The drama alternates between the difficult and poverty-stricken life of Fausta (Magaly Solier), who works as a housekeeper for a painter, and carnival-like scenes in which several couples and their guests celebrate their weddings at a service organised by Fausta's relatives.

In addition to Claudia Llosa's success, Héctor Gálvez's **Paradise** (*Paraíso*) and Javier Fuentes-León's **Counterstream** (*Contracorriente*) participated (respectively) in the festivals of Venice and San Sebastián. Both films were directorial

debuts and have yet to be released in Lima.

Terrorism and violence also featured in Fabrizio Aguilar's sophomore feature, **Tarata**, whose similarly themed debut, *Paper Dove*, was set in the Peruvian Andes. By contrast, *Tarata* unfolds in the context of the worst terrorist attack in Lima, in 1992, and focuses on a family who live near the site of the car bomb. Although they survive the experience, a sense of threat and fear creeps into their lives. Like *The Milk of Sorrow*, the film reflects on the civil war the country lived through following the rise of the guerrilla movement, Shining Path (Sendero Luminoso).

Fabrizio Aguilar's **Tarata**

Four

Four (*Cu4tro*) is a portmanteau film directed by four young graduates of the University of Lima: Frank Pérez-Garland, Christian Buckley, Bruno Ascenzo and Sergio Barrio. Each episode deals with themes of loss, absence, and mourning, the most remarkable of which is the first, directed by Frank Pérez-Garland and starring Vanessa Saba, one of the country's best actresses.

The Award (*El premio*) was directed by Alberto Durand, one of the country's most experienced filmmakers. His sixth feature follows a young man's desire to leave his small-town home and experience life in the city. With a storyline that lacks originality and a screenplay that fails in its attempt to offer a critical perspective on consumerism and modern life, *The Award* lacked the sharpness it needed in order to convince.

Eduardo Schuldt's The Dolphin

In terms of attracting commercial success, no film in the last year was marketed as much as Eduardo Schuldt's animated film, **The Dolphin** (*El Delfín*), based on the bestseller by Sergio Bambarén. The film adopts the book's air of new ageiness, but lacks enough adventure to make it a Peruvian *Finding Nemo*.

One of the most disappointing films of the last year was *Motor and Motive* (*Motor y Motivo*), about the cumbia band Grupo 5, who are popular in the poorer regions of the country. The film purported to be a thriller with an element of comedy thrown in, but the narrative is extraneous to what was ultimately little more than a travelogue of the band's tour around various Peruvian cities.

Several releases have been announced for the next few months, which highlights the level of support being offered by the Cinematography National Council (CONACINE). The council also offers incentive awards for filmmakers. In addition to these benefits, films can receive further financial aid through the grants supplied by European foundations and agencies such as IBERMEDIA.

Audience figures have increased significantly over the last year. *The Milk of Sorrow*, *Tarata* and *Motor and Motive* have been seen by almost two hundred thousand people. However, the box-office figures for *The Dolphin* will certainly exceed that. The film has been picked up by Fox, who will release it across 22 countries, marking another first in an excellent year for Peruvian cinema.

The year's best film
The Milk of Sorrow (Claudia Llosa)

Directory
All Tel/Fax numbers begin (+51)
Consejo Nacional de Cinematografia (CONA-CINE), Museo de la Nación, Avenida Javier Prado 2465, Lima. Tel/Fax: 225 6479.

ISAAC LÉON FRÍAS is a film critic and Professor of Language and Film History at the University of Lima. From 1965 to 1985 he was director of *Hablemos de Cine* magazine and from 1986 to 2001 ran Filmoteca de Lima.

Poland Barbara Hollender

Paradoxically, it is in a time of crisis that Polish cinema caught a new, fresh breath. The economic meltdown had little impact on the funds of the Polish Film Institute (PISF), which had at its disposal a decent, at least for Poland, €34.2 million, €21 million of which was allocated for production.

The financial collapse did hit Public Television (TVP). A powerful producer and the main partner of PISF, instead of €6.3 million, it had only €1.2 million for feature production. In addition, over 50% of this amount had to be used to pay off liabilities from 2008. This accounts for why several high-profile projects that were supposed to be co-produced by TVP failed to materialise. What did get made was a record number of modest movies (around 60 productions), because producers successfully topped up their budgets with the help of distributors, non-public television stations and private investors.

Artists of all generations managed to see their productions reach fruition. There have been films by Andrzej Wajda and Janusz Morgenstern as well as Agnieszka Holland, Krzysztof Zanussi, Robert Gliński and Feliks Falk. Above all, however, a new generation of filmmakers caught a break. These debuting and sophomore directors are the ones helping to refresh Polish cinema, bringing their energy and an often unconventional view of the world, as well as a new approach to cinema language, to the screen.

This year witnessed the release of two biographical films. Rafał Wieczyński's **Popiełuszko: Freedom is Within Us** (*Popiełuszko. Wolność jest w nas*) presented the life of Jerzy Popiełuszko, a priest murdered

Rafał Wieczyński's **Popiełuszko: Freedom is Within Us**

in 1984 by the communist secret service (SB). Ryszard Bugajski's **General Nil** (*Generał Nil*) told how the Stalinist secret police (UB) persecuted and arrested a war hero, one of the Home Army leaders, General Fieldorf, who was sentenced to death in a fixed trial in 1952 and was executed in 1953.

The most important historical films, however, were ones that explored the complexity of the past and avoided any clichéd representations of it. In his directorial debut, **Reverse** (*Rewers*), which received the Golden Lions award at the Polish Film Festival, Borys Lankosz presented a story set during the Stalinist era, featuring Sabina, a love-hungry spinster from an educated family, who becomes the object of desire for

Borys Lankosz's **Reverse**

a handsome man. He turns out to be a secret police (UB) agent who tries to blackmail his sweetheart into informing on her co-workers. Lankosz's film, though occasionally grotesque, accurately captures life in 1950s Poland, with black-and-white camerawork by Marcin Koszałka enhancing the sense of realism.

Wojciech Smarzowski followed his debut, *The Wedding*, with **The Dark House** (*Dom Zły*), which revisits the years 1978–82, in which a crime reveals a hidden political agenda. In this bleak world, where vodka flows like water, everything is in moral decline. The authorities shamelessly flaunt their impunity from any action, and blackmail and denunciation are rampant. Janusz Morgenstern's **The Lesser Evil** (*Mniejsze zło*) is also set during the same period, but in Warsaw and amongst the intelligentsia environment of 'Solidarity'. A young poet, who becomes involved with the opposition by coincidence, is a fraud, stealing others' texts, and a scoundrel, abusing women. Morgenstern shows that the wind of history elevates not only heroes, but also those unworthy of respect. The film is a cautionary tale about conformism, reminding us that it is easier to change the political system than people's mentality.

Borys Szyc and Leslaw Zurek in Janusz Morgenstern's **The Lesser Evil**

Krzysztof Zanussi's **Revisited** (*Rewizyta*) looked at further developments in the lives of several characters from his earlier films: *Family Life*, *The Constant Factor* and *Camouflage*. The same actors appeared in the parts they performed ipreviously and the resulting film highlights not only their fate, but looks at the changes each person can undergo in specific

circumstances, as well as detailing the intricacies of life and the merciless progress of time.

Paweł Borowski's **Zero**

A higher quality of storytelling and sensitivity also appeared in contemporary stories. The feature debut by Paweł Borowski, **Zero** (*Zero*), is a well-made, multi-layered narrative concerning the shallowness of relationships and how unfulfilled people are in the 21st century. In a film about loneliness and missed connections, because of the constant rush of modern life, the film moves with dizzying speed, the camera remaining with the person who spoke the last line in a scene. There are more than 20 main characters and their lives intertwine throughout.

Marcin Wrona's **My Flesh My Blood** (*Moja krew*) is the story of a dying ex-boxer who wants to make a mark. He talks a young Vietnamese immigrant into having a baby with him in return for marriage and citizenship. The film, an account of brutal times where only winners seem to count, is also about longing for something that you can base your life on.

Marcin Wrona's **My Flesh My Blood**

Xavery Żuławski's **Snow White and Russian Red**

Xavery Żuławski made **Snow White and Russian Red** (*Wojna polsko-ruska*) based on a novel by Dorota Masłowska – a young writer honoured with one of the most prestigious Polish literary awards, Nike. In a very dynamic form, it shows people whose lives, devoid of moral guidance, a sense of community and any chances for success, have fallen apart.

Two interesting pictures about underage prostitution were produced. Robert Gliński's **Piggies** (*Świnki*) tells a story of paedophilia on the Polish-German border, while in Katarzyna Rosłaniec's **Mall Girls** (*Galerianki*), young teenage girls sell themselves to middle-aged men at city malls in return for a dress, fashionable shoes or the latest mobile phone.

Katarzyna Rosłaniec's **Mall Girls**

Two films offered thoughts on grander subjects. Andrzej Wajda, the master of Polish cinema, in his beautiful **Sweet Rush** (*Tatarak*), told a story about death and how life goes on after it. The film was also about the acting profession; how much a performer gives of him or

herself to their art. An adaptation of Jarosław Iwaszkiewicz's story interweaves with the story of the making of a film and the confession of an actress, played by Krystyna Janda, who talks about her husband's death. A shocking, moving film, made in a very modern way.

Andrzej Wajda's **Sweet Rush**

Piotr Dumała's **The Forest** (*Las*) resembles a philosophical treatise. The first film with live actors by this excellent animator, it looks like a work of art. Slow moving, with sublime camerawork by Adam Sikora, it makes a subversive use of the myth of Isaac and Abraham, at the same time becoming a magical story about the father-son relationship, sacrifice and the emptiness caused by the loss of someone close.

On the commercial side, **The Magic Tree** (*Magiczne drzewo*) was made by the distinguished children's film director, Andrzej Maleszka. And there were comedies. Film critics are invariably negative about them, pointing out naïve screenplays and weak acting – mostly by actors from TV soap operas. But cinemagoers support these films. **Love and Dance** (*Kochaj i tańcz*) and **The Perfect Guy for My Girlfriend** (*Idealny facet dla mojej dziewczyny*) dominated the year's top ten. There were also devoted viewers of **God's Little Village** (*U Pana Boga w ogródku*), Jacek Bromski's warming countryside story, which is set in eastern Poland.

And somewhere between art and entertainment there was the new movie by

Agnieszka Holland and Kasia Adamik's **Janosik. The True Story**

Agnieszka Holland and Kasia Adamik, **Janosik. The True Story** (*Janosik. Prawdziwa historia*). The legend of a highland robber from the Tatras, who 'took away from the rich and gave to the poor', it was filmed as a tragic story about a young man who cannot find a place for himself in life after returning home from war.

This year has revived hopes concerning Polish films and sharpened audience appetites. What will the next year bring? Andrzej Wajda has announced he is making a film about Lech Wałęsa, but there is no screenplay as yet. Jan Jakub Kolski's **Wenecja** (*Venice*) sounds interesting – an adaptation of a short story by Odojewski, about a boy who, hiding in a cellar during World War Two, dreams about a trip to Venice. Janusz Majewski will go back to post-war times to make an autobiographical movie, **Junior High School Exam 1947** (*Mała matura 1947*). Filip Bajon is preparing an adaptation of Aleksander Fredro's comedy, **Maidens' Vows** (*Śluby panieńskie*). Dorota Kędzierzawska is finishing her film about two young immigrants from Russia, **Tomorrow Will Be Better** (*Jutro będzie lepiej*). But the most anticipated films are those by new filmmakers. And again, there will be a fair few of them. The '30 minutes' programme started by the Polish Filmmakers Association obviously does find the real talent out there.

BARBARA HOLLENDER is a Warsaw-based journalist and film critic for the daily *Rzeczpospolita*. She covers many major film festivals, and has written, among other works, a study of *Studio Tor* (2000).

The year's best films
Reverse (Borys Lankosz)
Sweet Rush (Andrzej Wajda)
Zero (Paweł Borowski)
The Dark House (Wojciech Smarzowski)
Snow White and Russian Red (Xawery Żuławski)

Quote of the year
'I don't know who an average moviegoer is. I don't think there is someone like that. I believe in an intelligent moviegoer.' BORYS LANKOSZ *talking about* Reverse.

Directory
All Tel/Fax numbers begin (+48)
Polish Film Institute, 00-071 Warsaw, ul., Krakowskie Przedmieście 21/23. Tel: (22) 421 0518. Fax: (22) 421 0241. pisf@pisf.pl www.pisf.pl.
Polish Filmmakers Association, 00-068 Warsaw, Krakowskie Przedmieście 7. Tel: (22) 556 5440, (22) 845 5132. Fax: (22) 845 3908. biuro@sfp.org.pl. www.sfp.org.pl.
National Chamber of Audiovisual Producers, 00-724 Warsaw, ul., Chełmska 21 bud.28. Tel: (22) 840 5901. Fax: (22) 840 5901. kipa@kipa.pl. www.kipa.pl.
National Film Archive, 00-975 Warsaw, ul., Puławska 61. Tel: (22) 845 5074. Fax: (22) 646 5373. filmoteka@fn.org.pl. www.fn.org.pl.
Media Desk Poland, 00-724 Warsaw, ul., Chełmska 19/21 p. 229. Tel/Fax: (22) 851 1074, Tel. (22) 559 33 10. biuro@mediadeskpoland.eu. www.mediadeskpoland.eu.

Bartłomiej Topa in Wojciech Smarzowski's **The Dark House**

Portugal Martin Dale

Portuguese cinema is caught in a
quandary. While some national films
are revered by certain international
film connoisseurs and shunned by their
compatriots, other local works attempt to go
'mainstream' but tend to resort to clichés and
hackneyed formulae.

Portugal's generalist TV broadcasters, RTP, SIC
and TVI (the latter in particular), have made
major strides in recent years by producing
TV fiction – primarily tele-novellas – that have
weaned audiences away from the traditionally
dominant Brazilian soaps.

However, local filmmakers continue to face
an uphill struggle, centred on two distinct
challenges: how to build on the country's
'poetic cinema' reputation and secure more
international prizes and presence in foreign
markets; and how to chime with national
audiences and break beyond the current 2-3%
barrier of the domestic box office. Portugal still
lags behind certain European countries, such
as Denmark, who have succeeded in winning
major festival awards and market presence
both domestically and abroad.

Centagenarian Manoel de Oliveira maintains a
breathtaking rhythm of one film per year. His
most recent work, **Eccentricities of a Blonde-
Haired Girl** (*Singularidades de uma Rapariga
Loira*), which was produced by Filmes do Tejo
and premiered at the Berlinale, is a dreamlike
adaptation of the realist novel by Eça de
Queiros, about an earnest man who becomes
disenchanted with the object of his infatuation.
Oliveira is now in pre-production on his next
film, **The Strange Case of Angelica**, based on
a script he wrote in 1952, about a photographer
commissioned to take pictures of a dead girl.

Manoel de Oliveira's **Eccentricities of a Blonde-Haired Girl**

Doomed Love, produced by Paulo Branco and
directed by accomplished cinematographer
Mario Barroso, played at Locarno in 2008 and
was Portugal's 2009 Foreign Language Oscar
entry. A contemporary take on the tragic love
triangle of the classic nineteenth-century novel
by Camilo Castelo Branco, the film features
excellent cinematography, but at times feels
distant and anachronistic.

João Pedro Rodrigues' **To Die Like a Man**
(*Morrer como um Homem*) screened in Un

João Pedro Rodrigues' **To Die Like a Man**

Certain Regard at the 2009 Cannes Film Festival. It's a mesmerising yet tortuous exploration of the lives of drag queens in Lisbon. Pedro Costa's fascinating behind-the-scenes music documentary about French actress-turned-singer, Jeanne Balibar, **Ne Change Rien**, played in the festival's Directors' Fortnight.

French-American director Eugene Green's **The Portuguese Nun** (*A Religiosa Portuguesa*) is an intriguing and atmospheric tale inspired by the 'Letters of a Portuguese Nun' by the Count of Guilleragues, which plays like a love letter to Lisbon.

Eugene Green's **The Portuguese Nun**

João Mário Grilo's **Two Women** (*Duas Mulheres*) portrayed the social repercussions of a married woman, Joana (Beatriz Batarda), falling in love with another woman (Débora Monteiro). The film had its world premiere at the Estoril Film Festival. The festival also featured veteran director Fernando Lopes' latest work, **The Smiles of Destiny** (*Os Sorrisos de Destino*), a digitally shot adulterous tale set in contemporary times. But there was a sense that we have been over this territory before.

In terms of new talent, the year revealed an upcoming young auteur, João Salaviza, whose **Arena** won the Palme d'Or for Best Short Film at Cannes. It is about a young man imprisoned at home and featured non-professional actors from one of Lisbon's poorest inner-city neighbourhoods. Salaviza is now working on a follow-up short, **Rafa**.

In parallel – almost in opposition – to such productions, Portugal has also spawned a

series of films deliberately targeted at a wider domestic audience. Many were financed by a new investment fund, FICA, which combines funds from broadcasters, cable TV operators and the Ministry of the Economy, with a 5-year budget of €83 million. FICA invests in two ways: individual films and production slates. With regard to the latter, the fund signed a five-year financing deal with Utopia Filmes, run by Alexandre Valente, whose 2005 film, *The Crime of Father Amaro*, directed by Carlos Coelho da Silva, remains Portugal's biggest box office hit (380,000 admissions). Valente's films use a strong erotic charge in order to attract spectators, but his latest outing, **Second Life**, was a disappointment, notwithstanding a high-profile cast that included footballer Luis Figo, with admissions only reaching 90,000. The slick project, about a film producer found dead in his swimming pool after a raunchy birthday party, features glossy cinematography courtesy of Acácio de Almeida and an attractive soundtrack by accomplished composer Bernardo Sassetti, but is weak on plot, character and story.

Sandra Barata Belo in Carlos Coelho da Silva's **Amália**

Carlos Coelho da Silva has since teamed up with VC Filmes, who have also signed a five-year financing deal with FICA, to direct Portugal's biggest local hit of the last 12 months (213,000 admissions), **Amália**, about the world-famous Fado singer. With a somewhat confusing narrative structure, the film cuts back and forth between different moments in the singer's life. Its main strengths are the Fado songs that use original recordings by Amália Rodrigues and the portrayal of the diva, by Sandra Barata Belo, as a free spirit in a time of constraints and repression. The film was severely criticised by some members of the Rodrigues family as being wildly inaccurate.

Coelho da Silva's next production for VC Filmes was **Adventure in a Haunted House** (*Uma Aventura na Casa Assombrada*), an action-thriller based on the popular 'Aventura' children's novels. The film opened in December across 50 screens.

Joaquim Leitão's **Hope is Where You Least Expect It** (*A esperança está onde menos espera*) was an intelligent tale about a family forced to move from a plush suburb to a tough inner-city neighbourhood. It generated 40,000 admissions. British director Mark Heller's **Star Crossed** was an ambitious attempt to recreate Shakespeare's *Romeo and Juliet* against the backdrop of two rival football teams in Oporto. Excellent visuals, including impressive football sequences, were dampened by lacklustre performances, leading to a poor performance at the box office.

Joaquim Leitão's Hope is Where You Least Expect It

At the other end of the spectrum, the micro-budget and somewhat amateurish production, **100 Volta**, directed by and starring 'Zé Galinha' (Daniel Sousa), managed to generate 7,685 admissions. The film threw wacky characters, goofy car chases and soft porn into its heady mix.

Overall, Portuguese cinema maintains a distinctively eclectic mix of films, some of which are willing to tackle difficult subjects in terms of intellectual complexity and underlying social issues. The next step is to consolidate these skills in order to achieve a more forceful presence at international festivals and the domestic box office.

Jeanne Balibar appears as herself in Pedro Costa's Ne Change Rien

The year's best films
Arena (João Salaviza)
Ne Change Rien (Pedro Costa)
Hope is Where You Least Expect It (Joaquim Leitão)
The Portuguese Nun (Eugene Green)
Amália (Carlos Coelho da Silva)

Quote of the year
'The future of cinema will increasingly revolve around linguistic zones rather than territories. Language will be the key factor.' *Producer* TINO NAVARRO.

Directory
All Tel/Fax numbers begin (+351)
Cinemateca Portuguesa, Rua Barata Salgueiro 63, 1269-059 Lisbon. Tel: (21) 359 6200. Fax: (21) 352 3180. www.cinemateca.pt.
Institute of Cinema, Audiovisual & Multimedia (ICAM), Rua de S Pedro de Alcântara 45, 1°, 1250 Lisbon. Tel: (21) 323 0800. Fax: (21) 343 1952. mail@icam.pt. www.icam.pt.

MARTIN DALE has lived in Lisbon and the north of Portugal since 1994 and works as an independent media consultant and a contributor to *Variety*. He has written several books on the film industry, including *The Movie Game* (1997).

Romania Cristina Corciovescu

Statistically and quantitatively speaking, Romanian cinema has seen few significant changes in the last year. There are still only 10–12 domestic releases each year and about as many films again in various stages of production. Some of the completed films are so far unreleased, with producers waiting for the right moment to premiere them (i.e. a major festival competition). Only after that will they be screened for the Romanian public.

As in previous years, domestic audiences play hard to get when it comes to local films, as can be seen in the box-office statistics, which in 2008 only featured US releases in the top ten. Even the Romanian media pretty much ignores cinema (there hasn't been one single film magazine for ten years). Newspapers, magazines and television stations only ever talk about Romanian films in special circumstances and a film review can only be found in a few cultural publications, whose circulation is, at best, limited.

Looking forward, there may be a decline in the production of Romanian films. The global financial crisis has obviously played a part, but there have also been local problems. The National Centre for Cinematography recently suspended the annual project competitions (there were two each year, one in spring and the other in autumn). The reason given was to improve the competition regulations, a move prompted by younger filmmakers who were unhappy with its structure. On the other hand, there are more and more film festivals – over 15 – that, at least in theory, should draw people back into cinemas and, at the same time, revive their appetite for films with less commercial appeal than the Hollywood product that dominates the box office.

The achievements of the past few years, peaking in 2007 with Cristian Mungiu's *4 Months, 3 Weeks & 2 Days* winning the Palme d'Or, have set a high – if not completely unattainable – benchmark for young filmmakers to aspire to. But what course will the careers of the recent 'new wave' directors take? And what about the filmmakers following in their footsteps? And will there be a return to more genre-based films, albeit set in contemporary situations? The last year has hopefully brought forth some answers.

Corneliu Porumboiu's **Police, Adjective**

Without a doubt, the cinematic event of the year was the new film by Corneliu Porumboiu, **Police, Adjective** (*Politist, adj.*), which picked up the Un Certain Regard Jury Prize at the Cannes Film Festival. Further proof, if any were needed, of the exceptional talent of this filmmaker, who pushes his minimalist aesthetic to the extreme, the film centres on the conflict between conscience and law, even though, from a traditional cinematic perspective, the film is almost devoid of conflict. A cop follows three students who smoke weed behind their college during breaks, but refuses to organise a sting operation that would end the case because he fears that it would ruin their lives. Among the many highlights the film has to offer, its humour draws out the subtleties of language, while there are impressive performances by the leads, whose most insignificant looks and gestures are laden with meaning.

The Legend of the Official Visit *from* Tales from the Golden Age

Cristian Mungiu's return as writer, co-director and co-producer of **Tales from the Golden Age** (*Amintiri din epoca de aur*) was highly anticipated. Five directors are credited with working on the film, although it was decided not to identify which director was responsible for individual segments. Each story humorously recalls typical situations that took place in 1980s Romania: in *The Legend of the Official Visit*, there are fervent preparations in a village that the General Secretary of the Communist Party's car is going to pass through; in *The Legend of the Party Photographers*, there is tension in the office of a major newspaper, where pictures of the aforementioned General Secretary are

The Legend of the Zealous Activist *from* Tales from the Golden Age

to be artificially modified in order to make him look taller and more distinguished; both *The Tale of the Greedy Policeman* and *The Legend of the Chicken Driver* deal with the shortage of food (including ordinary items such as eggs or pork meat), which occasionally results in unfortunate consequences; in *The Legend of the Zealous Activist*, a young man goes to ridiculous lengths to bring old people into a school in order to help eradicate illiteracy; and in *The Legend of the Air Sellers*, an ingenious, though not quite legal, plan is hatched in order to generate money. For Mungiu, this return to short features was merely an interlude. For the other co-directors, the omnibus was another step forward (Hanno Hofer, Constantin Popescu) or the first step (Ioana Uricaru, Razvan Marculescu) towards a promising career.

Radu Jude's The Happiest Girl in the World

Radu Jude directed **The Happiest Girl in the World** (*Cea mai fericita fata din lume*), which received the CICAE Award at Berlin and FIPRESCI prize at Sofia. It is the story of a provincial high-school student who wins a car that her parents want to sell in order to start a business. Jude builds his film out of an ordinary family dispute, interspersed with scenes of the girl talking to camera, during which she repeats the same line and employs the same gestures. Andrei Gruszniczki's **The Other Irene** (*Cealalta Irina*) was the FIPRESCI award winner at Pecs, while Bobby Paunescu directed **Francesca**. Both films were more conventional dramas: one of a man who cannot believe that his wife has lied and

Monica Barladeanu in Bobby Paunescu's **Francesca**

cheated on him, while the other features a woman who hopes that her migration to a new country might offer a new perspective on life.

Veteran filmmakers also returned to the screen. As well as Sergiu Nicolaescu's docu-drama, **Carol I**, there was Stere Gulea with **Weekend with My Mother** (*Week- end cu mama*), about a mother who finds her daughter after years of searching, only to lose her forever, and Mircea Daneliuc with

Adela Popescu in Stere Gulea's **Weekend with My Mother**

Marilena, the adaptation of a novel that deals with how one woman, played by Cecilia Bârbora, is perceived by three men. They do not see her for what she is. Instead, the film portrays her as some kind of victim because all the men see is an object to have sex with.

The last year also saw the involvement of HBO Romania in film production, which stimulated the documentary scene and supported films such as Tudor Giurgiu's **Weddings, Music and Videotapes** (*Muzici, nunti si casete video*), about the wedding planning industry, Alexandru Solomon's **Apocalypse on Wheels** (*Apocalipsa dupa soferi*), about traffic problems in Bucharest, and Claudiu Mitcu's **Australia**, about the Homeless World Cup.

The year's best films

Police, Adjective (Corneliu Porumboiu)
Tales from the Golden Age (Cristian Mungiu, Ioana Uricaru, Hanno Hofer, Constantin Popescu, Razvan Marculescu)
The Other Irene (Andrei Gruszniczki)
Francesca (Bobby Paunescu)
The Happiest Girl in the World (Radu Jude)

Directory

All Tel/Fax numbers begin (+4)
Centrul National al Cinematografiei, Str. Dem I Dobrescu nr. 4-6, sector 1, 010026, Bucuresti. Tel: 021 310 43 01. Fax: 021 310 43 00. www.cncinema.ro.
Uniunea Cineastilor, Str. Mendeleev nr. 28-30, sector 1, Bucuresti. Tel: 021 316 80 83. Fax: 021 311 12 46. www.ucin.ro.
Arhiva Nationala de Filme, Soseaua Sabarului nr. 20, com Jilava. Tel/Fax: 021 450 12 67. anf@xnet.ro.

CRISTINA CORCIOVESCU is a film critic and historian, and the author of several specialised dictionaries.

Russia Kirill Razlogov

The last year could be considered 'the hour of truth' for Russian cinema. At the end of 2008, private money deserted the film industry, practically halting production on the majority of feature-length films. As a result, state support in 2009 went almost entirely towards completing these productions, with very few new projects funded. The number of completed and released films dropped by almost 50%, even if the overall box-office figures remained optimistic. The rate of growth might have slowed, but there appears to be no threat of a decrease. Two reasons account for this: cinema attendance remains stable and ticket prices have increased, particularly in the more state-of-the-art venues, where prices have jumped from US$5 to US$6.80. Nevertheless, a large chunk of revenue goes to Hollywood, with the Russian share of the market, after a glorious 30% in 2008, declining – the result of fewer local successes.

As forecast, the year's biggest domestic hit was Fyodor Bondarchuk's **Inhabited Island: Part One** (*Obitayemyi ostrov. Film. Pervyi*). Its total gross in the CIS was almost US$22 million, coming in third after *Ice Age 3* with $44 million and *2012*, reaching US$34 million within just a few weeks of its release. Bondarchuk's sequel, **Inhabited Island: The Combat** (*Obitayemyi ostrov. Skhvatka*), only grossed US$6 million, its failure attributable either to the impact of the financial crisis or, I suspect, audiences' disappointment with the first part. This adaptation of the Strugatsky Brothers' politically orientated science fiction was transformed into an old-fashioned, 1980s-style Hollywood saga. The only qualities in this obsolete fantasy tale were a number of interesting performances, in particular by Alexei Serebryakov and Bondarchuk himself.

The body-switch sequel, **Lovey-Dovey 2** (*Lybov'-morkov' 2*), in which children become grown-ups and vice versa, grossed more than $17 million. Equally successful was Igor Zaytsev's **High Security Vacation** (*Kanikuly strogovo rezhima*), a comic mixture of summer-camp adventure and prison labour-camp romanticism.

Oleg Fomin's **The Very Best Film 2** (*Samyi luchshyi fil'm 2*) was better than the original, but the box office still declined to US$12 million following the audience's disappointment with the first instalment. These films marked the entry of Fox into the Russian film market, soon followed by Disney, who co-produced Vadim Sokolovsky's **The Book of Masters** (*Kniga masterov*) with Nikita Mikhalkov's Tri-Te Studio. At the time of writing, the film was still performing well at the box office.

Oksana Akinshina in Valery Todorovsky's **Hipsters**

One of the sensations of the year was Valery Todorovsky's **Hipsters** (*Stilyagi*), a musical about young rebels in late 1950s Moscow, which featured hit songs from the 1980s. The film grossed almost $17 million and succeeded in attracting critical praise as well as audiences. Parents and grandparents relived the joys of youth, while younger audiences appreciated the provocative energy of the protagonists.

Official cultural policy currently supports expensive historical blockbusters and literary adaptations glorifying Russia's past, be it politically or culturally. The results were uneven. Vladimir Bortko's **Taras Bulba**, a nationalistic adaptation of a Gogol story, became a box-office hit with US$17 million, but was severely criticised by liberal critics, although it featured brilliant performances by Ukrainian actor Bogdan Stupka in the title role, Polish classical actor Daniel Olbrychsky as the villain and young Igor Petrenko as the son who betrays his country for a Polish princess.

Vladimir Bortko's **Taras Bulba**

Pavel Lungin's **Tsar** fared poorly at the box office, grossing just $5 million, but did represent Russian cinema in Cannes in Un Certain Regard and opened the Moscow International Film Festival. The director avoided comparisons with Eisenstein's masterpiece, *Ivan the Terrible*, by changing the dynamic to a conflict between the tsar (played by former rock star and present mystic Petr Mamonov) and metropolitan Filip (Oleg Yankovsky), and between worldly and spiritual power. The performance by Yankovsky – tragically his last – is a highlight of the film. He was also impressive as the betrayed Karenin in Sergei Soloviov's **Anna Karenina**. Both films were made simultaneously just prior to the actor's death.

The religious trend, revived by Lungin's *Island*, was not just limited to *Tsar*. Vladimir

Alexander Proshkine's **The Miracle**

Khotinenko directed **Pop** (the name for an orthodox priest in slang), with Sergei Makovetsky as the title character, a hero in the Second World War. The film has understandably been compared with works in the Christian hagiographic tradition. Alexander Proshkine's **The Miracle** (*Chudo*) is more radical, at least aesthetically. Based on a legend from the region of Samara, on the Volga River, the film details a tragic event that took place in the late 1950s when a girl was petrified with an icon for sins such as dancing, drinking and partying in a period of religious abstinence. The reconstruction of country life in the opening stages is excellent, but the discussions around the miracle and, even more dubiously, a visit by Nikita Khrushchev, are ridiculous. It is a frustrating result for an ambitious project that won a special jury award at the Moscow Film Festival.

The main Saint George Award at the festival went to Nikolai Dostal's **Pete on the Road to Heaven** (*Petya po doroge v tsartstvie nenesnoye*), a 1950s-set melodrama featuring one woman and the three men in her life: her KGB husband, her lover-colleague and a young married manager she is in love with.

The jurors of the Moscow Film Festival were severely criticised for giving four of the five awards to Russian-language films (three Russian and one Ukrainian). The best actor award went to Vladimir Il'in in Karen Shakhnazarov's adaptation of Chekhov's **Ward #6** (*Palata nomer 6*). This modernised and controversial version has been nominated as Russia's entry for the Academy Awards for Best Foreign Language Film.

The best actress, Elena Kostyuk, was not an actress at all but a small girl portraying another small girl in the utterly pessimistic **Melody for the Barrel-Organ** (*Melodiya dlya sharmanki*), an anti-Christmas tale by the cult director Kira Muratova, Romanian based in Odessa. The best director prize went to Mexican filmmaker, Mariana Chenillo, for *Five Days Without Nora*.

Andrei Khrzhanovsky's **Room and a Half**

The Mar del Plata Film Festival, which awarded *Five Days Without Nora* the main prize, also gave Andrei Khrzhanovsky's **Room and a Half** (*Poltory komnaty ili sentimental'noe puteshestvie na Rodinu*) two special mentions, one from the main jury and the other from Argentinean critics. The film is an ironic and lyrical biography of the poet Joseph Brodsky, in which he returns, on a fictitious visit, to St Petersburg, from where he has been banished, never to return in his lifetime. Incorporating Brodsky's texts, documentary, animated footage (Khrzhanovsy is a great animation filmmaker) and docu-drama, it became a sensation on the international festival circuit and scored something of a record at home, playing in one Moscow cinema for six months.

So, what of the younger generation? They have been as active as before, if not more so, with many of their films presented at the 'Kinotavr' National Film Festival in Sochi. The main festival award went to **Wolfy** (*Vochok*), the

debut film of theatre playwright and director Vasily Sigarev. The original play centred on a mother/daughter love-hate relationship. Sigarev maintained the play's structure and preserved the theatricality of the piece in an attempt to emphasise the horrors of life. However, what may have been ambitious on stage came across as pretentious on film. A similar fate befell another director of the so-called 'New Drama' movement, Ivan Vyrypayev, with **Oxygen** (*Kislorod*), which underwent severe re-editing before being released.

In **Minnesota**, Alexander Proshkin Jr. constructed a hockey parable about the difficult relations between two brothers. After *Heart of Stone*, Alexei Mizgirev presented **Buben Baraban**, marking the return of the legendary actress Natalia Negoda. This dark provincial tale was acclaimed at several international festivals. The popularity of darker, critical views of Russian society at festivals was confirmed by the selection of Nikolai Khomeriki's **Tale in the Darkness** (*Skazka pro temnotu*) for Un Certain Regard at Cannes. Featuring the former ballet dancer Alisa Khazanova, the sad tale unfolds in Vladivostok, in the far east of Russia. Meanwhile, *Koktebel* director Boris Khlebnikov's **Help Gone Mad** (*Sumasshedshaya pomoshch*) was a tricky social thriller.

Boris Khlebnikov's **Help Gone Mad**

There was also the adaptation by Alexei Balabanov, one of the 'lost generation' of Russian filmmakers, of a short story by Mikhail Bulgakov, **Morphia** (*Morfyi*). Long in gestation,

Leonid Bichevin in Alexei Balabanov's **Morphia**

this project was originally the brainchild of Sergei Bodrov Jr., finally arriving on the screen as a startling account of drug addiction.

This pessimistic trend in many Russian films, corresponding to the mood of the most important European film festivals, encountered severe criticism from all sides: from political leaders to the older generation of filmmakers, such as Nikita Mikhalkov, Stanislav Govorukhin, whose **Passenger** (*Passazhirka*) was savaged by younger critics, and Sergei Soloviov.

The only film that attracted universal acclaim was **One War** (*Odna Voyna*), directed by the actress Vera Glagoleva. It told the dramatic story of Russian single mothers who bore the children of the German soldiers that occupied the country during the Second World War.

The future might not be as bleak as it seems. The official promise of 4.9 billion rubles for the film industry in 2010 still holds, even if the mechanisms for distributing this money have yet to be finalised. So the battle between filmmakers for state financing will continue.

KIRILL RAZLOGOV is Director of the Russian Institute for Cultural Research and Programme Director of the Moscow International Film Festival. He has written 17 books on cinema and culture and hosts Kultura's weekly TV show, *Movie Cult*.

The year's best films
Room and a Half (Andrei Khrzhanovsky)
Morphia (Alexei Balabanov)
One War (Vera Glagoleva)
Pete on the Road to Heaven (Nikolai Dostal)
Tale in the Darkness (Nikolai Khomeriki)

Quotes of the year
'How was it possible that out of 100 feature films funded by the Ministry of Culture only 50 were finalised and only 20 really released?' NIKITA MIKHALKOV, *defending the new system of state film financing in Orenburg.*

'I won't go to the next "Kinotavr", the last one is more than enough! I had to eat so much shit sitting in the screening room that I have to say – No. If that is the new cinema, I'll stay with the old one.' STANISLAV GOVORUKHIN, *actor, director and deputy of the State Duma about the programme of the main national film festival.*

Directory
All Tel/Fax numbers begin (+7)
Alliance of Independent Distribution Companies, Tel: 243 4741. Fax: 243 5582. felix_rosental@yahoo.com.
Ministry of Culture (without Mass Communications) of the Russian Federation, 7, Maly Gnezdnikovsky Lane, Moscow 103877. Tel: 495-923-2420 and 629-7055.
National Academy of Cinema Arts & Sciences, 13 Vassilyevskaya St, Moscow 123825. Tel: 200 4284. Fax: 251 5370. unikino@aha.ru.
Russian Guild of Film Directors, 13 Vassilyevskaya St, Moscow 123825. Tel: 251 5889. fax: 254 2100. stalkerfest@mtu-net.ru.
Russian Guild of Producers, 1 Mosfilmovskaya St, Moscow 119858. Tel: 745 5635/143 9028. plechev@mtu-net.ru.
Union of Filmmakers of Russia, 13 Vassilyevskaya St, Moscow 123825. Tel: 250 4114. Fax: 250 5370. unikino@aha.ru.

Serbia & Montenegro Goran Gocić

For a few years, *Shock Corridor*, Aleksandar Radivojevic and Nenad Bekvalac's television show about cinema, regularly preached more gore, more perversion, more violence and more Takashi Miike in Serbian cinema. Looking at some film releases over the last year, someone may have been listening.

Emilio Rosso in Milan Todorovic and Milan Konjevic's **Zone of the Dead**

Among the first Serbian premieres in 2009 was **Zone of the Dead** (*Zona mrtvih*), a zombie horror film shot in English (in the notoriously polluted Belgrade suburb of Pancevo), with a local crew and starring Ken Foree (who appeared in George A. Romero's *Dawn of the Dead*). This Serbian-Italian-Spanish co-production, directed by Milan Konjevic and Milan Todorovic, was one of the few original franchises made here. It was followed by Mladen Djordjevic's **The Life and Death of a Porn Gang** (*Zivot i smrt porno bande*), a smart, socially conscious slasher that smacked of early John Waters. A bunch of losers decide to hit the road and present their porn theatre in the Serbian backwaters. Their luck changes when a German businessman asks them to make snuff movies. And finally, Aleksandar

Srdjan Todorovic in Srdjan Spasojevic's **A Serbian Movie**

Radivojevic's own **A Serbian Movie** (*Srpski film*) was about an unemployed actor who strays into the Serbian porn underworld. Radivojevic significantly contributed to the trend with his masterful stage play, *Suicidal Hook*, starring Bekvalac, which premiered in 2009. It seems that a self-styled horror genre has finally forced its way into the Serbian cinema.

Here and There (*Tamo i ovde*), an excellent debut feature by Darko Lungulov (a Serbian-US-German co-production), was awarded the New York Best Narrative prize at the Tribeca Film Festival. Told with unusual subtlety, it is the story of a down-and-out American musician, played by David Thornton, who is involved in a fake marriage scheme to a Serbian woman. Singer Cyndi Lauper features in a cameo role. **The Belgrade Phantom** (*Beogradski fantom*), a Serbian-Hungarian-

Jovan Todorovic's **The Belgrade Phantom**

Bulgarian co-production directed by Jovan Todorovic, is a drama-documentary about a notorious Belgrade driver who, in the 1970s, teased the local police for weeks in a stolen white Porsche 911. Made for television, it performed surprisingly well in cinemas, even entering the top ten at the box office. Vladimir Perisic's **Ordinary People** (*Obicni ljudi*), a Serbian-French-Swiss co-production, was screened at the Critics' Week in Cannes and was awarded the Best Film prize at Cottbus Film Festival. It deals with the moral conundrum faced by soldiers in an unnamed location who are ordered to execute men and boys in civilian clothing for no given reason. **The Ambulance** (*Hitna pomoc*), a Serbian-German-Greek co-production, was written and directed by the documentary filmmaker, Goran Radovanovic. All of these ambitious newcomers succeeded, miraculously, in securing finance from abroad.

Aleksa Gajic's **Technotise – Edit and I**

There remained a few home-grown films. The most impressive and unique was **Technotise – Edit and I** (*Technotise – Edit i ja*), a highly accomplished animated sci-fi drama set in Belgrade in 2074. It was written and directed by Aleksa Gajic. Zelimir Zilnik's **The Old School of Capitalism** (*Stara skola kapitalizma*) is a funny account of the state of Serbian companies, while writer-director

Zelimir Zilnik's **The Old School of Capitalism**

Miroslav Momcilovic's **Wait for Me, and I Surely Won't Come** (*Cekaj me, a ja sigurno necu doci*) is a modern variation on Chekhov's *The Seagull*, set in New Belgrade's projects, where everybody is in love but no one is able to reciprocate.

Vladimir Paskaljevic's (son of filmmaker Goran) cruel urban drama, **Devil's Town** (*Djavolja varos*), Marko Novakovic's series of stories about abortion, **Someone is Still Waiting** (*Neko me ipak ceka*), and Milos Pasic's **Autumn in My Street** (*Jesen u mojoj ulici*), a day in the life of two twentysomethings, felt more like films made for television (Novakovic's was, but RTS decided on screenings at a number of festivals first) and this was reflected in the audience response. They preferred Rade Markovic's Second World War spoof, **Comrade Black in WW2** (*Drug Crni u NOB-u*).

In **The Tour** (*Turneja*), writer/director Goran Markovic presented a similar idea to *The Life and Death of a Porn Gang*. Its protagonists are stage actors in a multi-ethnic troupe on tour around Yugoslavia in the early days of the civil war. Markovic's Serbian-Bosnian co-production was released late in 2008 and received Serbian critics' majority vote as the best film of the year. It also performed relatively well at the box office, just outside the top ten, even though it was released so late in the year. **Honeymoon** (*Medeni mesec*), directed by Goran Paskaljevic, premiered at the Venice Film Festival. The first Serbian-Albanian co-production, it is another story from the troubled Balkan border. **Besa**, written and directed by Srdjan Karanovic, is a First World War tale about forbidden love, whose finance came from six countries around the region.

The most eagerly expected premiere and the year's biggest box-office success was Srdjan Dragojevic's costly **St. George Shoots the Dragon** (*Sveti Georgije ubiva azdahu*). With a budget in the region of €4.5 million, it is one of the most expensive domestic films ever made. Based on Dusan Kovacevic's famous stage play (he also wrote the screenplay), it is about a group of invalids forced to stay at home following the introduction of the draft at the start of the First World War. When they begin to take advantage of the women in the villages and towns, the authorities are left with no choice but to send the injured men to the front.

Albanian characters are apparently chic this season, as was seen in *Honeymoon*, *Besa* and **Serbian Scars**, directed by Brent Huff. A US action movie without finance from Serbia, but not without compassion for the Serbian cause, it was written by Vladimir Rajcic, who also produced and played in it, alongside Mark Dacascos and Michael Madsen.

It seems that Serbia is becoming the new shooting location for international productions. It is cheaper then Hungary or Bulgaria and American money has created the Serbian Film Commission for the purpose of expanding opportunities in the country. Rian Johnson's *Brothers Bloom* was shot here and Ralph Fiennes announced he would film his version of *Coriolanus* here in 2010.

The year's best films
Here and There (Darko Lungulov)
Technotise – Edit and I (Aleksa Gajic)
The Life and Death of a Porn Gang (Mladen Djordjevic)
The Old School of Capitalism (Zelimir Zilnik)

Quote of the year
'Boring, pathetic and vapid state-funded films are done by people who don't know first thing about cinema. They are, however, generously

David Thornton in Darko Lungulov's **Here and There**

supported by bureaucratic foreign film funds which stick to their politically correct manuals to produce inarticulate treatises about transition and peace-making. We had enough of sad rubbish about ethnic girls with matches. That's why I activated my old noir idea about a porn actor who is drawn into narco-snuff hell. Director Srdjan Spasojevic established a production house symbolically called Counterfilm and we launched a crusade to complete this project.' *Screenwriter* **ALEKSANDAR RADIVOJEVIC** *explains the genesis of* **A Serbian Movie**.

Directory
All Tel/Fax numbers begin (+381 11)
Film Center Serbia, Zagrebacka 9/III, 11000 Belgrade. Tel: 262 51 31. Fax: 263 42 53. fcs.office@fcs.rs. www.fcs.rs.
Yugoslav Film Archive, Knez Mihajlova 19, 11000 Belgrade. Tel/Fax: 262 25 55. kinoteka@org.rs. www.kinoteka.org.yu.
Faculty of Dramatic Arts, Bulevar Umetnosti 20, 11070 Belgrade. Tel: 213 56 84. Fax: 213 08 62. fduinfo@eunet.rs. www.fdubg.com.
Film in Serbia, Dalmatinska 17, 11000 Belgrade. Tel/Fax: 329 20 24. info@filminserbia.com. www.filminserbia.com.

GORAN GOCIĆ is a broadcast and print journalist whose works have been published by over 30 media outlets in eight languages. He has written chapters in 15 books on the mass media, edited several magazines, authored studies on Warhol, Kusturica and pornography and directed two feature-length documentaries.

Singapore Yvonne Ng

As far as quality is concerned, 2009 was a muted year for Singaporean cinema. It began with considerable media hype surrounding two commercially oriented Chinese releases. **The Wedding Game** (*Da xi shi*) by Thai-born, Singapore-based Ekachai Uekrongtham featured real-life celebrity couple Fann Wong and Christopher Lee as movie stars who fake their romance for fame and profit. The US$1.5 million romantic comedy pitted its star power against the less glamorous **Love Matters** (*Xing fu wan sui*), co-directed by veteran filmmaker Jack Neo and newcomer Gilbert Chan for under US$1 million. It revolves around three couples of varying ages coping with romantic and sexual problems.

Comedies and horror continued to be staples of mainstream Singapore cinema. Jack Neo, co-directing with Boris Boo, combined the two genres in the Chinese-language **Where Got Ghost?**. Comprising three separate tales, the film sported Neo regulars and retained his trademark humour and sentimentality. Another ghostly yarn was Glen Goei's **Blue Mansion**, an English-language black comedy that owed a debt to Agatha Christie whodunits, which featured a Singapore-Malaysian cast of well-known

Jack Neo and Boris Boo's **Where Got Ghost?**

stage names. A pineapple tycoon returns as a ghost at his own wake and attempts to uncover the cause of his death. Though the script could have been better, the visuals were highly polished. The US$2 million independent production was shot in a nineteen-century UNESCO heritage mansion in Penang, Malaysia.

Chai Yee Wei's feature debut, **Blood Ties** (*Huan hun*), is based on his eponymous short. The gory, non-linear narrative tells the story of a murdered policeman whose spirit returns to possess his younger sister in order to exact revenge on his killers. It was the first film completed under the Singapore Film Commission's feature-film fund.

Independent features offered more contemplative fare. Jason Lai's **Brother No. 2** was a thought-provoking documentary about those who suffered under the Khmer Rouge regime in Cambodia, as represented by the story of Soy Sen, a prison-camp survivor. The film included an interview with Nuon Chea, Pol Pot's second-in-command, now awaiting trial by an international tribunal.

Kan Lume's **Female Games** examined female friendship and rivalry through two naive young Singapore models, who venture into neighbouring Malaysia to advance their careers. The film traces their relationship, from strangers to friends and ultimately enemies, culminating in a vicious catfight. The film's Sapphic finale was censored, causing it to be withdrawn from the 2009 Singapore International Film Festival.

Though the censors are now more tolerant of homosexuality, it is still a sensitive subject, particularly when the authorities themselves are depicted. Boo Junfeng's **Tanjong Rhu** and Loo Zihan's **Threshold**, two short films based on real-life police-entrapment exercises and the subsequent arrest of gay men, were inexplicably pulled out of the government-supported Sixth annual Short Cuts Film Festival. Both films were rated R21 and passed uncut. **For Two** (*Er Ren*) by Tan Shijie was another short film inspired by true events. Shot without dialogue, this 17-minute study of a fragile relationship revolves around a widower living in an apartment and a woman who secretly shares the flat with him. It competed at the Venice Film Festival.

A sense of entrapment and a desire to escape was a theme that ran through several low-budget, independent productions, including **Invisible Children**. The first feature of 29-year-old multimedia artist Brian Gothong Tan, it owed a debt to Eric Khoo's *12 Storeys* through its public housing block setting and the depiction of the empty, joyless lives of those who live in it.

Multimedia artist Ho Tzu Nyen took the idea of inner and outer imprisonment a step further in his original experimental first feature, **Here**. A man called He Zhiyuan strangles his wife and is sent to the Island hospital for the criminally insane. There, he and other inmates undergo a 'videocure' as part of their treatment. Ho's sensitivity to visual design and sound is apparent. The film premiered at the 41st Directors' Fortnight at Cannes. Ho also created **Earth**, a 41-minute, unique tableau vivant on the fate of the Earth, which screened at Venice.

At Cannes, the Media Development Authority announced three initiatives as part of the Singapore Media Fusion Plan. In addition to the US$358 million already committed to interactive digital media research and development, another US$165 million has been allocated to an International Film Fund to encourage local-foreign partnerships to make films with global appeal, as well as the production of stereoscopic 3D films and the development of Mediapolis@one-north, a state-of-the-art studio with sound stages, digital production, broadcast and distribution facilities.

Ho Tzu Nyen's **Here**

The year's best films
Here (Ho Tzu Nyen)
Brother No. 2 (Jason Lai)
For Two (Tan Shijie)
Tanjong Rhu (Boo Junfeng)

Quotes of the year
'I had to make the film 100 times in my own mind. While writing the script, I was also planning the camera moves and editing points.' HO TZU NYEN *on completing* **Here** *in 11 days.*

'Unless you have the resources for it, making films like that in Singapore would be akin to trying to construct the Empire State Building in your backyard.' *Filmmaker* KAN LUME *on never trying to compete with Hollywood.*

Directory
All Tel/Fax numbers begin (+65)
Cinematograph Film Exhibitors Association, 13th & 14th Storey, Shaw Centre, 1 Scotts Rd, Singapore 228208. Tel: 6235 2077. Fax: 6235 2860.
Singapore Film Commission, 140 Hill St, Mita Bldg #04-01, Singapore 179369. Tel: 6837 9943. Fax: 6336 1170. www.sfc.org.sg.
Singapore Film Society, 5A Raffles Ave, #03-01 Marina Leisureplex, Singapore 039801. Fax: 6250 6167. ktan@sfs.org.sg. www.sfs.org.sg.

YVONNE NG is on the editorial board of *KINEMA*. She is co-author of *Latent Images: Film in Singapore* (2000), *Latent Images: Film in Singapore CD-ROM* (2003) and *Latent Images: Film in Singapore Second Edition* (2009).

Slovakia Miro Ulman

S lovak films continued the success they experienced in 2008. The country also adopted the Euro as its national currency and the long-awaited Law on the Audiovisual Fund came into effect. The financing that derives from it is expected to provide €8 million, double the state's current budget for film.

Six fiction films and two full-length documentaries were completed last year, with nine other films involving some level of input from Slovakia. Despite the financial crisis, the first nine months of the year saw 3.13 million admissions, an increase of 25% over 2008 and the largest audience figures for 13 years. Slovak film production accounted for 13% of market share, with an increase in admissions aided by the opening of nine digital cinemas.

Jaro Vojtek's **The Border**

Peter Kerekes' **Cooking History**

Slovak documentaries continue to be of high quality. Peter Kerekes' **Cooking History** (*Ako sa varia dejiny*) looked at army cooks and how the everyday dietary needs of thousands of troops play an important role. It was nominated for the EFA Documentary 2009. Marko Škop's **Osadné** (*Osadné*), a subtle story

about the local leaders of a small Slovak village on the border of the European Union, who take the opportunity to gain experience from the more expansive arena of the European political scene, was awarded the Best Documentary prize at the Karlovy Vary Film Festival. Jaro Vojtek's **The Border** (*Hranica*) focused on the village of Slemence, which, one night in 1946, was forever changed when the imposition of the Czech–Soviet Union border split it in half. This absurd border still divides families up to this day. The film won the Best East European Documentary Award at the Jihlava Documentary Film Festival.

Slovak feature films are also gaining momentum abroad. The Slovak submission for the 2010 Academy Awards is Jiří Chlumský's **Broken Promise** (*Nedodržaný sľub*), the true story of a Jewish boy (played by Best Actor Award winner at Festroia Film Festival, Samuel Spišák) who escaped deportation to a concentration camp thanks to his extraordinary skills as a footballer, as well as a series of lucky circumstances.

Three recent Slovak titles ranked as some of the most successful local releases over the last 15 years. Vlado Balko's debut, **Soul at Peace** (*Pokoj v duši*), a contemporary story

Vlado Balko's **Soul at Peace**

about childhood friends and the crises they experience, was the first Slovak feature in five years to appear in competition at Karlovy Vary. Agniezka Holland and Kasia Adamik's **Jánošík: A True Story** (*Jánošík. Pravdivá história*) was one of the most expensive Slovak film projects – a co-production with Poland – with over €2 million of state support. Meanwhile, 21-year-old Jakub Kroner's low-budget **Bratislavafilm** (*Bratislavafilm*), featuring a hip-hop soundtrack, was an uncompromising account of what big, city life is like for young people.

Agniezka Holland and Kasia Adamik's **Jánošík: A True Story**

Laura Siváková's second feature, **Heaven, Hell... Earth** (*Nebo, peklo... zem*) detailed the complex relationships in one woman's life. Ivan Vojnár's **My Husband's Women** (*Ženy môjho muža*) reflected on the life of a married couple who are no longer in love with each other. Finally, Miloslav Luther's tragicomedy, **Mosquitoes' Tango** (*Tango s komármi*), told the story of two pre-1989 emigrants returning for a brief visit to Slovakia after spending many years in Spain.

There were two minority co-productions made by young female Slovak directors. Diana Fabiánová's **Moon Inside You** (*Mesiac v nás*) looked at the taboo – for some – subject of menstruation, while Mira Fornay's **Foxes** (*Líštičky*) focused on the problematic relationship between two sisters who have emigrated to Ireland.

There are currently 18 productions in various stages of limbo due to a lack of financing. It is hoped that the Audiovisual Fund will begin awarding grants in spring 2010. As a result, the only Slovak premiere slated for release in the first half of the year will be Mariana Čengel-Solčanská's debut, **Flying Cyprian** (*Lietajúci Cyprián*), inspired by the eighteenth-century monk who invented a flying machine.

The year's best films
The Border (Jaro Vojtek)
Broken Promise (Jiří Chlumský)
Cooking History (Peter Kerekes)
Osadné (Marko Škop)
Soul at Peace (Vlado Balko)

Quote of the year
'The charisma of Václav Jirácek is similar to that of the young Tom Cruise or Robert Redford.' **AGNIESZKA HOLLAND**, *about the main actor of her film,* **Jánošík: A True Story**.

MIRO ULMAN is a freelance journalist. He works for the Slovak Film Institute and is a programmer for the Art Film Festival Trenčianske Teplice – Trenčín.

Jiří Chlumský's **Broken Promise**

ABU DHABI FILM COMMISSION

Slovenia Ziva Emersic

With an annual budget of just €4.7 million underwriting the Slovenian Film Fund, local production has shown surprising stamina, offering up an eclectic selection of features. The national film festival in Portoroz, which takes place at the beginning of October, screened 23 features and some 50 other formats, of varying lengths, which were supported by the Fund, RTV Slovenia, international co-productions and private sources.

Igor Sterk reinforced his reputation as Slovenia's most form-orientated filmmaker, with his bleak drama, **9:06**, an artistic, almost wordless thriller concerned with identity. A cop (Igor Samobor) investigates the mystery suicide of a musician, only to take on the victim's life as his own. The film was awarded 12 of the 17 prizes at the national festival, but still awaits a theatrical release.

Damjan Kozole presented his gloomy drama, **Slovenian Girl** (*Slovenka*), about a young student who offers sexual services to wealthy older men. Kozole has often been accused of picking controversial subjects and *Slovenian*

Damjan Kozole's **Slovenian Girl**

Girl was no exception. The film was overlooked by the national festival jury, but received a warm welcome from local audiences. Lead actress Nina Ivanisin received the best actress award at the Valencia Film Festival.

Janez Lapajne's **Personal Luggage**

Janez Lapajne, an ambitious and energetic filmmaker, wrote a strong script for his third feature, **Personal Luggage** (*Osebna prtljaga*). For the nouveau riche family of a plastic surgeon, this personal luggage turns out to be the overwhelming angst of a wealthy Ljubljana suburb. The interaction of the characters and their concerns and fears were evocative of Eric Bogosian's *Suburbia*, but the tone remained Slovenian, linked to the country's troubled past, particularly the civil conflict that followed the Second World War.

TV Slovenia showed some muscle in new drama, producing five feature films, as well as a film for younger audiences, **Distortion** (*Distorzija*), by Miha Hocevar. **Playing with Pairs** (*Igra s pari*) was written and directed by Miran Zupanič, whose recent documentary, *Children from Petricek Hill*, was highly acclaimed. The film offers a portrait of marital relations, love, betrayal and boredom, with Polona Juh giving a chilling performance as a fragile but steely-minded and manipulative woman.

Maja Weiss' **Angela Vode – A Secret Memory**

Angela Vode – A Secret Memory (*Angela Vode – skriti spomin*) was yet another television production that attracted public controversy because of its chosen topic. Based on the diaries of a devoted female communist member who was later cast out by her own comrades, veteran director Maja Weiss shot an historically accurate yet bloodless film, despite the powerful central performance of Silva Cusin.

Jan Cvitkovic, who is currently preparing his next feature film, **Archeo**, screened his third short, **This is Earth, My Brother** (*To je zemlja, brat moj*). A philosophical essay on the essence of things, it did not match the critical acclaim of his debut, *Heart is But a Piece of Meat.*

The new, award-winning star of Slovenian literature, Goran Vojnovic, directed the short, **The Chinese Are Coming** (*Kitajci prihajajo*). It was a bitter-sweet picture about the harsh lives of the unemployed in Slovenia, who blame the Chinese for their misfortune. Vojnovic's debut novel will soon be adapted for the screen.

One of the more surprising achievements of the year was Miha Knific's animated feature, **The Cloud Catcher** (*Lovec na oblake*). This eco-fable is a shocking vision of a parched, sun-burned Earth in 2147, where the seas have long disappeared and the only way to access water is by chasing the clouds. Beside the impressive animation, the highlight of the film was the camerawork of Emir Kusturica's cinematographer Vilko Filac, who passed away in November.

Slovenian film seems to be more alive than ever. Despite the fact that few filmmakers, producers or critics are entirely happy with the current subsidies system, production is surprisingly persistent and displays a maturity that comes with years of experience in an unstable and relatively small national market.

The year's best films
The Cloud Catcher (Miha Knific)
Slovenian Girl (Damjan Kozole)
The Chinese Are Coming (Goran Vojnovic)

Quote of the year
'Slovenian movies are good, but there is no sign of happiness or hope in the stories. They are watchable but desperately dark.'
JOZE DOLMARK, *selector of the Slovenian Film Festival Portoroz 2009.*

Directory
All Tel/Fax numbers begin (+386)
Association of Slovenian Film Makers, Miklošičeva 26, Ljubljana. dsfu@guest.arnes.si.
Association of Slovenian Film Producers, Brodišče 23, Trzin, 1234 Mengeš. dunja.klemenc@guest.arnes.si.
Slovenian Cinematheque, Miklošičeva 38, Ljubljana. Tel: 434 2520. silvan.furlan@kinoteka.si.
Slovenian Film Fund, Miklošičeva 38, 1000 Ljubljana. Tel: 431 3175. info@film-sklad.si.

ZIVA EMERSIC is a film critic, a former programme director of Slovenian National Film Festival in Portoroz, and currently the head of documentary film production at TV Slovenia.

South Africa Martin P. Botha

The past year has been characterised by two contrasting developments in South African filmmaking. On the one hand, government funding in the form of grants by the South African National Film and Video Foundation (NFVF) remains hopelessly inadequate. The institution currently needs in the region of US$44 million per year to do a proper job. Unfortunately, its annual allocation in 2009 has been a mere US$5.2 million with which it has to cover its administrative expenditure, as well as funding obligations. The non-renewal of a special feature-film fund by the Department of Arts and Culture a few years ago also stifled feature-film production. The result is that many exciting new and veteran filmmakers have to rely on their own resources to finalise projects.

In stark contrast to the limited role of the NFVF are the remarkable individual achievements by a new generation of South African filmmakers, who have managed to secure alternative funding for their projects. In several cases these young filmmakers also succeeded in reaching significant South African audiences on the mainstream circuit.

Since its inception in 2005, the Department of Trade and Industry's (DTI) film and television production and co-production scheme has been instrumental in growing the film indus-try. More than 37 features, including South African-born Neill Blomkamp's international hit, **District 9**, benefited from this rebate incentive scheme. Blomkamp's sci-fi spectacle about aliens who, their spaceship stranded above Johannesburg, have to endure a daily routine of unemployment, gangsterism and xenophobia in a squalid Johannesburg shantytown, shot straight to number one at the US box office,

Neill Blomkamp's **District 9**

earning US$37 million in its opening weekend. At the time of writing, this allegorical film about recent xenophobia in post-apartheid South Africa had raked in over US$200 million from around the world. The film undoubtedly drew international attention to the talent and skills to be found in the South African film industry.

To date, DTI's film and television production incentive programme has approved 81 productions for a total rebate of US$52 million, including the local box-office hit, **White Wedding**. Director Jann Turner's romantic comedy about a groom and his best man who race against time to get to a wedding ceremony in Cape Town, opened the Cape Winelands Film Festival to great acclaim, receiving a standing

Jann Turner's **White Wedding**

ovation. During its first week of release on the circuit, the film grossed over US$148,000 at the box office. It has since run for 11 consecutive weeks in a total of 43 cinemas in South Africa. The film is South Africa's official selection for entry into the Foreign Language Category of the 2010 Academy Awards.

Oliver Hermanus' **Shirley Adams**

Madoda Ncayiyana's **My Secret Sky**

Shot in Durban and Inanda, director Madoda Ncayiyana's **My Secret Sky** (*Izulu Lami*) tells the story of two orphan children, Thembi and Khwezi, who travel to Durban to find a priest who admired their mother's hand-woven mats and encouraged her to enter them in a craft competition. However, when they arrive in the city, they encounter a group of tough street children led by Chilli-Boy (Tshepang Mohlomi), learning the hard way that the city is a dangerous place. The film won several international prizes, including the Dikalo Award for Best Feature Film at the Pan African International Film Festival in Cannes, the Audience Award for Best Feature Film at Spain's Cinema Africano de Tarifa Film Festival and the Best Actress Award for Sobahle Mkhabase, who was ten years old when the film was shot, as well as the SIGNIS Award for Best Film, at the Zanzibar International Film Festival.

Among the year's outstanding films is **Shirley Adams**, a feature-length project co-produced by the London Film School (LFS) with Centropolis Entertainment and South African production house DV8. It is the final LFS project of Oliver Hermanus, who graduated in 2009 with the film. Set in Mitchell's Plain in Cape Town, it is the sensitive story of a mother

who struggles to rehabilitate her son after he is paralysed by a gunshot wound. Denise Newman's portrayal of the mother is one of the highlights of recent South African cinema. Hermanus scooped the prizes for Best South African Feature Film and Best First Feature Film at the Durban International Film Festival (DIFF) and Newman picked up the Best Actress Award.

Another cinematic jewel of 2009 was Claire Angelique's **My Black Little Heart**. It is a beautifully shot tale of a heroin user stuck in a Durban seaside vortex of decrepit flats and abandoned office blocks, littered with self-mutilators, ex-cons, gangsters, street delinquents, hustlers and addicts. There was also the South African-Australian co-production, **Disgrace**, starring John Malkovich. Steve Jacobs' award-winning adaptation of J.M. Coetzee's novel about a Cape Town professor who settles with his daughter in the Eastern Cape and becomes enmeshed in the complexities of post-apartheid racial relationships, divided local film critics because of its representation of race.

Steve Jacobs' **Disgrace**

لجنــة أبـوظبـي للأفـلام
ABU DHABI FILM COMMISSION

One of the country's leading film directors, Regardt van den Bergh, received international recognition for his lifetime contribution to South African cinema. He was awarded a Global Film Award at the 7th Ischia Global Film and Music Festival. His latest film, the poetic **Tornado and the Kalahari Horse Whisperer**, was screened at the festival. It tells the story of Pierre (Quintin Krog), a depressed and damaged young man, and Tornado, his emotionally disturbed horse. Sensing Tornado's potential, Pierre travels to Noenieput, in the Groen Kalahari, to find Barrie Burger (Danny Keogh), a horse whisperer. With Barrie's advice, Pierre and Tornado embark on a journey of healing and self-discovery.

A highlight of the Global Film and Music Festival was an exhibition on the 113-year history of South African cinema. A unique collection of film stills, posters and DVD clips was the result of a collaboration between the director of the Cape Winelands Film Festival, Leon van der Merwe, and the South African National Film Archives. The exhibition on South Africa's film heritage demonstrated to an international audience that, among the decades of cinematic escapism, racist films and government propaganda, South Africa has produced some beautiful works of art.

The year's best films
Shirley Adams (Oliver Hermanus)
District 9 (Neill Blomkamp)
Disgrace (Steve Jacobs)
My Black Little Heart (Claire Angelique)
Tornado and the Kalihari Horse Whisperer (Regardt van den Bergh)

Quote of the year
'Through a meticulously observed minimalism, the film tackles numerous relevant social issues with both subtlety and a mature sensitivity. Its themes of love, human endurance, and forgiveness are universal, and give it audience appeal both locally and abroad. *Shirley Adams* is a special movie in which the director takes a number of risks. Moving his camera around as if it was an extra

character in the story, he follows his main actress ceaselessly. The result is a powerful movie with great emotions that works all the more since the emotions mostly stay beneath the surface. And these emotions are definitely felt by the viewer.' *The statement of the JURY at the Durban International Film Festival, where* **Shirley Adams** *won three awards.*

Directory
All Tel/Fax numbers begin (+27)
Cape Film Commission, 6th Floor, NBS Waldorf Bldg, 80 St George's Mall, Cape Town 8001. Tel: (21) 483 9070. Fax: (21) 483 9071. www.capefilmcommission.co.za.
Independent Producers Organisation, PO Box 2631, Saxonwold 2132. Tel: (11) 726 1189. Fax: (11) 482 4621. info@ipo.org.za. www.ipo.org.za.
National Film & Video Foundation, 87 Central St, Houghton, Private Bag x04, Northlands 2116. Tel: (11) 483 0880. Fax: (11) 483 0881. info@nfvf.co.za. www.nvfv.co.za.
South African Broadcasting Co (SABC), Private Bag 1, Auckland Park, Johannesburg 2006. Tel: (11) 714 9797. Fax: (11) 714 3106. www.sabc.co.za.

MARTIN P. BOTHA has published five books on South African cinema, including an anthology on post-apartheid cinema entitled *Marginal Lives and Painful Pasts: South African Cinema After Apartheid*. He is a professor of film studies in the Centre for Film and Media Studies at the University of Cape Town. He was awarded a Global Film Award at the Ischia Global Film and Music Film Festival for his lifetime contribution to the South African film industry.

Regardt van den Bergh's **Tornado and the Kalahari Horse Whisperer**

South Korea Nikki J. Y. Lee

The Korean box office hit a new high during the first half of 2009. The steady growth of the local film market is led by Hollywood blockbusters and the unwavering popularity of domestic titles. Seventy-one Korean films were released theatrically, and according to statistics published by KOFIC (Korean Film Council), by October 2009 domestic films accounted for 51.2% of the total market share. In spite of the financial crisis, the film industry could still sustain its profit margins, thanks to the expansion of the multiplex cinema chains. (The number of screens increased from 720 in 2000 to 2,081 in 2008.)

Some Korean critics have noted the increasing tendency of certain releases to cover safe subjects, thus entertaining a wider demographic. Likewise, audiences are increasingly reluctant to watch films that offer a challenge to simple entertainment. This helps explain why Park Chan-wook's **Thirst** (*Bakjeui*) and Bong Joon-ho's **Mother** (*Madeo*), the two most anticipated Korean films of 2009, garnered far lower box-office takings than expected. Park's *Thirst* is based

upon Emile Zola's *Thérèse Raquin*, but it was transformed into a strange horror tale in which a Catholic priest turns into a vampire and kills the husband of his mistress. Like Park's popular *Oldboy* and *Lady Vengeance*, it is a dark and sensuous film with a twisted sense of humour. However, it met with polarised responses from critics and audiences alike, ultimately failing to match the appeal of the director's earlier works. Indeed, some audiences complained that *Thirst* was superficial and pretentious. Released on 462 screens, it attracted 2.2 million people and by October ranked ninth among the year's domestic films at the box office.

Kim Hye-ja in Bong Joon-ho's **Mother**

Bong's *Mother* followed the lone struggle of a woman attempting to clear her son of a murder charge. It also dealt with the terrifying consequences of the character's unconditional, almost primal, maternal love. Bong's *Memories of Murder* and *The Host* were both box-office hits and, for this reason, it was anticipated that *Mother* would become one of the biggest smashes of the year. The film had also been the focus of public attention because it featured actress Kim Hye-ja, known for playing a typically Korean maternal figure on countless prime-time television soap

Song Kang-ho and Kim Ok-bin in Park Chan-wook's **Thirst**

operas over the last two decades, as well as local heartthrob Won Bin. When it was released on 648 screens in late May, the film drew viewing figures of less than three million and by October ranked just seventh among the year's most popular releases.

Yun Je-gyun's **Tidal Wave**

If these films' dark and uncompromising qualities are taken into consideration, then their performance at the box office cannot be considered that poor. Statistics show that the brand names of Park and Bong might no longer dominate Korean cinema, yet they still have large appeal. Nevertheless, it is clear that the local film culture, developed through the expansion of multiplex cinema chains, has more affinity with more populist films than Park's and Bong's. Other domestic films in the list of top-ten box-office hits confirm this tendency. Yun Je-gyun's **Tidal Wave** (*Haeundae*), another record-breaking Korean blockbuster, topped the box office with an audience of more than ten million. Drawing upon memories of the 2004 tsunami, the film imagines a similar disaster hitting Haeundae, a popular beach in Pusan. For the

Shin Jeong-won's **Chaw**

all-important special effects, the filmmakers collaborated with Hans Uhlig, CG supervisor on the Hollywood smash *The Day after Tomorrow*. (Uhlig also worked on the CGI for Shin Jeong-won's **Chaw** [*Chau*], which features a people-eating wild pig). The disaster film is a new genre for Korean cinema and *Tidal Wave* succeeded through its blending of a Hollywood genre with a destination popular with audiences.

Park Geon-yong's **Lifting King Kong**

Kim Yong-hwa's **Take Off** (*Gukgadaepyo*) was the second most successful film, with an audience of eight million. It was released at the end of July, one week after *Tidal Wave* and during the peak summer season (both films stayed in cinemas until the end of September). Inspired by a true story, the film is a typical sports drama concerning five young men who participated in the ski-jumping event at the 1998 Nagano Winter Olympics. Once again, CGI was employed for the spectacular ski-jumping scenes. Sport-related films have shown a great deal of stamina at the local box office, with 2008's *Forever the Moment*, about a female handball team, performing well and, more recently, Park Geon-yong's **Lifting King Kong** (*Kingkongeul Deulda*), a touching film about six high-school girls on a weightlifting team.

In contrast to the high-concept blockbusters that topped the box office, the films that followed them were mid-budget, light-hearted romantic comedies. Shin Terra's **My Girlfriend is an Agent** (*Chilgeup Gongmuwon*), perhaps a little too reminiscent of *Mr and Mrs Smith*,

Shin Terra's **My Girlfriend is an Agent**

is a spy film about a young couple who, unbeknown to each other, both work for a secret national agency. In Kang Hyeong-cheol's **Scandal Makers** (*Gwasokseukaendeul*), a thirtysomething ex-pop star receives a surprise visit from a young woman who insists that she is his daughter and the young boy accompanying her is his grandson. The unexpected box-office success of this comedy was perhaps due to strong word of mouth, which helped it stay in cinemas long enough to attract family audiences over the Chinese New Year holiday period.

The rest of the year's biggest-grossing domestic releases covered other genres that appeal to large audiences. Yu Ha's **A Frozen Flower** (*Ssanghwajeom*) combined two popular elements of current Korean cinema: erotic period drama and homoerotic relationships among *flower-beauty* male actors. Following the formula of the successful 2006 film, *King and the Clown*, the film adds fictional

Kang Hyeong-cheol's **Scandal Makers**

characters and stories to its real historical setting. The melodrama, which also features some action scenes, unfolds in the late Goryo period (AD918–1392) and concerns the love triangle between the King, Gong-min, his young male lover and the Queen. Lee Yeon-woo's **Running Turtle** (Geobugi Dallinda) starred Kim Yun-suk as a loser cop desperately chasing a serial murderer through the countryside. Kim had played a similar role in *The Chaser*, but in contrast to that film's disturbingly ominous atmosphere, Yeon-woo opted for a warm and comical human drama. Park Dae-min's **Private Eye** (*Geurimja Sarin*) is a detective story set during the Japanese imperial period and concerns a serial murder case. Clearly, Korean films' fascination with the first decades of the twentieth century, as well as the popularity of the thriller genre, continues. Finally, there was Lee Chung-ryoul's **Old Partner** (*Wuonangsori*). Initially released in mid-January on just 20 screens, this low-budget, independent documentary, about a yellow cow and its elderly owner, exerted its slow magic and, by late February, it had taken the top position at the box office.

Lee Chung-ryoul's **Old Partner**

The success of *Old Partner* also increased the public's interest in other independent films such as Yang Ik-joon's **Breathless** (*Ttongpari*) and Noh Young-Seok's **Daytime Drinking** (*Natsul*). The former concerns an extremely violent low-life who thrives on his hatred for his abusive father, while the latter presents a series of silly episodes in the life of a young man who travels to a remote mountain area.

Noh Young-Seok's **Daytime Drinking**

The increase of women-oriented films, some of which were also directed by women, continued to refresh the local film scene. They widened the spectrum of female characters beyond the limited stereotypes presented by mainstream, male-oriented films. **Goodbye Mom** was a gentle comedy-drama about a ruthless 29-year-old woman and her relationship with her mother. Park Chan-ok's second feature, **Paju**, touched upon the complicated emotions experienced by a young woman who falls in love with her late older sister's husband. Kang Hye-jung (of *Oldboy*) played the role of a strangely attractive, homeless young woman in Hwang Soo-ah's **Why Did You Come to My House?** (*Urijibe woe woattni?*), while in **Sisters on the Road** (*Jigeum Idaeroga Joayo*) two half-sisters with very different personalities go travelling, following the death of their mother, in order to uncover an untold secret held by one of their fathers. Goh Tae-jeong's **The Room Nearby** (*Geunyeodeurui Bang*) juxtaposed the lives of a young, poor woman who is struggling to find a place to live, and an older, rich woman who has lost her family and lives on her own in a large house.

Among the films released in autumn, popular titles included Jang Jin's comedy about three different presidents, **Good Morning President** (*Gudmorning prejident*), and Hur Jin-ho's romance about a Korean man and a Chinese woman who meet again in China, **A Good Rain Knows** (*Housijeol*), which has been dubbed the Korean *Before Sunset*.

The most anticipated titles due to come out at the end of the year include Choi Dong-hun's sci-fi martial-arts blockbuster, **Jeon Woo Chi, The Taoist Wizard** (*Jeonuchi*), and Park Shin-woo's **White Night** (*Baegyahaeng – Hayan Eodum Sogeul Geotda*), adapted from the best-selling Japanese mystery thriller.

The most exciting new titles slated for next year include remakes of two 1960s classics – Kim Ki-young's grotesque 1960 psycho-thriller *The Housemaid* and Lee Man-hui's 1966 masterpiece *Full Autumn*, a love story about a female prisoner on three-day parole and a young man on the run.

The year's best films
Bandhobi (Shin Dong-il)
Distrust Hell (Lee Yong-ju)
Grandmother's Flower (Mun Jeong-Hyun)
Mother (Bong Joon-ho)
The Room Nearby (Goh Tae-jeong)

Quote of the year
'I can't really admit that *Thirst* is incomprehensible. I don't think it's true that people don't understand it. They may simply have a different taste.' PARK CHAN-WOOK, *talking about* Thirst.

Directory
All Tel/Fax numbers begin (+82)
Korean Film Archive, 700 Seocho-dong, Seocho-gu, Seoul 137-718. Tel: (2) 521 3147. Fax: (2) 582 6213. www.koreafilm.or.kr.
Korean Film Council (KOFIC), 206-46, Cheongnyangni-dong, Tongdaemun-gu, Seoul 130-010. Tel/Fax: (2) 958 7582. www.kofic.or.kr.

Dr. NIKKI J.Y. LEE is a film researcher based in the UK. She has published articles on Korean directors like Park Chan-wook and Im Kwon-taek and on Korean films like Bong Joon-ho's *The Host*.

Spain Jonathan Holland

'Spanish film,' declared veteran director José Luis Cuerda in 2009, 'is dead'. The early part of the year bore him out. In 2008, Spain produced 174 films, with only a 15% local market share, which compares unfavourably with Europe's other major territories. Throughout early 2009, this figure dwindled to less than 10%. Something had to be done. The answer appeared in the form of a controversial overhaul of the subsidy system, which many believe is the reason for the dreadful figures.

Under the new order, designed to give Spanish cinema more commercial appeal, subsidies will begin at 75,000 admissions, and only films costing USD$2.86 million or more will benefit. The result will lead to an increasingly two-tiered system of higher-budget films and smaller, micro-budgeted releases. The proposed measure has met with opposition from many in the sector and, at the time of writing, Brussels has blocked it, effectively leading to a temporary subsidy freeze, whose effects will ripple through the industry during early 2010.

Further legislation likely to be approved shortly will drop broadcasters' legally imposed 5%

investment in European films to 3%, which in these cash-strapped times could be damaging.

There is an increasing awareness among film producers that Spanish film should focus on telling powerful human stories without losing commercial appeal – combining, in other words, a European interest in character with Hollywood's interest in telling a good story. The new subsidy regulations look likely to give this model institutional heft.

In what appears to be a forerunner of the new regulations, the end of year did see a number of box-office records broken. 2009 appeared to be the year in which 2001's record $165.3 million takings, the best in decades, might be beaten. For only the second time since that year, Spanish films topped the rankings for six weeks running. They were backed by large marketing campaigns, so no change there. The surprise was that they were actually good films. And each fulfilled, in its own way, the new Euro/US brief.

One was Daniel Monzón's powerful, testosterone-fuelled prison drama, **Cell 211** (*Celda 211*), starring Alberto Ammann as a guard who finds himself trapped on the

Daniel Monzón's **Cell 211**

wrong side of the bars during a riot. Luis Tosar's performance as the convicts' ringleader was the most explosive Spanish screen performance of the year.

The other was the long-awaited, English-language **Agora**, Spain's costliest live-action feature and the biggest opener of 2009, which saw Alejandro Amenábar again switch genres with an old-fashioned – though strongly revisionist – sword-and-sandals epic. Starring Rachel Weisz, the film was a vastly ambitious project that drew praise for its scale, scope and spectacle, but also some criticism for its lack of an easy emotional hook. A film about the sufferings of the female philosopher Hypatia in Alexandria in the fourth century, which some saw as a criticism of religion, was always going to be a tough US sell, so sounds of relief were audible when, on the back of remarkable domestic business, it finally found American distribution towards the end of the year.

Until the arrival of these big hitters, the year belonged to two juvenile projects aimed at

Alejandro Amenábar on the set of **Agora**

exploiting the transitory fame of faces on loan from television. **Sex, Party and Lies** (*Mentiras y gordas*) was a messy, depressing exploration of the sex-and-drug-addled lives of a group of teens with few redeeming features (movie and teens both). The fact that it was co-scripted by the now head of the Spanish Ministry of Culture, Ángeles González-Sinde, hardly inspired hope. Equally dispiriting was **Brain Drain** (*Fuga de cerebros*), a so-called comedy about a gang of Spanish dimwits let loose in Oxford.

Borja Cobeaga's **The Friend Zone**

Far better was Borja Cobeaga's witty, good-hearted, unlucky-in-love comedy, **The Friend Zone**, a Spanish *Gregory's Girl* for which word-of-mouth recommendations worked like a charm. These projects, following 2008's *Chef's Special*, have sold well internationally, suggesting that, with an improvement in production values, there is a growing market for such fare. Javier Ruiz Caldera's **Spanish Movie**, a gags-driven parody of recent Spanish film successes à la *Scary Movie*, was due for release in December 2009 and looked set to improve the Spanish box-office bonanza.

For many years, Spanish genre films have looked like a pale imitation of their American originals. But of late, scriptwriters have been finding ways of fusing Spanish themes with US narrative models to powerful effect. Two fine examples of recent Spanish thrillers were **Just Walking** (*Solo quiero caminar*), Agustin Diaz Yanes' genre-bending, Mexican-set thriller about a gang of women hell-bent on revenge, and Patxi Amexcua's low-budget, high-energy

Patxi Amexcua's **25 Carat**

25 Carat (*25 kilates*), about the criminal underworld in Barcelona. Both suffered undeservedly at the box office.

Argentinean Juan José Campanella showed how genre-blending worked with the magnificent **The Secrets in the Eyes** (*El secreto de sus ojos*). Romance, a noirish thriller and an investigation into historical memory came together in a story about a court official, played by a superb Ricardo Darín, investigating an old unsolved crime. The fact that it was made with mostly local money is a credit to the Spanish industry. However, it does throw up the question of why so few scripts of similar quality are being produced.

Away from genre exercises, the year delivered the usual sprinkling of edgier, more experimental fare. Of particular interest was Javier Rebollo's **Woman Without Piano**, a beautifully composed, highly stylised study of 24 hours in the drab life of a Madrid housewife, which featured a wonderful performance from Carmen Machi. And while the major issues in Spanish politics – unemployment and immigration – continue to be dealt with only fitfully by scriptwriters, Isaki Lacuesta's slow-burning, intense **The Damned** (*Los condenados*) at least dealt, albeit obliquely, with the way that past violence breeds present consequences, as a former guerrilla heads back to the jungle for the excavation of a colleague's grave.

Another low-key gem was Galician Mario Iglesias' compelling, intimate **Stories** (*Relatos*),

featuring a superb performance from a non-professional actor, Concepción González, as a childless woman in middle age who writes fiction to fend off her demons.

Daniel Sánchez Arévalo's **Gordos**

Other offbeat projects that attracted praise for their daring were Antonio Naharro and Álvaro Pastor's debut, **Me Too** (*Yo tambien*), about a man with Down's Syndrome seeking the love of a woman who is not interested in him. Potentially a tightrope walk in terms of its tone, the film managed to be both serious and humorous, and moving without being sentimental. Pablo Pineda's partly autobiographical central performance also attracted critical acclaim. The tyranny of our bodies was also the subject of Daniel Sánchez Arévalo's **Gordos**, which explored the trials of a group of overweight people to wonderfully stylish, but dramatically uneven, effect.

Outside Spain, the country is attracting a reputation (with Juan Antonio Bayona's *The*

REC 2

Orphanage leading the pack) for being the home of horror. Following up on the international success of its predecessor, remade in the US as *Quarantine*, **REC 2** returned with a further dose of Blair Witchcraft, again helping to prop up the end-of-year box-office figures.

Another big hitter in 2009 was Pedro Almodóvar's **Broken Embraces** (*Los abrazos rotos*). But there are increasing signs at home that the relationship between the Manchegan maestro and Spanish audiences is becoming strained. The beautiful but hollow film – a subtly structured piece about a film director who goes blind – received a less than rapturous reception at home, both critically and (by Almodóvar's standards) commercially. In the 2009 box-office stand-off, Amenábar was the clear winner. And even offshore, the adulation of Pedro was starting, for the first time in a decade, to sound a little muted.

Pedro Almodóvar's **Broken Embraces**

Films by female directors continued to represent a tiny percentage. As a result of the gender imbalance, a positive discrimination law was mooted in 2009, making it financially more viable to subsidise films directed by women.

Isabel Coixet's disappointing **Map of the Sounds of Tokyo** (*Mapa de los sonidos de Tokyo*), dealing with a female assassin who falls for her target, was pretty enough, but failed to make an impact with audiences. On the other hand, Mar Coll's directorial debut, **3 Days with the Family** (*3 días con la familia*), was a beautifully nuanced portrait of a Catalan

Isabel Coixet's **Map of the Sounds of Tokyo**

family reunited at a funeral. For many, it was the strongest debut of the year.

On the animation front, the last twelve months saw only two projects of distinction. One was the charming, eco-friendly **The Missing Lynx: Paws on the Run**, directed by Manuel Sicilia and Raul Garcia, about the escapades of one of Spain's endangered species. The other was the most expensive film in Spanish film history, the long-awaited Spain/US/UK co-production **Planet 51**, directed by Jorge Blanco, Javier Abad and Marcos Martinez. In it, an American astronaut lands on an alien planet only to find that he's the alien. Attracting mixed reviews, the film opened strongly on its US release, which further bolstered Spanish coffers.

Jorge Blanco, Javier Abad and Marcos Martinez's **Planet 51**

Spanish filmmakers continued to provide high-quality documentaries, which found their way onto the festival circuit. Oriol Porta's **A War in Hollywood** (*Hollywood comtra Franco*) grippingly examined the US film industry's portrayal of the Spanish Civil War and the life of screenwriter Alvah Bessie, one of the

Hollywood Ten. Carlos Balagué examined the life and unpleasant times of Spain's most notorious serial killer in **Arropiero, the Tramp of Death** (*Arropiero, el vagabundo de la muerte*), while mental illness of a different kind came under scrutiny in Abel García Roure's touching, powerful **A Certain Truth** (*Una cierta verdad*), about the experiences, over several years, of six patients in a Barcelona mental hospital.

Spanish projects to watch out for in 2010 are led by Bayona's follow-up to *The Orphanage*, which should be Telecinco Cinema's big 2010 release. The film production wing of the broadcaster Telecinco, the company was also responsible for *Pan's Labyrinth*, *Agora* and *The Orphanage*, making it by some distance Spain's most successful production outfit. Other projects of note are **Verbo**, an adventure story about the adolescent inside us all, directed by Eduardo Chapero-Jackson, whose shorts have won numerous festival awards. There is also Julio Medem's **Room in Rome** (*Habitación en Roma*), an intimate account of the life-changing encounter between two women in a Rome hotel. With it, the director will probably be seeking to consign to the past the commercial failure of his last outing, the daring *Chaotic Ana*. Also worth waiting for will be Oskar Santos' high-profile, Amenábar-produced debut **The Evil Of Others** (*El Mal Ajeno*), a psychological thriller, with fantasy elements, about a doctor accused of driving a patient to suicide.

But let's keep things in perspective. Grotesque bureaucratic wrangling apart, it's still the case that only a minority of films make a difference at the Spanish box office and that, of 160 films released in 2009, only 15 returned more than $1 milllion. That means over 90% of Spanish films are of little or no interest to Spanish people. It is a division between producers and public that urgently needs to be addressed. Spanish cinema may not, as José Luis Cuerda claims, be dead. But the injection of oxygen represented by the new subsidy laws is looking increasingly like its last chance of resuscitation.

The year's best films

25 Carat (Patxi Amexcua)
Agora (Alejandro Amenábar)
Cell 211 (Daniel Monzón)
Stories (Mario Iglesias)
Pagafantas (Borja Cobeaga)

Quotes of the year

'This job is shit. Today you're a genius and tomorrow you're either an idiot, or old and useless.' RICARDO DARÍN, *Argentinean actor.*

'I hate glamour. It makes me vomit.' MARIO CAMUS, *veteran film director.*

Directory

All Tel/Fax numbers begin (+34)

Escuela de Cinematografia y de la Audiovisual de la Comunidad de Madrdid (ECAM), c/Juan de Orduña, Km 2200, 28223 Madrid. Tel: (91) 411 0497. www.ecam.es.

Federation of Associations of Spanish Audiovisual Producers (FAPAE), Calle Luis Bunuel 2-2º Izquierda, Ciudad de la Imagen, Pozuelo de Alarcón, 28223 Madrid. Tel: (91) 512 1660. Fax: (91) 512 0148. web@fapae.es. www.fapae.es.

Federation of Cinema Distributors (FEDICINE), Orense 33, 3ºB, 28020 Madrid. Tel: (91) 556 9755. Fax: (91) 555 6697. www.fedicine.com.

Filmoteca de la Generalitat de Catalunya, Carrer del Portal de Santa Madrona 6-8, Barcelona 08001. Tel: (93) 316 2780. Fax: (93) 316 2783. filmoteca. cultura@gencat.net.

Filmoteca Espanola, Calle Magdalena 10, 28012 Madrid. Tel: (91) 467 2600. Fax: (91) 467 2611. www.cultura.mecd.es/cine/film/filmoteca.isp.

Filmoteca Vasca, Avenida Sancho el Sabio, 17 Trasera, Donostia, 20010 San Sebastián. Tel: (943) 468 484. Fax: (943) 469 998. www.filmotecavasca.com.

JONATHAN HOLLAND has lived in Madrid for 20 years. He is a university lecturer and *Variety*'s critic in Spain.

Sweden Gunnar Rehlin

With the film versions of deceased author Stieg Larsson's *Millennium* trilogy, Swedish film in 2009 experienced its biggest success ever. The first film, the tense and well-made **The Girl with the Dragon Tattoo** (*Män som hatar kvinnor*), directed by Niels Arden Oplev, opened in Sweden in February and went on to conquer the world. In France it opened on more than 500 prints in May, and when lead actors Michael Nyqvist and Noomi Rapace visited the Cannes Film Festival, they were treated like royalty.

Noomi Rapace in Niels Arden Oplev's **The Girl with the Dragon Tattoo**

Film number two, **The Girl Who Played with Fire** (*Flickan som lekte med elden*), directed by Daniel Alfredson, opened across Scandinavia in the middle of September and had even larger opening figures than the first film. Number three, **The Girl Who Kicked the Hornet's Nest** (*Luftslottet som sprängdes*), directed by Daniel Alfredson, opened locally at the end of November. With even longer television and DVD versions to follow, the *Millennium* success story will continue long into 2010.

Another long story is the Ingmar Bergman heritage. In the fall, both his belongings and his home on Fårö island were up for auction.

The belongings sold for a record sum of 2.5 million dollars – his old waste basket sold for 1,500 dollars! The Ingmar Bergman Foundation wanted to buy his home and make it a haven for scholars and film students, but it was highly unlikely that the foundation could meet the auction's demands, despite appeals to Bergman admirers such as Woody Allen.

The Girl with the Dragon Tattoo had its premiere at the Berlin Film Festival, as did Lukas Moodysson's **Mammoth**. A highly anticipated film, the director's first in English, it was about a successful US businessman who travels to Asia and undergoes life-shattering experiences. Inexplicably, the well-made and fascinating film was 'killed' by international critics, leaving the Swedish film industry wondering what happened. Moodysson himself shrugged off the hostile reception.

Lukas Moodysson's **Mammoth**

A better reception was given by Berlinale critics to Fredrik Wenzel and Henrik Hellström's meditative film about a young boy observing the different characters in his neighbourhood, **Burrowing** (*Man tänker sitt*), and Fredrik Edfeldt's **The Girl** (*Flickan*), about a young girl left alone at home one summer.

Fredrik Edfeldt's **The Girl**

The Swedish film industry has been trying to encourage a greater number of female directors, with the result that some of the best films from the last year were made by women. Lisa Siwe directed **Glowing Stars** (*I taket lyser stjärnorna*), based on a novel about a teenage girl whose mother is dying of cancer. It successfully avoided sentimentality without sacrificing the emotional power of the story. The same went for the gripping **In Your Veins** (*I skuggan av värmen*), directed by Beata Gårdeler, about a female security guard who tries to hide her heroin addiction. It featured Malin Crepin and Joel Kinnaman, two of Sweden's rising young stars.

One of the biggest hits of the summer was Peter Magnusson's comedy, **The Summer with Göran** (*Sommaren med Göran*), about a young man looking for love at a high-society summer party.

There were four Swedish films in the official selection of the Venice Film Festival, although none was in competition. The most talked about of the four was Erik Gandini's **Videocracy**, an anti-Silvio Berlusconi documentary that implies that the Italian prime minister uses his TV empire to provide simple-minded, sexist entertainment in order to dumb down the nation. The film went on to open in more than 70 Italian cinemas.

The other films in Venice were Jesper Ganslandt's **The Ape** (*Apan*), the captivating story of a man trying to come to terms with a terrible crime he has committed, Jörgen

Bergmark's **The Rational Solution** (*Det enda rationella*), a talky but well-made black comedy about two adult couples moving in with each other, and Tarik Saleh's dystopian animated feature, **Metropia**, about a future society where the big companies rule. All films received fair, if not overwhelmingly positive, reviews and opened locally in autumn.

Jörgen Bergmark's **The Rational Solution**

In September, the Swedish Film Institute announced that Ruben Östlund's **Involuntary** would be the year's contender for the 2010 Academy Awards. Although it is a solid film, even Östlund considered his chances of winning very slim.

For those who have said for years that Ulf Malmros, the man behind *Slim Susie*, is one of Sweden's finest and most underrated directors, **The Wedding Photographer** (*Bröllopsfotografen*), proved them right. An emotionally engaging comedy-drama about a young man from the countryside who discovers the downside of life amongst the upper echelons of Stockholm society, it was both funny and moving, with Kjell Bergqvist

Ulf Malmros's **The Wedding Photographer**

Helena Bergström's **So Different**

giving a career-best performance as an actor down on his luck. Another acclaimed performer, Helena Bergström, premiered her sophomore directing effort, the comedy **So Different** (*Så olika*).

Looking forward to 2010, a number of films look interesting. For the first time in years, Josef Fares has made a comedy, although it remains untitled. February also sees the premiere of Göran Brisinger's highly anticipated **Among Us** (*Änglavakt*), starring Michael Nykvist and Izabella Scorupco as a married couple who hope for a miracle when their child is taken gravely ill.

Spring will see the premiere of Kristian Petri's horror film **Bad Faith** (*Ond tro*), and the director will soon take the reins on an adaptation of John Ajvide Lindqvist's **Handling the Undead** (*Hanteringen av odöda*). Lindqvist previously wrote the novel *Let the Right One In*, which Tomas Alfredson made into a worldwide hit film. That success has now given Alfredson two Hollywood movies to direct. First up is Nicole Kidman in **The Danish Girl**, which will be followed by a feature adaptation of John Le Carré's **Tinker, Tailor, Soldier, Spy**.

Another Swedish success story, in other words.

The year's best films
Mammoth (Lukas Moodysson)
Princess (Teresa Fabik)
The Girl (Fredrik Edfeldt)
The Wedding Photographer (Ulf Malmros)
Glowing Stars (Lisa Siwe)

Quote of the year
'I feel like I'm in some sort of bloody *Harry Potter*.' Millennium *actor* MICHAEL NYQVIST *after touring Europe, giving interviews and being hunted by paparazzi.*

Directory
All Tel/Fax numbers begin (+46)
Cinemateket, Swedish Film Institute, Box 27126, SE-102 52 Stockholm. Tel: (8) 665 1100. Fax: (8) 666 3698. info@sfi.se. www.sfi.se.
Swedish Film Distributors Association, Box 23021, SE-10435 Stockholm. Tel: (8) 441 5570. Fax: (8) 343 810.
Swedish Film Institute, Box 27126, SE-10252 Stockholm. Tel: (8) 665 1100. Fax: (8) 666 3698. info@sfi.se.
Swedish Film Producers Association, Box 27298, SE-102 53 Stockholm. Tel: (8) 665 1255. Fax: (8) 666 3748. info@frf.net.
Swedish National Archive for Recorded Sound & Moving Images, Box 24124, SE-10451 Stockholm. Tel: (8) 783 3700. Fax: (8) 663 1811. info@ljudochbildarkivet.se.

GUNNAR REHLIN is a Swedish journalist who is the Nordic correspondent for *Variety* and contributor to a string of Scandi magazines. In the film *Sex, Lies and Videoviolence*, he had his head blown off by Quentin Tarantino's favourite Swedish actress, Christina Lindberg.

Lisa Siwe's **Glowing Stars**

Switzerland Marcy Goldberg

The last year has been very solid for Switzerland. The film industry has clearly emerged from the slump of 2008 and the upswing shows every indication of continuing into 2010. There is also an emerging generation of new filmmakers. Whether presenting a first feature or following up on a promising debut, these directors – many of them graduates of the film schools established here within the past two decades – seem set on taking Swiss cinema in new directions. At the same time, the Swiss documentary tradition is returning to its former strength after several years of underfunding and neglect on the part of federal film policy.

Ursula Meier's **Home**

Two of the rare highlights of 2008 went on to even greater success in 2009. Ursula Meier's first feature, **Home**, a somewhat surreal drama starring Isabelle Huppert and Olivier Gourmet as a couple whose family life spirals into crisis when a superhighway is built next to their house, collected over 20 awards from festivals around the world, as well as attracting extensive international distribution. The Swiss-French-Belgian co-production was also hailed by Swiss audiences across the linguistic divide, with a 2009 release in

German-speaking Switzerland matching 2008's box-office success in the francophone region.

2009 also brought an Academy Award nomination for best live-action short for Reto Caffi's *On the Line*, a hit at festivals and the winner of over 50 awards.

Lionel Baier's **Another Man** (*Un autre homme*) premiered at the Locarno Film Festival in 2008 but did not hit its stride until 2009, with numerous international festival appearances, foreign distribution deals, a domestic cinema release and much critical acclaim. Shot in black and white in homage to the Swiss and French New Waves of the 1960s and 70s, *Another Man* tells the bitingly satirical story of a naive literature graduate faking his way through a job as film critic for a small-town Swiss newspaper by plagiarising an obscure Marxist broadsheet. Baier, already known to international festival audiences for his exploration of gay Swiss identity in *Stealth*, *Comme des voleurs (a l'est)*, *Stupid Boy* and the documentary *The Parade, Our Story*, is one of the country's most innovative, refreshing and mischievous young filmmakers and definitely a name to watch.

Robin Harsch in Lionel Baier's **Another Man**

Another promising young director is Micha Lewinsky. Following up on the unexpected success of his first feature, *The Boyfriend*, Lewinsky scored another surprise hit in 2009 with **The Civil Registrar** (*Die Standesbeamtin*), a film originally produced for Swiss public television. The light romantic comedy became one of the year's domestic box-office successes and launched the career of Marie Leuenberger. She plays the film's eponymous civil servant, a bumbling but lovable registry office clerk faced with the prospect of having to marry the love of her life to someone else.

Christoph Schaub's **Julia's Disappearance**

speaking market. Further examples of this trend included veteran Christoph Schaub's comedy of manners about aging, **Julia's Disappearance** (*Giulias Verschwinden*), starring Corinna Harfouch and Bruno Ganz. There was also internationally acclaimed visual artist Pipilotti Rist's feature debut. A Swiss-Austrian co-production, **Pepperminta** is a colourful but rather plotless romp that references *Pippi Longstocking*, *Yellow Submarine* and the artist's own video installations. Also noteworthy in the

Micha Lewinsky's **The Civil Registrar**

Bettina Oberli, who directed the 2006 comedy hit *Late Bloomers*, returned this year with the German-Swiss co-production, **Tannöd**, a sombre adaptation of Andrea Maria Schenkel's true-crime bestseller, itself based on a series of decades-old unsolved murders in rural Bavaria. Shot in Germany with a mainly German cast, *Tannöd* may prove to be part of a new Swiss trend in co-production for the larger German-

Pipilotti Rist's **Pepperminta**

Kit Hung's **Soundless Wind Chime**

co-production category was Kit Hung's Swiss-Chinese debut, **Soundless Wind Chime**. The semi-autobiographical drama about a Chinese man's search for his lost European lover is set in Beijing, Hong Kong and Switzerland. It was an international festival success, primarily on the Queer/LGBT circuit.

Christian Frei's **Space Tourists**

2009 saw the return of two of Switzerland's most respected non-fiction filmmakers, each with a feature documentary about space exploration. In **Space Tourists**, Christian Frei juxtaposed a space-shuttle journey by Iranian-American millionaire, Anousheh Ansari, with the dilapidated remains of the former Soviet space programme and the impoverished shepherds who scavenge rocket debris in the Kazakhstan steppes. With **Mars Dreamers**, Richard Dindo, Switzerland's best-known documentary filmmaker, extended his long-running fascination for utopian dreamers to the motley community of American

scientists, writers and adventurers eager to colonise Mars.

Another documentary veteran, Peter Liechti, blurred the boundaries between truth and fiction with his experimental feature, **The Sound of Insects: Record of a Mummy**, a gripping and poetic chronicle of a suicide by starvation. Liechti adapted his film from a novella by Japanese author Shimada Masahiko, who ostensibly based his text on an authentic diary found next to a mummified corpse. *The Sound of Insects* premiered at Rotterdam, where Liechti was also the subject of a well-deserved retrospective, and has gone on to win several significant awards, including the European Film Academy's Prix Arte.

Peter Liechti's **The Sound of Insects: Record of a Mummy**

2009 was also the year of tributes to Alain Tanner, whose 1976 arthouse hit *Jonah Who Will Be 25 in the Year 2000* remains the most successful and best-loved Swiss film. In honour of the director's 80th birthday, retrospectives were held in Paris, Poland, India and Thailand, with further events planned for 2010.

Richard Dindo's **Mars Dreamers**

Séverine Cornamusaz's **Coeur Animal**

End-of-year premieres included Séverine Cornamusaz's **Coeur Animal**, a hard-hitting drama set in an Alpine farming milieu, and Stascha Bader's painstakingly researched music documentary **Rocksteady: The Roots of Reggae**.

Stascha Bader's **Rocksteady: The Roots of Reggae**

MARCY GOLDBERG is a film historian and independent media consultant based in Zurich.

The year's best films
The Sound of Insects: Record of a Mummy
(Peter Liechti)
Another Man (Lionel Baier)
Tannöd (Bettina Oberli)
Home (Ursula Meier)

Quote of the year
'There are two words I strictly avoid when talking about my films: "art" and "experiment". Between us we can say that we see ourselves as artists. But hopefully no one will hear us!' *Filmmaker* PETER LIECHTI, *interviewed in the newspaper Tages-Anzeiger.*

Directory
All Tel/Fax numbers begin (+41)
Swiss Films, Neugasse 6, P.O. Box, CH-8031 Zurich. Tel: (43) 211 40 50. Fax: (43) 211 40 60. info@swissfilms.ch. www.swissfilms.ch.
Swiss Films Genève, Maison des Arts du Grütli, 16, rue Général Dufour, CH-1204 Genève. Tel: (22) 308 12 40. Fax: (22) 308 12 41. geneva@ swissfilms.ch. www.swissfilms.ch.

Bettina Oberli's **Tannöd**

Taiwan David Frazier

In the year and a half since pro-China politician Ma Ying-jeou took over Taiwan's presidency, in May 2008, both Chinese and Taiwanese in nearly every field have begun probing new possibilities for cooperation. In film, the idea of a consolidated Greater China Market, including Taiwan, Hong Kong, China and Chinese-speaking communities in Singapore and Malaysia, seems to many to be inevitable, though still at some vague point in the future. In 2009, Taiwan's two main film festivals, the Taipei Film Festival and the Golden Horse Film Festival – which is not only the oldest in Asia, its pan-Chinese awards ceremony also boasts the most prestigious red carpet for the region's film stars – both went so far as to host conferences on this convergence trend, featuring Hou Hsiao-hsien as well as other heavyweight directors, studio heads and government film bureau chiefs from Hong Kong, China and Taiwan.

That said, the number of Taiwan-China co-productions has not yet skyrocketed, numbering only four in the last year (though several other films on both sides involved Hong Kong partners). Talk of co-productions is nevertheless more common and a sense of how the trend may take shape is beginning to emerge. To wit, China's large market will best support the economies of scale needed for blockbusters, so it will naturally exert its gravitational pull on the region's top directors, stars and technicians. The industry will then form one big triangle, with China as its LA, Hong Kong perhaps as New York, and Taiwan as a Toronto or Vancouver (at least in terms of studio output – stars will still prefer to live in Hong Kong or Taipei). This has already begun to happen and, at the Taipei Film Festival, Chu Yen-ping, a Taiwanese director who has worked

between the three regions, noted China's dominant position. 'Last year [2008], the historical action film *Red Cliff* and the romantic comedy *If You Are the One* grossed over RMB 300 million each in Chinese theatres,' he said. Both were Chinese films, and one prominently featured Taiwanese actors. 'If you put them together, you have *Cape No. 7* five times over.' *Cape No. 7*, a 2008 romantic comedy, was Taiwan's largest-grossing film ever, raking in just over US$16 million in Taiwan and another US$3 million in China.

Politics remains something of an impediment and film has at times become a political battleground. *Cape No. 7* became a political issue when China delayed its release in December 2008 over concerns that the film's vision of Taiwanese identity would undermine Chinese nationalism. After the express urgings of Taiwan's president Ma, the film was finally given a Valentine's Day release on the mainland. An even greater furor was stirred up by **The 10 Conditions of Love**, a US-Australia-produced documentary on a controversial leader of China's western Muslims. The drama began in July at the Melbourne Film Festival, which received threats from Beijing officials

Hsiao-tse Cheng's **Miao Miao**

for merely scheduling the film. When it was announced that screenings would go ahead (now to a huge crowd in a larger venue), all Chinese films were pulled from the festival. One Hong Kong distributor, Fortissimo Films, obsequiously followed Beijing's lead and pulled its entries, including the Hsiao-tse Cheng Hong Kong-Taiwan co-production **Miao Miao**, a smartly conceived teen romance. This angered Taiwan's government, which had funded a significant chunk of *Miao Miao's* production costs and demanded a refund. It was certainly a tangled web of political tensions, and further entanglements were to come. In October, when *The 10 Conditions of Love* was slotted into the Kaohsiung Film Festival in south Taiwan, Beijing again complained. This time, Taiwanese politicians were divided, with some in the president's pro-China party pushing for censorship. The film was eventually shown, however, and the main result was a boycott by Chinese tourists of Kaohsiung, the festival's host city.

Politics aside, it was a slow year for Taiwanese cinema, with around 25 films produced. Lacking the blockbusters of the previous two years – *Lust, Caution* in 2007 and *Cape No. 7* in 2008 – Taiwanese films only managed to attain 2% of the national box office, with another 1.5% going to Hong Kong and Chinese films, and the remaining 96% shared by foreign, mainly Hollywood, fare. (All totals are through to September 2009.) Yet even this was an improvement on a decade ago, when Taiwanese films often failed to take even 1% of national receipts. Increased government funding and major hits of recent years have led to a guarded optimism as well as more commercially geared films. Almost every Taiwanese production receives government funding – up to half of the budget. Chief funding sources are the national-level Government Information Office, followed by the Taipei Film Commission (Taipei City) and the Kaohsiung City Government. In May, the national government announced it would continue its support, injecting US$228 million into the nation's film industry over the next five years.

Christina Yao's **Empire of Silver**

The four China-Taiwan co-productions were bigger, slicker and more star-studded, if not always as deeply felt as Taiwan's home-grown art-house features. **Empire of Silver** (*Bai Yin Di Guo*) showed a fascination with the evolution of China's silver guilds into an early form of bank. Unfortunately, characterisation was weak, but the grandiose style now expected of Chinese historical epics was good enough to merit it second place in the year's domestic box-office listings. **The Message** (*Feng Sheng*), a mostly China-made film by Taiwanese director Chen Kuo-fu, was a 1930s period thriller that revisited the intrigue of *Lust, Caution*, albeit insipidly and with all traces of politics neatly excised. **Forever Enthralled** (*Mei Lan Fang*), a biopic of the

Chen Kaige's **Forever Enthralled**

Clara Law's **Like a Dream**

20th century's most famous Peking Opera singer, was directed by one of the icons of China's Fifth Generation, Chen Kaige, with the participation of a Taiwan production house. Lastly, Clara Law's romantic comedy **Like a Dream** (*Ru Meng*) was a late-year release and all expectations pointed to it performing well, alongside its nine nominations at the Golden Horse Awards.

Ang Lee on the set of **Taking Woodstock**

Of Taiwan's internationally famous directors, Ang Lee returned to Hollywood to make the 1960s period piece **Taking Woodstock**, while Hou Hsiao-hsien is still in pre-production on his highly anticipated martial-arts epic, **The Assassin** (*Nie Yin Niang*), which will reportedly feature big-name stars Shu Qi and Chang Chen. Tsai Ming-liang did manage to complete **Face** (*Visage/Lian*), a magical-realist interpretation of the biblical story of Salome. It was the first film in a new series funded by the Louvre, which contributed €775,000, or about 20% of the budget. But Tsai's films are falling into a pattern and, for at least three or

four films, many reviewers have felt compelled to offer the caveat: 'for Tsai Ming-liang fans only'. I count myself a fan, but despite Tsai's continued genius for visual metaphors, a complete absence of narrative development made sitting through this one hard work.

Tsai Ming-liang's **Face**

Taiwan's auteur tradition is hardly dead, however, as a new generation rises through the ranks. **Yang Yang**, a college girl's coming-of-age story by sophomore director Cheng Yu-chieh, was shot and edited with an intimacy that defies convention and is rarely seen in cinema. Leon Dai's **No Puedo Vivir Sin Ti** (*Bu Neng Mei You Ni*) wowed critics and was awarded the top prize at the Taipei Film Festival. A social-realist story of a lowly dock worker fighting state bureaucracy to keep custody of his daughter, it was shot in black and white in a style reminiscent of Truffaut. **A Place of One's Own** (*Yi Xi Zhi Di*) by Lou Yi-an, was a well-scripted rock'n'roll drama, while Chung Mong-hong's **Parking** (*Ting Chi*)

Cheng Yu-chieh's **Yang Yang**

ABU DHABI FILM COMMISSION

Chung Mong-hong's **Parking**

managed a Taipei-style black comedy with shades of Jim Jarmusch circa Mystery Train. Veteran director Chang Tso-chi, who was known for rolling takes and an understated pathos during the 1990s, made **How Are You Dad?** (*Ba Ni Hao Ma?*), a moving, one-man omnibus of father-son stories.

Wi Ding Ho's **Pinoy Sunday**

Looking ahead, the most eagerly anticipated film of 2010 has to be **Seediq Bale**, the latest from *Cape No. 7* director Wei Te-sheng. In terms of budget and scope, it will become Taiwan's largest historical epic in decades, telling the story of a battle between native Taiwanese and Japanese colonials at the beginning of 20th century. Also highly anticipated are veteran actor-director Doze Niu's 1980s-era gangster film **Mongo** (*Meng Jia*), and Wi Ding Ho's **Pinoy Sunday**, a tale of Filipino labourers in Taiwan, featuring some of the Philippines' biggest stars.

The year's best films
Yang Yang (Cheng Yu-chieh)
No Puedo Vivir Sin Ti (Leon Dai)
Empire of Silver (Christina Yao)
A Place of One's Own (Lou Yi-an)
Parking (Chung Mong-hong)

Quote of the year
'Last year, the historical action film *Red Cliff* and the romantic comedy *If You Are the One* grossed over RMB 300 million each in Chinese theatres. If you put them together, you have *Cape No. 7* five times over.' *Taiwanese director* CHU YEN-PING, *comparing two typical Chinese blockbusters with Taiwan's largest-grossing film of all time.*

Directory
All Tel/Fax numbers begin (+886)
Chinese Taiwan Film Archive, 4F, 7 Chingtao East Rd, Taipei. Tel: (2) 2392 4243. Fax: (2) 2392 6359. www.ctfa.org.tw.
Government Information Office, Department of Motion Picture Affairs, 2 Tientsin St, Taipei 100. Tel: (2) 3356 7870. Fax: (2) 2341 0360. www.gio.gov.tw.
Motion Picture Association of Taipei, 5F, 196 Chunghwa Rd, Sec 1, Taipei. Tel: (2) 2331 4672. Fax: (2) 2381 4341.
Taipei Film Commission, 4F, #99, Section 5, Civic Blvd., Taipei. Tel: (2) 2528-9580. Fax: (2) 2528-9580. www.taipeifilmcommission.org.

DAVID FRAZIER is a freelance journalist, film critic, art critic, rock'n'roll promoter and director of the Urban Nomad Film Fest for indie shorts and documentaries. He has lived in Taipei since 1995.

Leon Dai's **No Puedo Vivir Sin Ti**

Thailand Anchalee Chaiworaporn

The global economic downturn and domestic political upheavals severely affected the Thai film industry in the first eight months of 2009. The result was a downturn in domestic revenue figures, the emergence of fewer new directors, with some filmmakers being forced to turn to television to earn money. One such example was veteran director Nonzee Nimibutr, who oversaw two successful action series.

There were 50 releases across the year, slightly lower than 2008. However, as political riots soared through the country, in light of the Internal Security Act, only three domestic films actually performed well, earning more than US$1.45 million.

God Bless Trainees (*Saranae Hao Peng*) earned US$2.67 million, despite the poor quality of images and sound. Audiences flocked to see how famous people react to various set-ups, in the style of candid camera, as they have done for a decade with the television series, *Saranae*. Another comedy, Mum Jokmok's **The Dynasty** (*Wong Kham Lao*), also topped the box office, with US$2.55 million. The former star chose to parody a famous and frequently adapted Thai novel, *The Golden Sand House*, about a young girl fighting against her cousins, who occupy a higher social status. Piyapan Choopetch's **My Ex** (*Fan Kao*) was a horror film about a man who discovers that he and his current girlfriend are being pursued by the ghost of his ex. Lead actor Shakrit Yamnam had apparently made a comment about his co-star's breasts, which he denied during a teary press conference. But the revelation was enough to send audiences rushing to the cinema to watch the film.

Of the few new directors to emerge over the last year, most of the films they produced aimed at commercial success. It was not surprising that Naruebordee Wechakum was involved with *God Bless Trainees*, as he had also directed the original television series. Thakaew Ruengrut directed the horror film **Death Happens** (*6.66 Tai Mai Dai Taay*), which was financed by the television production company Work Point Entertainment. Only one film edged more towards an artistic statement. Genwaii Thongdeenok, produced by Sahamongkol Film, with whom he has long been associated, directed **The Happiness of Kati** (*Kwaamsuk Khong Kati*), an adaptation of a novel about a ten-year-old girl attempting to hold her life together as her mother is dying.

Kao Jeerayu in **Phobia 2**

By September, the general situation was improving. GTH released **Phobia 2** (*Haa Praeng*) and **BTS Bangkok Traffic Love Story** (*Rodfaifa Maha Na Ther*). *Phobia 2* was widely expected to build on the success of *Phobia*, which had dominated the local box office and performed well internationally. The sequel was divided into five stories, directed by Paween Purijitpanya, Songyos Sugmakanan, Banjong Pisanthnakun, Parkpoom Wongpoom, and

Adisorn Tresirikasem's **BTS Bangkok Traffic Love Story**

Wisoot Poolvorarak. It looked set to become Thailand's top grossing domestic box-office hit of the year, with more than US$3.3 million. However, the combination of male star Theeradet Wongpuaphan and a romantic comedy was more than enough to see audiences flock to *BTS Bangkok Traffic Love Story*. The film was the first to be set on the capital's skytrain and, at the time of writing, the film had grossed an impressive US$4.21 million.

Hollywood-backed Columbia Tristar Buena Vista Film (Thailand) Co Ltd officially announced plans to distribute Thai films for the first time, but will focus only on productions from the new studio overseen by Princess Ubonrat, Oriental Eyes. So far, its slate includes three projects covering the popular horror and action genres, as well as an epic.

Artistically speaking, 2009 was a painful year, both in the mainstream and independent circles. Among the few memorable entries, there was New Thai Cinema pioneer Pen-Ek

Wanida Termthanaporn in Pen-Ek Rattanaruang's **Nymph**

Rattanaruang's **Nymph** (*Nang Mai*). His ninth film challenged the popularity of horror by presenting a silent ghost story, exploring the jealousy of an adulterous wife who believes her husband is having an affair with a ghost. It officially opened in Cannes in Un Certain Regard section and an homage was paid to the film's Dutch producer, Wouter Barendrecht, who had recently passed away.

Arak Apakad in Kongkiat Khomsiri's **Slice**

Nymph's local producer, Five Star Productions, made another of the year's best films with Kongkiat Khomsiri's **Slice** (*Chuen*), a dark thriller based on a story by Wisit Sasanatieng. A young man is released from prison in order to help a cop investigate a serial murder case. His return to his hometown brings up ghosts from the past. The studio also produced Wisit Sasanatieng's **The Red Eagle** (*Insee Daeng*), a remake of the classic 1973 Thai action film, *Insee Thong*, which saw the lead actor die suddenly during shooting.

Uruphong Raksasad's **Agarian Utopia**

In a quiet year for independent films, only Uruphong Raksasad's agriculture-themed documentary **Agarian Utopia** (Sawan

Anocha Suwichakornpong's **Mundane History**

Banna), and Apichatpong Weerasethakul's shorts, **A Letter to Uncle Boonmee** and **Phantoms of Nabua**, travelled to festival circuits. Apichatpong's works were part of the multimedia **Primitive** projects, about a village in a communist country.

At the end of the year, Anocha Suwichakornpong finished her experimental debut, the silent **Mundane History** (*Jao Nokkrajok*), in which she questions the current political climate through the relationship of a father and his son.

It is likely that film production in 2010 will see traction in two directions. The industry will encourage more commercially successful genre films, particularly comedies, considering their success over the last year. The independent scene will also be more lively. In addition to *Mundane History*, Apichatpong Weerasethakul and Aditya Assarat have begun shooting their new films: a feature-length version of *A Letter to Uncle Boonmee* and **Hi-So**, derived from Assarat's experience of being a Thai ex-pat in his own home.

The year's best films
Mundane History (Anocha Suwichakornpong)
Agrarian Utopia (Urupong Raksasad)
Slice (Kongkiat Khomsiri)
Nymph (Pen-Ek Rattanaruang)
Preta (Paween Purijitpanya), a section of the omnibus horror film, **Phobia 2**

Quote of the year
'The fact that we stand out from the rest has its price – we make fewer movies and have difficulties raising funds. Everyone likes our freedom. Does this mean that we are New Wave?' PEN EK-RATANARUANG, *talking about the Thai New Wave.*

Directory
All Tel/Fax numbers begin (+66)
Federation of National Film Association of Thailand, 31/9 UMG Theatre 2 Fl., Royal City Avenue, New Petchburi Road, Bangkapi, Bangkok 10310. Tel: (2) 6415917-8. www.thainationalfilm.com.
National Film Archive, 93 Moo 3, Phutthamonthon Soi 5 Phutthamonthon, Nakorn Prathom 73120. Tel: (2) 4822013-5. www.nfat.org.
Office of Contemporary Arts and Culture, Ministry of Culture, 666 Baromrajchonnanee Road, Bangplad, Bangkok 10700. Tel: (2) 4228819-20. http://www.ocac.go.th.

ANCHALEE CHAIWORAPORN contributes to both local and international journals, and won 2000's Thai Best Film Critic award. She now runs a bilingual website on Thai cinema, www.thaicinema.org.

Tunisia Maryam Touzani

The lack of film production in Tunisia is suffocating the industry. Closing cinemas, the crisis in distribution sectors and the growth in piracy add to the problem. To revive its industry, the country has taken a series of decisions that appear to suggest a real desire for change.

The Committee of Aid to Production has anticipated two annual committees instead of one, which should give the opportunity for a larger array of projects to see the light of day. The creation of a National Commission for the Reform and the Development of Cinema and the Audiovisual Sector also seems to be a step forward.

Finding sources of funding remains a huge obstacle for producers and filmmakers. The contribution made by the Ministry of Culture and Heritage is the only budget guaranteed for a national production and is far from sufficient. Production companies have found themselves strapped financially, and attracting private funding to support projects is not an easy task. Co-productions are generally the only way out and Tunisian films rely heavily on them. Despite the existing difficulties, once in a while a successful film emerges, which boosts the image of Tunisian cinema.

Raja Amari's *Satin Rouge* earned her great acclaim in Tunisia and beyond. Her second feature, **Buried Secrets**, a story of incomprehension and confrontation between two different worlds, affirmed the promise of her debut and appeared in the Orrizonti section of the 2009 Venice Film Festival. Faithful to her style, Amari skilfully portrays a searching psychological portrait of Aicha, Radhia and their mother, who exist away from the real world,

Raja Amari's **Buried Secrets**

in the servants' quarters of an abandoned house. Their calm existence is disrupted when a young couple move into the house. Afraid of eviction, the three women hide from their co-habitants. But the youngest sister is attracted to Salma, a young, vivacious woman who represents everything she wishes to be. One day, Salma discovers them and they decide to lock her away. Tunisian actress Hafsia Herzi is revelatory as Aicha. Her previous performance in Abdellatif Kechich's award-winning *Couscous* won her international acclaim and various awards at festivals.

In Mohamed Zran's documentary **Being Here** (*Vivre Ici*), a grocery shop in the small southeastern Tunisian city of Zarzis is the unlikely ground for significant political and philosophical discussions. Simon is a Jewish grocer who has always been the local confidant. In his store, a marriage-fixer, a taxi driver, an artist and others debate life, love and politics, sharing their particular vision of the world. Zran

Mohamed Zran's documentary, **Being Here**

gives a say to ordinary people, 'listening to the world' through their voices and proving that the most significant opinions need not come out of the mouths of intellectuals. The filmmaker has distinguished himself in the past with *Song for the Millennium*, which won him the prize for Emerging Documentary Feature Filmmaker at the 2003 Tribeca Film Festival.

Tunisia is trying to revive its documentary production. Doc in Tunis Festival was created four years ago and in 2009 screened films from 17 countries. Karim Souaki's first feature-length documentary, **Silence**, is a portrait of Jimmy, who has been diagnosed with HIV and who leads a daily struggle against discrimination, as he tries to create awareness about the disease in his neighbourhood. Faouzi Chelbi, who works for Tunisian Television, directed **Son of the Sun** (*Le Fils du Soleil*), in which Ahmed Kouissem, an elderly man who was condemned to death by the French colonial powers but escaped execution, recounts his story.

Tunisia's film production tends to revolve around its biennial film festival, the Journées Cinématographiques de Carthage, where local films await screenings. Since most films made their appearance in last year's festival, the scarcity of films this year comes as no surprise. However, recent years have seen an increase in the production of short films. This is due in part to the advent of digital production, which has helped democratise cinema and given inspiration to many young filmmakers, who are the key to the future of Tunisian cinema.

Among this year's shorts is Nadia Touijer's **Crossing** (*La Traversée*), the story of eight-year-old Amin, who lives in a working-class suburb on the hills of Tunis and travels to the city for a day, with unexpected results. In Mourad Ben Cheikh's **A Season between Heaven and Hell** (*Une Saison entre l'Enfer et le Paradis*), Ala, a drunken professor of Arabic literature, enters a delirious state in a bar and relives a poem written more than a thousand years ago. Malik Amara's **The Drowned Fish** (*Le Poisson Noyé*) recounts the fable of the successive resurrections of an old fishmonger in a Mediterranean village.

Although the industry has many weaknesses, its assets are noteworthy. It enjoys international recognition, with Tunisian films and filmmakers of worldwide repute. The country supports its cinema by grants and not by an advance of revenue. It also features favourable film legislation and tax incentives. In addition to this, its diverse geography could make it a hub for international productions. Nonetheless, these are no guarantees of an immediate change in the industry's circumstances.

In the 1960s, Tunisia had 100 cinemas. Today, less than 20 remain. It is yet to be seen whether the coming years will witness the rebirth of a national cinema.

The year's best films
Buried Secrets (Raja Amari)

Quote of the year
'I wanted to build a story around the path of a character that becomes aware of her femininity and of her identity; a journey of freedom and liberation.' RAJA AMARI, *director of* **Buried Secrets.**

MARYAM TOUZANI is a freelance journalist based in Morocco and working internationally, specialising in art and culture.

ABU DHABI FILM COMMISSION

Turkey Atilla Dorsay

It has been a good year again for Turkish cinema, both in terms of box office and critical acclaim, with films picking up awards at many international festivals. Cinema attendance increased from 31 million in 2008 to over 38 million. Of the 250 films screened, 50 were domestic releases. Nevertheless, they attracted 23 million people, again an increase of 50% on the previous year.

Mahsun Kirmizigül's **I Saw the Sun**

Cem Yilmaz's **A.R.O.G.**

The main attractions were comedies. Togan Gökbakar's **Recep Ivedik 2** attracted 4.5 million viewers, breaking previous attendance records. Once again, it featured the director's brother, popular comedian Sahan Gökbakar. **A.R.O.G.** (*Bir Yontma Tas Filmi*) was another sequel, to 2004's *G.O.R.A.*, starring the Turkish TV and media golden boy, Cem Yilmaz, who also wrote the screenplay and co-directed the film with Ali Taner Baltaci. More than three million people turned out for the film. The smaller **Alone** also performed well. The surprise box-office success, a low-key love story set in Istanbul, was directed by Cagan Irmak.

More sombre and serious political films were also transformed into box-office gold. The popular singer-composer Mahsun Kirmizigül's **I Saw the Sun** (*Günesi Gördüm*) called for

peace and mutual understanding as it tackled the ongoing Kurdish problem with a story that underlined the human elements of a tense political situation. Focusing on a family whose two sons have become political enemies, it has seen Kirmizigül, who is a Kurd, became regarded by some as the new Yilmaz Güney. It attracted an audience of 2.5 million and is the Turkish entry for the 2010 Academy Awards. Levent Semerci's debut, **Breath: This Above All** (*Nefes: Vatan Sagolsun*), was equally successful. It explored the military side of the Kurdish conflict, focusing on the events that took place in 1993 when a group of young soldiers were caught in a Kurdish trap and had to fight for their lives amongst the mountains of the country's eastern border. More of an anti-war statement than a piece of nationalistic

Levent Semerci's **Breath: This Above All**

or military propaganda, it focuses on the absurdities of conflict. It was still playing to large audiences as the year drew to a close.

Other successes were generally comedies, such as Zübeyir Sasmaz's gangster parody, **Muro**, and popular humourist Gani Müjde's **The Ottoman Republic** (*Osmanli Cumhuriyeti*), which asked what life would be like had Mustafa Kemal Atatürk not become leader and, following the disaster of the First World War, if the English and their allies had assumed control of the country.

Gani Müjde's **The Ottoman Republic**

A wide variety of films attracted very different audiences. The well-known journalist and television director Can Dündar made **Mustafa**, a docu-drama about Mustafa Kemal Atatürk, normally an untouchable subject for the majority of the Turks, with even a few realistic observations and criticisms attracting considerable ire. However, the film attracted more than one million spectators. Another veteran from television production, Tomris Giritlioglu, directed **Autumn Ache** (*Güz Sancisi*). Her film dealt with the dark period around 1955, when shops and apartments belonging to the Greek community in Istanbul's Pera district were attacked and plundered. The attacks were sparked by a false rumour that the house Mustafa Kemal was born in, in Thessaloniki, had been burned down. It was the first Turkish film to tackle this subject and, although it was not actually very good, Giritlioglu's courage was praised and it was quite popular with audiences (more in Turkey than Greece).

Documentary filmmaker Tolga Örnek's first feature, **Cars of the Revolution** (*Devrim Arabalari*), was also popular with audiences and critics. It focused on the period of the Turkish industrial revolution in the 1960s when, thanks to the passion of a group of engineers, the country first began to produce cars.

Atalay Tasdiken's directorial debut, **Mommo, My Sister** (*Mommo*), was about a pair of siblings experiencing the sadness of a broken family, while documentary filmmaker Pelin Esmer's feature **10 To 11** (*11'e 10 Kala*) explored the relationship between an old collector and his doorman. Both films smacked of naïvete, but nevertheless collected prizes at local and international festivals. Two other debuts, Selim Evci's **Two Lines** (*Iki Cizgi*), an Antonioni-like chronicle of a couple solving their marital problems during a car trip to the Aegean coast, and Mahmut Fazil Coskun's **Wrong Rosary** (*Uzak İhtimal*), about a Muslim man and Catholic woman who has ambitions to be a nun, were far more interesting.

Selim Evci's **Two Lines**

Murat Saracoglu's second film, **The Piano Girl** (*Deli Deli Olma*), was about the fractious relationship between two elderly people belonging to a Russian tribe that immigrated to Turkey a century ago. It reunited the actors who played the couple in Yilmaz Güney's *Yol*, Tarik Akan and Serif Sezer.

A number of prestigious directors also produced work. Zeki Demirkubuz's **Envy** (*Kiskanmak*) was adapted from a classic novel of tortured love that unfolds in a remote region of Anatolia in the

Reha Erdem's **My Only Sunshine**

1930s. Demirkubuz's first period piece, featuring many of his personal touches, was criticised by some for betraying its source. Reha Erdem's **My Only Sunshine** (*Hayat Var*), the chronicle of a 14-year-old girl and her experiences along the Bosphorus, was an exceptional piece of cinema, with its emphasis on character complemented by extraordinary editing and sound design, creating a remarkable example of cinematic poetry. His new film, **Cosmos**, which won an award at the Antalya National Film Festival and is scheduled for release next year, is likely to surprise even more.

Among other films worthy of interest, there was Ümit Ünal's peculiar **The Shadowless** (*Gölgesizler*), a literary adaptation that blurred the lines between reality and fiction. Aslı Özge's **Men on the Bridge** (*Köprüdekiler*) is a kind of semi-documentary that sees a group of actors interact amongst real people on a bridge across the Bosphorus. Orhan Eskiköy and Özgür Dogan's **On the Way to School** (*İki Dil, Bir Bavul*) is about a young teacher in a small village primary school trying to teach Kurdish children who don't speak one word of Turkish, while he has no knowledge of Kurdish. It perfectly suited the political mood, at a time when the country's government was attempting to put an end to conflict and resentment amongst ethnic groups.

Documentaries also had a good year. A new festival, 1001 Documentaries, began in Istanbul and achieved great success. And some local efforts have been commercially released with reasonable results. In addition to Dündar and Esmer's films, there was Nesli

Cölgecen's **The Last Meeting** and Handan Öztürk's **Mine and Roza's Autumn**.

The year's best films
My Only Sunshine (Reha Erdem)
Breath: This Above All (Levent Semerci)
Cars of the Revolution (Tolga Örnek)
Wrong Rosary (Mahmut Fazil Coskun)
I Saw the Sun (Mahsun Kirmizigül)

Quote of the year
'Albert Camus said: "A man is human not with what he says, but with what he hides." When we were writing our film, that has been our "tagline". And instead of a series of dialogues as in every Turkish film, we used the silence.'
MAHMUT FAZIL COSKUN, *writer-director of* **Wrong Rosary**.

Directory
All Tel/Fax numbers begin (+90)
CASOD (The Association of Actors), Istiklal Caddesi, Atlas Sinemasi Pasaj- C Blok 53/3 - Beyoglu/ Istanbul. Tel: 212 251 97 75. Fax : 212 251 97 79. casod@casod.org.
FILM-YÖN (The Association of Directors), Ayhan Isik Sokak, 28/1- Beyoglu/ Istanbul. Tel: 212 293 90 01.
IKSV- Istanbul Kültür ve Sanat Vakfi (The Istanbul Culture and Arts Foundation), Sadi Konuralp Caddesi No 5/ Deniz Palas, Evliya Çelebi Mahallesi- 34433, Sishane/ Istanbul. Tel: 212 334 07 00. Fax: 212 334 07 02. film.fest@istfest.org.
SIYAD- Sinema Yazarları Dernegi (The Association of Film Critics), Erol Dernek Sokak No 7/1-A, Beyoglu 80600/ Istanbul. Tel: 212 251 56 47. Fax: 212 251 63 27. denizyavuz@superonline.com.
TÜRSAK (The Turkish Cinema and Audiovisual Culture Foundation), Gazeteci Erol Dernek Sokak, 11/2 Hanif Han- Beyoglu/ Istanbul. Tel: 212 244 52 51. Fax 212 251 67 70. tursak@superonline.com.

ATILLA DORSAY has been a film critic since 1966 and has published over 30 books, including biographies of Yilmaz Güney and Türkan Soray. Founder and honorary president of SIYAD-Association of the Turkish critics, he is also one of the founders and consultants of the Istanbul Film Festival.

Ukraine Volodymyr Voytenko

The Ukrainian film industry has suffered badly under the burden of the global economic crisis. Accordingly, one can see the diminishment of the state funding of national cinema. In the place of the 2008 budget of approximately US$6.25 million of state financing, the last year saw a mere US$625,000 reaching the film industry's coffers. As a result, the weight placed on independent film projects has grown and there is currently a situation that prompts the question: how possible is it to consider the development of national cinema compared to previous years?

There is a certain irony in the fact that an industry coping with little state financing sports a number of features that are directly linked to statesmen. Oleksandr Kyrienko's 2008 production, *Illusion of Fear*, based on the book by Oleksandr Turchynov, Vice-Prime Minister of Ukraine, was nominated for a Best Foreign Language Film Oscar. It was an unconvincing attempt to reflect on the social psychology of the Ukraine's 'wild capitalism'. And Valeriy Yamburskiy's feature debut, **The Day of the Defeated** (*Den' peremozhenykh*), was based on a book about the public's ambivalent attitude to its totalitarian past, written by Volodymyr Yavorivskiy, the Deputy of the Parliament majority.

A divergence in public attitudes on politics, which Ukrainian politicians have taken advantage of, particularly the populace's not having built upon the achievements of the Orange Revolution of 2004, are to inform the new work by graphic artist Ihor Podol'chak. He has almost completed the hallucinatory **Delirium**, which depicts either the private history of a psychiatrist's madness or perhaps one that is being experienced by the entire world.

A Mysterious Island (*Tainstvenniy ostrov*) by Volodymyr Tykhiy, which develops as a pseudo-thriller about an ominous island where a businessman's wife disappears, was another Ukrainian film about an individual's psyche within a collective 'darkness'. Tykhiy was also the producer and one of the directors of the low-budget omnibus, **F***kers. Arabesques** (*Mudaky. Arabesky*), a biting satire on Ukrainians' 'mental defects', which hamper their civilised development.

Vira Yakovenko's **Contract**, which revolts against the conventions of television's melodramatic aesthetics, gained resonance through its story of the murder of a provincial journalist fighting against corruption in Eastern Ukraine at the beginning of the decade. The problem of the spread of AIDS was the theme of the short film **Diagnosis** (*Diahnoz*) by Myroslav Slaboshpytskiy, which participated in Competition at the 2009 Berlinale. Roman Bondarchuk's short, **Taxi-Driver** (*Taksyst*), was poetic in its presentation of life in the lower depths of southern Ukraine. While Maryna Vroda, currently preparing her feature debut, directed **Family Portrait** (*Simeyniy portret*),

Maryna Vroda's **Family Portrait**

a short psychological drama. And first-time documentary filmmaker Maksym Vasyanovych presented his profound and powerful philosophical film **Mommy Died on Saturday in the Kitchen...** (*Mama pomerla v subotu na kukhni...*).

Roman Shyrman's **An Awesome Tale**

Feature debuts **An Awesome Tale** (*Prykolna kazka*) by Roman Shyrman and **Once I Will Not Sleep** (*Odnoho razu ya prokynus*) by Maryna Kondrat'yeva offered audiences inventive fantasies. And for audiences interested in animation, there was **Niki Tanner** (*Nikita Kozhemyaka*) by Misha Kostrov and Serhiy Havrylov, and the adaptation of Jaroslav Hašek's tale of stolen dogs, **The Good Soldier Schweik** (*Pryhody bravoho voyaka Shveyka*), directed by Rinat Gazizov and Manuk Depoyan.

Ukrainian co-productions were actively and successfully continued by producer Oleh Kokhan. The recent success of his company, Sota Cinema Group, which worked on Shirin Neshat's Venice prize winner, **Women Without Men** (*Zanan-e bedun-e mardan*), shows that there is a modicum of hope for 2010.

The year's best films
Mommy Died on Saturday in the Kitchen...
(Maksym Vasyanovych)
Taxi-Driver (Roman Bondarchuk)
Family Portrait (Maryna Vroda)
*F**kers. Arabesques* (Volodymyr Tykhiy)

Quote of the year
'As far as I know modern cinema, there is such a trend: modern cinema moves towards modern art and modern art moves towards modern cinema. And it seems to me, I am in the trend.' IHOR PODOL'CHAK, *the director of* Las Meninas *and* Delirium.

Directory
All Tel/Fax numbers begin (+380)
National Oleksandr Dovzhenko Center (State Film Archives), 1 Vasylkivska St, Kyiv 03040. Tel: 257 7698. Fax: 201 6547.
Central State Archives of Film, Photo & Sound Documents, 24 Solomyanska St, Kyiv 03601. Tel: 275 3777. Fax: 275 3655. tsdkffa@archives.gov.ua.
Institute of Screen Art, Kyiv National University of Theatre, Cinema and Television, 40 Yaroslaviv Val St, Kyiv 01034. Tel: 272 1032. Fax: 272 0220. info@knutkt.kiev.ua. http://knutkt.kiev.ua.
Ukrainian Cinema Foundation, 6 Saksahansky St, Kyiv 01033. Tel/Fax: 287 6618. info@ucf.org.ua. www.ucf.org.ua.
Ministry of Culture and Tourism of Ukraine, State Cinema Service, 19 Ivan Franko St, Kyiv 01601. Tel/Fax: 234 4094, 234 6951. ros@mincult. gov.ua. http://dergkino.gov.ua/.
Kyiv International Film Festival Molodist, 6 Saksahansky St, Kyiv 01033. Tel/Fax: 461 9803. info@molodist.com. www.molodist.com.
Krok International Animated Film Festival, Suite 208, 6, Saksagansky St, Kyiv 01033. Tel/Fax: 287 52 80. krokfestival@gmail.com. www.krokfestival.com.

VOLODYMYR VOYTENKO is a film critic, editor-in-chief of Internet portal www.kinokolo. ua presenter of the weekly programme about art cinema at the national TV channel 1+1.

Maksym Vasyanovych's **Mommy Died on Saturday in the Kitchen...**

United Kingdom Jason Wood

I n an economically precarious climate, cinema continues to be defined by the prominence of digital technology and the potential democratisation of the filmmaking process. The UK is a market saturated with films and distributors fighting to release them, with the demand on screen space remaining paramount. So, in an effort to ensure that their films can actually be seen, distributors and producers have begun to engage in a direct dialogue with the consumer, an environment in which cinemas may play only a cameo role.

R.J. Cutler's **The September Issue**

The independent sector has long since acknowledged that in certain cases there is little to be gained from demanding that the traditional theatrical window be adhered to. This less militant approach has led to an impressive diversity of films to be found in UK cinemas (one of the peculiar was Lucky Akhurt's **Morris: A Life with Bells On**), and some significant financial successes (R.J. Cutler's **The September Issue**, which became a genuine box-office phenomenon despite appearing on DVD just seven days after its theatrical release). It has also led to a re-thinking of the ways in which films are actually shown. Single screenings, frequently accompanied by live or even satellite Q&As have proved popular

and in many cases strengthened the notion of cinemagoing as a communal activity. Should the screenings meet with unexpected demand, another benefit of the UK's advanced digital capabilities (the UK has more digital screens than any other European country – 310 and counting) means that surplus screenings can easily be facilitated.

Specialising in issue-related documentaries, Dogwoof have reaped particular dividends by releasing their films in this fashion, with Franny Armstrong's climate change despatch, **The Age of Stupid**, grossing almost €200,000. More innovative still in its strategy of seeking to connect with a potential audience, whilst also

Through our Prints
and Advertising fund
we support the distribution
of foreign language and
independent films and
documentaries

Giving more choice to
UK cinema audiences

UK FILM | COUNCIL
LOTTERY FUNDED

www.ukfilmcouncil.org.uk

Franny Armstrong's **The Age of Stupid**

remaining acutely aware of its radical properties, Sally Potter's **Rage**, a starry, talking-head
snapshot of the fashion industry, appeared in
cinemas whilst also becoming the first feature
to premiere on iPhones and iPod devices, via
a collaboration with Babelgum, the independent Web and mobile content platform. What
audiences actually expect to see in cinemas
has certainly mutated, with alternative content,
including live and recorded opera and theatre
productions, becoming increasingly popular.

Sally Potter's **Rage**

With the parlous economic state and many
scheduled Hollywood productions set to film
in the UK suffering cancellations and delay,
it is clear that government aid is going to be
essential to both the survival and development
of British cinema, specialised or otherwise.
The introduction of a new Digital Economy Bill,
placing a statutory commitment on Channel 4 to
invest in film, brought welcome relief, especially
in the wake of the closure of the distribution
arm of Pathé. Ironically, this was announced in
the immediate aftermath of Pathé's release of
Slumdog Millionaire. Confirming Danny Boyle's
reputation as one of Britain's most versatile

directors, the film triumphed at the Academy
Awards and the BAFTAs, going on to gross €30
million in the UK alone.

Perhaps the most newsworthy item of 2009,
and one which set alarm bells ringing, was
the recent announcement that the UK Film
Council (UKFC) and the British Film Institute
(BFI) were to be merged into a single flagship
body to support film and benefit both the film-
going public and the industry. The proposed
merger, the exact details of which are still to
be finalised at the time of writing, has been
proposed with the intent of establishing better-
coordinated public support for film, with more
of the available funding channelled directly to
frontline services through an organisation with
both a cultural and economic remit. The merger
has also been described as an attempt to
reduce gaps and overlaps. With both UK Film
Council Chairman Tim Bevan and Greg Dyke,
Chair of the BFI, presenting a united front,
UK Film Minister Siôn Simon commented in a
press statement that 'Film in Britain is highly
valued, both for its tremendous contribution
to our cultural life and its economic success.
Thanks to the work of the UK Film Council,
as an industry it contributes €4.3 billion to our
economy [up by 44% since 2000, when the
UK Film Council was created], with British
films taking 15% of the global box office last
year. And buoyant attendances show that after

Greg Dyke © Paul Archer

more than a century, cinema is still seen as a great night out'. With regards to the proposed merger, Simon added, 'A new, streamlined, single body that represents the whole of the film sector will offer a better service both for filmmakers and film lovers. There are practical issues which we need to resolve to ensure that this proposed merger brings about the benefits we want without impacting on the work currently done by the BFI and UKFC. DCMS [The Department for Culture, Media and Sport] will now work closely with both the BFI and the UKFC to deliver a better service for film.'

The repercussions of the merger have still to be realised, particularly with regards to how the British Film Institute will be affected. However, what has already become clear is that, as lottery funds are being siphoned off from the cultural and arts arena to pay for the cost of hosting the 2012 Olympics, there will be a significant downsizing of the UKFC's production and development fund. This comes with the announcement of the loss of 22 UKFC jobs, but also with the production of a consultation document entitled, 'UK Film: Digital innovation and creative excellence', which outlines new funding priorities from April 2010 to March 2013. This new €15 million film production fund is focused on the pursuit of creative excellence and puts more emphasis on first- and second-time filmmakers. Other significant highlights of the new UKFC initiatives include:

- A producer equity position in all UK Film Council-funded feature films.
- A minimum 25% target for non-London-originated film production.
- A new €5 million Innovation Fund, to promote new business models and ensure UK film's successful transition into a fully digital age.
- Sustained investment in the BFI, to support the conservation of UK film heritage and improve access to film culture.
- A renewed emphasis on attracting inward investment to the UK film sector and underlining the continued importance of the Film Tax Relief.

- Prioritising skills training for new technologies and post-production.
- Additional funding to support the industry in combating film theft.
- Continued support for film distribution and audience-focused initiatives.
- An ongoing commitment to achieving a more diverse and inclusive workforce and film culture.

This emphasis on a commitment to sustaining and nurturing first- and second-time filmmakers comes as particularly welcome news in the light of a growing diaspora of British directors, including Ben Hopkins and Thomas Clay (whose **Soi Cowboy** offered an improvement on his flawed but fascinating *The Great Ecstasy of Robert Carmichael*), forced to work under foreign flags. Relocating to the Pyrenees after labouring for almost ten years to make the film in Britain, Andrew Kötting's remarkable **Ivul**, a visceral, innovative and ultimately moving tale of a family feud is set for release in 2010. But perhaps the greatest sense of triumph over adversity came with Peter Strickland's

Andrew Kötting's **Ivul**

Peter Strickland's **Katalin Varga**

Berlin prize-winning **Katalin Varga**. Made with inheritance money in Hungary and Romania after Strickland had been turned down by just about everybody in the UK, the film, set in the Carpathian mountains, is a harrowing yet beautifully rendered tale of redemption informed by the debutant director's love of *Night of the Hunter* and Paradjanov's *Shadows of Our Forgotten Ancestors*.

Gideon Koppel's **Sleep Furiously**

These filmmakers are also evocative of a continuing purple patch in British arthouse cinema. Having accrued festival acclaim for their *Civic Life* television series, Joe Lawlor and Christine Molloy completed a successful segue into features with the visually and sonically mesmerising **Helen**. A tale of emotional transference that intelligently utilises a non-professional cast, the film's low-budget origins were in marked contrast to its high-end production values. A poetic and profound journey into a world of endings and beginnings, Gideon Koppel's similarly beguiling **Sleep Furiously** was undoubtedly one of the year's standout films. Set in a small farming community in mid-Wales, which

provided a home for Koppel's refugee parents, the film resists any traditional documentary-style structure, instead presenting an impressionistic observation on a changing way of life. And the Aphex Twin soundtrack proved to be a perfect accompaniment. Though generally less rapturously received, Duane Hopkins' gritty urban drama, **Better Things**, suggested that the promise of the director's shorts would one day be fully realised.

Duane Hopkins' **Better Things**

Though Andrea Arnold has just two features to her name, she already feels like an industry veteran. Picking up another Cannes Grand Jury Prize, **Fish Tank** placed the famously uncompromising Arnold at the vanguard of contemporary British filmmakers. An intense story of love, lust and family, this poignant and authentic portrait of contemporary London life through the eyes of a 15 year-old outcast features at its core a phenomenal turn from teenager Katie Jarvis, who was discovered whilst in the midst of a furious argument with her boyfriend at an East London underground

Andrea Arnold's **Fish Tank**

station. As the surrogate father figure/lover who comes into her life, Michael Fassbender cements his position as one of the UK's most versatile actors. In a not dissimilar vein to *Fish Tank*, though a little rougher around the edges, Edinburgh Film Festival favourite **Kicks** augurs well for the future of director Lindy Heymann and fledgling stars Nichola Burley and Kerrie Hayes. Although the film flounders a little under the weight of a script that in its latter stages errs too closely to convention, there is still much to admire.

Duncan Jones' **Moon**

There were also notable, albeit strikingly disparate, debuts from Duncan Jones and Eran Creevy. Jones found critical and commercial success with the low-key sci-fi drama, **Moon**. Paradoxically, this beautifully rendered tale of a lonely astronaut yearning to return home from a three-year work contract harvesting energy for the earth, which synthesises some of the more cerebral entries of the genre (*Dark Star*, *Silent Running* and *2001*), managed to be refreshingly original. Based on Creevy's own teenage experiences and funded by the innovative, low-budget Microwave scheme, **Shifty** employed humour and candour to engage with pressing contemporary social issues, perhaps most pertinently hard drugs and the temptations offered by a life of crime. Microwave is currently working with an incredible roster of young talent and their next projects are awaited with anticipation.

Though experienced in other fields and disciplines, notable first features also emerged from Turner Prize-winning artist Sam Taylor

Wood, fashion guru Tom Ford, and leading satirist and creator of TV's *The Thick of It*, Armando Iannucci. Resisting the austerity of fellow artist Steve McQueen's *Hunger*, Taylor Wood's **Nowhere Boy** presents an intriguing look at a 15 year-old John Lennon (newcomer Aaron Johnson). Though largely conventional in form, the film, scripted by *Control*'s Matt Greenhaigh, wisely resists a whistle-stop tour of Beatles iconography, instead observing Lennon's troubled family life and complex relationship with the two key women in his life: the domineering Aunt Mimi (Kristin Scott Thomas), and his flighty mother (Anne-Marie Duff). With another musical biopic, Mat Whitecross takes an entirely different tack in **Sex & Drugs & Rock and Roll**, bolting on an over-zealous visual style to a fine lead performance from Andy Serkis in the account of The Blockheads' frontman Ian Dury's life.

Taylor Wood's **Nowhere Boy**

Tom Ford's **A Single Man**, a sumptuous adaptation of Christopher Isherwood's novel, in which a college professor mourns the recent death of his gay lover, has been described as

Armando Iannucci's **In the Loop**

Mad Men by way of *Far From Heaven*. With Colin Firth and Julianne Moore on fine form, this is a deftly acted and intelligent drama about status and grief. Impeccably designed – to within an inch of its life in fact – it feels somewhat churlish to mention the nagging sense of emotional vacuity that an initial viewing of the film invoked. Seemingly created to justify the existence of the phrase 'razor-sharp political comedy', Armando Iannucci's **In The Loop** re-locates potty-mouthed political strategist Malcolm Tucker to Washington where an inexperienced Secretary of State for International Development (Tom Hollander) is winning friends by advocating war. Frequently hilarious and extremely dexterous in its invention of new ways to both use four-letter words and reveal the Machiavellian nature of politics, Iannucci's film also acts as a very tasty appetiser for Chris Morris's forthcoming terrorist satire, **Four Lions**. His film emerges from the increasingly significant Warp stable, whose recent productions include Shane

Tom Hooper's **The Damned United**

Meadows' shot on-the-hoof **Le Donk and Scor-say-see** and the Mighty Boosh movie that wasn't, Paul King's *Withnail and I*-inspired **Bunny and the Bull**.

From a clutch of upmarket, middlebrow UK-financed projects dealing with real-life figures (a select roll call of which includes **Creation**, **The Young Victoria**, and **Me & Orson Welles**) Tom Hooper's **The Damned United** and Jane Campion's **Bright Star** stood out. An adaptation of David Peace's fictional account of Brian Clough's doomed 44-day tenure as the manager of Leeds United, *The Damned United* softened the portrait of Clough, yet still failed to appease Clough's surviving family. A pity, for this darkly humorous tale – for which no appetite for football is required – captures a brilliant and conflicted character who may well be the most charismatic sporting figure of modern times. Needless to say, Michael Sheen excels in the central role. A UK/Australian co-production directed by the New Zealand-born auteur, Campion's *Bright Star* is a ravishing period drama based on the three-year romance between nineteenth-century poet John Keats (Ben Whishaw) and Fanny Brawne (Abbie Cornish), which was cut tragically short by Keats' untimely death aged just 25. Incredibly sensuous and sensual, the film ranks amongst the highest achievements of Campion's estimable career.

Jane Campion's **Bright Star**

Equally accomplished, if for different reasons, Lone Scherfig's tilt at journalist Lynn Barber's account of coming to age under the wing of an urbane and cultured suitor found a sympathetic

...

Lone Scherfig's **An Education**

translator in novelist-turned-screenwriter Nick Hornby. A work rich in period detail without being suffocated by it, **An Education** also marked the breakthrough performance of Carey Mulligan. Another director who found favour working on British shores was Danish auteur Nicolas Winding Refn whose **Bronson** offered a nihilistic, stylistically intrepid depiction of the inner psychology of serial British prison lifer Michael Peterson, a.k.a. Charlie Bronson (an unrecognisable Tom Hardy).

Terry Gilliam's **The Imaginarium of Doctor Parnassus**

It proved a mixed year for veteran directors. Reuniting the *Dangerous Liaisons* dream team of Stephen Frears, writer Christopher Hampton and Michelle Pfeiffer, **Chéri** largely failed to recapture that earlier film's magic. A handsomely mounted adaptation of Colette's novel about an ageing courtesan who falls in love with a younger man, the film entertained but never truly sparkled. Similar sentiments could be expressed about Terry Gilliam's characteristically ambitious and visually audacious **The Imaginarium of Doctor**

Parnassus. Though dramatically flawed, it should be applauded for overcoming with aplomb and sensitivity the premature death of Heath Ledger during its production.

Undoubtedly the biggest non-event in the UK film calendar proved to be Richard Curtis's **The Boat That Rocked**. A critical and commercial disaster, the 60s pirate-radio comedy proved that no amount of marketing can mask a lacklustre script and poor direction.

Ken Loach's **Looking For Eric**

With Mike Leigh's next project not scheduled for release until late 2010 (the last of Leigh's works to be produced by Simon Channing Williams, who also tragically died in 2009), it was left to Ken Loach to carry the baton. Infused with Loach and regular writing collaborator Paul Laverty's trademark humanism, humour and compassion, **Looking For Eric** also signalled the most unlikely collaboration of the year, through the spirited involvement of former Manchester United legend Eric Cantona. The tale of a Manchester postman (Steve Evets) whose midlife crisis is narrowly averted following a few philosophical aphorisms from a very special life coach, this engaging and surprisingly accessible work gave Loach his biggest box-office hit since *Kes*.

JASON WOOD is a film programmer and contributor to *Sight and Sound* and *The Guardian*. He has also published several books on cinema.

The year's best films

Sleep Furiously (Gideon Koppel)
Helen (Joe Lawlor and Christine Molloy)
Katalin Varga (Peter Strickland)
Fish Tank (Andrea Arnold)
Ivul (Andrew Kötting)

Quote of the year

'I'd been making a nuisance of myself throughout the 90s, but nobody paid much attention.
There were some great times to be had doing
home movies on Super 8 and various projects
with a small group of friends, but I was limited in
terms of what I was able to achieve. Some ideas
just need money, so when you find yourself with
an inheritance from a close relative, you know
you'll kick yourself forever if you do something
sensible like put a deposit on a house.' Katalin
Varga *director* PETER STRICKLAND.

Directory

All Tel/Fax numbers begin (+44)

**British Academy of Film & Television Arts
(BAFTA)**, 195 Piccadilly, London, W1J 9LN.
Tel: (20) 7734 0022. Fax: (20) 7734 1792.
www.bafta.org.

British Actors Equity Association, Guild House,
Upper St Martins Lane, London, WC2H 9EG.
Tel: (20) 7379 6000. Fax: (20) 7379 7001.
info@equity.org.uk. www.equity.org.uk.

British Board of Film Classification (BBFC),
3 Soho Square, London W1D 3HD.
Tel: (20) 7440 1570. Fax: (20) 7287 0141.
webmaster@bbfc.co.uk. www.bbfc.co.uk.

British Film Institute, 21 Stephen St, London,
W1T 1LN. Tel: (20) 7255 1444. Fax: (20) 7436 7950.

sales.films@bfi.org.uk. www.bfi.org.uk.
Directors Guild of Great Britain (DGGB), Acorn
House, 314-320 Grays Inn Rd, London, WC1X 8DP.
Tel: (20) 7278 4343. Fax: (20) 7278 4742.
guild@dggb.org. www.dggb.org.
National Film & Television Archive, British Film
Institute, 21 Stephen St, London W1P 1LN.
Tel: (20) 7255 1444. Fax: (20) 7436 0439.
Scottish Screen Archive, 1 Bowmont Gardens,
Glasgow G12 9LR. Tel: (141) 337 7400.
Fax: (20) 337 7413. archive@scottishscreen.com.
www.scottishscreen.com.
Scottish Screen, 249 West George St,
2nd Floor, Glasgow, G2 4QE. Tel: (141) 302 1700.
Fax: (20) 302 1711. info@scottishscreen.com.
www.scottishscreen.com.
UK Film Council, 10 Little Portland St, London,
W1W 7JG. Tel: (20) 7861 7861. Fax: (20) 7861
7862. info@ukfilmcouncil.org.uk.
www.ukfilmcouncil.org.uk.
UK Film Council International, 10 Little Portland
St, London, W1W 7JG. Tel: (20) 7861 7860. Fax:
(20) 7861 7864. internationalinfo@ukfilmcouncil.
org.uk. www.ukfilmcouncil.org.uk.

لجنة أبوظبي للأفلام
ABU DHABI FILM COMMISSION

United States Tom Charity

'Just relax and let your mind go blank…' That's the instruction Jake Sully (Sam Worthington) hears as he settles into his groove in James Cameron's 3D blockbuster **Avatar**, possibly the most expensive film ever made (The *New York Times* put the budget at US$500 million, though more sober sources settled for about half that figure).

More on Cameron's long-awaited end-of-decade opus anon, but the same advice would well serve anyone confronted with 90 percent of the output from American filmmakers over the last year.

Perhaps the most significant film of 2009 was one that didn't get made. In June, Sony Pictures pulled the plug on Steven Soderbergh's **Moneyball** just three days before the US$50 million production was due to start shooting, leaving the director and star Brad Pitt hanging, and in effect writing off US$10 million the studio had already invested in the project.

Whatever the rights and wrongs behind this fiasco (studio boss Amy Pascal balked after reading Soderbergh's rewrite of Steve Zaillian's screenplay), such a drastic about-face is indicative of the tectonic shifts rippling through Hollywood as it struggles to adjust to new market realities.

Among the criteria Pascal must have considered: *Moneyball* was a story about

Major League Baseball, a sport of little inherent interest to most film territories around the world; Soderbergh's unimpressive box-office record since the twin triumphs of *Traffic* and *Erin Brockovich* in 2000, *Ocean's Eleven*, *Twelve* and *Thirteen* excepted (2008's diptych *Che* being the latest commercial misfire); declining ancillary revenues from the shrinking DVD market and the reluctance of consumers to upgrade to Blu-Ray in these recessionary times.

Above all, there is that hefty US$50 million price tag, at the cheaper end of the scale for an A-list studio picture these days, but a figure that does not cover the expensive business of releasing and marketing the film. Pascal only had to look at the box-office numbers for three of the five best picture nominees from 2008: *Milk*, *Frost/Nixon* and *The Reader* all struggled to recoup costs in North America. Brad Pitt's *The Curious Case of Benjamin Button* made twice as much as those three put together, but it cost considerably more.

These returns were put to shame by the small UK production *Slumdog Millionaire*, which cost just US$15 million to make and grossed US$141 million in North America, and US$236 million elsewhere.

Steven Soderbergh's **The Girlfriend Experience**

Soderbergh, more than most, seems open to finding other ways of making American films. In the can before *Moneyball* imploded, he had one low-budget digital film, **The Girlfriend Experience**, with porn star Sasha Grey as a

Manhattan escort, and a studio picture, **The Informant!**, with Matt Damon as a real-life corporate whistle-blower.

The latter was actually the more playful and experimental of the two, a dizzily unpredictable comedy masquerading as a social conscience thriller that audiences and critics didn't know what to make of (the North American gross was US$33 million). Of course, Soderbergh's eclecticism and adventurousness make him unreliable in some eyes, and may have counted against him as Amy Pascal weighed her options.

Matt Damon in **The Informant!**

Put simply, the middle has dropped out of the Hollywood industrial model. Studios remain confident in the profitability of staple lower budget genre fare – teen comedies, horror films, action thrillers – and continue to bank heavily on big-budget blockbuster 'tentpoles' (more expensive than ever now that CGI and 3D are primary selling points), but mid-priced middle-brow dramas aren't a good fit for today's default business plan, which involves a fast-and-wide release supported by saturation TV advertising.

None of this is new, but the studios' rush to get out of 'indiewood', eliminating or cutting back subdivisions like Paramount Vantage and Warner Independent in a year that looked likely to post a record-breaking, billion-dollar box-office tally tells its own story.

The once proud Miramax brand (a subdivision of Disney) was summarily slashed, with mass redundancies, the loss of president Daniel

Greg Mottola's **Adventureland**

Battsek and projections of a much-reduced slate of just three films a year. Battsek's 2009 output included Greg Mottola's superior teen comedy **Adventureland** (a minor success), Mike Judge's patchy satire **Extract**, and the well-crafted but fatally bland tearjerkers **The Boys are Back** (with Clive Owen as a laissez-faire single dad) and **Everybody's Fine** (Robert De Niro in a remake of Giuseppe Tornatore's Marcello Mastroianni vehicle). None found a wide audience. As Disney acknowledged, Battsek had brought much prestige to the company, but the bottom line was the bottom line.

The times were equally tough for the Weinstein Company, led by Miramax founders Harvey and Bob Weinstein and fighting off rumours of impending insolvency for most of the year. The one bright spot for the Weinsteins came from Quentin Tarantino's long-awaited World War Two film, **Inglourious Basterds**, which garnered strong reviews and, more importantly, restored his box-office lustre after the disastrous *Grindhouse*.

Quentin Tarantino's **Inglourious Basterds**

In the director's outrageous revisionist revenge fantasy, not only do the Jews resist Hitler – in the form of a crack US guerrilla unit operating behind enemy lines and outside official jurisdiction – but they terrorise the German army with the bloodcurdling ferocity of their reprisals. Led by Brad Pitt's Lt Aldo Raine, this Dirty Dozen redux turns out to be the sketchiest component in an elaborate design dominated by Christoph Waltz's arch villain, Colonel Hans Landa. The long, long, first sequence – or 'chapter', as Tarantino terms it – is essentially a 20-minute two-hander between Landa and a French farmer (played by Denis Menochet), where the SS man most graciously presumes on his host's wary hospitality, flattering him and his family, even complimenting his milk… The man is a tease, but a deadly one. With every perfectly enunciated phrase he turns the screws tighter and tighter, up to the point where the poor farmer is ready to tell him everything. It's a brilliant scene, bleakly comic and horribly suspenseful, and as bold in its way as anything Tarantino has done before. (Who starts an adventure film with 30 pages of dialogue?) Before it is over we have developed a powerful antipathy towards this brilliant, vicious fellow, Landa; it is clear that, like so many of the most memorable screen villains, he is a man we will love to hate.

Nine

How far the film's US$120 million North American gross will stretch only time will tell. For the Weinsteins, much is riding on the company's big-budget, all-star musical, **Nine**, a Broadway riff on Fellini's *8 1/2* which pundits are

Joel Coen's **A Serious Man**

On the surface, *A Serious Man* seems to be a modest venture – it doesn't feature any stars and it appears to be a relatively banal story about a physics professor, Larry (Michael Stuhlbarg), barely coping with the news that his wife is leaving him just as a work promotion hangs in the balance. Yet from these domestic tribulations the Coens have fashioned a film that is, on the one hand, a probing examination of mortality, faith, and guilt, and, on the other, a bitingly acidic black comedy about middle-American Jewish mores in the late 1960s. 'Why is this happening to me?' the beleaguered Larry keeps asking. 'I haven't *done* anything.' Yet it's this sin of omission that will precipitate his downfall, and maybe – if we can take a hint from the bracingly doom-laden ending – our own. At the time of writing, after ten weeks on release, *A Serious Man* had North American receipts totalling US$8.5 million.

Kathryn Bigelow's highly acclaimed Iraq war movie, **The Hurt Locker**, also bottomed at around $13 million, despite the most

Katherine Bigelow's **The Hurt Locker**

enthusiastic reviews of the year. Intensely suspenseful but also authentically harrowing, the film avoided direct political commentary, but left audiences to draw their own conclusions from the death-wish bravado of protagonist William James (Jeremy Renner), a bomb-disposal expert who is only happy when he's dicing with imminent extinction.

As often happens, one of the year's biggest box-office hits failed to earn critical respect. Michael Bay's US$250 million sequel, **Transformers: Revenge of the Fallen**, was far and away the summer's biggest blockbuster (with worldwide grosses in the region of US$833 million), but this inane exercise in demolition overdrive rated a mere 19 percent 'fresh' on the critical aggregator site Rotten Tomatoes, putting it among the worst-reviewed films of the year. Quite right, too. This idiotic monstrosity was a sexist, homophobic, xenophobic, militaristic and mind-numbingly overblown commercial pitching war-toys for boys.

The Twilight Saga: New Moon

Much better, but hardly Oscar-bait, **Harry Potter and the Half-Blood Prince** was another confident entry in J.K. Rowling's saga – a commercial dead cert that Warner Bros will be sorry to see the end of. (The last novel has been pragmatically split into two films.) Meanwhile, Paramount owed heaps of gratitude to J.J. Abrams, the smart operator behind the TV hit *Lost* and handi-cam horror *Cloverdale*, who single-handedly revitalised an all-but-moribund franchise with his cheeky, time-travelling prequel, **Star Trek**. Would that other sequels and remakes – among them **Terminator: Salvation, X-Men Origins: Wolverine** and **The Twilight Saga: New Moon** – had anything like the same affectionate intuition for what makes pop culture pop. (As a side note, it seems that numbering sequels is out of fashion – presumably because there are so many of them now.)

Nora Ephron's **Julie and Julia**

Historically speaking, 2009 was a banner year for female filmmakers. Why this should be is hard to explain, unless it was an unexpected side effect of the prominence of Hilary Clinton and Sarah Palin in the presidential campaign of the previous year. In addition to Kathryn Bigelow's taut thriller, Jane Campion's fulsomely romantic **Bright Star** was heralded as a return to form and looked like an important stepping-stone for Australian actress Abbie Cornish. Nora Ephron had her biggest success since *Sleepless in Seattle* with **Julie and Julia**, with a lovely, plummy performance from Meryl Streep as the doyenne of French cooking, Julia Child. Streep's co-star in that film, Amy Adams, also had a minor hit opposite rising star Emily Blunt in Christine Jeffs' **Sunshine Cleaning**.

Robin Wright Penn shone in Rebecca Miller's **The Private Lives of Pippa Lee** and Sandra Bullock scored three straight hits with **All About Steve, The Blind Side** and Anne Fletcher's rom-com **The Proposal**. Admittedly Mira Nair and Karyn Kusama (**Jennifer's Body**)

had a tough time of it, but Drew Barrymore made a promising directorial debut with the roller-derby comedy **Whip It**, starring Ellen Page, and there were art-house hits for Lone Scherfig (**An Education**), Lynn Shelton (**Humpday**) and Anne Fontaine (**Coco Before Chanel**).

And then there was **Precious: Based on the novel 'Push' by Sapphire**. Marked as a potential breakout as early as Sundance (where it won the Jury prize as *Push*), this bruising, independently made adaptation of a popular teen novel about abuse and empowerment hit paydirt with its mixture of Jerry Springer-style emotional exhibitionism, alternately harrowing and uplifting melodrama, and a clutch of authentic performances from such unlikely sources as the mountainous newcomer Gabourey Sidibe, comedienne Mo'nique as her mother, and singers Mariah Carey and Lenny Kravitz as a social worker and a nurse, respectively. With its sledgehammer inspirationalism this was the quintessential Oprah film, and indeed the powerful talk-show host was quick to jump on board as an executive producer and cheerleader.

Precious: Based on the novel 'Push' by Sapphire

One area where quality and commerce did overlap to a remarkable degree was animation. For 15 years now the Pixar company has been the most reliable imprimatur in Hollywood, and so it proved again with **Up**, their tenth feature and the first in 3D. Written by Bob Petersen and directed by Petersen and Pete Docter – both Pixar veterans – *Up* mixes allegory with adventure and dumb imaginative exuberance. It is the story of Carl, a grumpy old man deeply attached to his home of many decades. When the developers won't take no for an answer, he ups and leaves, but he takes the house with him courtesy of several hundred helium balloons. His destination is Paradise Falls, a kind of South American Shangri-la, the dream location he'd always planned to visit with his beloved wife but somehow never found the opportunity. What Carl hasn't reckoned with is an inadvertent stowaway, a plucky cub scout by the name of Russell. No less than the previous Pixar films, it's impossible to imagine *Up* as a live-action film. It may begin grounded in reality, but it soon takes off into the fantastic. There are fabulous goofy creatures, talking dogs, and vertiginous flights of fancy.

Bob Petersen and Pete Docter's **Up**

The trick of the film, and of Pixar generally, is that the filmmakers respect both sides: the mature aspect that Carl represents and the youthful innocence of Russell. Which is not to say that youthful curiosity and the spirit of adventure don't win out over cynicism and disenchantment, but still, the arrogance of youth must be tempered with the sagacity of experience. No wonder Pixar films have universal appeal. Indeed, *Up* was the third-highest grosser of the year.

Disney animation (now under the leadership of Pixar's John Lasseter) enjoyed another hit with **The Princess and the Frog**, a loving throwback to the studio's traditional hand-drawn musical fairytales, with one significant

Disney's **The Princess and the Frog**

difference: Tiana, the hardworking waitress who smooches with an aristocratic amphibian was Disney's first African-American heroine.

Two outstanding stop-motion animated features edged closer to an adult sensibility. Adapted by Henry Selick from Neil Gaiman's novella, **Coraline** is a contemporary fairytale about a bored, blue-haired 11-year-old who scuttles through a tunnel at night to find a fabulous mirror image of her own home, right down to an identical mom and dad. Identical, except that these parents give her pancakes, presents and their full attention. That, and the buttons stitched into their skulls where their eyes should be. Tapping into primal fantasies and fears with a disturbing intensity, the film also echoes classic fairytales: the Brothers Grimm, Lewis Carroll and L. Frank Baum. The tunnel suggests the rabbit hole Alice fell down, and the crazy-mirror manner in which the 'other' world reflects back on reality reminds us of the doubling of actors in *The Wizard of Oz*, as well as Jean Cocteau's surreal *Orphée*.

Henry Selick's **Coraline**

Wes Anderson's **Fantastic Mr Fox** also dressed up adult concerns in the guise of a family film. Taking Roald Dahl's story as a starting point, Anderson reconceived the reckless red fox as another of his irresistible, incorrigible and tragically immature alpha males, a furry cousin to Gene Hackman's fraudster in *The Royal Tenenbaums* and Bill Murray's egotistical ichthyologist in *The Life Aquatic with Steve Zissou*. Mr Fox's bravado has potentially terrible ramifications for his family and friends, as he ruefully comes to admit, yet this is his nature and he cannot be otherwise. The same is true of Anderson, whose signature remains indelible even in this context. Yet the switch to stop-motion has inspired his most visually lovely film, and freed up Anderson's comic imagination. It's jam-packed with delicious non-sequiturs and merrily absurd inventions, like the tube sock Fox's boy pulls over his head in lieu of a professional bandit hat, or the star-spangled button eyes that repeatedly signal a poor opossum's blank incomprehension.

Spike Jonze's **Where the Wild Things Are**

Wes Anderson's **Fantastic Mr Fox**

In a curious coincidence, Anderson's excursion into kid-lit corresponded with the arrival of another long-delayed project from his near-contemporary Spike Jonze, who brought Maurice Sendak's much-loved bedtime story **Where the Wild Things Are** to the screen. Ever the eccentric, Jonze went the live-action route and his wild things were actors in full body costumes, albeit with computer-rendered facial expressions. Working without screenwriter Charlie Kaufman for the first time (he brought in novelist Dave Eggers to collaborate), Jonze gave us a poignant, strange picture about

loneliness, fantasy and failure, constantly teetering on the edge of failure itself – and slipping more than once – but shot through with moments of piercing emotional truth.

If Anderson and Jonze mined children's stories to explore the kind of growing pains that stay with you into middle age, James Cameron set his sights on an infinitely wider scope.

In *Avatar*, his first feature since 1997's box-office champ *Titanic*, Cameron imagines a distant planet, Pandora, and an indigenous population menaced by heavily armed Earthlings intent on extracting a rare mineral. One marine, Sully, switches his allegiance to the tall, blue-skinned natives – the Na'vi – after spending months in their company, learning their ways, in the guise of his avatar, an organic being created in the image of the Na'vi from a combination of human and alien DNA.

An eco fable drawing on influences as disparate as the original sixties TV show *Star Trek* and Kevin Costner's western *Dances With Wolves*, *Avatar* wears its anti-imperialist heart on its sleeve (the trigger-happy humans spout Bush-era 'War on Terror' slogans to underline the point). With its seamless synthesis of live

James Cameron's **Avatar**

action and computer-generated effects – as well as the vividly rendered depth and detail of Pandora's flora and fauna, and its exhilarating 3D action scenes – *Avatar* measures up as the epochal fantasy film that Cameron intended. Yet its immediate ramifications are most likely to fuel still further the inflationary, winner-takes-all blockbuster mentality that equates size, spectacle and sensory overload with success.

The year's best films

A Serious Man (Joel Coen)
Inglourious Basterds (Quentin Tarantino)
Coraline (Henry Selick)
Two Lovers (James Grey)
Fantastic Mr Fox (Wes Anderson)

Quotes of the year

'The cinema as we know it is falling apart. It's a period of incredible change. We used to think of six, seven big film companies. Every one of them is under great stress now. Probably two or three will go out of business and the others will just make certain kinds of films like *Harry Potter* – basically trying to make *Star Wars* over and over again, because it's a business.' FRANCIS FORD COPPOLA.

'Tickets sell $15 in 3-D and $12 in 2-D, so movies – whether it's *Avatar* or any other movie – are still the best value for your money, and the ratio of the bargain goes up the higher the budget of the film, which is why Hollywood has become a blockbuster business. The independent business is not a great business – you have a few breakout films every year that you make some money with, but the rest... it's not a business for these studios anymore,

unfortunately, which is sad, it's a sad thing. The reality is the type of film I make is the type of film that's keeping Hollywood alive in rough times.' JAMES CAMERON.

Directory

All Tel/Fax numbers begin (+1)
Academy of Motion Picture Arts & Sciences, Pickford Center, 1313 North Vine St, Los Angeles, CA 90028. Tel: (310) 247 3000. Fax: 657 5431. mpogo@oscars.org. www.oscars.org.
American Film Institute/National Center for Film & Video Preservation, 2021 North Western Ave, Los Angeles, CA 90027. Tel: (323) 856 7600. Fax: 467 4578. info@afi.com. www.afi.com.
Directors Guild of America, 7920 Sunset Blvd, Los Angeles, CA 90046. Tel: (310) 289 2000. Fax: 289 2029. www.dga.org.
Independent Feature Project, 104 W 29th St, 12th Floor, New York, NY 10001. Tel: (212) 465 8200. Fax: 465 8525. ifpny@ifp.org. www.ifp.org.
International Documentary Association, 1201 W 5th St, Suite M320, Los Angeles, CA 90017-1461. Tel: (213) 534 3600. Fax: 534 3610. info@documentary.org. www.documentary.org.
Motion Picture Association of America, 15503 Ventura Blvd, Encino, CA 91436. Tel: (818) 995 6600. Fax: 382 1784. www.mpaa.org.

TOM CHARITY is film critic for CNN.com and Lovefilm, and a regular contributor to *Sight & Sound* and *CinemaScope*. He also programmes the Vancity Theatre in Vancouver.

James Grey's **Two Lovers**

Venezuela Martha Escalona Zerpa

The development of Venezuelan cinema production continued solidly in 2009. On the one hand, there was a noticeable commitment of financial support on the part of the Ministry of the Popular Power for the Culture, the CNAC (Centre for National Cinematography) and Villa del Cine (Filmstudios by Caracas) towards film production, mainly of a documentary, nationalistic, patriotic or historically revisionist nature. On the other hand, there has been a diversification of content and genres, which has never been seen before in the country's cinema. As part of that, a new and young generation of local talent, living both in the country and abroad, is emerging. Their interests include the expression of different, specific aspects of Venezuelan reality.

Alejandra Szeplaki's **The Orange Day**

There are a number of fine examples of this new, young talent. Alejandra Szeplaki's **The Orange Day** (*Dia Naranja*) is the story of three Latin American women who, simultaneously, face the decision to become mothers, in three distinct locations. The plot takes place over 12 hours, from an intense orange dawn to twilight. **A Distant Place** (*Un lugar lejano*) by

Efterpi Charalambidis' **Liberator Morales, the Ambassador of Justice**

Jose Ramon Novoa chronicled a photographer's search for himself in the Argentine Patagonia. Haik Gazariàn explored a Caribbean-Venezuelan perspective during the Second World War in his film **Venezzia**, during which Venezuela was the oil supplier for the English allies. **Be Careful of Your Dreams** (*Cuidado con lo que sueñas*) was a commendable drama by Geyka Urdaneta, whose characters, a collection of immigrant women and Venezuelan nationals, meet in a hairdressing salon and, in spite of their differences, present a portrait of the country. Efterpi Charalambidis' **Liberator Morales, the Ambassador of Justice** (*Libertador Morales, el justiciero*) recounted the eventful journeys of an ex-cop who works as a motorcycle-taxi driver in Caracas, while Hernan Jabes' **Macuro, the Force of a Village** (*Macuro, la fuerza de un pueblo*) narrated the rebellion of a fishing town when faced with the adverse effects of the continuous interruption of their electrical service.

Among the documentaries, there was Ana Cristina Enriquez's **Lands of Sweet Water** (*Tierras de agua dulce*), which centred on a peasant from the tropical plains and her bond with nature. In **Red Wine, The Film**, (*Vino tinto, la película*), Miguel New narrated the most exciting moments of the Venezuelan National

Football Team during the 2001–02 season. **America Has a Soul** (*América tiene alma*), by the legendary documentary filmmaker Carlos Azpúrua, looked at one of the most important celebrations of Bolivian indigenous resistance, the 'Carnivals of Oruro'. **Zamora, Land and Free Men** (*Zamora, tierra y hombres libres*), by veteran director Román Chalbaud, looked at Venezuela in the middle of the nineteenth-century, when it was downtrodden, socially and politically, by the War of Independence from Spain. The polarisation of liberals and conservatives marked the political agenda, and the inequalities of colonial society kept peasants and slaves under the yoke of an oligarchy. Out of this world came Ezequiel Zamora who, driven by the desire for freedom, fought to erase social inequalities and to divide the land equitably. Finally, Andres Agusti's **Memories of Expressions** (*Memorias del gesto*) presented an interesting portrait of a modern and sophisticated Venezuela.

A movement towards co-productions with other countries in the Latin American region is currently under way. The participation of Venezuelan productions of different formats (short, medium-length and feature film) in film festivals locally and internationally also helped promote the national cinema on the world stage. Film analysts and critics are beginning to speak of a fundamental new boom in Venezuelan cinema as a result of these new developments. In 2009, ten Venezuelan films were released commercially, with many others in various stages of post-production.

If 2008 was marked by the visit of Sean Penn and Danny Glover, the visit of Benicio Del Toro (who came to present the film *Che* by Steven Soderbergh) and of Oliver Stone in 2009 produced various headlines within the country and abroad. Stone unveiled his documentary **South of the Border** (*Al Sur de la Frontera*), which was scripted by British/Pakistani author Tariq Ali and is a non-critical portrait of President Chavez from the point of view of other Latin-American heads of state sympathetic to his ideology. It featured Lula da

Silva, Raúl Castro, Evo Morales, Rafael Correa and Néstor Kirchner and Cristina Fernández de Kirchner. The premiere took place at the Venice International Film Festival.

Translation from Spanish by Ina Martinucci and Kerstin Mozuch

The year's best films
Orange Day (Alejandra Szeplaki)
Liberator Morales (Efterpi Charalambidis)
America Has a soul (Carlos Azpúrua)
Zamora, Land and Free Men
(Román Chalbaud)
Venezzia (Haik Gazariàn)

Quote of the year
'This film shows the new face of the Venezuelan cinema which is now on an even level with the rest of the world.' ALEJANDRA SZEPLAKI *talking about her film* **Orange Day**.

Directory
All Tel/Fax numbers begin (+58)
Centro Nacional Autónomo de Cinematografía (CNAC), Avenida Diego Cisneros, Edificio Centro Monaca, Ala Sur, Piso 2, Oficina 2-B Urb. Los Ruices, 1071 Caracas. comunicación@cnac.org.ve. www.cnac.org.ve.
Ministerio del Poder Popular para la Cultura, Av. Panteón, Foro Libertador, Edif. Archivo General de la Nación, PB. Tel: (212) 509 5600. mppc@ministeriodelacultura.gob.ve. www.ministeriodelacultura.gob.ve.
Distribuídora Nacional de Cine Amazonia Films, Av. Francisco de Miranda, Edif. Meine Grande, Piso 10, Ofic. 10-3 y 10-4, Los Palos Grandes, Caracas. Tel: (212) 286 9241. Fax: (212) 286 6856. www.amazoniafilms.gob.ve.
Villa del Cine, www.villadelcine.gob.ve. Consejo Directivo: consejodir@villadelcine.gob.ve. Presidencia: presidencia@villadelcine.gob.ve, direjecutiva@villadelcine.gob.ve.

MARTHA ESCALONA ZERPA is a journalist and psychologist with a PhD from the Humboldt University. She has lived in Berlin since 1989.

Additional Countries

ANGOLA

Since the end of the civil war in 2002, filmmaking in Angola has slowly recovered from a long period of inactivity. Richard Pakleppa's documentary, **Angola: Saudades from the One Who Loves You**, provided a vivid portrait of a country recovering from a devastating war. Pakleppa took his camera onto the streets of Angola to capture stories from all sections of society and find out how the country has recovered from a conflict that raged for three decades. A group of street urchins, a teacher, a priest, a fishmonger, a model and a rapper all talk about the war and the changes they are currently experiencing. One person leads an affluent life, the other still eats using a piece of cardboard; one is cynical, the other optimistic, claiming 'democracy is still shy here, but it's on the rise'.

The stories of various people, from petrol-sniffing children to oil barons, allow Pakleppa the opportunity to address various facets that colour society, from jurisprudence and oil, to landmines, poverty and micro-credit. The images of the landscape and its people are accompanied by a voiceover set against a wistful musical backdrop: 'We are children lost in the mud, we are the children of the bullets.'

Phil Grabsky's documentary, **Escape from Luanda**, also deals with life after the civil war. In Luanda, one of the world's poorest and most dangerous areas, three students from Angola's only music school work towards their end-of-year concert. The Music School is the country's first and only school of its kind. It houses some 80 students, most of them desperately poor. Many face disapproval and outright rejection from their families, who can't see a future in music. This film asks if musical passion can overcome the terrible hardships

Phil Grabsky's **Escape from Luanda**

of a long civil war. Joana, one of the students, brightly comments, 'Art is life!' She and the other students know this only too well, as music seems to be the only thing that drives them. To each of the students, it offers a new life, a hope for a new future, or simply a dream of what could be. Each of the students tell heart-breaking tales of their own experiences. They can carry on because they have music as their focus. – *Martin P. Botha*

BURKINA FASO

As with many African countries, the opportunity to screen a film in one of the continent's major festivals is cause for filmmakers to ensure that their films are completed on time. Such was the case with film production in Burkina Faso this year.

The Pan African Festival of Cinema and Television of Ouagadougou (FESPACO), held from 28 February to 7 March, scored a record level of participation. Celebrating its 40th edition, the festival received 664 films. Unfortunately, there were some organisational problems. Some directors who had been invited could not travel, journalists found themselves working under difficult conditions and there were also problems with the screening of some films.

Selected for the official competition, Missa Hébié's **The Armchair** (*Le fauteuil*) called for an improvement in the image of working women. His story is about a woman who takes control of a company and faces prejudice and dirty tricks in an attempt to undermine her. Although the screenplay is far from original, the performances and photography make for a solid film.

Sacred Dance in Yaka (*Danse sacrée à Yaka*) is the best film of the year. Its director, Guy Désiré Yaméogo, looks at the conflict between tradition and modernity through a forced marriage. A modern girl, Bineta, is married to an old man who dies, but she refuses to submit to a sacred dance in order to ward off bad luck.

HONORÉ ESSOH is a journalist who works for media outlets in West Africa. He started a filmmaking career two years ago and directed his first short film, about clandestine immigration in Senegal, in 2008. He is presently working on his first feature film, which is about Internet scams in Ivory Coast.

BURUNDI

As Leonce Ngabo, Burundi's most prominent filmmaker, who currently lives in Belgium, confirmed, very little film activity is currently taking place in Burundi, which has only recently come out of a 13-year civil war. The exceptions are a number of developmental films and commercial projects, which are almost entirely supported by Menya Media and Burundi Film Centre (BFC). Menya Media is a non-governmental organisation run by Belgian activist Jean-Luc Pening, while BFC is a media development project launched by three Canadian filmmakers.

BFC has trained 36 youths in basic film production and produced five dramatic shorts. The absence of a developed media sector has crippled the country's ability to operate as a democracy and highlights the need for professional journalism and artistic expression through audio-visual media.

Menya Media, founded in 2001, exists to bring about development through communication. The group works to create initiatives aimed at making the populace more sensitive, conscientious and responsive to development issues. Everything from posters, songs and videos to concerts and radio broadcasts have been used to educate against the spread of HIV/AIDS and in the promotion of peace, democracy, human rights, health and social well being. Menya Media's 'promoting artists and Burundian culture' initiative includes an audiovisual media studio that can also be let out to interested parties.

Although the country has no film school or film festivals, there is a film club at the French Cultural Centre and at the University of Burundi.

OGOVA ONDEGO is a Nairobi-based writer and cultural practitioner who specialises in socio-cultural and audiovisual media issues. He publishes ArtMatters.Info and runs Lola Kenya Screen film festival for children and youth in eastern Africa.

CAMBODIA

Although the film industry in Cambodia remains far from healthy, two films released in 2009 proved that there is a commercial film market in the country and that audiences are ready for something more than the low-quality horror films they are usually served.

Khmer Mekong Films' thriller **Vanished** (*Bakluon*) centres on a radio station where the disappearance of a staff member is followed by theft and murder. A modest production, Cambodian director Tom Som's film perfectly captures contemporary office life in Phnom Penh, while maintaining suspense to the very end. Shown in three cities, it attracted a record 30,000 viewers.

Tom Som's **Vanished**

Who Am I (*Kyom Chear Nak Na*) prompted discussion on a topic hardly broached in the country. It was the first Cambodian film to feature a lesbian love affair. Producer-director Poan Phoung Bopha's ending – one woman is shot by the prospective groom of her lover, who then commits suicide – attracted some criticism, but the film was a commercial success.

The Cambodian Ministry of Culture and Fine Arts postponed the national film festival until 2010, due to the small number – 33 up to July 2009 – and poor quality of films produced over the last two years. One studio, Chlang Den Production, was forced to close down, blaming its revenue loss on pirated DVDs sold openly on the streets and the government's lax approach to copyright.

However, according to Sin Chan Saya, the Ministry's cinema director, what ails the film industry is far more complex. Producers lack capital and therefore make low-quality movies that yield small box-office revenues, and they make low-quality movies because the film professionals they cannot afford to hire have left the business. He stated that the ministry is working with foreign film schools to train a new generation of film professionals.

The Cambodia Film Commission, created in 2009 with support from the French Development Agency in order to promote film locations in the country, is also training Cambodians to assist future international crews, training which will benefit the country's

national industry, Executive Director Cedric Eloy said.

MICHELLE VACHON is a journalist based in Cambodia who mainly covers the arts, culture and archeology.

CAMEROON

This year, documentaries took the lead in terms of quantity and quality. Gérard Désiré Nguélé Amougou's **They Are Called My Beauty** (*Elles s'appellent Majolie*) unearthed the scandal of antiretroviral drug trials by a US pharmaceutical company. These tests were conducted between 2004 and 2005 on prostitutes in Cameroon. Amougou thoroughly explored the issues through research and interviews with key participants.

Osvalde Lewat's **An Issue of Negroes**

Produced in 2007 and released in France this year, Osvalde Lewat's **An Issue of Negroes** (*Une affaire de Nègres*) told the story of the Cameroonian special police unit who, in 2000, killed more than one thousand people with total impunity. Lewat's film openly denounced the injustice and showed great sensitivity in her interviews with the victims' parents.

French filmmaker Jean-Daniel Bécache, who is closely associated with Cameroon, completed his fourth film in the country. **Yellow Fever** (*Fièvre jaune*) covered the massive Chinese immigration into Cameroon and its impact

This is set to change with the arrival of Sham Said Productions, a Congolese outfit that has previously operated as the publisher Editions Sham Said in South Africa. The company relocated to DRC in 2008 and has turned to film production with the hope of re-opening the country's many cinemas. It has consequently co-produced a feature film, **The Last Laugh in Kinshasa**, with the national broadcaster, RTNC. The film premiered in December 2008.

The film is about a man who loses his job and misses the chance to be a millionaire when his wife steals his winning lottery ticket just before the winning numbers are announced. His hope of reviving his career and re-invigorating his marriage are dashed when the wife, rich from the winnings of the stolen ticket, decides to seek a younger lover, a move instigated by her sister.

RTNC managing director Emmanuel Kipolongo said the process of filming *The Last Laugh in Kinshasa* had enabled his organisation to assess the kind of talent available and was a way of energising the Congolese film sector. RTNC supplied the equipment, technical crew and office space, while Sham Said brought in the financing, script and cast.

Whether *The Last Laugh in Kinshasa* will generate excitement in a country dominated by Nigerian, American and French movies is yet to be seen.

In the eastern part of the country, a Kampala-based Congolese national, Petna Ndaliko Katondolo, has stated that his Yole! Africa and Uganda International Film Foundation are exploring ways of running a regional multi-city video festival called East African Video Hall Film Festival. It will unfold simultaneously in Kampala, Nairobi, Dar es Salaam and Goma. Katondolo, who runs the annual Salaam Kivu International Film Festival in Goma, says the project will also seek to establish a regional distribution network.
– *Ogova Ondego*

EL SALVADOR

The murder of documentary filmmaker Christián Poveda shocked the film community in El Salvador. A respected journalist, he was a reporter during the civil war in the 1980s and had just completed his film, **La vida loca**, which touched on one of the fundamental issues in Salvadorian society – the widespread problem of gangs or 'maras'.

Edwin Arévalo, a Salvadorian filmmaker who lives in the US, is finalising his latest film, **Tres caminos**, a drama that deals with alcoholism and Nietzsche's eternal recurrence theory, in which time is viewed as cyclical and not linear. The film has so far screened in the US, France, Mexico and El Salvador. Just as well, then, that the artistic and technical team was composed of Americans, Mexicans and Salvadorians. The film was screened in the ICARO Festival in Guatemala.
– *Maria Lourdes Cortés*

Christián Poveda's **La vida loca**

ERITREA

Eritrea's capital Asmara may have palm-lined boulevards with stylish cafés and cinemas, but Eritrea can hardly be described as a great film nation.

With largely self-taught filmmakers, due to the absence of film and drama schools, local films are formulaic and lack imagination and original- ity. They are generally romances or patriotic films, the latter resulting from the conflict against Ethiopia that raged for three decades that ended in 1991 and saw Eritrea emerge two years later as Africa's newest state.

In April 2009, Human Rights Watch published a damning report on the Eritrean government's serious human rights violations, including severe restrictions on freedom of expression since 2001, when the country cracked down on political opposition and the mass media. The government's actions had serious implications for the filmmaking community. Since January 2008, all films have had to pass through the Eri- trean Film Rating Committee, which is charged with 'protecting Eritrean culture and identity'. Once the rating is issued, it cannot be changed.

Anna Little, a British journalist who was based in Eritrea for seven years and is now based in Ethiopia, made the 25-minute documentary, **Eritrea, A Nation Held Hostage**. The film tells the story of appalling and unrelenting abuse committed by the government in Eritrea by the government.

Shekorinatat screened at the Cannes Film Festival in the Women Film Directors section. It was directed by Rahel Tewelde, an employee of the Film and Drama Branch of the Cultural Affairs Bureau of the People's Front for Democracy and Justice (PFDJ).

Some of the current Eritrean films and their creators included: **Menyu TeHatati** by Elsa Kidane and Gizenesh Mengis; **Shiyakh** by Jemal Saleh; **Burkuta** by Mem. Teame Arefayne; **Efoyta** by Ghirmay Ghebrelul; **Eti**

Hitsan by Nahom Abraham; **Motin MerAn** by Awol Said; **Girat Fereka** by Zewongel Tekle; **Nrim** by Fitwi Teklemariam; **Gurhi'do Eshinet** by Megos Angesom; **Guramayle** by Abrar Abdelhakim; **Nobel** by Nahom Abraham; **Trikolata** by Alamin Alimuz; **Asmait** by Kesar Zaid; **Wazema** by Daniel T/amariam & Kibra Tsegay; **Adhineni** by Efrem Andebrhan; **Roza** by Ghidey Ghebretatios; **Harmony** by Efrem Kahsay; **Nayhilmey Wedi** by Saleh Said Rizqey; and **Nigsti Alem** by Tesfit Abraha.

Eritrea has three annual film festivals, the China-Eritrea Film Week, the European Film Week and the French-Eritrean Film Festival.

The third China-Eritrea Film Week took place at Cinema Asmara, October 14–20. It showcased five Eritrean and seven Chinese films. The Chinese film **One Person's Olympic** was presented in the local Tigrinya language at the opening ceremony. Eritrean films that were shown alongside Chinese ones were **Sheyak**, **Adheneni**, **Eta Adde**, **Ablel**, and **Hdget**.

The 7th European Film Week opened at Asmara's Cinema Roma in November. It featured 25 films selected from EU-member countries represented in Eritrea. Organised by the Delegation of the European Union and the Embassies of the European Union Member States, this festival sought to reach a broader audience. It also took place in Keren, Massawa and Dekemhare before arriving in Asmara. – *Ogova Ondego*

ETHIOPIA

With the awareness that film could play a major developmental role in Ethiopia, there have been calls for the authorities to assist in developing an infrastructure for film, with professional crews, equipment, knowledge and experience. Although the number of films shot in Ethiopia has been limited, with those that have been produced generally directed by established Ethiopian filmmakers trained and living abroad, some local figures have started to make films.

American, European, Indian and Arabic films are the main films screened at cinemas or watched on DVD or video. They are widely available through distributors in urban areas. This should change with several initiatives proposed by the private sector.

The Ethiopian Film Initiative (EFI) was created to support filmmakers, the development of a film industry, and the provision of training and advice on production management, marketing and distribution. It conducted the workshop 'Making Short Television Documentaries' in June 2009. The aim was to help participants develop their treatments in order to successfully embark on the filming and editing phases of their projects. As a result, three documentaries are to be realised. They deal with recycling by street children in Addis Ababa, the impact of charcoal burning on the environment, and recollections of the elite military academy in Ethiopia.

Another important development was the result of a comprehensive and detailed feasibility study conducted in 2007 by Ragnhild Ekthe for Global Film Expression (GFE) an initiative set up by the International Emerging Talent Film Festival (IETFF), in Monaco. The idea behind the initiative was to identify not only the problems but also offer tangible solutions to the film industry in the country.

Perhaps it was in response to this that Ethiopia's celebrated filmmaker and scholar, the US-based Professor Haile Gerima, began developing an institution to support African films, in Addis Ababa. Along with four colleagues, he formed the company Gebbette Entertainment Information Technology Plc, which is in the process of constructing a new film production centre. The four-storey building will house four cinemas, a convention centre and support services for film production. Its goal is to attract Ethiopian and other African filmmakers to create films that focus on Africa.

Three other organisations have been formed. The Ethiopian Filmmakers Association,

Ethiopian Producers Association and Alatinos Association were all created to help the local industry move forward.

The 3rd Addis Ababa International Film Festival, which focused on human rights, took place 20– 29 March in the 450-seat Sebastopol Cinema. The Indian Documentary Film Festival, held 15–19 June, was organised by the Embassy of India at the Italian Cultural Institute. And from 23–29 November, the Ethiopian International Film Festival was staged, with the theme 'Lost and Found'.

The government also passed its most liberal regulations regarding work permits and visas for international filmmakers.

On the production front, Aida Ashenafi made **The Journey** (*Guzo*), a 35mm feature documentary about two young, middle-class Addis Ababa residents staying for three weeks in the Ethiopian countryside. Following its success at the Addis Ababa International Film Festival, it became the first domestic film to be shown on Ethiopian Airlines. It has since screened in New York City and in Washington DC, receiving positive reviews. Unfortunately, it lost money during its eight-day run at the 1,500-seat Ambassador Cinema in Addis Ababa, where it attracted jut 200–300 viewers per screening.

The most successful film was Professor Gerima's **Teza**. It won the Golden Stallion Yenenga prize for the best film at the Pan

Professor Gerima's **Teza**

African Film and Television Festival of Ouagadougou (FESPACO), the Golden Tanit for the best film at the Carthage Film Festival, Special Jury and Best Screenplay awards at the Venice Film Festival, and various other awards at international festivals.

Illusions and Realities, a 40-minute film by Daniel Worku, was another documentary highlight of the year. It received the best short film award at Addis International Film Festival. The film dealt with immigration from Ethiopia to Germany and aimed to illustrate the socio-cultural mechanisms and psychological implications of leaving one's home country to settle in another. – *Ogova Ondego*

GABON

Unlike the television industry, which is dynamic in Gabon, very few films were produced in the last year. One that attracted attention was the first feature film from Patrick Bouémé, **A Rose in the Slum** (*Une rose dans les Matitis*). It dealt with the complicated story of two lovers who belong to different social classes. It was a well-made film, with perhaps a little too much emphasis on dialogue.

Frenchman Jean-Christian Chavihot's documentary **Gullah** was a great success. Not a surprise considering the resources available and the skill of this fine filmmaker. Told through the eyes of a Gabonese doctor, the film offered an insight into the lives of the Gullah people, natives of Gabon, who were deported for slavery to South Carolina in the US.

Gabon continues to be at the forefront of film production in Africa, with some titles recently winning awards. Young directors Manouchka Labouba Kelly and André Côme Ottong, the latter sadly passing away this year, were given awards at film festivals in Cameroon and Burkina Faso.

After his blockbuster *The Shadow of Liberty*, Imunga Ivanga, one of the best-known

Gabonese filmmakers, is working on two feature projects: **A Love in Libreville** (*Un amour à Libreville*) and **The Colour of the Gods** (*La Couleur des dieux*). – *Agnes Thomasi*

GHANA

In a bold move towards a picture-perfect situation, Ghanaian producers and film institutions focused on a few quality productions in 2009, as a way of giving the fledgling industry some much needed impetus.-
It was also the year in which popular actors like Van Vicker, Nadia Buhari, Majid Michael and Jackie Appiah-Agyemani firmly established themselves as Ghana's current hit makers, starring in practically every popular release of the year.

Shirley Frimpong-Mansu's **Perfect Picture**

Sparrow Productions' **Perfect Picture**, a romantic drama set in contemporary Accra, was the year's market leader, premiering with a great deal of fanfare in April and screening in all major cinemas across West Africa. Director Shirley Frimpong-Mansu improved on her 2008 production, *Scorned*, which received two nominations at the AMAA awards for its raw depiction of fast living in Accra, to tell a far more appealing story –actually, three different stories – about three women, set against the background of urbane Accra. Also noteworthy was director Leila Djansi's poetic illustration of Ghana's past and present reality, **I Sing of a Well**, which premiered at the end of October.

The year was not without its controversy, with Frank Rajah's **Heart of Men**, a sexy, urban thriller that was described as Ghana's first pornographic film. The controversy obviously worked well for sales.

In their fight for more investment for production and distribution, forums were held to deliberate the future of the industry. The Real Life Documentary Film Festival, coordinated by Professor Awam Amkpa, was one such event.

Works-in-progress include **Red Soil**, a documentary about the influence of the IMF on the agricultural sector in Ghana, and Akofa Edjeani-Asiedu's **Tulips**, a dramatic tale of a girl who witnesses her father's murder.
– *Steve Ayorinde*

GUATEMALA

There was only one Guatemalan film in the last year. Produced by filmmakers Elias Jimenez and Rafael Rosal's Casa Comal company, **La**

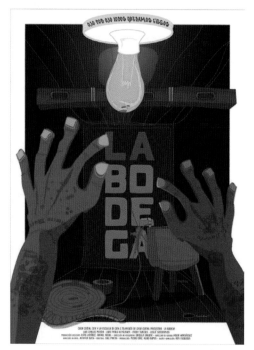

The provocative poster for Ray Figueroa's **La Bodega**

Bodega was a critique of violence and its destructive impact on Guatemalan society. When a member of his family is attacked, a man kidnaps a member of the gang responsible, knowing that any revenge will exact a further toll. The film premiered in August.

In its association with Escuela Internacional de Cine y Televisión (EICTV) in Cuba, Casa Comal set up a film institution that offers more opportunities to local producers. In the past, the two organisations created the Central American festival ICARO, which recently celebrated its twelfth edition. In 2008, responsibility for the festival was assumed by the government.

Forthcoming projects include Julio Hernández Cordón's **Polvo** and Alejo Crisóstomo's **Fe**. Both films received support from international institutions. – *Maria Lourdes Cortés*

GUINEA

The military coup that took place in the country has been a blow to the Guinean film world. The grant that the filmmakers normally receive, which is a minimal sum, has been reduced again. Only directors based outside the country are now able to get a break to make films. Such is the case for Mama Kéïta, who lives in France and directed the feature **The Lack** (*L'absence*). Kéïta talks about Africans living abroad who are torn between their countries of origin and their current homes. Shot in the Senegalese capital, Dakar, the film is intriguing, although it features unnecessary scenes of nudity. It won the best screenplay award at FESPACO in Burkina Faso and the first prize at the Festival de Cine Africano de Tarifa, in Spain.

After the success of his first feature film, *Clouds Over Conakry*, Cheick Fantamady Camara returned with **Morbayassa**. It is the story of a woman who goes in search of the daughter she abandoned at birth who has become a prostitute.

The only film-related event in the country was the first International Festival of Short Films. It was organised by the Association Sogua Nene and the French Cultural Centre in Guinea (DBFO) in Conakry on 30 April.
– *Agnes Thomasi*

HONDURAS

With the economic and political crisis the country suffered following the overthrow of President Manuel Zelaya, Honduras still, miraculously, succeeded in producing a film, only the fifth in the country's history.

Mathew Kodath and Hernán Pereira's **Amor y frijoles**, which premiered in May, is a social comedy about a woman who believes her husband is cheating on her. To catch him out, she enlists the help of a neighbourhood friend who follows him about the countryside, which gave the filmmakers the opportunity to show off their country's magnificent scenery.

In the pipeline, but very much dependent on the volatile situation in the country, is Katia Lara's **Como si Dios fuera negro**.
– *Maria Lourdes Cortés*

KENYA

The film festival circuit in Kenya began on 13 May with the 18 European Film Festival, which screened 23 features. It was followed by Lola Kenya Screen, the audiovisual media festival, production workshop and market for children and youth in Eastern Africa, which is held in Nairobi during the second week of August.

Lola Kenya Screen gave everyone, from three-year-old pre-schoolers to senior citizens, a chance to watch a variety of films from 50 nations and featuring 33 languages. Over three thousand people attended the six-day event. Sixteen children were equipped with the basics in documentary filmmaking, with two documentaries and one fiction film completed.

Events unfolding at lola Kenya Screen

Five children were trained in creative journalism and reported on the festival. Two children were guided on how to organise and present events, and were in charge of the festival as MCs. And six other children were guided on how to critique, judge and award films. They went on to hand out the Lola Kenya Screen Golden Mboni Award for the best children's film and the 14-Plus Award for the best youth film.

To ensure that when the children grow up they will continue to make child-friendly, creatively produced films, six youths went through a week of intensive training in television drama for children and youth. Together they realised one film, **It's My Life**, a thought-provoking drama on the tough environments modern children are forced to grow up in, with pressures ranging from peer pressure to drug abuse, while striving to excel in school.

Films made by children aged 6–15 years during Lola Kenya Screen film production workshops were nominated for the all-Africa Movie Academy Awards (AMAA) in Nigeria in April. Lola Kenya Screen films have been screened at festivals and special events around the world.

The last year also saw the first film summit for independent producers in Eastern Africa (Kenya, Uganda, Tanzania, Rwanda, Burundi, Somalia, Djibouti, Eritrea, Ethiopia and Sudan), which was held with the support of UNESCO's Communication and Development Division in Paris. The summit's aims were to debate and prepare a detailed plan of action to strengthen networking between producers, broadcasters and UNESCO, and to set up an Independent Producers Organisation in Eastern Africa. The summit also conducted some training for independent producers on creating quality content for broadcast and distribution, as well as the marketing of independent productions.

The main outcome of the summit was the adoption of the Africa Independent Audiovisual Media Practitioners Plan of Action (the Nairobi Declaration).

Jitu Films, a subsidiary of Vivid Features, which was established in 1996 by Nick Hughes from the UK, along with his Kenyan partner, John Gatibaru, introduced the idea of mass producing locally made feature films on VCD/DVD. Jitu will help create a dependable market for Kenyan films by encouraging a cinema-going and DVD-buying culture for local Kenyan films. To get around the problem of piracy, Jitu have made their films available for approximately US$1 in major supermarkets.

Over the next two years, Lola Kenya Screen, in collaboration with Africalia of Belgium, will go on the road with a mobile cinema. Dubbed CineToile, it will show a series of high-quality educational and entertaining development-related films to children and youths in five Nairobi neighbourhoods. It will also train children and youths in film production and the critical appreciation of film. – *Ogova Ondego*

KYRGYZSTAN

Unfortunately, 2009 saw a decline in film production in Kyrgyzstan. The financial crisis had a major impact on the film industry, with just one full-length feature completed: **A Thief in Love**, directed by Ernest Abdyzhaparov. Whilst in Kazakhstan, at the private film studio Tanaris, another Kyrgyz director, Aktan Arym Kubat, completed **Mother's Paradise**. There were a few films made by amateurs on the video format, but they add little to the development of film in Kyrgyzstan.

Mother's Paradise is based on the screenplay by one of Iran's most famous film directors, Mokhsen Makhmalbaf. It is set in contemporary Tajikistan, but since it was being produced through Kazakhstan, it concerned an international family in which the father is a Kazakh who has left home to earn money in Russia, but the family never hears from him again. The mother, a Russian with two young children and elderly parents, is forced to become a prostitute to earn money. For all the skill of Aktan Arym Kubat's direction and Makhmalbaf's fine screenplay, the film nevertheless lacks a local dimension.

Aktan is close to completing a film in Kyrgyzstan, **Light** (*Svet*), produced by Chedomyr Kolar, from an idea that has been in development for a number of years. It is about an electrician who goes from house to house providing electricity for people. He also brings light via the warmth of his personality and kindness. But when the electricity supply stops, for all his kindness, the people he has helped become angry and want to take revenge against him.

Aktan Arym Kubat's **Light**

Abdyzhaparov's interesting *A Thief in Love* is a crime drama that opens in the distant past, when a horseman is killed by an arrow. At the gates leading to the afterworld, a prophetess tells the main character that he has one more chance to redeem himself back on Earth. We are then transported to the present day, where the man has become the head of a criminal organisation.

Ernest Abdyzhaparov's **A Thief in Love**

There are two films currently in production. Marat Sarulu's **Ak Zhol** tells of the adventures experienced by an old man and his grandson in one day, while Marat Alykulov and Emil Dzhumabaev's **Paradise** is set in the slums of Bishkek. – *Gulnara Abikeyeva*

LEBANON

In the past few years, Lebanese cinema's presence was often limited to festivals and cultural events. But in 2009, despite this country's socio-political turmoil, domestic releases began to increase, with the aim of gaining some hold at the local box office.

The year began with two films being released after their long tenure at festivals. Borhane Alaouié's award-winning *Khalass* succeeded in striking a chord with Lebanese audiences, in telling the story of two young lovers whose dreams of a bright future are shattered by the outbreak of civil war in 2007. In the same context, director Philippe Aractingi's *Under the Bombs* found a mother, Zeina, trying to locate her young son, lost when the war ignited during his summer holiday. Samir Habchi's **Beirut Open City** (*Dokhan Bela Nar*) was yet another political thriller, starring Khaled Nabawy as an Egyptian photojournalist who, while shooting newsreels, is caught in the crossfire with his girlfriend, played by Lebanese singer Cyrine Abdelnour. The film was released in Arab countries to a mixed response.

On a lighter note, Last year's releases also included successful comedies such as **Abu-Riad**, an Egyptian-Turkish-Lebanese production about an amusing grandfather (Adel Karam) and his comical encounters with friends and family. Also, **Christmas Eve** (*Leila Eid*) saw Rita Persona playing a famous singer who accidentally witnesses the flipside of this celebration in a poor Beirut alley.

On the avant-garde front, Marc Abu-Rashed's **Help** shed some light on Beirut's underground club scene. But due to an explicit sex scene featuring the film's co-stars, Joanna Andrews and Paul Chahine, the movie had to be cut to secure an adult certificate.

Produced by Palestinian filmmaker Rachid Masharawi, the documentary **What Happened?** (*Chou sar?*) was supported by European funds, as many other Lebanese films are. Filmmaker De Gaulle Eid returned to Lebanon to investigate the assassination of his family in the 1980s, only to discover some hideous contemporary realities about his home city, Edbel. – *Sherif Awad*

MALI

In recent years, the National Centre for Cinematography of Mali (CNCM) embarked on a revitalisation of the sector. As a result, CNCM produced three documentaries directed by Assane Kouyate: **The Masters of Banco** (*Les maîtres du banco*), **The Goldsmiths of Clay** (*Les orfèvres de l'argile*) and **From Cotton to Weaving** (*Du coton au tissage*). The documentaries dealt with, respectively, crafts that are becoming extinct in contemporary Mali: traditional masonry, pottery, and weaving.

The Malian family of filmmakers was saddened by the death of director Adama Drabo on 15 July. A major figure in the film industry, his most famous film, 1997's *Taafé Fangan*, won prizes at film festivals in Cannes, Tokyo, Ouagadougou and Namur.

Souleymane Cissé's **Tell Me Who You Are**

The veteran director Souleymane Cissé returned to filmmaking 14 years after his last feature, *Waati*, with **Tell Me Who You Are** (*Min Ye*), the only African film selected for competition at the Cannes Film Festival. In it, he deals with daily problems experienced by an African filmmaker and his wife.
– *Honoré Essoh*

MAURITANIA

This year, the Mauritanian association of filmmakers (referred to as the House of Film-makers) engaged in a series of activities that have helped keep cinema alive in the country. They included three training sessions for young filmmakers, enabling them to produce 33 short films. The works were presented at the National Film Week, from 23 to 30 October.

The most high-profile Mauritanian film at festivals was Djibril Diaw's documentary **1989**, which saw him revisit the massacres that took place in the country. The film excelled through extensive research and an emotional distance from its subject.

Less technically impressive was Zinealabidine Mohamed Almokhtar's documentary, **My Disappeared Friend** (*Mon ami disparu*), which nevertheless has some merit in its attempt to deal with young suicide bombers, a growing reality of Mauritanian life.

French director Thierry Nutchey also covered a controversial topic with **Crude Under the**

Canoes (*Du brut sous les pirogues*), which revealed the problems caused by the recent discovery of oil in Mauritania, emphasising the environmental damage to the area.
– *Agnes Thomasi*

MONTENEGRO

Montenegrin filmmakers have rarely chosen local settings for their works. One of the reasons has probably been its minuscule market (the country has 678,177 inhabitants). Cecil B. DeMille made more films set in Montenegro (*The Captive* and *The Unafraid*) than the best-known Montenegrin filmmakers. Likewise, Brad Pitt made one of his earliest films there (*Dark Side of the Sun*, released in 1997, but shot in 1988), whereas actresses Milena Vukotic or Milla Jovovic, who are of Montenegrin descent, have never worked here. Yet this small and underdeveloped republic in the Eastern Adriatic, which regained its independence in 2006, is an exceptionally proud nation.

Its biggest claim to cinematic success has been Dusan Vukotic, an Academy Award winner for his animated short – the first non-American to win in this category. That said, his 1961 film, *The Substitute*, which was a mixture of Joan Miro and absurdist humour, featured little that one would recognise as Montenegrin.

Similarly, of his 13 features, Montenegrin maverick Veljko Bulajic only set one in Montenegro itself (1979's *The Man to Kill*). Bulajic's most recent film, 2006's *Libertas*, about renaissance writer Marin Drzic, was a Croatian production. Several contemporary Montenegrin filmmakers, such as Bozidar Nikolic or Marija Perovic, are based in Serbia. Bulajic chose to move to Croatia, like Vukotic (1927–1998) who worked there throughout most of his life.

This has left the contemporary Montenegrin film scene pretty much high and dry, with virtually no studios or post-production facilities and very few old masters to emulate.

However, since 2003, the Montenegrin Ministry of Culture has been allocating funds for film production. As a result, some films have been produced locally: *Packing the Monkeys, Again* in 2004, *I Have Something Important to Tell You* and *A View from the Eiffel Tower* in 2005, and, most recently, Marija Perovic's **Look at Me** (*Gledaj me*).

Olga Pakalovic in Marija Perovic's **Look at Me**

A Montenegrin-Croatian co-production, *Look at Me* is based on novelist Ksenija Popovic's *The Boy from Water*. A psychological thriller, it deals with violence within the family circle in a small Montenegrin port. It received a decent festival run, winning the prize for the best new director at the Alexandria Film Festival.

There has also been Drasko Djurovic's comedy **Invasion on Prcevo** (*Desant na Prcevo*), a 50-minute spoof about the 2006 referendum on Montenegrin independence, which surfaced unexpectedly at the New York International Independent Film and Video Festival last year.

The Greek-owned Sters Cinema multiplex in Belgrade opened a similar venue in the Monte-negrin capital, Podgorica. Between December 2008 and June 2009 the multiplex had 176,000 admissions – not bad for a city with a mere 140,000 inhabitants. The country as a whole has only six cinemas with 13 screens. Distribution rights for the country are bound up with Serbia. It takes 10% of the total revenue. – *Goran Gocić*

NAMIBIA

Aside of its importance as a location for international productions, Namibia has a small domestic film industry. The short film **Desert Soul** formed part of **Untold**, a series of nine short films from nine Southern African countries: Botswana, Lesotho, Malawi, Mozambique, Namibia, South Africa, Swaziland, Zambia, and Zimbabwe.

The series was a cross-border regional collaboration, led by the Soul City Institute for Health and Development Communication, and is an effort to act as a region to help deal with the HIV epidemic. Over an 18-month period, producers, scriptwriters, and directors from each of the nine countries were trained in filmmaking and the 'edutainment' process. In each country, local NGOs, many of whom are partners of the Soul City Regional Programme, worked with the filmmakers to produce each film. The *Untold* series deals with a range of issues, including HIV testing, teacher-student abuse, friendship, loyalty, fidelity, gender-based violence, growing up and making choices, living with HIV, and AIDS orphans.

Desert Soul is set in a funky hair salon in Windhoek. A friendship is put to the test when the wealthy, smooth-talking boyfriend of one of the characters makes a move on her friend and business partner. Facing financial pressures due to an ailing father, she needs to make a choice between money and maintaining her friendship.

On the production services side, Namib Film facilitated an international production, **The People of the South**, which will result in a documentary, **The Herero and German Colonial War**. – *Martin P. Botha*

NEPAL

This year has been something of a relief for the Nepali film industry, which has experienced hard times for almost a decade. There has been an increase in the number of films made, newcomers have entered the industry, and traditional approaches have been challenged by experiments in film practice.

Love stories have continued to win the hearts of the audience this year. Rajendra Uprety's love triangle, **The Continuation** (*Silsila*), attracted a positive response from audiences early in the year, as did Deepak Shrestha's **The Fate** (*Takdir*).

Simos Sunuwar's innovative and experimental **Mission Money** (*Mission Paisa*) was praised, but its critical success was not reflected commercially. It focused on Nepalis living in Hong Kong and the problems with contemporary society's emphasising the importance of material wealth.

Experienced directors seemed to fall short when compared with their younger colleagues. **Life and Death** (*Jiban Mrityu*) by Ramesh Budhathoki and Akash Adhikari's **The Protector of Gurkhas** (*Gorkha Rakshak*) failed commercially, while Sagar Lamichhane made a feature about the popular serial character, **Iku Iku** (*Jungle man*), which made money due to the film's small budget.

There has been an increasing trend in artists investing money in productions. **Where Can Be Met** (*Kaha Vetiyela*) was funded by popular actor Shri Krishna Shrestha and went on to become one of the most successful films of the year. Directed by Shiva Regmi, it involved a woman who struggles to find her lover. Regmi's other film, **Arjundev**, was another local hit.

Two relatively new directors, Nirak Poudel and Sudarshan Thapa, continued their success. Poudel's **Kusume Rumal**, a remake of a film

Nirak Poudel's **Kusume Rumal**

made 25 years ago, was satisfying and his **It Will Be a Sin If You Leave** (*Chhodi Gaye Pap Lagla*) also played well with audiences. Thapa's modern love story, **I Have a Friend** (*Mero Euta Sathi Chha*), was noteworthy for attracting a middle-class audience.

Sudarshan Thapa's **I Have a Friend**

Besides the feature films, some documentaries also proved popular with audiences. Kschen Chheten's **In Search Of Real** looked at Nepali labourers working in the Gulf countries, while Amanda Burel's **The Forgotten Refugees** was based on the predicament of the Bhutanese refugees and this author's **Journey Beyond the Himalayas** was based on a journey to Upper Mustang.

The improvement witnessed in the film industry over the last year is a positive sign for the future of film in Nepal.

PRABESH SUBEDI is a freelance journalist and documentary maker. He is also the editor of the e-magazine *Filmnepal.com*.

NICARAGUA

Last year, for the first time in 21 years, the Nicaraguan film industry produced a fiction feature (the last was Ramiro Lacayo's *El espectro de la Guerra* in 1988, produced when Film Nicaraguan Institute (INCINE) still existed). Florence Jaugey's **La Yuma** premiered at the Biarritz Film Festival in France.

The film is about a young woman from a very poor neighbourhood who takes up boxing, one of the country's most popular sports. Her reasons for entering the sport include a desire to break out of a neighbourhood riddled with drugs and gang violence. She also wants to escape from her dysfunctional family, including a stepfather who wants to molest both her and her little sister.

Jaugey, together with her husband, cameraman Frank Pineda, had previously produced a number of works, including the acclaimed Berlinale award winner, C*inema Alcázar. La Yuma* was their first attempt at a feature. – *Maria Lourdes Cortés*

NIGER

While the prospect of greater state involvement in the Niger film renaissance looms on the horizon, filmmakers continue to rely on private funds to produce their works, which are dominated by short films.

One of the best films of the year was the documentary **Fati Hamidou or the Victory of Disability** (*Fati Hamidou ou la victoire sur le handicap*), co-directed by Amadou Souley and American Jenna MacLellan. It is the story of a young woman who, despite her disability, is constantly active. She is a tailor, an international athlete and a feminist activist.

Women were also honoured in **Two Women, One Passion** (*Deux femmes, une passion*), directed by Mariama Seydou Namata. It was the portrait of two women who dare to publicise their passion for football in a Muslim country. The joy of life and the sincerity of these women makes for a refreshing film.

Lompo Edouard Amadou's **Book City** details the lives of young rappers who find and sell items found on a dump and who oppose authorities that want to close it. The rhythm of the film is slow but lead actor Bilal Keit, a local rap star, is captivating.

Authorities have announced that the National Centre for Cinematography will commence in late 2010, now that all necessary equipment has been purchased. It is hoped that the centre will revive local cinema considerably. – *Honoré Essoh*

PALESTINE

Due to low admissions at local venues and a weak infrastructure, New Palestinian Cinema is still unable to continue without foreign funding. Due to the sensitivity of many Palestinian viewers, films dealing with issues of occupation, settlement and refugees generate more interest at international festivals and art-house cinemas internationally.

2009 witnessed a global focus on Palestinian cinema in the context of Jerusalem's role as the capital of Arab culture. Many of the new Palestinian films, whether made by Palestinians from the diaspora or based locally, presented various viewpoints in depicting the Israeli-Palestinian conflict and other related topics.

Best known for *Divine Intervention*, writer-director Elia Suleiman returned to the Cannes Film Festival's Official Competition with the similarly poetic and semi-autobiographical **The Time That Remains** (*Al Wakt Al Motabaki*). The Nazareth-born Suleiman also starred, as a filmmaker who recounts in four segments the story of his family through the diaries of his father, a resistance fighter, and the letters of his mother to others in exile.

Elia Suleiman's **The Time That Remains**

Najwa Najjar's **Pomegranates and Myrrh**

In the award-winning **Pomegranates and Myrrh** (*Al-mor wa al rumman*), writer-director Najwa Najjar created a love story against the backdrop of the occupation. While her husband Zaid faces an extended jail sentence, free-spirited dancer Kamar (Yasmine Elmasri) falls in love with Kais (Ali Suliman), the new choreographer who has just returned to Ramallah.

Following his award-winning *Laila's Birthday*, Rashid Masharawi went to Baghdad to shoot the documentary **Little Wings** (*Al ajniha assaghira*), which focused on young children forced to work in post-war Iraq. Masharawi faced the same trauma in Gaza's refugee camp.

Premiering at the Dubai Film Festival, Michel Khleifi's **Heretic** (*Zendeeq*) was controversially received by critics, due to its avant-garde approach in portraying contemporary Ramallah from the viewpoint of a Palestinian filmmaker returning to shoot a new documentary. In naming his protagonist 'M', Khleifi echoed Costa Gavras's *Z*, in a complex and occasionally surreal depiction of a homecoming, which marks a new direction in the filmmaker's work.
– *Sherif Awad*

PANAMA

It has now been 60 years since Panama last produced a feature film (Rosendo Ochoa's *Cuando muere la illusion*). The country has served as an ideal location for international productions, the most recent case being the last Bond film, Marc Forster's *Quantum of Solace*, in 2008.

However, this lack of local production changed last year, thanks to the involvement of Ibermedia. The first film was Abnaer Benain's **Chance**, which premiered at the Huelva Film Festival, in Spain. The director described the story as being 'a black comedy about two maids who, being poorly treated and badly paid, decide to take action. They work for an aristocratic Panamanian family, where appearance is very important. The film explores the conflict over social status as a comedy.' It was based on a true story that took place in Brazil, when two maids took control of a house.

Abnaer Benain's **Chance**

Cuban actor Francisco Gattorno and Panamanian Rosa Lorenzo played the leads, with Colombian performers Isabella Santo Domingo and Aída Morales adding to the cast. The story developed from a documentary Benaim was making. 'There were thousands of stories and some of the best ones were impossible to cover in a documentary, so I decided that I had to write a fictional story.'

Luis Franco is currently preparing **El suspiro de la fea**, which will feature Panamanian singer, actor and politician, Ruben Blades.
– *Maria Lourdes Cortés*

RWANDA

Rwanda, like her southern neighbour, Burundi, has provided the backdrop for films by individuals and organisations interested in genocide-related subjects.

Anne Aghion's **My Neighbour, My Killer**

My Neighbour, My Killer is a documentary about Rwanda's Gacaca open-air citizen hearings, which were instituted in 2001 as a way for the Rwandan people to participate in a system of justice over the crimes committed in the 1994 genocide. It premiered at the Cannes Film Festival in France in Un Certain Regard. The film also won the Human Rights Watch Nestor Almendros Prize for courage in filmmaking.

My Neighbour, My Killer was the fourth film by Emmy Award-winning documentary filmmaker Anne Aghion, who began filming ordinary Rwandans in 1999. Her previous films were *Gacaca: Living Together in Rwanda?*, *In Rwanda We Say: The Family That Does Not Speak Dies* and *The Notebooks of Memory*.

The Public Affairs Office of the United States of America in Kigali hosted a two-day documentary-filmmaking workshop in July 2009. The independent documentary filmmaker and film professor, Karen Kramer, conducted the sessions.

Some 15 students have undergone training in basic filmmaking at the Rwanda Film Institute, a project of Eric Kabera's Rwanda Cinema Centre, which also runs the annual Rwanda Film Festival. The institution is currently creating a three-year degree course in filmmaking.

The Rwanda Film Festival, presented by the Rwanda Cinema Centre in collaboration with the Ministry of Sports and Culture, was held in Kigali, March 21–28.

Rwanda Cinema Centre, a community-based organisation founded in 2003, remains the main audiovisual media player in Rwanda and works with a host of international partners across many countries. – *Ogova Ondego*

SENEGAL

Film production in Senegal has increased over the last year, with documentaries dominating, in addition to a small collection of impressive features.

Mansour Sora Wade's sophomore feature, **The Fires of Mansaré** (*Les feux de Mansaré*), dealt with interfaith dialogue through the amorous rivalry between two childhood friends and featured a remarkable performance by Senegalese actor Ibrahima Mbaye. The film also acted as a metaphor for Africa, as represented by a young woman who is coveted by everyone.

Filmmaker and former journalist Ben Diogaye Bèye directed the docu-drama **Dakar... the Public Street** (*Dakar … la rue publique*), which denounced the disorder and the unsanitary environment of the Senegalese capital. Adam Sie exposed the 'gangrene' of Senegalese society – the large population of street children – in **Stolen Innocence** (*Innocence volée*), which details the difficult lives of these children, who face crime, begging, drugs and sexual violence.

A documentary about the life of the late Senegalese filmmaker Sembène Ousmane has been announced for 2010. The project will be overseen by filmmaker and Sembène biographer, Samba Gadjigo.

The Ministry of Culture also announced that in 2010 the Promotion Funds Organisation and the Technical Centre will be launched, which will hopefully reinvigorate national film production. – *Honoré Essoh*

SWAZILAND

The most significant production of the past year was the short film, **Tell Them** (*Batjele*), a drama set in the foothills of Manzini. Shot in SeSwati with English subtitles, director Samkeliso Nxumalo presented the story of a young Swazi girl, Nkululeko, who has to stand up to an abusive teacher. The film was groundbreaking for three reasons: it was the first film produced regionally in Swaziland by Swazis; the filmmakers exposed an issue that few people want to talk about openly, namely sexual abuse in the school environment; and finally the producer, Thembumenzi Mabuza, is female.

Samkeliso Nxumalo graduated from the American University in Paris in 2001 with a double major in international communications and European cultural studies, which included some exposure to the film industry. After much social and family pressure, Samkeliso decided to follow his own instincts and started a video production company. Since 2002, his company has produced a variety of material, including music videos, documentaries, promos and magazine programmes for television. He has served in a variety of roles on these productions, from direction and camerawork to editing and scripting. *Batjele* is his first dramatic production. – *Martin P. Botha*

TAJIKISTAN

Private studios remain the most active element of the film industry in Tajikistan. It is clear that most films are made on video, but digital technologies have become a useful tool for cheap and mobile film production.

Nosir Saidov's **Apparent Noon** takes place at the beginning of 90s. It is a story of unconsumated love due to a border that emerges between the houses of the central characters. The idea of a border is used to mean many things: the boundary between people, nations, cultures and civilisations. Iranian director Mohsen Makhmalbaf took an active role in the production process. He invited his colleagues from Iran, including actors, a sound director and assistant director to participate. He donated time and equipment, knowing that there are few opportunities to produce professionally made films in Tajikistan.

Under the auspices of the national studio, Tajikfilm, Saidjon Kodiri directed **Spring Time of One Street**. Set during the Second World War, a family man leaves his wife, son and daughter to head out to the front. Soon after, the mother receives notification that he has been killed in battle, information she decides to hide from her children.

To-to, directed by Iskander Usmonov, could be regarded as a truly Central Asian film. The script was written by Kyrgyz author Alisher Niyazov and was shot with the help of two Kazakh film directors, Arman Kuanov and Erlan Nurmukhambetov. It tells the story of a seven-year-old mute boy, Umed, who is forced, in order to ensure happiness and harmony for his mother, to live in the orphanage for deaf-and-mute children. The photograph of an Italian singer, Toto Cutugno, gives him hope that happy times for his family may soon arrive. Interestingly, the film was made possible through the financial support of the Open Society Institute (USA) and Foundation of Cooperation for Documentary and Experimental Film (Iran).

Safarbek Soliyev's **The Moon Bracelet** was a co-production with Kyrgyzstan. The main characters of the film fall in love with each other recklessly and with disregard for their different nationalities and religious beliefs. It is only as their marriage approaches that the couple's love shatters against these unconquerable obstacles. – *Gulnara Abikeyeva*

TANZANIA

Despite the existence of copyright legislation, Tanzania remains the leading country in terms of piracy in the southern and eastern African region. Broadcasters tend not to pay for the music and films they use.

Tanzania has no formal film distribution system or a film training school. Moreover, Tanzanian filmmakers appear to favour the practice of working without scripts, while the idea of criticism is frowned upon as a destructive impediment to creativity. This approach arguably has its basis in the praise-singing culture that was rooted in the Ujamaa socialist system of Julius Kambarage Nyerere, the founding president of the Tanzanian nation.

Except for Mfuko wa Utamaduni (the Tanzania Culture Fund), there is virtually no public funding for filmmaking in Tanzania. Under such a scenario, it is difficult, if not impossible, for art to thrive.

Zanzibar-based ZIFF remains among the largest arts and culture festivals in Africa. It serves films, music, literature, and the visual arts. Screenings and performances take place near the historic UNESCO world heritage site of Stone Town. The festival features numerous strands, including: Main Panorama, Women's Panorama, Children's Panorama and Village Panorama. Each panorama features any combination of art form to explore specific issues and action plans for addressing them.

The American actor Danny Glover attended ZIFF last year, where his films **Namibia: the Struggle for Liberation** and **Gospel Hill** were screened. He was also present at several youth-related events, including the UNICEF child-education camp run by ZIFF, and the Children's Film Panorama, run by the Danish Film Institute. – Ogova Ondego

THE GAMBIA

Production continued last year in The Gambia, but at a very low rate. The scene is dominated by producer/director Ebou Waggeh, who has been working on feature films since 1998. Since then, he has produced films on a

variety of topics, from Goodness of a Man's focus on male circumcision and the rites of passage among young Gambian men in 2001 to Improving Community Skills in The Gambia, a 2008 production looking at how various institutions have developed programmes for improving skills in communities and the impact of such programmes.

His latest production, **Promoting Excellence in the Sciences**, brought to light the impact of assistance given every year to science students in senior secondary schools by The Gambia Ports Authority.

Ebou Waggeh is the main promoter of a registered organisation of filmmakers in The Gambia, known as G-FACT. He also runs the independent production company, WAX Media, who make documentary films and commercials. – Agnes Thomasi

UGANDA

The demand for locally made films in Uganda is very high. While a Hollywood or Nollywood film on VCD costs approximately US$0.60 and a DVD US$1.25, a Ugandan film on both VCD and DVD costs in the region of US$2.50. Compare this to the country's only cinema, which screens only Hollywood and Bollywood films and charges an equivalent $2.50 per show. The country's 2,000 video halls screen mainly pirated Hollywood films at $0.10 per ticket.

Although Uganda has 105 radio stations, 15 newspapers and seven television stations, it is rare to find any of these media outlets tackling issues related to local films. There is no formal film distribution network, while television stations demand a fee to air local product. Only NBS TV has a weekly programme dedicated to reviewing local films.

Ashraf Simwogerere Mayanja, perhaps Uganda's most prolific independent filmmaker, was trained as a dentist and has been a full-time filmmaker since 2003. Some of his feature-length films include *The Passion of the Ugandan Martyrs* and *The Honourable*.

Winnie Gamisha, a promising screenwriter and film director fresh from the London Film School, recently completed **The Painter**, a 25-minute fiction film on the scars of political brutality and repression during the dictatorship of General Idi Amin Dada and the healing effect of art. It takes the viewer through the life of a young artist whose community does not understand his aspirations. 'This film explores how political brutality and poverty shape people's personalities in making them introverts, but how persistent love can be in bringing the best out of people like Kefa [the main character] and letting it flourish. It also suggests a way of protecting these gifts and talents from envious relatives and neighbours who will seek to destroy creativity if they cannot directly benefit from it,' said Gamisha. The film was produced by the Goethe-Institute, the London Film School and Andreas Frowein Films.

Matthew Bishange (popularly known as Matt Bish) was one of five African filmmakers to win US$10,000 from Focus Features' Africa First Programme for short films. This initiative offers eligible and participating filmmakers the chance to be awarded financing for pre-production, production and/or post-production of a fiction short made in continental Africa and tapping into the resources of the local film industry. Bish's winning project, **A Good Catholic Girl**, addresses questions of religion and marriage in Christian and Arab communities. – *Ogova Ondego*

UZBEKISTAN

Uzbek cinemas unveiled local premieres almost every week last year. Most were made on video with a budget that rarely exceeded US$100,000, which meant that private studios could recoup their costs within two weeks of a film opening, often going on to earn twice the film's budget.

The main genre of Uzbek commercial films, which feature their own local star system, are melodrama, which often highlight social imbalances within the country. Comedy and action films are also popular.

To produce serious films or to shoot on 35mm, the support of national agency, Uzbekkino, is necessary, They produce ten to twelve films a year and, from these, a number travel to various international festivals.

One of the best films of the year was Djakhongir Kasymov's **For Water** (*Suv Yokalab*), which presented one day in the life of an old man, who sets out with his sons to collect water for his garden. However, the water never reaches its destination as the man shares it with neighbours on his way home, emphasising the importance of community and neighbourliness. The man may lack water for his garden, but he is happy.

Djakhongir Kasymov's **For Water**

Metaphor is critical to the domestic cinema in terms of any criticism of the state. It is no surprise then that Yelkin Tuychiev named his most recent film **The Silence** (*Sukhunat*). In it, the two main characters lose their hearing and memory. They represent a community that has chosen to forget the past and is deaf to the needs of individuals.

Several films deal with the topic of terrorism. Khilola Nasymov directed **The Threat** (*Tagdid*), in which the main character discovers that

Yelkin Tuychiev's **The Silence**

what he thought was a piece of shrapnel lodged in his body is actually a bomb. In Mansur Abdukholykov's **The Strayed** (*Arosat*) a man changes his religious beliefs only to be ostracised by his community, which leads to serious consequences.

Some of the most interesting domestic releases tend to be those that grapple with the Uzbek mentality or notions of the 'exotic' East. In **Oidinoy**, Nazym Abbasov tells the story of a six-year-old girl who dreams of going to school and starting her studies. It details village life, with its open market and the importance of the village school in teaching children the Uzbek way of life. In Jacques Debs' co-production between Uzbekistan and France, **Boskachi**, the main characters are a horseman and an Eastern beauty. The mysticism of the narrative is combined with a documentary style and draws from elements of contemporary art. – *Gulnara Abikeyev*

ZAMBIA

Zambia's first female filmmaker, Musola Cathrine Kaseketi, completed her debut film, **Faith** (*Suwi*), an international co-production with Finland. The 80-minute 'edutainment' feature won an award from the International Labour Organisation (ILO) for its strong human rights and labour law message. Filmed in English, Nyanja and Bemba, *Faith* details how a young woman, Suwi, and AIDS orphan, Bupe, find each other after a drastic change in their lives.

Kaseketi's optimistic narrative about disability, determination, tradition, orphans, street life, HIV/AIDS and child sexual abuse originated from her 1988 stage play, *Rejection of Reality*. It was screened by the Zambia National Broadcasting Corporation as a television play in 1991. She has been working on the adaptation of the stage play for the screen since 2004, but only managed to shoot it in 2008, with a budget of €125,000. A graduate of Johannesburg's Newtown Film and Television School, Kaseketi has been a pioneering force in the Zambian film industry, creating the country's first ever international film festival.

The documentary, **Tikambe**, made with USAID funding, captured how the stigma against people with HIV/AIDS affects the lives of ordinary Zambians. *Tikambe*, which means 'let's talk about it', is one of two films that chronicle the experiences of two Zambian families. One of the principal characters is Harriet Mulenga, who tested positive for HIV soon after her husband, a minibus driver, died of tuberculosis. When she was no longer able to care for herself, she moved in with her mother, but her reception was less than warm. After a month in a hospice, Harriet started taking antiretroviral drugs. In this period, her mother learned how to care for a person with the disease. Harriet recovered her strength, reconciled with her mother, and found the courage to go public. She told her neighbours how to protect themselves from the disease, and her 'HIV-positive' shirt announced that she would hide no longer. 'Finding families willing to go public was difficult,' said film producer Carol Duffy Clay, who lived in Zambia for five years. 'Hopefully, this film will help break down some of the stigma that is at the very centre of the HIV/AIDS epidemic.'

The film, developed for the Zambia Integrated Health Programme, a project run by Johns Hopkins University's School of Public Health for USAID, will be shown throughout Zambia, including on Zambian television.
– *Martin P. Botha*

ZIMBABWE

World headlines continued to carry the news of the dire situation in Zimbabwe, which ranges from Robert Mugabe's complete disregard for basic human rights, which threatens the stability of the fragile unity government, to an economy that struggles to get back on its feet after suffering the highest inflation rate in the world.

A recent documentary, which was funded by CIVICUS (World Alliance for Citizen Participation), portrays the disintegration of the country and the tragic impact on the people of Zimbabwe. **Time 2 Act** was shot during December 2008. It depicts a bleak Christmas, characterised by despair, desperation and destitution, with a particularly devastating impact on women and children. The film focuses on the lives of ordinary Zimbabweans and how they cope with conditions in a country that has reached a critical state. The filmmakers also expose the crackdown on basic freedoms and the breakdown of government structures, exemplified by the abduction and intimidation tactics of ZANU-PF, targeting civil and political activists. The film was shot by Rikhado Makhdo, a film student from South Africa. It was screened in SADC (South African Development Community) countries, to the South African president and various NGOs, and on YouTube.

Lucy Bailey and Andrew Thompson's documentary **Mugabe and the White African** also details the terror of Mugabe's regime. Winner of the Sterling World Award at the Silverdocs Documentary Film Festival, the film is an intimate and moving documentary, charting one family's extraordinary courage in the face of a relentless campaign of state-sanctioned terror. Michael Campbell is one of the few hundred white farmers left in Zimbabwe since Mugabe began his violent land-seizure programme in 2000. Since then, the country has descended into chaos, the economy brought to its knees by the reallocation of formerly white-owned farms

Mike Campbell (centre right) and Ben Freeth (middle back) with some of their farm workers in Lucy Bailey and Andrew Thompson's **Mugabe and the White African**

to ZANU-PF friends and officials with no knowledge, experience or interest in farming. Mike, like hundreds of white farmers before him, has suffered from years of multiple land invasions and violence at his farm.

In 2008, Mike, 75 years old and a grandfather – unable to call upon the protection of any Zimbabwean authorities or to rely on the support of his fellow white farmers, who all faced the same brutal intimidation – took the unprecedented step of challenging Mugabe before the SADC international court, charging him and his government with racial discrimination, as well as the violation of human rights. The film is an insider's account of one family's astonishing bravery in the face of brutality, in a fight to protect their property, their livelihood and their country.
– *Martin P. Botha*

Festival Focus: Berlinale

Berlinale – 60 Years
by Andrea Dittgen

Alfred Hitchcock's **Rebecca**

Twelve days of new films, crowds cheering the stars, even the Golden Bear – everything you know about the Berlinale was there from the beginning – thanks to American Film Officer Oscar Martay, who had the idea of launching a film festival amongst the remains of Berlin, still in a poor state six years after the end of the Second World War.

Of course, the creation of the Berlinale was a political act, also supported by the British Film Office and the Berlin Senate, but it was not born out of fascism (like Venice) or as reaction to fascist policy (like Cannes). The Berlin International Film Festival, directed by film historian Alfred Bauer, marked a fresh start as 'showcase of the free world', directed at the public as well as the international film business.

The first festival in 1951 featured 114 films from 21 countries, opening on 6 June with Alfred Hitchcock's *Rebecca*. Its location made the festival an ideal cultural meeting point for East and West – it was the Cold War and films from communist countries were not widely available. Meanwhile, Berliners' hunger for glamour – they extended a warm welcome to Gina Lollobrigida, Jean Marais, Federico Fellini, and Walt Disney – was distinctive of the festival's atmosphere in the 1950s. Because the audience decided on the awards in the first five years, it took until 1956 for the Berlinale to receive official A-list status (which depends, among other things, on the presence of an international jury), but the inclusion of the ordinary festivalgoer from the get-go might also be responsible for the fact that Berlin remains the A-list festival with the largest audience up to this day.

Berlin programmed its first film of the French new wave in 1959: *The Cousins* by Claude Chabrol. Godard, Truffaut and the other new wave directors would make appearances in subsequent years. Consequently, in 1960, a representative showcase of countries was introduced, which was a precursor of the film market.

Claude Chabrol's **The Cousins**

1965 Golden Bear winner, Jean-Luc Godard's **Alphaville**

Struggling not only with the building of the Berlin Wall and the Oberhausen Manifesto in 1962, but also with too many mediocre films, the decision in 1967 to officially disconnect the Berlinale from politics and to integrate film critics, such as Ulrich Gregor, in the selection process, made it easier to invite Eastern European countries. Due to the Germans' habit of discussing a lot and doing little, the Berlinale was spared from cancellation in 1968 (like Cannes), when the European-wide solidarity for striking students and workers reached Berlin.

However, crisis arrived two years later with a German film: *O.K.* by Michael Verhoeven, about the rape and murder of a Vietnamese girl by US soldiers during the ongoing war. The jury resigned and no Bears were awarded. After this incident, new sections were created, following the example of Cannes. The International Forum of New Cinema (with Ulrich Gregor and Manfred Salzgeber in the selection committee) wanted 'to inform and promote avant garde and progressive developments in film from all countries, as well as support these developments'. The critics proposed to show German films of the past 12 months, which eventually led to the section, 'German Films'. Bauer agreed, but couldn't help prevent a certain rivalry between the Competition and Forum. In the 1970s, the Forum sharpened its profile, showing art-house films and continuing to expand.

The Competition welcomed a film from the Soviet Union for the first time in 1974, Radion Nahapetov's *At the World's Limit*. This opened the door for a new aspect of the Berlinale: until the fall of the Berlin Wall, no other top festival showed more films from Eastern Bloc countries.

The 1970s, arguably the most turbulent decade of the Berlinale, is also remembered for the heated discussion about Nagisa Oshima's *Empire of the Senses*, which was confiscated by the District Attorney for being pornographic.

Nagisa Oshima's **Empire of the Senses**

Film journalist Wolf Donner took over from Alfred Bauer, who retired in 1977. Donner made the most important changes the festival had seen up to that point. He executed Bauer's plan to move the Berlinale from June to February, positioning it before Cannes and allowing it to expand its film market and to profit from films produced in the second half of the previous year. The festival poster of 1978, the first Berlinale opening in February, showed the bobble hat that became an icon. Though Donner resigned unexpectedly a few weeks before the festival in 1979, for a new job in journalism, his reforms freed the festival from its rigidity. He created new sections for German and children's film and opened the festival up for more diverse and younger audiences.

Donner's successor, Moritz de Hadeln, took over in 1980 – together with Ulrich Gregor as the director of the Forum, in an equal position. He would succeed in winning back the Russians who, in 1979, had pulled their films from competition and went home after the screening of Michael Cimino's *The Deer Hunter*, declaring their solidarity with the

Michael Cimino's **The Deer Hunter**

people of Vietnam, and then in 1980, when they protested against films in the Billy Wilder retrospective (including the Cold War screwball comedy *One, Two, Three*) and withdrew their films. But, most of all, de Hadeln had to win domestic fights against ministries and film directors who didn't approve of his insistence on including German films perceived as 'difficult'. Initiating the biggest changes in the festival's organisation, de Hadeln introduced new directors to the film market, the Children's Film Festival and the Info Showcase, renamed Panorama in 1986.

Each section expanded in the second half of the 80s, underlining the Berlinale's reputation as the place to go for the film business as well as the film buff. The projectors were running 18 hours a day and rarely a year went by without the screening of some revelatory, formerly banned film from Eastern European countries; from Russia, then Poland, East Germany, Czechoslovakia and Bulgaria. The Market, renamed the European Film Market (EFM), grew bigger. The Forum, already appreciated around the globe for its interesting audience discussions after the screenings,

1982 Golden Bear winner, R.W. Fassbinder's **Veronika Voss**

established a new sidebar for overlong films, starting in 1986 with Claude Lanzmann's Holocaust-documentary *Shoah*, which ran to 566 minutes. The Forum regularly presented new films by Aki Kaurismäki, Peter Greenaway, Manoel de Oliveira and other European writer-directors of the art-house scene.

1987 Golden Bear winner, Gleb Panfilov's **The Theme**

Meanwhile, the Panorama sharpened its profile, featuring neighbouring countries in a Mediterranean Panorama, Black Sea Panorama, Baltic Sea Panorama and a focus on gay and lesbian films of all kinds and formats. With two large retrospectives each year and about 800 films to watch in twelve days, the Berlinale offered a selection no other festival could match.

A new highlight came shortly after the fall of the Berlin Wall. In 1990, the festival took place in both parts of the city and showed the entire output of East German cinema from 1966–67 – a sensation, because those films were originally banned for political reasons and could now be seen by the East German public for the first time.

But as it became obvious that Berlin would lose its status as a window for Eastern European films, the most difficult decade in the festival's history began. Country focuses (mainly in the Forum) championed countries often overlooked – including Serbia, Africa, Mexico, and Burma. With more documentaries than ever in Forum and Panorama, and alternating the dominance

1997 Golden Bear winner, Milos Forman's **The People Vs. Larry Flynt**

of US and European films in competition, the Berlinale quite accurately reflected the tendencies of cinema in the 1990s. However, severe budget cuts (one million D-Mark in 1993, another 500,000 in 1994) led to a reduction in the number of films screened.

With the long-awaited move to Potsdamer Platz in 2000, everything changed. The cool architecture and the multiplexes created a decidedly different atmosphere, while the short distance between venues intensified communication. There were more cinemas for repeat screenings and some of the old cinemas, such as Zoo Palace, Royal Palace and Delphi, were still in use to ease the abrupt change of location. The constant presence of Asian films in 2001 and a certain taste for sex and intimacy became obvious in the multifaceted farewell programme of Moritz de Hadeln (after 22 years) and Ulrich Gregor (after 30 years) in 2001.

The recent rise in the quality of German films was reason enough for Dieter Kosslick, appointed Festival Director in 2002, to confidently create the new section, Perspectives of German Cinema, and to show

2002 Golden Bear winner, Hayao Miyazaki's **Spirited Away**

at least three German films in competition from that year on. Kosslick tightened cooperation between the sections, especially with new Forum director Christoph Terhechte, focusing on contemporary trends of filmmaking. The creation of the Berlinale Talent Campus – inviting 500 young talents to learn professional skills from experienced filmmakers – in 2003 was a great and novel idea. However, its launch was a little overshadowed by American guests such as Spike Lee, Martin Scorsese and Oliver Stone, who were vocal in their criticism of President George W. Bush.

2009 Golden Bear winner, Claudia Llosa's **The Milk of Sorrow**

The Forum and the Panorama screened films digitally for the first time and the Children's Film Festival expanded with the new series, 14plus. Some improvements were achieved by giving the short films a better standing, creating a co-production market to help the financing of new films and moving the still expanding EFM to the more spacious Martin Gropius Building in 2006. Together with excellent programming in all sections, the Berlinale annually beats its own records, with more than 15,000 accredited guests from 136 countries, 6,300 participants at EFM and more than 270,000 tickets sold in 2009, setting the benchmark for the 60th edition of the festival.

ANDREA DITTGEN is a film critic and editor of the daily newspaper *Die Rheinpfalz* and a contributor to the magazine *Filmdienst*. She is also a member of the board of the German Film Critics Association and web editor for the International Federation of Film Critics (www. fipresci.org).

Berlinale – Milestones

1951 – The Berlinale opens on 6 June with Alfred Hitchcock's *Rebecca*; Festival director: film historian Alfred Bauer. Two Sections: Competition, Retrospective.

1953 – New: Cultural Films.

1955 – New: Competition for Short Films

1956 – Received the so-called 'A-status' by the International Federation of Film Producers (FIAPF). Two juries: Feature Films and Documentaries.

1957 – The Zoo Palace Theatre becomes the festival centre.

1962 – Staged for the first time in a divided city. Discussions focus on the Oberhausen Manifesto.

1965 – The festival takes over choosing jurors. New: Showcase of Countries (film market).

1968 – Students protest.

1969 – Counter festival organised by The Friends of the German Cinemathek.

1970 –Michael Verhoeven's competition entry *O.K.* causes protests and the resignation of the Jury. No awards handed out.

1971 – New section following the scandal of 1970: International Forum of New Film.

1975 – East Germany (GDR) in competition with Frank Beyer's *Jacob the Liar*. *Ninotchka* by Ernst Lubitsch is withdrawn from the retrospective out of consideration for the Soviet delegation.

1976 – Confiscation of Nagisa Oshima's *Empire of the Senses* by the District Attorney.

1977 – New Festival Director: film journalist Wolf Donner. New: German Films, Info Schau, a retrospective organised independently by the German Cinemathek.

1978 – First Berlinale in winter. New: Children's Film Festival.

1979 – After the screening of Michael Cimino's *The Deer Hunter*, Soviet-controlled countries pull their films from the Competition and go home.

1980 – New Festival Director: Moritz de Hadeln. Aina Bellis becomes head of the Film Market, Manfred Salzgeber of the Country Focus (Info Schau). The Competition and Forum share equal status.

1986 – Reinhard Hauff's *Stammheim* wins the Golden Bear. Jury President Gina Lollobrigida breaks her pledge of secrecy: 'I was against this film.' Info Schau becomes Panorama. Gaby Sikorski takes over the Children's Film Festival. New prize: Berlinale Camera.

1987 – Berlinale becomes a forum for new Soviet cinema.

1988 – A film from Asia, *Red Sorghum* by Zhang Yimou, wins the Golden Bear for the first time. Beki Probst takes over the renamed European Film Market. Renate Zylla takes over the Children's Film Festival.

1990 – Three months after the fall of the Berlin Wall, the festival takes place in both parts of the city.

1993 – Wieland Speck takes over the Panorama.

1994 – Children's Film Festival offers a competition.

2000 – For its 50th anniversary, the Berlinale moves to the rebuilt Potsdamer Platz, the new centre of Germany's capital.

2002 – New festival director: Dieter Kosslick. New Forum director: Christoph Terhechte. Co-operation between the sections for the first time. New: Perspectives German Cinema (Director: Alfred Holighaus).

2003 – New: Berlinale Talent Campus. American guests such as Spike Lee, Martin Scorsese and Oliver Stone used the Berlinale as a platform to express their disapproval of the policies of George Bush. New director: Thomas Hailer (Children's Film Festival). Festivals shortened from 12 to 11 days.

2004 – First projections with the latest digital technology. New: Berlinale Specials and 14plus in the Children's Film Festival.

2006 – New: Berlinale Shorts. European Film Market moves to the Martin Gropius Building.

2007 – Talent Campus moves to the Theatre Hebbel am Ufer. Children's Film Festival renamed Generation.

Berlinale – Portraits

DIETER KOSSLICK,
Film Festival Director

Born in Pforzheim in 1948. Promoting German cinema is his life's passion. He was the first director of the Berlinale with a background not in film culture but in film finance, starting in 1983 with the Hamburg Film Funding Office. Kosslick is a co-founder of the European Low Budget Forum and co-founder of the European Film Distribution Office (EFDO, 1988–1996). In 1992, he became CEO of the Filmstiftung NRW (North Rhine-Westfalia) and turned it into the most powerful regional film fund in Germany, spending over 30 million Euros annually. Taking over the Berlinale in 2001, Kosslick expanded the Film Market and promoted German cinema as well. He was the first festival director to select three or four German films for the Competition and initiated the new section Perspectives of German Cinema. Kosslick will be head of the Berlinale until 2013.

CHRISTOPH TERHECHTE,
Head of Forum

Born in 1961 in Münster. As a film critic in the 80s and 90s, writing for the daily newspaper *taz*, and an editor for the Berlin-based magazine *tip* (1991–2001), he expressed a fondness for films that were offbeat and outside the norm, selecting titles from all over the world. He joined the Forum selection committee in 1997 and was appointed head of Forum in 2001, after Ulrich Gregor retired. He continues to search for new trends in all genres, and followed the tradition of having long discussions after the screenings to create a direct link between young directors

Dieter Kosslick

Christoph Terhechte

and experienced directors. Following the introduction of digital screenings, the Forum expanded in 2007.

WIELAND SPECK,
Head of Panorama

Born in Freiburg in 1951. He joined the Panorama team in 1982. The former student of the San Francisco Art Institute was a talented actor in films of colleagues such as Ulrike Ottinger (*Freak Orlando*, 1981) and directed the

feature film *Westler* (1985) about a gay couple living in East and West Berlin. His work as a director, author, actor, producer and exhibitor helped him in his first ten years as assistant of Panorama Director Manfred Salzgeber, whom he succeeded in 1992. Speck continued the gay/lesbian focus of Panorama and has also kept an eye on the zeitgeist, programming films dealing specifically with social problems. He introduced the Panorama audience award in 1999.

Beki Probst

BEKI PROBST,
Head of the European Film Market

Born in Istanbul. The former Turkish journalist became a cinema owner and manager in Switzerland in the 1960s. From 1981 to 1988, she was the Berlinale delegate for Turkey and Greece. She was appointed director of the film market in 1998, which she renamed European Film Market (EFM). Her biggest concern is the structural growth of the market. Under her management, the EFM has grown bigger each year. Among the new features of the market, she introduced a second market venue in 2008 with the EFM Marriott Offices and booths, and the EFM Industry Debates, promoting digital cinema and digital home cinema, as well as raising awareness of documentaries with 'Meet the Docs' seminars.

Wieland Speck

THOMAS HAILER,
Head of Children's Film Festival

Born in 1959 in Öhringen. His roots were in theatre, but in 1995 he began working with children's films as advisor for funding at the Kuratorium Junger Deutscher Film, later as the director of studies of the Academy for Children's Media. Appointed head of the Berlinale Children's Film Festival, he subscribes to a simple motto: he wants children to start watching good films early on, because they are the audience and filmmakers of tomorrow. To introduce older children to the cinema, he expanded the section in 2004 with the 14plus competition, which was renamed Generation in 2007.

Alfred Holighaus

Thomas Hailer

ALFRED HOLIGHAUS,
Head of Perspective German Cinema

Born in 1959 in Dillenburg. He started writing on film in the 1980s, since 1984 as editor for the Berlin-based magazine *tip* and was eventually promoted to head of the publication in 1986. He already had experience in promoting and producing film before he joined the Berlinale in 2001, when he was tasked with the promotion and presentation of the German films in the various sections. To promote German Cinema, he was appointed head of the new section, Perspective German Cinema, in 2002. He chose 12 feature films and some shorts each year, mostly from newcomers, to support the Berlinale's aims as a champion for

the quality and quantity of German films. He leaves the Berlinale in 2010 for a new position at the German Film Academy.

HEINZ BADEWITZ,
Head of German Cinema

Born in 1941 in Hof. He studied film at the Munich Film School HFF and directed some shorts before becoming the most active local promoter for German cinema, creating the Festival Internationale Hofer Filmtage in 1967, which he has established (and is still running) as one of the most acclaimed German film festivals, with its own distinct traditions. He is responsible for the Berlinale programme German Cinema (integrated into the EFM) since 1977. His unique skill for finding young, talented German directors is legendary, as are his worldwide contacts.

Heinz Badewitz

GOLDEN BEAR WINNERS 1952–2009

1952 **One Summer of Happiness**
(Arne Mattsson, Sweden)

1953 **The Wages of Fear**
(Henri-Georges Clouzot, France)

1954 **Hobson's Choice** (David Lean, UK)

1955 **The Rats**
(Robert Siodmak, Federal Republic of Germany)

1956 **Invitation to the Dance** (Gene Kelly, US)

1957 **12 Angry Men** (Sidney Lumet, US)

1958 **Wild Strawberries**
(Ingmar Bergman, Sweden)

1959 **The Cousins** (Claude Chabrol, France)

1960 **El Lazarillo de Tormes** (César Ardavin, Spain)

1961 **La Notte** (Michelangelo Antonioni, Italy)

1962 **A Kind of Loving** (John Schlesinger, UK)

1963 **The Devil** (Gian Luigi Polidoro, Italy)

1964 **Reflections** (Metin Erksan, Turkey)

1965 **Alphaville** (Jean-Luc Godard, France)

1966 **Cul-de-Sac** (Roman Polanski, UK)

1967 **Le depart** (Jerzy Skolimowski, Belgium)

1968 **Who Saw Him Die?** (Jan Troell, Sweden)

1969 **Early Works** (Želimir Žilnik, Yugoslavia)

1970 No Prize Given

1971 **The Garden of the Finzi-Continis**
(Vittorio De Sica, Italy)

1972 **The Canterbury Tales**
(Pier Paolo Pasolini, Italy)

1973 **Distant Thunder** (Satyajit Ray, India)

1974 **The Apprenticeship of Duddy Kravitz**
(Ted Kotcheff, Canada)

1975 **Adoption** (Márta Mészáros, Hungary)

1976 **Buffalo Bill and the Indians, or Sitting
Bull's History Lesson** (Robert Altman, US)

1977 **The Ascent** (Larisa Shepitko, Soviet Union)

1978 **Trout** (José Luis García, Spain),

Ascensor (Tomas Munoz, Spain),

The Worlds of Max
(Emilio Martínez Lázaro, Spain)

1979 **David** (Peter Lilienthal, West Germany)

1980 **Heartland** (Richard Pearce, US),

Palermo or Wolfsberg
(Werner Schroeter, West Germany)

1981 **Hurry, Hurry!** (Carlos Saura, Spain/France)

1982 **Veronika Voss**
(R.W. Fassbinder, West Germany)

1983 **Ascendancy** (Edward Bennett, UK),

The Beehive (Mario Camus, Spain)

1984 **Love Streams** (John Cassavetes, US)

1985 **Die Frau und der Fremde**
(Rainer Simon, East Germany),

Wetherby (David Hare, UK)

1986 **Stammheim** (Reinhard Hauff, West Germany)

1987 **The Theme** (Gleb Panfilov, Soviet Union)

1988 **Red Sorghum** (Yimou Zhang, China)

1989 **Rain Man** (Barry Levinson, US)

1990 **Music Box** (Costa-Gavras, US),

Larks on a String
(Jiri Menzel, Czechoslovakia)

1991 **The House of Smiles** (Marco Ferreri, Italy)

1992 **Grand Canyon** (Lawrence Kasdan, US)

1993 **Woman Sesame Oil Maker**
(Xie Fei, China),

The Wedding Banquet
(Ang Lee, Taiwan/US)

1994 **In the Name of the Father**
(Jim Sheridan, UK/Ireland)

1995 **The Bait** (Bertrand Tavernier, France)

1996 **Sense and Sensibility** (Ang Lee, UK/US)

1997 **The People Vs. Larry Flynt**
(Milos Forman, US)

1998 **Central Station** (Walter Salles, Brazil/France)

1999 **The Thin Red Line** (Terence Malick, US)

2000 **Magnolia** (Paul Thomas Anderson, US)

2001 **Intimacy** (Patrice Chereau, UK / France/
Germany/Spain)

2002 **Spirited Away** (Hayao Miyazaki, Japan),

Bloody Sunday (Paul Greengrass, UK/Ireland)

2003 **In This World** (Michael Winterbottom, UK)

2004 **Head-On** (Fatih Akin, Germany/Turkey)

2005 **U-Carmen eKhayelitsha**
(Mark Dornford-May, South Africa)

2006 **Esma's Secret: Grbavica**
(Jasmila Žbanic, Bosnia and Herzegovina)

2007 **Tuya's Marriage** (Wang Qaun'an, China)

2008 **The Elite Squad** (José Padilha, Brazil)

2009 **The Milk of Sorrow** (Claudia Llosa, Brazil)

Era New Horizons goes from strength to strength

Era New Horizons International Film Festival, whose 10th edition runs from 22 July – August 1, is held in the town of Wrocław (south-western Poland). The largest film festival in Poland, it is accredited by FIAPF and is regarded as one of the most important film events in Central Europe.

As the festival's name suggests, it is an exploration of new horizons in film language, expression and storytelling that goes beyond the borders of conventional cinema. The international programme of films can provoke extreme reactions and emotions, controversies and discussions, applause and protests. The films in competition offer audiences a chance to see works that might otherwise have no chance of being screened for a Polish audience.

The festival's 2010 programme will include retrospectives of the films of Jean-Luc Godard, recent Turkish cinema, Polish filmmaker Wojciech Jerzy Has and the Quay Brothers. The festival will also feature a retrospective of films by acclaimed academic Laura Mulvey.

The festival sections are:
New Horizons International Competition – the most important competitive section of the festival – consists of 14 bold and original Polish premieres. It is meant to pose a question: is there a place in 21st century cinema for directors who go against the grain – for individuals with their own style and inimitable language? The winner of this competition is awarded the Grand Prix (€20,000), the festival's highest honour. The winners of the

Left Agnès Varda, director of **The Beaches of Agnes** *and Festival Director Roman Gutek*

Grand Prix, Audience Award and Film Critics Award are guaranteed distribution in Poland.

Films on Art International Competition – launched at the 2009 edition of the festival, this is sure to become an important section of the programme. Entries are works on the borderline of cinema and visual arts. There are 14 feature-length documentaries, with the winner taking the Best Film Prize (€10,000), which will guarantee distribution in Poland.

New Polish Films Competition – both features and documentaries are eligible, offering foreign professionals and festival audiences an opportunity to assess the latest and most interesting productions from recent Polish cinema. An international jury awards the Wrocław Film Prize (€25,000), and the Best New Director Prize (€10,000). In 2009 the competition consisted of 13 films, four of which were world premieres. This section reinforces the festival's importance as a showcase for new Polish films.

New Polish Short Films Competition – short and medium-length films are eligible. It is also a unique occasion for younger filmmakers to present their works to an international audience. This section is an essential strand for programmers from other international short film festivals.

European Short Films Competition – aimed at students and young filmmakers. Debut films of a length not exceeding 20 minutes compete for the Best Film Prizes (€1,000 each) in three categories: fiction films, documentaries and animation.

The Third Eye is a cycle of special screenings, presenting films made by visual artists for whom cinema is a means of expression. The section allows audiences to see films previously shown in art spaces rather than cinemas.

A recent addition to the festival was the educational series **New Horizons of Film Language**, which was organised to last several years and is aimed at drawing the audience's attention to how film as a work of art has changed over the last 10–15 years. Programming ten films each year, the key aim of this series is to allow

audiences to appreciate the formal aspects of original works – this will be done through screenings, lectures and discussions.

There are also retrospectives championing the films of national cinemas and also bodies of work by master directors; reminiscence series and cinema lessons; open-air screenings at the Wrocław Market Square for almost two thousand spectators; unique installations and expositions; and, finally, the opportunity to take part in meetings with artists and in discussions.

In 2009, a Polish-Swedish Co-Production Forum took place. It featured one-on-one pitching sessions, lectures and a case study of the film *Miracle Seller*, which was a Polish-Swedish co-production premiered at the festival. Market screenings of new Swedish films were prepared for Polish distributors and TV buyers. The Andrzej Wajda Master School of Directing and Göteborg Film School participated in workshops devoted to film directing, with masterclasses conducted by Jacek Bławut and Johan Palmgren.

biggest film festival in poland

era new horizons
international film festival
wrocław 22.07—01.08.2010
www.enh.pl

Since its inception, the festival has become one of the leading film music events. Every year it presents large outdoor concerts, silent films with live music featuring artists as diverse as Marianne Faithfull, Michael Nyman, Eleni Karaindrou, Wim Mertens, Meredith Monk, Jocelyn Pook, Tibor Szemzö and many others.

Era New Horizons is financed by the city of Wroclaw and the corporate sponsor, ERA, the major mobile operator in Poland, the MEDIA Programme of the European Union, the Ministry of Culture and National Heritage and Lower Silesia Voivodship.

Zlin is 50 and Zeman is 100!

This year, the International Film Festival for Children and Youth in Zlin will celebrate its 50th anniversary. And amongst its many celebrations, there will be an opportunity to look at the work of the great Czech filmmaker, Karel Zeman, with the commemoration of 100 years since his birth.

Zlin is the oldest festival for children and youth cinema. It is also the biggest, screening the most films of any similarly themed festival. It was originally created solely to be a showcase for Czech and Slovak films for children. However, since 1989 it has widened its focus to include international productions. It has also increased in size since 2000, not to mention prestige.

The main competitive sections are for children and for youth, as well as a section of short

Actor Tim Curry in front of the Zlin Film Festival main theatre

animated films and two sections for an older audience: European Debuts and films from the Visegrad countries. The 2010 edition will also see non-competitive sections: Night Horizons, targeted at films about problematical and provocative issues related to teenagers; and the return of the popular Japanese Anime section.

The 50th anniversary will be celebrated with a strong focus on Czech and Slovak cinema. This showcase will also present a retrospective of one of the most innovative Czech filmmakers, Karel Zeman, to commemorate 100th anniversary of his birth.

European Film Awards 2009

The 22nd European Film Awards took place on 12 December 2009 in the heart of Germany's industrial Ruhr area. It was a unique change from the norm, which normally sees the European Film Awards hosted in Berlin – the home of the European Film Academy – every two years.

Michael Haneke's *The White Ribbon* was the big winner of the evening, garnering the three top prizes: European Film, Director and Screenwriter. Haneke called his film 'a truly European production'. He was accompanied on stage by the film's Austrian, German, French and Italian co-producers.

Another favourite of the evening, *Slumdog Millionaire*, received two awards; director Danny Boyle accepted the People's Choice Award, voted for by film fans across the continent, and Anthony Dod Mantle's Cinematographer Award for his diverse work on both *Slumdog Millionaire* and Lars von Trier's *Antichrist*.

Stephen Daldry, the recently appointed European Film Academy ambassador, accepted the award for European Actress on behalf of Kate Winslet for her performance in his adaptation of the bestselling novel, *The Reader*.

The award for European actor went to newcomer Tahar Rahim for his role as a

Winners and presenters at the 22nd European Film Awards
Picture: EFA/jens-braune.de

prisoner forced to kill another inmate in Jacques Audiard's *A Prophet*. The prison drama also took home the European Film Academy Prix d'Excellence, which went to the film's sound designers, Brigitte Taillandier, Francis Wargnier, Jean-Paul Hurier and Marc Doisne.

Broken Embraces composer Alberto Iglesias was awarded European Composer, while Swiss filmmaker Peter Liechti's *The Sound of Insects – Report of a Mummy*, an account of a man starving himself to death, received the European Film Academy Documentary – Prix Arte. The European Co-Production Award – Prix EURIMAGES went to producers Diana Elbaum and Jani Thiltges.

Two awards went to Poland: Marcel Lozinski's *Poste Restante* was awarded European Short Film and this year's Critics' Award, the Prix FIPRESCI, went to Andrzej Wajda for *Tatarak*.

For the first time in its history, the Academy gave an award for Best Animated Feature,

which went to Jacques-Rémy Girerd for *Mia and the Migoo*.

How much of cinema comes down to the passion and enthusiasm of individual artists was rarely more apparent than in the nominees for European Discovery for Best Debut. Like his four co-nominees, British director Peter Strickland, who shot his disturbing revenge drama *Katalin Varga* in Romania with Hungarian-speaking actors, fought for his film for years before he completed it.

French actress Isabelle Huppert, who received the award for European Achievement in World Cinema from German director Volker Schlöndorff, spoke emotionally when she opined that the language that unites Europe is cinema.

One of the most moving moments of the ceremony was when surprise guest Eric Cantona took the stage in honour of Ken Loach, who received the Lifetime Achievement Award from the star of his latest film, *Looking for Eric*. The football legend hailed Loach as 'a genius' and added: 'For five decades he has not stopped tackling social issues and always with realism, humour, love and modesty.'

The 2010 Awards Ceremony will take place in Tallinn, Estonia's beautiful capital, on the banks of the Gulf of Finland, the easternmost arm of the Baltic Sea. The event will be an early highlight of Tallinn's European Capital of Culture tenure in 2011. The 23rd European Film Awards are scheduled for 4 December 2010.

Tampere Film Festival celebrates its 40th Anniversary

Located in southern Finland and surrounded by two beautiful lakes, the Tampere International Short Film Festival celebrates its 40th anniversary in March 2010.

The Opening Jubilee will look back at some of the best and most memorable films screened at previous festivals, while in the Rake Special: Harvest programme, there will be a chance to savour some of the finest Finnish shorts of all time.

International Jury 2009: Ngo Phuong Lan (Vietnam), Maike Mia Höhne (Germany), William Sloan (United States), Montserrat Guiu Valss (Spain) and Kristiina Pervilä (Finland). Photo: Wilhelmiina Saikkonen

Opening reception at Bravo Plaza. Photo: Markus Nikkilä

Two screenings of the extensive ¡Viva el Corto! programme will be devoted to Uruguayan short films. There will also be plenty of chance to catch up with other Mexican, Spanish and Ibero-American films throughout the whole festival.

Besides the actual short film programme the festival bursts with related events and activities. On Saturday, Yo-talo gathers friends of indie filmmaking to the Trash Film Festival

tenth anniversary gala. Videotivoli, International Children and Youth Video festival, will be held for the seventh time. And FestArt, a media art exhibition held in TR1 at Väinö Linna Square, will be open from February 14th.

The retrospective sections will champion the work of Laila Pakalnina, Patrik Eklund, Gustav Deutsch, Julien Temple and Gustavo Taretto. Meanwhile, the Fortress Europe programme will focus on the complex issues surrounding immigration in European societies through new short films and debates.

The competition programme has always had strong international appeal, with the 2009 Grand Prix awarded to Pablo Lamar for *Ahendu nde sapukai*, which was the first Paraguayan film to feature in the festival. Professionals can participate in the comprehensive Film Market, and can join filmmakers, guests and audience members later at the unforgettable Sauna Party. Tervetuloa Tampereelle!

Cottbus celebrates 20 years of their Festival

With an anniversary that almost coincides with the fall of the Berlin Wall, FilmFestival Cottbus will celebrate its 20th edition in November 2010. Over two decades, FilmFestival Cottbus has become the world's most renowned Festival of East European Cinema. Each year, it provides a comprehensive programme of recent productions from the Baltics to the Balkans and from Central Europe to Central Asia.

Originally founded to offer young filmmakers from Eastern Europe a platform for their work, the festival now presents a wide variety of new and recent feature films from the region. In addition to the competition features and short films, there are sections dedicated to regional blockbusters, experimental work and countries particularly active in the film business. In many cases, the festival serves as a stepping-stone towards a theatrical release in Germany and other countries.

The festival closed its 2009 edition with a record attendance of 18,900 visitors, who attended 140 films from 35 countries, including Russia, the Czech Republic, Poland, Azerbaijan, Hungary, Croatia and Serbia, who were all represented in the main competition programme. 'We're no longer a special-interest section,' stated Festival Director Roland Rust. 'Meanwhile Cottbus may be regarded as home of Eastern-European film,' he added. The 2010 edition will include a programme of films representing how the world views

The Opening Night of the Cottbus Film Festival

contemporary Eastern Europe. It is hoped that this view will span the globe, offering audiences the opportunity to see how Eastern and Central Europe looks from inside and out.

The East-West co-production market, Connecting Cottbus, is the festival's industry section. It supports the development of new films that go on to achieve recognition at festivals around the world. Artistic Director Gabriele Brunnenmeyer should have much to look forward to in 2010, following the success of last year's event: 'The 14 presented ideas for feature films showed an astonishing variety... accordingly high was the interest of producers and financiers. This gives us reason to hope that many projects will be realised from this year's market.'

As well as the many screenings, there is an extensive supporting programme, with exhibitions, parties and concerts by Eastern European bands, which all work towards promoting the culture of the filmmaking countries in focus.

valCottbus Festival des osteuropäischen Films / Festival of East European Cinema **2.–7.11.2010 20.**
ival des osteuropäischen Films / val of East European Cinema **2.–7.11.2010 20. FilmFestiva**
mFestivalCottbus Festival des osteuropäischen Films / Festival of East European Cinema **2.–7.11.20**
20. FilmFestival Cottbus Festival des osteuropäischen Films / Festival of East European Cinema **2**
ival des osteuropäischen Films / val of East European Cinema **2.–7.11.2010 20. FilmFestiva**
lmFestivalCottbus Festival des osteuropäischen Films / Festival of East European Cinema **2.–7.11.20**
valCottbus Festival des osteuropäischen Films / Festival of East European Cinema **2.–7.11.2010 20.**
ival des osteuropäischen Films / val of East European Cinema **2.–7.11.2010 20. FilmFestival**Cottbus Festival des osteuropäischen Films / Festival of East European Cinema **2.–7.11.20**
www.filmfestivalcottbus.de 2.–7.11.2010 20. FilmFestival Cottbus Festival / Festival o

20. **Film Festival** Cottbus
2.–7.11.2010
Festival des osteuropäischen Films
Festival of East European Cinema

IFG Inspiration Award Winners

The 40th Door Wins at Cottbus

Elchin Musaoglu was the recipient of the Cottbus Film Festival's first IFG Inspiration Award, for his moving drama *The 40th Door*. Set in the director's home city of Baku, Azerbaijan, it tells the story of a young boy, Rustam, whose father is murdered while working in Russia. Taking it upon himself to become the breadwinner, he soon experiences the tough-side of life on the street, encountering thieves, bullies and discovering a society that appears to have forgotten how to care. In its simplicity, the film tells a universal tale of enduring hope through the bleakest of circumstances.

Elchin Musaoglu

Elchin Musaoglu was born 11 July 1966 in Baku, Azerbaijan. He is a graduate of the Azerbaijan State Institute of Arts and Culture, Faculty of Directors (1983-1989), the State Institute of Theatre and Arts, Faculty of Directors, Moscow, Russia (1989-1990). Elchin is also the founder of the Society of the Development of Documentary Films and Authorial Programmes and author of more than 50 documentaries. In 2009 *The 40th Door* received the Gold Remi Award for Foreign films at the Houston International Film Festival and the East of the West award at the Karlovy Vary International Film Festival.

René Wins at London's East End Festival

One of the documentary highlights of the year and winner of the IFG Inspiration Award at London's East End Film Festival, Helena Třeštíková's powerful *René* is the story of one man and his life as a habitual criminal, whose way of living has been forged by his experiences in prison. Starting with offences committed at the age of eighteen and following him over the course of the next two decades, Třeštíková builds a powerful portrait against a backdrop of social upheavals, when the political map of Europe was forever changed.

Born in 1949, Helena Třeštíková graduated in documentary direction from the Prague Film School (FAMU) in 1974. Since then, she's made some 30 films, specialising in long-form observational studies that follow their subjects over many years. Previous features have included *Marcela*, *Sladke stoleti* and *Lida Baarova's Bittersweet Memories*.

Helena Třeštíková's **René**

Film Festivals Calendar

November

December

Leading Festivals

American Film Market
November 3–10, 2010

The business of independent motion-picture production and distribution – a truly collaborative process – reaches its peak every year at the American Film Market. Over 8,000 leaders in motion-picture production and distribution – acquisition and development executives, agents, attorneys, directors, financiers, film commissioners, producers and writers – converge in Santa Monica for eight days of screenings, deal-making and hospitality. The AFM plays a vital role in global production and finance. Each year, hundreds of films are financed, packaged, licensed and green lit, sealing over $800 million in business for both completed films and those in pre-production. With the AFM-AFI FEST alliance, attendees capitalise on the only festival-market combination in North America. *Inquiries to:* 10850 Wilshire Blvd, 9th Floor, Los Angeles, CA 90024-4311, USA. Tel: (1 310) 446 1000. e: afm@ifta-online.org. Web: www.americanfilmmarket.com.

Amiens International Film Festival
November 12–21, 2010

A competitive festival in northern France for shorts, features, animation and documentaries. Also retrospectives, tributes and the 'Le monde comme il va' series, which includes works from Africa, Latin America and Asia. 'Europe, Europes' presents new works from Young European Talents (Shorts, Documentaries and Animation). *Inquiries to:* Amiens International Film Festival, MCA, Place Léon Gontier, 80000 Amiens, France. Tel: (33 3) 2271 3570. e: contact@filmfestamiens.org. Web: www.filmfestamiens.org.

Amsterdam-International Documentary Film Festival (IDFA)
November 18–28, 2010

The world's largest documentary festival, built up over 22 years, IDFA 2009 opened with Dariusz Jablonski's *War Games and the Man Who Stopped Them*. Over the following ten days, IDFA screened 309 documentaries and sold over 165,000 tickets. In addition to the regular sections, IDFA featured several competition programmes. The big winner of the 2009 festival was *Last Train Home* by Lixin Fan, which won the VPRO IDFA Award for Best Feature-Length Documentary. The festival also featured daily talk shows, debates and masterclasses by, amongst others, Frederick Wiseman and Eyal Sivan. IDFA has two markets: the FORUM, a market for international co-financing; and Docs for Sale, which stimulates the sales and distribution of creative documentaries. Since December 2008, Docs for Sale has also boasted an online marketplace, where new as well as older documentaries can be viewed throughout the year. Docs for Sale Online is a place where sales agents and producers can show

Guests arrive for the opening night of IDFA 2009 at Tuschinski cinema.
Photo: Felix Kalkman

their documentaries to potential buyers and exhibitors online, even after IDFA is over. *Inquiries to:* International Documentary Film Festival Amsterdam, Frederiksplein 52, 1017 XN Amsterdam, Netherlands. Tel: (31 20) 627 3329. Fax: 638 5388. e: info@idfa.nl. Web: www.idfa.nl.

AWARDS 2009
VPRO IDFA Award for the Best Feature-Length Documentary: **Last Train Home** (Canada/China), Lixin Fan.
VPRO IDFA Special Jury Award: **The Most Dangerous Man in America** (USA), Judith Ehrlich and Rick Goldsmith.
NPS IDFA Award for Best Mid-Length Documentary: **Iron Crows** (South Korea), Bong-Nam Park.
NPS IDFA Award for Best Short Documentary: **Six Weeks** (Poland), Marcin Janos Krawczyk.
IDFA Award for First Appearance: **Colony** (Ireland/USA), Ross McDonnell and Carter Gunn.
Dioraphte IDFA Award for Dutch Documentary: **The Player**, John Appel.
Nederland 2 IDFA Audience Award: **The Cove** (USA), Louie Psihoyos.
IDFA Award for Student Documentary: **Redemption** (Germany), Sabrina Wulff.
IDFA DOC U! Award: **The Yes Men Fix the World** (France/USA), Andy Bichlbaum and Mike Bonanno.

Report 2009
Frederick Wiseman: In honour of his 80th birthday, this year's IDFA devoted special attention to his work. Wiseman has directed and produced dozens of documentaries (including *Welfare*, *Titicut Follies* and *High School*), which often focused on social relations within American institutions. He is regarded as one of the major exponents of Direct Cinema. Alongside a retrospective programme compiled by him, a screening of his latest film and a masterclass, the festival also looked at Wiseman's work as a theatre director. In his masterclass, Wiseman deconstructed selections from his extensive oeuvre, with comments and questions from

international
documentary film festival
amsterdam

idfa

IDFA www.idfa.nl
18 – 28 November 2010
Deadlines for entry: 1 May and 1 August

the FORUM
22 – 24 November 2010
Deadline for entry: 1 September

the FORUM online
Deadlines for entry see **www.idfa.nl**

Docs for Sale
19 – 27 November 2010
Deadline for entry: 1 October

Docs for Sale online
Deadlines for entry see **www.idfa.nl**

IDFAcademy
19 – 21 November 2010
Deadline for accreditation: 10 October

Jan Vrijman Fund
New application deadlines:
15 January 2010 and 15 May 2010

Frederick Wiseman receives a Living Legend Award from Festival Director Ally Derks at the opening night of IDFA 2009. Photo: Felix Kalkman

a rapt audience. **Eyal Sivan masterclass:** A discussion was held with the great and controversial Israeli filmmaker (including *Izkor*, *Slaves of Memory*, *The Specialist*, *Jaffa* and *The Orange's Clockwork*) about his creative process, his critics and his IDFA retrospective. **Ira Glass Presentation:** Ira Glass, a special guest of this year's Doc Lab programme, is one of the most unique and best-loved documentary storytellers in America. The radio version of his documentary programme *This American Life* (there is also a television version) attracted no less than 1.8 million listeners a week and won just about every non-fiction award going since starting out in 1995. The bizarre, moving and brilliant documentary stories presented each week by Glass on the radio have now also resulted in a dozen feature films (most recently, *The Informant!* by Steven Soderbergh). In his afternoon lecture, Glass showed the way to bring a story to life on the radio and how, with the right techniques, you can transform a small anecdote into a big, exciting documentary story. **IDFA Media Fund Lecture by Julien Temple:** The first annual IDFA Media Fund Lecture was given by Julien Temple, the British director of documentaries, music videos and fiction films. His work includes the new film *Oil City Confidential*, *The Great Rock 'n' Roll Swindle*, *The Secret Policeman's Other Ball*, *Stones at the Max*, *The Filth and the Fury*, and music videos for artists such as David Bowie, Depeche Mode, Janet Jackson, Duran Duran, Neil Young, Paul McCartney, The Rolling

Stones and The Sex Pistols. **Happy Days – a theatrical event with Frederick Wiseman and actress Catherine Samie:** Frederick Wiseman and French actress Catherine Samie took part in a special theatrical event, based on *Happy Days*, a play by Samuel Beckett. The event was a mixture of live performance, lecture, film fragments and a discussion of Wiseman's version of the play, which he produced for the Comédie Française in the Théatre du Vieux-Colombier, Paris.
- Cathalijne de Wilde, IDFA Communication.

Austin Film Festival
October 21–28, 2010

For 17 years, the Austin Film Festival has been dedicated to celebrating the art of storytelling through film. The event comprises a four-day conference, eight days of films and parties, with networking opportunities for filmmakers, screenwriters and film buffs. The festival programme shows narrative, animation and documentary features and shorts, including premieres, advanced screenings and independent films. Film screenings are complemented by lively and informative Q&A sessions with cast members and filmmakers. The conference provides over 80 inspiring and interactive panels, round tables and 'get to know you sessions' with established screenwriters and filmmakers. *Inquiries to:* Austin Film Festival, 1801 Salina Street, Austin, TX 78702, USA. Tel: (1 512) 478 4795. e: info@austinfilm.com. Web: www.austinfilmfestival.com.

Bergen International Film Festival
October 20–27, 2010

Norway's beautiful capital of the fjords launches the eleventh BIFF in 2010. The festival, which is largest of the Norwegian film festivals in terms of content, has a main International Competition of about 15 films, as well as an International Documentary Competition. The documentary section makes BIFF one of the Nordic countries' largest annual documentary events. The festival has sidebars with international arthouse films, Norwegian Shorts Competition as well as premieres of the upcoming winter and Christmas theatrical releases, through extensive collaboration with Norway's distributors. Also hosts seminars and other events. *Inquiries to:* Bergen International Film Festival, Georgernes verft 12, NO-5011 Bergen, Norway. Tel: (47) 5530 0840. e: biff@biff.no. Web: www.biff.no.

AWARDS 2009

Jury Award-Cinema Extraordinaire Competition: **No One's Son** (Croatia/Slovenia), Arsen O. Ostojic.
Documentary Award: **Afghan Star** (UK), Havana Marking.
Audience Award: **Bring Childrn From Streets** (Norway), Espen Faugstad and Eivind Nilsen.
Visjon Vest Award for Young Talent: Espen Faugstad & Eivind Nilsen.
Youth Documentary Award: **The Cove** (USA), Louie Psihoyos.
Norwegian Short Film Award: **Skylapjenta** (Norway), Iram Haq.

Berlin –
Internationale Filmfestspiele Berlin
February 11–21, 2010

Interest in the Berlinale 2009 among visitors from both the film industry and the general public has been greater than ever: more than 20,000 accredited visitors from 136 countries, including 4,000 journalists, attended the 59th Berlin International Film Festival. Approximately 490,000 cinemagoers have attended the festival, with roughly 270,000 tickets sold. Altogether, 389 films were

Photo Jan Windszus © Internationale Filmfestspiele Berlin

shown in 950 screenings. Besides the 'regular sections' – Competition, Panorama, Forum, Generation, Perspektive Deutsches Kino and Berlinale Shorts. Special events, including the comprehensive '70 mm – Bigger Than Life' Retrospective and the Homage to Maurice Jarre, as well as the Berlinale Special and the Culinary Cinema events, were almost completely sold out. Under Jury President Tilda Swinton, Christoph Schlingensief, Henning Mankell, Gaston Kaboré, Isabel Coixet, Alice Waters and Wayne Wang brought glamour, passion and expertise to the Berlinale 2009. *Inquiries to:* Internationale Filmfestspiele Berlin, Potsdamer Str 5, D-10785 Berlin, Germany. Tel: (49 30) 259 200. Fax: 2592 0299. e: info@berlinale.de. Web: www.berlinale.de.

AWARDS 2008

Golden Bear: **The Milk of Sorrow** (Peru/Spain), Claudia Llosa.
Jury Grand Prix Silver Bear: **Everyone Else** (Germany), Maren Ade and **Gigante** (Argentina/Germany/Uruguay), Adrián Biniez.
Silver Bear for Best Director: Asghar Farhadi for **About Elly** (Iran).
Silver Bear for Best Actress: Birgit Minichmayr for ***Everyone Else*** (Germany).
Silver Bear for Best Actor: Sotigui Kouyate for **London River** (Algeria/France/UK).
Golden Bear for Best Short: **Please Say Something** (Republic of Ireland), David O'Reilly.
Silver Bear for Best Short: **Jade** (UK), Daniel Elliott.

St. George Bank Brisbane International Film Festival
End July/mid August, 2010

Since its inception in 1992, this annual celebration of film has evolved to become one of Australia's most highly respected and celebrated festivals, delighting the Brisbane community with quality programming and cutting-edge events. BIFF showcases a range of entertaining and thought-provoking films from Australia and around the world. The critically acclaimed programme offers a feast of about 200 films that include features, documentaries, shorts, experimental and retrospectives. It showcases a number of awards and competitions including the Chauvel and Kinetone Awards, as well as the Queensland Short Film Competition and Queensland New Filmmakers Awards. In addition, BIFF hosts three major film Juries including FIPRESCI, NETPAC and Interfaith. Translink Cine Sparks – the Australian Film Festival for Young People – provides quality world cinema and masterclasses to school-groups and young people. *Inquiries to:* St George Bank BIFF, GPO Box 15094, Brisbane City East, Queensland 4002, Australia. Tel: (61 7) 3007 3003. e: biff@biff.com.au. Web: www.stgeorgebiff.com.au.

AWARDS 2009

Queensland Short Film Competition Audience Favourite Award: **Behind Blue Eyes** (Australia), Martin Moynihan.
Queensland Short Film Competition Critics Choice Award: **Seersucker** (Australia), Mairi Cameron.
TransLink Cine Sparks Award – Junior Jury: **It's Not Me, I Swear!** (French), Philippe Falardeau.
TransLink Cine Sparks Award – Senior Jury: **Ben X** (Netherlands), Nic Balthazar.
Fipresci Jury Award: **Balibo** (Australia), Robert Connolly.
Interfaith Jury Award: **Balibo** (Australia), Robert Connolly.
NETPAC Jury Award: **Agrarian Utopia** (Thailand), Uruphong Raksasad.
NETPAC Jury Award: **About Elly** (Iran), Asghar Farhadi.
Kinetone Award: Jackie McKimmie.
Showtime Top Ten Award Features: **Balibo** (Australia), Robert Connolly.
Showtime Top Ten Award Documentaries: **Yes Madam, Sir** (Australia), Megan Doneman.

Report 2009

St.George Bank Brisbane International Film Festival's milestone 18th year has been marked with commercial success and audience acclaim. Twenty-seven cinema

sessions in the 11-day programme were sell-outs – the highest number and proportion in its history. Average session attendances were also up 42% on last year, contributing to sales targets being exceeded by 18.5%. *Balibo* was the most popular and highly awarded film of the festival, winning two of the festival's five jury prizes as well as the number-one spot on the Showtime Top Ten (the audience's favourites). **– Julie Byth**, Publicist.

Buenos Aires International Independent Film Festival
April 7–18, 2010

BAFICI was created in 1999 and is renowned as an essential form of promotion for independent film output, where the most innovative, daring and committed films are shown. The comprehensive programming of the festival reflects the variety of cultural interests and gathers together acclaimed directors and new talents within a dynamic atmosphere. With its wide range of films, including Argentinean, Latin American and worldwide premieres, as well as retrospectives, BAFICI is one of the most prestigious events for independent cinema in Latin America. BAFICI also programmes sections dedicated to outstanding directors. *Inquiries to:* Buenos Aires Festival Internacional de Cine Independiente, Avenue Roque Saenz Peña 832, 6 Piso, 1035 Capital Federal, Buenos Aires, Argentina. Tel: (54 11) 4393 4670. e: prensa@bafici.gob.ar. www.bafici.gob.ar.

AWARDS 2009
FIPRESCI Award: **Everyone Else** (Germany), Maren Ade.
International Official Selection
Best Feature Film: **Aquele Querido Mês de Agosto** (Portugal), Miguel Gomes.
Special Jury Mention: **Todos Mienten** (Argentina), Matías Piñeiro.
Special Jury Award: **Gasolina** (Guatemala), Julio Hernández Cordón.
Distinction to Best Argentine Film:
Todos Mienten (Argentina), Matías Piñeiro.

Cape Winelands Film Festival
March 17–27, 2010

The Cape Winelands Film Festival (CWFF) is one of the largest film events on the African continent. Since its first edition, it has grown significantly in size and international participation. The 2010 edition will feature 300 screenings in open-air amphitheatres and cinemas in the scenic Winelands district of Stellenbosch, as well as in the historic independent art cinema of the Labia Theatre, in the beautiful city centre of Cape Town. The festival aims to build a rich film culture among South African audiences by celebrating great achievements of the past and present. Aside of existing partnerships with the City of Cape Town, the Cape Film Commission, M-Net's African Film Library and the Centre for Film and Media Studies at the University of Cape Town, the festival organisers have formed new partnerships with the following institutions and individuals: the International Film Guide, The African Film Festival of Leuven in Belgium, the African Cinema Unit at the University of Cape Town, the Cape Town Film Studio and the Cape Town Carnival. In collaboration with these partners, the following main focus areas are planned for 2010: M-Net Lifetime Achievement Award for a great artist from the African continent, which will include a retrospective of the individual's work; a tribute to Terence Davies, including a retrospective and the director's participation in workshops at UCT and Stellenbosch; a tribute to Alain Resnais, who received a lifetime achievement award at the 2009 Cannes film festival, which will include screenings of such

Braam Muller (Jury), Constantinos Soulious (Consul of Greece in Cape Town), Lilian Baksalevowicz (Jury) Kleber Mendonça Filho (Jury)

classic films as *Hiroshima mon amour* and *My American Uncle*, as well as recent films by this great filmmaker. There will also be a tribute to Koos Roets, one of South Africa's greatest cinematographers. It will be the first tribute to a local cinematographer at a South African film festival. There is also a focus on new voices in South African cinema. A strong competition component of selected features, documentaries and shorts from around the world will include a look at the recent films from Russia, Estonia, Latvia and Lithuania. The next edition will also establish the 'Green Carpet Club' (GCC) in order to further develop the festival's environmental initiatives. Open to filmmakers and film industry figures, the GCC aims to promote activities that will help preserve the environment, raise awareness of ecological issues and raise funds that will be donated to organisations with green initiatives. Film fans can participate in the GCC's many planned 'green' activities, such as screenings of movies with 'green' power,

the Earth Conference, and so on. *Inquiries to:* Cape Winelands Film Festival, 1 Waterkant, 52 Arum Rd, Bloubergrandt, Cape Town 7441, South Africa. Tel: (27 21) 556 3204. e: director@films-for-africa.co.za. Web: http:// films-for-africa.co.za.

AWARDS 2009
Best Feature Film: **The First Day of Winter** (Italy), Mirko Locatelli.
Best Documentary: **Accidental Son** (Bosnia), Robert Zuber and Tomislav Mrsic.
Best Short Film: **The Toes** (Belgium), Laurent Denis.
Audience Award Best Film: **My First War** (Israel), Yariv Mozer.

Report 2009
Over 70 features, documentaries and short films from over 35 countries appeared in competition, with more than 130 screenings in the festival programme. The sheer diversity of film cultural offerings at the 2009 festival was acknowledged by many film critics. Highlights during 2009 included a focus on the cinemas of Egypt, Israel, Brazil, Italy, Iran, as well as the former Yugoslavia. The extensive World Panorama section of the festival included the work of many great directors. The festival also celebrated the exciting work by new voices in World Cinema. A strong component of the 2009 festival was the short films, which included numerous award winners from other festivals around the world. Aside from several South African features, shorts and documentaries in the competition, the festival included a special focus on recent South African cinema, with short films by exciting new voices in the film industry. These screenings of graduate work were well attended by students from all of the film courses in Cape Town. The festival had premieres of various South African productions including the comedy *White Wedding* (which enjoyed a highly successful opening night), and *Tornado and the Kalahari Horse Whisperer*, the new feature by acclaimed director Regardt van den Bergh.
– Leon van der Merwe, Festival Director.

Cartagena International Film Festival
February 26–March 6, 2010

Celebrating its 50th anniversary in 2010, the festival promotes cultural diversity and has become the focus for films from Latin American and Caribbean countries that compete for the India Catalina Award. The festival features shorts, documentaries, tributes to Latin American directors and a film and TV market. *Inquiries to:* Cartagena International Film Festival, Centro, Calle San Juan de Dios, Baluarte San Francisco Javier, Cartagena, Colombia. Tel: (57 5) 664 2345. e: info@festicinecartagena.org. Web: www.festicinecartagena.org.

Chicago International Film Festival
October 7–21, 2010

The Chicago International Film Festival is among the oldest competitive events in North America. It spotlights the latest work by established international directors and newcomers, showcasing over 100 features and more than 40 short films during the festival. It bestows its highest honour, the Gold Hugo, on the best feature in the International Competition, with separate prizes for documentaries, student films and shorts. Chicago is one of two US sites to award the FIPRESCI prize for first- and second-time directors, judged by top international critics. *Inquiries to:* Chicago International Film Festival, 30 E Adams St, Suite 800, Chicago, IL 60603, USA. Tel: (1 312) 683 0121. e: info@chicagofilmfestival.com. Web: www.chicagofilmfestival.com.

AWARDS 2009
International Feature Film Competition
Gold Hugo for Best Film: **Mississippi Damned** (USA), Tina Mabry.
Silver Hugo Special Jury Award: **Fish Tank** (UK), Andrea Arnold.
Silver Hugo for Best Director: Marco Bellocchio for **Vinere**, (Italy).
Silver Hugo for Best Actress: Giovanna Mezzogiorno for **Vinere**, (Italy).
Silver Hugo for Best Actor: Filippo Timi for **Vinere**, (Italy).

Gold Plaque for Best Supporting Actress:
Jossie Harris Thacker for **Mississippi Damned**
(USA).
Gold Plaque for Best Supporting Actor:
Michael Fassbender for **Fish Tank** (UK).
Gold Plaque for Best Screenplay:
Tina Mabry for **Mississippi Damned** (USA).
Gold Plaque for Best Cinematography:
Daniele Ciprì for **Vinere**, (Italy).
Gold Plaque for Best Art Direction:
Hipsters (Russia), Valery Todorovsky.

Cinekid Festival
October 20–29, 2010

Cinekid Festival is an annual Film, Television
and New Media Festival for Children that is
held in Amsterdam, in the Netherlands. Every
year, more than 50,000 children are given an
opportunity to attend one or more of the 500
media productions that Cinekid presents:
feature films, children's documentaries, short
films, animation, TV series and single plays,
cross-media productions and interactive
installations, as well as workshops. The main
festival is held in Amsterdam, but approximately
30 satellite festivals are held in cities all over the
Netherlands. Cinekid for Professionals is the
place to be for anybody involved with children
and media. There are readings, seminars, a
chance to meet fellow professionals, screenings
of the best and latest international productions
and all the information needed about them, and
an opportunity to be kept up to date with the
very latest developments and trends: at Cinekid
for Professionals it's all possible. *Inquiries to:*
Cinekid Festival, Korte Leidsedwarsstraat 12,
1017 RC Amsterdam, Netherlands. Tel: (31 20)
531 7890. Fax: 531 7899. e: info@cinekid.nl.
Web: www.cinekid.nl.

AWARDS 2009
Film
Cinekid Lion Jury Award: **A Brand New Life**
(France, South Korea), Ounie Lecomte.
Cinekid Lion Audience Award: **The Crocodiles**
(Germany), Christian Ditter.
MovieSquad Award Cinekid: **The Crocodiles**
(Germany), Christian Ditter.

Television
Cinekid Kinderkast Jury Award Fiction: **Tales
from Zoutvloed** (Netherlands), Iván López
Núnez, Ineke Houtman and Ties Schenk
(VPRO).
Cinekid Kinderkast Jury Award Non-Fiction:
Letters from Nicaragua (Netherlands), Stef
Biemans (VPRO).
Cinekid Kinderkast Audience Award Fiction:
Puppy Patrol (Netherlands), Annemarie
Mooren (Nickelodeon).
*Cinekid Kinderkast Audience Award Non-
Fiction:* **Laura & Anne 4 Ever** (Netherlands),
Susan Koenen (RKK/KRO).
Golden Cinekid Kinderkast: **Applecore,
Episode 'What To Do If You Fall Through the
Ice'** (Netherlands), Uif Putters, Leo de Groot
and Kees Prins (NPS).
New Media
Cinekid New Media Jury Award: **Children for
Children Karaoke** (Netherlands), VARA and
Lost Boys.
Cinekid New Media Audience Award: **SpangaS**
(Netherlands), NCRV and Shop Around.

Report 2009
Cinekid 2009 was a huge success, welcoming
the most visitors ever. The festival opened
with two films, Philippe Falardeau's *It's Not
Me, I Swear!* (Canada), which won both the
jury prize and the children's jury prize at the
Berlin International Film Festival, and Laurent
Tirard's *Le Petit Nicolas* (France), based on
the famous French children's book by René
Goscinny and Jean-Jacques Sempé. The
film competition programme consisted of
15 films from 16 different countries. In the
television section, many Dutch children's

Aaron Springer giving a workshop in the Medialab at Cinekid 2009

series, like *13 in de Oorlog, Tien Torens Diep*, and six youth documentaries made in the Kids & Docs project premiered. The Cinekid Medialab housed 12 installations, different games and over 150 workshops for children. The festival welcomed important guests from all over the world, including Dave Burgess, Head of Character Animation at DreamWorks, and Aaron Springer, writer and director of *Spongebob Squarepants*. Burgess gave a master class and Springer spoke at the seminar 'Scriptwriting for Animation'. Both also attended the Cinekid Medialab and gave workshops for children. The members of the Cinekid 2009 juries were: Film Jury: Michael Hegner (Denmark), Marion Creely (Ireland), Marlene Edmunds (US, Netherlands), Danckert Monrad-Krohn (Norway) and Dorien van de Pas (Netherlands). Television Jury: Mieke de Jong (Netherlands), Remy van Heugten (Netherlands), Marijn van de Jagt (Netherlands), Ingeborg Jansen (Netherlands) and Chris Silos (Netherlands). New Media Jury: Carla Hoekendijk (Netherlands), Christine van de Horn (Netherlands), Remco Pijpers (Netherlands), Henk Loorbach (Netherlands) and Rutger Verhoeven (Netherlands). – **Elvira Pouw**, Assistant Marketing & Communications.

Cinéma Tous Ecrans
October 31–November 7, 2010

Cinéma Tous Ecrans (cinema for any screen) is an international film festival focusing on fiction films for cinema, television, the web, cell phones and urban screens. The only one of this kind in Switzerland, the festival celebrates the evolution of cinema and continues to open itself up to all existing types of screens, those of today and tomorrow, promoting the idea that visual supports are beyond artistic hierarchy. *Inquiries to:* Claudia Durgnat, Director, Cinéma Tous Ecrans, Maison des Arts du Grütli, 16 rue Général Dufour, CP 5730, CH-1211 Geneva 11, Switzerland. Tel: (41 22) 809 6918. Fax: 329 3747. e: info@cinema-tous-ecrans.ch. Web: www.cinema-tous-ecrans.ch.

AWARDS 2009
International Competition
Reflet d'Or for Best Film: **Lost Persons Area** (Belgium/Hungary/Netherlands), Caroline Stubbe.
Reflet d'Or for Best Direction: **Tamo I Ovde** (*Here & There*), (Germany/Serbia/USA), Darko Lungulov.
Prix Tudor Best Female Performance: Adèle Haenel for **Déchaînées** (Switzerland).
Prix Tudor Best Male Performance: Riz Ahmed for **Shifty** (UK).
Prix Titra Film SA for the Encouragement of Theatrical Distribution: **Tamo I Ovde** (*Here & There*), (Germany/Serbia/USA), Darko Lungulov.
FIPRESCI Award: **Tamo I Ovde** (*Here & There*), (Germany/Serbia/USA), Darko Lungulov.
Youth Jury Award: **Shifty** (UK), Eran Creevy.
Youth Jury Special Mention: **Tamo I Ovde** (*Here & There*), (Germany/Serbia/USA), Darko Lungulov.
Audience Award: **Un Ange à la Mer** (Belgium/Canada), Frédéric Dumont.
Regards d'Aujourd'hui Competition
Reflet d'Or for Best Film: **Backyard** (Mexico), Carlos Carrera.

Caroline Stubbe's **Lost Persons Area**, *winner of the Reflet d'Or for Best Film at Cinéma Tous Ecrans*

Actua Films Award: **Fortapasc** (Italy),
Marco Risi.
*International Series, Collections & Long
Dramas Competition*
Reflet d'Or for Best Series: **Klass: Elu Pärast**
(*The Class: Life After*) (Estonia), Ilmar Raag and
Gerda Kordemets.
Reflet d'Or for Best Collection & Long Drama:
Blood and Oil (UK), David Attwood.
Audience Award for Best Series:
Les Invincibles (France), Alexandre
Castagnetti and Pierric Gantelmi d'Ille.
New Screens for Drama Competition
Reflet d'Or for Best Online Series: **Enjoy the
Silence** (France), Jean Auguste François and
Marc Laine.
Reflet d'Or for Best Web Fiction:
The Hunt for Gollum (UK), Chris Bouchard.
*Reflet d'Or for Best Interactive Multimedia
Fiction:* **The Time Machine** (USA), Chad
Villela, Matt Bettinelli-Olpin, Rob Polonsky and
Jonah Goldstein.
Grand Award Pacte Multimedia: **Les Valaisans
dans l'Espace** (Switzerland), Hatman.
*Prix TV5 Monde for Best French Speaking
Fiction:* **Déchaînées** (Switzerland),
Raymond Vouillamoz.
Swissperform Award for Best TV Film:
Déchaînées (Switzerland),
Raymond Vouillamoz.
*Swissperform Award for Best Female
Performance:* Marie Leuenberger for
Die Standesbeamtin (Switzerland).
*Swissperform Award for Best Male
Performance:* Bastien Semenzato for
Les Caprices de Marianne (Switzerland).
Swiss Short Films Competition
Reflet d'Or for Best Swiss Short Film:
Schönzeit, Irene Ledermann.
*Swisscom Audience Award for Best Swiss
Short Film:* **Signalis**, Adrian Flückiger.
*Taurus Studio Incentive Award for Best Swiss
Short Film:* **Signalis**, Adrian Flückiger.
European Short Films Competition
Reflet d'Or for Best European Short Film:
Gestreept (Belgium), Toon Mertens and Jonas
Baeckland.
Special Mention: **Left Right** (Greece),
Starvos Raptis and Argiris Germanidis.

TSR Award for Best European Short Film:
The Last Day of Bulkin I S (Russia),
Alexey Andrianov.
Other Awards:
Cinema Tout Mobile: (Mobile phone screens
competition: see www.cinematoutmobile.ch
for details.
Cinema Tout Dooh: (Urban screens
competition: see www.cinematoutdooh.com
for details.

Clermont-Ferrand Short Film Festival
January 29–February 6, 2010

International, National and 'Lab' competitions
for 35mm films and digital works on DigiBeta
and Beta SP, all completed after 1 January,
2009, of 40 minutes or less. All the entries
will be listed in the Market catalogue. Many
other side programmes (retrospectives and
panoramas). The 31st edition attracted more
than 137,000 admissions and welcomed 3,000
professionals. *Inquiries to:* Clermont-Ferrand
Short Film Festival, La Jetée, 6 Place Michel-
de L'Hospital 63058 Clermont-Ferrand Cedex
1, France. Tel: (33 473) 916 573. e: info@
clermont-filmfest.com. Web: www.clermont-
filmfest.com.

AWARDS 2009
Grand Prix
International: **Everyday Everyday** (Malaysia),
Chui Mui Tan.
National: **Forbach** (France), Claire Burger.
Lab: **Muto** (Italy), Blu.
Audience Prize
International: **Andong** (Philippines),
Milo Talentino.
National: **Séance Familiale** (France, Taiwan),
Cheng-Chui Kuo.
Lab: **Yellow Sticky Notes** (Canada),
Jeff Chiba Stears.

Copenhagen Film Festivals

BUSTER September 10–20, 2010
CPH:DOX November 5–14, 2010
CPH:PIX April 15–25, 2010

Copenhagen Film Festivals is the Danish
capital's festival powerhouse, with the country's
three major international film festivals: CPH
PIX – the new feature film festival launched
in 2009 after the merger of the Copenhagen
International Film Festival and the NatFilm
Festival; BUSTER – the international film
festival for children and youth launched in 2000;
CPH:DOX – the international documentary film
festival launched in 2004. *Inquiries to:* Øster
Farimagsgade 16B, DK-2100 Copenhagen Ø,
Denmark. Tel: CPH:PIX (45) 3312 0005, BUSTER
(45) 3312 0005, CPH:DOX (45) 3393 0734.
e: info@cphpix.dk, buster@buster.dk, info@
cphdox.dk. Web: www.cphfilmfestivals.dk.

AWARDS 2009

CPH PIX
New Talent Grand PIX: Peter Strickland,
Katalin Varga (Romania).
Politiken Audience Award: **It's Not Me I Swear**
(Canada), Philippe Falardeau.
BUSTER
Best BUSTER (Children's Jury):
Die Perlmutterfarbe (Germany),
Marcus H Rosenmüller.
Best Film For Children (International Jury):
The Other Bank (Georgia), George Orvashvili.
Best Film For Youth (Youth Jury):
My Suicide (USA), David Lee Miller.
CPH:DOX
DOX:AWARD: **Trash Humpers** (USA),
Harmony Korine.

NEW: VISION Award: **O'er the Land** (USA),
Deborah Stratment.
Politiken's Audience Award: **Into Eternity**
(Denmark), Michael Madsen.

Cork Film Festival

November 7–14, 2010

Cork Film Festival is Ireland's oldest film
festival. Now in its 55th year, the eclectic
programme includes World Cinema, Documentary Panorama and Irish Showcase strands. In
particular the festival celebrates the art of the
short film. Short Film Competition includes
awards for Best International Short, Best European Short and Best Irish Short. The festival's
side-bars include retrospectives, programmes
of experimental work, 'live cinema' and films
from the Mediterranean countries (EuroCin-
eMed). *Inquiries to:* Corona Cork Film Festival,
Emmet House, Emmet Place, Cork, Ireland.
Tel: (353 21) 427 1711. Fax: 427 5945. e: info@
corkfilmfest.org. Web: www.corkfilmfest.org.

AWARDS 2009

Best Irish Short: **Free Chips Forever!**
Claire Dix.
*Claire Lynch Award for Best First-Time Irish
Director:* **Questions**, Mark Noonan.
Best International Short: **Muto** (Italy), Blu.
*Cork Short Film Nominee for the European
Film Awards:* **Joseph's Snails** (France),
Sophie Roze.
Audience Award for Best International Short:
Moore Street Masala (Ireland),
David O'Sullivan.
Audience Award for Best Irish Short: **Bye Bye
Now**, Ross Whitaker and Aideen O'Sullivan.

Festival director, Mick Hannigan, Councillor Dara Murphy, Lord Mayor, and P.S. Raghavan, Ambassador of India. Photo: Sarah Cadogan

Award of the Festival for Best Short: **Elephant Skin** (Austria), Severin Fiala and Ulrike Putzer.
Youth Jury Award for Best International Short: **Lesh Sabreen** (Palestine), Muayad Alayan.
Outlook Award for Best LGBT Short: **Bombshell** (Australia), Kim Farrant.
'Made In Cork' Award for Best Short: **My Beamish Boy**, Mike Hannon.

Report 2009

The 54th edition of Cork Film Festival attracted some 30,000 admissions to a wide-ranging programme of screenings, talks, masterclasses and events. Guests included Julian Temple, presenting his latest film *Oil City Confidential*; Swiss animator Georges Scwizgebel, subject of the festival retrospective; Austrian avant-garde filmmaker Peter Tscherkassky; Vancouver-based filmmaker Alex MacKenzie; artist Qasim Riza Shaheen presenting the world premiere of his installation, 'Stains and Stencils', and Edward

Julien Temple, director and Stephen Malit, producer of **Oil City Confidential**. *Photo: Sean Moriarty*

De Bono giving a workshop on 'Creativity and Innovation'. The festival also welcomed a host of documentary and short film directors and producers. The Festival Focus was on Indian shorts, and new films from the Mediterranean and Arab territories were also highlighted. New Irish productions of shorts, documentaries and features were screened.
– Sean Kelly, Festival Manager.

FilmFestival Cottbus:
Festival of East European Cinema
November 2–7, 2010

With an upcoming 20th anniversary, FilmFestival Cottbus has developed as the world's leading festival of East European cinema. Each year in November, it presents a representative survey of contemporary feature-films and short features from the Central and Eastern European area. While the programme centres around the feature-film competition, different sections are dedicated to National Hits, Spectrum – different artistic approaches, Retrospective or Children's and Youth film. A Focus every year casts a spotlight upon a special region. With almost 19,000 visitors in 2009 and a total prize value of 77,000 Euros, the festival attracts actors and producers who also gather at the Cottbus receptions in Karlovy Vary and Sarajevo, as well as many visitors from the region.
Inquiries to: FilmFestival Cottbus, Werner-Seelenbinder-Ring 44/45, D-03048 Cottbus, Germany. Tel: (49 355) 431 070. Fax: 431 0720. e: info@filmfestivalcottbus.de. Web: www.filmfestivalcottbus.de.

AWARDS 2009
Feature Film Competition
LUBINA for Best Film: **Ordinary People** (Serbia), Vladimir Persisic.
LUBINA for Best Director: Alexey Mizgirev for **Buben Baraban** (Russia) and Zvonimir Juric and Goran Devic for **The Blacks** (Croatia).
LUBINA for Outstanding Actress: Anna Karczmarczyk for **Mall Girls** (Poland).
LUBINA for Outstanding Actor: Relja Popovic for **Ordinary People** (Serbia).

The opening night of the Cottbus Film Festival

IFG Inspiration Award: **The 40th Door**
(Azerbaijan), Elchin Musaoglu.
Short Feature Competition
Main Prize: **Coming Out** (Hungary), Pici Papai.
Special Prize: **Interieur, Apartment, Night**
(Croatia), Sasa Ban.
Promotion prize of the DEFA Foundation:
Dreams of the Lausitz (Germany),
Bernd Sallmann.
Prize for Best Debut Film:
Mall Girls (Poland), Kasia Roslaniec.
Audience Award: **Farewell, Gulsary!**
(Kazakhstan), Ardak Amirkulov.
FIPRESCI: **The Blacks** (Croatia), Zvonimir Juric
and Goran Devic.
Prize of the Ecumenical Jury: **Buben Baraban**
(Russia), Alexey Mizgirev.
Don Quijote-Prize:
Alive! (Albania), Artan Minarolli.
Dialogue Prize for Intercultural Communication:
Foxes (Czech Repubic/Slovakia), Mira Fornay.
Cottbus Discovery Award: **Folds and Cracks**
(Georgia), Zaza Rusadze.

Report 2009
By no means simply a stopgap year, wedged
between the 18th edition ('coming of age')
and the planned 20th anniversary, the 19th
FFC managed to increase both the programme
and audience numbers. Additional to the
'Russian Day', the festival introduced 'Salem
Kazakhstan!' and 'Polskie Horyzonty', the
latter being a tribute to a new cooperation
with Era New Horizons Festival in Wroclaw.
Round tables with the Russian, Kazakh and
Black Sea industry, as well as the East-West
co-production market Connecting Cottbus,

were forums for exchange. While the Balkan
countries dominated the competition, films
from Georgia as well as filmmakers Nana
Djordjadze, Zaza Rusadze and others proved
the secret stars of this year´s festival.
– **Cornelia Kaestner**, Press Officer.

Crossroads Film Festival
April 16–18, 2010

The Crossroads Film Festival is the largest
film festival in Mississippi and celebrates
its eleventh anniversary in 2010. Founded in
1999 in the capital city of Jackson – known as
'The Crossroads of the South' – the festival
was designed as a place where the strands
and influences of art, theme, and culture
come together. Every event celebrates film,
music, and food, along with the great culture
and heritage of Mississippi. Each year, the
festival provides a cross-cultural backdrop of
screenings, concerts and receptions, as well as
young filmmakers' workshops and filmmaker
forums. It has celebrated filmmakers with ties
to Mississippi, beginning with Robert Altman in
its premiere year and including native Morgan
Freeman, resident Joey Lauren Adams, and
Vicksburg native Charles Burnett. Crossroads is
a top Mississippi stop for many films made in
the state: *Prom Night in Mississippi, Ballast, Big
Bad Love, The Rising Place, I'll Fly Away, Cries
of Silence, Red Dirt* and *Blossom Time* among
them. *Inquiries to:* Crossroads Film Festival, PO
Box 22604, Jackson, MS 39225, USA. Tel: (1
601) 510 9148. e: info@crossroadsfilmfestival.
com. Web: www.crossroadsfilmfestival.com.

AWARDS 2009
Feature: **Goodbye Solo** (USA), Ramin Bahrani.
Documentary: **Life of a Legend** (USA),
Jim Dollarhide.
Short Documentary: **Creative Crossroads**
(USA), Tristan Wheelock, Win Graham and
Sichendra Bista.
Short: **Small Collection** (USA),
Jeremiah Crowell.
Student: **Symphony** (USA), Erick Oh.
Animation: **A Long Distance Call** (China),
Joe Chang.

Experimental: **An Unquiet Mind** (USA),
Chihwen Lo.
Music Video: **Gentleman Auction House's
'The Book of Matches'** (USA), Steve Kozel.
Adam Ford Youth Filmmaking: **Unrenewable**
(USA), Philip Heinrich.
The Ruma: **Leaves Flutter** (USA),
Clay Hardwick.
Director's Choice Award: **I Ran Against Us**
(USA), N T Bullock and Jared Hopkins.
Audience Choice Award: **Prom Night in
Mississippi** (Canada, USA), Paul Saltzman.

Starz Denver Film Festival
November 11–21, 2010

The Starz Denver Film Festival presents more
than 175 films from around the world and
plays host to over 125 filmmakers. Including
new international features, cutting-edge
independent fiction and non-fiction works,
shorts and a variety of special programmes,
the Starz Denver Film Festival also features
the best in student work with the inclusion
of the First Look Student Film section. SDFF
pays tribute to established film artists with
retrospective screenings of their works.
Entry fee: $40 ($20 for students). The Denver
Film Society also programmes the Starz
FilmCenter, Colorado's only cinematheque,
daily throughout the year. *Inquiries to:* Denver
Film Society at the Starz FilmCenter, 900
Auraria Parkway, Denver, Colorado 80204,
USA. Tel: (1 303) 595 3456. e: dfs@denverfilm.
org. Web: www.denverfilm.org.

Dubai International Film Festival
Mid-December 2010

The Dubai International Film Festival (DIFF),
the leading festival in the region, was launched
with its theme of 'Bridging Cultures/Meeting
Minds' in 2004. DIFF reflects Dubai's cosmopolitan and multicultural character and its
mission for global understanding and intercultural dialogue. The festival showcases a wide
selection of features, shorts and documentaries from around the world. It continues to
act as a platform for showcasing excellence in
Arab Cinema and contributing to the development and growth of the regional industry and
talent. The Muhr Awards for Excellence in Arab
Cinema, in its third successful year, gained
a sibling prize in 2008, the Muhr Asia Africa
Competition, with an aim of recognising filmmakers originating from these markets. The
Muhr Awards applaud the perseverance and
talent of young and independent filmmakers
and encourage creativity from Asia, Africa and
the region. The 2008 festival built on the successes of the past years and introduced strong
new initiatives, such as the revolutionary Dubai
Film Market, a state-of-the-art content-trading
platform that spurred several high-level agreements between regional and international film
professionals. For more information please
log on to www.dubaifilmfest.com. *Inquiries
to:* Dubai Media City, PO Box 53777, Dubai,
United Arab Emirates. Tel: (971 4) 391 3378.
e: diffinfo@dubaimediacity.ae. Web: www.
dubaifilmfest.com.

Edinburgh International Film Festival
June 17–28, 2009

Edinburgh International Film Festival devotes
itself to discovering and promoting the very
best in international cinema and to embracing,
celebrating and debating changes and developments in the global film industry. Key to the
EIFF mission is the identification, exposure and
development of the filmmaking legends of the
future. *Inquiries to:* Edinburgh International Film
Festival, 88 Lothian Rd, Edinburgh EH3 9BZ,
Scotland. Tel: (44 131) 228 4051. e: info@edfilm-
fest.org.uk. Web: www.edfilmfest.org.uk.

AWARDS 2009
*Michael Powell Award for Best New British
Feature:* **Moon** (UK), Duncan Jones.
*PPG Award for Best Performance in a British
Feature Film:* Katie Jarvis for **Fish Tank** (UK).
Skillset New Director's Award: Cary Joji
Fukunaga for **Sin Nombre** (Mexico, USA).
Best New International Feature: **Easier With
Practice** (USA), Kyle Patrick Alvarez.
Best Documentary Award: **Boris Ryzhy**
(Netherlands), Aliona Van Der Horst.

Standard Life Audience Award: **The Secret of Kells** (Belgium, France, Ireland), Tomm Moore.
The Rotten Tomatoes Critical Concensus Award: **Humpday** (USA), Lynn Shelton.
UK Film Council Award for Best British Short Film: **After Tomorrow** (UK), Emma Sullivan.
McLaren Award for Best New British Animation in Partnership with BBC Film Network: **Photograph of Jesus** (UK), Laurie Hill.
European Film Academy Short Film - Prix UIP: **Princess Margaret BLVD** (Canada), Kazik Radwanksi.
Short Scottish Documentary Award Supported by Baillie Gifford: **Peter In Radioland** (UK), Johanna Wagner.

Era New Horizons
International Film Festival
July 22–August 1, 2010

Era New Horizons International Film Festival is the biggest film festival in Poland and regarded as one of the most important film events in Central Europe, visited each year by an increasing number of cinema lovers from Poland and abroad. The festival presents films which go beyond the borders of conventional cinema. Its main objective is to present uncompromising, innovative and original cinema from all over the world. The festival's name suggests an exploration of new horizons in film language, expressions and storytelling. The festival belongs to the elite group of festivals accredited by FIAPF – the International Federation of Film Producers Associations.
Inquiries to: Era New Horizons International Film Festival, 1 Zamenhofa Street, 00-153 Warsaw, Poland. Tel: (48 22) 530 6640. Fax: 831 0663. e: festival@enh.pl. Web: www.enh.pl.

AWARDS 2009
New Horizons International Competition
Grand Prix: **Hunger** (United Kingdom), Steve McQueen.
Film Critics: **Hunger** (United Kingdom), Steve McQueen.
Audience Prize: **Oxygen** (Russia), Ivan Vyrypayev.

Films on Art International Competition
Best Film Award: **FLicKeR** (Canada), Nick Sheenan.
Jury Special Mention: **Double Take** (Belgium/Germany/The Netherlands), Johan Grimonprez.
New Polish Films Competition
Wrocław Film Award: **Snow White and Russian Red** (Poland), Xawery Żuławski.
Best New Director Prize: **Mall Girls** (Poland), Katarzyna Rosłaniec.

Report 2009
For its ninth edition, the festival presented 545 films from 45 countries, including 250 feature titles of which 120 had their Polish premieres in Wrocław. The 2009 festival attracted over 122,000 spectators. Films in competition, country focuses, director retrospectives and Polish-Swedish Film Meetings highlighted the festival's 2009 platform. The festival organisers presented opportunities for audiences to discover emerging filmmakers from around the world, while savouring the classic work

Screening of the 1919 Swedish masterpiece **Sir Arne's Treasure** *at the Wrocław Opera with live music composed for the festival by Leszek Możdżer*

of established film artists. During the festival, five competitions were held: Festival's flagship – New Horizons International Competition; premiering in 2009, Films on Art International Competition; New Polish Films Competition; European Short Films; and Polish Short Films Competition. The prizes awarded came to a value of over 70,000 Euros. An important part of the programme of the festival presents retrospectives of national cinematography of different countries. The 2009 festival focused on Swedish cinema, presenting new films and a retrospective of films by Jan Troell, contemporary Canadian cinema (including a retrospective of Guy Maddin) and the Hungarian New Wave. The festival also showcased directors' retrospectives, devoted to Tsai Ming-Liang, Jennifer Reeves, Guy Maddin, Jan Troell, Krzysztof Zanussi and Piotra Dumała. The Polish-Swedish Film Meetings brought together producers, distributors, sales agents, film schools and other professionals from Sweden and Poland to select eight projects from both countries seeking co-producers and funding. Over three days, the participants took part in seminars, one-to-one pitching sessions and informal meetings. International sales agents, among them TrustNordisk, Svensk Filmindustri, Wide Management and The Coproduction Office presented their latest films to the Polish distributors and acquisition executives from Polish broadcasters. The special events of the festival included screenings of silent films with live music at the Wrocław Opera House as well as art installations and video-installation such as Erotic Space by Tsai Ming-Liang. Over 11 days, the festival hosted over 350 international and 550 guests from Poland, including prestigious directors, producers, distributors and film critics. There were many outstanding artists among them: Agnès Varda, Peter Greenaway, Mike Figgis, directors of films presented in the competitions and filmmakers presented in the retrospectives such as Guy Maddin, Jan Troell, Tsai Ming-Liang, Jennifer Reeves, Krzysztof Zanussi and Piotr Dumała. Some 355 journalists and film critics from Poland and abroad were accredited at the festival.

- **Agnieszka Wolak**, Public Relations Director.

Espoo Ciné International Film Festival
August 21–29, 2010

Espoo Ciné has established itself as the annual showcase of contemporary European, primarily long-feature, cinema in Finland. The 21st Espoo Ciné festival will take place in Espoo, Finland 21–29 August, 2010. The traditional section should appeal to every movie buff in Finland, and the growing fantasy selection should attract those hungry for stimulation of the imagination. Annual special programmes present, for example, Spanish and Italian gems, films from Eastern Europe, documentaries, gay films and US indies, not to forget the best of contemporary Finnish cinema, outdoor screenings, retrospectives, sneak previews, seminars and distinguished guests. Estimated amount of screenings: 150–200. Estimated attendance: 27,000. For entry regulations see the website. *Inquiries to:* Espoo Ciné, PO Box 95, FI-02101 Espoo, Finland. Tel: (358 9) 466 599. Fax: 466 458. e: office@espoocine.fi. Web: www.espoocine.fi.

The outdoor screening of **Mamma Mia** *at Espoo Ciné on 20 August 2009. Photo: Matti Näränen*

Fajr International Film Festival
January 25–February 4, 2010
Iranian International Market for Films and TV Programmes
January 27–February 1, 2010

In the international programme of the festival, there are three different competitive sections: International Competition, Competition of Spiritual Cinema (emphasising cinema's role as a rich medium for the expression of the essence of religious faith) and Competition of Asian Cinema (organised with the aim of promoting film art and industry in Asian countries). The non-competitive sections include 'Festival of Festivals' (a selection of outstanding films presented at other international festivals), 'Special Screenings' (films of documentary or narrative content which introduce cinema or cultural developments in certain geographical regions), retrospectives, etc. Coinciding with the international programme, the Iranian Film Market (IFM) provides not only a friendly atmosphere for cutting deals, but also a unique showcase for new Iranian productions with English subtitles or simultaneous translation, premiered for the international participants. In the national programme, there are different competitive sections as well. Director: Mahdi Masoud Shahi. *Inquiries to:* Fajr International Film Festival, No. 19, 2nd Floor, Delbar Alley, Toos St, Valiye Asr Ave, Tehran 19617-44973, Iran. Tel: (98 21) 2273 5090/4801. Fax: 2273 4801. e: office@fajrfestival.ir. Web: www. fajrfestival.ir.

AWARDS 2009
International Competition:
Best Film: **Snow** (Bosnia and Herzegovina/ France/Germany/Iran), Benny Dreschel, Karsten Stoter, François d'Artemare and Elma Tataragic.
Special Jury Prize: **Pandora's Box** (Belgium/ France/Germany/Turkey), Yesim Ustaoglu.
Best Director: Aida Begic for **Snow** (Bosnia and Herzegovina/France/Germany/Iran).
Best Script: **9mm** (Belgium/ France), Taylan Barman and Kenan Gorgun.

Aida Begic, Bosnian filmmaker, accepts her prize for **Snow** *from International Jury of Fajr 2009*

Best Performance: Derya Alabora, Ovul Avkiran and Tsilla Chelton for **Pandora's Box** ((Belgium/France/Germany/Turkey).
Best Technical or Artistic Achievement: **Divine Weapon** (South Korea), Yu-jin Kim.
Best Short Film (jointly): **Why Dogs Hate Cats?** (Iran), Lida Fazli; **Amin** (France/Germany/The Netherlands), David Dusa.
Competition of Spiritual Cinema:

Best Film: **Every Night, Solitude** (Iran), Rasoul Sadr Ameli.
Best Director: **Orphanage** (Mexico/Spain), Juan Antonio Bayona.
Best Script: **Walking My Life** (Japan), Satsuo Endo.
Competition of Asian Cinema:
Best Film: **With a Girl of a Black Soil** (France/South Korea), Soo-il Jeon.
Best Director: **Kabuli Kid** (Afghanistan/France), Barmak Akram.
Best Script: **Best Wishes for Tomorrow** (Japan), Takashi Koizumi and Roger Pulvers.

Aida Begic's **Snow**

Fantasporto
February 26–March 6, 2010

The 30th edition of the Oporto International Film Festival takes place in the cinemas of Oporto and in the north of Portugal, mostly at the Rivoli – Teatro Municipal, Teatro Sá da Bandeira and Warner Lusomundo Theatres (around 5,000 seats in total). Aside from the Competitive Sections (Fantasy, Directors' Week, Orient Express) the Festival also includes the sections, 'Panorama of the Portuguese Cinema', 'Anima-te' for younger audiences, 'Première' for previews and vintage features, and 'Love Connection'. The Retrospectives will include the Portuguese director Luis Galvão Telles, among others. Director: Mário Dorminsky. *Inquiries to:* Fantasporto, Rua Anibal Cunha 84, Sala 1.6, 4050-048 Porto, Portugal. Tel: (35 1) 222 058 819 Fax: 222 058 823. e: info@fantasporto. online.pt. Web: www.fantasporto.com.

AWARDS 2009
Official Fantasy Section
Best Film: **Idiots and Angels** (USA), Bill Plympton.
Special Jury Award: **Hansel and Gretel** (South Korea), Phil-Sung Yim.
Best Direction: James Watkins for **Eden Lake** (UK).
Best Actor: Jack O'Connel for **Eden Lake** (UK).
Best Actress: Macarena Gomez for **Sexykiller** (Spain).
Best Screenplay: Bill Plympton for **Idiots and Angels** (USA).
Best Cinematography: James Hawkinson for **The Unborn** (USA).

Best Fantasy Short: **Next Floor** (Canada), Denis Vileneuve.
Special Mention of the Jury: **Astropia** (Finland/Iceland/UK), Gunnar Gudmundsson.
19th Director's Week
Best Film Award and Manoel de Oliveira Award: **Moscow, Belgium** (Belgium), Christhope van Rompaey.
Best Director: Bent Hamer for **O'Horten** (France/Germany/Norway).
Special Jury Prize: **Palermo Shooting** (France/Germany/Italy), Wim Wenders.
Best Actor: Brian Cox for **The Escapist**, (Republic of Ireland/UK).
Best Actress: Mamatha Bhukya for **Vanaja** (India/USA).
Best Screenplay: Sergey Rokotov and Yevgeniy Nikishow for **The Vanished Empire** (Russia).
Orient Express Competitive Section
Best Film Award: **Hansel and Gretel** (South Korea), Phil-Sung Yim.
Special Jury Award: **The Chaser** (South Korea), Hong-Jin Na.
Méliès D'Argent Awards
Méliès D'Argent Feature: **Absurdistan** (Germany), Veit Helmer.
Méliès D'Argent Short Film: **Mama** (Spain), Andy Muschietti.
Homage: Galician Cinema (Spain).
Critics Award: **Delta** (Hungary), Kornel Mundruczo.
Audience Award: **The Wrestler** (USA), Darren Aronofsky.
Career Awards: José Fonseca e Costa, Wim Wenders and Paul Schrader.

Report 2009
With a selection that was praised by juries,

Wim Wenders and Paul Schrader on the boat tour of Fantasporto's social programme for guests

audiences and critics, the 29th edition of the Oporto International Film Festival has again been a huge moment for film in Portugal. German director Wim Wenders, who was one of the honorees with a Career Award from the festival, also presented a film in competition, *The Palermo Shooting*. The film received the Special Jury Prize of the 19th Directors' Week. Other Career Awards recipients were Paul Schrader and Portuguese director José Fonseca e Costa, who was also honoured with a full retrospective of his work. Galicean Cinema and German director Jorg Buttgereit also received retrospectives. The festival also showcased a full programme dedicated to 'Architecture and the Cinema'. Celebrated architects Sou Fujimoto (Japan) and Marcos Cruz (UK/Portugal) presented their own visionary creations to complete the film programme, which was attended by nearly 2,000 people. *Idiots and Angels*, by American animation master Bill Plympton, won the Best Film Award of the Fantasy competition. The film also won the Best Screenplay Award. British director James Watkins won the best director award for his

horror film, *Eden Lake*, with the Best Actor Award going to Jack O'Connell, as the leader of a gang of very fierce teenagers. South Korean director Phil Sung-Yim's *Hansel & Gretel* ran in two sections and won the Special Prize of the Fantasy competition and the Best Film award of the Orient Express programme. The 19th Directors' Week, a favourite of the festivalgoers, gave its major award to *Moscow, Belgium* by Christophe Van Rompaey. Van Rompaey had previously won two short film awards at Fantasporto. The Critics Award went to the Hungarian film *Delta*, by Kornél Mundruczo, while the Audience Award went to Darren Aronofsky's *The Wrestler*. The festival closed with the traditional Vampire's Ball, attended by nearly 10,000 people. The festival budget was €4 million. The 30th edition of the Oporto International film festival will take place 26 February to 6 March in the world heritage city of the north of Portugal.
– **Mário Dorminsky**, Festival Director.

Far East Film Festival
April 23–May 1, 2010

Created in 1998, the Far East Film Festival is the most highly anticipated annual event in Udine. A popular festival, it has gradually forged a unique place for itself, presenting International and European Premieres of films from Japan, China, Hong Kong, Thailand, the Philippines, Indonesia, Malaysia, South Korea, Taiwan, Vietnam and Singapore. With an overall attendance of over 50,000, Far East Film has seen, year after year, an increase in interest from the international, national, and local public, including over a thousand accreditation

APRIL 23rd/MAY 1st 2010
Teatro Nuovo/Visionario
Udine, ITALY
www.fareastfilm.com

Far East Film Festival president Sabrina Baracetti (left), with director Ann Hui (centre), and festival coordinator, Thomas Bertacche (right)

requests from journalists coming from Europe, Asia and America... all of whom are now loyal FEFF fans. *Inquiries to:* Centro Espressioni Cinematografiche, Via Villalta 24, 33100 Udine, Italy. Tel: (39 04) 3229 9545. Fax: 3222 9815. e: fareastfilm@cecudine.org, Web: www. fareastfilm.com.

AWARDS 2009
Audience Award First Prize: **Departures** (Japan), Takita Yojiro.
Audience Award Second Prize: **Scandal Makers** (South Korea), Kang Hyeoung-chul.
Audience Award Third Prize: **The Rainbow Troops** (Indonesia), Riri Riza.
Black Dragon Award First Prize: **Departures** (Japan), Takita Yojiro.
Black Dragon Award Second Prize: **4BIA** (Thailand), Yongyooth Thongkongtoon.
Black Dragon Award Third Prize: **Connected** (Hong Kong), Benny Chan.

Report 2009
This year, the Udinese Festival exceeded its threshold of 50,000 spectators, bringing together the greatest number of applicants ever to participate in the event: 1,200 from over ten different countries, along with the 200 plus journalists and 30 representatives from international festivals. The festival's annual international visionary showcase, 'Ties That Bind', was transformed this year into an audiovisual workshop, where producers and distributors from Europe and Asia came to exchange news, views and ideas. The workshop, set up with EAVE, is

a key instrument for the European Union's MEDIA programme, and is exclusively reserved for professionals working in the field. **– Gianmatteo Pellizzari and Federica Manaigo**, Press Office.

Festival Des 3 Continents
November 23–30, 2010

The only annual competitive (with fiction and documentary) festival in the world for films that originate solely from Africa, Asia, and Latin and Black America. It's one of the few festivals where genuine discoveries may still be made. From Hou Hsiao-hsien or Abbas Kiarostami in the 1980s, to Darejan Omirbaev or Jia zang Ke more recently, unknown great authors have been shown and acknowledged in Nantes. For more than 30 years, F3C has also charted the film history of the southern countries through retrospectives (genres, countries, actors and actresses), showing more than 1,200 films and bringing to light large pieces of an unrecognised part of the world's cinematographic heritage. *Inquiries to:* Philippe Reilhac, General Manager, Festival des 3 Continents, BP 43302, 44033 Nantes Cedex 1, France. Tel: (33 2) 4069 7414. e: festival@3continents.com. Web: www.3continents.com.

Filmfest Hamburg
September 23–October 2, 2010

Under the direction of Albert Wiederspiel, the renowned film festival takes place every year in the fall. Around 130 international films are screened as German or world premieres in the following sections: Agenda, Eurovisuell, Voila!, Vitrina, Nordlichter, Deluxe, TV Movies in cinema and Michel Children's and Youth Filmfest. The many facets of the programme range from highbrow arthouse films to innovative mainstream cinema. The Douglas Sirk Award honours outstanding contributions to film culture and business. There are 38,000 admissions and about 1,000 industry professionals attend. Filmfest Hamburg also sees itself as a platform for cultural exchange and dialogue: in the past years, the festival has, among other things, shed light more especially on productions from Asia (from Iran to Japan and Korea) and Europe (from the UK and Scandinavia to France, Spain and Eastern Europe). *Inquiries to:* Filmfest Hamburg, Steintorweg 4, 20099 Hamburg, Germany. Tel: (49 40) 3991 9000-0. e: info@filmfesthamburg. de. Web: www.filmfesthamburg.de.

Fort Lauderdale International Film Festival
October 22–November 11, 2010

The festival features more than 200 films from around the globe during the world's longest film event, with screenings in Miami, Palm Beach and Fort Lauderdale. Awards include Best Film, Best Foreign-Language Film, Best American Indie, Best Director, Actor, Screenplay, Best Florida Film and Kodak Student prizes for Narrative (over 20 minutes), Short Narrative (20 minutes or under), Documentary and Experimental. *Inquiries to:* The Fort Lauderdale International Film Festival, 1314 East Las Olas Blvd, Suite 007, Fort Lauderdale, FL 33301, USA. Tel: (1 954) 760 9898. e: info@fliff.com. Web: www.fliff.com.

Fribourg
March 13–20, 2010

The festival promotes and supports independent cinema and young filmmakers from Asia, South America and Africa. The core of the festival is the high-level competition of feature-length fiction and documentary films, which attracts every year audacious, artistic and visionary pictures. The official selection is complemented by a short-film programme. Furthermore, special sections and retrospectives offer the possibility of going deeper into a cinematographic topic, genre or period. *Inquiries to:* Fribourg International Film Festival, Ancienne Gare, Case Postale 550, CH-1701 Fribourg, Switzerland. Tel: (41 26) 347 4200. e: info@fiff.ch. Web: www.fiff.ch.

AWARDS 2009
Grand Prix Le Regard d'Or: **My Magic** (Singapore), Eric Khoo.
Talent Tape Award: **La Nana** (Chile), Sebastián Silva.
Special Jury Award: **Intimidades de Shakespeare y Victor Hugo** (Mexico), Yulene Olaizola.
Audience Award: **Ramchand Pakistani** (Pakistan), Mehreen Jabbar.
Ecumenical Jury Award: **Be calm and Count to Seven** (Iran), Ramtin Lavafipour.
FIPRESCI Jury Award: **Intimidades de Shakespeare y Victor Hugo** (Mexico), Yulene Olaizola.
IFFS Jury 'Don Quijote Award': **Intimidades de Shakespeare y Victor Hugo** (Mexico), Yulene Olaizola
Ex-Change Award: **Breathless** (South Korea), Yang Ik-june.

Ghent International Film Festival
October 12–23, 2010

Belgium's most prominent annual film event, which attracts an attendance of 125,000 plus and is selected by *Variety* as one of the 50 'must attend' festivals due to its unique

Composer of the Year Alexandre Desplat accepts his award at the World Soundtrack Awards, which takes place during the Ghent Film Festival. Photo: Luk Monsaert

focus on film music. This competitive festival awards grants worth up to $120,000 and screens around 130 features and 50 shorts, most without a Benelux distributor. Besides the official competition, focusing on the impact of music on film, the festival includes the following sections: Festival Previews (World, European, Benelux or Belgian premières), World Cinema (films from all over the world, mainly without a distributor), retrospectives, a programme of media art, film music concerts, seminars and a tribute to an important international film maker. The festival's Joseph Plateau Awards are the highest honours in the Benelux. Presented for the first time in 2001, the festival also hands out the World Soundtrack Awards, judged by some 270 international composers. Every year in October, the Ghent Film Festival is the meeting point for film music composers and fans worldwide. *Inquiries to:* Ghent International Film Festival, 40B Leeuwstraat, B-9000 Ghent, Belgium. Tel: (32 9) 242 8060. Fax: 221 9074. e: info@filmfestival. be. Web: www.filmfestival.be. and www. worldsoundtrackacademy.com.

AWARDS 2009

Impact of Music on Film Competition
Grand Prix for Best Film: **Eyes Wide Open** (Israel), Haim Tabakman.
Georges Delerue Award for Best Music: **A Rational Solution** (Finland/Germany/Italy/ Sweden), Jörgen Bergmark.
SABAM Award for Best Screenplay: **Zion and His Brother** (France/Israel), Eran Merav.
Special Jury Prize: **Min Dit-The Children of Diyarbakir** (Germany/Turkey), Miraz Bezar.
Mine Xplore Award: **Ajami** (Germany/Israel), Scandar Copti and Yaron Shani.
National Lottery Award for Best Belgian Short: **A Gentle Creature** (Belgium), Marc Roels.
ACE Award for Best Flemish Student Short: **Helden van de Harmonie** (Belgium), Nele De Cat.
Prix EFA GHENT: **Amor** (Norway), Thomas Wangsmo.
Port of Ghent Audience Award: **The Cove** (USA), Louie Psihoyos.
CANVAS Audience Award: **The Stoning of Soraya M** (USA), Cyrus Nowrasteh.

Report 2009

The 36th Ghent International Film Festival focused on Asia and was once again a highlight for film music lovers. The Brussels Philharmonic performed music by Shigeru Umebayashi, Marc Streitenfeld, Marvin Hamlisch and Alexandre Desplat. The latter received the award for Best Film Composer and Best Soundtrack during the World Soundtrack Awards ceremony and Hamlisch received a Lifetime Achievement Award. A.R. Rahman received a World Soundtrack Award for Best Song written for Film. More music came from American actor Kevin Costner who performed with his rock band, Modern West, in a sold out Handelsbeurs. Other special guests at the Ghent fest were actor Andy García (for *City Island*) and French director Claude Miller (for Marching Band) who both received a Joseph Plateau Honorary Award. The international jury (Chinese director Wang Quan'an, Belgian actor Filip Peeters, Hungarian director Laszlo Nemes, Swiss composer & jury president Niki Reiser) gave kudos to *Eyes Wide*

Open by Haim Tabakman (Best Film), *Zion and His Brother* by Eran Merav (Best Script) and *A Rational Solution* by Jörgen Bergmark (Best Music). **– Wim De Witte**, Programmer.

Giffoni International Film Festival (Giffoni Experience)
July 12–25, 2010

Located in Giffoni Valle Piana, a small town about 40 minutes from Naples, the Giffoni International Film Festival for Children and Young People was founded in 1971 by Claudio Gubitosi to promote films for youthful audiences and families. It now includes five competitive sections: Elements +6 (animated and fiction feature-length films and short films that tell fantastic stories, judged by 500 children aged six to nine); Elements +10 (animated and fiction feature-length films and short films, mainly fantasy and adventure, judged by 500 children aged 10 to 12); Generator +13 sees 450 teenagers (aged 13 to 15) assessing features and shorts about the pre-adolescent world; Generator +16 has 400 jurors (aged 16 to 19) and takes a curious look at cinema for young people. Troubled Gaze has 100 jurors (from 19 years old) and is the section that explores the relationship between children and parents. *Inquiries to:* Giffoni Film Festival, Cittadella del Cinema, Via Aldo Moro 4, 84095 Giffoni Valle Piana, Salerno, Italy. Tel: (39 089) 802 3001. e: info@giffoniff.it. Web: www.giffoniff.it.

AWARDS 2009
Gryphon Award-Best Film Elements +6 Section: **Carlitos and the Chance of a Lifetime** (Spain), Jesus Del Cerro.
Gryphon Award-Best Short Film Elements +6 Section: **Fishing with Sam** (Norway), Atle S. Blakseth.
Gryphon Award-Best Film Elements +10 Section: **A Time to Love** (Iran), Ebrahim Forouzesh.
Gryphon Award-Best Short Film Elements +10 Section: **Il Mio Ultimo Giorno di Guerra** (*My Last Day of War*) (Italy), Matteo Tondini.
Gryphon Award-Best Film Generator +13

Section: **Broken Hill** (Australia/USA), Dagen Merrill.
Gryphon Award-Best Short Film Generator +13 Section: **See You** (Denmark), Jesper Waldvogel Rasmussen.
Jury Grand Prix-Generator +13 Section: **Accidents Happen** (Australia/UK), Andrew Lancaster.
Gryphon Award-Best Film Generator +16 Section: **My Suicide** (USA), Davide Lee Miller.
Gryphon Award-Best Short Film Generator +16 Section: **The Ground Beneath** (Australia), René Hernandez.
Jury Grand Prix-Generator +16 Section: **My Suicide** (USA), Davide Lee Miller.
Gryphon Award-Best Short Film Troubled Gaze Section: **Bisesto** (*Leap Day*) (Italy), Giovanni Esposito and Francesco Prisco.

Gijón International Film Festival
November 18–27, 2010

One of Spain's oldest festivals (48th edition in 2010), Gijón is now at the peak of its popularity. Having firmly established itself as a barometer of new film trends worldwide, it draws a large and enthusiastic public. Gijón has built on its niche as a festival for young people, programming innovative and independent films made by and for the young, including retrospectives, panoramas, exhibitions and concerts. Alongside the lively Official Section, sidebars celebrate directors who have forged new paths in filmmaking. *Inquiries to:* Gijón International Film Festival, PO Box 76, 33201 Gijon, Spain. Tel: (34 98) 518 2940. e: info@gijonfilmfestival.com. Web: www.gijonfilmfestival.com.

AWARDS 2009
Official Section
Best Feature Film: **La Pivellina** (Austria/Italy), Tizza Covi and Rainer Frimmel.
Best Director: Lynn Shelton for **Humpday** (USA).
Best Actor: Mark Duplass and Joshua Leonard for **Humpday** (USA).
Best Actress: Patrizia Gerardi for **La Pivellina** (Austria/Italy).
Best Script: Philippe Lioret, Emmanuel Courcol

Inaugural gala of the 47th edition of the Gijón International Film Festival. Photo: Palmira Escobar

and Olivier Adam for **Welcome** (France).
Best Art Direction: Gustavo Ramírez for **Mal Día Para Pescar** (Spain/Uruguay).
Special Prize of the Jury: **Le Roi de L'Evasion** (France), Alain Guiraudie.
Cortometrajes
Best Short Film: **Bingo** (The Netherlands), Timur Ismailov.
Special Mention: **Pablo** (Spain), Nely Reguera.
Non Fiction Documentary
Best Film: **Border** (Armenia/The Netherlands), Harutyun Khachatryan.
Audience Prize Special Competition Rellumes:
Barking Water (USA), Sterlin Harjo.
FIPRESCI: **Francesca** (Romania), Bobby Paunescu.
Young Jury Prize for Best Feature Film:
Welcome (France), Philippe Lioret.
Young Jury Prize for Best Short Film:
L'Homme Est El Seul Oiseau Qui Porte Sa Cage (France), Claude Weiss.
'Enfants Terribles' for Best Feature Film for audiences under 13 years-old: **Les Enfants**

de Timpelbach (France/Luxembourg), Nicolas Bary.
'Enfants Terribles' for Best Feature Film for audiences over 12 years-old: **Turn It Loose** (USA), Alastair Siddons.

Report 2009
Fourteen feature films participated in the Official Section competition and prizes were awarded by the International Jury formed by Lenny Abrahamson, Kiko Amat, Lucía Puenzo, Christine Dollhofer and Andres Gertrudix. Specific juries were also formed for the Short Film Section in Competition and the Non-Fiction/Documentary section and the public awarded the main prizes at the Rellumes competition and the Enfants Terribles section. Gijón also hosted a FIPRESCI Jury for the main competition made up of Spanish premieres. Alvaro Brechner's first feature *Mal Día Para Pescar* was the national representative in a programming that highlighted the latest relevant productions from all the corners of earth. Harmony Korine introduced his latest film *Trash Humpers* along with the retrospective dedicated to his films. Other tributes were held for such prestigious directors as Fatih Akin from Germany but of Turkish origin and Russian Alexey Balabanov.
- **María José Alvarez Sierra**, Press.

goEast Festival of Central and Eastern European Film
April 21–27, 2010

goEast has been celebrating and promoting the diversity of Central and Eastern European Film since 2001. Presented by the German Film Institute, DIF, goEast presents films made by our Eastern neighbours to an interested audience, at the same time exploring the wider cultural landscape and providing a specialist forum for dialogue between East and West. The festival centres on films otherwise seldom screened in Germany, the promotion of young filmmakers from East and West, and on cultural dialogue. Rapidly changing developments – not just in Central and Eastern Europe – raise important questions and give rise to debates in which European identity can be experienced

directly. News travelled fast about the ambitious goEast programme and the special atmosphere offered by attractive locations such as the Caligari festival cinema and the festival centre in Villa Clementine. Over the years, goEast has established its place on the domestic and international cultural calendar, as evidenced by the wide variety of international guests and wide general audience who flock to Wiesbaden each spring for the festival and its films. The festival hosts FIPRESCI Jury. *Inquiries to:* Deutsches Filminstitut - DIF, goEast Film Festival, Schaumainkai 41, 60596 Frankfurt, Germany. Tel: (49 69) 9612 20650. Fax: 9612 20669. e:info@filmfestival-goeast.de. Web: www.filmfestival-goeast.de.

AWARDS 2009

The Škoda Award for Best Film - the 'Golden Lily' and FIPRESCI Prize: **The Other Bank** (Georgia, Kazakhstan), George Ovashvili. *Documentary Award - 'Remembrance and Future':* **I Love Poland** (Poland), Joanna Sławińska, Maria Zmarz-Koczanowicz. *Award of the City of Wiesbaden for Best Director:* **Help Gone Mad** (Russia), Boris Chlebnikov. *Award of the Federal Foreign Office:* **Morphia** (Russia), Aleksej Balabanov.

Report 2009

At the 9th goEast Film Festival, more than 110 feature-length and short films were presented and supplemented by a range of talks, panel discussions, and a rich

At the 9th goEast opening ceremony in the Caligari FilmBühne (left to right): Prof. Dr. Hilmar Hoffmann, Patron of goEast, Claudia Dillmann, Director of the Deutsche Filminstitut – DIF and new Festival Director Nadja Rademacher.

programme of accompanying events. An international jury chaired by Jerzy Stuhr awarded four prizes worth €29,500. The homage to Ukrainian director Kira Muratova, a tribute to Krzysztof Komeda-Trzciński and the Students Competition, in which invited film schools presented their latest films in the categories of Short Feature, Documentary and Animated/Experimental Film, all witnessed an impressive turnout and response from audiences. For the third time at the festival, the Robert Bosch Foundation awarded their Co-Production Prize for young German and Eastern European Filmmakers. Three projects were chosen and supported with a total sum of €194,300. Further highlights of the Festival included a portrait of Czech filmmaker Jan Svěrák, the Symposium, 'After Winter Comes Spring – Film Presaging the Fall of the Wall', and a reading with the Polish writer Dorota Maslowska. Workshops and master classes held by film experts like Martin Blankemeyer and Maciej Karpinski were highly appreciated by the participants and underlined the high quality of the goEast Young Professionals Programme. goEast 2009 counted around 9,000 visitors over the course of the festival and accompanying programme.
– Stefan Adrian, Festival Manager.

Göteborg International Film Festival
January 29–February 8, 2010

Now in its 33rd year, Göteborg International Film Festival is one of Europe's key film events. With a large international programme and a special focus on Nordic films, including the Nordic Competition, GIFF is Scandinavia's most important film festival. International seminars, master classes and the market place Nordic Film Market attract buyers and festival programmers to the newest

Scandinavian films. The 30th jubilee, in 2007, introduced a new international competition – the Ingmar Bergman International Debut Award (TIBIDA). Some 1,800 professionals attend and more than 124,000 tickets are sold to 450 films from around 70 countries. *Inquiries to:* Göteborg International Film Festival, Olof Palmes Plats, S- 413 04 Göteborg, Sweden. Tel: (46 31) 339 3000. e: info@giff.se Web: www.giff.se.

AWARDS 2009
Winner of TIBIDA: **Parque Vía** (Mexico), Enrique Rivero.
Best Nordic Film: **The Visitor** (Finland), Jukka-Pekka Valkeapää.
The Kodak Nordic Vision Award: Tuomo Hutri (Finland) for **The Visitor**.
The Church of Sweden Film Award: **The Blessing** (Denmark), Heidi Maria Faisst.
The Fipresci Award: **The Blessing** (Denmark), Heidi Maria Faisst.
Best Swedish Short: **My Life As A Trailer** (Sweden), Andreas Öhman.
Viewers Choice Award, Feature: **Mommy is at the Hairdresser's** (Canada), Léa Pool.
Viewers Choice Award, Short: **Attached to You** (Sweden), Cecilia Actis, Karin Bräck and Mia Hulterstam.

Report 2009
The 33rd edition attracted 32,000 visitors and for the third year in a row a new record in ticket sales was broken – 124,500. Among the most popular films in the programme were the opening film *The Queen and I* by Nahid Persson Sarvestani, Sam Mendes' *Revolutionary Road* and Valdis Oskarsdottir's

Country Wedding. The Country in Focus was Turkey and the Animator in Focus was Bill Plympton. Notable guests included Claire Simon, Nathalie Baye, Marco Tullio Giordana and Bille August (a member of the TIBIDA jury). Head of Nordic Jury: Vinca Wiedemann. **– Ulf Sigvardson**, Festival Editor.

Haugesund –
Norwegian International Film Festival
New Nordic Films: August 18–21, 2010
The Amanda Awards Ceremony:
August 20, 2010
The Norwegian International Film Festival:
August 21–26, 2010

Film Festival
Situated on the west coast of Norway, our charming festival, often called the 'Nordic Cannes', is a gateway to the Norwegian film and cinema industry. With Liv Ullmann as Honorary President, the Norwegian Film Festival assembles the complete Norwegian film industry and press corps for red-carpet screenings, festival parties and events, which feature our most famous actors and actresses.
Amanda
The Amanda Awards ceremony – the Norwegian 'Oscar' – will celebrate the previous year's Norwegian film production during a live TV show.
The New Nordic Films Market brings together film professionals from all over the world. The market programme consists of films at three different levels in the production phase: screening of the best completed Nordic films from 2010; a showcase for works in progress; and a successful co-production and

Norwegian International Film Festival Amanda Awards winners Mads Sjøgård Pettersen and Agnes Kittelsen. Photo: Helge Hansen

film-financing forum. Festival Director: Gunnar Johan Løvvik. Programme Director: Håkon Skogrand. Honorary President: Liv Ullmann. *Inquiries to:* PO Box 145, N-5501 Haugesund, Norway. Tel: (47 52) 743 370. e: info@ filmfestivalen.no. Web: www.filmfestivalen.no.

AWARDS 2009

Film Critics Award: **Fish Tank** (UK), Andrea Arnold.
The Ray of Sunshine: **Looking for Eric** (Belgium/France/Italy/Spain/UK), Ken Loach.
Audience Award: **Up** (USA), Pete Docter and Bob Peterson.
Andreas Award: **The White Ribbon** (Austria/France/Germany/Italy), Michael Haneke.

Helsinki International Film Festival – Love & Anarchy
September 16–26, 2010

The largest film festival in Finland, which achieved a record-breaking attendance in 2009 of over 51,000 admissions. Organised annually since 1988, the festival has found its place as the top venue for the new and alternative in cinema and in popular culture. The festival has a memorable subtitle, 'Love & Anarchy', adopted from a Lina Wertmüller film from the 70s; it has become a symbol of cutting-edge films over the years, films with a spark of something different, which fearlessly plunge into unexplored frontiers. The winner of the Finnkino Prize, voted for by the audience, receives distribution by the leading operator of multiplex theatres, Finnkino.

Inquiries to: Helsinki International Film Festival, Mannerheimintie 22-24, PO Box 889, FI-00101 Helsinki, Finland. Tel: (358 9) 6843 5230. e: office@hiff.fi. Web: www.hiff.fi.

AWARDS 2009
Finnkino Prize: **A Year Ago in Winter** (Germany), Caroline Link.

Report 2009
This year's festival included 425 screenings, of which 96 were sold out. Among the most popular films were *(500) Days of Summer, Il Divo, The September Issue, An Education, Synecdoche, New York, Hierro, The Cove, Humpday, Heaven's Heart, The Girlfriend Experience, Mary and Max, Calamari Union (Seattle remake), Food Inc., Ponyo on the Cliff* and the festival closing film, *Bright Star.* The screenings of John Woo's historical spectacle *Red Cliff I-II* were also very popular. *Red Cliff I-II* was screened as the original, five-hour version, for the first time in the West.
– Press Department.

Hof International Film Festival/ Internationale Hofer Filmtage
October 26–31, 2010

The Hof International Film Festival – often nicknamed 'The German Telluride' – was founded in the northern Bavarian town of Hof in 1968 by current festival director Heinz Badewitz and several up-and-coming filmmakers of the day (Wim Wenders, Volker Schloendorff, Werner Herzog and Rainer-

Actor and director Lou Castel arrives at the Hof Film Festival for a retrospective of his work

Werner Fassbinder among them). It has since gone on to become one of the most important film festivals in Germany, concentrating both on German films by the new filmmaking generation and on independent films from abroad. There is a retrospective that so far has been dedicated to directors as varied as Monte Hellman, Mike Leigh, Lee Grant, John Sayles, Brian De Palma, Peter Jackson, Roger Corman, John Cassavetes, Costa-Gavras, and Wayne Wang. It's a festival that attracts not only cinemagoers and critics, but also producers, distributors and the media – not to forget the filmmakers themselves. *Inquiries to:* Hof International Film Festival, Altstadt 8, D-95028 Hof, Germany. Fax: (49) 9281 1441 434 e: info@hofer-filmtage.de. Web: www. hofer-filmtage.de.

Report 2009

Whilst the festival itself does not give awards to films because the festival judges all films to have the same importance, the following prizes, which are chosen by different juries, were awarded in the course of the 43rd Hof

IFF, 2009: the City of Hof Award is given by the City of Hof to a German director/actor close to the festival and Hof and is chosen by the City of Hof and festival director Heinz Badewitz. The winner receives the honour and a porcelain sculpture created in the Hof region. It went to director Christian Petzold. The Young German Cinema Award is awarded by Bavaria Film, Bayerischer Rundfunk/Bavarian Broadcasting and HypoVereinsbank. It is given for an outstanding artistic performance in a German film screened in Hof and it may be given to a young person in any production category (excluding directors and actors). The award includes prize money of €10,000. It went to *Ceasefire*, directed by Lancelot von Naso, for its outstanding production design, editing, cinematography and sound design. The Eastman Award for Young Talents is awarded by Kodak Germany and includes €4,000's worth of film stock. It is given to a young German director whose film screened at the festival. It went to director Marc Rensing for *Parkour*. The Best Art Direction Award is awarded by S/F/K Production Design/Costume Design and the

THE HOF SOCCER DREAM TEAM:

1 Atom Egoyan
2 John Sayles
3 Volker Schloendorff
4 Werner Herzog

5 George A. Romero
6 David Lynch
7 Roberto Benigni
8 Monte Hellman

9 David Cronenberg
10 Jim Jarmusch
11 John Carpenter
12 Brian de Palma
13 Tom Tykwer

14 John Waters
15 Wim Wenders
16 Gavin Hood

Coach: Sam Fuller

SUBSTITUTES:
Jack Sholder
Christian Petzold
Michael Winterbottom
Sönke Wortmann
Hans-Christian Schmid
Detlev Buck
Alex Cox
Percy Adlon
Florian Henckel von Donnersmarck

44th Hof International Film Festival

October 26th to 31st, 2010

Please contact:

Heinz Badewitz, Director

Mobile: ++49 171 61 92 743
FAX: ++49 89 123 68 68
h.badewitz@hofer-filmtage.de

For more information please visit www.hofer-filmtage.de

Director Cary Joji Fukunage presents **Sin Nombre** *at Hof Film Festival*

HFF-University of Television and Film Munich. It went to Annemarie Otto and Tobias Maier for *Freunde von Fruher*, directed by Tim Moeck. **– Rainer Huebsch.**

Hong Kong International Film Festival
March 21–April 6, 2010

The Hong Kong International Film Festival Society is a non-profit, non-governmental organisation which develops, promotes and encourages creativity in the art and culture of film through the presentation of the annual Hong Kong International Film Festival (HKIFF). The Society is also committed to organising regular programmes and other film-related activities throughout the year in order to promote the art and creativity of cinema, with an international dimension and outlook. Today, the HKIFF has grown to be Hong Kong's largest cultural event and is one of Asia's most reputable platforms for filmmakers, film professionals and filmgoers from all over the world to launch new work and experience outstanding films. Screening over 300 titles from 50 countries in 11 major cultural venues in Hong Kong, the HKIFF reaches an audience of over 580,000 and 4,500 business executives attending the Hong Kong International Film and TV Market (FILMART). The Society further demonstrates its commitment to the development of a vibrant film culture by organising the Hong Kong-Asia Film Financing Forum (HAF) and the Asian Film Awards (AFA). *Inquiries to:* Hong Kong International Film Festival Office, 21/F, Millennium City 3, 370

Kwun Tong Road, Kowloon, Hong Kong. Tel: (852) 2970 3300. e: info@hkiff.org.hk. Web: www.hkiff.org.hk.

Huelva Latin American Film Festival
November 2010

The Latin American Film Festival in Huelva, which celebrated its 35th edition in 2009, is one of the most important competition festivals of its kind. The most outstanding films from both shores of the Atlantic get together in the third week of November in Huelva, to make up one of the main Latin American cultural events. Due to its international vocation, the festival aims to open the European film market to up-and-coming talents from the Latin American sector. It also hosts the Latin American Co-Production Forum, where outstanding producers, directors and distributors meet. The best film is awarded the Golden Colombus prize. *Inquiries to:* Casa Colon, Plaza del Punto s/n, 21003 Huelva, Spain. Tel: (34 95) 921 0170. e: festival@festicinehuelva.com. Web: www.festicinehuelva.com.

Independent Film Week
September 19–23, 2010

Formerly known as the IFP Market, Independent Film Week is the oldest and largest forum in the US for the discovery of new projects in development and new voices on the independent film scene. It is qualitatively and quantitatively the best and biggest opportunity in the nation for an independent filmmaker to find funding or a producer. Annually, IFP invites approximately 125 new works-in-development. Projects are accepted into one of three sections: Emerging Narrative, No Borders International Co-Production Market, and Spotlight on Documentaries. A wide range of industry decision-makers make Independent Film Week their annual meeting point in New York to discover new documentaries and narrative feature projects. Strategically positioned between the Toronto and New York Film Festivals, it is an efficient week for meetings, screenings and re-connecting with colleagues. *Inquiries to:* Independent Film Week, 68 Jay Street Room 425 Brooklyn, NY 11201, USA. Tel: (1 212) 465 8200. Web: www.ifp.org and www.independentfilmweek.com.

International Film Festival and Forum on Human Rights (FIFDH)
March 5–14, 2010

The inspiration and impetus behind the International Film Festival and Forum on Human Rights (FIFDH) came from human rights defenders, filmmakers, representatives from the media and the University of Geneva. The FIFDH coincides with the UN Human Rights Council and is a platform for all public and private actors defending human dignity. The festival is an International Forum on Human Rights that informs and denounces violations wherever they take place. Situated in the heart of Geneva, the International Capital for Human Rights, the festival also serves as a go-between for all human-rights activists. For one week, it offers debates, original film screenings and solidarity initiatives. With its concept 'a film, a subject, a debate', the aim of the FIFDH is to denounce attacks on human dignity and to raise public awareness through films and debates in the presence of filmmakers, defenders of human rights and recognised specialists. *Inquiries to:* Leo Kaneman and Yaël Reinharz Hazan, Directors, FIFDH Maison des Arts du Grütli, 16 rue Général Dufour, CP 5730 CH 1211 Geneva 11, Switzerland. Tel: (41 22) 800 1554. Fax: 329 3747. e: contact@fifdh.ch. Web: www.fifdh.ch.

AWARDS 2009
Grand Prix FIFDH: **The Choir**, (Australia), Michael Davie.
Special Mention of the Jury: **To Make an Example** (Turkey), Necati Sonmez.
Foundation Barbara Hendricks Award in Honour of Sergio Vieira de Mello: **Kassim the Dream** (USA), Kief Davidson.
OMCT Award: **En Terre étrangère** (France), Christian Zerbib.
Special Mention of OMCT: **Gaza-Sderot, Chroniques d'Avant Guerre**, (France/Israel/Palestine), Serge Gordey, Robby Elmaliah and Khali al Muzayyen.
Youth Jury Award: **Barcelone Ou la Mort** (France), Iurissa Guiro.

Report 2009
Once again, the International Film Festival and Forum on Human Rights has played a role as agent provocateur, opening minds to fresh ideas. By the time this year's edition ended, more than 16,000 spectators had

2001 Nobel Prize winner, Economist Joseph Stiglitz at FIFDH 2009. Photo: Miguel Bueno.

watched the festival's films and participated in the accompanying debates. The festival was organised around 14 themes, of which 'Another World is Possible', 'Women as Change Agents', 'Humanitarian Interventionism', 'Algeria Gagged' and 'Freedom of Expression' provoked enormous excitement and interest. Among the festival's 50 guests, Micheline Calmy-Rey, Leila Chahid, Elie Barnavi, Stéphane Hessel, Rony Brauman, Abderrahmane Sissako, Charles Berling, Patrice Leconte and, of course, Nobel economics prize-winner Joseph Stiglitz, were the high-profile personalities who attracted large crowds of festival-goers keen to debate crucial civil-society issues with them – precisely the kind of exchange needed if people are to mobilise in support of human-rights victims and further the cause of human rights. The 2009 Jury, comprised Jury President Louise Arbour, former UN High Commissioner for Human Rights, Florence Aubenas, journalist and Algerian author and playwright Slimane Benaïssa.
- **Jeffrey Hodgson**, General Adminstrator.

International Film Festival of India
Late November/early December 2010

Annual, government-funded event recognised by FIAPF and held in Goa under the aegis of India's Ministry of Information and Broadcasting. Comprehensive 'Cinema of the World' section, foreign and Indian retrospectives and a film market, plus a valuable panorama of the year's best Indian films, subtitled in English. *Inquiries to:* The Directorate of Film Festivals, Sirifort Cultural Complex, August Kranti Marg, New Delhi 110049, India. Tel: (91 11) 2649 9371. e: dir.dff@nic.in. Web: www.iffi.nic.in.

The International Short Film Festival Winterthur
November 10–14, 2010

The International Short Film Festival Winterthur is Switzerland's most significant short-film event. The festival takes place each year in November and attracts over 14,000

spectators. It is a popular audience event and an important platform for European short films and filmmakers. During five days, over 200 films are shown from all over the world. The core of the festival is the International and National Competition, where the latest short film productions contend with each other for prizes worth 46,000 CHF (30,450 EUR). In addition, the festival offers a rich and varied supporting programme that includes thematic film programmes, panel discussions, special events and concerts. At the Swiss Film School Day and the Producers' Day, filmmakers can meet important contacts from the film industry and participate at special industry events. *Inquiries to:* The International Short Film Festival Winterthur, Steiggasse 2, CH-8402 Winterthur, Switzerland. Tel: (41 52) 212 1166. Fax: 212 1172. e: info@kurzfilmtage.ch. Web: www.kurzfilmtage.ch.

AWARDS 2009
Grand Prize of the International Competition: **Please Say Something** (Germany/Ireland), David O'Reilly.
Promotional Award of the International Competition: **Believe** (UK), Paul Wright.
Prize for the Best Swiss Film: **Ich Bin's Helmut** (Germany/Switzerland), Nicolas Steiner.
Swiss Cinematography Award: **Lorenz Merz for Schonzeit** (Switzerland), Irene Ledermann
Audience Price: **Wagah** (Germany/India/Pakistan), Supriyo Sen.
Shortrun Award: Sahar Suliman for **Muselé** (Documentary Project).

Report 2009
In 2009, 14,000 spectators visited the festival – a new record attendance for the festival, which shows that the interest in it has been greater than ever before. The greatest audience draws were the competition

Theater Winterthur, Sunday 8th november 2009. Photo: Eduard Metzler

programmes, as well as the programme series about 'political short films'. The Producers' Day, which allowed filmmakers to get in contact with industry representatives, counted over 800 entries. The members of this year's jury included Vanja Kaludjercic, Mário Micaelo, Patricia Mollet-Mercier, Oliver Rhis and Shane Smith. The festival was visited by many directors, including Fredi Murer, Jürg Hassler and the Oscar-nominated Reto Caffi.
– Delphine Lyner.

Istanbul International Film Festival
April 3–18, 2010

The only film festival that takes place in a city where two continents meet, the Istanbul International Film Festival boasts the largest attendance in Turkey, with 162,000 in 2009. In its 29th year the Festival will hold the fifth of its industry events, 'Meetings on the Bridge', with the third edition of the feature-film development workshop in its framework. The Festival will also take on a distinctively European character due to Istanbul being designated as the European Capital of Culture in 2010. The Festival programme focuses on features dealing with the arts and the artist, or literary adaptations in its main competition, the Golden Tulip. There are also selections from world festivals, with other thematic sections such as 'The World of Animation', 'Mined Zone', 'Women's Films', 'Documentary Time', 'Human Rights in Cinema' with the Council of Europe Film Award, FACE, 'Young Masters' and a comprehensive showcase of Turkish cinema with emphasis on new talents and innovative

approaches. The deadline for submissions is December 31, 2009. *Inquiries to:* Ms Azize Tan, Istanbul Foundation for Culture and Arts, Istiklal Caddesi 146, Beyoglu 34435, Istanbul, Turkey. Tel: (90 212) 334 0721. e: film.fest@iksv.org. Web: www.iksv.org/film/english.

AWARDS 2009
International Competition
Golden Tulip: **Tony Manero** (Brazil/Chile), Pablo Larrain.
Special Prize of the Jury: **A Film With Me In It** (Ireland), Ian Fitzgibbon.
FIPRESCI Prize: **Milk** (France/Germany/Turkey), Semih Kaplanoglu.
FACE Award: **Birdwatchers** (Brazil/Italy), Marco Bechis.
FACE Award Special Prize of the Jury: **Firaaq** (India), Nandita Das.
People's Choice Awards: **Milk** (Turkey), Semih Kaplanoglu.
National Competition
Special Prize of the Jury: **10 to 11** (France/Germany/Turkey), Pelin Esmer.
FIPRESCI Prize: **My Only Sunshine** (Turkey), Reha Erdem.
Golden Tulip: **Men on the Bridge** (Germany/Turkey), Asli Özge
Best Turkish Director of the Year: Mahmut Fazıl Coşkun for **Wrong Rosary**.
Best Actress: Derya Alabora for **Pandora's Box**.
Best Actor: Nadir Sarıbacak for **Wrong Rosary**.
Best Screenplay: Tarik Tufan, Görkem Yeltan and Bektas Topaloglu for **Wrong Rosary**.
Best Director of Photography: Özgür Eken for **Milk**.
Best Music: Nail Yurtsever for **Ali's Eight Days**.
People's Choice Awards: **Children of the Other Side**, Aydin Bulut.
Meetings On The Bridge Feature Film Project Development Workshop Award: **Come To My Voice!** by Hüseyin Karabey.

Report 2009
With a diverse programme of 200 films from 49 countries, shown in 455 screenings at seven theatres, with renowned guests and many events, the Istanbul International Film Festival attained an attendance of 162,000.

The Festival for the first time included in its programme a selection of recent video art works from Turkey, under the title '(very) Small Distortions in the Order'. The International Jury was led by Goran Paskaljevic, while the National Jury was presided over by Kutlug Ataman. Highlights of the 2009 Festival included master classes by John Malkovich, Bill Plympton, Cristian Mungiu and Peter Greenaway. Guests included François Ozon, Andrei Khrzhanovsky, Jerzy Skolimowski, who received the Lifetime Achievement Award, Ventura Pons and Nandita Das, amongst many others who presented their films.
– **Yusuf Pinhas**, Festival Editor.

Jerusalem International Film Festival
July 8–17, 2010

Celebrating its 27th Anniversary this year, the Jerusalem International Film Festival, Israel's most prestigious cinematic event, offers an alternative Middle East headline – that those of all faiths, ethnicities, and political positions have the opportunity to sit side by side in the shadow of the silver screen, to be moved, to share discourse and to hope. Our Opening Gala event attracts over 6,000 spectators, under the stars, in the shadow of the ancient Jerusalem Walls. The festival's programme will present 150 films, to over 70,000 spectators, in a wide spectrum of themes and categories focusing on: the Best of International Cinema; the Best of New Israeli Cinema; and Human Rights and Social Justice. Other categories include: Documentaries; Animation; Jewish Themes; Retrospectives; Avant Garde; Restorations; Television; Special Tributes and Classics. The festival has become the largest local market for international films, where distributors from all over the world have the opportunity to bring the finest examples of World Cinema to the growing and increasingly influential Israeli audience. Israeli filmmakers set the world première of their films at the festival knowing that a strong local reaction is tantamount to a new Israeli film success throughout Europe and the world. International distributors increasingly look to the Festival

27th JERUSALEM FILM FESTIVAL

President: Lia van Leer

July 8-17, 2010

as a guide to new Israeli film – knowing that a success in Jerusalem means a success worldwide. The festival offers dozens of professional events and seminars designed to promote and assist local filmmakers and to connect Israel to the European and international industry. It has become not only the harbinger of and launching point for new and cutting-edge Israeli Cinema, but also an active and proud promoter. Programmes include *'The Jerusalem Pitch Point'*: a meeting place for Israeli filmmakers and producers with key members of the European and international film industry whose aim is to encourage and promote co-

Actress Ayelet Zurer and Founder and President of JFF Lia van Leer at the Opening Event of the Jerusalem International Film Festival at Sultan's Pool – 9 July. Photo: Nir Sha'anani

productions with Europe, and beyond, of Israeli full-length feature films. Submission deadline: April 1, 2010. *Inquiries to:* Jerusalem Film Festival, Hebron Road 11, Jerusalem 91083, Israel. Tel: (972 2) 565 4333. Fax: 565 4334. e: daniel@jff.org.il. Web: www.jff.org.il.

AWARDS 2009

Wolgin Awards for Israeli Cinema given by Jack Wolgin, patron and long-time supporter of the art of cinema in Israel
Best Full-Length Feature Film: **Ajami**, Scandar Copti and Yaron Shani.
Honourable Mention: **Eyes Wide Open**, Haim Tabakman.
Best Actress: Hana Rita Zohar for **Mrs Moskowicz and the Cats**.
Best Actor: Zohar Strauss for **Eyes Wide Open**.
Best Documentary Film: **Diplomat**, Dana Goren.
Best Short Film: **Guided Tour**, Benjamin Friedenberg.
Awards for Israeli Drama in Memory of Anat Pirchi
Best Animation: **Wings**, Sasha Bushuev.
Best Single Drama: **Freeland**, Gur Bentwich.
Best Documentary Series: **Baderech Ha'baita**, Tomer Heymann.
Best Documentary Short: **Tales of the Defeated**, Yael Reuveny.
'In the Spirit of Freedom' Awards in Memory of Wim van Leer: **Yodok Stories** (Norway/Poland), Andrzej Fidyk and **Burma VJ – Reporting from a Closed Country** (Denmark/Sweden/UK), Andreas Østergaard.
FIPRESCI International Critics' Award: **Burma VJ – Reporting from a Closed Country** (Denmark/Sweden/UK),Andreas Østergaard.
Lia Award: **The Last Krasucky** (Israel), Y A Krasucky.
Avner Shalev Yad Vashem Chairman's Award: **Human Failure** (Germany), Michael Verhoeven.
Forum for the Preservation of Audio-Visual Memory Award: **Harlan - In the Shadow of the Jew Süss** (Germany),Felix Moeller.
The Israeli Video Art and Experimental Cinema Awards
First Prize: **In Between**, Tamar Shippony.
Second Prize: **Beton**, Yuval Yefet.

Karlovy Vary International Film Festival
July 2–10, 2010

Founded in 1946, Karlovy Vary is one of the most important film events in Central and Eastern Europe. It includes Official Selection – Competition, Documentary Films in Competition, East of the West – Films in Competition and other programme sections that offer the unique chance to see new film production from all around the world. Film entry deadline: April 2, 2010. *Inquiries to:* Film Servis Festival Karlovy Vary, Panská 1, CZ 110 00 Prague 1, Czech Republic. Tel: (420 2) 2141 1011. e: program@kviff.com. Web: www.kviff.com.

AWARDS 2009
Grand Prix- Crystal Globe: **Angel at Sea** (Belgium/Canada), Frédéric Dumont.
Special Jury Prize: **Twenty** (Iran), Abdolreza Kahani.
Best Director: Andreas Dresen for **Whisky with Vodka** (Germany).
Best Actress: Paprika Steen for **Applause** (Denmark).
Best Actor: Olivier Gourmet for **Angel at Sea** (Belgium/Canada) and Paul Giamatti for **Cold Souls** (USA).
Special Mention: Filip Garbacz for **Piggies** (Germany/Poland).
Best Documentary Film Under 30 Minutes: **Wagah** (Germany/India/Pakistan), Supriyo Sen.
Special Jury Mention: **Till It Hurts** (Poland), Marcin Koszałka.
Best Documentary Film Over 30 Minutes: **Osadné** (Czech Republic, Slovak Republic), Marko Škop.
Special Jury Mention: **We Live in Public** (USA), Ondi Timoner.
East of the West Award: **Room and a Half** (Russia), Andrey Khrzhanovsky.
Special Mention: **Scratch** (Poland), Michał Rosa.
Award for Outstanding Artistic Contribution to World Cinema: Isabelle Huppert (France), John Malkovich (USA) and Jan Švankmajer (Czech Republic).
Festival President's Award: Antonio Banderas (USA).

Pravo Audience Award: **A Matter of Size**
(France/Germany/Israel), Erez Tadmor and
Sharon Maymon.

Krakow Film Festival
May 31–June 6, 2010

Krakow Film Festival is devoted to
documentary, short and animated films.
One of the oldest film events in Europe,
the festival celebrates its 50th anniversary
in 2010. For 50 years the festival has gained
many distinguished friends. Documentary
filmmakers such as Krzysztof Kieslowski,
Andrzej Fidyk and Marcel Łozinski presented
their debuts here, while Pier Paolo Pasolini,
Werner Herzog, Mike Leigh, Kenneth Branagh
and Oscar winners Jan Sverak and Zbigniew
Rybczynski also screened their films at the
festival. For 50 years, thousands of people
have visited the festival. Each year it hosts over
500 accredited guests – filmmakers, journalists
and festival representatives, in addition to
17,000 viewers. The festival is divided into
three sections: International Documentary Film
Competition (new), International Short Film
Competition and the National Competition.
The diverse programme also includes
retrospectives, thematic cycles and masters'
screenings. It is accompanied by the Krakow
Film Market and Dragon Forum (for pitching) –
a magnet bringing many film professionals to
Krakow. *Inquiries to:* Krakow Film Festival, Ul
Morawskiego 5/434, 30-102 Krakow, Poland.
Tel: (48 12) 294 6945. e: info@kff.com.pl. Web:
www.kff.com.pl.

*The opening night of the 49th Krakow Film Festival. (from left) Jeff
Kanew, Andrzej Wajda, Paul Mazursky. Photo: Tomasz Korczyński.*

AWARDS 2009
*Feature Length Documentary Competition -
The Golden Horn:* **Unmistaken Child** (Israel),
Nati Baratz.
International Competition - The Golden Dragon:
Pizza in Auschwitz (Israel), Moshe Zimerman.
*National Competition - The Golden Hobby -
Horse:* **Rabbit a la Berlin**, Bartek Konopka.
The EFA Nomination Krakow 2009:
Poste Restante (Poland), Marcel Łoziński.
*Dragon of Dragons Special Prize for Lifetime
Achievement:* Jerzy Kucia (Poland).

Report 2009
The 49th Krakow Film Festival was held
between 29 May and 4 June 2009. Of the
2,200 films submitted, some 90 were shown
in competition. The festival was opened by
Paul Mazursky, who introduced his film,
Yippee, A Journey to Jewish Joy, a travel
theme that returned throughout the festival.
There was a full retrospective of the films
of Jerzy Kucia, the laureate of Dragon of the
Dragons Award for Lifetime Achievement.
Out-of-competition screenings included
new documentaries (Krakow Documentary
Premieres), music documentaries (Sound of
Music) and thematic cycles (Jewish Roots). For
the fourth time the event was accompanied
by the digital Krakow Film Market and Dragon
Forum Pitching. **– Barbara Orlicz-Szczypula**,
Director of Programme Office.

La Rochelle International Film Festival
June 25–July 5, 2010

Our world-renowned Festival is non-
competitive and features more than 250

original and new releases from all over the world, before a large audience (81,349 in 2009) of very enthusiastic film buffs. The festival includes: tributes to contemporary directors or actors, often in their presence (last year saw Ramin Bahrani, Nuri Bilge Ceylan, Jacques Doillon and Bent Hamer); a panorama of a national cinema (in 2009 it was Malaysia); retrospectives devoted to the work of past filmmakers (last year: Joseph Losey, Jacques and Pierre Prévert, and Ladislas Starewitch); Here and There – a selection of unreleased films from all over the world; From Yesterday till Today – premieres of rare films restored; Carpets, Cushions and Video – video works projected on a ceiling above spectators; and Films for Children. The festival ends with an all-night programme of five films, followed by breakfast in cafés overlooking the old port. *Inquiries to:* La Rochelle International Film Festival, 16 rue Saint Sabin, 75011 Paris, France. Tel: (33 1) 4806 1666. e: info@festival-larochelle.org. Web: www.festival-larochelle.org. Director: Mrs Prune Engler; Artistic Director: Mrs Sylvie Pras; Managing Director: Mr Arnaud Dumatin.

Las Palmas de Gran Canaria International Film Festival
March 12–20, 2010

The festival is proud of its role as a defender of creative and independent productions from outside the mainstream. Films that at first seemed bizarre or on the fringe in Spain are now firmly established in the culture of quality productions. The Lady Harimaguada is the award received by the winners at the Festival and is a replica in miniature of the sculpture that local artist Martín Chirino made in 1995. It is awarded in three categories: the Golden Lady Harimaguada to the Spanish distributor of the winning film, the Silver Lady Harimaguada and the Honorific Lady Harima-guada in bronze. *Inquiries to:* León y Castillo, 322, 4ª Planta, 35007 Las Palmas de Gran Canaria. Tel: (34 928) 446 833. e: laspalmas-cine@hotmail.com. Web: www.festivalcinelas-palmas.com.

Leeds International Film Festival
November 4–21, 2010

Presented by Leeds City Council, the Leeds International Film Festival is the largest regional Film Festival in the United Kingdom. The Film Festival programme will feature Official Selection, Cinema Versa, Fanomenon, Thought Bubble, Short Film City and Cherry Kino. In addition, Leeds Film organises year-round exhibition with partner organisations in the city, education programmes, and delivers the Leeds Young People's Film Festival. *Inquiries to:* Leeds International Film Festival, The Town Hall, The Headrow, Leeds, LS1 3AD, UK. Tel: (44 113) 247 8398. e: filmfestival@leeds.gov.uk. Web: www.leedsfilm.com.

Locarno International Film Festival
August 4–14, 2010

Founded in 1946, located right in the heart of Europe in a Swiss-Italian town on Lake Maggiore, the Locarno International Film Festival is one of the world's top film events, offering a panoramic view of the full range of current cinematic expression. With its three competitive sections (International Competition, Filmmakers of the Present and Leopards of Tomorrow) the Festival takes stock of new approaches and perspectives in filmmaking; throughout its 62 year history, Locarno has often discovered or confirmed directors who now enjoy a widespread recognition. The Festival also provides a showcase for major new films of the year from around the world: every night the famous open-air screenings offer prestigious premieres to an audience of up to 8,000 people in the extraordinary setting of Piazza Grande. The Locarno Festival has also established itself in recent years as an important industry showcase for auteur filmmaking, a perfect networking opportunity for distributors, buyers and producers from all countries with over 3,000 film professionals and 1,000 journalists attending – together with 160,000 filmgoers. *Inquiries to:* Festival Internazionale del film Locarno, Via Ciseri 23, CH-6601 Locarno,

Locarno Film Festival Leopard of Honour recipient William Friedkin.
Photo: Jannuzzi Smith

Switzerland. Artistic Director: Olivier Père.
Tel: (41 91) 756 2121. Fax: 756 2149. e: info@
pardo.ch. Web: www.pardo.ch.

AWARDS 2009
International Competition
Golden Leopard: **She, A Chinese**
(France/Germany/UK), Xiaolu Guo.
Special Jury Prize & Leopard for the Best
Director: Alexei Mizgirev for **Buben.Baraban**
(Russia).
Best Actress: Lotte Verbeek for **Nothing**
Personal by Urszula Antoniak (Republic of
Ireland/Netherlands).
Best Actor: Antonis Kafetzopoulos for
Akadimia Platonos by Filippos Tsitos
(Germany/Greece).
Filmmakers of the Present Competition
Golden Leopard: **The Anchorage** (Sweden/
USA), CW Winter & Anders Edström.
CinéCinéma Special Jury Prize: **Piombo Fuso**
(Italy), Stefano Savona.
Other Awards
Best First Feature: **Nothing Personal** (Republic
of Ireland/Netherlands), Urszula Antoniak.
Prix du Public UBS (Audience Award): **Giulias**
Verschwinden (Switzerland), Christoph Schaub.
Variety Piazza Grande Award: **Same Same But**
Different (Germany), Detlev Buck.

Report 2009
Highlights of the 62nd Festival included: the
Manga Impact project on Japanese animation,
which featured some of the grand masters of
the genre, such as Isao Takahata; major names
in world cinema in conversation with festival-

goers at the Forum, from US director William
Friedkin (Leopard of Honour – Swisscom)
to French producer Martine Marignac (Best
Independent Producer Award), plus star Italian
actor Toni Servillo (Excellence Award – Moët
& Chandon); or the Open Doors co-production
lab for new projects by a dozen filmmakers
from Greater China. **– Alessia Botani**, Head of
Editorial Content.

BFI London Film Festival
Late October 2010

The UK's largest and most prestigious public
film festival presented at the BFI Southbank,
West End venues, and at cinemas throughout
the capital. The programme comprises around
200 features and documentaries as well as
showcasing over 100 short films. There is a
British section and a very strong international
selection from Asia, Africa, Europe, Latin
America, US independents and experimental
and avant-garde work. More than 1,600
UK and international press and industry
representatives attend and there is a buyers/
sellers liaison office. *Inquiries to:* Emilie
Arnold, London Film Festival, BFI Southbank,
Belvedere Road, South Bank, London SE1 8XT,
UK. Tel: (44 20) 7815 1305. e: emilie.arnold@
bfi.org.uk. Web: www.bfi.org.uk/lff.

AWARDS 2009
Star of London
Best Film: **A Prophet** *(France),*
Jacques Audiard.
Best British Newcomer: Screenwriter Jack
Thorne for **The Scouting Book For Boys** (UK).
The Sutherland Trophy Winner: **Ajami** (Germany/
Israel), Scandar Copti and Yaron Shani.
The Times BFI London Film Festival Grierson
Award: **Defamation** (Austria/Denmark/Israel/
USA), Yoav Shamir.
BFI Fellowships: Souleymane Cissé and
John Hurt.

Report 2009
The Times BFI 53rd London Film Festival
opened with the world premiere of Wes
Anderson's *The Fantastic Mr Fox* and rounded

The London film Festival's open air screening on Trafalgar Square.

off another highly successful year with the world premiere of Sam Taylor-Wood's *Nowhere Boy*. The Festival hosted 193 feature films and 113 short films from 46 countries including 15 world premieres. There were 515 screenings and 553 filmmakers, with 277 of the filmmakers from outside the UK. With 874 industry delegates accredited, the Festival exceeded last year's figures and reports the highest-ever audience attendance in excess of 124,000 filmgoers, compared to 115,00 in 2008. **–Tim Platt**, Festival Marketing Manager.

Los Angeles Film Festival
June 17–27, 2010

The Los Angeles Film Festival showcases the best of American and international independent cinema. With an expected attendance of over 100,000, the festival screens over 175 narrative features, documentaries, shorts, and music videos. Now in its 15th year, the festival has grown into a world-class event, uniting new filmmakers with critics, scholars, film masters, and the movie-loving public. *Inquiries to:* Los Angeles Film Festival, 9911 W Pico Blvd, Los Angeles, CA 90035, USA. Tel: (1 310) 432 1200. e: lafilmfest@filmindependent.org. Web: www. lafilmfest.com.

Málaga Film Festival
April 16–24, 2010

The Málaga Film Festival, together with the Goya prizes, have grown to become the two fundamental appointments for the whole audiovisual sector of Spanish Cinema. A festival that brings together all industry professionals, both to present their films and to debate questions affecting the audiovisual sector. In addition, the Festival has created three audiovisual markets, Málaga Markets: Málaga Screenings (Spanish Film Market); TV Market (Market for Spanish Fiction and Animation Productions for Television); and MercaDoc (European and Latin-American Documentary Market). *Inquiries to:* Málaga Film Festival, Calle Ramos Marín 2, 29012 Malaga, Spain. Tel: (34 95) 222 8242. e: info@festivaldemalaga.com. Web: www.festivalmalaga.com.

International Filmfestival Mannheim-Heidelberg
November 2010

The festival of independent new film artists presents around 40 international new features, of which around 75% are fiction, with documentaries and short films also occupying places in the two main sections, International Competition and International Discoveries. Our films are genuine premieres as we do not screen any films that have already been seen at other big festivals such as Cannes, Berlin, Venice, Locarno or at any German festival. The selection process is a radical one: they have to be really outstanding new art-house films by new directors. The Mannheim Meetings offer a unique and innovative concept of one-to-one business meetings for different players in the art-house arena: film producers, distributors, and sales agents. The international co-production market is one of only four worldwide (alongside Rotterdam, New York and Pusan). The sales & distribution market is dedicated to distributors and sales agents. More than 60,000 filmgoers and 1,000 film professionals attend. *Inquiries to:* Dr Michael Koetz, International Filmfestival Mannheim-Heidelberg, Collini-Center, Galerie, D-68161 Mannheim, Germany. Tel: (49 621) 102 943. e: info@iffmh.de. Web: www.iffmh.de.

Mar del Plata International Film Festival
November 2010

The festival's President is acclaimed filmmaker José Martínez Suárez. It is the only A-grade film festival in Latin America with an Official Competition, usually comprising around 15 films, with around two from Argentina. Other sections include Latin American Films, Out of Competition, Point of View, Near Darkness, Soundsystem, Heterodoxy, Documentary Frame, Argentine Showcase, Memory in Motion and The Inner Look. *Inquiries to:* Mar del Plata International Film Festival, Hipólito Yrigoyen 1225 (C1085ABO), Buenos Aires, Argentina. Tel: (54 11) 4383 5115. e: info@ mardelplatafilmfest.com. Web: www. mardelplatafilmfest.com.

Melbourne International Film Festival
July 23–August 8, 2010

MIFF is regarded unequivocally as the most significant film event in Australia. It has the largest and most diverse programme of screenings and special events in the country, in addition to the largest audience. There is also growing international regard for MIFF as a film marketplace, with a steady increase in sales agents attending. The longest-running festival in the southern hemisphere, showing more than 400 features, shorts, documentaries and new media works, presented in five venues. *Inquiries to:* PO Box 4982, Melbourne 3001, Victoria, Australia. Tel: (61 3) 8660 4888. e: miff@melbournefilmfestival.com.au. Web: www.melbournefilmfestival.com.au.

Miami International Film Festival
March 5–14, 2010

The Festival is a world-class platform for film and filmmakers promoting Miami as an educational and international film destination. It presents the best of emerging and established film to the local and international community within an educational framework. *Inquiries to:* Miami International Film Festival, 25 NE 2nd Street, Suite 5501, Miami, Florida 33132, USA. Tel: (1 305) 237 3456. e: info@miamifilmfestival.com. Web: www.miamifilmfestival.com.

AWARDS 2009
World Cinema Competition Knight Grand Jury Prize: **The Past is a Foreign Land** (Italy), by Daniele Vicari.
Ibero-American Competition Knight Grand Jury Prize: **Historias Extraordinarias** (Argentina), Mariano Llinás.
Dox Competition: **Shakespeare and Victor Hugo's Intimacies** (Mexico), Yulene Olaizola.
Shorts Competition: **First Love** (Hungary), Ildikó Enyedi.
Cutting the Edge Competition: **On War** (France), Bertrand Bonello.
International Film Guide Inspiration Award: **The Maid** (Chile/Mexico), Sebastián Silva.

Middle East International Film Festival
October 14–23, 2010

The Middle East International Film Festival (MEIFF) was established in 2007 and is presented annually in Abu Dhabi, the United Arab Emirates, by the Abu Dhabi Authority for Culture and Heritage (ADACH). MEIFF's mission is to affirm the key place Abu Dhabi holds as an emerging cultural centre and to foster the growth of its local film community. The Festival celebrates cinema in all its forms by creating a vibrant forum for storytellers from the Middle East and around the world. *Inquiries to:* MEIFF, c/o ABACH, PO Box 2380, Abu Dhabi, UAE. Tel: (971 2) 417 444. Fax: 443 6076. e:contact@meiff.com. Web: www.meiff.com.

AWARDS 2009
Narrative Feature Competition
Black Pearl Award for Best Narrative Film: **Hipsters** (Russia), Valery Todorovsky.
Black Pearl Award for Best New Narrative Director: Glendyn Ivin for **Last Ride** (Australia).
Black Pearl Award for Best Middle Eastern Narrative Film: **The Time That Remains** (Belgium/France/ Italy/Palestine/UK), Elia Suleiman.

Elia Suleiman accepts the Black Pearl Award for Best Middle Eastern Film for **The Time that Remains** *at MEIFF 2009 Closing night ceremony. Photo: Pamela Gentile*

Black Pearl Award for Best New Middle Eastern Narrative Director: Pelin Esmer for **10 to 11** (France/Germany/Turkey).
Black Pearl Award for Best Actor: Hamed Behdad for **No One Knows About Persian Cats** (Iran).
Black Pearl Award for Best Actress: Alicia Laguna and Sonia Couoh for **Northless** (Mexico).
Jury Special Mention: **Northless** (Mexico), Rigoberto Pérezcano.
Documentary Feature Competition
Black Pearl Award for Best Documentary Film: **The Frontier Gandhi: Badshah Khan, A Torch for Peace** (Afghanistan/ India/Pakistan/USA), TC McLuhan.
Black Pearl Award for Best New Documentary Director: Johan Grimonprez for **Double Take** (Belgium/Netherlands).
Black Pearl Award for Best Middle Eastern Documentary Film: **On the Way to School** (Turkey), Orhan Eskiköy and Özgür Doğan.
Black Pearl Award for Best New Middle Eastern Documentary Director: Mohamed Zran for **Being Here** (Tunisia).

Jury Special Mention: **The Age of Stupid** (UK), Franny Armstrong.
Short Film Competition
Black Pearl Award for Best Narrative Short: **The Six Dollar Fifty Man** (New Zealand), Mark Albiston and Louis Sutherland.
Black Pearl Award for Best Documentary Short: **Wagah** (Germany/India/Pakistan), Supriyo Sen and Najaf Bilgrami.
Black Pearl Award for Best Middle Eastern Short: **Tripoli, Quiet** (Lebanon), Rania Attieh and Daniel Garcia.
Black Pearl Award for Best Student Short - First Prize: **Anna** (Denmark), Runar Runarsson.
Black Pearl Award for Best Student Short - Second Prize: **Kasia** (Belgium), Elisabet Llado.
Black Pearl Award for Best Student Short - Third Prize: **Schautag** (Germany), Marvin Kren.

Report 2009
MEIFF's 3rd edition marked some major innovations, including separate competitions for Narrative Features (the jury was chaired by Abbas Kiarostami) and Documentary Features (with James Longley as chair). Half the entries in each were from the Middle East, and included a number of exciting world premieres. Sidebars focused on recent Turkish cinema and environmental issues, while the World Cinema Showcase lived up to its title. Short films of all types were judged by a jury headed by Yousry Nasrallah. Attendance at festival screenings doubled from 2008, signalling the Festival's fast-growing reputation. Master classes explored the role of music and scoring in film, while other highlights included conversations with Naomi Watts, Oscar-winning composer A.R. Rahman and fashion designer Jason Wu. Stars on hand included Orlando Bloom, Golshifteh Farahani, Eva Mendes, Demi Moore, Khaled Abol Naga, Freida Pinto, Maggie Q, Hend Sabry and Hilary Swank.
– Peter Scarlet, Executive Director.

Mill Valley Film Festival
October 7–17, 2010

Known as a filmmakers' festival, the Festival offers a high-profile, prestigious, non-competitive and welcoming environment, perfect for celebrating the best in independent and world cinema. MVFF presents over 200 films from 50 countries featuring a wide variety of high-calibre international programming, in beautiful Marin County, just across the Golden Gate Bridge. Celebrating its 33rd year in 2010, the festival includes the innovative Vfest, Children's Film Fest, celebrity tributes, seminars and special events. *Inquiries to:* Mill Valley Film Festival/ California Film Institute, 1001 Lootens Place, Suite 220, San Rafael, CA 94901, USA. Tel: (1 415) 383 5256. e: mvff@cafilm.org. Web: www.mvff.com.

Report 2009
The 2009 MVFF was one of our best years ever: our spotlights and tributes were star-studded and thoughtful, with honorees including Clive Owen, Uma Thurman, Woody Harrelson and Jason Reitman. Daniel Lee's *Precious* was one of two opening night features and the festival closed out with *Looking for Eric* and *The Young Victoria*. Other notables included Andrea Arnold's *Fishtank*, Lone Scherfig's *An Education*, Andre Techine's *The Girl on the Train*, Sebastian Silva's *Maid*, Valery Todorovsky's *Hipsters*, Judith Elrich and Rick Goldsmith's *The Most Dangerous Man in America*. Various guests included John Woo, Henry Selick, Seymour Cassel, Lone Scherfig, Daniel Ellsberg, Scott Hicks, Stacy Keach, Valery Todorovsky, Lee Daniels, Paula Patton, Gabourey Sidbe and Emily Blunt. In total, films from some 41 countries were shown, including 24 premieres. There were some great panels too: a distribution discussion with Bob Berney, Ryan Werner, Ira Deutchman, and Howard Cohrn and Eric d'Arbeloff, Co-Presidents of Roadside Productions.
– **Mark Fishkin**, Festival Director.

Montreal World Film Festival
August 26-September 6, 2010

The goal of the festival is to encourage cultural diversity and understanding between nations, to foster the cinema of all continents by stimulating the development of quality cinema, to promote filmmakers and innovative works, to discover and encourage new talents, and to promote meetings between cinema professionals from around the world. Apart from the 'Official Competition' and the 'First Films Competition', the festival presents 'Hors Concours' (World Greats), a 'Focus on World Cinema' and 'Documentaries of the World', plus tributes to established filmmakers and a section dedicated to Canadian student films. *Inquiries to:* Montreal World Film Festival 1432 de Bleury St, Montreal, Quebec, Canada H3A 2J1. Tel: (1 514) 848 3883 e: info@ffm-montreal.org. Web: www.ffm-montreal.org.

AWARDS 2009
Feature Films
Grand Prix des Americas: **Freedom** (France), Tony Gatlif.
Special Grand Prix of the jury: **Weaving Girl** (China), Wang Quan'an.
Best Director: Kichitaro Negishi for **Villon's Wife** (Japan).
Best Actress: Marie Leuenberger for **Will You Marry Us?** (Switzerland).
Best Actor: Cyron Melville for **Love and Rage** (Denmark).
Best Screenplay: Alain Le Henry for **I'm Glad That My Mother Is Alive** (France).
Best Artistic Contribution: **Saint George Shoots The Dragon** (Bosnia/Bulgaria/Serbia), Srdjan Dragojevic.
Innovation Award: **Fire Keeper** (Iran), Mohsen Amiryoussefi.
Short Films
1st Prize: **Pigeon Impossible** (USA), Lucas Martell.
Jury Award: **Attached To You** (Sweden), Carin Bräck, Cecilia Actis and Mia Hulterstam.
Zeniths for the Best First Fiction Features Films
Golden Zenith: **You Will Be Mine** (France), Sophie Laloy.
Silver Zenith: **When The Lemons Turned Yellow** (Iran), Mohammadreza Vatandoost.
Bronze Zenith: **Riff Raff** (Ecuador), Cristina Franco, Jorge Alejandro Fegan, Diego Coral López and Nataly Valencia.

Moscow International Film Festival
June 2010

The large competition remains international in scope, covering Europe and the CIS, South East Asia, Latin and North America. The Media-Forum (panorama and competition) is devoted to experimental films and video art. There is a wide panorama of recent Russian films and the special documentary cinema programme 'Free Thought'. 2009 Moscow FF also included the programmes 'Asian Extreme', 'Focus on Bulgarian cinema', 'Indian Panorama', '8 S films', Georgian cinema from the 'Vow to Repentance', 'Russian Trace', 'Socialist Avant-Gardism', retrospectives of Marco Ferreri , Shyam Benegal, Pavel Lungin and Jerzy Skolimowski. Industry Co-Production Forum. *Inquiries to:* Moscow International Film Festival, 11 Maly Kozikhinsky Pereulok, Moscow 123001, Russia. Tel: (7 495) 699 0625. e: info@moscowfilmfestival.ru. Web: www.moscowfilmfestival.ru.

AWARDS 2009
Golden George: **Pete on a Way to Heaven** (Russia), Nikolai Dostal.

Napa Sonoma Wine Country Film Festival
September 16–26, 2010

World cinema, culture and conscience gather in the heart of California's premium wine region, Napa and Sonoma Valleys, just 50 miles from the Golden Gate Bridge. Films are screened during the day in select theatres and at night under the stars in spectacular

(left and right) Cellin Gluck and Rinko Kikuchi present **Sideways** *(re-imagined) at Closing Night of the 2009 Napa Sonoma Wine Country Film Festival, and Festival Director Stephen Ashton (centre).*

vineyard settings. The festival is gently paced, mainly non-competitive and accepts features, documentaries, shorts, and animation. All genres are welcome. Programme categories are: World Cinema, US Cinema, EcoCinema (environment), Arts in Film and Cinema of Conscience (social issues). *Inquiries to:* PO Box 303, Glen Ellen, CA 95442, USA. Tel: (1 707) 935 3456. e: wcfilmfest@aol.com. Web: www.wcff.us.

AWARDS 2009
Best of the Festival: **The Good Life** (Chile), Andres Wood.
Best World Cinema: **The Anarchist's Wife** (Germany/Spain), Marie Noelle and Peter Sehr and **Zen** (Japan), Takahashi Banmei.
Best Eco Cinema Drama: **Pradolongo** (Spain), Ignacio Vila.
Best Eco Cinema Doc: **Food Beware - That Should Not Be** (France), Jean-Paul Jaud and **Pirate For the Sea** (USA), Ron Colby.
Best Documentary International: **Which Way Home** (Mexico/USA), Rebecca Camissa.
Best Cinema of Conscience: **Viva Mandela: A**

Hero For All Seasons (South Africa), Catherine Meyburgh and **Taking Root: The Vision of Wangari Maathai** (USA), Lisa Merton & Alan Dater.
Mondavi Award for Peace and Cultural Understanding Dramatic: **I, The Other** (Italy), Mohsen Melliti.
Mondavi Award for Peace and Cultural Understanding Documentary: **The Billboard From Bethlehem** (USA), Bruce Barrett.

Report 2009

Shifting this international film festival from mid-summer dates to the wine country's fabulous harvest season proved successful. Over 5,000 moviegoers packed the outdoor and indoor theatres to see the US premiere of *Capitalism: A Love Story*, and world premieres of *The Invention of Lying* – which won Best US Cinema – and *Sideways*, the new Japanese version of Alexander Payne's film, shot almost entirely on location in the Napa Valley. Best Director Awards went to Nana Djordjadze's stunning *The Rainbowmaker* (Georgia) and Manijeh Hekmat for *3 Women* (Iran). The festival's David L. Wolper Best Documentary, *No Subtitles Necessary: Lazlo & Vilmos*, preceded a master class with Vilmos Zsigmond. **– Justine Warner**, Public Relations.

Netherlands Film Festival, Utrecht
September 22–October 1, 2010

Since 1981, The Netherlands Film Festival (NFF) has presented the latest crop of Dutch feature films, documentaries, short films and television films to the Dutch public as well as an audience of international and Dutch-based professionals. Many of these productions are world premieres, of which a selection compete for the grand prize of Dutch cinema, the Golden Calf for Best Film. During the festival each genre is allotted its own special day. Retrospectives and special programmes offer audiences a chance to review films from previous years. Furthermore, the festival screens films made by talented young filmmakers from the Dutch audio-visual institutes, as well as short and long

films from neighbouring Flanders. Talkshows, workshops, parties and exhibitions make the festival complete – a unique platform that highlights the very best of Dutch cinema. The Holland Film Meeting (HFM) is a sidebar of the Netherlands Film Festival that provides a series of business-oriented events for the international professionals in attendance. The HFM consists of the Benelux Screenings, the Netherlands Production Platform (NPP), professional workshops and panels, the Variety Cinema Militants Programme and the Binger-Screen International Interview. *Inquiries to:* Netherlands Film Festival, PO Box 1581, 3500 BN Utrecht, Netherlands. Tel: (31 30) 230 3800. Fax: 230 3801. e: info@filmfestival.nl. Web: www.filmfestival.nl.

AWARDS 2009
Country of Origin for all shown:
The Netherlands
Best Short Film: **Sunset From a Rooftop**, Marinus Groothof.
Best Short Documentary: **I Wanna Be Boss**, Marije Meerman.
Best Full-Length Documentary: **Outfoxed**, Jan Musch and Tijs Tinbergen.
Best TV Drama: **Anvers**, Martijn Maria Smits.

The Goden Calf, made by Theo Mackaay, in front of the city Theatre of Utrecht during the 29th Netherlands Film Festival, September 2009. Photo: Felix Kalkman

Best Production Design: **Winter In Wartime**,
Floris Vos.
Best Photography: **Nothing Personal**,
Daniël Bouquet.
Best Sound Design: **Nothing Personal**,
Jan Schermer.
Best Editing: **Can Go Through Skin**,
Esther Rots.
Best Score: **Carmen of the North**, Perquisite.
Best Male Supporting Role: Raymond Thiry for
Winter In Wartime.
Best Female Supporting Role: Pleuni Touw for
Bride Flight.
Best Actor: Martijn Lakemeier for **Winter In
Wartime**.
Best Actress: Rifka Lodeizen for **Can Go
Through Skin**.
Best Screenplay: Alex van Warmerdam for
The Last Days of Emma Blank.
Best Director: Urszula Antoniak for
Nothing Personal.
Best Full-Length Feature Film:
Nothing Personal, Reinier Selen and Edwin
van Meurs (Rinkel Film and TV).
Special Jury Award: The entire crew and cast
of **Can Go Through Skin**.
Film 1 Audience Award: **Upstream**,
Danyael Sugawara.
Dutch Film Critics Award: **Boris Ryzhy**,
Aliona van der Horst.

Report 2009
At this year's event, the festival introduced
Dutch Angle. This programme emphasised
a series of films by talented and innovative
Dutch authors, which have been selected for
some of the leading international festivals but
remain relatively unknown among domestic
audiences. This year's festival pulled in a
record number of 151,000 visitors. The
NOFF and Festival TV attracted 1.8 million
visitors. Furthermore, Willemien van Aalst
was appointed director of the Netherlands
Film Festival as of October 3, 2009. She took
over from Doreen Boonekamp, who has
worked for the festival for 20 years and was its
festival director since 2002. **– Esther Bendijk**,
Marketing & Communications.

The New Zealand International Film Festival

Auckland July 8–25, 2010
Wellington July 16–August 1, 2010

In 2009, the 41-year-old Auckland International
Film Festival and 38-year-old Wellington
Film Festival – operating under the same
umbrella since 1984 – dropped their individual
identities to become known as the New
Zealand International Film Festival. The
Festival provides a non-competitive New
Zealand premiere showcase and welcomes
many international filmmakers and musicians.
Highlights of its programme, brimming with
animation, art-house, documentary and
retrospective programmes, toured in 2009
to a further 14 New Zealand centres. Festival
Director: Bili Gosden. *Inquiries to:* New
Zealand International Film Festivals, Box 9544,
Marion Square, Wellington 6141, New Zealand.
Tel: (64 4) 385 0162. Fax: 801 7304. e: festival@
nzff.co.nz. Web: www.nzff.co.nz.

Visions du Réel, International Film Festival – Nyon

April 15–21, 2010

Visions du Réel is a unique international
festival, providing an overview of the best
of cinema du réel, with films challenging
boundaries, made by independent filmmakers
and producers who take risks with radical
choices, strong writing and new forms of
storytelling. As part of Visions du Réel, Doc
Outlook-International Market, with its Pitching
Sessions, Market Screenings and Panels
attracts more than 770 professionals from
all over the world (41 countries in 2009).
The success has definitely given notice to
the festival and the Town of Nyon to ensure
it continues: a new cinema will be provided
to meet everybody's expectations. Entry
deadlines: Festival: 5 January 2010. Market: 10
March 2010. *Inquiries to:* Visions du Réel, 18
Rue Juste-Olivier, CH-1260 Nyon, Switzerland.
Tel: (41 22) 365 4455. Fax: 365 4450.
e: docnyon@visionsdureel.ch.
Web: www.visionsdureel.ch.

VISIONS DU RÉEL
NYON

VISIONS DU RÉEL
INTERNATIONAL FILM FESTIVAL
DOC OUTLOOK-INTERNATIONAL MARKET
NYON, 15-21 APRIL 2010

THE FINE FESTIVAL IN THE HEART OF EUROPE
WITH ITS FAMOUS SECTIONS OPEN TO
THE SUPERB DIVERSITY OF FILMS DU RÉEL...

THE MARKET WITH A PREMIUM SELECTION,
COPRODUCTION MEETINGS, PACE MAKER
FOR TENDENCIES IN NEW MEDIA...

NYON: THE SPRING OF FESTIVALS!

ENTRY FORMS AND REGULATIONS
WWW.VISIONSDUREEL.CH
Deadlines for entries
Festival: 5 January 2010
Market: 10 March 2010

AWARDS 2009

International Competition
Grand Prix La Poste Suisse - Visions du Réel:
L'Encerclement - La Democratie Dans Les Rets Du Neoliberalisme (Canada), Richard Brouillette.
Prix SRG SSR Idée Suisse: **Die Frau Mit Den 5 Elefanten** (Germany/Switzerland), Vadim Jendreyko.
Audience Prize: **Les Damnes de la Mer** (Belgium/Morocco),Jawad Rhalib.
Inter-religious Jury Prize: **Mental** (Japan/USA), Kazuhiro Soda.
Special Mention: **Die Frau Mit Den 5 Elefanten** (Germany/Switzerland), Vadim Jendreyko.
Young Audience Prize: **Petropolis - Aerial Perspectives on the Alberta Tar Sands** (Canada), Peter Mettler.
Special Mention: **Twenty Show Le Film** (France), Godefroy Fouray and François Vautier.
Regards Neufs: **Cash and Marry** (Austria/Macedonia), Georgiev Atanas and **Babaji, An Indian Love Story** (The Netherlands), Jiska Rickels.
Special Mention: **18 Ans** (Belgium/France), Frédérique Pollet Rouyer.
Cinéma Suisse
Prix George Foundation Best Newcomer Film:
Familientreffen - Marthaler Theater Im Grand Hotel (Switzerland), Sarah Derendinger.
Prix Suissimage/Société Suisse des Auteurs SSA: **Die Frau Mit Den 5 Elefanten** (Germany/Switzerland), Vadim Jendreyko.
All Sections
Prize "Regards Sur le Crime": **The Soldier's Tale** (France), Penny Allen.
Prize "Buyens-Chagol": **El Olvido** (Germany/The Netherlands), Heddy Honigmann.

Report 2009
Anniversary Highlights: 40 Years Festival Nyon, 15 Years Visions Du Réel, 20 Years Since the Fall of the Berlin Wall and 10 Years Eurodoc. *Ateliers* with Joana Hadjithomas and Khalil Joreige (France/Lebanon) and Sergey Kvortsevoy (Kazakhstan). *Seances Speciales:* 20 Years Since the Fall of the Berlin Wall, Doc Alliance, Eurodoc and Docweb Kowalski – Camera War. *Guest of Reprocessing*

Richard Brouillette, winner of the Grand Prix La Poste Suisse – Visions du Réel. Photo: Laetitia Gessler

Reality: Susan Mogul (USA). *Professional Events:* Doc Outlook Breakfasts, Podium Swiss Broadcasting Company - Arte, Panel Association Suisse des Journalistes: Festivals, Est-Il Encore Reellement Question de Cinema?, Agora: Authenticite, Verite, Archive, Document (with MEDIA, SRG SSR, idée suisse and Sunny Side of the Docs), Federal Office of Culture: Production Agreement Between Germany, Austria and Switzerland, Docweb, Workshop - Tape and File Based Workflow With Final Cut Pro (Schweizer Video AG & Apple Solution Expert Video & Broadcast).
Festival Facts and Figures: The festival was held over seven days with 1,800 films submitted, 143 films selected, 43 nationalities, 47 world premieres, 37 international premieres, four theatres, 203 screenings, 32,000 entries, 1,350 accreditations, 145 filmmakers and 164 journalists. *Doc Outlook International Market Facts and Figures:* 770 professionals, 239 films selected, 30 VOD viewing booths, 3,576 viewings and 41 production countries. **– Brigitte Morgenthaler**, Communication & Partnerships.

Oberhausen
International Short Film Festival
April 29–May 4, 2010

The International Short Film Festival Oberhausen, one of the leading short-film festivals in the world, is known for its open attitude towards short formats and its focus on experimental works. The traditional competitions – International,

German, Children's Shorts and Music Video
– provide an extensive overview of current
international short-film and video production.
A fifth competition for regional films (NRW
Competition) was introduced in 2009. The
2009 thematic programme UNREAL ASIA took
a look at current short films from South East
Asia, featuring a characteristically wide range
of works from NGO-sponsored documentaries
to artist videos, intended for gallery contexts.
Oberhausen also continued its PODIUM series
of lively and very well-attended discussions.
Retrospectives of the works of Matsumoto
Toshio and the Sarajevo Documentary
School were among the other highlights of
the festival. Deadline for entries: 15 January
2010. Entry forms and regulations can be
downloaded at www.kurzfilmtage.de from
October 2009. Festival Director: Dr Lars Henrik
Gass. *Inquiries to:* Oberhausen International
Short Film Festival, Grillostrasse 34, D-46045
Oberhausen, Germany. Tel: (49 208) 825
2652. e: info@kurzfilmtage.de. Web: www.
kurzfilmtage.de.

Lichtburg Filmpalast, main festival cinema of the Oberhausen
International Short Film Festival

AWARDS 2009
International Competition
Grand Prize of the City of Oberhausen:
A Letter to Uncle Boonmee (Thailand),
Apichatpong Weerasethakul.
Two Main Prizes: **Ketamin - Hinter dem Licht**
(Germany), Carsten Aschmann and **True Story**
(USA), Robert Frank.
ARTE Prize for a European Short Film:
Bernadette (UK), Duncan Campbell.
German Competition
Prize for the Best Contribution (ex aequo): **N.N.**
(Germany), Michel Kloefkorn, and **Please Say
Something** (Germany), David O'Reilly.

Odense International Film Festival
August 2010

Denmark's only international short-film festival
invites the best international unusual short
films with original and imaginative content.
Besides screenings of more than 200 national
and international short films and Danish documentaries, Odense Film Festival offers a number of exciting retrospective programmes and
viewing of all competition films in the Video
Bar. The festival hosts a range of seminars for
the film professionals, librarians and teachers, educates children and youth in the field
of forceful, alternative film experiences and is
a meeting place for international film directors and other film professionals in the field of
short films and documentaries. *Inquiries to:*
Odense Film Festival, Odense Slot, Nørregade
36-38, DK-5100 Odense C, Denmark. Tel: (45)
6551 2823. e: filmfestival@odense.dk. Web:
www.filmfestival.dk.

**Oulu International
Children's and Youth Film Festival**
November 15–21, 2010

Annual festival with competition for full-length
feature films for children and youth, it screens
recent titles and retrospectives. Oulu is set
in northern Finland, on the coast of the Gulf
of Bothnia. *Inquiries to:* Oulu International
Children's and Youth Film Festival, Hallituskatu
7, FI-90100 Oulu, Finland. Tel: (358 8) 881 1293.

Fax: 881 1290. e: eszter.vuojala@oufilmcenter.
inet.fi. Web: www.oulunelokuvakeskus.fi/lef.

AWARDS 2009

Kaleva Award: **The Crocodiles** (Germany),
Christian Ditter.
CIFEJ-Prize: **The Magic Tree** (Poland), Andrzej
Maleszka.
*Media Foundation of the Evangelical Lutheran
Church Prize:* **Forbidden Fruit** (Finland) Dome
Karukoski.
POEM's Little Bear Award: Niina Veittikoski.

Report 2009

The competition consisted of 12 films. The
other sections were Kaleidoscope, Growing

*Vilma, the mascot of Oulu International Children's and Youth Film
Festival. Photo: Jari Haavikko.*

Pains, Finnish Survey and Childhood is Luxury.
The guest of honour was Finnish children
and youth-film director Raimo O Niemi. To
commemorate the Swedish Cultural Year
there was a programme entitled the Classics
of Swedish Chilrden's Film. The theme of the
Media Seminar this year was The Creative
Class. The Sami Children's Chanel held an
exhibition entitled Unna Junná and attracted
several children.
– Eszter Vuojala, Festival Director.

Palm Springs International Film Festival
January 4–18, 2010

Palm Springs, celebrating its 21st edition
in 2010, is one of the largest film festivals
in the US, hosting 120,000 attendees for a
line-up of over 230 films at the 2009 event.
Special sections of the festival have included
Cine Latino, New Voices/New Visions, Gala
Screenings, Awards Buzz (Best Foreign
Language Oscar Submissions), World Cinema
Now, Modern Masters and the True Stories
documentary section. The festival includes
a Black Tie Awards Gala on January 5, 2010
– 2009 honorees include Clint Eastwood,
Leonardo DiCaprio, Kate Winslet, Ron Howard,
Anne Hathaway, and Alexandre Desplat.
Inquiries to: Darryl MacDonald, 1700 E Tahquitz
Canyon Way, Suite 3, Palm Springs, CA 92262,
USA. Tel: (1 760) 322 2930. e: info@psfilmfest.
org. Web: www.psfilmfest.org.

AWARDS 2009

Audience Award for Best Narrative Feature:
Departures (Japan), Yojiro Takita.
*Audience Award for Best Documentary
Feature:* **Visual Acoustics: The Modernism of
Julius Shulman** (USA), Eric Bricker.
*FIPRESCI Award for Best Foreign Language
Film:* **Revanche** (Austria), Götz Spielmann.
FIPRESCI Award Best Actor: Natar Ungalaaq
for **The Necessities of Life** (Canada).
FIPRESCI Award Best Actress:
Martina Gusman for **Lion's Den** (Argentina).
New Voices/New Visions Award: **Hooked**
(Romania), Adrian Sitaru.
John Schlesinger Award for Outstanding First

Feature: **Captain Abu Raed** - (Jordan) -
Amin Matalqa
Bridging the Borders Award:
Waltz with Bashir (Israel), Ari Folman.

Pesaro Film Festival
June 19–27, 2010

The Mostra Internazionale del Nuovo
Cinema/Pesaro Film Festival was founded
in Pesaro in 1965 by Bruno Torri and Lino
Miccichè and since 2000 has been directed
by Giovanni Spagnoletti. The Pesaro Film
Festival, in addition to being known for
the dynamic and original documentation it
offers, is synonymous with discoveries, with
showcasing emerging cinematographers, with
re-readings, with 'Special Events'. *Inquiries
to:* Mostra Internazionale del Nuovo Cinema/
Pesaro Film Festival, Via Faà di Bruno 67, 00195
Rome, Italy. Tel: (39 06) 445 6643/491156.
e: info@pesarofilmfest.it. Web: www.
pesarofilmfest.it.

AWARDS 2009
New Cinema Competition: **Non è ancora
domani/La pivellina** (Austria/Italy), Tizza Covi
and Rainer Frimmel.
Amnesty Italia/Cinema and Human Rights:
Vietato Sognare/Forbidden Childhood
(Italy), Barbara Cupisti.
Pesaro Cinemagiovane: **Fixer: The Taking of
Ajmal Naqshbandi** (Afghanistan/USA),
Ian Olds.
Special Mention: **Eoddeon Gaien Nal** (Korea),
Lee Suk-gyung.
Public's Award: **La fisica dell'acqua** (Italy),
Felice Farina.

Pordenone Silent Film Festival
October 2–9, 2010

The world's first and largest festival dedicated
to silent cinema, now in its 29th year. The
event sees an annual invasion by archivists,
historians, scholars, collectors and enthusiasts
from around the world, along with cinema
students chosen to attend the internationally
recognised 'Collegium'. Year by year the

festival consistently succeeds in rediscovering
lost masterpieces from the silent years, all
accompanied by original live music. Festival
Director: David Robinson. *Inquiries to:* Le
Giornate del Cinema Muto c/o La Cineteca
del Friuli, Palazzo Gurisatti, via Bini 50, 33013
Gemona (UD), Italy. Tel: (39) 0432 980458.
Fax: 970542. e: info.gcm@cinetecadelfriuli.
org. Web: www.giornatedelcinemamuto.it.

Report 2009
Highlights of the 2009 festival include Erich
von Stroheim's *The Merry Widow*, with
a new score by Maud Nelissen, and the
international première of *Ukulelescope*,
performed by The Ukulele Orchestra from the
UK. Important restorations were presented by
the Nederlands Filmmuseum (Abel Gance's
J'accuse!) and the Cinémathèque Française
(Albatros collection). Jay Weissberg curated
a series on Sherlock Holmes, revealing the
influence of Conan Doyle on silent cinema.
Rarities of divas Francesca Bertini, Asta
Nielsen and Pola Negri were also showcased.
Guests of honour included John Gilbert's
daughter Leatrice Gilbert Fountain and Max
Linder's daughter Maud (recipient of the Jean
Mitry Award). **– Giuliana Puppin**, Press.

*The orchestra directed by Maud Nelissen accompanying Erich von
Stroheim's* **The Merry Widow**, *the opening event of the 28th Pordenone
Silent Film Festival. Photo: Paolo Jacob*

33RD PORTLAND INTERNATIONAL FILM FESTIVAL

Portland International Film Festival
February 11–28, 2010

Portland International Film Festival is an invitational event, presenting more than 100 films from 30 plus countries to 35,000 people from throughout the Northwest. Along with new international features, documentaries and shorts, the festival will feature showcases surveying Hispanic film and literature, Pacific Rim cinema and many of the year's foreign-language Oscar submissions. *Inquiries to:* Northwest Film Center, 1219 SW Park Ave, Portland, OR 97205, USA. Tel: (1 503) 221 1156. Fax: 294 0874. e: info@nwfilm.org. Web: www.nwfilm.org.

Filmmaker Bill Plympton goofs off at the 32nd Portland International Film Festival. Photo: Jason E. Kaplan

Pusan International Film Festival (PIFF)
October 2010

PIFF is known as the most energetic film festival in the world and has become the largest film festival in Asia. This world-class event has been promoting Asian and Korean cinema worldwide in particular and screens over 350 films from over 70 countries of which around 140 are world and international premieres. Also, retrospectives, special programmes in focus, seminars, master classes and other related events are presented annually. In addition, its

project market – Pusan Promotion Plan (PPP) – has been a platform for moving Asian film projects forward in the international marketplace, along with its own talent campus, Asian Film Academy (AFA), offering various filmmaking programmes for young talent from all over Asia. *Inquiries to:* 1st Floor, 6 Tongui-dong, Jongno-gu, Seoul 110-062, Korea. Tel: (82 2) 3675 5097. e: publicity@piff.org. Web: www.piff.org.

Raindance Film Festival
September 29–October 10, 2010

Raindance is the largest independent film festival in the UK and aims to reflect the cultural, visual and narrative diversity of international independent filmmaking, specialising in first-time filmmakers. The festival screens around 100 feature films and 150 shorts as well as hosting a broad range of workshops, masterclasses and workshops. *Inquiries to:* Festival Producer, Raindance Film Festival, 81 Berwick St, London, W1F 8TW, UK. Tel: (44 20) 7287 3833. e: festival@raindance.co.uk. Web: www.raindance.co.uk/festival.

AWARDS 2009
Best UK Feature: **Down Terrace** (UK), Ben Weathley.
Best International Feature: **25 Kilates** (Spain), Patxi Amézcua and **My Suicide** (USA), David Lee Miller.
Best Debut Feature: **Redland** (USA), Asiel Norton.
Best Documentary: **A Normal Life Please** (Japan), Tokachi Tsuchiya.
Best Micro Budget Feature (Documentary or Fiction): **Colin** (UK), Marc Price.
Best UK Short: **Infidel** (UK), George Milton.
Best International Short: **Of Best Intentions** (Ireland), Brian O'Malley and Brian Durnin.
Film of the Festival: **The Slow Game** (Italy), Paolo Sorrentino.

Reykjavík International Film Festival
September 23–October 3, 2010

The festival is one of the most exciting film events in Northern Europe, as well as Iceland's major annual film event. The main purpose of the festival is to offer a wide selection of alternative, independent cinema. The festival's intention is to celebrate cultural diversity, to provoke the public's interest in independent cinema, to impart film's social importance and to encourage discussions. The festival emphasises the relationship between film and other art forms, with art exhibitions, concerts, etc. The festival's main award, the Discovery of the Year, the Golden Puffin Award is dedicated to new filmmakers. *Inquiries to:* Reykjavík International Film Festival, Fríkirkjuvegur 1, 101 Reykjavík, Iceland. Tel: (354) 4117055. Web: www.riff.is.

Milos Forman receives his RIFF 2009 Honorary Award at Bessastadir, the President's residence in Iceland, September 20th 2009

AWARDS 2009

The Golden Puffin, Discovery Award:
I Killed My Mother (Canada), Xavier Dolan.
FIPRESCI Award: **The Girl** (Sweden),
Fredrik Ekdfelt.
The Church of Iceland Award: **Together**
(Norway), Matias Armand Jordal.
RIFF Audience Award: **The Gentlemen**
(Iceland), Janus Bragi Jakobsson.
The Icelandic Red Cross Human Rights Award:
Umoja: Where Men Are Forbidden (France),
Jean Marc Sainclair and Jean Crousillac.
RIFF Environmental Award:
The Dancing Forest (Togo/UK), Brice Lainé.
*The Golden Egg, RIFF 2009 Talent Laboratory
Award:* **Footnotes** (Spain), Anna Bofarull.

Report 2009

The Festival opening was of Xavier Dolan's remarkable debut feature, *I Killed My Mother*, which was awarded the Festival's Grand

Prize, the Golden Puffin, for Discovery of the Year. Milos Forman, this year's recipient of the Honorary Award for Lifetime Achievement in Cinema, attended sold-out screenings of three of his films, participated in Q&As and gave a masterclass. Danish actress Iben Hjejle was President of this year's all-female Jury, and RIFF 2009 enjoyed record attendances of over 22,000 guests. **– Jon Agnar Olason**, Marketing & PR.

Rome International Film Festival
October 29–November 6, 2010

The city of Rome provides a magnificent backdrop to the festival, with the Auditorium Parco della Musica and the Cinema Village being the main nerve centre. The festival offers films, retrospectives, meetings and major international stars, which attracts movie lovers as well as being a great event for all those who work for cinema, show cinema and tell us stories through cinema. The festival has now established itself as a truly unique occasion with the people flocking to the events, exhibitions, encounters and screenings, offering proof of a great passion and interest in culture. The Business Street, which is a five-day-long Roman film market for accredited professionals provides a setting for producers, distributors and all film professionals to meet, debate, share their experiences, and do business, with a special focus on Europe. *Inquiries to:* Rome International Film Festival, Viale Pietro De Coubertin 10, 00196 Rome, Italy. Tel: (39 06) 4040 1900. e: press. international@romacinemafest.org. Web: www.romacinemafest.org.

AWARDS 2009

Golden Marco Aurelio Jury Award Best Film:
Brotherhood (Denmark), Nicolo Donato.
Silver Marco Aurelio Award Best Actress:
Helen Mirren for **The Last Station**
(Germany/Russia).
Silver Marco Aurelio Award Best Actor:
Sergio Castellitto for **Alza la Testa** (Italy).

International Film Festival Rotterdam
January 27–February 7, 2010

With its adventurous, original and distinctive
programming, Rotterdam highlights new
directors and new directions in contemporary
world cinema, exemplified by its Tiger
Awards Competition for debut and second
feature films; the annual showcase of films
from developing countries that have been
supported by the festival's Hubert Bals Fund,
supporting innovative and original film projects
from developing countries; the CineMart, the
international co-production market developed
to nurture the financing and production of
new cinema. *Inquiries to:* International Film
Festival Rotterdam, PO Box 21696, 3001 AR
Rotterdam, Netherlands. Tel: (31 10) 890 9090.
e: tiger@filmfestivalrotterdam.com. Web:
www.filmfestivalrotterdam.com.

AWARDS 2009

VPRO Tiger Awards: **Be Calm and Count to
Seven** (Iran), Ramtin Lavafipour, **Breathless**
(South Korea), Yang Ik-June and **Wrong Rosary**
(Turkey), Mahmut Fazil Coskun.

*Rotterdam VPRO Tiger Award Winners Ramtin Lavafipour (left), Yang
Ik-June (centre) and Mahmut Fazil Coskun.*

Tiger Awards for Short Film: **A Necessary
Music** (UK), Beatrice Gibson, **Despair** (Russia),
Galina Myznikova and Sergey Provorov and
Bernadette (UK), Duncan Campbell.

San Francisco International Film Festival
April 22–May 6, 2010

The longest-running film festival in the
Americas, in its 53rd year, San Francisco
continues to grow in importance and
popularity. It presents more than 150
international features and shorts and plays
host to more than 80,000 film lovers, and
hundreds of filmmakers, journalists and film
industry professionals, throwing sensational
parties, launching new digital initiatives like
International Online, celebrating Bay Area film
culture and showcasing new technologies.
Special awards include the New Directors
Award, the Golden Gate Awards and the
FIPRESCI Prize. *Inquiries to:* San Francisco
International Film Festival, Programming Dept,
San Francisco International Film Festival,
39 Mesa St, Suite 110, The Presidio, San
Francisco, CA 94129, USA. Tel: (1 415) 561
5014. e: gga@sffs.org. Web: www.sffs.org.

AWARDS 2009

New Directors Award - First Narrative Feature:
Snow (Bosnia and Herzegovina), Aida Begic.
FIPRESCI Prize: **Everything Strange and
New** (USA), Frazer Bradshaw.
Golden Gate Awards
Investigative Documentary: **Burma VJ:
Reporting from a Closed Country** (Denmark),
Anders Østergaard.
Documentary Feature: **Nomad's Land**
(Switzerland), Gaël Métroz.
Bay Area Documentary Feature: **D Tour** (USA),
Jim Granato.
Documentary Short: **Tongzhi in Love** (USA),
Ruby Yang.
Bay Area Short: **Immersion** (USA),
Richard Levien.
Narrative Short: **Angels Die in the Soil** (Iran),
Babak Amini.
Animated Short: **Kanizsa Hill** (USA),
Evelyn Lee.

New Visions: **Circles of Confusion** (USA), Phoebe Tooke.
Work for Kids and Families: **Mutt** (Australia), Glen Hunwick.
Youth Works: **No Light at the End of the Tunnel** (USA), Charlotte Burger.
Youth Work Honourable Mention:
Poetry in the Dark (USA), Daniel Kharlak.
Adobe Youth Film for Change Award:
A Generation of Consolidation (USA), Samantha Muilenburg and Brooke Noel.
TV Narrative: **Artemisia** (Taiwan), Chiang Hsiu-chiung.
Audience Award for Best Narrative Feature:
Don't Let Me Drown (USA) Cruz Angeles.
Audience Award for Best Documentary Feature: **Speaking in Tongues** (USA) Marcia Jamel and Ken Schneider.

San Sebastian International Film Festival
September 17–25, 2010

Held in an elegant Basque seaside city known for its superb gastronomy and beautiful beaches, the San Sebastian Festival remains the Spanish-speaking world's most important event in terms of glamour, competition, facilities, partying, number of films and attendance (1,077 production and distribution firms, government agencies and festival representatives from 53 countries, and accredited professionals and 1,053 journalists from 38 countries). Events include the Official Competitive section, Zabaltegi, with its €90,000 cash award, Kutxa-New Directors for first or second long features in Zabaltegi – New Directors or the Official Section, Horizontes Latinos with its €35,000 cash award and meticulous retrospectives. In partnership with the Rencontres Cinémas Amérique Latine in Toulouse, the Films in Progress industry platform aims to aid the completion of Latin American projects. Cinema in Motion 5 is a place to discover projects by filmmakers from from Magreb and Portuguese-speaking African countries, and developing Arab countries, presented to professionals only, in partnership with Amiens Film Festival

and Fribourg Film Festival. *Inquiries to:* San Sebastian International Film Festival, Apartado de Correos 397, 20080 Donostia, San Sebastian 20080, Spain. Tel: (34 943) 481 212. e: ssiff@sansebastianfestival.com. Web: www.sansebastianfestival.com.

AWARDS 2009
Golden Shell for Best Film:
City of Life and Death (China), Lu Chuan.
Special Jury Award:
Le Refuge (France), François Ozon.
Silver Shell for Best Director: Javier Rebollo for **La Mujer sin Piano** (France/Spain).
Silver Shell for Best Actress: Lola Dueñas for **Yo, También** (Spain).
Silver Shell for Best Actor: Pablo Pineda for **Yo, También** (Spain).
Jury Award for Best Photography:
Cao Yu for **City of Life and Death** (China).
Jury Award for Best Screenplay:
Andrews Bowell, Melissa Reeves, Patricia Cornelius and Christos Tsiolkas for **Blessed** (Australia).
Kutxa - New Directors Award:
Le Jour Où Dieu Est Parti En Voyage (Belgium), Philippe Van Leeuw.
Horizontes Award: **Gigante** (Uruguay), Adrián Biniez.

Seattle International Film Festival
May 20–June 13, 2010

The largest film festival in the US, SIFF presents more than 250 features, 50 documentaries, and 100 shorts annually. There are cash prizes for the internationally juried New Directors Showcase and Documentary Competition, and for Short Films in the categories of: Live Action, Documentary, and Animation. Festival sections include: Alternate Cinema, Face the Music, FutureWave, Films4Familes, Contemporary World Cinema, Emerging Masters, Documentary Films, Tributes, and Archival Films. *Inquiries to:* Seattle International Film Festival, 400 Ninth Avenue North, Seattle, WA 98109, USA. Tel: (1 206) 464 5830. e: info@siff.net. Web: www.siff.net.

AWARDS 2009
New Directors Showcase
Grand Jury Prize: **The Other Bank**
(Georgia/Kazakhstan), George Ovashvili.
Documentary Competition
Grand Jury Prize: **Talhotblond** (USA),
Barbara Schroeder.
Special Jury Prize: **Manhole Children** (Japan),
Yoshio Harada.
Short Awards
Narrative Grand Jury Prize: **Short Term 12**
(USA), Destin Daniel Cretton.
Narrative Special Jury Prize: **Lowland Fell**
(Ireland), Michael Kinirons and **Next Floor**
(Canada), Denis Villeuneuve.
Documentary Grand Jury Prize:
The Herd (Ireland), Ken Wardrop.
Animation Grand Jury Prize:
Photograph of Jesus (UK), Laurie Hill.
Futurewave
WaveMaker: **A Generation of Consolidation**
(USA), Samantha Muilenberg.
Special Jury Award: **If U Want 2 Get Technical**
(USA), Riaebia Robinson.
FutureWave Shorts Audience Award:
A Generation of Consolidation (USA),
Samantha M.
*Youth Jury Award for Best FutureWave
Feature:* **My Suicide** (USA), David Lee Miller.
Special Jury Award: **Sounds Like Teen Spirit**
(USA), Jamie J Johnson.
Golden Space Needle Audience Awards
Best Film: **Black Dynamite** (USA), Scott Sanders.
Best Documentary: **The Cove** (USA),
Louie Psihoyos.
Best Short Film: **Wallace and Gromit:
A Matter of Loaf and Death** (UK), Nick Park.
Best Director: **The Hurt Locker** (USA),
Kathryn Bigelow.
Best Actor: **Moon** (United Kingdom),
Sam Rockwell.
Best Actress: **Séraphine** (France/Belgium),
Yolande Moreau.

Seville European Film Festival
November 2010

The Festival is established as one of the best,
showcasing the finest films in Europe, with
more than 170 of the most prestigious long
feature films, documentaries and short films
produced from 34 different countries, including
the United Kingdom, Spain, Germany, France,
Italy and Belgium. The festival attracts more
than 69,500 spectators and, thanks to them,
some 126 screenings were sold out. In 2009,
as a result of the festival's international success,
the European Film Academy (EFA) signed
an agreement in Cannes in conjunction with
ICAS to hold the ceremony for announcing the
European Film Awards nominations in Seville
as part of the Festival. The agreement will be
in force until 2012 and will enable the festival
to screen a selection of the films competing
for nomination, as well as the short films
nominated for the European award. In addition,
the Seville Festival has become a patron of the
Academy, supporting all its activities. In another
step towards its internationalisation, the
Festival is proud to announce that its 2008 jury
president, Danish producer Vibeke Windelow,
has agreed to join its Advisory Board. The
Festival also signed a new collaboration
agreement with the main European fund for
aiding co-production, Eurimages, whose general
secretary, Roberto Olla, participated in activities
at the 2009 Festival. Along with the official and
parallel sections of film screenings, the Festival
continues to strengthen the initiative begun in
2008 to become a meeting place for industry
professionals and also includes seminars,
master classes, lectures, exhibitions and public
presentations. *Inquiries to:* Seville European
Film Festival, Pabellón de Portugal, Avenida Cid
1, 41004 Seville, Spain. Tel: (34 955) 115 586.
Fax: 115 587. e: info@festivaldesevilla.com.
Web: www.festivaldesevilla.com.

AWARDS 2009
Golden Giraldillo Official Section: **Lourdes**
(Austria/France/Germany), Jessica Hausner.
Silver Giraldillo Official Section:
Nothing Personal (Ireland/The Netherlands),
Urszula Antoniak.
Special Jury Prize: **44 Inch Chest**
(United Kingdom), Malcolm Vevnville.
Best Director: Roland Vranik for **Transmission**
(Hungary).

Golden Giraldillo for Best Documentary:
Garbo, The Spy (Spain), Edmon Roch.
Eurimages Award: **Tears of April**
(Finland/Germany/Greece), Aku Louhimies.
Audience Choice Award: **A Prophet** (France),
Jacques Audiard.

Shanghai International Film Festival
June 12–20, 2010

After the amazing 12th Shanghai International
Film Festival 2009, 2010 will be an even
greater edition for SIFF, with the Shanghai
EXPO being held during the festival. SIFF,
as China's only A-category international
film festival, is mainly composed of the
competition section (Jin Jue Award, Asian
New Talent Award and International Student
Shorts Award), SIFF Mart (Film Market, China
Film Pitch and Catch, Co-production Film Pitch
and Catch), SIFFORUM and International
Film Panorama. Sign up either your films or
projects at www.siff.com to showcase in
this glorious film festival in 2010. *Inquiries to:*
Shanghai International Film Festival, 11F, B,
STV Mansions, 298 Wei Hai Road, Shanghai
200041, China. Tel: (86 21) 6253 7115. Web:
www.siff.com.

AWARDS 2009
Jin Jue Awards
Best Feature Film: **Original** (Denmark/
Sweden), Antonio Tublén and Alexander
Brøndsted.
Jury Grand Prix: **The Search** (China),
Pema Tseden.
Jury Award: **Empire of Silver** (China/Hong
Kong/Taiwan, China), Christina Yao.
Best Director: Julius Sevcik for **Normal** (Czech
Republic/Macedonia).
Best Actor: Sverrir Gudnason for **Original**
(Denmark/Sweden).
Best Actress: Simone Tang for **Aching Hearts**
(Denmark).
Best Screenplay: Fabio Bonifacci and Giulio
Manfredonia for **We Can Do That** (Italy).
Best Cinematography: Nicolas Guicheteau
and Hans Meier for **Nowhere Promised Land**
(France).

Best Music: Hyoung-woo Roh for **Rough Cut**
(Korea).
Asian New Talent Awards
Best Director: Zhao Ye for **Jalainur** (China).
Best Film: **Scandal Makers** (Korea),
Hyung-chul Kang.
Jury Prize: **Be Calm and Count to Seven**
(Iran), Ramtin Lavafipour.

Sheffield Doc/Fest
November 3–7, 2010

For five days, Sheffield Doc/Fest brings the
international documentary family together to
celebrate the art and business of documentary
filmmaking. Combining a film festival, industry
sessions and market activity, the festival offers
pitching opportunities, controversial discussion
panels and in-depth filmmaker masterclasses,
as well as a wealth of inspirational documentary
films from across the globe. Around 140
documentary films are screened, mainly from
a call for entries made in March. Around 50
debates, discussions, case studies, interviews
and masterclasses are presented and there
are a number of well-attended social and
networking events. The MeetMarket takes
place over two days of the festival. It is a highly
effective initiative; pre-scheduled one-on-one
meetings where TV commissioning editors,
executive producers, distributors and other
financiers meet with independent producers
and filmmakers to discuss documentary
projects in development that are seeking
international financing. The film programme is
also open to the public. *Inquiries to:* Sheffield

*Special Jury members R.J. Cutler, A.J. Shnack and Claire Aquilar at The
Sheffield Doc/Fest Awards Ceremony*

Doc/Fest, The Workstation, 15 Paternoster Row, Sheffield, S1 2BX, UK.
Tel: (44 114) 276 5141. e: info@sidf.co.uk.
Web: www.sheffdocfest.com.

AWARDS 2009
Special Jury Award: **Videocracy** (Denmark/Sweden), Erik Gandini.
Sheffield Innovation Award: **LoopLoop** (Canada), Patrick Bergeron.
Sheffield Green Award: **The Blood of The Rose** (Germany/Japan/UK) Henry Singer.
The Youth Jury Award: **Sons of Cuba** (UK), Andrew Lang.
The Wallflower Press Student Doc Award: **Arsy - Versy** (Slovakia), Miro Remo.
Sheffield Doc/Fest Audience Award: **Junior** (USA), Jenna Rosher.
Sheffield Inspiration Award: Adam Curtis.

Report 2009
A high point this year was the screening of Michael Moore's new film: *Capitalism: A Love Story.* Moore gave valuable advice about what not to do in order to avoid becoming

The Opening night screening of **Moving to Mars** *at the Sheffield Doc/Fest. Photo: Jacqui Bellamy, Pixelwitch Pictures*

like America, in his live skype Q&A session. The three-year Japanese project concluded this year and included Hara Kazuo's *Extreme Private Eros,* a searingly personal portrait of Hara and his relationship to Japan's outsiders in the 1970s. The Junior screening saw the director, Jenna Rosher and subject, Eddie Belasco, appear before an enthusiastic crowd. The audience voted it their favourite of 2009's official programme. – **Hussain Currimbhoy**, Film Programmer.

SILVERDOCS: AFI/Discovery Channel Documentary Festival
June 16–20, 2010

Silverdocs is an international film festival and conference (June 16–19) that promotes the art of documentary film. Silverdocs takes place at the AFI Silver Theatre, one of the premiere film exhibition spaces in the country, and the top art-house cinema in the Washington, DC region. Anchored in the US capital, where important global and national issues are the daily business, Silverdocs is marked by its relevance, broad intellectual range, and wide public appeal. Among its numerous special programmes is the Charles Guggenheim Symposium which, in 2009, honoured legendary film director Albert Maysles. Past recipients include Spike Lee, Martin Scorsese, Barbara Kopple and Jonathan Demme. *Inquiries to:* AFI Silver Theatre and Cultural Center, 8633 Colesville Road, Silver Spring MD 20910, USA. Tel: (1 301) 495 6720. e: info@ silverdocs.com Web: www.silverdocs.com.

AWARDS 2009
Sterling US Feature Award: **October Country** (USA), Donal Mosher and Michael Palmieri.
Sterling World Feature Award: **Mugabe and the White African** (UK) Lucy Bailey and Andrew Thompson.
Sterling Short Award: **12 Notes Down** (Denmark) Andreas Koefoed.
Music Documentary Award: **RiseUP** (USA) Luciano Blotta.
Witness Award: **Good Fortune** (USA) Landon Van Soest.
Writers Guild of America Documentary Screenplay Award: **Off and Running** (USA) Nicole Opper.
Feature Audience Award: **The Cove** (USA) Louie Psihoyos.

Singapore International Film Festival
April 15–21, 2010

The largest international film festival in Singapore, SIFF has become significant in the Singapore arts landscape because of its dynamic film programming and commitment to the development of film culture and local cinema. The Festival screens over 200 films annually of all genres, with a focus on groundbreaking Asian cinema. Under the umbrella of the Silver Screen Awards, SIFF recognises excellence in Asian cinema with its three awards categories – Asian Film Competition, Singapore Short Film Competition and the Singapore Film Awards introduced in 2009. *Inquiries to:* Singapore International Film Festival, 554 Havelock Road, Suite 02-00A Ganges Centre, Singapore 169639, Singapore. Tel: (65) 6738 7567. e: filmfest@pacific.net.sg. Web: www.filmfest.org.sg.

Sitges
International Film Festival of Catalonia
October 2010

Sitges is one of the leading fantasy film festivals in the world. It is considered one of Europe's leading specialised festivals and is an essential rendezvous for movie lovers and audiences eager to embrace a stimulating universe of encounters, exhibitions, presentations and screenings of fantasy films from all over the world. *Inquiries to:* Sitges Festival Internacional de Cinema Fantastic de Catalunya, Calle Davallada 12, 3rd Floor, CP:08870 Sitges, Barcelona, Spain. Tel: (34 93) 894 9990. e: festival@cinemasitges.com. Web: www.cinemasitges.com.

Slamdance Film Festival
January 21–28, 2010

Slamdance is organised and programmed exclusively by filmmakers for filmmakers, and the sole aim is to nurture, support and showcase truly independent works. In doing so, Slamdance has established a unique reputation for premiering new films by first-time writers and directors working within the creative confines of limited budgets. This Academy qualifier also attracts and launches established artists, with world-class alumni including Steven Soderbergh, Christopher Nolan, Marc Forster and Jared Hess. The Festival has helped hundreds of films find distribution, including *The King of Kong*, *Weirdsville*, *Mad Hot Ballroom* and the recent breakout success, *Paranormal Activity*. Slamdance supports self-governance amongst independents and exists to deliver what filmmakers go to festivals for – a chance to show their work and a launching point for their careers. *Inquiries to:* Slamdance Inc, 5634 Melrose Ave, Los Angeles, California 90038, USA. Tel: (1 323) 466 1786. e: mail@ slamdance.com. Web: www.slamdance.com.

Solothurn Film Festival
January 21–28, 2010

Since 1964, the Solothurn Film Festival has presented an overview of the previous year's entire output of Swiss filmmaking. It is the popular rendezvous for the film media branches and a large public audience. Aside from the main focus on current national film productions of all genres and lengths, with many premieres of new Swiss films, the festival programme includes a retrospective of prominent filmmakers or actors, the music-clip section 'Sound & Stories' and the 'Invitation' section, with a selection of films produced in countries bordering Switzerland. Young talents can be discovered in the film-school section. The screenings are accompanied by a variety of daily round-table discussions, talk shows, film industry meetings and seminars. *Inquiries to:* Solothurn Film Festival, PO Box 1564, CH-4502 Solothurn, Switzerland. Tel: (41 32) 625 8080. Fax: 623 6410.
e: info@solothurnerfilmtage.ch.
Web: www.solothurnerfilmtage.ch.

Festival Director Ivo Kummerr and Swiss-Canadian filmmaker Léa Pool.

45th Solothurn Film Festival
January 21 – 28 2010   www.solothurnfilmfestival.ch

Report 2009
The 44th Solothurn Film Festival hosted around 1,500 professionals and over 46,000 cinemagoers, who enjoyed 300 films in different programme sections. The festival opened with the feature *Du Bruit dans la Tete* by Vincent Pluss. Three hundred films in the festival programme highlighted the thematic and stylistic spectrum of Swiss filmmaking, with works ranging from political and documentary films like *La Forteresse* by Fernard Melgar, to comedies such as *Tandori Love* by Oliver Paulus, and socio-critical films like Handl Klaus' *Marz*. The festival lived up to its reputation as the showcase for Swiss film production. Film talks, special programmes and controversial discussions about film and politics made up the frame of the festival. The retrospective, called 'Recontre', was devoted to the Canadian Swiss director, Lea Pool, who won the audience award for her latest film, *Mama N'est Chez le Coffieur*. The jury award for the best music clip went to Simon Jaquemet for Nacht. The first recipients of the new jury prize 'Prix de Soleure' was awarded to film director Fanny Brauning. She was honoured with the award, endowed with CHF60,000 for *No More Smoke Signals*, a moving documentary film about today's situation of the Lakota Indians in South Dakota and their struggle for justice.
– Ivo Kummer, Festival Director.

South by Southwest Film Festival
March 12–21, 2010

The festival explores all aspects of the art and business of independent filmmaking. The Conference hosts a five-day adventure in the latest filmmaking trends and new technology, featuring distinguished speakers and mentors. The internationally acclaimed festival boasts some of the most wide-ranging programming of any US event of its kind, from provocative documentaries to subversive Hollywood comedies, with a special focus on emerging talents. *Inquiries to:* South by Southwest Film Festival, Box 4999, Austin, TX 78765, USA. Tel: (1 512) 467 7979. e: sxsw@sxsw.com. Web: http://sxsw.com.

Stockholm International Film Festival
November 17–28, 2010

The Stockholm International Film Festival, which this year launches its 21st festival, is one of Europe's leading cinema events. Recognised by FIAPF and hosting a FIPRESCI jury, it is also a member of the European Coordination of Film Festivals. The festival welcomed 130,000 visitors during 2009, 1,000 accredited journalists and industry officials and it hosts around a hundred directors, actors and producers every year. In 2009, some 180 films from 50 different countries were presented. Susan Sarandon, Wong Kar-Wai, Charlotte Rampling, Wes Anderson, Jason Schwartzman, Oliver Stone, David Cronenberg, Gena Rowlands, Park Chan-wook, Ang Lee, Quentin Tarantino and Lauren Bacall were some of the distinguished guests. Since 2006 the festival also offers distribution over the Internet through VOD, video on demand. *Inquiries to:* Stockholm International Film Festival, PO Box 3136, S-103 62 Stockholm, Sweden. Tel: (46 8) 677 5000. Fax: 200 590. e: info@stockholmfilmfestival.se. Web: www.stockholmfilmfestival.se.

Sundance Film Festival
January 20–30, 2011

Long known as a celebration of the new and unexpected, the Sundance Film Festival presents the best in independent film from the US and around the world. For ten days in January, audiences in darkened theatres will discover the 125 feature films and 80 shorts that Festival programmers have scoured the world to find. The critically acclaimed Festival presents features and documentaries from the US and around the world, and competition films are combined with nightly premieres of works by veteran film artists, for a programme that inspires, challenges, delights, startles and moves festival goers. Archival gems by early independent filmmakers, animation of every kind, cutting-edge experimental works, midnight cult films, and a jam-packed schedule of panel discussions at Prospector Theatre, Filmmaker Lodge and New Frontier on Main, live shows at the Music Café and a host of spirited parties and events up and down historic Main Street make for a complete film experience that celebrates the art and community of independent filmmaking. Continuing the tradition of sharing the Festival with online audiences, www.sundance.org/festival takes both original content and the nuts and bolts of Festival going beyond the streets of Park City. With short films from the Festival, filmmaker interviews, and breaking news, combined with film listings, box-office information and travel tips, Sundance Film Festival Online is a single online source for experiencing the Sundance Film Festival both on the web and on the ground. *Inquiries to:* John Cooper, Director, Festival Programming Department, Sundance Institute, 8530 Wilshire Blvd, 3rd Floor, Beverly Hills, CA 90211-3114, USA. Tel: (1 310) 360 1981. e: institute@sundance.org. Web: www.sundance.org.

AWARDS 2009
Grand Jury Prize Documentary:
We Live in Public (USA), Ondi Timoner.
Grand Jury Prize Dramatic: **Push: Based on the novel by Sapphire** (USA), Lee Daniels.
Audience Award Documentary: **The Cove** (USA), Louie Psihoyos.
Audience Award Dramatic: **Push: Based on the novel by Sapphire** (USA), Lee Daniels.
World Cinema Jury Prize Documentary:
Rough Aunties (UK), Kim Longinotto.
World Cinema Jury Prize Dramatic:
The Maid (Chile), Sebastián Silva.
World Cinema Audience Award Documentary:
Afghan Star (Afghanistan/UK), Havana Marking.
World Cinema Audience Award Dramatic:
An Education (UK), Lone Scherfig.

Tallinn Black Nights Film Festival (PÖFF)

PÖFF Main Programme
26 November–5 December, 2010
Children and Youth Film Festival Just Film
November 11–14, 2010
Animation Film Festival Animated Dreams
November 17–21, 2010
Student and Short Film Festival Sleepwalkers
November 20–27, 2010
Nokia Mobile Phone Film Festival MOFF
September 1–December 2, 2010
Baltic Event co-production market 2010:
December 1–3, 2010
Black Market Industry Screenings will take
place during the first days of December 2010

In 2010, the Tallinn Black Nights Film Festival
(founded in 1997) will celebrate its 14th
edition. PÖFF, recognised by FIAPF, is a
unique event that combines a feature film
festival with sub-festivals, a film industry
gathering called the Baltic Event and Black
Market Industry Screenings. The PÖFF
main programme has three international
competitions – EurAsia, Tridens Baltic feature
film competition and competition of North
American *indie* films – along with Panorama,
Forum and several special programmes. All
competing films are judged by international
and local juries, including the FIPRESCI jury
that awards the best Baltic films. The Student
and Short Film Festival, Sleepwalkers, includes
an international competition for student
films – fiction, documentary or animation
films; national competition of Estonian short
films, and various special programmes.
Animation Film Festival, Animated Dreams,
holds an international competition of short
animation. Its additional non-competitive
programmes include a retrospective of a
filmmaker and focus on a country. Children
and Youth Film Festival, Just Film, includes
the competition of children's and youth films,
and non-competitive special programmes.
Nokia Mobile Film Festival, MOFF, organises
a competition of short films made with
mobile phones. The Baltic Event Film and
Co-production Market screens the latest
feature films from the Baltic countries, along

with a co-production market open for projects
from the Baltic countries, Central and Eastern
Europe, Russia and Scandinavia. In 2010, Black
Market Industry Screenings will take place
in Tallinn during the first days of December,
together with the Baltic Event Co-production
Market. The film market is mainly focusing on
the new films from neighbouring regions and
smaller film industry countries: the Baltics,
Central and Eastern European countries,
Nordic countries, Russia and Central-Asian
countries such as Georgia, Ukraine, Romania,
Armenia, Kazakhstan, Uzbekistan, Kyrgyzstan
and Tajikistan. In addition, the literary rights
market, Books To Films, will present film
literature from Estonia, Latvia, Lithuania,
the Nordic countries, Russia and other
neighbouring countries, to producers and
filmmakers looking for new ideas. The goal is
to enhance audiovisual cooperation on both
sides of the Eastern border of the European
Union and Nordic countries, as well as giving
filmmakers greater visibility and access to the
bigger audiovisual markets around the world.
The timing of the screenings and meetings
at the beginning of December will help to
summarise the year and prepare for the next
one. The European Film Awards ceremony
will come to Tallinn in 2010. It will be the
cornerstone and a launch pad of Tallinn's year
as European Culture Capital in 2011. The event
is organised simultaneously with the 14th

*Closing Ceremony of the 2009 Tallinn Black Nights Film Festival
(PÖFF), Bahman Ghobadi, director of the feature film* **No One Knows
About Persian Cats** *(Iran) and Head of the NETPAC Jury Krishnan
Hariharan. Photo: Rivo Sarpaik.*

Tallinn Black Nights Film Festival, offering many possibilities to enhance the regular events of both the festival and the Award ceremony. Together with Black Nights, the Black Market (film market), the Baltic Event (co-production market) and Books to Film (literature market), along with our regular programme (250 films and 600 screenings, receptions and parties each day of the festival, seminars, concerts and many other cultural events), it is the perfect chance to discover the great essence of the festival and to make contacts and carry out work. *Inquiries to:* Tallinn Black Nights Film Festival (PÖFF), Telliskivi 60A, 10412 Tallinn, Estonia. Tel: (372) 631 4640. e: poff@poff.ee. Web: www.poff.ee.

AWARDS 2009
Grand Prix for Best Eurasian Film:
Ajami (Germany/Israel), Scandar Copti and Yaron Shani.
Best Director: Klaus Häro for **Postia Pappi Jaakobille** (Finland).
Best Actor: David Dencik for **Broderskab** (Denmark).
Best Actress: Maria Bonnevie for **Engelen** (Norway/Sweden/Finland).
Special Jury Prize: **Nunta in Basarabia** (Luxembourg/Moldova/Romania), Napoleon Helmis.
Best Baltic Film: **Duburys** (Lithuania), Gytis Lukšas.
FIPRESCI Award for Best Baltic Film:
Disko Ja Tuumasõda (Estonia), Jaak Kilmi.
Best North American Independent Film:
Untitled (USA), Jonathan Parker.
FICC Jury Award: **Kasi Az Gorbehaye Irani Khabar Nadareh** (Iran), Bahman Ghobadi.

NETPAC Jury Award: **Kasi Az Gorbehaye Irani Khabar Nadareh** (Iran), Bahman Ghobadi.
Audience Award: **Kim Ssi Pyo Ryu Gi** (South Korea), Lee Hey-jun.

Report 2009
The festival had around 56,000 admissions in 2009, and together with the Baltic Event and Black Market Industry Screenings, it hosted 273 international guests. The 13th edition of the festival screened around 500 films, of which 260 were full-length features, in nine cities and 21 cinemas. Tallinn Black Market Film Festival launched a new annual and regional cinema and audiovisual market called Black Market Industry Screenings. In addition, the literary rights market Books to Films was also launched for the first time in 2009.
– **Anneli Vask**, Marketing Manager.

Tampere Film Festival
March 10–14, 2010

The Festival is the oldest and the largest short film festival in Northern Europe. It celebrates its 40th Anniversary in 2010. The festival programme consists of the International and Finnish short film Competitions, and the special thematic programme. It is famous for its excellent and innovative programming, magnificent festival atmosphere and, of course, the Finnish Sauna Party. Besides the 120 screenings, the festival is bursting with various seminars, panel discussions and meetings for film professionals and enthusiasts. The Festival promotes up-and-coming filmmakers – it is an event to find future masters of cinema. The high-quality

14th Tallinn Black Nights Film Festival **PÖFF**
November 11 – December 5, 2010

European Film Academy in Tallinn
December 3 – 5, 2010

Film Market has over 4,000 titles from all over the world. The special thematic programmes for our 40th anniversary edition include the highlights of Ibero American short film, focusing especially on Spanish and Uruguayan short film. Other themes include documentaries from the Finnish Film Archive and the Canon of Short Film, which is a project carried out by eight major short-film festivals. The aim is to collect, discuss and screen the best and most influential short films of all times. Videotivoli, the international event for films made by children and young people will take off on the festival week. Videotivoli offers a colourful section of genres and cinematic means of expression with topics ranging from fairy tales and fantasies to serious life experiences and global issues. *Inquiries to:* Tampere Film Festival, PO Box 305, FI-33101 Tampere, Finland. Tel: (358 3) 223 5681. Fax: 223 0121. e: office@tamperefilmfestival.fi. Web: www.tamperefilmfestival.fi.

AWARDS 2009

International Competition
Grand Prix: **Ahendu Nde Sapukai** (Paraguay), Pablo Lamar.
Best Animation: **Photograph of Jesus** (UK), Laurie Hill.
Best Fiction: **Arayeshgar E Bagh Dad** (Iran), Massoud Bakhshi.
Best Documentary: **Was Übrig Bleibt** (Germany), Andreas Gräfenstein and Fabian Daub.
EFA Nominee Tampere: **Szklana Pulapka** (Poland), Pawel Ferdek.
Diplomas of Merit: **Planet A** (Japan), Momoko Seto and **Between Dreams** (Finland/France/Russia), Iris Olsson and **Zeestan** (Iran), Mahmoud Falavarjani.
Audience Award: **KJFG NO. 5** (Hungary), Alexei Alexeev.

Report 2009

The audience interest in Tampere Film Festival remained high: the festival gathered nearly 30,000 film professionals and enthusiasts together. There were over 800 accredited guests and members of the press, including

MoMa screening at Tullikamari. Photo: Markus Nikkilä

some 140 international guests. Ten screenings had sold out by Sunday, including, in addition to competition screenings, *Terra Femina 3*, Finnish Film Archive screening *Valentin Vaala 100 Years*, Pavel Koutsky's animated works and the Carte Blanche screening assembled by Marja Pallassalo. The Grand Prix of Tampere Film Festival's International Competition was awarded to Pablo Lamar's fictional film *Ahendu Nde Sapukai*. The film made history by being the first Paraguayan film to participate in the International Competition. The international Jury members were Maike Mia Höhne (Germany), Ngo Phuong Lan (Vietnam), Kristiina Pervilä (Finland), William Sloan (United States) and Montserrat Guiu Valss (Spain).
– Katariina Pasuri, Marketing Coordinator.

Telluride Film Festival
September 3–6, 2010

Each Labour Day weekend, more than 3,000 passionate film lovers ascend to the high Colorado mountain village of Telluride for four days of movie heaven. True to long-time Telluride tradition, the programme is kept a secret until opening day, when audiences discover the 20–25 new narrative and documentary features, with directors, actors and writers in attendance. The Festival also showcases rare archival restorations, silent films with live scores, short-film programmes, special events and tributes. The 36th Festival included tributes to German actor and director Margarethe von Trotta, who previewed her latest directorial work, *Vision*; French actress Anouk Aimee; and Hollywood leading man Viggo Mortensen.

Previous tributes have included: director David Fincher, actress Jean Simmons, and director Jan Troell in 2008; actor Daniel Day Lewis, composer Michel Legrand and Indian director Shyam Benegal in 2007; editor Walter Murch, actress Penelope Cruz and Australian director Rolf de Heer in 2006. Each year a Guest Director presents an eclectic series of films. 2009 featured American film director Alexander Payne, curating forgotten Hollywood gems as well as rare foreign films from Spain, Italy and Japan. Additionally, the 36th festival spotlighted Russian animator and first-time feature director Andrey Khrzhanovsky, honoured film critic and painter Manny Farber and paid special tribute to film preservationist and showman, Serge Bromberg, of Lobster Films. In partnership with the Italian Silent Film Festival, 'Pordenone Presents' offered the glorious French film *Les Nouveaux Messieurs* along with acclaimed musician Stephen Horne providing the score.

Jens Meurer and director Michael Hoffman at Telluride for the screening of **The Last Station***. Photo: Michael Caulfield.*

Each year there are surprise sneak previews, intimate conversations, seminars in the park and a lively student programme, all book-ended by the Opening Night Feed and the Labour Day Picnic. Screened in nine venues, including the Abel Gance Outdoor Cinema, the festival presentations meet the highest technical standards, using top projectionists. Telluride is a non-competitive festival. Complete past programmes and information about entering features and shorts, programmes for high-school and college students can be found on the festival's website. *Inquiries to:* Telluride Film Festival, 800 Jones Street, Berkeley, CA 94710 USA. Tel: (1 510) 665 9494. e: mail@telluridefilmfestival.org. Web: www. telluridefilmfestival.org.

Thessaloniki International Film Festival
November 12–21, 2010
Thessaloniki Documentary Festival
March 12–21, 2010

In its 50th year, the oldest and the most important film event in South-East Europe targeted a new generation of filmmakers as well as independent films by established directors. The International Competition (for first or second features) awarded the Golden Alexander (€40,000) to Scandar Copti and Yaron Shani for their film *Ajami* (Germany/Israel) and the Silver Alexander (€25,000) to Calin Netzer for *Medal of Honour* (Romania). Other sections include Balkan Survey, the informative section Independence Days, the thematic section Focus, Greek Films, retrospectives, plus master classes, galas and exhibitions. As always, the festival's market, Agora, acted as an umbrella service for film professionals who benefited from the services of the Balkan Script Development Fund, Crossroads Coproduction Forum, Agora Film Market and Salonica Studio Student Workshops. The Thessaloniki Documentary Festival – Images of the 21st Century is Greece's major annual non-fiction film event. Its sections include 'Views of the World' (subjects of social interest), 'Portraits – Human Journeys' (highlighting the human contribution to cultural, social and historical developments) and 'Recording of Memory' (facts and testimony of social and historic origin). The festival also hosts the third-largest documentary market in Europe, the Thessaloniki DocMarket. *Inquiries to:* Thessaloniki International Film Festival, 9 Alexandras Ave, 114 73 Athens, Greece. Tel: (30 210) 870 6000. e: info@filmfestival. gr. Web: www.filmfestival.gr. Director: Despina Mouzaki. Inquiries to: Thessaloniki Documentary Festival (address, website and Tel number as above). Artistic Director: Dimitri Eipides. e: eipides @filmfestival.gr.

AWARDS 2009
Thessaloniki International Film Festival
Artistic Achievement Award: **Missing Person** (South Korea), Lee Seo.
Best Screenplay Award: **Ajami** (Germany/ Israel), Scandar Copti and Yaron Shani and **Medal of Honour** (Romania), Tudor Voican.
Best Actress Award: Ruth Nirere for **Le jour où Dieu Est Parti en Voyage** (Belgium/France).
Best Actor Award: Victor Rebengiuc for **Medal of Honour** (Romania).
Best Director Award: Rigoberto Perezcano for **Norteado** (Mexico/Spain).
Silver Alexander Award: **Medal of Honour** (Romania), Calin Netzer.
Golden Alexander Award: **Ajami** (Germany/ Israel), Scandar Copti and Yaron Shani.

AWARDS 2009
Thessaloniki Documentary Festival - Images of the 21st Century
Hellenic Red Cross Audience Award for a Greek film over 45 minutes: **Ethnikos Kipos**, Apostolos Karakasis.
Hellenic Red Cross Audience Award for a foreign film over 45 minutes: **Burma VJ - Reporting from a Closed Country**, (Denmark), Anders Ostergaard.
Hellenic Red Cross Audience Award for a Greek film under 45 minutes: **Vgikame Apo Ta Rouha Mas**, Elli Zerbini.
Hellenic Red Cross Audience Award for a foreign film under 45 minutes: **Flowers of Rwanda** (Spain), David Munoz.

Tokyo International Film Festival
October 23–31, 2010

Over the nine days of the 22nd Tokyo International Film Festival (TIFF), films from a variety of genres were screened in several intriguing programmes: *'Competition'*, which selects the winner of the Tokyo Sakura Grand Prix from a carefully chosen ensemble of premiere films directed by first-timers and recognised directors; *'Special Screenings'*, which premieres highly entertaining films prior to their public release in Japan; *'Winds of Asia–Middle East'*, which boasts the largest number of films and audience numbers of all the TIFF screenings; *'Japanese Eyes'*, which showcases a broad range of independent Japanese films for the worldwide audience; *'natural TIFF'*, with a theme of the *'symbosis between nature and mankind'*. TIFFCOM, an entertainment content business market affiliated with TIFF, is expanding every year to establish its position as one of the major business opportunities in Asia. *Inquiries to:* Unijapan/TIFF Office, 5F Tsukiji Yasuda Building, 2-15-14 Tsukiji Chuo-ku, Tokyo 104-0045, Japan. Tel: (81 3) 3524 1081. e: tokyo@tiff.net. Web: www.tiff-jp.net.

Torino Film Festival
November 26–December 4, 2010

Torino Film Festival is one of Europe's most important cinematographic events and is known for its discoveries as well as for its unique retrospectives. The festival constitutes a meeting point for contemporary international cinema and pays particular attention to emerging cinemas and filmmakers and promotes awareness of new directors whose work is marked by strong formal and stylistic research. Its programme includes competitive sections for international features, Italian documentaries and Italian shorts, as well as spotlights and premieres. *Inquiries to:* Torino Film Festival, Via Montebello 15, 10124 Torino, Italy. Tel: (39 011) 813 8811. e: info@torinofilmfest.org. Web: www.torinofilmfest.org.

Toronto International Film Festival
September 9–18, 2010

The Toronto International Film Festival presents one of the world's largest annual showcases of Canadian film, with the Canada First!, Short Cuts Canada and Canadian Open Vault programmes. The festival screens over 300 films from more than 60 countries and attracts thousands of Canadian and international industry delegates, as well as over 1,000 international media. The Festival consistently strives to set the standard for excellence in film programming with audiences shown the work of emerging talent and masters of the cinema craft from around the world. As always, the Festival remains committed to supporting Canadian filmmakers and has been a platform for Canada's artists. *Inquiries to:* Toronto International Film Festival, 2 Carlton St, 16th Floor, Toronto, Ontario, M5B 1J3, Canada. Tel: (1 416) 967 7371. e: proffice@tiff.net. Web: www.tiffg.ca.

Tribeca Film Festival
April 22–May 3, 2010

The Tribeca Film Festival was founded in 2002 by Robert De Niro, Jane Rosenthal and Craig Hatkoff, to spur the economic and cultural revitalisation of Lower Manhattan through an annual celebration of film, music and culture. The Festival's mission is to help filmmakers reach the broadest possible audience, enable the international film community and general public to experience the power of cinema and promote New York City as a major filmmaking centre. Since its founding, the Festival has attracted over 2.4 million attendees from the US and abroad and has generated close to US$560 million in economic activity for New York City. The Festival is anchored in Tribeca with additional venues throughout Manhattan and includes film screenings, special events, concerts, a family street fair, and 'Tribeca Talks' panel discussions. *Inquiries to:* Tribeca Film Festival, 375 Greenwich St, New York, NY 10013, USA. Tel: (1 212) 941 2400. e: festival@tribecafilmfestival. org. Web: www.tribecafilmfestival.org.

A drive-in at Tribeca Film Festival. Photo: Tribeca Film Festival

AWARDS 2009
Best Narrative Feature: **About Elly** (Iran), Asghar Farhadi.
Best New Narrative Filmmaker: **North** (Norway), Rune Denstad Langlo.
Best Documentary Feature: **Racing Dreams** (USA), Marshall Curry.
Best New Documentary Filmmakers: **Fixer: The Taking of Ajmal Naqshbandi** (USA), Ian Olds.
Best Actress in a Narrative Feature: Zoe Kazan for **The Exploding Girl** (USA).
Best Actor in a Narrative Feature: Ciarán Hinds for **The Eclipse** (Ireland).
'Made In NY' - Narrative: **Here and There** (Germany/Serbia/USA), Darko Lungulov.
'Made In NY' - Documentary: **Partly Private** (Canada), Danae Elon.
Heineken Audience Award: **City Island** (USA), Raymond De Felitta.
Best Narrative Short: **The North Road** (France), Carlos Chahine.
Best Documentary Short: **Home** (USA), Matthew Faust.
Student Visionary Award: **Small Change** (Australia), Anna McGrath.

Tromsø International Film Festival
January 18–23, 2011

Norway's largest film festival for the audience, with 50,000 admissions in six days, Tromsø International Film Festival presents cutting-edge international art-house cinema, screening more than 180 titles. This includes a feature competition and several exciting sidebars, among them 'Films from

An outdoor screening at Tromsø International Film Festival. Photo: Ingun A Mæhlum

the North', with new shorts and docs from arctic Scandinavia, Canada and Russia. The festival is also an important meeting place for industry professionals. *Inquiries to:* Tromsø International Film Festival, PO Box 285, N-9253 Tromsø, Norway. Tel: (47) 7775 3090. Fax: 7775 3099. e: info@tiff.no. Web: www.tiff.no.

AWARDS 2009

Aurora Prize: **Revanche** (Austria), Götz Spielman.
Norwegian Peace Film Award:
Waltz With Bashir (Israel), Ari Folman.
FIPRESCI Prize: **Revanche** (Austria), Götz Spielman.
Don Quijote: **It's not Me, I Swear** (Canada), Philippe Falardeau.
Tromsø Palm: **Cairn** (Norway), Hanne Larsen.
Audience Award: **Shooting the Sun** (Norway), Pål Jackman.

Report 2009

Götz Spielman's psychological thriller *Revanche* won the FIPRESCI award as well as TIFF's own Aurora prize at the 19th edition of Tromsø International Film Festival. Norwegian Pål Jackman's opening night film, *Shooting the Sun*, starring Norwegian veteran actor Bjørn Sundqvist in one of his greatest roles on the screen, also attracted a great deal of attention. TIFF '09 also featured a new sidebar for children, with outdoor screenings on the main square of Tromsø. – **Håvard Stangnes**, Public Relations. Manager.

Valencia International Film Festival – Mediterranean Cinema
October 2010

The Valencia Mostra Film Festival – Mediterranean Cinema celebrated its 30th anniversary edition in 2009 and continues to promote cinema from Mediterranean countries on an international level. After the retirement of the Valencian veteran, Juan Piquer Simón, the role of director at the Mostra festival was taken over by Salomón Castiel. Mostra shows the most popular and interesting films that have been produced in Mediterranean countries over the previous year and aims to promote an intercultural dialogue and understanding between the different cultures from the Mediterranean area. Mostra provides an international platform for those films that often don't get the opportunity for exhibition and distribution outside their own country and is organised by the Fundación Municipal de Cine. *Inquiries to:* Fundación Municipal de Cine, Plaza de la Almoina 4, Puertas 1,2 and 3, 46003 Valencia, Spain. Tel: (34 96) 392 1506. e: festival@mostravalencia.com. Web: www.mostravalencia.org.

Valladolid International Film Festival
Last week in October, 2010

One of Spain's key events, the festival spotlights the latest work by established directors and newcomers. Competitive for features, shorts and documentaries. Also offers retrospectives, a selection of recent Spanish productions and a congress of new Spanish directors. *Inquiries to:* Valladolid International Film Festival Office, Teatro Calderón, Calle Leopoldo Cano, s/n 4ª Planta, 47003 Valladolid, Spain. Tel: (34 983) 426 460. Fax: 426 461. e:festvalladolid@seminci.com. Web: www.seminci.com.

AWARDS 2009
International Jury Awards
Prix UIP Valladolid: **Ampelmann** (Germany), Giulio Ricciarelli.
Golden Spike for Short Film: **Ampelmann** (Germany), Giulio Ricciarelli.
Silver Spike for Short Film: **The Six Dollar Fifty Man** (New Zealand), Mark Albiston and Louis Sutherland.
Best Director of Photography Award: Camilla Hjelm Knudsen for **Lille Soldat** (Denmark).
Music: Gabriel Yared for **Le Hérisson** (France) and **Adam Resurrected** (USA).
Script: Gilles Taurand, Serge Le Peron and Robert Guédiguian for **L'Armée du Crime** (France).
Actress: Trine Dyrholm for **Lille Soldat** (Denmark).
Actor: Alberto San Juan for **La Isla Interior** (Spain).
Pilar Miró Prize for Best New Director: Adán Aliaga for **Estigmas** (Spain).

Special Jury Prize: **L'Armée du Crime** (France), Robert Guédiguian.
Golden Spike for Feature Film: **Honeymoons** (Albania/Serbia), Goran Paskaljevic.
Silver Spike for Feature Film: **Lille Soldat** (Denmark), Annette K Olesen.

Vancouver International Film Festival
September 30–October 15, 2010

The Vancouver International Film Festival is among the largest film festivals in North America and is one of the largest cultural events in Canada. An autumn fixture on the international film festival calendar, this outstanding festival is a microcosm of its home city: cosmopolitan, innovative, friendly, culturally complex and very accessible. The festival shows over 600 screenings of more than 350 films from 80 countries with around 160,000 people attending. Founded in 1982, the festival's mandate is to encourage the understanding of other nations through the art of cinema, to foster the art of cinema, to facilitate the meeting in British Columbia of cinema professionals from around the world, and to stimulate the motion-picture industry in British Columbia and Canada. *Inquiries to:* VIFF, 1181 Seymour St, Vancouver, British Columbia, Canada V6B 3M7. Tel: (1 604) 685 0260. e: viff@viff.org. Web: www.viff.org.

Venice International Film Festival
September 1–11, 2010

The Festival offers an overview of world cinema, in a spirit of freedom and tolerance, under Marco Müller's directorship. The Festival

includes competitive and out of competition sections, in addition to retrospective sections, tributes and parties galore, plus exquisite art exhibitions around downtown Venice. The official line-up of the 67th edition will be announced in a press conference that will take place in Rome at the end of July 2010. *Inquiries to:* La Biennale di Venezia, Palazzo del Cinema 30126 Lido di Venezia, Italy. Tel (39) 041 521 8711. Fax: 521 8815. e: ufficiostampa@labiennale.org. Web: www.labiennale.org/en/cinema.

AWARDS 2009

Golden Lion for Best Film: **Lebanon** (France/Germany/Israel), Samuel Maoz.
Silver Lion for Best Director: Shirin Neshat for **Zanan Bedone Mardan** (Austria/France/Germany).
Special Jury Prize: **Soul Kitchen** (Germany), Fatih Akin.
Coppa Volpi for Best Actor: Colin Firth for **A Single Man**, (USA).
Coppa Volpi for Best Actress: Ksenia Rappoport for **La doppia Ora** (Italy).
Marcello Mastroianni Award for Best New Young Actor or Actress: Jasmine Trinca for **Il Grande Sogno** (Italy).
Osella for Best Technical Contribution: Sylvie Olive for **Mr Nobody** (France).
Osella for Best Screenplay: Todd Solondz for **Life during Wartime** (USA).

Victoria Independent Film & Video Festival

January 29–February 7, 2010
February 4–13, 2011

Whether it is the controversial cinema, Oscar-winning drama, provocative documentary or the list of special guests attending the Victoria Film Festival, this romp through the world of film is

Barry Pepper, Charles Martin Smith, BJ Cook at the 2009 Victoria Film Festival Patron's Reception. Photo: Margaret Hansen

the event you don't want to miss! With historic architecture and fabulous vistas, downtown streets are lined with theatres, shops, museums and cafes that provide the perfect backdrop for the home of the *boutique schmooze*. The Festival screens 150 films at four downtown venues. As Vancouver Island's biggest and longest-running film festival it's the place to see the best of independent cinema in one of the top destinations in the world, according to Condé Nast. A great package at the legendary Fairmont Empress is available. The 16th Annual Victoria Film Festival presents the most exclusive industry event of the year. SpringBoard features masterclasses along with talks by the top young filmmakers of the day. Online registration and information can be found at www.victoriafilmfestival.com. *Inquiries to:* Victoria Film Festival, 1215 Blanshard St, Victoria, British Columbia, V8W 3J4 Canada. Tel: (1 250) 389 0444. Fax: 389 0406. e: festival@victoriafilmfestival.com Web:www.victoriafilmfestival.com.

AWARDS 2009

Star!TV Award for Best Feature: **Hunger** (UK), Steve McQueen.
Best Canadian Feature: **Before Tomorrow** (Canada), Marie-Hélèn Cousineau, Madeline Piujuq Ivalu.
Canwest Award for Best Documentary: **Inside Hana's Suitcase** (Canada), Larry Weinstein.
Cineplex Entertainment Award for Best Short Animation: **Yellow Sticky Notes** (Canada), Jeff Chiba Sterns.
Best Short Awards: **My Inventions** (Canada), Robert Holbrook.
Audience Favourite Award: **Stone of Destiny** (Canada), Charles Martin Smith.

InVision Award for Best Student Film:
Ogopogo (Canada), Christian Amundson.

Report 2009

Victoria Film Festival broke all records and jumped 22% at the box office, as attendance climbed to over 20,500. The introduction of the Top 20 emerging talents in Canada and a roster of industry insiders rounded out a new event – the salon-inspired Springboard – and brought a unique networking element to the Festival. Guests at the Festival included Tony award winner Don McKellar, actor Barry Pepper and *Star Wars* concept designer Iain McCaig. The underground-style Opening Gala had the crowd going late into the night. **– Kathy Kay**, Festival Director.

VIENNALE –
Vienna International Film Festival

October 21–November 3, 2010

The Viennale is Austria's most important international film event, as well as being one of the oldest and best-known festivals in the

Viennale Festival Director Hans Hurch and Guest of Honour, Tilda Swinton. Photo: Robert Newald.

German-speaking world. It takes place every October in Vienna's historic centre, offering an international orientation and a distinctive urban flair. A high percentage of the 94,800 visitors to the festival are made up of a young audience. In its main programme, the Viennale shows a carefully picked selection of new films from all over the globe, as well as new films from Austria. The choice of films offer a cross section of bold filmmaking that stands apart from the aesthetics of mainstream conventionality, and is politically relevant. Aside from its focus

on the newest feature films of every genre and structural form imaginable, the festival gives particular attention to documentary films, international short films, as well as experimental works and crossover films. The Viennale receives regular international acclaim for its large-scale historic retrospective in collaboration with the Austrian Film Museum, its numerous special programmes, as well as its tributes and homages, dedicated to prominent personalities and institutions in world cinema. *Inquiries to:* Siebensterngasse 2, 1070 Vienna, Austria. Tel: (43 1) 526 5947. Fax: 523 4172. e: office@viennale.at. Web: www.viennale.at.

Report 2009

With a total of 94,800 Viennale-goers, the 2009 festival has again seen a considerable increase in the number of visitors. The festival's attendance figures rose from 76.80% in 2008 to 79.60% at the Viennale 2009. While the number of film showings more or less remained the same with a total of 345 screenings, the number of sold-out screenings rose to 124. There were tributes to Tilda Swinton and Lino Brocka, the former considered one of the highlights of this edition of the festival. The Viennale would like to thank festivalgoers who, through their curiosity, openness and joy of discovery, contributed in realising and supporting the festival. **– Katharina Sekulic**, Head of Press Department.

Zlín International Film Festival for Children and Youth
May 30–June 6, 2010

Zlín is the oldest and also the biggest film festival for children and youth in the world. This year the festival celebrates the 50th anniversary of its foundation, in 1961. The main focus will be on Czech and Slovak films for children, as Zlín used to be one of the major producers of features and animation for children. This showcase will also present a retrospective of one of the most innovative Czech filmmakers, Karel Zeman, to commemorate the 100th anniversary of his birth. The festival programme will consist of five main competition sections

Actor Tim Curry meets Festival Director Petr Koliha in front of the Zlin Film Festival main theatre.

(for children, for youth, short animated films, European debuts and films from the Visegrad countries). Two other supplementary programmes will take place during the festival – Rainbow Marble (a competition of commercials targeted at children) and Zlin Dog (echoes of students' film festival). In the non-competition informative section, full-length features, short animation and documentaries will be screened. A rich supporting programme full of entertainment for the youngest audiences will also be offered across the whole festival week. *Inquiries to:* FILMFEST s.r.o., Filmová 174, CZ-76179 Zlín, Czech Republic, Tel: (420 5) 7759 2275. Fax: 7759 2442. e: festival@zlinfest.cz. Web: www.zlinfest.cz.

AWARDS 2009
Golden Slipper for Best Feature Film for Children: **Who Is Afraid of the Wolf** (Czech Republic), Maria Procházková.
Golden Slipper for the Best Feature Film for Youth: **Max Embarrassing** (Denmark), Lotte Svendsen.
The City of Zlín Award - Honorable Mention for a Feature Film for Children: **A School Day with a Pig** (Japan), Tetsu Maeda.
The Miloš Macourek Award - Special Recognition for a Feature Film for Youth: **It´s Not Me, I Swear** (Canada), Philippe Falardeau.
Joint International Jury of Children and Adults for Animated Films
Golden Slipper for Best Animated Film: **Post!** (Germany), Christian Asmussen and Matthias Bruhn.
The Hermína Týrlová Award for Young Artists Aged Under 35: **Paul and the Dragon**

(Netherlands), Albert ´t Hooft and Paco Vink.
The Europe Award for the Best European Debut: **Pa-ra-da** (France/Italy/Romania), Marco Pontecorvo.
International Expert Jury for European Debuts Special Prize: **City of the World** (Germany), Christian Klandt.
The Czech Minister of Culture Award for the Best Film from Visegrad Countries: **Music** (Slovakia), Juraj Nvota.
The Don Quixote Award: **Cowards** (Spain), José Corbacho and Juan Cruz.
Ecumenical Jury Award: **Max Embarrassing** (Denmark), Lotte Svendsen.
The Recognition of Ecumenical Jury: **Little Robbers** (Austria/Latvia), Armands Zvirbulis.
Main Prize of the Children Jury for Best Feature Film for Children: **Hell with Princess** (Czech Republic), Miloslav Šmídmajer.
Main Prize of the Children Jury for Best Feature Film for Youth: **It´s Not Me, I Swear** (Canada), Philippe Falardeau.
Spectator´s Prize: Golden Apple - for Best Feature Film: **Hell with Princess** (Czech Republic), Miloslav Šmídmajer.
Golden Apple - for Best Animated Film: **Carrot on the Beach** (Estonia), Pärtel Tall.
Recognition of Creative Contribution in Filmmaking for Children and Youth: Lubomír Lipský.

Report 2009

The 49th edition of the festival brought 473 movies from 44 countries (almost 100 screened within the five competitions). The total number of visitors was 96,441. The showcase focused on Spanish cinematography with 43 screenings in eight sub-sections (Films for Children, Films for Youth, Spanish Spaghetti Western, Spanish Animation for Children, Barcelona Film School, Treasures of Spanish Cinema, Tribute to Luis and Juan-Luis Buñuel, Tribute to Vicente Aranda). The guests of the Spanish section included, among others, Juan Luis Buñuel, Imanol Uribre and young shooting star, Clara Lago. The biggest stars of this edition of the festival were Tim Curry, Gábor Csupo, Luce Vigo and Anna Sophia Robb.
– **Rudolf Schimera**, Programme Coordinator.

FILM FESTIVAL ZLÍN

50th International Film Festival for Children and Youth

100th anniversary of Karel Zeman's birth

Days of Czech and Slovak Cinema

70mm Film Show

100th anniversary of Mark Twain's death

Come and celebrate our big 50th anniversary with us in Zlín!

May 30 – June 6, 2010
Zlín, Czech Republic

50 FILM FESTIVAL ZLÍN
International Film Festival for Children and Youth

www.zlinfest.cz

Other Festivals and Markets of Note

ALCINE – Alcalá de Henares/Comunidad de Madrid Film Festival, Plaza del Empecinado 1, 28801 Alcalá de Henares, Madrid, Spain. Tel: (34 91) 887 0584. e: festival@alcine.org. Web: www.alcine.org. *(Competition for Spanish short films, European short films and New Spanish directors full-length films. Several international sidebars and music sections – Nov.)*

Almería International Short Film Festival, Diputación de Almería, Area de Cultura, Calle Navarro Rodrigo 17, 04001 Almeria, Spain. Tel: (34 950) 211 100 e: jefadeprensa@almeriaencorto.es. Web: www.almeriaencorto.net. *(Competition for international shorts with professional meetings and complementary cultural activities – early Dec.)*

Anima: Brussels Animation Film Festival, Folioscope, Ave de Stalingrad 52, B-1000 Brussels, Belgium. Tel: (32 2) 534 4125. e: info@folioscope.be. Web: www.animatv.be. *(Over 150 films in the international competition (shorts and features, commercials, music videos), retrospectives, exhibitions, lessons, workshops for the kids, the Futurama professional days, round-table discussions, numerous guests and film concerts make Brussels an international appointment not to be ignored. It's also the place to find out about Belgian animation with a national competition and screenings in panorama – Feb 12–20, 2010.)*

Ann Arbor Film Festival, PO Box 8232, Ann Arbor, MI 48107, USA. Tel: (1 734) 995 5356. e: info@aafilmfest.org. Web: www.aafilmfest.org. *(Cutting-edge, lovingly crafted and artistically inspired films are showcased in the longest-running independent film festival in North America within the genres of experimental, animation, documentary, music video and narrative from all over the world – March 23–28, 2010.)*

Annecy/International Animated Film Festival and International Animated Film Market (MIFA), CITA, 18 Ave du Trésum, BP 399, 74013 Annecy Cedex, France. Tel: (33 4) 5010 0900. e: info@annecy.org. Web: www.annecy.org. *(Annecy has been showcasing the very best in animation for 50 years, making it one of the industry's leading international animation competitive festivals with a useful sales/distribution market (MIFA) – Festival: June 7–12, 2009; MIFA: June 9-11, 2010.)*

Arab Film Festival, 300 Brannan St, Ste 508, San Francisco, CA 94107, USA. Tel (1 415) 564 1100. e: info@aff.org. Web: www.aff.org. *(The festival screens films from and about the Arab World that provide realistic perspectives on Arab people, culture, art, history and politics – late Oct.)*

Art Film Fest International Film Festival, PO Box 62, Bajkalska 212, 820 12 Bratislava, Slovakia. Tel: (421 2) 2085 5100. e: info@artfilm.sk. Web: www.artfilm.sk. *(Competitive sections for International features and shorts with cult classics, classic comedies and much more – June 18–26, 2010.)*

Aspen Filmfest, 110 E Hallam, Ste 102, Aspen, CO 81611, USA. Tel: (1 970) 925 6882. e: info@aspenfilm.org. Web: www.aspenfilm.org. *(Shortsfest: Short subject competition showcasing the great filmmakers of tomorrow and introducing a rich variety of current productions from around the world – April 7–11 2010; Filmfest: Feature-length invitational which champions independent film at its eclectic, thoughtful, and often inspiring best – late Sept/early Oct, 2010.)*

Atlantic Film Festival, 1601 South Park St, Halifax, NS, B3J 2L2, Canada. Tel: (1 902) 422 3456. e: festival@atlanticfilm.com. Web: www.atlanticfilm.com. *(With a distinctive focus on film and music, the festival screens some of the best international, Canadian and Atlantic Canadian films, with opportunities to hear some of the best artists the region offers. In addition to screening films from around the world and across Canada,* and providing a platform for showcasing the finest Atlantic Canadian films, AFF programmers scour the world for unique films for an AFF audience. Whether it's inspiring documentaries, off-beat film noir, the latest Hollywood has to offer or beautifully crafted animation, there will be a favourite film for everyone – Sept 16–25, 2010.)

Augsburg Children's Film Festival, Filmtage Augsburg, Schroeckstrasse 8, 86152 Augsburg, Germany. Tel: (49 821) 153 078. e: filmbuero@ -t-online.de. Web: www.filmtage-augsburg.de. *(International features for children – late April/early May, 2010.)*

Baltic Film Festival Berlin, c/o Gudrun Holz, Graefestrasse 4, 10967 Berlin, Germany. Tel: (49 176) 6753 3733. e: info@balticfilmfestivalberlin. net. Web: www.balticfilmfestivalberlin.net. *(Since it was founded in 2004, the festival has seen a continuously growing number of visitors and has been very much appreciated by a young and mobile audience, interested in a an innovative cinema that deals with new topics and new forms of expression. In 2010 we will celebrate the 6th birthday of the BFFB. The six-day annual festival will be dedicated to current films produced in the three states of Estonia, Latvia and Lithuania. Films from the following categories are admitted to the festival: feature films, animations, short films and documentaries. The programme 'New Baltic Features' offers a striking selection of new feature films from the last two years. The industry event 'Meet the Baltics!' aims at inspiring new international*

film projects and co-operations in the context of the festival. The documentary programme 'Opposite Screens' presents productions that are dedicated to the tension-filled processes in the civil societies, both in the Baltic States as well as in their neighbouring countries. The programme 'Hommage' honours one filmmaker each year who dominates the film scene as far as style is concerned. The section 'Animania' covers the latest animated films. The programme 'Baltic Classics' shows cult films and classics in restored versions, which play a significant role in safeguarding the cultural heritage of the Baltic States – Oct 22–28, 2010).

Banff Mountain Film Festival, Mountain Culture at The Banff Centre, Box 1020, 107 Tunnel Mountain Drive, Banff, AB, T1L 1H5, Canada. Tel: (1 403) 762 6675. e: banffmountainfilms@banffcentre.ca. Web: www.banffmountainfestivals.ca. *(International competition for films and videos related to mountains and the spirit of adventure; Aug 3 deadline for entries – Oct 30–Nov 7, 2010.)*

Bangkok International Film Festival, 31/9 2nd Floor Royal City Ave, New Petchaburi Rd, Bangkapi, Huay Khwang, Bangkok, Thailand. Tel: (66 2) 203 0624. e: info@bangkokfilm. org. Web: www.bangkokfilm.org. *(The festival showcases more than 80 feature and short films, representing the works of filmmakers from Thailand, the ASEAN region, plus a selection of some of the most exciting and innovative films from around the world. There are two competitive sections: Main Competition for films by first and second time directors, and the Southeast Asian Competition for films from the region – Sept).*

*German premiere of the feature film **Vasha** at BFFB 2009. Director Hannu Salonen, Festival Director Gudrun Holz, Actor Tim Seyfi. Photo: Christine Kisorsy*

the discovery of new and emerging film artists and presents a dynamic event of 200 international films with over 400 film artists, technologists, and professionals from 34 countries in attendance – Feb 23–March 7, 2010.)

CineVegas Film Festival, 170 South Green Valley Parkway, Henderson, NV 89012, USA. Tel: (1 702) 952 5555.e: info@cinevegas.com. Web: www. cinevegas.com. (The festival is a platform for artists and art lovers who are drawn to the edge. Held at the Palms Casino Resort and Brenden Theatres amidst the unique, unpredictable and intoxicating environment that is Las Vegas, the festival pushes the boundaries of cinema presenting work by innovative, uninhibited, and renegade artists to an audience of local and national film lovers, journalists, and film industry representatives – June 9–14, 2010.)

Cleveland International Film Festival, 2510 Market Ave, Cleveland, OH 44113-3434, USA. Tel: (1 216) 623 3456. e: marshall@clevelandfilm. org. Web: www.clevelandfilm.org. (Ohio's premier film event features over 240 films originating from close to 60 countries. Visiting filmmakers, panel discussions, and student screenings are all CIFF highlights. Organised by the Cleveland Film Society whose aim is to help the world discover the power of the film arts to educate, entertain and celebrate the human experience – March 18–28, 2010.)

Coca-Cola Cinemagic International Film & Television Festival, 49 Botanic Ave, Belfast, BT7 1JL, Northern Ireland. Tel: (44 28) 9031 1900. e: info@ cinemagic.org.uk. Web: www.cinemagic.org.uk. (The largest film festival for young people in the UK and Ireland runs an action-packed programme of fascinating events. Film and TV enthusiasts have a wealth of screenings, masterclasses with film and television industry guests, workshops for schools, a young film jury and Q&As to choose from. All of these aim to inspire, entertain, motivate and create opportunities for young people aged from 4 to 25. Young people aged 16 to 25 who are interested in finding out more about working in the media industry can do just that via the 'Talent Lab' event. The Cinemagic Outreach and Education department works throughout the year with school and youth groups across Northern Ireland, offering a packed programme of exciting and hands-on educational opportunities for teachers and students, ranging from careers events to production training and from film criticism to media literacy workshops with top industry professionals – Nov 11–Nov 26, 2010.)

Crossing Europe Film Festival Linz, Graben 30, 4020 Linz, Austria. Tel: (43 732) 785700. info@ crossingeurope.at. Web: www.crossingeurope.at. (The European Competition showcases European young cinema dealing with contemporary subjects and is open to first, second or third films from a director. The European Panorama is non-competitive and includes features and documentaries that have been highly acclaimed and distinguished with awards at international festivals. The festival grants a central place to the diversity and richness of the cultural distinctiveness of young European cinema. Apart from the competitions the festival offers a full programme of tributes to outstanding film directors; film evenings centring on music and youth cultures, plus much more – April 20–25, 2010.)

Cyprus International Film Festival, PO Box 70, Anapafseos & Anonymou, Agioi Theodoroi, Corinthia, Greece. Tel: (357) 9979 8112. e: ciff@ cyiff.com. Web: www.cyprusfilmfestival.org. (The festival offers new and upcoming directors the opportunity to showcase their talent in front of a jury of internationally acclaimed cinema experts, directors and actors. Animation, feature films, music videos, short films and video art – Oct 13–22, 2010.)

Dhaka International Film Festival, 75 Science Laboratory Rd, 3rd Floor, Dhaka-1205, Bangladesh. Tel: (88 2) 862 1062. e: amzamal@ bdcom.com . Web: www.dhakafilmfest.org. (The festival will screen approximately 100 films from some 30 countries. There is a competitive section for Asian cinema and categories include: Retrospective, Tributes, Cinema of the World, Children's Film, Focus, Bangladesh Panorama, Women Filmmakers, Independent Films Section and Spiritual Films Section – Jan 14–22, 2010.)

Divercine, Canelones 2226 Apt 102, Casilla de Correo 5023, 11200 Montevideo, Uruguay. Tel: (59 82) 401 9882. e: ricardocasasb@gmail.com. Web: www.divercine.com.uy. (Children's festival – July.)

Doclisboa, Largo da Madalena 1, 1°, 1100-317 Lisbon, Portugal. Tel: (351 21) 8 883 093. e: doclisboa@doclisboa.org. Web: www.doclisboa. org. (Competitive with the international section featuring a selection of some of the best documentaries from around the world, produced last season (2009–10). Some have already won awards and received critical acclaim, for others it will be their first screening – late Oct.

Doha Tribeca Film Festival, Web: www. dohatribecafilm.com. (The Festival will include a wide range of programming and include approximately 30 feature films, highlighting internationally acclaimed Arab films, plus the best of Hollywood, Bollywood, family films, documentaries, animation and world cinema. The films are screened at Doha's celebrated year-old Museum of Islamic Art and in cinemas across Doha and other choice venues around Doha. While uniquely Qatari in its identity, the festival is modelled on the success of Tribeca Film Festival's dedication to engaging the local community and helping to promote and support filmmaking talent – late Oct/early Nov.)

Durban International Film Festival, Centre for Creative Arts, University of KwaZulu-Natal, Durban 4041, South Africa. Tel: (27 31) 260 1145. e: cca@ukzn.ac.za. Web: www.cca.ukzn. ac.za. (Featuring more than 200 films from more than 95 countries. Screenings will take place throughout Durban, including township areas where cinemas are non-existent. The festival will also offer an extensive seminar and workshop programme featuring local and international filmmakers, and the return of the very successful Talent Campus Durban – July 22–Aug 1, 2010.)

Early Melons International Student Film Festival, Radlinského 2803/34, 811 07 Bratislava, Slovakia. Tel: (421 9) 0765 5146. e: info@ earlymelons.com. Web: www.earlymelons.com. (International student film festival established

to promote European student film production in Slovakia. The festival features an international competitive section in which an international jury will award prizes to films in the categories of Best Fiction, Best Animation, Best Documentary and the Grand Prix – March 17–20, 2010.)

East End Film Festival (EEFF), The Brady Arts Centre, 192–196 Hanbury St, London, E1 5HU, UK. Tel: (+44) 020 7364 7917. e: film@eastendfilm-festival.com. Web: www.eastendfilmfestival.com. (In 2010, The East End Film Festival will return for its 9th edition, spanning 9 days, over 11 venues and 3 London boroughs. The EEFF programme reflects the multi-cultural make-up of East London, with a strong emphasis on local, grassroots film exhibition and education; screenings of the 'new wave' of British, Asian and Eastern European cinema, and an innovative mix of experimental video art, live music and cross-arts events. EEFF aims to champion work that transcends political, cultural and artistic boundaries, provide a platform for undiscovered talent, and serve the vibrant local communities in the most exciting artistic hub in Europe – London's East End. In 2009 EEFF

Festival Director Alison Poltock with Steven Murray, Executive Producer at the 2009 East End Film Festival.

showcased more than 160 short and feature films, with free outdoor screenings, traditional cinema exhibition, alternative screening venues and galleries. Over 30,000 attended. In April 2010, EEFF will add an extra day to its schedule plus a UK Directors Focus to the billing. Film Award categories in 2010 will include Best Short Audience Award, Best Short Film, IFG Inspiration Award for Best Feature Documentary, Best UK First Feature and Best International First Feature – April 22–30, 2010.)

EcoVision Festival, Via Francesco Bentivegna 51, 90139 Palermo, Italy. Tel: (39 09) 133 2567. e: info@ecovisionfestival.com. Web: www.ecovisionfestival.com. *(International festival with the aim of promoting cinematographic and documentary production concerning any aspect of environment and nature – June 2010.)*

Edmonton International Film Festival, Edmonton International Film Society, Suite 201, 10816A-82 Ave, Edmonton, Alberta, T6E 2B3, Canada. Tel: (1 780) 423 0844. e: info@edmontonfilmfest.com. Web: www.edmontonfilmfest.com. *(The festival screens cinematic gems of all genres from around the globe and celebrates the unique voices in moviemaking such as directors, writers and producers – Sept 24–Oct 2, 2010.)*

Emden International Film Festival, An der Berufschule 3, 26721 Emden, Germany. Tel: (49) 4921 9155-35. e: filmfest@vhs-emden.de. Web: www.filmfest-emden.de. *(The main focus is on current film productions from North Western Europe, particularly Germany and the UK, with over 100 films screened. Emden is increasingly developing into a highly-regarded meeting place for numerous representatives of the German and North-West European film industry – June 2–9, 2010.)*

European Independent Film Festival (ÉCU), 108 Rue Damremont, Paris 75018, France. e: info@ecufilmfestival.com. Web: www.ecufilmfestival.com. *(Since its inception four years ago, the festival has established itself as a fantastic arena for independent filmmakers from around the world to screen their films to large audiences, made up of a cinema-loving public who are seeking*

alternatives to the offerings of major studios, as well as to agents, talent scouts, production company representatives, distributors and established producers looking for new projects and raw talent. Competitive – March 12–14, 2010.)

Expresión en Corto International Film Festival, Calle Nuñez 20, Centro San Miguel de Allende, San Miguel de Allende Guanajuato 37700, Mexico. Tel: (52 415) 152 7264. e: info@expresionencorto.com. Web: www.expresionencorto.com. *(The festival receives over 1,300 works from more than 70 countries in its international competition and screens around 400 films. The festival hosts an International Pitching Market which brings together international producers, distributors and diverse film financing institutions from around the world who are interested in participating in co-productions with the top Mexican feature and documentary projects currently in development as well as presenting a variety of films, conferences, workshops, tributes and activities – Late July/early Aug).*

FID Marseille, 14 Allée Léon Gambetta, 13001 Marseille, France. Tel: (33 4) 9504 4490 e: welcome@fidmarseille.org. Web: www.fidmarseille.org. *(The festival presents about 140 films, mostly international premieres, in a rich program made up of the official selection: (international competition, national competition, competition of first films plus parallel screens, round tables, etc. – early July.)*

Festival Dei Popoli, Borgo Pinti 82 Rosso, 50121 Firenze, Italy. Tel: (39 055) 244 778. e: festivaldeipopoli@festivaldeipopoli.191.it. Web: www.festivaldeipopoli.org. *(Partly competitive and open to documentaries on social, anthropological, historical and political issues – late Nov.)*

Festival du Cinema International en Abitibi-Temiscamingue, 215 Mercier Ave, Rouyn-Noranda, Quebec J9X 5WB, Canada. Tel: (1 819) 762 6212. e: info@festivalcinema.ca. Web: www.festivalcinema.ca. *(The Festival presents nearly 150 international shorts, medium and full-length features; animation, documentary and fiction from more than 30 countries – late Oct.)*

Festival International du Film Francophone de Namur, 175, Rue des Brasseurs, 5000 Namur, Belgium Tel: (32 81) 241 236. e: info@fiff.be. Web: www.fiff.be. *(Celebrating it's 25th Anniversary in 2010, the festival has promoted French-speaking film and diffuses French-speaking feature-length and documentary films and tries, for this purpose, to gather in Namur all the directors, producers, screenwriters, actors, distributors involved in French-speaking cinematographic creation. It is really a place of thinking and appointment by the means of conferences and professional meetings. The Festival also contributes to the education and the training of the young people offering teaching activities and personal spaces. The Bayards reward the happy prizes winner for the various competitions: feature films, short films and first works – Oct 1–8, 2010.)*

Filmfest Dresden, Alaunstrasse 62, D-01099, Dresden, Germany. Tel: (49 351) 829 470. e: info@filmfest-dresden.de. Web: www.filmfest-dresden.de. *(Filmfest Dresden is an international short film festival and includes short animated and fiction films as well as documentary and experimental films. Founded in 1989, it has developed into a major short film festival in Germany and hosts one of the best-funded short film competitions across Europe. The festival also organises workshops and seminars for young filmmakers. The main sections of the festival are the International and the National Competitions. These are accompanied by various other thematic events. Visitors, the press and film producers also use the festival as a meeting place and to exchange opinions and discuss new ideas with more than 21,000 people attending in 2009 – April 20–25, 2010.)*

Filmfest München, Sonnenstr 21, D-80331, Munich, Germany. Tel: (49 89) 381 9040. e: info@filmfest-muenchen.de. Web: www.filmfest-muenchen.de. *(Germany's largest summer festival screening over 200 films from more than 40 countries – June 25–July 3, 2010.)*

Films from the South (FFS), Dronningensgt. 16, N-0152 Oslo, Norway. Tel: (47 22) 8224 80/81/82. e: kjetil@filmfrasor.no. *(A unique international film festival based in the capital of Norway. Since 1991 the festival has presented the best films and filmmakers from Asia, Africa and Latin America to a diverse audience. Each year approximately 100 feature films and documentaries are screened, over ten festival days and 230 screenings – Oct.)*

Florida Film Festival, Enzian Theatre, 1300 South Orlando Ave, Maitland, Florida 32751, USA. Tel: (1 407) 644 5625 x 326. Web: www.floridafilmfestival.com. *(Showcases cutting-edge American independent and international film, plus educational forums, glamorous parties and other special events – April 9–18, 2010.)*

Focus on Asia Fukuoka International Film Festival, 1-8-1 Tenzin, Chuo-ku, Fukuoka 810-8620, Japan. Tel: (81 92) 733 5170. e: info@focus-on-asia.com. Web: www.focus-on-asia.com. *(Most of the films screened in the event every year are premieres and this valuable event promotes the discovery and cultivation of new talent, while introducing excellent films from Asia to the world and deepening understanding of Asia through cultural and international exchanges. Non-competitive – Sept.)*

Fredrikstad Animation Festival, PO Box 1405, N-1602 Fredrikstad, Norway. Tel: (47) 4024 9364. e: mail@animationfestival.no. Web: www.animationfestival.no. *(Competitive festival organised by the Norwegian Animation Forum which showcases Nordic, Baltic and international animation, including retrospectives and workshops – Nov.)*

Full Frame Documentary Film Festival, 324 Blackwell St, Suite 500, Washington Bldg, Bay 5, Durham, NC 27701, USA. Tel: (1 919) 687 4100. e: info@fullframefest.org. Web: www.fullframefest.org. *(Short and feature documentaries completed after January 1, 2008 are eligible for consideration. Regular deadline Oct 15; late deadline Nov 30 – April 8–11, 2010.)*

Future Film Festival, Via del Pratello 21/2, 40122 Bologna, Italy. Tel: (39 051) 296 0672. e: info@futurefilmfestival.org. Web: www.futurefilmfestival.org. *(The festival is dedicated to animation and special effects, and highlights* the changes in digital imaginary and analyses the evolution of cinema and animation. It hosts panels, international previews, special events and workshops – Jan 26–31, 2010.)

Galway Film Fleadh, 36D Merchants Dock, Merchants Road, Galway City, Ireland. Tel: (353 91) 562 200. Fax: 569 312. e: info@galwayfilmfleadh.com. Web: www. galwayfilmfleadh.com. ('The Galway Film Fleadh is a wonderful event. Might Rain. Doesn't matter!' – Anthony Minghella. The Galway Film Fleadh screens the best of New Irish Films, Feature Documentaries and World Cinema. It also platforms excellence in filmmaking, with retrospectives, public interviews, tributes and masterclasses. (Redmond Morris, Anjelica Huston Christopher Hampton, Michael Fassbender, Ted Hope, Peter O' Toole, Jessica Lange, Kathy Bates, Robert Towne, Paul Schrader, Mira Nair, Patricia Clarkson, Abbas Kiarostami, Paolo Taviani and many more). In addition, the Galway Film Fair, a transatlantic bridge for the European Film

Anjelica Huston and Redmond Morris were presented with the inaugural award 'The Galway Hooker'.

and Television Industry, hosts 600 one-on-one meetings for producers with projects and invited film financiers, seminars, networking breakfasts and other industry events – July 6–11, 2010.)

Gerardmer International Fantasy Film Festival, Le Public Système Cinéma, 40, rue Anatole France, 92594 Levallois-Perret Cedex, France. Tel: (33 3) 2960 9814. e: info@gerardmer-festival.com. Web: www.festival-gerardmer. com. (International fantasy, science fiction, supernatural, psychological thriller and horror films, with competition for features and French-speaking shorts – Jan 27–31, 2010.)

Glasgow Film Festival, 12 Rose St, Glasgow G3 6RB, UK. Tel: (44 141) 352 8613. e: info@glasgowfilmfestival.org.uk. Web: www.glasgowfilmfestival.org.uk. (The festival is now the third largest film festival in the UK. It is 11 days of great films, guests, events and parties catering to an audience of more than 28,000 people across 12 key city centre venues. The festival welcomes features, shorts and work in all genres, and is committed to supporting Scottish talent and providing audiences with the opportunity to see the best of world cinema – Feb 18–28, 2010.)

Glimmer: Hull International Short Film Festival, Suite 12 Danish Buildings, 44-46 High St, Hull, HU1 1PS, UK. Tel: (44) 01482 381512. e:office@hullfilm.co.uk. Web: www.hullfilm.co.uk. (Dedicated to showcasing the very best short films from across the world, of any genre that run up to a maximum of 45 minutes and were made after 1st January 2008. The wide and diverse selection of films include dramas, documentaries, artist's film, video and animation with over 200 films screened. Attended by special guests from the film world and with a host of great events for everyone to enjoy. Numerous competitions, masterclasses, and special programmes – April 19–25, 2010.)

Golden Apricot International Film Festival, Suite 3 Moskovyan St, 0001 Yerevan, Armenia. Tel: (374) 1052 1042. e: info@gaiff.am. Web: www.gaiff.am. (The festival takes place in the capital of Armenia, Yerevan, at the foot of biblical Mount

Ararat. The theme of the festival is 'Crossroads of Cultures and Civilization' and the aim is to build cultural bridges and foster dialogue in this very complex corner of the planet. Established in 2004, it has fast become a premier destination in the region for filmmakers of all genres, particularly those advancing universal values of peace, cultural harmony and mutual understanding. As one journalist wrote, the festival became a pleasant place for elite film meetings: 'Classics of the art house films can be understood: a fantastic country with such ancient history, dramatic presence and future perspective, naturally, interests any artist'. Internationally acclaimed filmmaker Atom Egoyan (Canada) is President of the Festival and noted filmmaker Harutyun Khachatryan (Armenia) is the Director. The festival includes two main competition sections: International Competition (Feature and Documentary) and Armenian Panorama National Competition. One Grand Prize 'Golden Apricot' and one Special Prize 'Silver Apricot' are awarded in each category. Other festival sections are: Directors Across Borders Regional Competition, retrospectives, master-classes etc. – July 11–18, 2010).

The main cinema of the Golden Apricot Film Festival in Yerevan. Photo: Zaven Sargsyan.

Guadalajara International Film Festival, Nebulosa 2916, Colonia Jardines del Bosque, Guadalajara, Jalisco, Mexico. Tel: (52 33) 3121 7461. e: info@festivalcinedgl.udg.mx. Web: www.guadalajaracinemafest.com. (Mexican and Ibero-American recent quality film productions, increasing the awareness of the world film industry by screening the work of noteworthy Ibero-American film directors and presenting other remarkable and innovative films by new filmmakers – March 12–20, 2010.)

Haifa International Film Festival, 142 Hanassi Ave, Haifa 34 633, Israel. Tel: (972 4) 8353 515. e: film@haifaff.co.il. Web: www.haifaff.co.il. (The festival attracts an ever-growing audience of over 60,000 spectators along with hundreds of Israeli and foreign professionals from the film and television industries. Some 180,000 people take part in the activities of the festival, including the outdoor events, screenings, workshops. During the festival around 150 new films from the best and most recent international productions are premiered with some 220 screenings in 7 theatres: feature films, documentaries, animation, short films, retrospectives and tributes – Oct.)

Hawaii International Film Festival, 680 Iwilei Rd, Suite 100, Honolulu, Hawaii 96813, USA. Tel: (1 808) 697 2463. e: info@hiff.org. Web: www. hiff.org. (Established in 1981, the festival seeks to promote cultural understanding between the peoples of Asia, the Pacific and North America through the medium of film. The festival screens an average of 150 features, documentaries and film shorts. Among them are world premieres, North American premieres, US premieres, experimental films, animation and digital works representing social and ethnic issues, and first features by new directors. HIFF also conducts seminars, workshops, special award presentation receptions with top Asian, Pacific and North American filmmakers participating – Oct.)

Heartland Film Festival, 200 S Meridian, Suite 220, Indianapolis, Indiana 46225-1076, USA. Tel: (1 317) 464 9405. e: info@heartlandfilmfestival. org. Web: www.heartlandfilmfestival.org. (The festival screens independent films from around the world and presents US$200,000 in cash prizes and Crystal Heart Awards to the Festival's top-judged submissions including Best Dramatic Feature, Best Documentary Feature and Best Short Film. The festival comprises student and professional films, a variety of special events and a one-of-a-kind experience in one of the Midwest's most inviting cities – Oct.)

Holland Animation Film Festival, Hoogt 4, 3512 GW Utrecht, Netherlands. Tel: (31 30) 233 1733. e: info@haff.nl. Web: www.haff.awn.nl. (International competitions for independent and applied animation; special programmes, retrospectives, student films, exhibitions – Nov.)

Hot Docs Canadian International Documentary Festival, 110 Spadina Ave, Suite 333, Toronto, Ontario, M5V 2K4, Canada. Tel: (1 416) 203 2155. e: info@hotdocs.ca. Web: www.hotdocs.ca. (North America's largest documentary festival, conference and market, which presents a selection of more than 150 cutting-edge documentaries from Canada and around the globe. Through its industry programmes, Hot Docs also provides a full range of professional development, market and networking opportunities for documentary professionals – April 29–May 9, 2010.)

Huesca Film Festival, Avenida del Parque 1,2, 22002 Huesca, Spain. Tel: (34 974) 212 582. e: info@huesca-filmfestival.com. Web: www.huesca-filmfestival.com. (Well-established shorts festival with official competitive sections composed of the Iberoamerican, International Shorts and European Documentary contests. The winners receive the Award Danzante and the winners of the Award Danzante in the Iberoamerican and International contest automatically qualify to enter the Short Films category of the Academy of Motion Picture Arts and Sciences in Hollywood for the concurrent season – June 4–12, 2010.)

Hungarian Film Week, Magyar Filmunió, Városligeti, Fasor 38, 1068 Budapest, Hungary. Tel: (36 1) 351 7760. e: filmunio@filmunio.hu. Web: www.hungarianfilmweek.com. (Well-established regular showcase presenting the former year's Hungarian film production to local and foreign professionals as well as to the Hungarian public. The event attracts internationally acclaimed journalists and critics, festival directors and programmers, producers and distributors. Competitive with Hungarian features, documentaries and short films – late Jan/early Feb.)

International Cinematographers Film Festival 'Manaki Brothers', 8 Mart 4, 1000 Skopje, Republic of Macedonia. Tel: (389 2) 3224 334. e: info@manaki.com.mk. Web: www.manaki.com.mk. (Held in remembrance of Yanaki and Milton Manaki, the first cameramen of the Balkans. The main part of the festival programme is Camera 300, the official competition for feature length films drawn from the most recent European and world production. There is also a short film programme, which is non-competitive and presents outstanding recent films. In addition, 'Manaki Brothers' is dedicated to young, talented filmmakers and features workshops, seminars and roundtable discussions – late Oct/early Nov.)

International Festival of New Latin American Cinema, Calle 2, Number 411 Entre 17 & 19 Vedado, Havana 10400, Cuba. Tel: (53 7) 552 841. Web: www.habanafilmfestival.com. (The festival screens animation, documentary and fiction films made in the preceding year – Dec.)

International Film Festival Innsbruck, Museumstrasse 31, A-6020 Innsbruck, Austria. Tel: (43 512) 5785 0014. e: info@iffi.at. Web: www.iffi.at. Director: Helmut Groschup. (Films about Africa, Latin America and Asia. Competitive – June 1–6, 2010.)

International Film Festival of Kerala, Mani Bhavan, Sasthamangalam, Trivandum, Kerala 695010, India. Tel: (91 471) 231 0323. Web: www.iffk.keralafilm.com. (The festival boasts an extremely popular Competition section for films produced or co-produced in Asia, Africa and Latin America within the last year of the festival cycle. The usual sections include world cinema, documentaries (in film formats), short fiction (in film formats), retrospectives, homages and tributes – Dec.)

International Leipzig Festival for Documentary and Animated Film, Grosse Fleischergasse 11, 04109 Leipzig, Germany. Tel: (49 341) 308 640. e: info@dok-leipzig.de. Web: www.dok-leipzig. de. *(The festival screens the best, most exciting, moving and artistically outstanding animated and documentary films from more than 50 countries. Competitive – late Oct/early Nov.)*

Israel Film Festival, Israfest Foundation, 6404 Wilshire Blvd, Suite 1240, Los Angeles, CA 90048, USA. Tel: (1 323) 966 4166. e: meir@ israelfilmfestival.org. Web: www.israelfilmfestival. com. *(The festival's aim is to showcase Israel's thriving film and television industry, providing an intercultural exchange that advances tolerance and understanding and enriches America's vision of Israel's impressive social and cultural diversity. It screens feature films, documentaries, television dramas and short films and has become one of the nation's leading foreign film festivals and the largest showcase for Israeli films in the United States, as well as a launching pad for several notable US premieres – 2010 dates: June in LA; Dec in NY and Miami.)*

Jameson Dublin International Film Festival, 50 Upper Mount St, Dublin 2, Ireland. Tel: (353 1) 662 4260. e: info@jdiff.com. Web: www.jdiff.com. *(One of Ireland's premiere feature film festivals, aimed squarely at the cinema-going public and presenting over 120 films from around the world. Irish Film Talent is celebrated as an integral part of the JDIFF programme each year by presenting Irish film in all its forms, from archival and documentary to the very latest Irish feature films from first time directors – Feb 18–28, 2010.)*

Jihlava International Documentary Film Festival, Jana Masaryka 16, PO Box 33, 58601 Jihlava, Czech Republic. Tel: (420 7) 7410 1656. e: office@dokument-festival.cz. Web: www.dokument-festival.cz. *(The festival shows work from around the world with screenings followed by after-film talks, plus an accompanying programme of workshops, panel discussions, theatre, authors' readings, concerts, and exhibitions. The festival has four competitive sections: 'Opus Bunim' for world documentaries of innovative themes and high aesthetic quality; 'Between the Seas' presents high quality films from the countries of Central and Eastern Europe; 'Czech Joy' surveys the newest Czech filmmaking; and the 'Fascinations' section focuses on experimental documentary. The festival is accompanied by one of the leading events of the year for film professionals: The East European Forum – an encounter of Eastern European documentary filmmakers with producers from prominent European TV stations. In addition, we also collaborate with the market of documentary film from Central and Eastern Europe: East Silver – Oct 26–31, 2010.)*

JumpCuts, 1215 Blanshard St, Victoria, BC, Canada, V8W 3J4. Tel: (1 250) 389 0444. e: communications@victoriafilmfestival.com. Web: www.victoriafilmfestival.com. *(JumpCuts is a youth oriented festival which celebrates the originality and diversity of young voices and the exciting and always popular programme is sure to delight, move and amaze you. This is an opportunity to witness the talent and enrich the creativity of young people ages 10–14. Free film screenings, free demonstrations, many workshops. Romp through the world of Animation, Acting, SFX Make-up, Composing, Screenwriting, Camera Techniques and much more! – June.)*

Kaunas International Film Festival, Antanavos G. 2-31, LT-46280 Kaunas, Lithuania. Tel: (370) 6550 6559. e: info@kinofestivalis.lt. Web: www. kinofestivalis.lt. *(Kaunas International Film Festival is one of Lithuania's most appreciated film festivals and the main film event in Kaunas, second largest city in the country. It presents*

KAUNAS INTERNATIONAL FILM FESTIVAL

October 1-17, 2010 Kaunas & Vilnius, Lithuania

A Kaunas International Film Festival Audience awaits the screening of Broken Embraces in 'Romuva', Lithuania's oldest cinema. Photo: Andrius Kriaučiūnas.

films that have been acclaimed worldwide and also looks for new discoveries. The main priority of Kaunas IFF is a combination of the artistic and social statements in film. In the Wide Angle section, acclaimed films are screened that reflect both modern tendencies in film art and social issues relevant to the global context. Kaunas IFF is the only film festival in the region to present a special section on music films with 'Music Moves the World' and films about art in the 'All the Muses'. These are the three main sections in the festival, with additional retrospective programmes and theme sections each year. Kaunas IFF invites all cineastes and film professionals to see the most interesting and noteworthy films created over the past few years and to use Kaunas IFF as a means of communication by participating in discussions, lectures and meetings with film professionals – Oct 1–17, 2010.)

London Turkish Film Festival, 52B Beatty Rd, London, N16 8EB. Tel: (44 20) 7503 3584. e: vedide@ltff.org.uk. Web: www.ltff.org.uk. (The growth of London's annual showcase for Turkish

films has mirrored the increasing international standing of Turkish cinema over the last 15 years with more showings and events in more venues across the capital. The LTFF Golden Wings Awards include the groundbreaking Digital Distribution Award, a €15,000 UK and Ireland cinema exhibition contract, alongside The People's Choice Award and The Lifetime Achievement Award – Autumn 2010).

On the Way to School, winner of the Golden Wings People's Choice Award directed by Orhan Eskiköy and Özgür Doğan.

Ljubljana International Film Festival, Cankarjev Dom, Prešernova Cesta 010, 1000 Ljubljana, Slovenia. Tel: (386 1) 241 7147. e: liffe@cd-cc.si. Web: http://en.liffe.si. (The festival provides an overview of contemporary world film production and shows over 90 feature films and 15 shorts films in more than 250 screenings. It also includes a film workshop, multi-media interactive projects, exhibition and other events. Competitive – Nov.)

Lucas International Children's Film Festival, c/o Deutsches Filmmuseum, Schaumainkai 41, 60596 Frankfurt/Main, Germany. Tel: (49 69) 9612 20670. e: info@ lucasfilmfestival.de. Web: www.lucasfilmfestival.de. (Germany's oldest children's film festival, which is dedicated to

showing independent films from all over the world for children aged from five to twelve – Sept 5–12, 2010.)

Margaret Mead Film & Video Festival, American Museum of Natural History, Central Park, West & 79th St, New York, NY 10024-5192, USA. Tel: (1 212) 769 5000. e: meadfest@amnh.org. Web: www.amnh.org/mead. (The longest running premiere showcase for international documentaries in the United States, encompassing a broad spectrum of work, from indigenous community media to experimental nonfiction – mid-Nov.)

Marrakech International Film Festival, BP 14212 Riad Larrouss, Marrakech, Morocco. Tel: (212 4) 324 93/94. e: ffifm@lafondation.ma. Web: http://en.festivalmarrakech.info. (Showcase for international feature films – Dec.)

Midnight Sun Film Festival, Kansanopistontie 5, 99600 Sodankylä, Finland. Tel: (358 16) 614 522. e: office@msfilmfestival.fi. Web: www.msfilmfestival.fi. (The festival is one of the most unique in the world, with internationally renowned film directors, young directors and an international audience meeting under the midnight sun, in the relaxed and informal 'spirit of Sodankylä'. The festival is informally divided in three sections: films by the most famous film directors of all time, pearls of the new cinema and silent movies with live music – June 16–20, 2010.)

Mipdoc, 11 rue du Colonel Pierre Avia, BP 572, 75726 Paris Cedex 15, France. Tel: (33 1) 4190 4580. e: info.miptv@reedmidem.com. Web: www.miptv.com. (Specialist international screening marketplace and conference for documentaries – April 10–11, 2010.)

Molodist – Kiev International Film Festival, 6 Saksahanskoho St, Kiev 01033, Ukraine. Tel: (380 44) 289 2335. e: info@molodist.com. Web: www.molodist.com. (The festival's main goal is to discover new young filmmakers from around the world. The competition programme consists of student films, first short film (animation, documentary, fiction film) and first full-length fiction film – Oct 23–31, 2010.)

Montpellier International Festival of Mediterranean Film (Cinemed), 78 Ave du Pirée, 34000 Montpellier, France. Tel: (33 4) 9913 7373. e:info@cinemed.tm.fr. Web: www.cinemed.tm.fr. (The best recent production with more than 120 films previously unscreened films in the official selection and more than €100,000 worth of prizes in cash, aid and services for the winners in the various competitions. Comprising features, shorts, documentaries and experimental films – late Oct.)

Montreal International Festival of New Cinema, 3805 Boulevard St-Laurent, Montreal, Quebec, Canada H2W 1X9. Tel: (1 514) 282 0004. e: info@nouveaucinema.ca. Web: www.nouveaucinema.ca. (Highlights the development of new trends in cinema and new media, providing a showcase for new, original works, particularly in the fields of independent cinema and digital creation. The festival welcomes Quebec, Canadian and international artists in a convivial atmosphere that prizes public and professional exchange – Oct.)

Mumbai Film Festival, Mumbai Academy of The Moving Image (MAMI), B 111, Crystal Plaza, New Link Rd, Andheri (W), Mumbai 400 053, India. Tel: (91 22) 4106 8223. e: mumbaifilmfest@gmail.com. Web: www.mumbaifilmfest.com. (The only independent film festival in India divided into five sections: International Competition for the First Feature Films of Directors, World Cinema, Indian Showcase, Mumbai Dimensions and Retrospectives – end Oct/early Nov.)

New Directors/New Films, Film Society of Lincoln Center, 70 Lincoln Center Plaza, New York, NY 10023, USA. Tel: (1 212) 875 5610. e: festival@filmlinc.com. Web: www.filmlinc.com. (One of the premiere international showcases for the work of emerging filmmakers. It is a non-competitive festival with no separate categories and no prizes awarded. Feature films and shorts are chosen according to quality from all categories: animated, experimental, documentary, dramatic etc. – March 24–April 4, 2010.)

New York Film Festival, Film Society of Lincoln Center, 70 Lincoln Center Plaza, New York,

NY 10023-6595, USA. Tel: (1 212) 875 5610. e: festival@filmlinc.com. Web: www.filmlinc.com. *(The festival shows new works by directors from around the world, featuring inspiring and provocative cinema by emerging talents and first-rank international artists, whose films are often recognised as contemporary classics – late Sept-early Oct.)*

NexT International Film Festival, 179 Traian St, 024043 Bucharest, Romania. Tel: (40 21) 252 4866. e: contact@nextproject.ro. Web: www. nextproject.ro. *(Created in memory of film director Cristian Nemescu and sound-designer and composer Andrei Toncu, emerging talents of Romanian cinema who tragically died in 2006, NexT IFF is focused on two main elements: film directing and sound design. NexT is one of the few festivals that pays special attention to sound design: a prize for best soundtrack, invited sound-designers and film composers of competition films give this festival a unique composition. NexT comprises a competition section (about 30 titles), several off-competition programmes (Countries in Focus, Festival Cities, NexT Kids, and They Were NexT Generation Too – a glance upon recent work/debut films of former competitors), and a series of seminars (mainly dedicated to film directing and sound-design, but also to production and distribution of shorts, screenwriting etc.) NexT IFF is part of a broader idea of creating a framework to support, to advise and guide young filmmakers, especially at the moment of taking the step from short to first full-length feature – April 13–18, 2010.)*

Nordic Film Festival, 75 rue General Leclerc, 76000 Rouen, France. Tel: (33 232) 767 322. e: festival.cinema.nordique@wanadoo.fr. Web: www.festival-cinema-nordique.asso.fr. *(Competitive festival of Nordic cinema, including retrospectives – March 10–21, 2010.)*

Nordic Film Forum Scanorama, Ozostrasse 4, Vilnius 08200, Lithuania. Tel: (370 5) 276 0367. e: info@kino.lt . Web: www.scanorama. lt. *(The festival screens a variety of genres including features, documentaries, shorts and experimental films from new and emerging talents that represent contemporary European film. From its beginning as a Nordic Film Forum crossing Lithuania from its capital to the coast, Scanorama has become a successful film festival embracing cinematographic achievements not only of the Nordic countries, but from the whole Europe – Nov.)*

Nordic Film Days Lubeck, Nordische Filmtage Lubeck, Schildstrasse 12, D-23539 Lubeck, Germany. Tel: (49 451) 122 1742. e: info@filmtage. luebeck.de. Web: www.filmtage.luebeck.de. *(The festival presents feature films, documentaries and short films from Denmark, Estonia, Finland, Iceland, Latvia, Lithuania, Norway and Sweden. There is an extensive children's and youth film programme, and a retrospective devoted to important eras, specific genres or icons of cinema. Accompanying the film programme are seminars, discussions and roundtable talks. Attendance exceeds 24,000 for more than 160 screenings – early Nov.)*

Open Air Filmfest Weiterstadt, PO Box 1164, D-64320 Weiterstadt, Germany. Tel: (49 61) 501 2185. e: filmfest@weiterstadt.de. Web: www. filmfest-weiterstadt.de. *(Mainly short films of all genres, formats and lengths although the programme has been extended to include feature films and documentaries. Attending filmmakers may camp in the forest, next to the festival area. Competitive, May 15 deadline for entries – Aug 12–16, 2010.)*

Osian's Cinefan – Festival of Arab and Arabian Cinema, B-35, Qutab Institutional Area, New Delhi-110016, India. Tel: 91 11 4174 3166. e: supriya@osians.com. Web: www.osians.com. *(The festival is one of Asia's leading film festivals, devoted principally to Asia and the Arab world, and enjoys an international reputation for the quality of films screened, complemented by panel discussions, one major seminar each time, the Auction of Popular Culture and Film Memorabilia, along with a number of exhibitions, a Talent Campus for budding young filmmakers from South Asia, and the presence and participation of film professionals from all over India and the world – mid July.)*

Palm Beach International Film Festival, 289 Via Naranjas, Royal Palm Plaza, Suite 48, Boca Raton, Florida 33432, USA. Tel: (1 561) 362 0003. e: info@pbifilmfest.org. Web: www.pbifilmfest. org. *(The Festival is committed to supporting emerging filmmakers of today and tomorrow, and screens American and international independent features, shorts, documentaries and large format. Competitive – April 22–26, 2010.)*

Palm Springs International Festival of Short Films & Film Market, 1700 E Tahquitz Canyon Way, Suite 3, Palm Springs, CA 92262, USA. Tel: (1 760) 322 2930. e: info@psfilmfest.org. Web: www.psfilmfest.org. *(Competitive shorts festival and market. Student, animation, documentary, live action and international competition with Audience and Juried Awards. Seminars and workshops – June.)*

Philadelphia Film Festival, Philadelphia Film Society, 4th Floor, 234 Market St, Philadelphia, PA 19106, USA. Tel: (1 215) 253 3599. e: info@ philadelphia.org. Web: www.phillyfests.com. *(The festival screens nearly 300 International and USA features, documentaries, shorts and animation from 50 countries to an audience of over 60,000. Usually held in Spring, the festival moved to Autumn in order to programme from a much wider and excellent selection of films, following their debuts at Cannes, Toronto, Venice etc – mid-Oct.)*

Polish Film Festival Gdynia, The Pomeranian Film Foundation in Gdynia, Armii Krajowej 24, 81-372 Gdynia, Poland. Tel: (48 58) 621 1509. e: biuro@festiwalgdynia.pl. Web: www. festiwalgdynia.pl. *(The Festival's aim is to popularise Polish film arts in Poland and internationally, and screens cinema and television feature films. Competitive, with special screenings, retrospectives, conferences and accompanying events – Sept.)*

Ravenna Nightmare Film Festival, Via Mura di Porta Serrata 13, 48100 Ravenna, Italy. Tel: (39 05) 4468 4242. e: ravenna@melies.org. Web: www.ravennanightmare.it. *(The festival revolves around Halloween weekend and features horror and fantastic film. The main event of the festival*

is the International Competition for features, which usually admits around 10–12 feature films, all of which are national premieres. The European Competition for short films screen around 15 films. Also features a number of special events out of competition, retrospectives, parties, music, and literature events featuring important writers of the horror genre – late Oct.)

River to River: Florence Indian Film Festival, Piazza Santo Spirito 1, 50125 Firenze, Italy. Tel: (39 055) 286 929. Web: www.rivertoriver.it. *(Indian cinema – Dec.)*

St Louis International Film Festival, 3547 Olive St, St Louis, MO 63103-1014, USA. Tel: (1 314) 289 4150. e: mailroom@cinemastlouis.org. Web: www.cinemastlouis.org. *(Showcases US and international independent films, documentaries and shorts, with the 2009 festival screening 250 films from more than 40 countries. Competitive – Nov.)*

St Petersburg International Film Festival, 10 Kamennostrovsky Ave, St Petersburg 197101, Russia. Tel: (7 812) 237 0072. e: info@filmfest. ru. Web: www.filmfest.ru. *(Non-competitive, showcasing the best films from around the world – June.)*

San Sebastian Horror and Fantasy Film Festival, Reina Regente 8, 20003 Donostia-San Sebastian, Spain. Tel: (34 943) 481 197. e: cinema_cinema@donostia.org. Web: www. sansebastianhorrorfestival.com. *(Cult, cutting-edge horror fantasy festival; short film and feature competition – Late Oct/early Nov.)*

San Sebastian Human Rights Film Festival, Donostia Kultura, Plaza de la Constitucion 1, 20003 Donostia-San Sebastian, Spain. Tel: (34 943) 481 471. e: cinederechoshumanos@ donostia.org. Web: www.cineyderechoshumanos. com. *(Short films and features about human rights – April 23–30, 2010.)*

Santa Barbara International Film Festival, 1528 Chapala St 203, Santa Barbara, CA 93101, USA. Tel: (1 805) 963 0023. Fax: 962 2524. e:info@

sbfilmfestival.org. Web: www.sbfilmfestival.org. *(Celebrating its 25th Anniversary in 2010 the festival screens over 250 international films and will host a plethora of parties, making it a spectacular entertainment experience – Feb 4–14, 2010.)*

São Paulo International Film Festival, Rua Antonio Carlos 288, 01309-010 São Paulo, Brazil. Tel: (55 11) 3141 0413. e: info@mostra.org. Web: www.mostra.org. *(Competitive festival that pays particular attention to new filmmakers and the most representative productions from around the world. It presents more 420 films, including a new filmmakers competition, retrospectives and tributes – Oct.)*

Sarajevo Film Festival, Zelenih beretki 12/1, 71000 Sarajevo, Bosnia and Herzegovina. Tel: (387 33) 209 411. e: programmes@sff.ba. Web: www.sff.ba. *(The festival presents a wide selection of competitive and non-competitive films, with a focus on Southeast Europe and it's filmmakers, who compete in Feature, Short and Documentary film sections – July 23–31, 2010.)*

Sarasota Film Festival, 1991 Main St, Main Plaza, Sarasota, Florida 34236, USA. Tel: (1 941) 364 9514. e: kathy@sarasotafilmfestival.com. Web: www.sarasotafilmfestival.com. *(Independent films, symposiums and events in a beautiful location; hospitable, inquisitive audiences plus a well-organised and publicised programme – April 9–18, 2010.)*

Short Shorts Film Festival Asia, 2F Hirakawacho Urban Bldg, 2-4-8 Hirakawacho, Chiyoda-ku, Tokyo 102-0093, Japan. Tel: (81 3) 5214 3005. Web: www.shortshorts.org. *(Film markets in Asian countries have been developing rapidly and are producing many great short films in various genres. Considering the successful growth in Asia's film industries, SSFFA has anchored itself as a unique exhibition of Asian short films and as a facilitator for cultural and artistic exchange between Japan and Asian countries. The festival presents over 90 short films and invites filmmakers from all over the world – June.)*

A screening at Silent Days Film Festival in Tromsø

Silent Film Days in Tromsø, PO Box, 285, N-9253 Tromsø, Norway. Tel: (47) 7775 3090. e: info@tiff.no. Web: www.tiff.no. *(The programme encompasses not only the great classics of silent film, but also many hidden treasures recovered from national and international archives – and here presented to a new audience. All films are screened with live music, composed and performed by international artists. The style of music ranges from the classical piano or organ accompaniment of the silent film tradition to jazz, rock and electronic music. The performers at last year's festival included legendary world music group Yath-Ka (Siberia, Russia), pianist Ben Model (USA) and*

Silent Film Days

Tromsø, Norway
September 2-5, 2010

www.tiff.no

electronic act Per Martinsen, Aggie Peterson and Sergey Suokas (Norway/Russia). The venue for the festival is Tromsø's original cinema, Verdensteatret, which opened in 1916 and was built expressly for the screening of silent films – Sept 2–5, 2010.)

Sofia International Film Festival, 1 Bulgaria Sq, Sofia 1463, Bulgaria. Tel: (359 2) 952 6467. e: office@sofiaiff.com. Web: www.sofiaiff.com. (Competitive festival showcasing new Bulgarian and Balkan films to international audiences. It includes the following sections: Official programme (international competition and special screenings), documentary programme (competition), Bulgarian feature films, Balkan films showcase, European screen, World screen, Bulgarian shorts, retrospectives, tributes and special events – March 4–14, 2010.)

Sonoma Environmental Film Festival, Sonoma Cinemas, Sonoma Woman's Club, Sonoma, CA 95442, USA. Tel: (1 707) 935 3456. e: wcfilmfest@aol.com. Web: www.seff. us. (Showcase of new eco-centric films, panel discussions, non-competitive. Seeks to raise awareness about our blue Planet and the green movement – Jan 20–23, 2011.)

Stuttgart Festival of Animated Film, Film- und Medienfestival GmbH, Schlosstrasse 84, 70176 Stuttgart, Germany. Tel: (49 711) 925 460. e: itfs@festival-gmbh.de. Web: www.itfs. de. (One of the largest events for animated film worldwide. The festival showcases a diverse range of animated film starting with artistic short films, through TV series and children's films and rounded off with feature-length animation. The festival focuses particularly on supporting talented young filmmakers with a special sponsorship award and the Young Animation competition – May 4–9, 2010.)

Sunny Side of the Doc, Résidence le Gabut Bâtiment E, 16 rue de l'Aimable Nanette, 17000 La Rochelle, France. Tel: (33 5) 4655 7979. e: info@sunnysideofthedoc.com. Web: www.sunnysideofthedoc.com. (International documentary market – June 22–25, 2010.)

Sydney Film Festival, PO Box 96, Strawberry Hills, NSW 2012, Australia. Tel: (61 2) 9318 0999. e: info@sff.org.au. Web: www.sydneyfilmfestival. org. (Broad-based event screening new Australian and international features and shorts – June 2–14, 2010.)

Taipei Golden Horse Film Festival, 7F, 196 Jhonghua Rd, Taipei City 10850, Taiwan, (ROC). Tel: (886 2) 2370 0456. e: info@goldenhorse. org.tw. Web: www.goldenhorse.org.tw. (The most prominent annual film festival in Taiwan, comprised of two parts. The Golden Horse Awards Competition encourages the development of Chinese-language films. The international programme is intended to introduce excellent films from around the world to Taiwanese audiences in order to stimulate an exchange of ideas and inspire creativity – late Nov/early Dec.)

Taormina Film Fest in Sicily, Corso Umberto 19, 98039 Taormina Messina, Italy. Tel Rome office: (39 064) 86808 e: press@taorminafilmfest. it. Web: www. taorminafilmfest.it. (With the aim of offering festival access to audiences around Sicily, finding extra screening space for its shows, increasing its impact in Sicily, offering a wide range of media stories and increasing tourism in the entire region, from 2009 the festival changed its name to become the Taormina Film Fest in Sicily. In addition to sharing Taormina's films and entertaining many of its actors, directors and journalists, each of the new locations around the island participate in the eight-day festival with their own exclusive film programme. The festival has a strong identity as a Mediterranean festival with strong ties to the US and world cinema and has chosen to remain a boutique showcase for a limited number of highly-selected films from the most recent production – June.)

Third Eye Asian Film Festival, Asian Film Foundation, Rajkamal Studio, Parel, Mumbai 400012, India. Tel: (91 22) 2413 7791. Fax: 2412 5268. e: info@affmumbai.com. Web: www. affmumbai.com. (Cinema arrived in Mumbai, (formerly Bombay) on the western coast of India, in July 1896, with the package of films

and divided culturally in the Middle East, West Asia, South Asia, Central Asia and the Far East, the Asian Cinema is as diverse and rich as its topography. The Asian countries share cultural similarities and a common socio-economic scenario being plagued by similar problems of poverty, illiteracy, population, lowly status of women. The Third Eye Asian Film Festival was established to create awareness about each other, amongst Asian countries, with cinema as the common bond bringing people together and fostering understanding between varied cultures. Chairman: Kiran Shantaram. Director: Sudhir Nandgaonkar – Oct 27–Nov 4, 2010).

Festival President Tudor Giurgiu, left, with Claudia Cardinale and Romanian actor Florin Piersic at the TIFF Gala. Photo Adi Marineci

Transilvania International Film Festival Cluj-Napoca (TIFF), Popa Soare 52, Sector 2, 023984 Bucharest, Romania. Tel: (40) 31 105 0187. e:info@tiff.ro. Web: www.tiff.ro. *(Founded in 2002, TIFF has grown rapidly to be the most important film-related event in Romania and one of the most spectacular annual events in the region. Over the years, TIFF has invited, as recipients of the Lifetime Achievement Award or special guests of the event, important figures from world cinema, including Claudia Cardinale, Catherine Deneuve, Julie Delpy, Fanny Ardant, Michael Radford, Annie Girardot, Udo Kier, Vanessa Redgrave, Nicolas Roeg and Franco Nero. In 2009, over 55,000 people attended the screenings in the 13 venues of Cluj Napoca, eager not to miss over 200 features and short films presented in the competitive and show-case sections. Having become a traditional premiere hub for domestic features, which are now landmarks of the evolution of the so-called*

made by the Lumiere brothers. By 2000, the Mumbai Film Industry had truly acquired the dimensions of an Entertainment Industry, catering to the entertainment needs of a nation of one billion. Although Asian Cinema has been winning accolades on the international film festival circuit, none of the SAARC countries screen Asian cinema commercially. The Asian Film Festival promotes Asian Cinema worldwide and aims to establish interaction amongst the Asian film fraternity and to create a dialogue with the West. Extending from Turkey to Japan,

Third Eye presented the Asian Film Culture Award to Amitabh Bachchan. (left to right) Kiran V. Shantaram, Chairman Asian Film Festival, Mr Bachchan received the trophy from the Chief Guest Ramesh Sippy.

Romanian New Wave of filmmakers, TIFF has also developed a market of Romanian work-in-progress feature fiction and documentary projects, scheduled in the frame of the Romanian Days (June 3–6, 2010) which take place during the festival – May 28–June 6, 2010.)

Trieste Film Festival, Via Donota 1, 34121 Trieste, Italy. Tel: (39 040) 347 6076. e: info@ alpeadriacinema.it. Web: www.alpeadriacinema. it. (Central and Eastern European Cinema – Jan 21–28, 2010.)

True/False Film Festival, 5 South Ninth St, Columbia, Missouri 65201, USA. Tel: (1 573) 442 8783. e: info@truefalse.org. Web: www.truefalse. org. (International documentary festival – Feb 25–28, 2010.)

Uppsala International Short Film Festival, PO Box 1746, SE-751 47 Uppsala, Sweden. Tel: (46 18) 120 025. e: info@shortfilmfestival.com. Web: www.shortfilmfestival.com. (Sweden's premiere arena for short film, having attained both national recognition of the Swedish Film Institute and genuine international renown. In addition, the festival is the most important international cultural event in Uppsala. Every year the festival shows more than 300 short films in five different sections exploring the diversity and richness of the short film – from new film to retrospective programmes, from fiction, documentary and experimental film to animation. Competitive – Oct 25–31, 2010.)

Uruguay International Film Festival, Lorenzo Carnelli 1311, 11200 Montevideo, Uruguay. Tel: (59 82) 419 5795. e: cinemuy@chasque.net. Web:

www.cinemateca.org.uy. (Presents independent and documentary films – Late Nov.)

USA Film Festival, 6116 N Central Expressway, Suite 105, Dallas, Texas 75206, USA. Tel: (1 214) 821 6300. e: usafilmfestival@aol.com. Web: www.usafilmfestival.com. (The festival features the best new American and foreign films, the Academy qualifying National Short Film and Video Competition and special tributes – April.)

Valdivia International Film Festival, Dirección Vicente Perez Rosales 787E, Valdivia, Chile. Tel: (56 63) 249 073. e: info@ficv.cl. Web: www.ficv. cl. (International feature contest, plus Chilean and international shorts, documentaries and animation – Oct.)

Viewfinders International Film Festival for Youth, PO Box 36139, Halifax, NS, B3J 3S9, Canada. Tel: (1 902) 422 3456. e: viewfinders@ atlanticfilm.com. Web: www.atlanticfilm.com. (Viewfinders is a five-day celebration of film, video and media, geared towards youth ages 3-18. The festival includes a comprehensive school programme complete with a guide for educators, as well as evening and weekend screenings and events for families and young adults. ViewFinders features films from around the world and includes a selection of films made by youth – April 20–24, 2010.)

Vila do Conde, Auditório Municipal, Praça da República, 4480-715 Vila do Conde, Portugal. Tel: (351 252) 638 025. e: submissions@curtas.pt. Web: www.curtasmetragens.pt. (National and International shorts competitions with special programme and retrospectives – July 3–11, 2010.)

Transilvania International Film Festival **09** MAY 28 – JUNE 6, 2010 CLUJ-NAPOCA

CALLS FOR ENTRIES deadline: 15 february 2010

www.tiff.ro

Festival director and honourable jury of 14th Vilnius International Film Festival after award ceremony. (left to right) Julia-Maria Köhler, Dexter Fletcher, Vida Ramaskiene, Pratibha Sastry, Andrius Mamontovas, Barr Potter. Photo: Inga Jankauskaite

Vilnius International Film Festival (Kino Pavasaris), Gedimino Pr 50, Vilnius 01110, Lithuania. e: info@kinopavasaris.lt. Web: www. kinopavasaris.lt. *(In 2010 Vilnius IFF celebrates its 15th anniversary and has become known for presenting high-quality films to Lithuanian and international filmmakers. Every year the festival presents more than 100 films which are divided into a number of programmes: the newest and critically acclaimed works of professional filmmakers (Masters), controversial films (Brave Vision), upcoming new filmmakers' works (Discoveries), important documentaries (Cinedocs), the newest works of Lithuanian filmmakers (Lithuanian Dreams), films of far, exotic and unknown foreign countries (Special Programme) as well as the best of cinema classics (Retrospective). The festival will again present the competition programme 'New Europe – New Names', which was held for the first time in 2009 and has now become an annual event. Only the best debut films from Eastern and Central Europe are in competition for 'The Best Film' Award chosen by an International Jury of leading film professionals – March 18–April 2, 2010.)*

Warsaw International Film Festival, PO Box 816, 00-950 Warsaw 1, Poland. Tel: (48 22) 621 4647. e: wff@wff.pl. Web: www.wff.pl. *(The programme includes over 140 full-length films and 115 shorts from more than 50 countries, many of them Polish premieres. It is a tradition of the WFF that meetings with filmmakers are held after screenings. The festival is held in the heart of Warsaw, with screenings at Multikino Złote Tarasy, Kinoteka, and Kultura. In 2009. the screenings brought in an audience of more than 108,000 people, a new attendance record – Oct 8–17, 2010.)*

Washington, DC International Film Festival (Filmfest DC), PO Box 21396, Washington, DC 20009, USA. Tel: (1 202) 274 5781. e: filmfestdc@ filmfestdc.org. Web: www.filmfestdc.org. *(Competitive festival celebrating the best in world cinema from over 30 countries – April 15–25, 2010.)*

ZagrebDox, Factum Centre for Drama Art, Nova Ves 18/3, 10 000 Zagreb, Croatia. Tel: (385 1) 485 4821. e: info@zagrebdox.net. Web: www. zagrebdox.net. *(International and competitive documentary film festival – Feb 28–March 7, 2010.)*

Zurich Film Festival, Spoundation Motion Picture GmbH, Bederstrasse 51, 8002 Zurich, Switzerland. Tel: (41 44) 286 6000. e: info@zurichfilmfestival. org. Web: www.zurichfilmfestival.org. *(The festival presents film premieres from all over the world, offers cinematic treats to a fascinated national and international audience, and facilitates direct on-the-spot exchange with the filmmakers. With numerous events and parties complementing the cinema programme, the festival offers an ideal platform for networking and exchanging ideas – Sept 23–Oct 3, 2010.)*

Index to Advertisers

International Liaison

Afghanistan: Sandra Schäfer
Algeria: Maryam Touzani
Angola: Martin P. Botha
Argentina: Alfredo Friedlander
Armenia: Susana Harutyunyan
Australia: Peter Thompson
Austria: Gunnar Landsgesell
Belgium: Erik Martens
Bolivia: José Sanchez-H.
Bosnia and Herzegovina: Rada Sesić
Brazil: Nelson Hoineff
Bulgaria: Pavlina Jeleva
Burkina Faso: Honoré Essoh
Burundi: Ogova Ondego
Cambodia: Michelle Vachon
Cameroon: Honoré Essoh
Canada: Tom McSorely
Chad: Agnes Thomasi
Chile: Hugo Díaz Gutiérrez
China: Luna Lin
Colombia: Jaime E. Manrique and
   Pedro Adrián Zuluaga
Costa Rica: Maria Lourdes Cortés
Côte D'Ivoire: Honoré Essoh
Croatia: Tomislav Kurulec
Cuba: Jorge Yglesias
Cyprus: Ninos Feneck-Mikelidis
Czech Republic: Eva Zaoralova
Democratic Republic of Congo:
   Ogova Ondego
Denmark: Christian Monggaard
Ecuador: Gabriela Aleman
Egypt: Sherif Awad
El Salvador: Maria Lourdes Cortés
Eritrea: Ogova Ondego
Estonia: Jaan Ruus
Ethiopia: Ogova Ondego
Finland: Antti Selkokari

France: Michel Ciment
Gabon: Agnes Thomasi
Georgia: Nino Ekvtimishvili
Germany: Andrea Dittgen
Ghana: Steve Ayorinde
Greece: Ninos Feneck-Mikelidis
Guatemala: Maria Lourdes Cortés
Guinea: Agnes Thomasi
Honduras: Maria Lourdes Cortés
Hong Kong: Tim Youngs
Hungary: John Cunningham
Iceland: Eddie Cockrell
India: Uma Da Cunha
Indonesia: Lisabona Raman
Iran: Kamyar Mohsenin
Ireland: Donald Clarke
Israel: Dan Fainaru
Italy: Lorenzo Codelli
Japan: Katsuta Tomomi
Kazakhstan: Gulnara Abikeyeva
Kenya: Ogova Ondego
Kyrgyzstan: Gulnara Abikeyeva
Lebanon: Sherif Awad
Lithuania: Ilona Jurkonytė
Luxembourg: Boyd van Hoeij
Malaysia: Norman Yusoff
Mali: Honoré Essoh
Malta: Daniel Rosenthal
Mauritania: Agnes Thomasi
Mexico: Carlos Bonfil
Montenegro: Goran Gocić
Morocco: Maryam Touzani
Mozambique: Martin P. Botha
Namibia: Martin P. Botha
Netherlands: Leo Bankersen
Nepal: Prabesh Subedi
New Zealand: Peter Calder
Nicaragua: Maria Lourdes Cortés

Niger: Honoré Essoh
Nigeria: Steve Ayorinde
Norway: Trond Olav Svendsen
Pakistan: Aijaz Gul
Palestine: Sherif Awad
Panama: Maria Lourdes Cortés
Peru: Isaac Léon Frías
Poland: Barbara Hollender
Portugal: Martin Dale
Romania: Cristina Corciovescu
Russia: Kirill Razglov
Rwanda: Ogova Ondego
Senegal: Honoré Essoh
Serbia: Goran Gocić
Singapore: Yvonne Ng
Slovakia: Miro Ulman
Slovenia: Ziva Emersic
South Africa: Martin P. Botha
South Korea: Nikki J. Y. Lee
Spain: Jonathan Holland
Swaziland: Martin P. Botha
Sweden: Gunnar Rehlin
Switzerland: Marcy Goldberg
Taiwan: David Frazier
Tajikistan: Gulnara Abikeyeva
Tanzania: Ogova Ondego
Thailand: Anchalee Chaiworaporn
The Gambia: Agnes Thomasi
Tunisia: Maryam Touzani
Turkey: Atilla Dorsay
Uganda: Ogova Ondego
Ukraine: Volodymyr Voytenko
United Kingdom: Jason Wood
United States: Tom Charity
Uzbekistan: Gulnara Abikeyeva
Venezuela: Martha Escalona Zerpa
Zambia: Martin P. Botha
Zimbabwe: Martin P. Botha

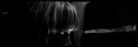  

VISIONS DU RÉEL
NYON

VISIONS DU RÉEL
INTERNATIONAL FILM FESTIVAL
DOC OUTLOOK-INTERNATIONAL MARKET
NYON, 15-21 APRIL 2010

THE FINE FESTIVAL IN THE HEART OF EUROPE
WITH ITS FAMOUS SECTIONS OPEN TO
THE SUPERB DIVERSITY OF FILMS DU RÉEL...

THE MARKET WITH A PREMIUM SELECTION,
COPRODUCTION MEETINGS, PACE MAKER
FOR TENDENCIES IN NEW MEDIA...

NYON: THE SPRING OF FESTIVALS!

ENTRY FORMS AND REGULATIONS
WWW.VISIONSDUREEL.CH

Deadlines for entries
Festival: 5 January 2010
Market: 10 March 2010

PARTNER
OF